PV

 St. Louis Community College

Forest Park
Florissant Valley
Meramec

Instructional Resources
St. Louis, Missouri

State and Local Public Finance

State and Local Public Finance

Ronald C. Fisher

Michigan State University

Scott, Foresman and Company
Glenview, Illinois   London

Acknowledgments

Cover photo left: Chicago's Michigan Avenue   Credit: Don & Pat Valenti
Cover photo right: Main Street, Middlebury, VT   Credit: © 1987 Frank Coco/
Vermont Stock Photo

Library of Congress Cataloging-in-Publication Data

Fisher, Ronald C.
  State and local government finance.

  Bibliography: p. 00
  Includes indexes.
    1. Finance, Public—United States—States.
2. Local finance—United States. 3. State-local relations—United
States. I. Title.
HJ275.F559   1988   336.73   88-29836
ISBN 0-673-18155-3

To the Folks at 30 Arrow

Preface

State and Local Public Finance is intended to be ideal for junior and senior undergraduates who are studying public finance and who have some knowledge of economic principles. It may be used either alone or with a reading supplement in courses specifically geared toward state–local government. For one-semester or year-long courses on public finance in general, two approaches are possible: the book may be used to supplement a general text, or it may become the basis for the course, with general theory illustrated by state–local examples. For instance, the general equilibrium analysis of capital taxes can be illustrated just as well by the property tax as by the corporate income tax. For the second approach, some supplement for the federal material (such as Pechman's *Federal Tax Policy*) would be advisable.

This book may also be of interest to undergraduate students studying political science, public administration, journalism, or prelaw, as well as students in master's degree programs in public policy analysis, public administration, or planning who wish to apply their knowledge of basic economics to subnational government policy issues. Additionally, government officials, applied economists in government and consulting, and graduate students in economics may also find this book useful as both a survey of and a reference to the economics literature on state–local finance issues.

There are at least two important reasons why a book devoted solely to state and local government fiscal issues is appropriate now. First, the subnational government sector has grown to be a substantial component of the U.S. economy, representing about 40 percent of the public sector and accounting for more than 10 percent of the gross national product. Furthermore, of all services provided through the public sector, those provided by the state–local governments—education, transportation, public safety, sanitation—are the most familiar to individuals and have the greatest effect on day-to-day life. Second, parallel to the growth in the economic activity of subnational governments over the past twenty-five years, there has been substantial growth and change in the economic analysis of subnational government finance.

This book provides what has been missing—an explanation and analysis of state–local government public finance practices and problems. It not only presents detailed descriptions of significant institutions when appropriate, but it applies modern economic theory to the way these institutions finance their services and it evaluates alternative policies. Although the emphasis is on American institutions and issues, much of the economic analysis can apply to any federal system.

Relatively sophisticated economic and political issues are examined using basic concepts. Readers are expected to have knowledge of the tools of introductory microeconomics but they do not have to know the theoretical tools usually associated with intermediate-level microeconomics. (In the few cases where these techniques add to the understanding of the material, they are presented in appendixes.) One should not confuse sophistication of methodology with level of analysis, however; some relatively sophisticated economic and policy issues are examined, albeit using basic tools. For instance, it is important that students learn economists' conclusions about the demand for state–local government services, even if they do not have a good understanding of the underlying utility theory or the econometrics upon which those conclusions were based. Although not a complete survey, the intent of *State and Local Public Finance* is to represent fairly the thinking of economists about state–local issues, much of which has been developed in the past twenty years or so.

/ Organization

The text is organized into five parts. An overview of the state-local sector, a discussion of the economic role of subnational governments, and a review of the microeconomic reasons for government provision comprise Part 1. The basic fiscal institutions and the core economic theory and analysis of state-local government finance are presented in Parts 2–4: interplay between the structure and the fiscal role of subnational governments is considered in Part 2; analysis of the various state–local revenue sources is presented in Part 3; and consideration of the provision of services—demand, costs, pricing, the role of grants—is examined in Part 4. (While these core chapters can be covered in any order, they contain cross-references to material in other chapters.) In Part 5 the institutional information and economic analyses from the core sections are applied to four policy issues.

/ Acknowledgments

Many individuals contributed to this project in direct and indirect ways. Several of my teachers—Byron Brown, the late Daniel Saks, and Milton Taylor at Michigan State University, and Vernon Henderson and Allen Feldman at Brown University—were instrumental in introducing economics to me and showing me how it could be profitably employed in understanding public-sector issues. I hope that my students will benefit as much from my teaching as I did from the teaching of these men.

John Shannon of the Advisory Commission on Intergovernmental Relations helped me in the early years of my career to learn how to bridge the gap between theory and policy, and Robert A. Bowman, State Treasurer of Michigan, gave me the opportunity later to practice what I had learned.

I wish to thank the following individuals who contributed by reviewing and commenting on all or part of the manuscript at various stages of production:

John E. Anderson	Eastern Michigan University
Jeff E. Biddle	Michigan State University
Kenneth D. Boyer	Michigan State University
Byron W. Brown	Michigan State University
Gerald S. Goldstein	Canadian Government
Larry E. Huckins	Baruch College
William A. McEachern	University of Connecticut
Sharon B. Megdal	University of Arizona
Peter Mieszkowski	Rice University
Pamela Moomau	University of New Orleans
Timothy Ryan	University of New Orleans
Rexford E. Santerre	Bentley College
Daniel B. Suits	Michigan State University
James H. Wycoff	University of Oklahoma

I want to particularly thank

R. Bruce Billings	University of Arizona
Douglas Holtz-Eakin	Columbia University
Mark J. Mazur	Carnegie-Mellon University
Michael J. Wolkoff	University of Rochester

for providing especially detailed comments that went beyond what is normally expected of reviewers.

I am also happy to thank the many students at Michigan State who contributed to this project, anonymously and in ways they did not realize, merely by their presence in my classes. Thanks also for fine research assistance goes to John Brown, Jeff Roggenbuck, Judy Temple, and Rob Wassmer, the latter two of whom provided answers to the end-of-chapter questions. Grateful appreciation also goes to the document librarians at Michigan State, headed by Eleanor Boyles, for patiently helping in the search for recent and appropriate data. As it is traditional to thank those responsible for typing the manuscript, I should thank Zenith Data Systems and Microsoft Corporation—producers of my word-processing setup—for making the task manageable for someone with as few technical skills as I. George Lobell and the staff at Scott, Foresman deserve special thanks for encouraging me, being patient, and producing a fine volume.

Finally, special thanks to my family—Cathy, Michael, and Charlie—who not only provided three additional important reasons why the book should be written, but who also shared in many ways in the cost of writing it. They have my special appreciation (but, of course, they always did).

Ronald C. Fisher

Contents

Part 1

Introduction

Every person has some familiarity with state and local government fiscal policies. We attend public schools; travel on streets, highways, and buses; receive clean water and dispose of dirty water; have our trash collected; enjoy the security of police and fire protection; use public hospitals; vacation at parks and public beaches; support the less fortunate with services and income maintenance; and we pay for these services. We pay property, income, and sales taxes; excise taxes on a variety of commodities such as alcohol, tobacco, and gasoline; a number of different user fees; and we buy lottery tickets. All this•encompasses state and local government finance. In this book, we will do more than reiterate personal experience, however. The task is to combine knowledge of the institutional details of fiscal policy with an analytical framework so that policy issues can be better understood.

The task begins in Chapter 1 first by providing a general overall view of those institutional facts. How large is the state and local government sector, and how has that size changed? What is the role of state and local governments compared to the federal government? What services do state and local governments provide, and how are those services financed? How are state and local governments organized? How representative is your experience, the way it is done in your state and community?

The analytical tools to analyze the institutional details and policy issues are presented in Chapter 2. Because this is an economics book, these facts are to be analyzed using standard economics methods. What is the economic role of government generally, and where do state and local governments fit in? What is meant by equity and efficiency, the traditional criteria for evaluating economic policy? What economic tools can state and local governments use to carry out their economic responsibilities in an equitable and efficient manner? From the general overview in this introductory section, the book proceeds to specific analysis of separate pieces of state and local finance and then returns, at the end, to more general analysis of broad policy issues.

1 / Why Study State and Local Government Finance?

> . . . It has become evident in recent years that the serious business of governing the United States is largely being done in the states.[1]
>
> *The Wall Street Journal*

The economic issues involved in the financing of state–local governments deserve and demand separate attention for three primary reasons: (a) The state–local government sector is now a substantial part of the U.S. economy, accounting for more than 10 percent of Gross National Product (GNP) and representing about one-third of the total government sector; (b) the major services provided by state–local governments—education, transportation, social services, and public safety—are those that most affect residents on a day-to-day basis; and (c) because of the *diversity* of state–local governments and the ease of *mobility* among them, the analysis of many economic issues is substantially different in the state and local arenas than for the federal government.

The importance of *diversity* and *mobility* for state–local government finance cannot be overemphasized. As you will learn in this book, there is tremendous diversity both in the structure of subnational government in different states and in the magnitude and mix of revenues and expenditures. In 1982 there were about 82,500 different state–local governments in the United States, each with independent functional responsibilities and revenue sources. Besides the fifty states, these included about 39,000 general-purpose local governments (counties, municipalities, and townships) and about 43,500 special-purpose local governments (school and other special districts). Because the boundaries of many of these jurisdictions overlap, any individual will be a member or resident of at least two subnational governments (a state and a locality) and more likely a resident of four or more (state, county, municipality, or township and at least one special district), each with separate elected officials and separate taxes and expenditures.

The division of responsibility among these different types or levels of subnational government varies by state or region. In some states such as Alaska and Hawaii, local governments play a relatively limited role with the state government being dominant. In others such as New Hampshire and New York, local governments account for the majority of state–local expenditures. The division of responsibility within the local sector also varies by state. In Maryland, for example, counties are

---

[1] Editorial. "Traverse City Whacks Washington." *Wall Street Journal*, 28 July 1987.

the dominant form of local government, collecting about 72 percent of local own-source revenue and making about 68 percent of all local government expenditures. At the opposite end of the spectrum, counties have no fiscal role at all in Connecticut where local government services are provided by 179 separate and nonoverlapping "towns." Perhaps a more common or typical structure is represented by that in Michigan where counties account for about 20 percent of local expenditures, municipalities and townships about 36 percent, and the rest by special districts, especially independent school districts.

In short, it can be very misleading to talk about "the services" provided by states, counties, cities, or local governments in general because there is no single structure. Similarly, even among governments that have responsibility for the same services, the quantity and quality of services provided can vary substantially. There is also great variety in the way in which subnational governments finance those services—that is, on which sources of revenue to rely. Indeed, this diversity is the essence of a federal, as opposed to unitary, system of government.

But it is the *ease of mobility* among these diverse subnational governments that causes the diversity to have economic implications. Diversity is largely uninteresting without mobility, and mobility is unimportant without the choice diversity creates. The notion of mobility here is not only physical mobility (the location of residences or businesses among different jurisdictions) but also economic mobility (the choice of where to consume or invest). In many cases, individuals can independently select the location of residence, work, investment, and consumption. Many individuals live in one city, work in another, and do most of their shopping at stores or a shopping mall in still another locality. In some cases, these activities cross state as well as local boundaries. And when individuals save through bank accounts or mutual funds, their money is invested in all kinds of projects located in many different states, localities, and even different countries. This economic mobility coupled with the choice provided by the diversity of subnational governments is largely the topic of this book.

/ Fiscal Characteristics of the Subnational Public Sector

/ Size and growth

In 1986 state–local governments spent nearly $455 billion of resources collected from their own sources (that is, excluding spending financed by federal aid), which represented almost 11 percent of GNP (Table 1.1). When spending financed by federal grants is included, state–local expenditures represent more than 13 percent of GNP. It is also interesting to compare the state–local sector to the federal government alone. For every dollar collected from its own sources and spent by the federal government in 1986, state–local governments collected and spent about $.44. In per-capita terms, state–local governments collected and spent about $1640 per person in 1986, while the federal government collected and spent (including grants to state–local governments) about $3730. If comparison is limited to spending for domestic programs by all levels of government, state–local governments col-

TABLE 1.1

The Relative Size of Federal, State, and Local Government, 1986

Government Level	Own-Source Expenditures[a]	Own-Source Expenditures as Percentage of GNP	Expenditures After Transfers[a]	Percentage of GNP
Federal	1030.2	24.5	926.2	22.0
State–Local	453.9	10.8	557.9	13.3
State	258.7	6.2	226.0	5.4
Local	195.2	4.6	331.9	7.9
Total	1484.1	35.3	1484.1	35.3

Source: ACIR, *Significant Features of Fiscal Federalism*, 1987b.

[a]Billions of dollars.

lected more than 42 percent of those funds and were responsible for spending more than 52 percent. By any of these measures, then, state–local governments are both an important component of the U.S. economy and a very large fraction of the entire government sector.

The current substantial relative size of the subnational government sector arose from a roughly twenty-five-year period of sustained rapid growth between the early 1950s and mid-1970s. This growth of total state–local government expenditures (either including or excluding spending financed by grants), both relative to GNP and in real per-capita dollars, is depicted in Figure 1.1. In 1949 total state–local spending from all sources represented slightly less than 8 percent of GNP, but by 1974 state–local spending had grown to about 14 percent of GNP. In other words, during those twenty-five years state–local spending had grown substantially faster than did the overall size of the economy. Even excluding federal grants, state–local spending from own-sources increased from about 7 percent of GNP in 1949 to about 11 percent in 1974. A similar pattern of growth is shown by per-capita, 1982 dollars, indicating that state–local spending also increased faster than population growth and inflation during this period. Not surprisingly, the pattern of growth in spending by state governments alone parallels the pattern for the entire state–local sector rather closely.

The relative growth of the state–local sector in this period is usually attributed to three factors. First, income in the United States increased rather substantially in these years; this caused an increase in demand for many different types of goods and services, some of which were largely provided by subnational governments. Second, growth in population and change in the composition of the population (especially the postwar "baby boom") also led to an increase in demand for state–local services (especially education). Third, substantial increases in manufacturing–labor productivity and thus manufacturing wages during this period created pressures to increase wages of state and local employees as well. This caused an increase in the relative cost of providing those services. In essence, spending rose faster than the economy grew because the population to be served (especially children) was

FIGURE 1.1 State–Local Expenditures, as Percentage of GNP (a) and per Capita in 1982 Dollars (b)

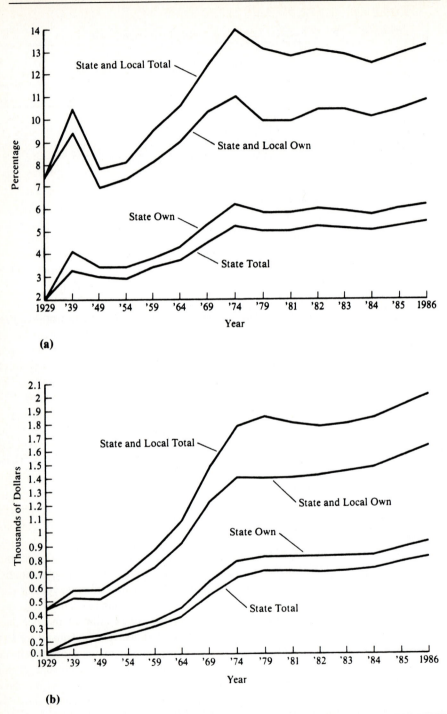

(a)

(b)

rising relatively fast, because the costs of providing state–local services were rising faster than average, and because consumers were demanding new or improved services from subnational governments.

Since the mid-1970s, however, the relative size of the state–local government sector has not changed substantially. In the decade from the late 1970s to the later 1980s, state–local government spending (either from all sources or only from own sources) has increased at about the same rate as the national economy. State–local government spending from all sources was about 13.1 percent of GNP in 1979 compared to about 13.3 percent in 1986; spending from own sources only was about 9.9 percent of GNP in 1979 and about 10.8 percent in 1986. A similar and clear slowdown in the growth of state–local government spending beginning in the latter 1970s is reflected by the graph of real per-capita spending in Figure 1.1b. The nearly flat growth of state–local spending (in relative terms) is particularly pronounced through 1984, with spending again having risen at a somewhat faster rate in the last several years.[2]

This pronounced change in the relative growth of state–local governments in the late 1970s has been attributed to several factors. First, income did not grow as fast in those years as previously because the economy weathered two rather long and deep recessions between 1974 and 1983. Second, the demand for school services lessened as the "baby boomers" completed school and delayed starting their own families. Third, state–local government costs, especially wages, did not increase relatively as fast in this period as previously. Fourth, federal grants to state–local governments did not grow in this period anywhere near as fast as in the previous period, although state–local spending from own sources also follows the same pattern of slowing growth. Finally, it has been suggested that the slowdown reflects a change in the tastes or preferences of consumers for government services, as reflected by the coordinated opposition to state–local taxes in the late 1970s and early 1980s—what has come to be called the "tax revolt." Whatever the combination of factors, it is clear that the past ten years or so have represented a very different environment for state–local finance than in the preceding twenty-five years.

/ *Expenditure categories*

Nearly half of the money spent by state and local governments in aggregate provides education or social services and income maintenance, as shown in Figure 1.2. In 1986 these two categories accounted for 48.3 percent of total state–local spending, with education accounting for about 30 percent and social services about 19 percent. Expenditures for transportation and public safety, the other main direct consumer services, represent about 7 to 8 percent of state–local spending, while interest on state–local government debt represents only about 5 percent of spending.

---

[2]In contrast to the state–local sector, federal government expenditures increased substantially faster than did GNP since 1979. Federal government expenditures, including grants paid to state and local governments, represented about 21 percent of GNP in 1979 and about 24.5 percent in 1986.

FIGURE 1.2 State–Local Government Expenditure and Revenue, 1985–86

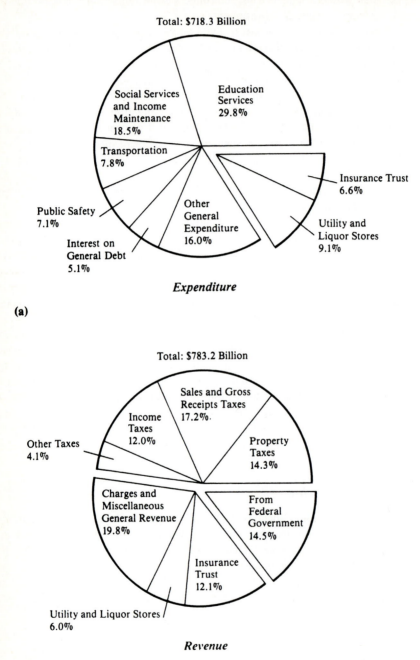

Total: $718.3 Billion

Education Services 29.8%

Social Services and Income Maintenance 18.5%

Transportation 7.8%

Public Safety 7.1%

Interest on General Debt 5.1%

Other General Expenditure 16.0%

Insurance Trust 6.6%

Utility and Liquor Stores 9.1%

Expenditure

(a)

Total: $783.2 Billion

Sales and Gross Receipts Taxes 17.2%.

Income Taxes 12.0%

Other Taxes 4.1%

Property Taxes 14.3%

Charges and Miscellaneous General Revenue 19.8%

From Federal Government 14.5%

Insurance Trust 12.1%

Utility and Liquor Stores 6.0%

Revenue

(b)

The distribution of spending by category for state–local governments together masks some differences between states and local governments, on average. Figure 1.3 shows the distribution of **general expenditure** for states and localities separately. (According to the Census definition, general expenditure includes all expenditures except those for government utilities, liquor stores, and employee-retirement funds.) Education is by far the largest category of spending for both states and localities (37 percent for states and 43 percent for localities). States also spend a relatively large fraction of their expenditures on welfare, highways, and health and hospital services, while the other major expenditure categories for local governments are social services, public safety, and transportation.

/ *Revenue sources*

State–local governments receive revenues from a wide variety of different sources, including a number of different types of taxes, as shown in Figure 1.2b. When all revenues to all state–local governments are added together, the five major sources, all of roughly equal importance, are charges and fees (19.8 percent of the total), sales taxes (17.2 percent), federal grants (14.5 percent), property taxes (14.3 percent), and income taxes (12.0 percent). In contrast, the predominant source of revenue for the federal government is income taxes, including the personal and corporate income taxes and the Social Security payroll tax.

The composition of revenues differs between states and local governments even more than the difference in expenditure patterns, as shown by Figure 1.4. Restricting the comparison to **general revenue** (excluding utility, liquor store, and employee-retirement revenue), states get nearly 75 percent of their revenue from sales taxes (about 29 percent), income taxes (21.7 percent from individual and corporate taxes), and federal grants (24 percent). The two dominant sources of general revenue for local governments accounting for about 60 percent of the total are state grants (about 33 percent) and property taxes (28 percent). From another perspective, grants from both the federal and state government provide about 39 percent of local government general revenue. It is worth noting that these are averages for all local governments; there is substantial variation by both type of local government and state.

/ *Diversity of Subnational Governments*

Although the statistics presented above for both the level and mix of expenditures and revenues characterize the overall state–local sector, they do not necessarily represent the fiscal picture in any individual state and local jurisdiction. As noted, diversity is the norm in subnational finance. Accordingly, some comparison of the fiscal environment in different states is shown by the data in Tables 1.2–1.4. It is not safe to simply compare the level of expenditures or revenues among states. Rather, it is necessary to standardize the data because of the different sizes and characteristics of the states. The two most common ways of standardizing are to compare the data in per-capita terms (per person) or as a percentage of income.

FIGURE 1.3   *General Expenditure of State and Local Governments, 1986*

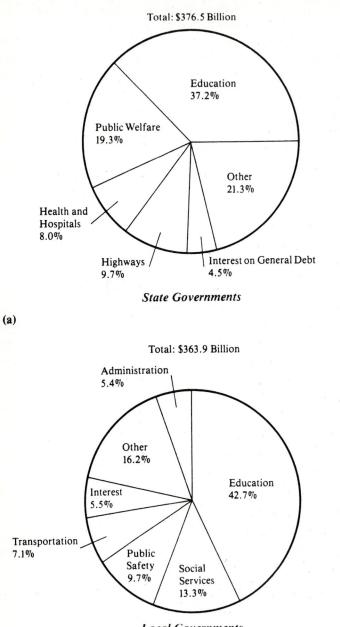

Total: $376.5 Billion

Education
37.2%

Public Welfare
19.3%

Other
21.3%

Health and
Hospitals
8.0%

Highways
9.7%

Interest on General Debt
4.5%

State Governments

(a)

Total: $363.9 Billion

Administration
5.4%

Other
16.2%

Education
42.7%

Interest
5.5%

Transportation
7.1%

Public
Safety
9.7%

Social
Services
13.3%

Local Governments

(b)

FIGURE 1.4   *General Revenue of State and Local Governments, 1986*

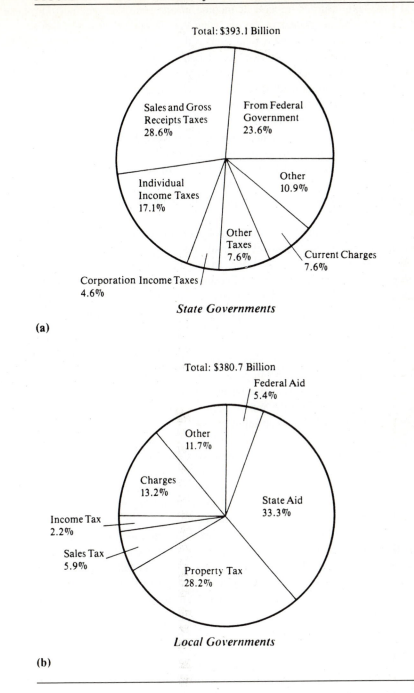

Total: $393.1 Billion

Sales and Gross
Receipts Taxes
28.6%

From Federal
Government
23.6%

Individual
Income Taxes
17.1%

Other
10.9%

Other
Taxes
7.6%

Current Charges
7.6%

Corporation Income Taxes
4.6%

State Governments

(a)

Total: $380.7 Billion

Federal Aid
5.4%

Other
11.7%

Charges
13.2%

Income Tax
2.2%

Sales Tax
5.9%

State Aid
33.3%

Property Tax
28.2%

Local Governments

(b)

But suppose that one state has higher per-capita expenditures than another or that expenditures take a larger fraction of income in one state than another. Do these mean that services are greater in the one state than the other? Not necessarily.

The rationale for per-capita comparisons is that it may require more expenditure and revenue to provide equal services to a larger population than to a smaller one. The degree to which that is true for different state–local services is not clear, however. If the production of state–local services exhibits **constant returns to scale**—that is, if the average cost of providing a unit of service to one consumer is constant—then total cost will increase proportionately to population. Equal per-capita amounts are then consistent with equal services, *if all other factors are the same between the jurisdictions being compared*. On the other hand, the production of some services may exhibit **increasing returns to scale,** which means that cost per person falls as the number of people served rises. In that case, equal services are consistent with lower per-capita expenditures in the larger jurisdictions, *all else the same*.

A similar analysis applies to interjurisdictional comparisons based on the fraction of income taken by state–local expenditures and revenues. Should one expect that two states, one rich and one poor, would have the same *percentage* of their income going to government services? The answer is yes only if the income elasticity of demand for those government services is one—that is, if demand for service increases proportionately with income. If not—if demand for state–local services increases slower or faster than income—then equal percentages of income going to state–local expenditures are not expected. In addition, this analysis requires that factors other than income be the same between the jurisdictions being compared.

What of those other factors? In general, differences in state–local expenditures or revenues among states may arise because of (a) different decisions about what services to provide through the public sector as opposed to the private sector in different states; (b) differences in input prices (especially labor) among the states; (c) differences in environment such as area, population density, or weather, which affect the cost of producing services; and (d) differences in demand for services from either population differences or income differences or differences in tastes. Standardization in per-capita terms may offset only the population effects, and standardization by state-income level offsets only the income effect on demand. With either standardization, differences in spending or taxes can remain, which do not reflect service differences. As a result, extreme caution is necessary in making interstate fiscal comparisons. A higher level of revenues and expenditures in one state may mean there are more services in that state, may reflect higher production costs in that state, or simply may mean that residents of that state have decided to provide some service (hospitals, for instance) through the government rather than privately.

/ Expenditures

With the cautions noted above in mind, the differences in state–local expenditure among the states are shown in Table 1.2. In 1985 state–local governments spent an average of $2321 per person, or about 18.3 percent of individuals' personal

TABLE 1.2

State–Local Government General Expenditures, by State, 1985[a]

State and Region	Per-Capita State–Local Expenditure	State–Local Expenditure as a Percentage of Personal Income	State Government Share of State–Local Own-Source Expenditure
United States	$2321	18.3%	57%
New England	$2352	16.4%	65%
Connecticut	2368	14.4	61
Maine	2111	19.6	63
Massachusetts	2445	16.6	70
New Hampshire	1816	14.1	47
Rhode Island	2550	20.0	68
Vermont	2410	22.5	68
Mideast	$2738	19.6%	50%
Delaware	2688	19.9	73
Maryland	2352	16.4	57
New Jersey	2486	16.2	58
New York	3355	23.5	44
Pennsylvania	2032	16.4	58
Great Lakes	$2234	17.6%	57%
Illinois	2173	15.8	54
Indiana	1853	15.8	61
Michigan	2505	19.9	54
Ohio	2120	17.1	57
Wisconsin	2561	20.6	60
Plains	$2279	18.2%	56%
Iowa	2316	18.9	59
Kansas	2220	16.8	50
Minnesota	2842	21.6	58
Missouri	1775	14.7	56
Nebraska	2256	18.1	51
N. Dakota	2696	21.8	75
S. Dakota	2214	20.1	55
Southeast	$1915	17.4%	60%
Alabama	1972	19.9	65
Arkansas	1695	17.4	65
Florida	1956	15.9	53
Georgia	1970	17.5	54
Kentucky	1798	17.5	70
Louisiana	2308	21.4	59
Mississippi	1784	20.4	62
N. Carolina	1785	16.7	66
S. Carolina	1782	17.9	70
Tennessee	1743	16.9	53
Virginia	1993	15.2	59
W. Virginia	1983	20.2	68

continued

TABLE 1.2 Continued

State–Local Government General Expenditures, by State, 1985[a]

State and Region	Per-Capita State–Local Expenditure	State–Local Expenditure as a Percentage of Personal Income	State Government Share of State–Local Own-Source Expenditure
Southwest	$2079	17.4%	53%
Arizona	2305	20.3	54
New Mexico	2536	25.2	77
Oklahoma	2034	17.5	61
Texas	2004	16.3	49
Rocky Mountain	$2468	20.9%	54%
Colorado	2420	17.8	49
Idaho	1869	18.6	61
Montana	2616	24.9	54
Utah	2327	23.8	61
Wyoming	4166	33.9	57
Far West	$2710	19.8%	64%
Alaska	9513	56.7	95
California	2647	18.8	63
Hawaii	2472	19.2	80
Nevada	2519	19.4	52
Oregon	2471	21.4	56
Washington	2521	20.0	62

Source: ACIR, *Significant Features of Fiscal Federalism*, 1987b, Table 15.3, 19.

[a]General expenditure includes all expenditure except utility, liquor store, and employee-retirement expenditure.

incomes. Eight states spent more than $2600 per person—Alaska ($9513), Wyoming ($4166), New York ($3355), Minnesota ($2842), North Dakota ($2696), Delaware ($2688), California ($2647), and Montana ($2616)—and seven states spent less than $1800 per person—Arkansas ($1695), Tennessee ($1743), Missouri ($1775), South Carolina ($1782), Mississippi ($1784), North Carolina ($1785), and Kentucky ($1798). A similar range exists in the fraction of income taken by state–local expenditures, from 56.7 percent in Alaska and 33.9 percent in Wyoming to 14.1 percent in New Hampshire and 14.4 percent in Connecticut. There is also very little of a regional pattern in the level of expenditures. Although per-capita spending is consistently below average in the Southeast and above average in the Far West, there is substantial variation within regions in the other cases.

Although there is a general correspondence between the rankings of states by per-capita spending and spending as a percentage of income, there are some important differences that stand out. In California, for example, per-capita spending is 14 percent greater than the national average, but spending relative to income is only slightly above the average. California's apparently high per-capita spending might be attributed to their above-average income. On the other hand, South Carolina is among the lowest states in per-capita spending, but its spending relative to income is just slightly below average. Here the relatively low income in the state may be holding per-capita spending down. And per-capita spending in Connecticut and Utah is almost exactly at the national average, but spending relative to income is about 22 percent below the national average in Connecticut and 30 percent above average in Utah.

By either measure, spending is way above average in Alaska. The explanation primarily lies in two factors—high costs for producing services and the collection of substantial amounts of oil-extraction revenue, which is distributed as royalties paid to residents.

The last column of Table 1.2 shows the fraction of state–local outlays generated by the state government in each state. The only obvious regional pattern is the relatively strong role played by state governments in New England (with the exception of New Hampshire). Otherwise there is quite a bit of variation within regions. State governments take a dominant role in Alaska (95 percent of own-source expenditures); Hawaii (80 percent); New Mexico (77 percent); North Dakota (75 percent); Delaware (73 percent); and Kentucky, Massachusetts, and South Carolina (all 70 percent). Local governments provide the majority of own-source funds in New York (44 percent of own-source expenditures by the state), New Hampshire (47 percent), and Colorado and Texas (both 49 percent).

/ Revenues

State levels of state–local revenues and taxes, both per capita and relative to income, are shown in Table 1.3. The relative state rankings in revenues are, not surprisingly, generally similar to the relative state positions in expenditures. Thus, the regional pattern shows relatively low revenues and taxes in the Southeast and substantial variation within most other regions. Besides taxes, state–local general revenue includes grants from the federal government as well as charges and fees. Generally, the level of taxes and level of general revenue is correlated, but not necessarily. A state with an unusually large amount of federal aid or charges may have average or above-average revenue but below-average taxes. For instance, Delaware (which receives substantial revenue from corporate license fees) has a relatively high level of general revenue but about average taxes.

It is important to note that these data refer to revenue and tax collections, *not* burdens. To the extent that states collect revenue from nonresidents (severance taxes, some sales taxes, some business taxes, property taxes on nonresident property owners), the taxes or fees do not represent a burden on residents. In those cases, standardizing by the resident population or income does not provide a very accurate or useful picture.

There is also substantial diversity in the **mix of revenue sources** used in different states, as shown in Table 1.4. The five major state–local revenue sources identified—property, sales, and income taxes; federal grants; and user charges—account for nearly three-quarters of state–local government general revenue on average, with each accounting for between 12 and 18 percent of revenue. The aggregate picture thus shows a diversified and balanced state–local revenue structure.

TABLE 1.3

State–Local Government Revenue, by State, 1985

State and Region	Per Capita		Percentage of Personal Income	
	General Revenue	*Taxes*	*General Revenue*	*Taxes*
United States	$2504	$1465	19.8%	11.6%
New England	$2574	$1627	18.0%	11.4%
Connecticut	2709	1816	16.5	11.0
Maine	2275	1328	21.2	12.4
Massachusetts	2663	1715	18.1	11.7
New Hampshire	1925	1126	14.9	8.7
Rhode Island	2654	1479	20.8	11.6
Vermont	2525	1392	23.6	13.0
Mideast	$3009	$1887	21.5%	13.5%
Delaware	3067	1558	22.8	11.6
Maryland	2575	1629	18.0	11.4
New Jersey	2737	1749	17.8	11.4
New York	3631	2334	25.4	16.3
Pennsylvania	2292	1420	18.5	11.2
Great Lakes	$2398	$1443	18.8%	11.3%
Illinois	2375	1474	17.2	10.7
Indiana	2047	1180	17.5	10.1
Michigan	2695	1609	21.4	12.8
Ohio	2255	1331	18.2	10.8
Wisconsin	2610	1611	21.0	12.9
Plains	$2409	$1352	19.2%	10.8%
Iowa	2290	1331	18.7	10.8
Kansas	2397	1357	18.2	10.3
Minnesota	3106	1767	23.6	13.4
Missouri	1908	1091	15.8	9.0
Nebraska	2316	1251	18.6	10.1
N. Dakota	2846	1357	23.0	11.0
S. Dakota	2168	1043	19.6	9.4
Southeast	$2059	$1134	18.7%	10.3%
Alabama	2029	990	20.5	10.0
Arkansas	1789	967	18.3	9.9
Florida	2109	1181	17.1	9.6
Georgia	2251	1181	20.0	10.5
Kentucky	1958	1033	19.0	10.0
Louisiana	2428	1298	22.6	12.1
Mississippi	1886	918	21.6	10.5
N. Carolina	1951	1144	18.2	10.7
S. Carolina	1920	1076	19.2	10.8
Tennessee	1848	996	17.9	9.6
Virginia	2121	1307	16.2	10.0
W. Virginia	2069	1203	21.1	12.3

continued

TABLE 1.3 Continued

State–Local Government Revenue, by State, 1985

State and Region	Per Capita General Revenue	Taxes	Percentage of Personal Income General Revenue	Taxes
Southwest	$2239	$1283	18.8%	10.8%
Arizona	2298	1376	20.3	12.1
New Mexico	2843	1249	28.2	12.4
Oklahoma	2244	1289	19.3	11.1
Texas	2173	1267	17.7	10.3
Rocky Mountain	$2678	$1418	22.7%	12.0%
Colorado	2538	1448	18.6	10.6
Idaho	1906	1022	19.0	10.2
Montana	2763	1383	26.3	13.1
Utah	2578	1258	26.4	12.9
Wyoming	5274	2580	42.9	21.0
Far West	$3399	$1690	23.8%	12.4%
Alaska	12,910	4585	77.0	27.3
California	2789	1645	19.8	11.7
Hawaii	2673	1652	20.8	12.9
Nevada	2602	1443	20.1	11.1
Oregon	2667	1420	23.1	12.3
Washington	2545	1435	20.2	11.4

Sources: U.S. Bureau of the Census, *Governmental Finances in 1984–85;* ACIR, *Significant Features of Fiscal Federalism,* 1987b.

TABLE 1.4

State–Local Revenue Sources, by State, 1985

State and Region	Percentage of State–Local General Revenue from Federal Aid	Property Tax	General Sales Tax	Individual Income Tax	User Charges
United States	17.8	17.4	14.1	11.7	12.5
New England	18.7	23.4	11.3	12.9	9.1
Connecticut	14.6	25.3	17.9	3.4	7.7
Maine	24.6	20.7	13.4	11.2	9.2
Massachusetts	19.1	21.3	9.3	20.4	9.6
New Hampshire	20.0	36.0	0.0	1.3	9.7
Rhode Island	20.6	22.2	10.7	11.0	9.4
Vermont	24.6	21.1	6.5	10.7	10.8
Mideast	18.0	18.9	11.4	16.7	9.3
Delaware	15.3	6.6	0.0	20.1	15.5
Maryland	16.3	15.8	9.7	22.9	9.8
New Jersey	15.0	26.2	10.9	9.4	9.9
New York	17.7	19.0	12.3	18.8	9.1
Pennsylvania	18.8	16.0	11.1	14.8	9.2

continued

TABLE 1.4 Continued

State–Local Revenue Sources, by State, 1985

	Percentage of State–Local General Revenue from				
State and Region	Federal Aid	Property Tax	General Sales Tax	Individual Income Tax	User Charges
Great Lakes	17.6	20.5	13.5	13.4	12.8
Illinois	18.1	22.1	15.4	9.5	9.3
Indiana	17.2	18.4	18.8	12.2	16.6
Michigan	17.4	23.0	10.4	13.9	13.9
Ohio	17.3	16.6	13.1	16.4	13.4
Wisconsin	17.9	21.8	11.7	16.1	13.5
Plains	17.4	17.6	12.9	12.4	14.6
Iowa	17.3	22.7	11.5	12.5	16.3
Kansas	14.8	20.9	11.4	10.3	13.5
Minnesota	16.0	16.0	10.4	17.1	13.8
Missouri	19.4	12.5	19.4	12.6	13.9
Nebraska	17.1	23.4	10.7	8.6	17.4
N. Dakota	21.0	11.9	9.6	3.9	17.9
S. Dakota	24.4	21.0	14.9	0.0	11.8
Southeast	19.1	12.7	16.7	8.7	15.8
Alabama	21.7	5.7	14.6	9.2	19.2
Arkansas	22.4	9.7	18.1	11.2	13.2
Florida	16.0	17.9	19.5	0.0	17.0
Georgia	20.2	13.1	14.8	12.8	18.8
Kentucky	22.5	9.3	11.2	13.4	11.1
Louisiana	17.3	7.3	20.2	4.8	13.8
Mississippi	24.0	11.2	18.9	5.3	19.9
N. Carolina	19.1	12.6	13.1	16.6	13.0
S. Carolina	19.6	12.5	15.7	13.2	16.6
Tennessee	22.0	11.8	25.6	0.7	16.7
Virginia	15.8	17.2	10.3	16.1	14.8
W. Virginia	21.2	9.6	19.8	12.6	11.6
Southwest	14.1	17.9	15.8	2.6	12.9
Arizona	12.8	16.0	22.2	8.3	11.6
New Mexico	16.7	5.3	17.4	2.1	9.6
Oklahoma	15.5	10.1	14.6	9.8	15.3
Texas	13.7	21.4	14.5	0.0	13.0
Rocky Mountain	18.0	18.3	13.1	9.2	12.6
Colorado	14.6	19.6	17.0	11.1	14.5
Idaho	21.8	14.7	12.5	13.5	15.1
Montana	22.9	22.9	0.0	7.9	9.6
Utah	20.4	13.4	16.0	10.2	11.5
Wyoming	17.5	20.9	8.2	0.0	9.4
Far West	17.9	15.1	15.8	12.0	12.4
Alaska	7.8	8.3	0.8	0.0	6.3
California	18.4	15.1	16.5	14.6	12.5
Hawaii	17.7	11.0	24.3	15.2	12.0
Nevada	13.9	12.1	19.0	0.0	17.4
Oregon	19.6	23.2	0.0	18.3	13.0
Washington	20.0	16.2	27.0	0.0	13.8

Source: ACIR, *Significant Features of Fiscal Federalism.* 1987b, 46.

But the picture is very different in some individual states. Most obviously, the general sales and individual income tax shares are zero in some cases. In a few states, these five revenue sources in aggregate represent a substantially smaller share of revenue than the average, indicating that there are some other substantial sources of funds in those special cases. For instance, these five sources account for only about 23 percent of revenue in Alaska (which receives substantial revenue from oil leases and severance taxes), for 56 percent in Wyoming (where severance taxes are important), for 57 percent in Delaware (which generates substantial corporate license fees as the official legal ''home'' state for many of the largest corporations), and for about 62 percent in Nevada and Texas (which receive substantial gambling revenue and severance taxes, respectively).

There is clearly more of a regional pattern in the reliance on different revenue sources than for the level of taxes and expenditures. For instance, property taxes are relied upon more than average in all of the New England states and less than average in all of the Southeastern states (except Florida). General sales taxes tend to be relied on more than average in the Southeast and Southwest, individual income taxes tend to be used to a relatively small degree in the Southwestern and Mountain states, and the use of user charges is relatively low in New England but relatively high in the Plains and Southeastern states. In some cases, these regional patterns result (a) from the relative fiscal importance of state as opposed to local governments, (b) from the nature of the economies in these states and regions, or (c) from historical factors coupled with inertia.

Geographic or regional competitive factors influencing revenue structures are often not decisive, however, as reflected by a number of regional anomalies— similar states located together with very different revenue structures. For instance, Oregon has no general sales tax and relatively high reliance on individual income and property taxes, whereas neighboring Washington has no individual income tax and high reliance on the sales tax. Among other similar cases, New Jersey relies heavily on property taxes and little on income taxes; Pennsylvania is just the opposite—heavy reliance on income taxes and little reliance on property taxes. New Hampshire has very high reliance on property taxes and has no sales tax and a very limited income tax; Vermont's tax structure is more similar to the national average with more balanced use of income and sales taxes and user charges. Finally, in two states dominated by the oil industry, property tax reliance is low in Oklahoma and income tax use about average, whereas there is no individual income tax and high property tax reliance in Texas.

While reflecting the great diversity in the world of state–local finance, these differences in revenue structure also raise the issue of whether there are any economic, as opposed to historical or institutional, explanations for these different fiscal decisions by various states. The one economic argument that consistently is offered to explain the choice of revenue structures is the opportunity to ''export'' tax and other revenue burdens to nonresidents. For instance, a recent analysis by Mary Gade (1987) of state government (only) revenue structures supports the idea that differences in the opportunity to export taxes go a long way toward explaining

states' choices of tax structure. For instance, Gade's analysis shows that states with a substantial tourist business tend to rely more on consumption taxes (after other factors are controlled for), that severance taxes are relied on heavily by states with an immobile resource base, and that taxes that are deductible against the federal income tax are used more intensively by states where a substantial number of taxpayers itemize deductions and face relatively high federal tax rates. (Through the deduction, state taxpayers lower their federal taxes forcing other federal taxpayers to pay a greater share.) On the other hand, Gade reports that states tend not to try to export tax burden by taxing manufacturing goods heavily, even if they are to be exported, apparently because of a fear of inducing a relocation of those manufacturing activities.

/ Fiscal Role of Subnational Governments

What is the appropriate economic role for subnational governments in a federal system? What responsibilities are better handled by the federal government, which by the subnational governments, and which can be shared among them? In what ways do the main characteristics of that sector—mobility and diversity—influence that role? Richard Musgrave has identified three traditional economic functions for government: maintaining economic stabilization, altering the distribution of resources, and obtaining an efficient allocation of society's resources. The conventional wisdom has been that state–local governments are limited in achieving the first two principally by the ease of mobility among them. Despite the fact that this notion suggests that stabilization and distribution are more appropriately federal government functions, it is apparent that many state–local services have substantial distributional implications and that the sheer size of the subnational government sector means that it may have macroeconomic effects. Thus, the conventional wisdom and some recent challenges to it are considered next.

/ Stabilization policy

Stabilization policy refers to the role of the government in maintaining employment, price stability, and economic growth through the use of fiscal and monetary policy. The conventional position is that state and local governments are inherently limited in influencing *the economic conditions in each specific subnational jurisdiction*— that is, a single state of municipality has little control over prices, employment, and the general level of economic activity in that jurisdiction. One reason is that state–local governments do not have any monetary authority (which rests with the Federal Reserve Board). Moreover, it is usually argued that states should not have monetary authority because separate state monetary decisions would increase the costs of transactions over boundaries and because each state would have an incentive to pay for trade by expanding its own "money supply," a large portion of which would be held by nonresidents.

A second factor is that the general openness of state–local jurisdiction economies restricts the opportunity for fiscal policy to be effective. Imagine a state or city attempting to expand economic activity by the traditional expansive fiscal policies—lowering local taxes, providing cash grants to residents, or expanding government purchases. As a result, residents are likely to increase consumption spending, but the ultimate effect of a substantial part of that consumption increase will occur in other jurisdictions where the goods and services are sold or produced. If your city borrowed $100 per resident and then gave each resident 100 "free" dollars to spend in any way, it is no different than if each resident borrowed $100. If the residents use the money to buy shirts, for example, the economic gain goes to the producers of shirts (and suppliers of their inputs), which may not be in your city. In addition, of course, the borrowed funds used to finance the expansive fiscal policy eventually must be repaid with a substantial portion of the funds (perhaps even all) having been borrowed from nonresidents.

There is a totally different stabilization issue as well, whether the aggregate fiscal position (taxes and spending) of the subnational sector influences the overall national economy. With subnational government spending accounting for 10 to 13 percent of the national economy, the expectation is surely that this sector does have an impact on national macroeconomic conditions. This factor has been noted most in two contexts. First, the state–local sector has an aggregate budget surplus in many years, which partly offsets the federal government budget deficits that have been the norm since 1970. In effect, the investment of surplus funds by state and local governments is a source of finance for both the federal government deficit and private-sector borrowing.

Second, there has been concern over whether state–local fiscal changes during national economic recessions or expansions might contribute to the national economic cycle. For instance, subnational government policy would be procyclical if states and localities reduce expenditures as a recession causes state–local revenues to decline (or increase less than was anticipated), thereby further reducing aggregate demand and slowing the economy more. A number of studies of this issue generally show that this does not occur, that state–local government fiscal policies tend to be countercyclical—states and localities respond to the revenue decrease caused by a recession by spending from reserves or by raising tax rates (see Bahl, 1984). The maintenance of state–local spending during a national economic contraction has a moderate countercyclical effect. Similarly, during economic expansions, state–local governments often build up reserves, thereby moderating the increase in aggregate demand. It is important to note that this conclusion applies to the aggregate state–local sector and not necessarily to every subnational jurisdiction and that the magnitude of this state–local countercyclical effect will vary for different recessions and expansions, depending on their length and other characteristics.

Regarding stabilization policy, then, the conclusions seem to be that while individual states and localities are limited in their ability to influence aggregate demand in their own jurisdictions, their collective fiscal decisions do have an impact on national economic conditions. It is incorrect, therefore, to focus only on the federal government's fiscal behavior in evaluating the macroeconomic implications of the public sector; state-local budgets matter as well.

/ Distribution policy

Distribution policy refers to the role of the government in obtaining and maintaining the socially preferred distribution of resources or income, in most cases by redistributing resources from rich to poor (there have been no serious claims that the economy, absent government intervention, generates too much income equality). Here the conventional wisdom has been very similar to the issue of stabilization. State–local governments are limited in their ability to redistribute resources because different jurisdictions select different amounts of redistribution and individuals and firms can easily move among the jurisdictions to frustrate any intended redistribution. If that is the case, then redistribution is also more appropriately carried out by the federal government (at least if international mobility is less than interjurisdictional mobility within the United States).

The conventional thought can be easily illustrated. Suppose that your city proposed to tax all families or individuals with income above $25,000 and to use the revenue to provide cash grants to individuals and families with income below $25,000. Such a pure redistributive policy would create an incentive both for higher-income taxpayers (those above $25,000) to move to a different city where such a redistributive tax did not exist and for lower-income individuals and families (those below $25,000) to move to your city to receive the grants. Paradoxically, if such moves occur, the program does result in a more equal income distribution in your city, but little redistribution from rich to poor. The existence of the incentive does not mean that all individuals will actually respond in this way—moving is costly and other locational factors may offset these redistributional incentives—but if some respond in this way, part of the program's intent is mitigated. One expects that the incentive will be greatest for very high- and very low-income individuals and when mobility is easiest. Moving among localities within the same area to avoid or take advantage of a local government redistribution program is expected in most cases to be easier or less costly than moving among states, and moving among nations more costly than moving among states. For these reasons, it has been argued that redistribution is best handled at the national level and, if not, at the states'.

But this conventional position flies in the face of several important facts. State governments administer two of the three major income-redistribution programs [Aid to Families with Dependent Children (AFDC) and Medicaid]. Other services provided by state–local governments, especially education, have important distributional implications. Finally, distributional concerns affect many state–local fiscal decisions, including the choice of tax structure. In the cases of explicit redistribution, AFDC and Medicaid, there is substantial diversity in the levels of support selected in different states even though the federal government typically pays about half the cost through a system of matching grants with higher matching rates for lower-income states. Edward Gramlich and Deborah Laren (1984) report that average AFDC benefits are roughly three times as high in the higher-benefit states as in the lower-benefit states. There are similarly wide differences in education services offered in different states and localities. Thus, despite the conventional notion that redistribution is best handled by the federal government, the actual fiscal structure leaves a substantial amount of redistribution to the subnational sector.

What accounts for the continuing distributional responsibility of subnational government and what are its effects? One possibility is that society has decided that redistribution should be a subnational government responsibility. This is reasonable if individuals only care about the welfare of other individuals who reside in their jurisdiction and if there is little mobility in response to redistributional policies. In that case, redistribution would be similar to, say, waste collection, and would be best handled at the local level where individual preferences could be satisfied. On the other hand, if individuals care about the welfare of lower-income individuals in the society regardless of what state or city they live in or if mobility frustrates local decisions, then some federal government involvement in redistribution policy is called for.

Indeed, the federal government is involved in the redistribution decisions of states through the federal grants for those programs. In theory, those grants could correct for the difficulties created by migration by reducing the cost of engaging in redistribution to residents who do not move. In effect, having federal grants pay for part of subnational government redistribution prevents higher-income individuals from avoiding some contribution. The available evidence seems to show, however, that few transfer recipients—on the order of 1 to 2 percent—actually do move to other states to receive higher welfare benefits annually (Gramlich, 1985b). However, the cumulative effect of a small number of moves in each year can be a substantial change in the geographic distribution of welfare recipients over time if the interstate pattern of benefits does not change. Even so, Edward Gramlich's analysis shows that the degree of mobility of recipients alone is not sufficient to justify the relatively large federal government share in welfare-program grants.

The conclusions, then, are that mobility of taxpayers among jurisdictions is not so severe as to preclude subnational redistributive policies, but that even with generous federal grants many states (representing about half of welfare recipients) choose very low welfare-benefit levels. In Gramlich's (1985b, 43) words, "voters in these low-benefit states appear to have little taste for redistribution. . . ." The issue about the appropriate level of government to carry out redistribution policy depends, then, on our attitudes about this variation in benefit levels. If the variation is tolerable, then the current structure (with perhaps less generous federal grants) is acceptable; if a more uniform standard for benefit levels is desired, then a direct federal income-redistribution program or at least a minimum benefit standard imposed by the federal government is called for.

/ Allocation policy

Government intervention in the market may also be necessary to ensure that society achieves its desired **allocation of resources**—that is, for specific goods and services to be produced in the desired quantities. Here the objective of government, at all levels, is to maintain market competition and to directly provide those goods and services that the private market fails to provide efficiently. The practical issues focus on what specific responsibilities fall into the category of private-market failure, how large government should be to meet those responsibilities, how should the government's resources be generated, and on what mix of services should those resources be spent. Because the government is providing these services as a result of the market's failure to do so in an efficient way, it is important to consider how government can most efficiently provide those services and whether government can in fact do a better job than the market. If a good or service is best provided through government, then the subsequent issue is which level or type of government—federal, state, or local—can most efficiently carry out that responsibility.

Given the conventional wisdom that state–local governments are inherently limited in carrying out stabilization and distribution policy, it is not surprising that the focus of economic analysis and research has been on the allocative role of subnational governments—their role, methods, and effectiveness in directly providing goods and services. That, too, is the primary focus of the rest of this book. Because of the importance traditionally assigned to the allocative role of subnational governments, the economic principles about market efficiency and market failure are first reviewed in Chapter 2 to provide a theoretical framework within which the institutions and practice of state–local government finance can be analyzed and evaluated.

/ Summary

Economic mobility coupled with the choice provided by the diversity of subnational governments is what makes analysis of state–local government finance interesting and different from that of the federal government.

The current substantial relative size of the subnational government sector—about one-third of the total public sector in the United States—arose from a roughly twenty-five-year period of sustained rapid growth between the early 1950s and mid-1970s. Since the mid-1970s, however, the relative size of the state–local government sector has not changed substantially.

Nearly half of the money spent by state–local governments in aggregate provides education or social services and income maintenance, with transportation and public safety being the next two largest categories of spending on direct consumer services. To finance these services, state–local governments receive revenue from five major sources, all of roughly equal importance: charges and fees (19.7 percent of the total), sales taxes (17.5 percent), federal grants (14.9 percent), property taxes (14.4 percent), and income taxes (12.4 percent).

The conventional wisdom is that state–local governments are inherently limited in carrying out stabilization and distribution policy. Therefore, the focus of economic analysis and research has been on the allocative role of subnational governments—their role, methods, and effectiveness in directly providing goods and services. Although individual states and localities are limited in their ability to influence aggregate demand in their own jurisdictions, their collective fiscal decisions do have an effect on national macroeconomic conditions. The mobility of taxpayers among jurisdictions is not so severe as to completely offset subnational redistributive policies, but even with generous federal grants many states (representing about half of welfare recipients) choose to provide a very small amount of income redistribution.

Discussion Questions

1. ''The state–local government sector stopped growing relative to the size of the economy in the late 1970s because of a decline in the amount of federal aid to states and localities.'' Do you think this is correct and why?

2. Although the diversity of subnational governments means that the notion of ''typical'' behavior is often not meaningful, it is still common in presentations of data, news reports, and political debate to compare a state or locality to the ''national average.'' How does the state–local sector in your state compare to that average in terms of (a) the structure of localities, (b) the level of expenditure, (c) the pattern of services provided, and (d) the mix of revenues sources? Do you know of any reasons why your case might differ from the ''national average''?

3. Some surveys show that citizens usually are quite aware of services provided by local governments but often not very certain of the services provided by state governments. Make a list of five services provided by your city/township and five provided by your state that *directly* benefit you. After thinking about how you directly pay for those services, do you believe you get your money's worth?

Selected Readings

Bahl, Roy. ''The Growing Fiscal and Economic Importance of State and Local Governments.'' In *Financing State and Local Governments in the 1980s,* 7–32. New York: Oxford University Press, 1984.

Gramlich, Edward M., ''Reforming U.S. Federal Fiscal Arrangements.'' In *American Domestic Priorities: An Economic Appraisal,* edited by J. Quigley and D. Rubinfeld, 34–69. Berkeley: University of California Press, 1985.

Oates, Wallace. ''An Economic Approach to Federalism.'' In *Fiscal Federalism,* 3–30. New York: Harcourt Brace Jovanovich, 1972.

2 / Microeconomic Analysis: Market Efficiency and Market Failure

The economic function left to state and local governments in the United States system is the allocation function, i.e., the determination of the amount and the mix of local public services to be offered.[1]

Roy Bahl

An important issue of microeconomics is when and why collective action, such as that by government, may be preferable to separate economic decision making by individual consumers and producers, what is usually referred to as the private market. In short, what is the economic rationale for government provision of some goods and services, and how can microeconomic tools be applied to evaluating the relative merits of government and private provision? As noted in Chapter 1, Richard Musgrave has argued that government's economic role may include attainment of a more efficient use of society's resources, alteration of the distribution of resources, and achieving macroeconomic stabilization. But the focus of microeconomic analysis and research concerning state and local governments has been on the first— their effectiveness in directly providing goods and services.

Before the potential for government provision can be evaluated against society's goals, the nature of economic efficiency and the reasons why government intervention may improve upon the results of private-market provision must be clearly understood. In this chapter then, the basic microeconomic principles of market operation and economic efficiency are reviewed, including why private markets may be efficient, the conditions under which private markets will not generate efficiency, the potential distributional concerns from private provision, and the ways government involvement generally in an economy (and not just state–local government) may improve efficiency or resource distribution compared to private markets.

/ The Efficiency of the Market

The concept of economic efficiency most often used in economics is called **Pareto efficiency,** or optimality (named after the Italian economist Vilfredo Pareto (1848–1923)

---

[1]Bahl, Roy. *Financing State and Local Governments in the 1980s*. Oxford, England: Oxford University Press, 1984, 25.

who proposed the definition), which states that *an economy is efficient if it is not possible to make at least one person better off without making someone else worse off.* This concept of economic efficiency is broader than what is often meant by everyday use of the word efficiency. Economic efficiency includes the idea of technical or engineering efficiency, requiring that goods be produced at lowest cost, but it also requires that the type and quantity of goods and services being produced are consistent with society's desires.

The test for efficiency, then, is to search for changes to the current economic situation that will improve the welfare or economic conditions of some people but not decrease the welfare of any others. If such changes are possible, the economy is not efficient; if those changes are not possible, then the original situation is efficient. If the gain to society from one small change is called the **marginal social benefit** and the cost of the change is the **marginal social cost,** then a general efficiency rule for evaluating changes can be stated. *If marginal social benefit is greater or less than marginal social cost, the economy is not efficient, and the proposed change would improve economic efficiency.* If marginal social benefit equals marginal social cost, then the economy is efficient because there is no net gain from any change.

Suppose, for example, that it is possible to produce more goods with the same resources by changing to a different (more efficient) production process. With more goods, the welfare of some (or even all) consumers could be improved at no cost to society. That economy was not producing goods efficiently. By ''welfare,'' economists mean the utility or satisfaction consumers receive from consumption. Because a consumer's utility depends on his or her own preferences—what he or she likes and dislikes—each consumer is the sole judge of his or her own welfare. To put it another way, more goods will not improve a consumer's welfare if that consumer does not like those goods.

As another example, suppose that society decides to produce fewer missiles and to use the freed-up resources to produce more education. If consumers in aggregate value the increased amount of education more than the lost missiles, the economy was not producing an efficient mix of consumer goods. The marginal benefit from providing more education is greater than the marginal cost. At least some consumers are made better off by the change, and any consumers who might be made worse off by the loss of missiles could be compensated (and thus not hurt) because the gain to consumers in aggregate is positive.[2]

This notion of economic efficiency has several advantages and one apparent weakness. The advantages are that value judgments about how much society ''cares'' for different types of consumers are not necessary and that no consumer need be opposed to changes to an inefficient economy. These both follow from the fact that if an economy is not Pareto efficient, no one need be hurt by a change to an efficient situation. The weakness of the definition is the narrow view of inefficiency. If a

---

[2]The efficiency definition only requires that it be *possible* to make some consumers better off without hurting anyone and does not address the issue of how any change actually is to be accomplished. If, in fact, no one is to be hurt by a change, then those who gain from that change would have to compensate those who lose.

potential economic change must hurt even one consumer while making all others better off, by the Pareto definition that situation *is* efficient. Because of that narrowness of definition, achieving Pareto efficiency would not resolve all social issues, but there appears to be no shortage of situations that could be resolved even by this narrow definition.

How do competitive markets satisfy this definition of efficiency? Although elegant mathematics are required to "prove" the efficiency of competitive equilibrium, the underlying principles are easily demonstrated. The long-run equilibrium of a competitive market is depicted in Figure 2.1a. The market demand for the product approximates the marginal benefit to consumers from consuming this good or service, and if producers act to maximize profits, the market supply corresponds to the marginal cost of producing the good or service. At the market equilibrium, then, the marginal cost of producing one more unit equals the marginal benefit— all the possible aggregate social gains from producing this good or service have been achieved. The equilibrium price P^* is equal to both the marginal cost and the marginal benefit.

From the point of view of a typical firm in this competitive market, the equilibrium price also equals the lowest possible production cost per unit—that is, the minimum of the average cost function (Figure 2.1b). At that price, firms are earning normal profits—that is, rates of return equal to those available elsewhere in the economy. Because investors are doing exactly as well in this business as they could in any other, there is no incentive for changes in output or prices.

The dollar magnitude of the gains to society from producing this good or service can also be approximated in Figure 2.1. **Consumer's surplus** is defined as the difference between the marginal benefit to consumers from a unit of the product

FIGURE 2.1   Competitive Market Equilibrium

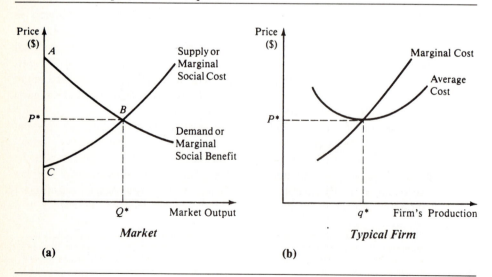

and the market price they actually pay, which is represented by area *ABP** in Figure 2.1a. **Producer's surplus** is defined as the difference between the price charged for the product and the marginal cost of producing a unit of the product, which is similarly represented by area *CBP** in Figure 2.1a. The net gain to society from producing *Q** units of this good or service can be measured by the sum of producer's and consumer's surplus. This is nothing more than the difference between the marginal cost and marginal benefit for each unit, summed for all the units produced.

If marginal social cost does not equal marginal social benefit for the amount of a good or service provided, then the outcome is not efficient, as depicted in Figure 2.2. If 100 units of this product are produced and consumed, the marginal benefit or gain to society from unit 101 is $10, while the cost to society of producing unit 101 is only $5. Production of one more unit of this product (beyond 100) would provide society a net gain in welfare worth $5. Conversely, if the market fails to provide unit 101, society effectively loses or foregoes that potential $5 welfare gain—the outcome is not efficient. Similarly, the marginal benefit is greater than the marginal cost for all the potential units of output between 100 and 200. If output and consumption are restricted to 100 units rather than the efficient quantity of 200, the welfare loss or welfare foregone by society can be measured by area *DEFG*, the sum of producer's and consumer's surplus.

The results in a competitive market when producers act to get the highest possible profits and consumers act to get the greatest possible satisfaction are as follows:

1. Marginal cost equals marginal benefit, with both equal to price.
2. Price equals the lowest possible production cost and producers earn normal profits.

FIGURE 2.2   *Efficiency Requires Equal Marginal Social Cost and Benefit*

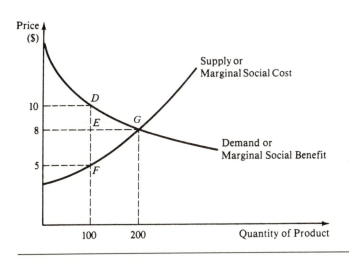

3. Because price equals both marginal cost and marginal benefit in all competitive markets—that is, $P_A^* = MC_A = MB_A$ and $P_B^* = MC_B = MB_B$,—it follows that the relative prices of different products reflect the relative production costs and relative marginal benefits in consumption or $P_A^*/P_B^* = MC_A/MC_B = MB_A/MB_B$.

/ When Markets Are Not Efficient

What might prevent provision through the private-market system from achieving economic efficiency? One possibility is that the marginal cost faced by producers does not reflect all the costs to society from additional production or that an individual consumer's marginal benefit does not equal society's benefit. If benefits accrue to other than the direct consumer or if private production costs do not reflect total social costs, then the competitive market choices may not be socially efficient choices. Although the competitive market sets marginal cost equal to marginal benefit, the costs and benefits are not properly measured. A second possibility is that a lack of competition, such as if economies of scale are present or entry of firms is blocked, may prevent the market from reaching the marginal cost equals marginal benefit equilibrium.

/ Externalities

One problem arises if consumption or production causes **external effects**—that is, if one person's consumption or one firm's production imposes costs or benefits on other consumers or producers. In essence, an **externality** exists if one economic agent's action (consumption or production) affects another agent's welfare and does so outside of changes in market prices or quantities. For instance, in the course of production, one firm (a steel mill) may discharge pollutants into a river, thereby increasing production costs for a downstream firm (a brewer) who must clean the water before using it in production. The pollution is an external effect because it is outside of the steel market—that cost is involuntarily transferred from the steel producer and consumers to the beer producer and consumers. In essence, there is no market or other mechanism to assign a price for river pollution to be paid by the polluter.

Externalities create an efficiency problem because the external costs or benefits usually will not be taken into account by the consumer or producer causing the external effect. If external costs are created by an activity, then the producer or consumer underestimates the social cost of the activity and chooses too much of that activity from society's viewpoint. If consumption or production generates benefits for others that are not considered, then the consumer or producer underestimates social benefits and chooses too little of that economic activity.

This issue is illustrated in Figure 2.3, which shows an individual's marginal benefit (demand) and marginal cost (price) from consuming a particular good or service. Constant marginal cost is assumed only to simplify the illustration. The quantity selected by consumers who equate marginal cost to marginal private benefits

FIGURE 2.3   Market Efficiency with External Benefits

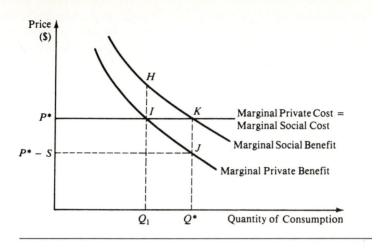

(their benefits) is Q_1. Because each unit of this good purchased by one consumer generates benefits for others as well, the marginal benefit to society is greater than to the direct consumers alone. In that case, the efficient amount of consumption is Q^*, where marginal private cost equals marginal social benefit. Because the direct consumers underestimate benefits, an inefficiently low amount of consumption from society's viewpoint is selected. When externalities are present, private choices by consumers and firms in private markets generally will not provide an economically efficient result. In this particular case, the benefits to other than direct consumers as a result of increasing consumption from Q_1 to Q^* are represented by area *HIJK*. The net gain to society from increasing consumption from Q_1 to the efficient amount is represented by area *HIK*, which is the difference between marginal social benefit and marginal cost.

Government may be able to intervene and create incentives so that private choices of consumers and firms will be efficient in the presence of externalities, however. If there are external costs, a tax equal to the marginal external cost will force the consumer or firm to include all costs in the economic decision, and thus the efficient quantity will be selected. Similarly, inefficiencies caused by external benefits can be corrected by a government subsidy equal to the marginal external benefit. If a consumer underestimates benefits by not considering those that accrue to others and thus chooses too little consumption, the subsidy will reduce private cost and induce an increase in consumption to the efficient amount. Returning to Figure 2.3, if marginal costs are reduced to $P^* - S$ by a subsidy of $\$S$ per unit, then the consumer is induced to choose consumption level Q^*. The externality has been eliminated, and the private market choice of the consumer is efficient.[3]

---

[3]This is exactly the rationale for many intergovernmental grants, to correct the externality that arises when state or locally provided public services provide benefits to nonresidents as well.

Externalities are common among the goods and services provided by state and local governments. Education, police and fire protection, transportation, and sanitation services all have benefits that accrue to those who are not direct consumers and to nonresidents of the communities providing those services. Negative externalities also are important for state and local governments because tax payments do not respect political boundaries. Nonresidents not only enjoy the benefits of services provided by a local government but also may pay part of that local government's cost through taxes.

/ Public goods

The term **public goods** is classically used to refer to goods or services that exhibit two properties. Public goods are *nonrival,* meaning that one additional person can consume the good without reducing any other consumer's benefit; once the good or service is produced, the marginal cost of an additional consumer is zero. Public goods are also *nonexcludable,* meaning that it is not possible (at least at reasonable cost) to exclude consumers who do not pay the price from consuming the good or service. The traditional example of a good said to exhibit both properties is national defense. Once a region is defended, there is no extra cost from adding one person to that region nor can any one individual in the region be excluded from protection. Another example is a lighthouse. Once a lighthouse is operating, an additional ship can be guided by the light while others are using it, and it could be very expensive (if not impossible) to enforce a "lighthouse use fee" on ships that come in view of the light.

If a good is nonrival, the marginal social cost of adding another consumer is zero, so efficiency requires a zero price. A zero price would obviously not provide revenue to cover any fixed costs, so these goods would not be provided in an efficient amount by private firms. Examples of nonrival goods include several usually provided by state–local governments, such as an "uncrowded" street, bridge, or park. If a park is not crowded, then another person can enter and use the park without reducing the enjoyment or benefit of any other user. To charge a fee to enter a park in that case is not efficient because the fee might induce some people not to use the park. Because the resources (mostly land) for the park have already been set aside, use of that resource at less than capacity is wasteful or inefficient from the viewpoint of the entire society. Of course, the problem of deciding on the amount of park services to provide and paying for acquiring those services remains.

The potential for government involvement in providing nonrival goods seems obvious. The task is to collect revenue to cover the fixed costs of a service (the cost of acquiring and operating the park) while maintaining the price for each use of the service equal to zero, that is, equal to the marginal cost. Government can use general taxes to pay the fixed costs, and because those general taxes do not depend on a taxpayer's use of the service, the price for each use is zero.

It is worth noting that nonrival or public goods may be thought of as a special externality case. A nonrival good for which another consumer may be added at no cost to others is simply a good with a substantial benefit externality. Everyone can benefit if only one consumer provides a nonrival good, so the external benefits simply are large compared to the private benefits that go only to the buyer. From this viewpoint, the major difference in an efficiency sense between a nonrival good and an external benefit is the *degree* of public compared to private impact.

If a good exhibits the nonexclusion property, so that it is not feasible to charge a price for consumption, then private firms will also be unable to collect revenue to cover costs. The tax power of government is needed to finance provision of these goods. If a commodity is both nonrival and nonexcludable, then individual consumers have no incentive to reveal their true demand for that good. Instead they can be free riders, benefiting, without paying, from the amount of goods purchased by others. Because all individuals have this incentive to understate their true demand, the quantity of these goods provided usually will be inefficiently low. And even if the efficient quantity of these goods can be determined, efficient use of the good may require prices that preclude private provision, as noted previously.

/ Increasing returns to scale

A final efficiency problem for competitive markets occurs if production of some commodities exhibits **increasing returns to scale**—that is, if a proportional change in all production inputs causes a greater than proportional change in output. For instance, if a doubling of the amounts of labor, land, and capital would cause output to more than double, then average production costs decrease as output increases. If

$$\text{Total Cost} = (\text{Price}_{Labor})\text{Labor} + (\text{Price}_{Land})\text{Land} + (\text{Price}_{Capital})\text{Capital}$$

and

$$\text{Average Cost} = \frac{\text{Total Cost}}{\text{Output}}$$

and the amounts of labor, land, and capital are doubled, then total cost doubles; but if twice as much of each input causes output to more than double, average cost falls.

A cost function reflecting increasing returns to scale is depicted in Figure 2.4. If average cost is decreasing, then marginal cost must be less than average cost at all output amounts (because average cost is decreased by more production if the extra cost of producing one more unit is less than the existing average cost). The usual explanation for this type of cost structure is the existence of fixed costs that are large compared to variable costs. Because fixed costs must be paid regardless of the level of output, a larger output allows those costs to be spread over more units, causing a decrease in cost per unit. This situation often applies to public utilities including electricity, natural gas, water, sewer, or transit services, all of which have large capital requirements even to serve a few customers. Industries with increasing returns to scale are often called **natural monopolies** because it

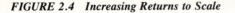

FIGURE 2.4 **Increasing Returns to Scale**

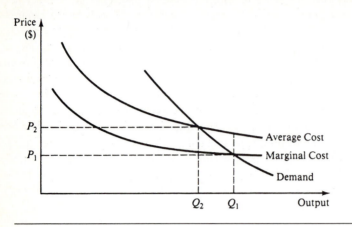

makes sense to have only one producer rather than duplicate the required infrastructure. Why have two separate but parallel water pipes if one is sufficient?

When increasing returns to scale exists, it is impossible to have price equal to marginal cost (which is required for efficiency) *and* have the producer earn a profit. With the demand for the product as shown in Figure 2.4, efficiency requires a price equal to P_1. But at that price and the resulting output Q_1, cost per unit is greater than revenue per unit, so the producer earns negative profits (that is, losses), and no firms would stay in business. In contrast, a price equal to average cost of P_2 allows producers to earn a normal profit or rate of return on investment, but output Q_2 is not efficient because too little of society's resources are applied toward producing this good. The inescapable problem is that with increasing returns to scale a price equal to marginal cost cannot generate enough revenue to cover total costs.

Government intervention may resolve this difficulty. One option is to have government become the producer. This is often done for water, sewer, and transit services but less often for electricity and gas production. The government can charge consumers a price equal to marginal cost and make up the revenue shortfall with general tax receipts. Also, sometimes more complicated pricing schemes can be used to cover the production-cost deficit while allowing the marginal price to equal marginal cost. This topic is expanded on in Chapter 16 in discussing how governments can set efficient user charges. An alternative to government production of goods with increasing returns to scale is regulated monopoly production, with government as the regulator. In that instance, government grants a firm a monopoly in the sale of the good, and attempts to regulate the price so that the producer earns normal profits. In either case, the outcome cannot be efficient because the taxes or regulation create other efficiency problems, so the preferable choice depends on whether government production or regulation works better practically.

/ Distributional Concerns

The standard competitive market analysis also can be used to explain the distribution of resources. The markets determine the prices of various types of labor, land, and capital goods, and those prices together with the quantities of the inputs supplied by individuals determine the resources available for market consumption by each individual. If society values highly the ability to pass a football effectively and if that skill is in short supply, then individuals with the skill will earn high wages and be able to enjoy substantial consumption. If society is not satisfied with the distribution of resources that results from that process, the alternatives are either to directly alter it through transfer payments or subsidies or to reject the market as a means of allocating consumer goods either by altering prices or substituting an entirely different allocation mechanism.

These distributional concerns with the outcome of markets provide another reason for government activity. If there is a social unhappiness with the distribution of resources (income or wealth) among individuals, then the efficient prices for commodities may not be attractive. The traditional economic solution is to transfer resources among individuals until the desired distribution is attained and then allow markets to allocate goods. If the process of redistribution does not have any costs, then that path may be preferable. But redistribution is not costless, because the taxes used to generate revenue and the receipt of transfer payments may alter behavior and create inefficiency and because the institution for redistribution, usually government, is costly itself. An alternative is to alter the prices of specific goods and services. As Peter Steiner (1983) has noted, even if it is practical to charge fees for park use, school bus transportation, and school lunches, it may not be desirable if society desires to alter the pattern of consumption as well as increase the level of consumption for some individuals. And in addition to these equity reasons, society may wish to alter the pattern of consumption for efficiency reasons because of the externalities involved.

/ Efficient Provision of Public Goods

The rule for efficient provision of goods is that the marginal social cost should equal the marginal social benefit. For goods involving externalities or public goods, social costs and benefits will differ from the costs and benefits of the direct consumers. Because all individuals consume a pure public good simultaneously, the **efficiency rule for public goods** is that the *marginal costs to society should equal the sum of the marginal benefits of all consumers,* which is the marginal social benefit.

To illustrate the application of this rule, consider a society with three different individuals (or groups of consumers) each with a different demand for the public good, as shown in Figure 2.5. Person A represents a small demand, Person B a medium level of demand, and Person C a high demand for this public good. A

FIGURE 2.5 *Efficient Quantity of a Public Good*

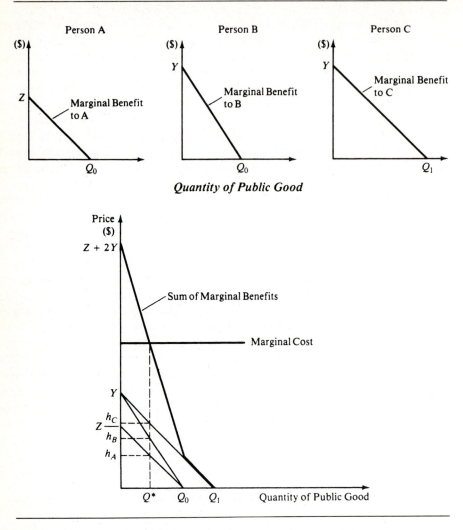

demand function for an individual shows the quantity demanded at *every* price, given that individual's tastes and income and the prices of substitute and complementary goods. The benefits to society equal the benefits to all three consumers together. In the bottom part of Figure 2.5, the marginal benefits of individuals A, B, and C have been added together to give the sum of marginal benefits for all three, labeled

$$\sum_i MB_i$$

which means $MB_A + MB_B + MB_C$.

In calculating this aggregate marginal benefit function, the individuals' marginal benefits are added *vertically*. For example, the demand by Person A shows that the marginal benefit of the first unit is Z; the first unit of national defense, police protection, or whatever provides Z worth of benefit to Person A. Similarly, the marginal benefit of the first unit of public good is Y for both Persons B and C. The marginal benefit of the first unit to all three individuals (that is, society) is therefore $(Z + 2Y)$. The aggregate marginal benefit curve is calculated in that way for every unit of the public good. Although all three consumers receive the same level of public good, only Person C values an amount between Q_0 and Q_1.

The efficient amount of this public good is $Q*$, for which the marginal cost to society equals the sum of individuals' marginal benefits. It is implicit in this rule that the marginal cost includes all the costs to the society, including opportunity costs generated by production (such as pollution). This rule is often called the **Samuelson rule,** or a Samuelson public goods equilibrium, reflecting economist Paul Samuelson's work in deriving the condition. Although the rule was illustrated for a pure public good, the rule also applies to any good involving externalities (recall that public goods are just special cases of external benefits). If consumption of a good by an individual imposes costs on or creates benefits for other individuals, those costs and benefits must be included to satisfy the efficiency rule that marginal social costs equal marginal social benefits.

/ Methods of government provision

An important topic of this book (and one to which we will return often) is how government might be able to achieve or provide for an efficient use of resources. Government can intervene in private markets in at least three ways: by directly providing goods and services, by creating incentives to alter economic decisions through the use of taxes and subsidies, and by regulating private economic activity. Government in the United States, including state and local government, uses all three methods. Government is the sole producer of some goods and services such as streets and highways and a parallel producer with the private sector of other services such as education, police and fire protection, and waste collection and disposal. A variety of taxes and subsidies are used in an attempt to curtail or expand different activities in view of their external effects. Intergovernmental grants, both offered by states to localities and by the federal government to the state–local sector, are one common example of these subsidies in the state–local government arena. In other cases, regulations are imposed on activities of the private sector, such as state regulation of public utilities or private schools, or on the activities of a different level of government, such as state regulation of local police agencies or local schools.

One should not assume, however, that every attempt by subnational governments to improve economic efficiency will be successful. Government provision involves substantial transaction costs, including the administrative costs of the government structure itself, the compliance costs to taxpayers and voters of making economic decisions collectively through government, and the information problems facing government in discerning the "public interest." As Peter Steiner (1983) and Richard Nelson (1987) have argued, the fact that private markets fail to provide goods or services efficiently may be of little relevance if government also cannot provide them efficiently. In that case, some different or at least broader analytical framework than the basic microeconomics reviewed in this chapter is necessary to evaluate the role of government. Society would select government to provide some goods and services, then, if government can better serve the "public interest," not defined solely by economic efficiency. Private provision may be selected for some goods even though the market is inefficient if government provision would be too costly or create other problems; government provision may be selected in other cases even if private-market inefficiencies are insignificant or nonexistent if society seeks another objective such as fairness or security.

Given these cautions about the emphasis on efficiency, it still is instructive to note one special government fiscal structure that may generate the efficient outcome. At the efficient amount of output shown on Figure 2.5, Q^*, the marginal benefits to Persons A, B, and C are labeled h_A, h_B, and h_C, respectively. If these individuals were charged a "price" for this public good equal to h_A, h_B, and h_C, the amount of public good demanded by each individual is Q^*, the efficient amount. Every consumer demands the same amount of government service, which is the efficient amount.

The particular characteristic of this situation that generates the efficient result is that each consumer is being charged a price equal to marginal benefit at the efficient quantity. Although this could perhaps be accomplished by user fees equal to marginal benefits, it is more common in the provision of government goods for the "price" to be the taxes a consumer pays. In that case, each consumer's taxes would have to equal marginal benefit, or at least the *share of taxes* paid by each individual should equal that person's *share of marginal benefits*. The shares for each consumer are

$$S_A = h_A/(h_A + h_B + h_C)$$
$$S_B = h_B/(h_A + h_B + h_C)$$
$$S_C = h_C/(h_A + h_B + h_C)$$
$$S_A + S_B + S_C = 1$$

These tax shares are very much like prices because they show the amount each person would have to pay to increase government spending by $1. For example, if $h_A = 20$ percent, $h_B = 30$ percent, and $h_C = 50$ percent and spending is to increase $1, taxes must also increase by $1, with Person A paying $.20 more, Person B $.30 more, and Person C $.50 more. The price to Person C for another dollar's worth of government service is $.50. If shares equal marginal benefits, then each is willing to pay the price up to the efficient amount. This situation, with tax shares equal to marginal benefit shares, is called a **Lindahl equilibrium** after the Swedish economist Erik Lindahl (1919–58). If consumers' marginal costs reflect their marginal benefits, then the efficient amount of public good will be demanded. Of course, it is not a simple matter to implement that solution.

First, marginal benefits must be measured and assigned to individuals or at least groups of individuals. But this may be an impossible or expensive task in part because consumers have little incentive to reveal their true demand. What, for instance, are the marginal benefits by income class of increasing police service spending by $1? Second, as previously noted, it may not be appropriate to charge marginal prices if the marginal cost of another user is zero. Third, it may not be feasible to exclude consumers from use if they refuse to pay the price set by the government. But the Lindahl equilibrium does offer the possibility of efficiency by converting taxes into a form of user charge with tax shares determined by benefit. This idea of benefit taxation and its efficiency properties is raised again in Chapters 4 and 8 concerning property taxes and in Chapter 16 with a more complete discussion of user charges.

/ Application to State and Local Governments

The problems of public goods, externalities, and increasing returns to scale provide reasons for government action to improve the efficiency of the economy, and many, although certainly not all, state and local government activities can be explained by these reasons. On the other hand, state–local government intervention is not used for all local goods or services that involve externalities or public good properties. Redistribution of society's resources can also be a legitimate and explicit objective of government policy, and although state and local governments may be limited in carrying out redistribution programs, it seems clear that distribution and equity concerns influence many (if not most) state–local government fiscal decisions.

Despite these qualifications, the framework outlined in this chapter does offer some explanation for common fiscal activities and behavior of many state–local governments. Why is government, particularly state and local government, deeply involved in the education business? (As explained in Chapter 1, education is by far and away the largest subnational government budget category.) First, education produces external benefits such as the gains to all from a literate and educated populous and the information generated by research at educational institutions (which is usually considered a public good). Second, education has the potential to be an important mechanism for income redistribution by affecting earnings potential. Third, education benefits cannot generally be confined to a particular geographic area or industrial sector, so intergovernmental arrangements may be called for. The education case may also illustrate reasons for government provision other than the classic economic efficiency arguments. Public education may be a way of implementing a basic notion of fairness—equal opportunity for all—and it has been a primary way society transmits social values and informal rules of behavior.

Similar arguments can be made about police and fire protection. These services are, to a large degree, nonrival and to a somewhat lesser degree, nonexcludable. There are also substantial interjurisdictional externalities (or spillovers) in the provision of these goods. Accordingly, some services of this type are publicly provided by almost every municipality or township in the United States. But these services are

---

/ APPLICATION 2.1
Efficiency and Equity in the Provision of Parks[4]

The potential for using the principles described in this chapter, even without the detail on taxes, user charges, and demand for government services discussed later in this book, is illustrated by this actual case regarding the use of a city's parks.

The city of Dearborn, Michigan, population 90,060 and home of the Ford Motor Company, shares a common border of roughly eleven miles with the city of Detroit, population 1,100,000. Among many significant differences between the cities, one stands out; Detroit's population is composed of more than 60 percent black residents while Dearborn has less than 0.1 percent black residents (83 out of 90,060 in 1985).

In the city election on November 5, 1985, Dearborn voters approved an ordinance restricting the use of the thirty-five city parks and playgrounds (except three) to residents and their guests only. Fifty-one percent of the city's registered voters voted on the issue, which was approved by a margin of 17,790 to 13,976; thus, 56 percent of those voting and 30 percent of the registered voters supported the ordinance. In July, the City Council had voted four to three *against* adopting the ordinance, a decision now overridden by the initiative vote. Accordingly, Dearborn police and park officials were instructed to check the identification of anyone using the parks who was suspected of being a nonresident.

The adoption of this ordinance had been preceded by a long and acrimonious uneasiness between black residents of the Detroit metropolitan area and a previous Dearborn city administration. Given that history, it was charged that the ordinance was primarily intended to exclude blacks from Dearborn parks. The Detroit branch of the NAACP and various civic and religious groups in Detroit initiated a boycott of retail establishments in Dearborn, including one of the major regional shopping malls, the Fairlane Center, for which 30 to 40 percent of the shoppers are black. The NAACP and the American Civil Liberties Union also filed suit in the Circuit Court of Wayne County, which includes both Dearborn and Detroit, seeking to have the ordinance declared unconstitutional. In November 1985, Dearborn agreed to

---

[4]*This section is based on various articles from* The Detroit Free Press *between November 1985 and September 1986. For instance, see Wylie Gerdes and M. Kim Heron, "Dearborn Agrees to Delay on Parks Law," 28 November 1985; and Brenda J. Gilchrist and Wylie Gerdes, "Judge Voids Non-residents Ordinance," 30 September 1986.*

---

also provided privately in the form of private security guards at businesses, private security patrols in some neighborhoods, and privately purchased and owned equipment such as locks, burglar alarms, and smoke detectors and fire extinguishers. Yet all of these activities also generate external effects. Largely for the economic reasons, government takes a central but not an exclusive role in providing these services.

Transportation provides a final illustration. State and local governments finance, own, and operate transportation facilities such as streets and highways, airports,

---

/ APPLICATION 2.1 Continued
Efficiency and Equity in the Provision of Parks

postpone enforcement of the ordinance until the court rendered a decision, in exchange for an end to the boycott.On September 29, 1986, the Wayne County Circuit Court ruled that the Dearborn ordinance was a violation of both the United States and Michigan Constitutions. The Court noted that Dearborn officials would have "totally unguided discretion as to when and where stops would be made, and as to whom they would stop." Given the very small number of Dearborn residents who are black and the large number of black Detroiters, there would be a tendency to check all black park users but not all white park users, which in the opinion of the Court constituted an unreasonable search and seizure. The Court also noted that Dearborn had a legal right to adopt an ordinance to correct overcrowding and rowdiness in its parks, but that enforcement must not be discriminatory.

This is, at least partly, an economic issue. A service spillover was involved because Dearborn residents were concerned that nonresident park users did not pay for acquiring or operating the parks. Dearborn residents were also apparently concerned about externalities within the parks due to crowding and unruly behavior. The ordinance was overturned due to its enforcement provisions rather than its intent. How might the Dearborn parks problem have been approached from an economic viewpoint?

Following the argument in this chapter that prices should equal marginal cost, one obvious solution would be an entrance or use fee for the parks. Differential fees could be charged to residents and nonresidents to reflect the fact that nonresidents generally pay less in city taxes than do residents to support the parks (nonresidents pay some, in part because Dearborn has a city income tax which applies to residents and nonresident workers). The fees could also differentiate between times when the parks are crowded (summer weekends) and when they are not. If the parks are truly not crowded, then no (or little) cost is incurred if anyone, resident or nonresident, uses the park. Perhaps the easiest solution, then, was to collect a park entrance fee only on evenings and weekends at times of the year when the parks are widely used, which could be greater for nonresidents. If such a proposal were not acceptable to the voters, then it would be clearer that the concern of the majority of voters is not paying for the parks or park congestion but racial discrimination.

---

and public-transit systems. The economic efficiency arguments again provide some explanation. If uncrowded, these goods are nonrival, requiring a zero price for efficiency. Benefit spillovers among different jurisdictions providing the facilities also are common, requiring some coordinating mechanism. Although state and local governments provide these facilities, they seldom produce them, rather usually contracting with or buying from private firms, thereby taking advantage of any economies of scale in production.

/ Summary

Some important aspects of microeconomics are reviewed in this chapter. An economy is Pareto efficient if it is not possible to make at least one person better off without making someone else worse off. Market efficiency requires that marginal social benefits equal marginal social costs.

Public goods are nonrival, meaning that one additional person can consume the good without reducing any other consumer's benefit. Once a nonrival good is produced, the marginal social cost of another consumer is zero, so efficiency requires a zero price.

An externality exists if one economic agent's action (consumption or production) affects another agent's welfare outside of the market. When externalities are present, private choices by consumers and firms in private markets generally will not provide an economically efficient result. Government may be able to intervene and create incentives through the use of taxes and subsidies so that private choices of consumers and firms will be socially efficient in the presence of externalities.

If production of some commodities exhibits increasing returns to scale, it is impossible to have price equal to marginal cost (which is required for efficiency) and have the producer earn a profit. Government may resolve this difficulty either by becoming the producer or by regulating monopoly production.

Many, although not all, state–local government activities can be explained by the problems of public goods, externalities, and increasing returns to scale. Redistribution of society's resources can also be a legitimate and explicit objective of government policy.

Discussion Questions

1. In parts of the country where snow is a regular occurrence, snow removal from public streets is almost always provided by a local government, but snow removal from public sidewalks is seldom provided by government. Sidewalk clearing is either left to individual choice or regulated by the government, perhaps by requiring that property owners clear the walks along their property. Yet the theoretical aspects of these two services are the same. What factors might explain why local governments typically don't plow sidewalks or, from the other point of view, why localities do not simply require property owners to clear snow from streets along their property? What does this imply about the standard externality/public goods argument justifying government intervention?

2. "For an efficient amount of a public good to be provided, the marginal cost of producing another unit of that good must equal the marginal benefit to each individual who consumes the good." Is this statement true or false, and why?

3. Explain why the existence of benefit spillovers across jurisdiction boundaries could lead the jurisdictions to provide too little of that service from society's

viewpoint. If the service in question is public safety, what might be the nature of common benefit spillovers?

Selected Readings

Bator, Francis M. "The Anatomy of Market Failure." *Quarterly Journal of Economics* 72 (August 1958): 351–79.

Samuelson, Paul A. "Diagrammatic Exposition of a Theory of Public Expenditure. *Review of Economics and Statistics* 37 (1955): 350–56.

Steiner, Peter. "The Public Sector and the Public Interest." In *Public Expenditure and Policy Analysis,* edited by R. Haveman and J. Margolis, 3–41. Boston: Houghton Mifflin, 1983.

Part 2

Public Choice and Fiscal Federalism

The most distinguishing feature of subnational governments is the sheer number of them and the ease of moving among them. These physical characteristics have economic implications, however, and perhaps none so important as the implications for tax and expenditure choice by those same subnational governments. That is the general topic of Chapters 3–5.

On one hand, the existing structure of a fiscal federalism—the comparative number and fiscal characteristics of cities, counties, and special purpose districts—must influence the fiscal choices of each subnational government. Tax competition among communities for new businesses and service competition for new residents are only the most obvious ways this influence is manifested. Given any existing federal structure then, the issue is whether the fiscal choices of those governments are likely to be efficient and, if not, whether realignment of fiscal responsibilities within that structure would improve things. For example, given a set of local governments in a metropolitan area, should one service, say police protection, be transferred from city to county government?

On the other hand, knowledge of the types and characteristics of the services to be provided may allow one to consider the best federal structure to provide those services. In that case, the issue is how many governments there should be, or equivalently how big they should be. At one end of the spectrum, some services may only require one government, in which case it would cover the entire nation. In contrast, some services may be better provided if there are many small governments.

The issue then is the optimal design of subnational governments or the optimal fiscal responsibilities among existing subnational governments. In the following three chapters, we explore what economics has to contribute about how individual choice about the activities of government affects the best structure for government to take.

3 / Public Choice Without Mobility: Voting

. . . The measurement of the preferences for [public] goods . . . cannot be subjected to individual consumer choice. The closest substitute for consumer choice is *voting*.[1]

Howard R. Bowen

/ Fiscal Choices

State and local governments face three fundamental fiscal choices. The first is the choice of revenue or tax structure—that is, what different types of revenue sources should be used and in what relative mix. The second choice is the level of total spending and thus the total amount of revenue required. Given a choice of tax structure, adjustments in the level of spending can be accomplished by moving all tax rates up or down as required without changing that basic revenue structure. Finally, the government must choose how to allocate total spending among the various goods and services demanded by voters. This is the decision of which services to provide in what quantity within the total spending goal.

Do not assume that these choices are made separately because the level of spending desired by an individual almost always depends on what he or she believes the money will be spent for. That is, the desired level of spending may depend on the mix of services provided. The level of spending desired also depends on the choice of revenue structure because the tax and charge system determines the cost or price of government spending to each individual. A person who is exempt from local taxes, for example, is likely to be more supportive of increased local spending than another person who expects to pay the resulting higher taxes.

It does appear, however, that governments make some of these decisions more often than others. The level of spending and taxes usually changes each year, sometimes more often, and commonly by a substantial amount. But the mix of government services may change only in a more gradual way as incremental adjustments are made in each budget cycle. Over a ten-year period, a city may find itself spending a larger fraction of its budget on public safety and less on education, but it is unlikely for that total change to have occurred in any one year. Finally, the revenue structure may be the most stable of all. Adoption of new taxes or fees

---

[1]"The Interpretation of Voting in the Allocation of Economic Resources." *The Quarterly Journal of Economics* 58 (Nov. 1943): 33.

or major structural changes to increase the reliance on one tax at the expense of another are relatively rare. More commonly, rates are adjusted for each budget to provide revenues sufficient for the spending plan.[2] Therefore, although we should recognize that these three fiscal decisions are interrelated, it may not be an unrealistic approximation to separate them in order to get the analysis started.

One important way that these fundamental state and local government fiscal decisions are made is by voting. Because these goods and services are not being sold in a traditional market, it is not possible for individuals to select and pay for the quantities of each which they desire. Unlike the choice of two hamburgers, fries, and a milk for $3.65, the city resident cannot order two police patrols per hour, a high school education emphasizing science, and one (unlimited) garbage collection per week for $1200 per year. Those choices are made collectively with the other city residents (or voters). And the use of voting to make these choices suggests that not all residents agree, so that voting becomes a method of resolving different desires.

Another way of resolving these differences in desired local government fiscal activity has similarities to individual shopping in private markets. If there are many different localities available for residential choice, individuals may select among them based on the package of taxes and services provided. For purposes of the current discussion, we assume that individuals are not mobile, that they must make fiscal decisions for the community in which they reside. The alternative to voting created by the mobility of residents will be explored in detail in Chapter 4.

In this chapter, the economic implications of several different types of voting on fiscal decisions are examined. We begin by examining the most common method, majority voting, and then consider how the outcome of majority voting may depend on the political characteristics of the government. This line of inquiry, which bridges economics and political science, is now almost a separate discipline called the study of public choice. Obviously, all public-choice issues cannot be covered in this one chapter, so the concentration is on those basic results that are most often applied to analyzing state and local government actions.

/ Desired government spending

It is almost axiomatic that not everyone desires the same things from government. To an economist, this suggests that individuals have different demand functions for government services. Individuals may have different demands for the same government service either because they have different incomes or because they value the service differently, that is, they have different tastes for that service.

To illustrate different demands, the example from Chapter 2 of three individuals (or groups), each with a different demand for government services, continues in Figure 3.1. Assuming that all three have the same tastes, then income differences

---

[2]It is an old debate in public finance whether governments "tax to spend," in which case all revenues generated by the existing structure are spent, or "spend to tax," in which case tax rates are set to fund the selected spending level. The characterization of three separate fiscal decisions for analytical purposes does not presume the answer to the debate nor which decisions "come first."

FIGURE 3.1   Demand For a Public Good

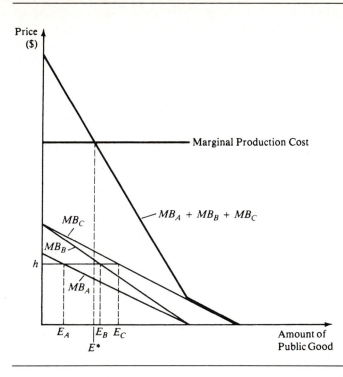

would be a reason for the different demands. If state and local government services are normal goods (which is usually the case), demand increases with income. For the example in Figure 3.1, it would require that Income$_A$ < Income$_B$ < Income$_C$. Alternatively, if Persons A, B, and C all have the same income, then demand differs because the three value the service differently, with Person C getting the greatest benefit from the service. Of course, it is also possible for demand to differ because both income and tastes vary among individuals.[3]

Even when an individual's demand function is known, to determine the desired amount or quantity of the government service one must know that individual's price. Individuals "buy" government services with the taxes and fees that they pay, so the tax structure determines each individual's price. Here we assume that this government has selected a tax structure that is not changed depending on the level of spending. The government adjusts the tax rates to generate more or less revenue as required, but the tax mix—the share of revenue from each source—remains the same.

_____

[3]It is useful to remember that because mechanisms to induce individuals to reveal their true demand for public goods are generally absent, these demands are not known. Thus, public officials cannot directly compute the desired level of services; voting is a mechanism for individuals to reveal their desires.

The price to each individual then is his or her share of total taxes. For instance, if the government finances services by a property tax, each individual pays an amount equal to the tax rate times the property value or Rate · Value$_i$. Each individual's share of taxes is equal to Rate · Value$_i$/Σ_i Rate · Value$_i$, which reduces to Value$_i$/Sum of values. Similar tax shares can be defined for any given tax structure.

To carry through the example, we assume the simplest tax structure in which each individual pays the same tax so that each has an equal tax share. In the example with three individuals, each pays one-third of the taxes collected by the government. In other words, the price to each individual of buying another dollar's worth of government services is \$.333.[4]

Given these different demands and the assumed tax shares, the price charged each person is one-third of marginal production cost, or h. The desired quantities of government service are E_A, E_B, and E_C, respectively. Because all taxpayers face the same tax price in this example, the differences in desired quantities are determined entirely by the differences in demand.

The problem for the government is choosing among the different desired quantities of government service that result from the combination of demand and tax shares. Because the nature of government goods is that one quantity is provided to all consumers, some compromise will be decided by voting. We turn now to a comparison of various voting methods.

/ Majority Voting

The most common voting method is majority voting. Sometimes voting is directly on budget issues such as in local government property tax–rate elections and sometimes voting is for officials who then make the allocation decisions for us. The victorious position or candidate in a majority vote is one that is supported by at least 50 percent plus one of the votes.

Returning now to the example in Figure 3.1, suppose that this government uses majority voting to choose among the three spending levels. Which one, if any, will receive majority support? If the government selects between E_A and E_B, Person A will vote for E_A, his preferred amount of spending, while Person B will vote for E_B. Of these two options, understanding that neither is his first choice, which will Person C select? Because Person C prefers an even greater amount of spending than either A or B, we expect that C will support level E_B because it is closer to the desired amount than E_A. Therefore, spending level E_B receives two votes and is selected by the community over A's preferred amount.

How does the community view E_B compared to the higher level E_C? Again, a majority vote would find Person B supporting E_B and Person C supporting E_C, while Person A would support B over C because spending level E_B is closer to the

---

[4]If incomes differ among the taxpayers, this is a regressive tax system because tax as a fraction of income would decline as income increased (see Chapter 6).

low level A prefers. Spending level E_B would be selected as the winner of the majority vote.

This simple example illustrates an important point about majority voting that is often misunderstood. Spending level E_B was selected not because a majority of the voters preferred it, but because it was the *only choice that could receive majority support*. If a low-spending level was proposed, Persons B and C could band together to defeat it, while, similarly, A and B could prevent the high-spending level from being selected. As a result of this majority vote then, Persons A and C are forced to compromise and accept a spending amount different from what they prefer. Only Person B is perfectly happy with the outcome. The results of this example can be, and have been, generalized.

/ Will there be only one winner of a majority vote?

One concern about majority voting is that there may not be a clear-cut winner or that the winner will be different depending on the order in which the choices are considered. This problem may occur if each voter does not have **single-peaked preferences**—that is, each voter does not have a clearly preferred alternative and does not continually get less satisfaction as one moves away from that alternative in either direction.

The potential difficulty with majority voting when preferences are not single-peaked is shown with this example. Again, suppose there are three possible spending levels denoted E_1, E_2, and E_3, going from low to high. Preferences toward those spendings levels are as follows:

Person	First Choice	Second Choice	Third Choice
A	E_1	E_2	E_3
B	E_2	E_3	E_1
C	E_3	E_1	E_2

Person C wants a high level of government spending most but a low level is his second choice; the medium amount of spending is least preferred. In a vote between levels 1 and 2, 1 receives two votes (from A and C) and wins. Similarly, in a vote between levels 1 and 3, 3 receives two votes (from B and C) and wins. It appears that spending level E_3 has been selected by majority vote and is most preferred. But suppose level E_3 is compared with E_2 in a vote. Surprisingly, 2 receives two votes (from A and B) and wins. The voting results are not consistent. Level 3 beats 1, level 1 beats 2, but level 2 beats 3. The implication is that the winner depends on the order in which the votes are taken. Level 3 wins if 1 is first put against 2 and the winner put against level 3, but level 1 wins if 2 is first put against 3 and the winner put against level 1.

This result occurs because Person C's preferences are not single-peaked. As spending is decreased from the most preferred high level, Person C becomes less and less happy until spending becomes very low, and C's happiness increases again. Person C is an extremist who is least happy with moderate positions. If preferences

FIGURE 3.2 Demand and Consumer Surplus

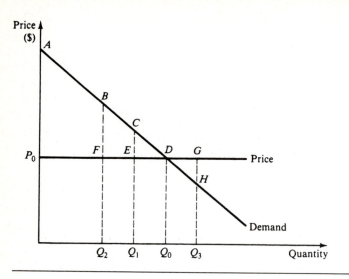

exhibit this property, then majority voting *may* be inconsistent (that is, the results are not transitive).

The potential for inconsistency may be a theoretical but not real problem in using majority voting to select amounts of government spending because standard downward-sloping demand curves imply single-peaked preferences. With the demand curve and individual price shown in Figure 3.2, Q_0 is the desired quantity. The consumer has consumer surplus—the difference between the maximum amount the consumer is willing to pay and the price—equal to the area ADP_0. As this consumer moves away from Q_0, the consumer's surplus, thus the consumer's happiness, continually decreases. At Q_1 the surplus is represented by the area $ACEP_0$; at the lower-quantity Q_2, the surplus is even smaller, represented as $ABFP_0$. If quantity is increased from Q_0 to Q_3, consumer's surplus would also decrease, being equal to area ADP_0 minus area DGH. In short, the desired quantity may be small or large, but if demand is always downward-sloping, then consumer happiness continually decreases the greater the distance from that desired amount. That is, preferences are single-peaked.[5]

In thinking about potential problems with majority voting, one must also consider the nature of the commodity for which preferences must be single-peaked. The commodity must be able to be characterized by a single, quantifiable and continuous parameter. In the case of government finance, government expenditure (in dollars) appears to be such a measure. But expenditure is really a measure of

---

[5]Of course, individuals still might have extremist positions regarding state–local finance issues— for instance, favoring a high level of education spending so that the public schools provide academic and extracurricular services to all students or, in the alternative, having all education done privately.

input purchases rather than goods and service production. If a government provides several services, a single expenditure amount is consistent with many different service combinations, so that total expenditure may not be an accurate parameter on which to base consumer preferences. The voting system must select the mix of services and the level of total spending. For that reason, the majority-voting model of government fiscal choice may be most applicable to single-purpose subnational governments such as school districts or separate utility, park, and transit districts.

Finally, the possibility of strategic behavior or collusion on the part of voters must be considered. If voters do not vote their true preferences in hopes of skewing the result or trading their vote on one issue for others' votes on a different issue, then majority voting again may be inconsistent. Although vote trading and negotiation may occur in legislative bodies, it is not expected to be as common in general voter elections because of the difficulty of arranging and enforcing collusion among a large number of people. Still, many if not most fiscal decisions are made by legislative bodies, which raises many other issues involving vote trading, lobbying, campaign contributions, and other ways of influencing the legislative outcome. In essence, then, the issue is whether state and local fiscal decisions can be represented *as if they were made by the participatory majority-voting process,* even if a more complex political process was actually involved.

/ The Median-voter theorem

A general rule of majority voting can now be stated: If voters' preferences are single-peaked, if the choice to be made by voting is represented along a single continuum, if all alternatives are voted on, and if voters act on their true preferences, then *the choice selected by majority vote is the median of the desired outcomes.* For those of you for whom statistics remain a mystery, the **median** is the potential outcome in the middle of the continuum—that is, the one with half of the potential choices lower and half-higher.

Applying this theorem to the choice of government expenditures suggests that if all individuals' demand curves for government services are downward-sloping, then the expenditure selected by majority vote will be the median of those individuals' desired expenditure amounts. In the simple example of Figure 3.1, the median is expenditure E_B, which is in the middle between E_A and E_C. Two other cases are shown in Figure 3.3, each with seven voters and seven different desired expenditure amounts. For case A, the median is expenditure amount 4, with three voters preferring a smaller amount and three preferring larger ones. Despite a very different structure of preferences for case B, the median, and thus the winner of a majority vote, is still the same expenditure amount 4.[6]

This illustrates an important point about the **median statistic** and thus the median winner of a majority vote. The median often does not change even if other

---

[6]It will be important to think about the economic characteristics of the median voter, particularly whether the median voter is the voter with median income. That issue and the use of the median-voter model for measuring demand are discussed in Chapter 14.

FIGURE 3.3 Illustration of Median-Desired Expenditure

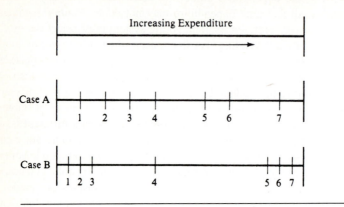

possible outcomes do change. Although voters 1, 2, and 3 prefer lower amounts in case B compared to case A and voters 5, 6, and 7 prefer higher amounts, the median is the same in both cases. The government expenditure level selected by majority vote, then, does not depend on the relative *strength* of the voters' preferences but only on their *order.*

All the examples so far have coupled each potential expenditure with only one voter, which may be somewhat unrealistic. What might be a more real-world characterization of preferences is shown in Figure 3.4, with the percentage distribution

FIGURE 3.4 Distribution of Desired Public Expenditure

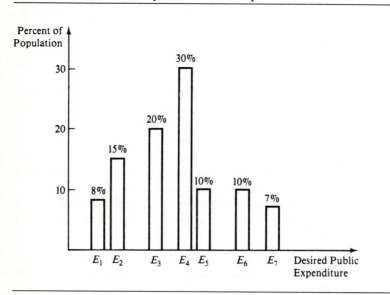

of voters shown for seven potential expenditure amounts. Thus, 15 percent of this jurisdiction's voters prefer expenditure amount E_2 while 20 percent prefer E_3 and so on. The median amount in this distribution is E_4 because if all the voters were counted in order of desired expenditure, the middle would come among the 30 percent who prefer E_4. This occurs despite the fact that 43 percent of the voters prefer an amount less than E_4 and 27 percent prefer a greater amount. Another way to look at the situation is that 60 percent of the voters prefer expenditures "close to" E_4 while 23 percent prefer much lower expenditures and 17 percent prefer much higher.

The discussion of majority voting to choose a government's expenditure has assumed an actual vote among taxpayers on the issue, what is usually called participatory democracy. But what of representative democracy, when voters elect representatives who then select the expenditure. Will the median-voter theorem still apply? In fact, it may. Suppose that candidates for a representative position campaign on the amount of government expenditure (and thus public service) they propose to implement. One candidate might campaign promising to restrict government spending (perhaps to amount E_2 in Figure 3.4) while another might propose new programs that would increase spending to amount E_6. If that happened, a third candidate could defeat those two by proposing spending amount E_4, the median amount. Remember that a majority of voters will always support E_4 over any alternative and thus should support a candidate proposing E_4 over candidates proposing any other amounts. The tendency for political candidates to try to stake out a moderate position in election campaigns is common.

In applying the median-voter model to analyze state and local government fiscal decisions, economists often assume that those decisions are made as if there had been a direct majority vote of the taxpayers. While political scientists and economists have examined in detail the conditions under which this will be true, the crucial factor for economists seems to be the amount of political competition. If elections are held often and if entry into the political wars is easy, then officials may be pushed toward the median choice to stay in power. This is the parallel of market competition (or potential competition) that pushes firms toward producing and setting prices at minimum average cost. More will be said on this question later in this chapter.

/ Characteristics of the median-voter result

The most fundamental characteristic of the median-voter choice of government expenditure is the inherent dissatisfaction among taxpayers with the outcome. For the example depicted in Figure 3.4, only 30 percent of the voters actually desire the outcome selected by majority vote while 70 percent are dissatisfied to some degree. In fact, it is possible that only *one* voter, the median voter, will be perfectly satisfied with the outcome of a majority vote. This characteristic is inherent in the model because the reason for voting in the first place is to choose among different desired outcomes with the resulting compromise requiring some dissatisfaction.

Indeed, this characteristic is one reason the median-voter model is attractive to economists. The model predicts what is apparently observed. As part of a series of public-finance surveys taken annually by The U.S. Advisory Commission on Intergovernmental Relations, respondents are asked, "Considering all government services on the one hand and all taxes on the other, which of the following comes closest to your view?" Respondents could answer "increase both," "decrease both," or "keep them about where they are." The results for three recent years are shown in Table 3.1.

The percentage finding the amount of taxes and spending "about right" varies from 42 to 52 percent while roughly 6 percent would prefer substantially greater amounts of spending (and taxes) and slightly more than one-third would prefer substantially less. Although this survey applies to all types of government spending together, similar results are obtained if this type of question is applied to a single state or local government. It is simply true that in almost every community there are some voters who want a smaller government, some who want a bigger one, and a substantial number, sometimes even a majority, who are approximately satisfied with the current state.

A second important characteristic of the median-voter model is that the amount of public expenditure selected will, in general, not be the economically efficient amount. Efficiency would result really only by accident. Moreover, there is no method for inefficiency to be removed. This is easily shown, for instance, by the example of Figure 3.1, in which the median amount chosen by majority vote, E_B, is not equal to the efficient amount E^*. As seen in Chapter 2, the efficient amount requires that the sum of individuals' marginal benefits equal marginal production cost while the median voters' desired amount (which becomes the community's selection) requires only that their marginal benefit equal their marginal tax cost.

Majority voting can lead to government spending greater than the efficient amount, as shown in Figure 3.1, but it is equally possible for majority voting to lead to too little. In general, it is not possible to predict which occurs, because the result depends on the relationship of tax price to marginal benefit and on the price elasticity of demand. But it is easy to understand *why* majority voting might not be efficient. Suppose that in a community of three voters one prefers school spending of $1000 per student, another $1500, and the third $5000. If tax shares are the

TABLE 3.1

ACIR Survey; Desired Changes in Taxes and Spending

| | Percentage Responding[a] | | |
Year	Increase	Decrease	Remain the Same
1982	8	36	42
1980	6	38	45
1977	4	31	52

[a]Totals do not add to 100 because a fourth possible response, "no opinion," is not shown.

same for all three, these amounts reflect only the relative benefits perceived by the three. The median is obviously $1500 per student. The choice of the efficient amount, however, recognizes that the third voter has a substantially higher marginal benefit than do the others at every amount, which causes the efficient amount to exceed the median. Majority voting does not take account of strength or magnitude of preference.

To summarize, if the amount of government spending by a state or local government is determined as if a majority vote were taken among the residents, the amount selected is the median of the residents' desired amounts. That median amount is not likely to be economically efficient, and a large number of voters, perhaps even a majority, will be dissatisfied with the choice.

There are two ways to reduce dissatisfaction: change prices or change tastes. If the government's tax system is altered so that the tax price increases for those voters who now prefer expenditure greater than the median, their preferred amount will decrease. And if, correspondingly, tax price decreases for those who want expenditure less than the median, their preferred amount will increase. Because the preferred expenditure amounts move toward the median, the unhappiness with government expenditure decreases. To eliminate the dissatisfaction totally requires that tax prices be proportional to marginal benefits so that each individual prefers the same amount. The difficulties with achieving such a benefit tax structure were noted in Chapter 2. Alternatively, tastes could change if the dissatisfied voters left this community for another while new residents with tastes similar to the current median voter's moved in. In that case, the differences in demand are eliminated and with them the dissatisfaction. That possibility is discussed in Chapter 4.

/ Monopoly Models of Fiscal Choice

Although majority voting is the most common public-choice method used and the median-voter model does predict some commonly observed conditions, many other fiscal-choice models have also been proposed. One of the most interesting of these other models is one in which the government has some monopoly power over fiscal decisions. The majority-voting/median-voter model implicitly assumes that the government's role is simply to implement voters' desires about government services and that it does so in a politically competitive environment. In contrast, these monopoly models assume that government officials attempt to implement their *own* preferences and try to get voters to go along. Officials or bureaucrats may be able to do that if they have more experience or more information than the voters and if they have and can maintain a political monopoly.

Monopoly models were first discussed by William Niskanen who proposed that bureaucrats attempt to maximize the size of their budgets subject only to a desire to remain in power. Since then, several different variants have arisen. There are several common assumptions among all the variants, however, so we examine these

FIGURE 3.5 A Monopoly Bureaucrat Model of Public Expenditure Choice

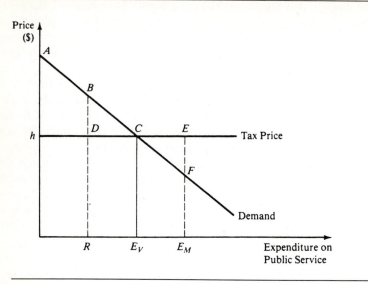

type of models by discussing the specific one proposed and used by Thomas Romer and Howard Rosenthal to analyze local government spending.[7]

The assumptions of the model are as follows:

1. Government officials have two objectives: maximize the amount of government spending and remain in office.
2. Government officials know the preferences of the residents of their communities.
3. The amount of government spending will be selected by majority vote of the residents. Importantly, there are a limited number of options that may be voted on and the government officials select those options.
4. If a majority of voters accepts none of the options proposed by the government, government spending reverts to a predetermined amount.

In essence, there is limited majority voting but the agenda from which voters may choose is determined by the government officials who wish to spend as much as possible.

The potential outcome of this monopoly, agenda control model is illustrated in Figure 3.5, which shows both the demand for government services and tax price of the median voter in the community. This voter prefers expenditure E_V, which is the amount chosen by majority vote of all the options and predicted by the median-

---

[7]See Niskanen (1968) and Romer and Rosenthal (1979a).

voter theorem. But suppose that if voters do not approve any of the amounts offered by the government in a limited number of votes, then expenditure automatically (because of some other law) is set at amount R, which is called the reversion amount. In other words, the reversion amount is the threatened or imposed expenditure if voters do not approve what government officials offer.

Suppose government officials, knowing all of this, propose a spending amount equal to E_M. If this voter understands that this is the only chance to vote, there is a quandry; the choice is effectively R or E_M. Given the conditions in Figure 3.5, this voter is indifferent about R and E_M. That is, this voter would get the same satisfaction from either expenditure amounts R or E_M, which would be less than from the most preferred amount E_V. At amount R, the consumer's surplus is represented by the area $ABDh$, which equals area ACh minus area BCD. At amount E_M, the consumer's surplus is represented by area ACh minus area CEF. The latter triangle is subtracted because for all amounts above E_V, the consumer's marginal benefit is less than the price, implying a loss of welfare. Finally, because triangle BCD equals triangle CEF by construction, the consumer's surplus at E_M also equals area $ABDh$. This voter would be equally hurt by less-than-desired government spending at R or more than desired at E_M.

If the alternative is R therefore, this voter would *prefer* any amount less than E_M. An expenditure proposal for a small amount less than E_M, even $1 less, would be approved by the voters rather than allow spending to fall to amount R, which would be worse. Because government officials want to spend as much as possible, they would propose spending $\$(E_M - 1)$. As a result, majority voting is used to choose expenditure, and the median voter's demand determines the outcome, but the amount chosen is greater than that most preferred by the median voter and that predicted by the median-voter model.

The crucial features that give this model its characteristics are the nature of the reversion amount and the absence of political competition. Consider each in turn. The simplest reversion is zero—that is, unless the voters approve a proposed expenditure, there will be no government service. Obviously, if voters believe this is a credible threat, it will be a powerful one. Most voters would be willing to accept some excess in government spending to prevent the loss of all government services. But in reality, reversions are usually not zero. In presenting the model, Romer and Rosenthal (1979a) suggest that it represents the situation in many school districts where residents vote on a proposed school budget (or taxes) with the reversion equal to either a state-mandated minimum school expenditure or the previous year's spending amount. As long as the reversion is less than the voter's desired expenditure, the lower is the reversion, the more monopoly government officials can exploit their positions to increase spending.

Therefore, those government officials also have a great interest in how and at what amount the reversion is set. Indeed, one of the weaknesses of this model is that the reversion amount is somehow predetermined, although it too must be selected by some type of fiscal-choice mechanism. One should also not get the idea that this method is riskless for government officials. Individuals' preferences can never be known exactly, and one is also not sure which residents will be voters. If government officials err in selecting the proposed expenditure and select too high, voters will decide to reject the proposal and effectively accept the reversion. As a result, government officials lose by having a smaller amount of government expenditure than the median voter preferred (remember that officials are assumed to be budget maximizers).

An absence of effective political competition is also crucial for the model's results. If government officials are successful in using a reversion expenditure as a threat to force voters to accept greater amounts of expenditure than they prefer, an opportunity is created for opponents in the next election to campaign on the promise of lower expenditure amounts. In effect, opponents can control the agenda in the election and by selecting a median position defeat incumbents. Of course, nothing is to prevent newly elected officials from playing the same game, except the danger of potential defeat at the subsequent election.

In other words, this model seems most applicable to governments dominated by a single political party or group, so that *effective* competition is absent. There have been notable examples. Erastus Corning, a Democrat, was mayor of Albany, New York, from 1942 until his death in 1983, a period of forty-two years. This surpasses even the twenty-two years Richard Daley, also a Democrat, was mayor of Chicago. Of course, it could be that these politicians stayed in office so long because they gave voters exactly what they wanted, and the fact that almost everyone recognizes these examples suggests that they are relatively uncommon. Proponents of monopoly fiscal-choice models must identify the institutional factors in each case where the model is to be used, which allow officials to *continually* not satisfy the voters' desires.

/ Summary

State and local governments face three fundamental fiscal choices, the choice of revenue or tax structure, the level of total spending, and how to allocate total spending among the various goods and services demanded by voters. Do not assume that these choices are made separately.

Individuals may have different demand for the same government service either because they have different incomes or because they value the service differently. The price to each individual is his or her share of total taxes. The problem for the government is choosing among the different desired quantities of government service, which result from the combination of demand and tax shares.

The most common voting method used to make government-allocation decisions is majority voting. The victorious position or candidate in a majority vote is the one that is supported by at least 50 percent plus one of the voters. If a spending amount is selected by majority vote, it is not necessarily because a majority of the voters preferred it, but because it was the only choice that could receive majority support.

If voters' preferences are single-peaked, if the choice to be made by voting is represented along a continuum, and if voters act on their true preferences, then the choice selected by majority vote is the median of the desired outcomes.

The most fundamental characteristic of the median-voter choice of government expenditure is the inherent dissatisfaction among taxpayers with the outcome. In almost every community, there are some voters who want a smaller government, some who want a bigger one, and a substantial number, although not always a majority, who are approximately satisfied with the current state.

A second important characteristic of the median-voter model is that the amount of public expenditure selected will, in general, not be the economically efficient amount. The efficient amount requires that the sum of individuals' marginal benefits equal marginal production cost while median voters' desired amount (which becomes the community's selection) requires only that their marginal benefit equal their marginal tax cost.

Monopoly models assume that government officials attempt to implement their own preferences and try to get voters to go along. Officials or bureaucrats may be able to do that if they have more experience or more information than the voters and if they have and can maintain a political monopoly. Proponents of monopoly fiscal-choice models must identify the institutional factors that allow officials to continually not satisfy the voters' desires.

Discussion Questions

1. "If school expenditures are selected by majority vote, then most of the voters in the school district will be perfectly happy with the selected amount of spending." Evaluate this statement.

2. "The efficient quantity of a public good is provided if the marginal production cost equals the sum of consumers' marginal benefits. That rule will be satisfied by majority voting about the level of government services." True, false, or uncertain? Explain.

3. Suppose that there are three quality-sized groups of voters in a community trying to select the amount of school spending per pupil. The options are to spend either $1000, $3000, or $5000 per pupil. The lowest level would allow only a bare-bones academic curriculum, the middle level would permit more varied academic courses and some transportation service, and the highest level would allow bus transportation for all students and extracurricular activities in addition to academics. The positions of the three voting groups are shown below:

Group	Most Preferred	Second Choice	Least Preferred
1	$1000	$3000	$5000
2	$3000	$5000	$1000
3	$5000	$1000	$3000

Thus, group 1 represents those trying to minimize government spending, group 2 are the middle-of-the-roaders, and group 3 represents the "all-or-nothing" viewpoint.

a. Plot the positions of the three groups on a diagram with level of preference on the vertical axis and level of expenditure on the horizontal axis. Connect the plots for each group with lines. Are the preferences of these groups single-peaked?

b. What level of spending will be selected by majority voting?

c. Can you think of any ways for this community to select a level of school spending and avoid the problem of majority voting?

Selected Readings

Holcombe, Randall G. ''Concepts of Public Sector Equilibrium.'' *National Tax Journal* 34, no. 1 (March 1980): 77–80.

Inman, Robert. ''Testing Political Economy's 'as if' Proposition: Is the Median Voter Really Decisive?'' *Public Choice* 33 (Winter 1978): 45–65.

Romer, Ted and Howard Rosenthal, ''Bureaucrats Versus Voters: On the Political Economy of Resource Allocation by Direct Democracy.'' *Quarterly Journal of Economics* 93 (1979): 563–87.

Appendix   Indifference Curve Approach to Voting Models

The economic analysis in this chapter was presented using individuals' demand curves and tax prices to determine desired amounts of government service. Welfare comparisons among alternative allocations were made using a simple measure of consumer's surplus. This technique is sufficient for a general understanding of the theory, but a better understanding and easier analysis of some more complex issues (to come later in the book) can result from examining how consumers' demand is determined. This requires some background in and use of what economists call consumer theory. This appendix does not provide a general introduction to that theory, rather it uses the theory to illustrate some of the conclusions of the chapter. For students having experience with the theory (probably a class in intermediate microeconomics), this and subsequent appendices to other chapters provide another way to view and understand the results.

Demand and Desired Government Service

In the simplest model, consumers choose between two types of commodities, private goods provided by the market and public goods provided by the government. Consumers pay for private goods directly through prices charged by the sellers and indirectly for public goods through taxes or fees collected by the government. Individual consumers are assumed to have no influence over prices, which are determined by the market in response to production cost and total consumer demand. Consumers are limited in the amount of both types of commodities they can consume by their available resources or budgets.

FIGURE 3A.1   *Indifference Curve Graph of Consumer Demand*

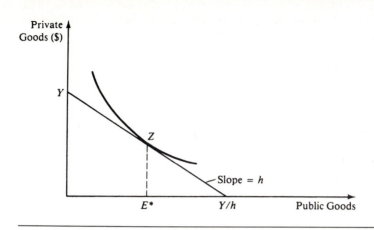

It is usually assumed that consumers can always choose among sets of these goods, that consumers' preferences for both types of goods are consistent (if A is preferred to B and B to C, then A is preferred to C), and that consumers can always be made better off by giving them more of at least *one* of the commodities. Finally, each consumer is assumed to choose the combination of commodities that provides greatest possible satisfaction or happiness (often called utility by economists). These assumptions are the standard ones used to analyze choice of private goods and are simply extended to public goods as well.

A graphical depiction of such a model is shown in Figure 3A.1. The amount of public good is represented on the horizontal axis, and total consumption of private goods is measured in dollars on the vertical axis. The convention of using dollars as the unit for private consumption is a way of combining all the different types of private goods into one measure. The consumer's resource or budget constraint is the line from point Y to point Y/hP_E, where Y equals the consumer's income, h is the consumer's share of taxes or tax price, and P_E is the cost of producing one unit of public good.[8] In other words, consumers can choose to spend all of their income on private goods, all on public goods, or some on each. If this consumer pays h percent of total taxes, then for each dollar of taxes he paid there will be $1/h$ dollars for public expenditure (if $h = 0.33$, this consumer pays one-third of total taxes; a \$1 tax bill means total taxes of \$3). The slope of the budget line in Figure 3A.1, which represents the relative cost of public and private goods to this consumer, is equal to the consumer's tax price h.

The consumer's preferences for private and public goods are represented by a set of indifference curves, one of which is drawn in Figure 3A.1. Indifference

---

[8] If P_E is assumed to equal 1, then the production of public goods is subsumed and the amount of public good measured by expenditure in dollars.

curves depict combinations of private and public goods from which the consumer gets equal satisfaction while each successively higher indifference curve (I_2 compared to I_1) shows combinations that provide greater satisfaction. The convex shape of the indifference curves results because of the assumptions about preferences noted above.

If the consumer tries to get the greatest possible satisfaction given the current conditions, the combination of goods (or bundle) on the highest reachable indifference curve is selected. That is, bundle Z in the figure. Because bundle Z includes public good amount E^*, we say that this consumer will *demand* E^* given income Y and tax price h. As the consumer's tax price is changed (because the government selects a different tax structure), the budget line will change, and there will be a different bundle similar to Z, which now maximizes the consumer's satisfaction. For each different price (holding income constant), there is a different desired amount of public good, which can then be represented as a demand curve.

Monopoly Models: An All-or-Nothing Choice

The latter part of the chapter included a discussion of how budget-maximizing government officials with political monopoly power could use a predetermined reversion amount to induce consumers to accept a larger amount of government expenditure than desired. That idea can also be understood using the indifference-curve/budget-line analysis outlined above.

Figure 3A.2 depicts the preferences and budget line for a consumer with desired consumption bundle Z and thus desired amount of public goods equal to E^*. If this individual is the median voter in the community—that is, E^* is the median of individuals' desired amounts—then that amount would be selected by an unrestricted majority vote. However, if government officials allowed only one vote and offered

FIGURE 3A.2   *Indifference Curve Representation of a Monopoly Bureaucrat Public-Choice Model*

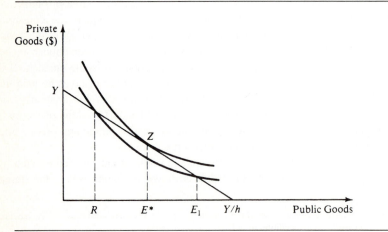

E_1 and if the amount of the public good would revert to R if the officials' proposal were rejected, this voter would be indifferent between E_1 and R. Both lie on the same indifference curve. It follows that any amount of public good just to the left of E_1 would be on a higher indifference curve and thus preferred by the consumer. Government officials could propose spending $E_1 - 1$, which would be accepted by this voter if the alternative is R.

This representation of the monopoly model also makes it clear how the maximum possible amount of public expenditure depends on the level of R. If R is less than the desired amount E^*, the maximum possible spending is greater the smaller is R. If R is greater than the desired amount, then the maximum possible spending equals R.

4 / Public Choice Through Mobility

Spatial mobility provides the local public-goods counterpart to the private market's shopping trip.[1]

Charles M. Tiebout

Since the publication in 1956 of "A Pure Theory of Local Expenditures" by Charles Tiebout, economists studying local governments have been fundamentally concerned with the possibility that consumer residential mobility among competing local communities may lead to efficiency in providing local public goods. The conventional wisdom regarding public goods is that because they may be consumed simultaneously by more than one consumer and because it may be difficult to exclude consumers from benefiting once the good is provided, individuals have an incentive to understate their true preference for the public good. They wish to be "free riders," benefiting from public goods provided by others without fully paying for them. It was this view that lead Paul Samuelson (1954, 388) to conclude that "no decentralized pricing system can serve to determine optimally these levels of collective consumption." But the work of Tiebout and others who have followed challenges this position by suggesting that a structure of many, small local governments may be a decentralized pricing system, which generates an optimal amount of public goods.

Tiebout's work also provides a contrast to the notion of public choice by voting. In the analysis in Chapter 3, consumers could not move among communities, so any differences in public-good demand had to be resolved by voting. In Tiebout's view, differences in public-good demand may also be resolved by moving or, more correctly, by grouping together consumers with the same demand. Consumers, then, may influence fiscal choices either by participating in the local political process (what political scientists call "voice") or by "voting with one's feet" (exit).

Probably no one paper in public finance has generated as much subsequent work as that by Tiebout. His model and results have implications not only for the efficiency of the public sector but also for the income-redistribution potential of local governments, the appropriate structure of intergovernmental grants, and need for policies to correct for fiscal disparities among localities. If stimulus to further inquiry and research is the measure, then perhaps no paper surpasses Tiebout's in importance for public finance. For that reason, this chapter reports the original

---

[1]"A Pure Theory of Local Expenditures," *Journal of Political Economy* 64 (Oct. 1956): 422.

Tiebout theory (although it does not substitute for reading the article) and considers some of the criticisms of and subsequent alterations to the concept. The theory and its implications are important for analyzing many issues considered throughout the book.

/ The Tiebout Hypothesis[2]

Tiebout's objective was to think of a way of achieving efficient public-goods provision and to characterize the specific conditions under which it would work. Tiebout's mechanism is easily stated. One factor individuals consider in choosing in which community to live is the tax and service package in the community—that is, the tax burden a resident will bear and the benefits from public services a resident will enjoy. If there are many localities, each with a different tax/service package, individuals will select the one that gives them the greatest satisfaction, presumably the one for which taxes and services are closest to their desired amount. In essence, individuals "shop" among localities and "buy" the one best for them. This analogy with private markets is important because it suggests that individuals *can* choose just what they want in the public sector and need not compromise through voting.[3]

The assumptions of the model spell out the conditions under which Tiebout believed this mechanism would work perfectly to bring about the efficient amount of public good in each community. It seems best to state those assumptions, followed by discussion:

1. Consumers are mobile and will move their residence to the community that best satisfies their preferences.
2. Consumers are completely knowledgeable about the differences in tax/service packages among the communities.
3. There are many communities from which to choose.
4. There are no restrictions or limitations on consumer mobility due to employment opportunities.
5. There are no spillovers of public service benefits or taxes among communities.
6. Each community, directed by a manager, attempts to attract the right-size population to take advantage of scale economies—that is, to reach the minimum average cost of producing public goods.

Tiebout concludes that under these conditions consumers will locate in the community that best satisfies their preferences. Further, if the production of public goods exhibits constant returns to scale (rather than assumption 6 above) and if there are enough communities, then consumers will move to the community that *exactly* satisfies their preferences. With constant returns to scale, communities of

---

[2]This section is obviously based on and adapted from Tiebout (1956).

[3]The government fiscal package need not be the only factor individuals consider in selecting where to live. Transportation cost, for example, and other factors may also be important.

FIGURE 4.1 Public-Service Demand in a Tiebout Community

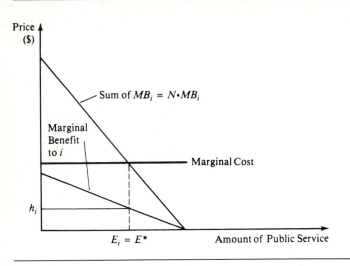

even one person can provide services at minimum average cost—community size becomes irrelevant.

The demand for public service in that case would appear as in Figure 4.1. Each individual selecting this community would have the same demand or marginal benefit schedule for public service, denoted as "marginal benefit to i" in the figure. The sum of all individuals' marginal benefits, then, is just the sum of all those identical demand curves. If all consumers pay an equal share of costs, shown as h_i, then the desired amount of public service is E_i, which is the same for all consumers in this community. Moreover, because each individual's share of marginal benefits equals each individual's share of costs (both equal to $1/N$, where N = the number of consumers), the amount of public service desired by each consumer is also the efficient amount of public service. In fact, the result of the Tiebout process in each community can be called a benefit tax equilibrium because everyone's cost reflects the marginal benefit. Unlike the equilibrium of majority voting without mobility, all consumers are perfectly satisfied with the amount of public service provided in their community, and that amount is the efficient quantity.

/ Evaluation of the Model

/ The assumptions

Tiebout, in the original article, noted the severity of these assumptions. Concerning the version in which consumer preferences are exactly satisfied, he wrote (1956, 421):

> . . . This model is not even a first approximation of reality. It is presented to show the assumptions needed in a model of local government expenditures, which yields the same optimal allocation that a private market would.

But although the assumptions characterize an "ideal" world, there is some validity in each.

The first three assumptions should be familiar to students of economics because these assumptions are the parallel of the standard assumptions of a perfectly competitive market. Consumers with complete knowledge of price and quality differences face many sellers of each product and make consumption choices in order to obtain the greatest possible satisfaction. As Tiebout noted, of these three the requirement of many communities may be the most troublesome. Because there must be enough jurisdictions to satisfy *every* preference, it is possible that as many communities as individuals may be required. Such one-person governments mean, of course, that public goods would be consumed as private goods. But, of course, that effectively eliminates government and collective consumption that would regenerate the efficiency problems for which government was created. Still, the number of different local communities in a given area or region is often large, as reflected by the data in Table 4.1. Thus, desires for many different combinations of public services can be accommodated, at least in larger metropolitan areas. The data in Table 4.1 suggest that choice from 100–150 general-purpose local governments and at least 50 different school districts is common even in medium-sized metropolitan areas.

In responding to this set of locational choices, there is little doubt that consumers do consider local government taxes and services in deciding where to live. Often the first question that a new or transferred employee will ask is "How are the schools around here?" Whether individuals have complete or even good knowledge about interjurisdictional tax and service differences is more problematic because collecting information is not costless. One private-market sector, the real estate industry, however, does specialize in acquiring and providing that information to prospective residents. And other, less formal networks, often through employers, also exist for transmitting the observations of current residents to prospective ones.

The assumption of no employment restrictions on residential mobility removes several potential problems including any difference in transportation cost between job location and alternative residential locations and the new costs created by the need to change job location for whatever reason. Tiebout envisioned someone living on capital income so that the amount of income was independent of where one lived. With that exception, and possibly one for certain types of self-employed individuals, this assumption will not be met in reality. But certainly some actual situations come closer to meeting this assumption than do others. For any given job and job location, individuals may have a choice of several or even a number of different communities in which to live, with equal transportation cost to that job. This is reflected in traditional urban economics models with a central business district or job center circled by suburbs at different distances. To the extent that there are a good number of such choices providing different tax/service packages in a given metropolitan area, this assumption may be approximated.

The most important assumption for the efficiency implications of the Tiebout model and yet the most troublesome is the absence of externalities or fiscal spillovers. As Tiebout (1956, 423) noted, "There are obvious external economies and diseconomies between communities." Indeed, as noted in Chapter 2 and elaborated

TABLE 4.1

Number of Local Governments in Selected Metropolitan Areas, 1982

| | | Number of | |
Area	Population (Millions)	Municipalities and Townships	School Districts
New York	9.120	142	135
Los Angeles	7.478	82	95
Chicago	7.104	374	313
Philadelphia	4.717	339	174
Detroit	4.353	209	107
Boston	3.663	147	31
San Francisco	3.251	59	88
Dallas	2.975	179	109
Nassau, N.Y.	2.606	108	128
Houston	2.410	94	54
Pittsburgh	2.264	312	92
Minneapolis	2.114	276	67
Atlanta	2.030	77	20
Newark	1.966	104	96
Cleveland	1.899	131	59
Denver	1.621	41	20
Seattle	1.607	46	34
Cincinnati	1.401	159	59
Milwaukee	1.397	90	48
Kansas City	1.327	118	51
Indianapolis	1.167	155	44
Columbus, Ohio	1.093	139	40
Rochester, N.Y.	.971	120	50
Albany, N.Y.	.795	99	50
Gary, Ind.	.643	52	25
Grand Rapids, Mich.	.602	58	28
Springfield, Mass.	.582	43	6
Lansing, Mich.	.472	100	40
Madison, Wis.	.324	64	16
Ann Arbor, Mich.	.265	28	11

Source: U.S. Department of Commerce, Bureau of the Census, *1982 Census of Governments*, Vol. 5, Local Government in Metropolitan Areas, Table 3.

on in Chapter 5, the existence of externalities is a primary reason why individual consumers *should* group together for collective consumption. If those externalities extend across jurisdiction boundaries and if the amount of public service selected in each community is efficient for that community (as in a Tiebout world), those amounts will not be efficient from the overall society's viewpoint.

There are several ways of correcting for the inefficiency caused by interjurisdictional externalities, two of which are most often discussed. First, externalities can be eliminated if governments are bigger (geographically and with larger population). If all those who benefit or pay for a public service are members of the same government, then there is no externality. But governments large enough to eliminate externalities may be too large to include only individuals with the same preferences for public service. This creates a potential trade-off of these two factors, which is discussed in greater detail in Chapter 5. Second, intergovernmental grants can be used to induce local governments to change their amount of public service to that which is socially efficient (discussed in Chapter 17). This can be accomplished without altering the size of those recipient governments.

Tiebout's final assumption poses a problem because it requires that each community attract just the right population to allow production of public services at minimum average cost. If population is too small, the marginal cost of adding one more person would be low but the average cost per resident very high. If population is too large, both the marginal and average costs would be high. With the optimal population, the community could produce at the minimum of average cost—where average and marginal cost are equal. But what happens if the number of people who desire a specific amount of public service is greater than the optimal population for the community? Another community providing the same quality of service would have to be created, but there may not be enough people to optimally populate two communities. In that case, community size must change. This difficulty is avoided if the number and geographic size of communities is not fixed or if there are constant returns to scale.

Recognizing the potential violations of the assumptions in actuality, it seems appropriate to note Tiebout's own conclusion (1956, 424):

> If consumer–voters are fully mobile, the appropriate local governments . . . are adopted by the consumer–voters. While the solution may not be perfect because of institutional rigidities, this does not invalidate its importance. The solution . . . is the best that can be obtained . . . .

In other words, because there are moving and information costs in reality, consumers may not move from a community because of relatively small differences between their desired public-service amounts and those provided. The Tiebout process may not lead to all consumers in a community having the *same* demand for public service, but they may have *similar* demand. By reducing the variance in public-sector demand, the Tiebout process may reduce the inherent dissatisfaction with a voted public-service amount.

/ Property taxes and stability of the model

A more fundamental criticism of the model than noting the severity of the assumptions is the possibility that *even if the assumptions are met* the process may fail to provide an efficient amount of local public goods. This possibility arises if the local public goods are financed by something other than benefit charges or head taxes. For example, property taxes remain the major locally generated source of revenue for local governments. In that case, in choosing to reside in a given community, an individual also selects the amount of public services to receive. But the amount of taxes that individual will pay toward those services (the tax price) depends on the *value* of the house the individual chooses to consume. In other words, with property tax financing, the choice of where to live and what type of house to consume must be analyzed together.

This potential difficulty with the Tiebout model is best shown by an example. Suppose that a metropolitan area is divided into two school districts with the following economic characteristics:

Example 4.1

Community A	Community B
Big houses, $100,000 value	Small houses, $40,000 value
Tax rate = 3% of value	Tax rate = 2.5% of value
Tax per house = $3000	Tax per house = $1000
One pupil per house	One pupil per house
Spending per pupil = $3000	Spending per pupil = $1000

Suppose also that these two governments were the result of the Tiebout process—that is, each family has selected the district that exactly satisfies their education preferences. In addition, families have also purchased the type of house they desire. Families in community A are *willing* to pay $3000 for a year of primary education while families in B are only willing to pay $1000. Given the assumptions of the Tiebout model (no externalities, no moving costs), both communities are providing the efficient amount of education service, and there is no consumer dissatisfaction in either community.[4]

The difficulty with the model is that this Tiebout equilibrium may not be stable because some individuals may be able to make themselves better off by moving. If one of the families in community B was to build a small, $40,000 house in community A, that family would consume the higher amount of education service in that district without paying its full cost. Given the 3-percent tax rate in community A, the tax on a $40,000 house would be $1200 rather than the $3000 paid by other residents. For that $1200 in taxes, this new family would enjoy slightly less than $3000 of per-pupil education spending.[5] While that family was not willing to pay $3000 to receive $3000 of education spending (or else they would have located in community A to begin with), they might very well be willing to spend $1200 to receive, say, $2990 of education spending. The trick is to own a house with below average value in a community providing a large amount of service.

In other words, even if a perfect Tiebout equilibrium could be achieved, tax financing generates an inherent instability. The incentive that induced this family to move from B to A exists, of course, for *all* the families in community B. If any

---

[4]Of course, expenditure on education may not measure the amount of education service, particularly if environmental conditions or prices vary between the communities. Here the assumption is that they do not differ. See Chapter 15 for more on this issue.

[5]The per-pupil spending in community A falls because one more pupil is added but only $1200 of new taxes are added. The amount of the anticipated decrease depends on the number of residents of A. For instance, if there were originally ten families in A, spending falls to $2836.36 ($31,200/11). If there are initially "many" families in A, the decrease in spending expected by a mover is insignificant.

one family makes this move, the efficiency of the Tiebout equilibrium is destroyed. The amount of education spending in community A is no longer equal to the efficient amount; dissatisfaction with the amount of government spending arises as consumers with different public-service demands enter the community.

There are two ways the homogeneity of demand characteristic of the Tiebout equilibrium could be restored. Community A could prevent a consumer from having a $40,000 house (discussed in the following section), or the original residents of A could exit to a third community. Indeed, the residents of A might face the same type of incentive as those of B do in the example, if, for instance, there is a community of $200,000 houses with per-pupil spending of $5000. It is this possibility that led Bruce Hamilton (1975) to note that the instability of the model could give way to a game of "musical suburbs" with everyone trying to move "up" to a wealthier community.

It is important to note that the instability of the model is not unique to property taxes but occurs with any tax other than a pure benefit charge or a head tax. If the local public good was financed by a proportional local income tax, for example, individuals from a lower-income/lower-spending community would similarly be made better off by moving to a higher-income/higher-spending community. The suggestion is that the difficulty arises unless *both* the demand for the public service and the demand for the private good that determines taxes (housing for a property tax, leisure for an income tax) are the same (or highly correlated) for all consumers in each Tiebout community. This is illustrated with a second example.

Suppose again that there are two communities, which comprise a Tiebout equilibrium, providing only education, with economic characteristics as follows:

Example 4.2

Community A	Community B
Big houses, $100,000 value	Small houses, $40,000 value
Tax rate = 3% of value	Tax rate = 7.5% of value
Tax per house = $3000	Tax per house = $3000
One pupil per house	One pupil per house
Spending per pupil = $3000	Spending per pupil = $3000

Unlike Example 4.1, both residents of A and B are willing to pay $3000 to enjoy $3000 of per-pupil educational service—that is, they have the same demand for educational service. But the residents of A and B have different demands for housing, which is the commodity that determines their tax payment. Residents of A like big houses while those in B prefer small ones. Although this could occur because residents of A have higher incomes than residents of B, it might also occur simply because residents of B prefer to spend their income on something else—vacations to Hawaii, for instance.

As in the first example, this equilibrium is not stable. If a resident of community B was to build a small, $40,000 house in A, taxes again would be $1200 to consume slightly less than $3000 of educational service. Although, in moving, this consumer would suffer a small decrease in government education spending, there would be a large decrease in tax cost. With the tax savings, the consumer could purchase other goods (including, of course, substitute private education service) to increase happiness.

/ Extensions of the Tiebout Model

/ Fiscal zoning

The potential efficiency of the Tiebout mechanism can be blocked if an individual can pay less than the average cost of local public goods. If public goods are to be financed by property taxes, this is accomplished by consuming a less-than-average value home. This difficulty would not arise if there was some method of preventing the consumption of lower-value housing in a community—that is, preventing the migration of consumers desiring small houses into communities of consumers who desire big houses as in the examples. It has been suggested that various forms of land-use restrictions or zoning laws may function, although imperfectly, as such a method.[6]

The simple solution is to merely prohibit consumption of housing with *value* less than that of the original houses in each community. Using the conditions of Example 4.1, individuals would not be allowed to move into community A unless they were willing to consume a $100,000 house. In that case, individuals from community B would not move because they would have to pay the full average cost of the education in A, which they revealed as less attractive by originally choosing community B. It is important to understand that it is the *value* of the house that matters because the value determines the property tax liability in any given community where everyone pays the same tax rate. Thus, individuals could consume small houses in community A if they were willing to have them valued as $100,000 houses.[7]

Of course, such explicit value-based zoning rules may not be possible, so the question becomes one of whether a set of rules defended for a nonexclusionary reason such as safety effectively serve the same purpose. For instance, rules on minimum lot size, minimum setback from streets, and required construction methods and materials serve to increase the production cost of housing and to impose a minimum ''type'' of house allowed in a community. Restrictions may also be imposed privately rather than by government. For example, a new suburban community may be built by one (or perhaps two) developers who effectively zone the community for housing value by building only similar-value houses. These styles can then be preserved through deed restrictions that prevent subsequent owners from altering the character of the community without the consent of all. This practice

---

[6]See, for example, Hamilton (1975) and Fischel (1978).

[7]Housing is the target of restrictions only because a property tax is presumed. If public services are financed by a beer tax, then minimum amounts of beer consumption would be required. Similarly, if local governments use an income tax, the residence restriction must be on income.

is common because many builders offer separate developments of "affordable," "family," or "executive" homes.

This use of fiscal zoning means that communities are cross-classified by both the amount of public good or service and housing values. If there are only two levels of desired government spending, High and Low, and two types of houses, Big and Small, fiscal zoning could be used to preserve four different communities, as shown in Example 4.3. Without fiscal zoning, households from the Small:Low community could benefit from moving to Big:High if they could consume a small house. Similarly, households from Small:High (Small:Low) could gain by living in Big:High (Big:Low) if they could consume a small house. That is prevented by house-zoning rules.

Example 4.3

Types of Tiebout Communities

	Government Spending	
Housing Type	*High*	*Low*
Big	Big:High	Big:Low
Small	Small:High	Small:Low

The separation of local communities by the demand for housing and public service and the maintenance of the separation by zoning also raises an important equity issue. Because the demand for both housing and public service tend to increase with income (in economic parlance, both are normal goods), the separation of communities by those demands may lead to communities classified by income. Using Example 4.3, households in community Big:High may have the highest incomes followed in order by communities Big:Low, Small:High, and Small:Low. In preventing a Small:Low household from occupying a small house in community Big:High by zoning, an explicit decision is made to maintain the satisfaction of the highest-income households and prevent an increase in the satisfaction of the lowest-income households to preserve efficiency. Although there may be other (perhaps even more effective) means of redistributing income, it may still be objectionable to a free society to legally limit where a person may live based on income.

More communities may be needed to achieve a Tiebout equilibrium as a consequence of property tax financing and fiscal zoning because each community must have residents with the same desired amount of public service *and* housing value. This creates another problem if the number of households with any particular combination of desired amounts is too small to achieve any scale economies in the production of the public good. It may be, for example, that only one household prefers combination Small:High. The choice then is to have a one-person community, which would be inefficient, or absorb that household into community Big:High, which also seems inefficient. There is, however, an economic response that may allow mixed housing types to coexist efficiently in the same community, as discussed in the next section.

/ Fiscal capitalization

The problems noted above of using zoning to ensure that all residents of a community desire not only the same amount of public service but also the same value housing may be alleviated by an economic response in the housing market. If the tax advantage of a small-house consumer in a big-house community is offset by a higher price for that small house, a process called tax or fiscal capitalization, then big and small houses can coexist in the same community as long as consumers still desire the same public service.

Suppose that one more community (call it Mixed:High) is added to the four in Example 4.3. This one has a High amount of spending ($3000 per pupil) but an equal number of big and small houses (houses that are valued at $100,000 and $40,000 in the homogeneous communities). If the values are the same in the mixed community, the average house value is $70,000, necessitating a tax rate of 4.2857 percent to generate $3000 of revenue per household. Big-house owners would pay $4285.70 in taxes and small-house owners would pay about $1714.30, although both would receive $3000 of educational service. The three communities are characterized below.

Example 4.4

Big:High	Mixed:High	Small:High
$100,000 houses	Half $100,000 and half $40,000 houses	$40,000 houses
Tax rate = 3%	Tax rate = 4.2857%	Tax rate = 7.5%
Tax = $3000	Tax, big = $4285.70	Tax = $3000
	Tax, small = $1714.30	

The conditions of Example 4.4 will not persist because small-house consumers pay less in the Mixed:High community than for the same amount of service in Small:High while big-house consumers pay more in Mixed:High than in Big:High. One expects therefore that small-house consumers would attempt to move to Mixed:High, increasing the demand for small houses in that community and increasing their price. Similarly, big-house consumers are expected to attempt to leave Mixed:High, decreasing the demand for big houses in the Mixed community and reducing their value. These changes are depicted in Figure 4.2. The changes in price are expected to continue until the higher price for small houses in the Mixed:High community, compared to the Small:High community, exactly offsets the lower taxes and until the lower price for big houses in the Mixed:High community, compared to the Big:High community, exactly compensates for the higher taxes.[8]

If this occurs, economists say that capitalization is complete or that the full amount of the tax difference has been capitalized into house values. Please note

---

[8]Of course, the supply of houses can also adjust, with more small houses and fewer big ones resulting from the change in prices. If this occurs, the tax difference is not capitalized into the value of the house but rather into the value of the land used for a particular type of house.

FIGURE 4.2 *Capitalization of Tax Differences*

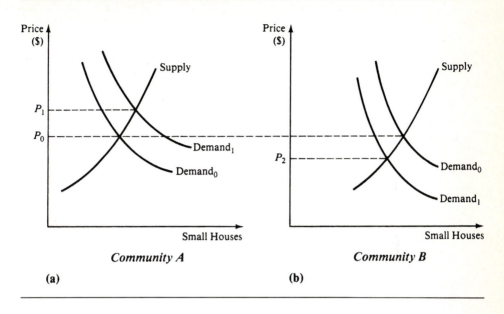

Community A (a)

Community B (b)

that *capitalization is nothing more than the change in the price of an asset due to a shift in demand.* For complete capitalization, the price of a small house in the Mixed:High community must increase by the present value of the tax difference between the homogeneous and mixed communities, while the price of a big house in the Mixed:High community must fall by a similar amount (they will be equal if there are an equal number of big and small houses in the Mixed:High community). Assuming a discount rate of 10 percent, small houses would be valued at $49,000 and big houses at $91,000 in the Mixed:High community. The equilibrium conditions for the three communities are shown in Example 4.5.[9]

Example 4.5

Big:High	Mixed:High	Small:High
$100,000 houses	Half $91,000 and half $49,000 houses	$40,000 houses
Tax rate = 3%	Tax rate = 4.2857%	Tax rate = 7.5%
Tax = $3000	Tax, big = $3900	Tax = $3000
	Tax, small = $2100	

The total residence cost in any community is the price of the house plus the present value of the future tax payments. The present value of future taxes equals

---

[9]Hamilton (1976b) derives the equations for full capitalization.

$$\frac{T_1}{1 + r} + \frac{T_2}{(1 + r)^2} + \frac{T_3}{(1 + r)^3} + \ldots + \frac{T_N}{(1 + r)^N}$$

where T = annual tax payment
   r = discount rate
   N = time period

If N is infinite and all tax payments are the same, this equals T/r. The total residence cost is the same for any given type of house regardless of the community. Assuming a 10-percent discount rate and an infinite house life, this is shown as follows:

Big houses in Big:High v. Big houses in Mixed:High
$100,000 + $30,000 = $91,000 + $39,000

Small houses in Small:High v. Small houses in Mixed:High
$40,000 + $30,000 = $49,000 + $21,000

The potential for capitalization of interjurisdictional differences in taxes or services has four important implications for the Tiebout hypothesis. First, if capitalization occurs, fewer communities are needed to achieve an efficient equilibrium. It is again only necessary to have a separate community for each desired amount of public service, not for every combination of desired public service and housing amount. Following Example 4.4, only two communities rather than four are needed, one providing a high amount of public service and one a low amount, with both having a mix of big and small houses.

Second, because communities need be homogeneous only in the desired amount of public service and can include households desiring the whole range of housing, the equity concerns about the Tiebout process may be mitigated. A small-house consumer (who is perhaps a low-income consumer) in a community of other small houses is not worse off than another small-house consumer in a mixed- or big-house community even though the *tax rate* is greater in the small-house community. In Example 4.5, the tax rate is 7.5 percent in Small:High and 4.2857 percent in Mixed:High for the same amount of service. But because (identical) small houses are less expensive in Small:High, small-house consumers are equally well off in either. Communities that include residents over the entire distribution of incomes can be Tiebout communities. Of course, this does not imply that society is necessarily satisfied with the overall distribution of income and might not want to use other tools to alter that distribution.

Third, complete capitalization means that the local property tax functions as a benefit tax with each household paying the full cost of the services in their community. Conversely, households cannot escape part of the public-service cost by consuming a less-than-average value house. This may seem strange because in the example, a small-house consumer in Mixed:High expects to directly pay $21,000 of tax in present-value terms ($2100 per year) while a big-house consumer pays $39,000 ($3900 per year). But the true cost of residing in the community and consuming its serices is not just the tax but also the difference in price for the type of house desired. The big-house consumer can buy that house in the mixed community for $9000 *less* than elsewhere while a small-house consumer must pay $9000 *more* for a small house than elsewhere. The true cost (in present-value terms) of consuming the mixed community's services is $30,000 for *both* types of housing consumers.[10]

Fourth, complete capitalization creates a difficulty for researchers seeking statistical evidence that capitalization has occurred. If every community provides a different amount of public service (and thus has a different amount of taxation) and if each has a complete mix of houses from low to high value, then there will be no statistical relationship between government expenditures (and taxes) and average house value.

/ Public Choice: Reality

What can be said about the comparative role of voting and migration as public-choice mechanisms in reality? No one believes that a perfect Tiebout equilibrium can be obtained because information and moving costs are not zero; even if it could be obtained, it would not be efficient because externalities are always present. Casual observation supports this view because community votes on fiscal matters are seldom (if ever) unanimous, which would be expected in a perfect Tiebout world.

Nevertheless, the Tiebout process does seem to apply up to the limits of those transaction costs, so that the greatest differences in desired public service are offset by residential choices. The Tiebout process serves to reduce but not eliminate the variance in desired government service within communities, thus the inherent dissatisfaction with the voted outcome. But because differences are not eliminated, voting is required and used to find a compromise position within those remaining differences of opinion. Rather than competing public-choice mechanisms, they are complementary. There is substantial evidence that residential choice is greatly influenced by the type of schools in a community. Families who choose to live in a community therefore are likely to generally approve of the amount of local school spending, but differences may still arise over the allocation of those funds between music and advanced math, for example.

Perhaps the most important legacy of the Tiebout idea is the emphasis on the welfare advantage of a decentralized government structure. But that advantage must be balanced against other economic forces that require a more centralized government to bring about economic efficiency. It is to that issue that we turn in Chapter 5.

/ Summary

If there are many localities, each with a different tax/service package, individuals will select the one that gives them the greatest satisfaction, presumably the one for

---

[10]For big-house consumers, the cost is $39,000 *minus* the $9000 house price advantage; for small-house consumers, the cost is $21,000 *plus* the $9000 house price addition.

which taxes and services are closest to their desired amount. This view, offered by Charles Tiebout, suggests that individuals *can* choose just what they want in the public sector and need not compromise through voting.

As a result of the Tiebout process, all consumers are perfectly satisfied with the amount of public service provided in their community and that amount is the efficient quantity.

Because there are moving and information costs in reality, consumers may not move from a community because of relatively small differences between their desired public-service amounts and those provided. The Tiebout process, then, may not lead to all consumers in a community having the *same* demand for public service, but they may have *similar* demand.

The Tiebout process may fail to provide an efficient amount of local public goods if public goods are financed by property taxes. By consuming a less-than-average value home, an individual can pay less than the average cost of those goods, thereby preventing the potential efficiency of the Tiebout mechanism.

The inherent instability caused by tax financing would not arise if there were some method of preventing the migration of consumers desiring small houses into communities of consumers who desire big houses. Various forms of land-use restrictions or zoning laws may function as such a method.

Because the demand for both housing and public service tend to increase with income (in economic parlance, both are normal goods), the separation of communities by those demands may lead to communities classified by income.

If the tax advantage of a small-house consumer in a big-house community is offset by a higher price for the small house, a process called tax capitalization, then big and small houses can coexist in the same community as long as the consumers desire the same public service.

With capitalization, the price of the house plus the present value of the future tax payments is the same for any given type of house regardless of the community. If capitalization is complete, a small-house consumer (who is perhaps a low-income consumer) in a community of other small houses is not worse off than another small-house consumer in a mixed- or big-house community even though the *tax rate* is greater in the small-house community.

Complete capitalization means that the local property tax functions as a benefit tax with each household paying the full cost of the services in their community. The true cost of residing in the community and consuming its services is not just the tax but includes the difference in price for the type of house desired.

The Tiebout process serves to reduce the variance in desired government service within communities. If the differences are not eliminated, voting is required and can be used to find a compromise position within those remaining differences of opinion.

Discussion Questions

1. The following data depict the fiscal characteristics of two school districts in a metropolitan area, each composed of identical single-family houses with one pupil per house:

School District A	Characteristic	School District B
$200,000	Per-pupil property value	$50,000
20	Property tax rate (in dollars per $1000 of value)	80
4,000	Per-pupil expenditure	4,000

The voters who have chosen to live in both districts desire and select $4000 of educational spending per pupil and collect property taxes to finance it. Because B has small (low-value) houses while A has big (high-value) houses, the tax rate in B is much higher than in A.

a. Would a voter in district B prefer to live in a big ($200,000) house in district A? Why?

b. Would a voter in B prefer to live in a small ($50,000) house in district A? Explain.

c. Suppose that there is a third school district to choose from with an equal number of big and small houses so that the average per-pupil value is $125,000. What tax rate is required in this district to spend $4000 per pupil? If small houses also cost $50,000 in this district, are small-house consumers better off here or in B? If big houses also cost $200,000 in this district, are big-house consumers better off here or in A?

d. Given your answers to part c, what do you expect will happen to the demand for big and small houses in this third district? What will happen to the prices of these houses in this mixed district?

e. Characterize the equilibrium that would allow all three districts to exist simultaneously. What does this imply about the equity implications of the Tiebout process? Do you think it is fair if some communities require higher tax rates than others to provide an equal amount of government spending?

2. The Tiebout process in this chapter represents an alternative to the majority-voting model described in Chapter 3 as a way of making public fiscal decisions. Compare these two alternative theories in terms of what they predict about the nature of local governments, including political characteristics and whether efficient public-good provision is likely to result.

3. Some people have suggested that political voting and voting with one's feet simultaneously apply in determining the amounts of local public services to provide. Discuss how this might happen. How might the limitations of the assumptions of the Tiebout theory contribute to a role for voting?

Selected Readings

Hamilton, Bruce W. "Zoning and Property Taxation in a System of Local Governments." *Urban Studies* 12 (June 1975): 205–11.

Hamilton, Bruce W. "Capitalization of Intrajurisdictional Differences in Local Tax Prices." *American Economic Review* 66, no. 5 (Dec. 1976): 743–53.

Tiebout, Charles M. "A Pure Theory of Local Expenditures." *Journal of Political Economy* 64 (Oct. 1956): 416–24.

5 / Organization of Subnational Government

> . . . It would be extremely desirable to find a mechanism to reduce the inefficiencies that arise from an imperfect correspondence in the provision of public goods.[1]
>
> *Wallace Oates*

The work by Tiebout and others emphasizes the advantage of decentralized government for satisfying the diverse public-service desires of consumers in an efficient way. But there are other economic factors that may require that governments be larger than those envisioned by Tiebout in order to have efficient provision of services. Among these are interjurisdictional cost or benefit externalities, economies of scale in the production of public goods, and the administration and compliance costs of government itself. The importance of these four factors will not be equal for all types of subnational government services. The issue, then, is what structure—size and number—for subnational governments is best to provide each type of service. Alternatively, once a federal system of national and subnational government is in place, the issue is which level of government in the federal system ought to have responsibility for each service.

/ The Economic Issues

/ Variations in demand

The greater are the variations in what individual consumers want from government and the more consumers with similar wants are grouped together, the stronger is the case for decentralized provision—that is, for having many small local governments. If all consumers desire the same amount and type of service, then there is no reason for more than one government, which would be a large one, to provide that uniform service. Conversely, if consumers with different demands for government service are served by a single government, many of those consumers will be dissatisfied because the amount of service provided by the government will be different than the amount desired. That dissatisfaction translates into a lower level of happiness or welfare for those consumers with like demand. It follows that the greater the number of different desired amounts of government service, the more

---

[1]*Fiscal Federalism*. New York: Harcourt Brace Jovanovich, 1972, 53.

governments required. And more governments mean smaller ones or provision at the most decentralized level of a federal system.

The existence of different demands for government service is not sufficient to justify decentralized provision unless consumers with similar demands are, or can be, located geographically together. Two separate government jurisdictions would not help if those with the same demand are not geographically together. If consumers can freely change residential location then the advantage of decentralized government is strengthened, as Tiebout emphasized.

/ Spatial externalities

A **spatial externality** (often called a spillover) occurs when the spatial distribution of the costs or benefits of government services is not confined to the jurisdiction boundaries of the providing government. Nonresidents either pay part of the costs or enjoy part of the benefits of a government's service. Spatial externalities can cause a government's choice about taxes and spending to be inefficient from the viewpoint of the entire society. If there is a spillover of costs, residents underestimate the true social cost and demand too much of the good or service, whereas a spillover of benefits causes residents to underestimate the true social benefit and demand too little. Of course, there can be simultaneous spillovers of costs and benefits, with the effect on the efficiency of provision depending on the relative size of each.[2]

Examples of spatial externalities involving subnational government services and taxes abound. When a nonresident landlord bears part of a city's property tax burden or a city business's property taxes are passed on to buyers of its product, some of whom are nonresidents, there is a spillover of local tax costs. Similarly, when a nonresident drives on the city's streets and finds traffic flowing smoothly and safely, there is a spillover of the city's transportation and public safety benefits. Or when a student is educated at public expense in the city and emigrates to another state or town, there is a spillover of educational service.

The classic economic solution to any externality problem is to internalize the externality—that is, to force the decision maker to consider the true social costs and benefits. A simple way to do this for spatial externalities involving government is to make the government's jurisdiction big enough to include all consumers who bear costs or enjoy benefits. If all consumers who benefit from services and pay taxes are residents, then there is no externality. The possibility of spatial externalities, then, can be a factor requiring a more centralized government structure composed of fewer, bigger subnational governments.

Indeed, spatial externalities are the reason for the general prescription that redistribution and stabilization policy can best be carried out by a central federal government. Expansionary fiscal policy by a state government to increase consumption, for instance, would generate benefits in other jurisdictions where the

---

[2]Reciprocal externalities may also occur—that is, both spillouts of costs and benefits from *and* spillins to a jurisdiction. Wallace Oates (1972) shows that such a condition is also likely to result in an inefficient allocation of resources.

consumer goods are produced. The state's residents would underestimate the benefits of that action and therefore fail to engage in an efficient amount of stabilization policy. Similarly, a state government is unable to internalize all the costs and benefits of an income-redistribution policy. The mobility of consumers and openness of subnational government economies create the spillovers that limit subnational government effectiveness in these areas.

/ Economies of scale

Economies of scale, in standard microeconomic usage, refers to a decrease in average cost as the quantity of output rises. But in reference to the optimal size for governments, the term usually refers to a decrease in cost *per person* for a given amount of service as population served increases. Economies of scale in that sense would exist, for instance, if the per-pupil cost of achieving a single degree of education was smaller for a 5000-pupil district than a 1000-pupil district. To put it another way, total cost or expenditure does not have to increase as much as population served to keep the service level constant. This concept of economies of scale is sometimes referred to as the advantage of joint consumption: Individual consumers can reduce their costs by sharing the good and its total cost with others.

An example of a good for which joint consumption might reduce per-person cost is a swimming pool. One household could purchase a swimming pool for its own use. That household could also join together with another household to jointly purchase the pool, reducing the per-household cost by half. If the sharing of the pool does not reduce the benefits by half, then the per-household cost of a unit of swimming service is reduced. As a special case, suppose that both households can swim as much and as easily in the shared pool as in singly-owned ones. In that case, the benefit of owning a shared pool is the same as a single one but the cost is half as great.

The evidence on the existence of this type of economies of scale for the goods and services usually provided by state and local governments in the United States is not conclusive. Of course, economies may exist for very small service populations but quickly be exhausted. The size where economies end is different for different services. The reasons most often given for potential economies are the elimination of duplication of inputs, increased coordination, and economies in purchasing. There are cases of services with capital extensive production, such as water, sewer, electric, and gas utilities, where substantial economies seem to exist. Indeed, government- or private-sector consolidation to produce those services is common to avoid duplication of expensive capital structures. But similar gains may be difficult for many subnational government services, which are very labor-intensive in character. In a recent review of the literature, Roy Bahl and Walter Vogt (1975, 13–14) conclude

> . . . Most positive findings of scale economies are based on statistical results that show a negative relationship between population size and per capita expenditures. There are great statistical and theoretical problems with interpreting such results as showing scale

economies, and about as many studies that find a negative relationship find a positive one.

In an earlier review, Werner Hirsch (1970) divides government services into those that are horizontally integrated, which results when existing units engaging in one stage of production are under common control, and those that are vertically integrated, which occurs if production and distribution are jointly provided. Hirsch suggests that traditional services such as police and fire protection are examples of horizontally integrated services, with many production "plants" under control of one government; utility services such as water and electricity provision are examples of vertically integrated services. Using this characterization, Hirsch concludes that scale economies appear to be substantial for vertically integrated services but not important for horizontally integrated ones, noting that "the average quasi-long-run cost function of horizontally integrated services tends to be reasonably horizontal over a wide range of operations" (p. 184).

The existence of scale economies may not be relevant to optimal government size anyway if provision of the good or service can be separated from the production of that good or service. Scale economies arise in the *production* phase. The primary role of the government is to *provide* a given amount of the good or service. Governments too small to achieve all economies of scale on their own can nevertheless take advantage of those economies by purchasing enough of the good or service for their residents from governments or private firms that are large enough to exhaust all economies.

Suppose, for example, that economies of scale exist for garbage-collection service up to 50,000 households served; that is, the per-household cost of a given quality of garbage collection (once per week, pick up at curb, trash bags required) is greater for a 25,000 household community than for larger ones. This might occur, for instance, if one standard garbage truck combined with one worker can serve exactly 50,000 households per week in this area. Communities with less than 50,000 households could find their truck idle for a portion of the week (unless they had some other use for it during those times or wished to change the quantity of service to more frequent weekly pick-ups). This difficulty can be resolved without making all governments bigger to include 50,000 households. One possibility is for one 25,000 household community to lease their truck to another 25,000 household community for half of each week. Another is for one 25,000 community to contract with another 25,000 community to pick up its garbage, subject to specific quality conditions. And still another is for all communities too small to take advantage of the economies in production to contract with a private firm for garbage pick-up in those communities at a quality of service specified by each community.

By contracting with private firms or other governments and through joint purchasing agreements, governments can provide the amount and type of services desired by a small population *and* enjoy the cost advantage of scale economies in production. In contracting, each individual government retains control over the amount of service to be consumed and finances the service by taxes or government fees, although the government does not directly produce the service. To the extent that such opportunities exist, scale economies are removed as an economic issue for the optimal size and structure of government.

Joint purchasing agreements among local governments are relatively common. A recent variant of those agreements applies to joint or pooled borrowing of funds by localities to conserve on the fixed (transaction) costs of bond sales. Contracting among governments or between a government and a private firm has also been common for some services, water and sewer services or public transportation, for instance. The use of contracting has been extended in recent years to police and fire dispatching under the 911 system, for example. In some areas, when residents of all communities dial 911 for emergency help, the relevant emergency unit from the caller's government is dispatched by a central dispatching office operated by one of the communities.

/ Administration and compliance costs

A final economic factor, which may be a reason for few subnational governments (and thus more centralization), is to conserve on the direct costs of administering those governments and what are largely the time costs for individuals to participate in the political process, called compliance costs. **Administrative costs** include the compensation paid to elected and appointed officials and staff and the overhead (buildings, supplies, utilities) accumulated in support of those officials. **Compliance costs** include such things as citizen costs of becoming informed on issues and candidate positions and the potential cash and time costs of registering an opinion, by participating in hearings, or voting for instance. The existence of fewer subnational governments *may* reduce these costs.

To argue that centralization will reduce administrative costs is to argue that there are economies of scale in administration of government, just as there may be economies in the production of public services. For instance, one might argue that a set of small cities each with a separate manager, finance director, and planning director is duplicative, that a single set of those officers could oversee all of the cities' operations simultaneously with no loss of efficiency. Those costs could therefore be reduced by consolidating those governments into a larger unit. But there is no guarantee that such opportunities will always, or even usually, exist. It could just as easily be argued that administrators become less effective the further removed they are from the people and operations they coordinate. In that case, **diseconomies of scale** result with larger governments requiring proportionally more administrators (perhaps with more layers in the administrative hierarchy) to run as well as smaller ones. Depending on the service (or set of services) provided, administrative scale economies could be a factor in favor of more or less centralization.

A relatively centralized subnational government structure (resulting from the consolidation of small government units perhaps) would reduce compliance costs only if the number of separate governments that each individual must deal with is reduced. For instance, if all city government functions are transferred to existing county governments and each county encompasses several cities, then each resident of the county will be a member of one rather than two local governments. This may reduce compliance costs because voters must participate in only one election and become informed about one set of candidates.[3]

In contrast, the consolidation of a set of school districts into one larger but independent district would not reduce compliance costs (although it might reduce or increase administrative costs as discussed above). Each individual would still be a member of one district. Similarly the transfer of only one or two city government functions to a higher-level government in the federal system, such as a county or state, would not reduce the *number* of separate governments serving each household and thus would not reduce compliance costs.

/ Optimal Government Size[4]

What follows is an attempt to develop a structure for applying the economic issues described above to actual decisions about government organization and the allocation of service responsibilities among levels of government in that organization. After examining the theory of optimal government size, some applications of that theory to actual policy cases are considered.

/ The correspondence principle

Suppose that governments provide a number of different public goods (nonrival goods), with the benefits of each confined to a fixed and known geographic area. Some of these goods benefit the entire nation (or world) once produced, whereas others benefit only a subset of the nation (perhaps even as small an area as that occupied by one household). For example, the defense advantages of a radar system can benefit the entire nation whereas a public television signal can be received only in a fifty-square-mile area around its origination. This type of public good, which can be simultaneously consumed in equal quantities by all but only in a limited spatial area, is often referred to as a **local public good.**

Further suppose that the population has no mobility, that the average cost of producing these goods is independent of the number of people served (or the size of government), and that there is some variation in the desired amounts of these public goods among the population. Under these conditions, the optimal government structure is a separate government for each area of benefit from a public good. There should be one central government to provide goods that simultaneously benefit all households, such as the defense radar system, and a set of separate subnational governments to provide each good that benefits only a limited number of households—for example, enough public-television governments to supply the good to all households (with each one serving a fifty-square-mile area). Wallace Oates has called this result the **correspondence principle** because the size of a government

---

[3]The gain from this example may be exaggerated. City and county elections may be held at the same time and place, and the ballot for the consolidated county election may be longer.

[4]This section is based on Oates (1972).

corresponds to the area of benefit from the goods it provides. As a result, each public good is provided in the smallest (that is, lowest-level) government consistent with no externalities.

The correspondence principle generates a federal system of governments along a spectrum from many small local governments to one national government. Variation in desired amounts of public goods is necessary to justify any subnational governments so that each one can provide a different amount of that good whose benefits are confined within its boundaries. Otherwise, it would be just as efficient to have one central government provide those goods to all using a number of different production plants. For instance, if all households desired the same amount of public television service, then it could be a national government function produced by many stations. The only reason to have each station operated by a separate government is to provide different amounts or types of service. But this raises another potential problem: The areas just consistent with no externalities may encompass households that desire different amounts of a good or service. Although the benefits of the radar system may go to all households in the nation, not all households may want the same amount of radar protection.

/ Preferences versus spillovers

The possibly conflicting objectives of having governments big enough to avoid cost or benefit spillovers but small enough to allow uniform desired amounts of public service suggests a trade-off between those two factors. For each public good or service, the optimal size government is the one that maximizes social welfare. As government size increases, the welfare gain from a reduced amount of spatial externality can be compared to the welfare loss due to increasing dissatisfaction among government members with the amount of public service selected. The optimal size government for each service is the one where the difference between the welfare gain and loss is greatest.

That choice of the optimal size government for some given service is shown in Figure 5.1. The cost function represents the cost or welfare loss that results as government size increases from combining individuals with different demand for public services. The total cost rises as government size increases, and the marginal cost of increasing government size—represented graphically as the slope of the cost function—also increases as size increases. This would occur if the new residents added first as government size increases are those with demands most similar to the original residents. The benefit function depicts the benefit or welfare gain from the reduction of spatial externalities as government size increases. Those benefits also rise as size increases although the marginal benefit of increasing government size—represented by the slope of the benefit function—decreases. That is, the largest gains from reducing externalities occur from the initial actions to form or enlarge local governments. For a public good or service with these characteristics, the optimal population size is N^*.[5]

---

[5]If the population is not mobile, then population size translates directly to a spatial area.

FIGURE 5.1   Optimal Jurisdiction Size for a Service

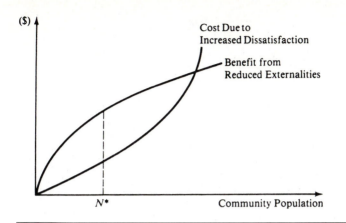

For other public goods and services, changes in the benefit and cost functions occur, with a resulting change in the optimal size. For example, if the differences in desired amounts for another service were much greater than the case in Figure 5.1, the cost function would rotate up having the effect of reducing the optimal N. On the other hand, if the problems of spatial externalities for another good were less severe—that is, a larger fraction of the externality is eliminated at smaller government sizes—the benefit function would rotate down and the optimal N would also decrease.[6]

In this manner, the optimal size government for every public good and service can be determined. Two examples are shown in Figure 5.2, one for a good requiring relatively small governments and one for a good with a larger, optimal-size providing government. This analysis is fully correct only if governments of any size can achieve all economies of scale in production of these goods by outside contracting and joint purchase agreements. If such arrangements are not possible, then the government size determined as above is a *minimum* size, with a larger size being optimal if further economies of scale can be achieved by expanding. Similarly, this analysis does not consider potential savings of administration and compliance costs, the issue to which we now turn.

/ Decision-making costs and clustering

If the optimal government size is determined by this procedure, it is possible, and even likely, that the optimal size will be different for each public good or service. As a result, as many levels of government would be required in a federal system as there are types of public goods and services. Every individual or household

---

[6]Note that the origin of each function should not change.

FIGURE 5.2 *Optimal Jurisdiction Size for Different Services*

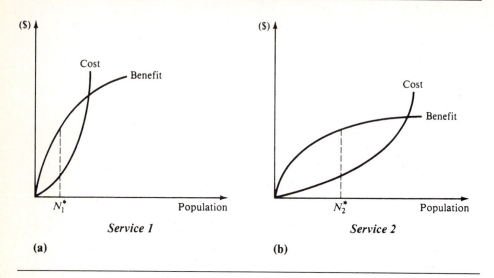

(a) Service 1

(b) Service 2

would be a member of that number of subnational governments. Such a structure may not be optimal, however, if consideration of the decision-making costs—that is, administration and compliance costs—is added to the externality and preference issues.

Suppose, for example, that there are eight different public goods to be provided by government, which can be denoted 1, 2, 3, . . ., 8. The optimal-size government to provide each is determined by comparing consumer welfare losses from grouping together consumers with different demands for each good against the welfare gains from a reduction of spatial externalities, as described above. Those optimal government sizes (measured by optimal population size N) are given in Figure 5.3. Good 1 requires the smallest size government, whereas at the opposite end of the spectrum, good 8 requires the biggest. To put it in terms of the required government structure, good 1 would be provided by many small local governments while good 8 would be provided by the federal government, with the other six provided by intermediate levels.

Oates (1972) has suggested that it is possible to reduce decision-making costs by *clustering* together goods with similar optimal sizes into single government units, reducing both the number of layers of government and the number of separate governments in each layer. For the example shown in Figure 5.3, goods 1, 2, and 3 might be clustered together for provision by government level A, goods 4 and 5 by larger governments at level B, and goods 6, 7, and 8 might be provided by the federal government at level C. Rather than eight levels of government there are only three, and rather than, say, five separate localities in the lowest level, there are three.

FIGURE 5.3 *Clustering of Jurisdictions by Size*

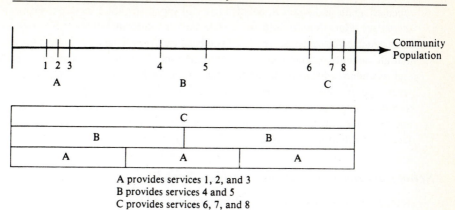

A provides services 1, 2, and 3
B provides services 4 and 5
C provides services 6, 7, and 8

Of course, this looks suspiciously like the government structure in the United States where the levels are the federal, state, and local governments, although the local government level in reality is more complex than suggested by this example (see Chapter 1). Given that such a structure exists, the common policy question is whether responsibility for providing the goods has been properly allocated.

/ Applications

Application of these principles in practice to the issue of the proper allocation of service responsibility among levels of government in a federal system usually comes down to a comparison of the importance of "local autonomy" versus concern about externalities, usually expressed as "what's best for all concerned."

For instance, consider a proposal to consolidate all local police departments into one metropolitan-area police authority. Because local governments would continue to provide other services, there would be no savings of political decision-making costs. There appear to be few economies of scale to be achieved, and if they do exist they may be captured without consolidation by cooperative agreements. Those opposing the consolidation would argue that local control would be lost, suggesting the concern that the consolidated authority would not provide the type or amount of police service desired as does the local department. This concern would be greater the more variation there is in the types of communities and police departments in the area. Those favoring the consolidation would argue that public safety is a metropolitan-area problem, that criminals do not recognize local government boundaries, perhaps even that the amount of police protection in some communities is "too low," in short that public safety is "too important to be left to localities."

This is a familiar refrain to those with experience in local government. It is repeated again and again in debates over all types of public services. Primary and secondary education ought to be a state government function because the benefits of an educated citizenry accrue to all and because everyone has an interest in ensuring that all students receive some minimum amount and type of education; or primary and secondary education should be a local function because each community knows what type of education is best for its students and because it would be dangerous to allow state bureaucrats to determine what students should learn. If the issues and principles involved are clear, the best way to measure the importance of these factors in actual cases is often not. One attempt to do that is reported next.

/ School district consolidation in New York[7]

Kenneth Greene and Thomas Parliament measured the potential welfare losses that could result from consolidation of twelve separate school districts in Broome County, New York, into one countywide district. Following the approach in this chapter and Chapter 4, these welfare losses would occur because the single amount of education to be provided by the consolidated district would be different than the amounts provided in many (or perhaps all) of the separate districts. If households were consuming their *desired* amounts of education service in each separate district, then consolidation would force some households to consume other than their desired amounts and thus suffer welfare losses. If consolidation is a good idea, these measured welfare losses would have to be offset by gains from fewer externalities or scale economies.

In measuring these welfare losses, Greene and Parliament suggest, however, that every household in each separate district may not be consuming the desired amount of education service. They assume, in other words, that the political choice in each district is represented by the median voter model rather than the Tiebout model. Because of costs and barriers to mobility, homogeniety of demand in each district is not expected. In that case, consolidation of education services will make some consumers better off by providing an amount closer to their desired amount of service. Thus, the potential welfare losses from consolidation are smaller than if one assumes a perfect Tiebout world to start.

Greene and Parliament's approach is represented in Figure 5.4, which shows the demands for education for three types of households in one of the separate school districts. The amount of education expenditure is selected by majority vote, so that the median amount E_B is chosen. Group A prefers less education expenditure while group C prefers more. The current welfare loss because A and C are not consuming their desired amounts is represented by areas *RST* and *SUW,* which measures the loss of consumer surplus for these groups.

Now suppose that consolidation occurs and the amount of expenditure chosen is the efficient amount of expenditure—the amount where the sum of marginal benefits equals marginal costs—E^*. Group A is made even worse off because the new

———————
[7]This example is from Greene and Parliament (1980).

FIGURE 5.4 **Welfare Effects of School District Consolidation**

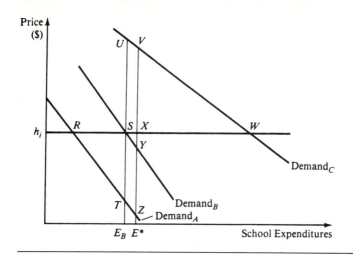

expenditure is even farther from their desired amount. Group B is also worse off because they no longer exactly consume their desired expenditure. Group C, however, is made *better off* because the new expenditure is closer to their desired one. In consumer-surplus terms, the new welfare loss to A is represented by area *RXZ*, the loss to B by area *SXY*, and the loss to C by area *XVW*. The change in welfare due to consolidation is represented by *SUVX − SXTZ − SXY*. This term may be positive or negative. If it is positive, it means that consolidation has *increased* welfare because the gain to group C offset the losses to groups A and B. In essence, the issue is whether consolidation moves the community toward the efficient level E^*, because at this level the sum of the consumer-surplus measures is maximized.

Greene and Parliament attempt to measure these welfare changes by first statistically estimating a demand curve for education based on all school districts in New York and then using that demand curve to predict both the amount of education expenditure that would be selected in the consolidated district and the desired amount for different income-class households. The estimated demand curve is:

$$\ln E = -1.21 - .343 \cdot \ln h + .697 \cdot \ln Y + .634 \cdot \ln N - .053 \cdot \ln P$$

where $\ln E$ = natural log of school-operating expenditures
$\ln h$ = natural log of tax price
$\ln Y$ = natural log of income
$\ln N$ = natural log of population
$\ln P$ = natural log of percentage of pupils in nonpublic schools.

This demand function, in combination with assumptions about the distribution of tax burdens by income, is used to measure the loss of consumer surplus for each of seven income-class households in each separate district that occurs because actual

TABLE 5.1

Welfare Costs of School-Expenditure Compromises

	Per-Capita Welfare Loss (in Dollars) Assuming	
	No Tax Exporting	Substantial Tax Exporting
After consolidation	116	63
Before consolidation	67	22
Change	49	41

Source: Greene and Parliament (1980).

expenditures in each district do not equal those households' desired expenditures. Those results are analogous to the loss to groups A and C in figure 5.4 when E_B is selected. Similar welfare losses are measured given the predicted expenditure for the consolidated district. These can be compared to show the cost due to the loss of political autonomy from consolidation.

The results are shown in Table 5.1 The average welfare loss for all twelve school districts initially (when they operate independently) is $67 per capita if no tax exporting is assumed or $22 per capital if there is substantial tax exporting. These numbers represent the average per-person cost because everyone in each district does not desire the same education expenditure. If all twelve districts are consolidated, the welfare losses increase to $116 per capita with no tax exporting or $63 with tax exporting. The change in welfare losses caused by consolidation—that is, the political cost of consolidation because households with greater differences in desired expenditures are grouped together—is then $49 per capita if no tax exporting is assumed or $41 with substantial tax exporting. If consolidation is to be economically desirable, there must be cost or welfare savings of that magnitude—perhaps from scale economies or reduced externalities—to be gained by the consolidation.

Greene and Parliament also calculated that the net change in per-capita welfare from consolidation is $64 if one assumed that the initial expenditure in each separate district was efficient. Therefore, the actual welfare losses from consolidation were much smaller than if efficiency in each locality had been assumed.

/ Service provision by contracting[8]

Contracting for service provision with another government or with a private firm is one way for localities to achieve any economies of scale in production of services. In fact, intergovernmental service contracts (under which one government pays another to provide a carefully specified service), private-service contracts (a government pays a firm or nonprofit agency to provide a service), and joint-service agreements (under which two or more governments join in financing and producing a service) are commonly used by local governments in the United States. In the first two types of contracting, provision decisions are retained by the contracting

---

[8]This section is based on ACIR (1985b).

government with production performed by the contractor; in the third case, both provision and production decisions are made jointly.

In 1983 the U.S. Advisory Commission on Intergovernmental Relations (ACIR) and the International City Management Association jointly undertook a survey of cities and counties, including all cities with population above 10,000, all counties with population above 50,000, and a sample of smaller jurisdictions, concerning use of intergovernmental service agreements. The survey showed that slightly more than half of all cities and counties contract with another government to provide some of their services and that 54 percent of cities and 60 percent of county governments enter into joint service agreements, as reported in Table 5.2. Moreover, intergovernmental service contracts and joint service agreements tend to be used to an even greater degree by larger cities and counties.

When contracts are used by cities, they most often contract with counties to have services provided; jails, sewage disposal, property tax assessing, animal control, and water supply are the services most commonly contracted out. County governments contract both with other counties and cities for such services as jails, fire protection, and computer and data-processing services. Joint-service agreements are used to provide police and fire communication, libraries, fire protection, and mental health services in addition to the services listed above. The survey also showed that 28 percent of cities and counties transferred production of some service to a private firm since 1976 and that 12 percent transferred some service responsibility to a nonprofit organization. Among the services whose production was transferred to the private sector were refuse collection and disposal, engineering, computer and data-processing services, and recreational facilities. (Private-service contracts are discussed in greater detail in Chapter 15.)

The dominant reason cited by these cities and counties for entering into both service contracts and joint agreements was to achieve economies of scale. That reason was cited by 52 percent of those using contracts and 51 percent of the

TABLE 5.2

City and County Use of Intergovernmental Service Arrangements

Jurisdiction Type	Percentage with Intergovernmental Service Contract	Percentage with Joint-Service Agreement
All Cities	52	54
Cities, population > 500,000	75	83
Cities, population < 500,000 and > 100,000	68	67
Cities, population < 100,000	51	53
All Counties	54	60
Counties, population > 500,000	54	72
Counties, population < 500,000 and > 100,000	55	63
Counties, population < 100,000	53	57

Source: ACIR (1985b, 26, 31).

governments participating in joint agreements. The second most cited reason (by 38 percent of those with contracts and 33 percent of those with joint agreements) stated that it was "more logical to organize services beyond jurisdictional or area limits," which seems to suggest that a larger service area would help reduce benefit spillovers. The most often cited fear about these intergovernmental agreements was a loss of local autonomy, particularly with joint agreements. In responding to the survey, an official from a city in Texas noted (ACIR 1985, 42):

> While joint service agreements have reduced the cost per unit of service delivered, there is a certain amount of control which is lost by the municipality in planning and meeting the city's goals.

Despite that caution, intergovernmental contracts, government/private-sector contracts, and joint agreements among governments for service provision appear to be commonly used by local governments for many services, primarily as a way of using economies of scale to lower service-production costs.

/ Summary

The greater are the variations in what individual consumers want from government and the more consumers with similar wants are grouped together, the stronger is the case for decentralized provision—that is, for having many small local governments.

The correspondence principle requires that the size of a government correspond to the area of benefit from the goods it provides. As a result, each public good is provided in the smallest (that is, lowest-level) government consistent with no externalities.

The possibly conflicting objectives of having governments big enough to avoid cost or benefit spillovers but small enough to allow uniform desired amounts of public service suggest a trade-off between these two factors. The optimal-size government for each service is the one where the difference between the welfare gain from fewer externalities and the loss from greater demand variety is greatest.

Economies of scale, in reference to the optimal size for governments, usually refers to a decrease in cost per person for a given amount of service as population served increases. Governments too small to achieve all economies of scale on their own can nevertheless take advantage of those economies by purchasing the good or service from governments or private firms that are large enough to exhaust all economies.

A final economic factor that may be a reason for few subnational governments (and thus more centralization) is to conserve on the direct costs of administering those governments and the costs to individuals of participating in the political process.

It may be possible to reduce decision-making costs by clustering together goods with similar optimal sizes into single-government units, reducing both the number of layers of government and the number of separate governments in each layer.

Application of these principles to the practical issue of the allocation of service responsibility among levels of government in a federal system usually comes down to a comparison of the importance of "local autonomy" versus concern about externalities, usually expressed as "what's best for all concerned."

Discussion Questions

1. "Unless there are economies of scale in the production of government goods and services, they should always be provided by the smallest available government units (that is, the lowest-level government in a federal hierarchy)." Evaluate this position.

2. Suppose that it is proposed to create a single local jurisdiction and government for your entire metropolitan area or region, to be called Metroland. It would replace all cities and/or towns that currently provide basic local services (such as public safety, streets, recreation services).

   a. Make the economic case *for* this consolidation into a metropolitan-area government (there are at least three potentially favorable economic reasons).

   b. Now suppose that you were hired as an economic consultant to advise about this change and your research uncovers three facts: (a) Currently, there is a big difference in per-capita spending among the municipalities to be consolidated, from $500 at the top to $200; (b) The variance in per-capita income for people living in the area is relatively large; (c) currently, many of these municipalities contract with the county (or state) government to have some services (such as jails, emergency dispatch, and parks) provided. Do these facts support or argue against the proposed consolidation? Explain your reasoning for each factor.

Selected Readings

Bahl, Roy W. and Walter Vogt. *Fiscal Centralization and Tax Burdens: State and Regional Financing of City Services.* Cambridge, Mass.: Ballinger, 1975.

Greene, Kenneth V. and Thomas J. Parliament. "Political Externalities, Efficiency, and the Welfare Losses from Consolidation." *National Tax Journal,* 33 no. 2 (June 1980): 209–17.

Oates, Wallace E. *Fiscal Federalism.* New York: Harcourt Brace Jovanovich, 1972. See especially Chapter 2.

Part 3

Revenue for State and Local Governments

State–local governments receive revenue from a variety of taxes and charges, from borrowing, from government production or sale of goods or services (such as electricity, liquor, and gambling), and from intergovernmental grants. The first three are sometimes referred to as ''revenues from a government's own sources'' and will be discussed in detail in Chapters 6–13. Intergovernmental grants are revenues collected by one government and transferred to another, usually at a different level of the federal government system. They are primarily intended to correct for economic inefficiencies resulting from the government structure by influencing the expenditure decisions of the recipient government. Accordingly, discussion of intergovernmental grants is included in Part 4 of the book concerning provision of government services.

In this part, we consider the traditional economic revenue issues of efficiency, equity, and administration, both by examining the institutional arrangements for these revenue sources and presenting the economic analysis of their effects. The key features of state–local government analysis—mobility and diversity—will be very much in evidence here. The relative ease of moving economic activity among subnational governments creates an additional avenue of escape from taxation that can substantially influence the expected economic effects of taxes. The great diversity of state–local government revenue systems both magnifies the influence of mobility and raises a question of just how state–local governments select their revenue structures.

This part begins in Chapter 6 with an overview of the basic tools of economic tax analysis, with emphasis on those issues that are most important for the state–local government situation. Although this overview is not intended to substitute for a more intensive study of the economic effects of taxes, it should provide a sufficient framework around which to organize the discussion of each specific revenue source. Thereafter, each revenue source is discussed in turn beginning with the ''big-three taxes''—property, income, and sales—and finishing with business taxes, borrowing, and government production and sale.

6 / Principles of Tax Analysis

> . . . No local, state, or federal government conducts its finances in an economy closed to the outside. . . . So there is little reason to believe either that all taxes are borne by residents of taxing regions or that the ultimate inter-regional distribution of these tax loads is very simple.[1]
>
> *Charles E. McLure, Jr.*

The basic economic issues and tools of tax analysis are introduced in this chapter. Readers should know and understand the methods and results in this chapter because they will be directly applied to specific taxes in the following chapters. For those readers who have never studied economic analysis of taxation, this should be sufficient introduction to allow a general analysis of the effects of different subnational government taxes. For other readers, this chapter may be a review.

/ The Economic Issues: Incidence and Efficiency

/ Tax incidence

Tax incidence is the analysis of which individuals bear the ultimate burden of taxes, that is, the burden after the economy has adjusted to any changes caused by the taxes. **Incidence** is usually defined as the change in private real incomes and wealth because of an adoption or change of a tax. Because individuals and firms may react to taxes by changing behavior, the taxpayers who bear the ultimate burden of a tax—that is, the economic incidence—may be different than the taxpayers from whom the tax is initially collected or levied upon, the statutory incidence of a tax. Incidence analysis usually considers the distribution of the amount of revenue generated by a tax, the revenue burden. But that burden must be compared to something, so incidence is usually a relative concept. One possibility is to compare the incidence of one tax to the incidence of another tax that generates an equal amount of revenue, the **differential incidence.** A second possibility is to compare

---

[1]"Commodity Tax Incidence in Open Economies." *National Tax Journal* 17 (June 1964): 187.

the incidence of the revenue of a tax to the incidence of the benefits of the goods and services financed by the tax, the **balanced-budget incidence**.[2]

The first step in doing incidence analysis is to determine which prices change and by how much as a result of the tax (or the tax and spending package). Of course, the prices of both consumer goods and services and factors of production can change, so a tax may affect individuals both from their uses of income (consumer purchases) and their sources of income (factor prices such as wages, rents, and interest). Suppose that such an analysis shows that the price of consumer good X rises and the price of factor of production Y falls because of a tax change. Thus, consumers of good X and suppliers of factor Y bear the burden of this tax. With this information, how can one determine the burden on a specific individual or a group of individuals, say those with incomes between $10,000 and $15,000? One must know the amounts of good X consumed and factor Y supplied by this individual or group of individuals. Those quantities, multiplied by the change in prices caused by the tax, show the magnitude of the tax burden imposed on each class. For instance, a person may bear none of the tax burden (if that person neither consumes X nor supplies Y), some of the tax burden (if that person consumes X but does not supply Y, or vice versa), or the full effect of the tax burden (if the person both consumes X and supplies Y).[3]

Once the burden of a tax change, because of the changes in prices of goods and services, is determined, that burden is usually characterized by its effect on income distribution. The terms *progressive, proportional,* and *regressive* are used to describe the effect of a tax on private-income distribution. Unfortunately, these terms can have more than one definition and meaning in tax analysis. In this book, we adopt the most common usage of these terms, describing tax burden as a percentage of income (unless a different specific definition is given). Those definitions are as follows:

> **Progressive tax**: Tax burden/income rises as income rises
> **Proportional tax**: Tax burden/income is constant as income rises
> **Regressive tax**: Tax burden/income falls as income rises

A progressive tax change therefore imposes a burden that is a greater fraction of income for higher-income persons than lower-income individuals. In contrast, a regressive tax change imposes a greater percentage burden on lower, as opposed to, higher incomes. Continuing the previous example, suppose that the amount spent on good X as a fraction of income is greater for higher-income than lower-income taxpayers, while suppliers of input Y are distributed equally throughout the income distribution. A tax change that increases the price of X and decreases the price of Y would be progressive. There is still some uncertainty with this definition, however, because income could be annual income or some longer-term measure

---

[2]A third possibility is **absolute incidence,** which is the incidence of a tax change when neither other taxes nor government spending are changed. The tax change would alter the government surplus or deficit and have macroeconomic effects.

[3]If input Y is also used to produce other products, then the analysis is still more complicated. Consumers of those other products could be affected.

such as lifetime income. The importance of these different measures of income will be considered in Chapter 8.

/ *Efficiency*

As discussed in Chapter 2, an economy is efficient if marginal social cost equals marginal social benefit for all goods. The efficiency cost of a tax change refers to changes in production and consumption of goods caused by the tax change so that marginal social cost and marginal social benefit are no longer equal. The tax revenue generated by the tax change does not represent an efficiency cost because that money is simply transferred from one part of the economy to another; the tax revenue is used to provide government goods and services that have corresponding benefits. The efficiency cost of a tax arises, rather, because individuals and businesses change their behavior due to the tax. By consuming different goods, which are less desirable than those that would be consumed in the absence of the tax, and by supplying different amounts of factors of production, the economy is moved to a less efficient or lower welfare position by the tax change.

The **efficiency cost** of a tax change refers therefore to the lost private welfare beyond that caused by the transfer of private income to tax revenue for the government. This is called the excess burden of taxation, that is, the burden over and above the revenue generated. The implicit assumption in this definition is that it may be possible to utilize some tax structure to collect a given amount of revenue at zero efficiency cost. Any other potential tax structure that can be used to generate the same revenue can be evaluated against this standard in terms of the efficiency cost, the welfare burden in addition to the revenue (which is the same for both tax structures).

/ *A general rule for tax analysis*

If there is one general rule for economic analysis of taxes, it is this: *The only way to (legally) avoid a tax is to change your behavior.* For instance, if a tax is imposed on the consumption of cigarettes, consumers can reduce their tax burden only by reducing the amount of cigarettes consumed or by purchasing cigarettes in a different (lower-tax) location. Similarly, a tax on the sale of gasoline can be avoided or shifted by firms only if producers sell less gasoline or sell it in a lower-tax jurisdiction. The rule also applies to broader-based taxes, in addition to specific excise taxes. An individual can reduce income tax liability only by earning less income or earning income in a lower-tax jurisdiction.[4]

This rule makes clear that tax incidence and tax efficiency are inherently connected. If individuals and businesses do not change their behavior in response to a tax change, then no efficiency cost is created and determination of tax incidence is simple—the tax change is a burden only for those directly taxed. If, on the other

---

[4]It is sometimes argued that businesses can also avoid a tax by raising prices. But higher prices are expected to reduce the amount demanded by consumers, requiring lower output. Thus the businesses would change production.

hand, individuals and businesses do change their behavior because of the tax-induced price changes, then the tax change will have an efficiency cost. And determination of tax incidence will be more complicated as individuals and businesses act to shift the tax burden to others.

There is an important corollary to this general rule. If the only way individuals and businesses can avoid tax burdens is by changing their behavior, it stands to reason that the more an economic agent is willing to change behavior, the more of the tax burden they can avoid. For instance, if an individual who drives a car stops driving entirely because of the imposition of a gasoline tax, that person obviously pays none of the tax. But an efficiency cost may have been created if the transportation method that this individual substitutes for driving is less preferred by that person.

/ Single-Market Tax Analysis

It is useful to consider how to apply the general principles outlined above to specific tax situations. The easiest way to illustrate those principles is to consider the effect of a tax on only one market, the market in which the tax is directly levied, called **partial-equilibrium analysis**.

/ A unit excise tax

Suppose that a tax of $\$t$ per gallon is to be imposed on the consumption of gasoline. Suppose also that gasoline is a commodity provided in a competitive market, as represented in Figure 6.1. Before the tax is imposed, the market is in equilibrium at price P_0 and quantity of gasoline G_0.

The imposition of a specific tax on a commodity can be analyzed either by shifting the demand curve down by the amount of the tax or by shifting the supply curve up by the amount of the tax—the methods are equivalent. In this case, because the tax is imposed on the consumers, we analyze the tax by shifting the demand curve down to Demand$_1$. If consumers are to consume the same amount of gasoline once the tax is imposed, the price the seller charges would have to fall by the amount of the tax so that consumers would still pay P_0. That is exactly what demand curve 1 represents. In essence, it shows the amount of gasoline demanded for different prices *charged by the seller,* whereas the original demand curve shows the amount demanded for different prices *paid by the buyer.* The two prices differ by the amount of the tax, so the two demand curves also differ by t.[5]

Once the tax is imposed, the new market equilibrium is shown by the intersection of supply and demand 1, the demand defined by the seller's price. As a result of the tax, the amount of gasoline sold falls to G_1, and the price charged by

---

[5]It is said that demand is shifted *down* (rather than to the left) because the change is of $\$t$ and dollars are measured vertically on this graph.

FIGURE 6.1 Incidence of a Unit Excise Tax

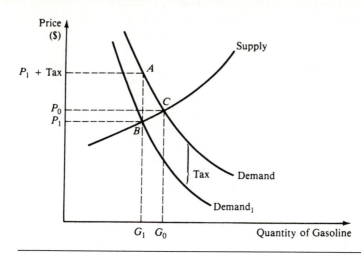

sellers falls to P_1. Remember, consumers must pay the seller's price plus pay the tax in this case, so the full price to a consumer is $P_1 + t$, which is shown on the graph as the price from Demand at quantity G_1. In sum the tax causes consumers to pay a higher price for gasoline and thus to buy less, while sellers also receive a lower price for gasoline than they did before the tax.

/ Incidence. Who bears the revenue burden of this tax? In this case, the revenue burden is borne both by consumers *and* sellers of gasoline. Due to the tax, the price consumers pay has risen from P_0 to $P_1 + t$, which is less than the amount of the tax. The price sellers receive has fallen from P_0 to P_1. The total tax revenue collected is tG_1, with the consumers' share being $(P_1 + t - P_0)G_1$ and the sellers' share equal to $(P_0 - P_1)G_1$. In this particular case, consumers bear a larger portion of the burden than sellers. You should understand, however, that the burden on sellers is a burden on *people,* not some business entity. The sellers' burden may result in lower profits to the owners, lower wages to employees, or lower prices for other factors of production. How the sellers' burden is divided among factors cannot be determined in single-market analysis.

What determines the division of revenue burden between consumers and sellers? Following the general rule noted above, the agents (consumers or sellers) who are less willing to change their behavior will bear the larger share of the burden. Willingness to change behavior as a tax alters prices is characterized by the price elasticity. If consumers are more willing to change behavior than sellers, then demand will be relatively more price elastic than supply, and sellers will bear the greater burden of any tax. In contrast, if sellers are more willing to change behavior, then supply will be more price elastic than demand, and consumers will bear the greater share of the revenue burden.

Following this rule, two special cases are presented in Figure 6.2. In Figure 6.2a, *supply is perfectly inelastic,* reflecting the fact that the same quantity will be supplied regardless of price; in essence, there is a fixed amount of this product. The imposition of a tax is shown by shifting the demand curve down by the amount of the tax, so price falls from P_0 to $P_0 - \text{tax}$. Because sellers will not change their behavior—that is, alter production—as the tax changes the price, sellers bear the full burden of this tax. In Figure 6.2b, just the opposite situation is depicted. If *demand is perfectly inelastic,* then consumers will not change their behavior as a tax alters price, so that the consumers' price rises by the full amount of the tax, and thus consumers bear the full burden of the tax.

FIGURE 6.2   *Incidence with Perfectly Inelastic Supply and Demand*

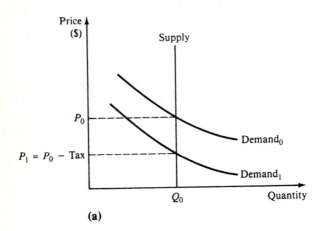

(a)

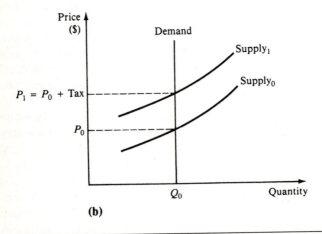

(b)

/ *Efficiency.*   This unit excise tax on gasoline also creates an efficiency cost. When the tax is imposed and the consumers' price rises, consumers move up along their demand curve and purchase less gasoline. Presumably, consumers are instead purchasing substitute fuels such as gasohol, they have substituted more fuel-efficient vehicles, they are traveling less, or they are still purchasing gasoline but in a different market, perhaps from stations in a neighboring locality. In any case, consumers have been induced to switch to less desirable alternatives, creating an efficiency cost. Similarly, as the tax causes the sellers' price to fall, sellers move down along their supply curve and produce less gasoline. Instead, those resources previously used for gasoline production are switched to the production of something else. If those resources cannot be used as efficiently in the production of those other commodities, an additional efficiency cost is created.

Measurement of the efficiency cost due to changes in consumers' behavior is depicted, for a simplified case, in Figure 6.3. In this case, the market-supply curve, which you may recall arises from the firm's marginal cost of production, is perfectly elastic (horizontal). The assumption of perfectly elastic supply means that any amount of the product can be supplied at the market price but that none will be supplied if the price falls below that market equilibrium. One example of such a situation is a product that is sold in many locations but whose price is set in a national or world market according to costs. For instance, once the world price of oil is determined, sellers need not sell oil in any market where the price is below that world price, because they can sell in other markets at the world price. This exact situation is common in the world of state-local government finance, with

FIGURE 6.3   *Efficiency Cost of a Unit Tax*

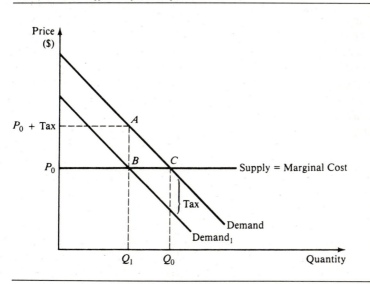

individual states or localities being small enough that they are price takers for goods sold in national (or world) markets.[6]

The imposition of a tax is analyzed by shifting the demand curve down by the amount of the tax. As a result, the quantity falls from Q_0 to Q_1, the sellers' price remains constant at P_0, and the consumers' price rises by the full amount of the tax to $(P_0 + \text{tax})$.[7] *The efficiency cost is the difference between the benefit to consumers and opportunity cost to society of each unit of the product foregone*— that is, the difference between marginal social benefit and marginal social cost. Assuming that one can approximate marginal social benefit by demand, the efficiency cost of the tax is the difference between demand and marginal cost for those units no longer produced due to the tax $(Q_0 - Q_1)$. Thus, the efficiency cost is represented graphically by triangle *ABC* in Figure 6.3. The tax generates revenue of tQ_1. The resources no longer needed to produce as much of this product, equal to $(Q_0 - Q_1)$ Marginal Cost, are shifted to the production of other products at no efficiency loss because marginal cost is constant.

The efficiency cost, which is represented by triangle *ABC,* can be computed with a simple formula. The area of any triangle is equal to $\frac{1}{2} \times$ the length $\times$ the height. Applying that formula to triangle *ABC* produces the result that

$$\text{Efficiency Cost} = \tfrac{1}{2}t^2EQ/P$$

where E = price elasticity of (compensated) demand.[8] In other words, the efficiency cost depends on the price elasticity of demand, the amount purchased, and the tax rate squared. This last factor is very important because as a tax rate is increased, the efficiency cost rises at a faster, quadratic rate.

There are three important warnings about the use of this formula to approximate efficiency costs. First, the formula applies exactly only if the demand curve is linear so that the efficiency cost is represented exactly by a triangle. Second, the formula applies only if the supply function is perfectly elastic (horizontal). If there is some elasticity to supply (the function is upward sloping), then the formula is more complicated and includes the price elasticity of supply. Third, the formula suggests that if the price elasticity of demand is zero (the demand curve is perfectly inelastic or vertical), then the efficiency cost would also be zero. This is generally

---

[6]Even for commodities sold in national markets, it is possible that prices may differ by location because of transportation costs, for instance. But for some, pricing strategies firms will bear transportation-cost differences and charge equal prices in all locations, such as the single "destination charges" used by automobile manufacturers. For a discussion of the theoretical issues, see Martin Beckmann (1968).

[7]Because supply is perfectly elastic, all of the tax burden is borne by the consumers. If the sellers' price fell below P_0, none of the product would be offered for sale, as the price would be less than marginal cost.

[8]The area is $\frac{1}{2}(AB)(BC)$, which equals $\frac{1}{2}t(Q_0 - Q_1)$. The price elasticity of demand E is the percentage change in quantity/the percentage change in price. That is, $E = [(Q_0 - Q_1)/Q_0]/(t/P_0)$. Solving for $(Q_0 - Q_1)$ and substituting into the equation for area gives the result.

FIGURE 6.4 Analysis of a Percentage Tax

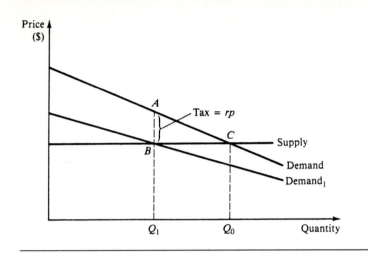

not correct. The problem arises because this is single-market analysis and thus ignores the behavior of consumers in other markets. Because the price of the taxed product has changed, consumers may alter their behavior in other markets (by purchasing less of some other product or by working less, for example), which would create an efficiency cost. This possibility is examined in the appendix to this chapter.[9]

/ How is a percentage tax different?

The above analysis is for a unit tax—that is, a tax of so many dollars per unit of product, such as $.15 per gallon of gasoline. The analysis of the more common percentage or *ad valorum* tax, such as a sales tax of 4 percent of the price, is only slightly different. As before, the tax can be analyzed by shifting the demand curve down by the amount of the tax per unit or by shifting the supply curve up. The difference is that the tax per unit depends on the price. If the tax rate is r percent, then

$$\text{Tax Revenue} = r(\text{Price})(\text{Quantity})$$

The tax per unit is then

$$\text{Tax Revenue/Quantity} = r(\text{Price})$$

Obviously, the higher is the price, the larger is the tax per unit in dollars, and the more the demand or supply curve must be shifted to reflect the tax. In Figure 6.4,

---

[9]For a good discussion, see Harvey Rosen (1988, 98–300).

the demand curve is shifted down by the amount of the tax with the distance being larger, the higher is the price.

While the analysis of the efficiency cost of this tax is exactly the same as for the unit tax, the formula to compute the approximate efficiency cost is different, as shown below:

$$\text{Efficiency Cost} = \frac{1}{2}r^2 EPQ$$

As before, the efficiency cost depends on the price elasticity of demand and the amount of the commodity purchased (now measured in dollars) and on the tax rate squared.[10]

/ Limitations of single-market analysis

While single-market analysis is very helpful in illustrating the general principles of tax analysis, it is often not very precise for two reasons. First, the effects in other markets, whether for other goods or for the same good in a different location, are not considered. Second, the manner in which any sellers' burden gets distributed among the various factors of production is not explicitly analyzed. While this may not be much of a problem in some cases where intermarket effects are small, it is often the case that intermarket effects can be substantial, particularly in the world of state-local governments, with relatively easy mobility among jurisdictions. Therefore, we turn now to multimarket analysis, effectively applying the same type of supply-and-demand analysis not only for the market in which the tax is directly imposed but also for other, closely connected markets.

/ Multimarket Analysis

/ Effects in parallel markets

Here we consider the effects of a tax levied in one market on other markets, including those for complementary or substitute goods. As an example, we can expand consideration of the effects of a unit tax of $\$t$ on gasoline to include those in the market for minibikes, assuming that cars and minibikes are substitutes. That situation is shown in Figure 6.5, with the simplifying assumptions of perfectly elastic supply of gasoline and minibikes. Given the national price for Best Unleaded Gasoline and Your Favorite Minibike, sellers will require that price in all markets in the long run. As before, the imposition of the unit tax on gasoline is represented by a downward shift in the demand for gasoline. As a result, the quantity of gasoline consumed decreases and the consumers' price rises, in this case by the full amount of the tax, because of the perfectly elastic supply. Consumers now purchase G_1 units of gasoline at a price of $P_0 + t$.

---

[10]Again, the area of the efficiency cost triangle is $\frac{1}{2}(AB)(BC)$, which equals $\frac{1}{2}rP(Q_0 - Q_1)$. Because $Q_0 - Q_1$ equals rEQ, the efficiency cost area equals $\frac{1}{2}r^2 EPQ$.

FIGURE 6.5   *Multimarket Analysis of a Unit Excise Tax with Constant Costs*

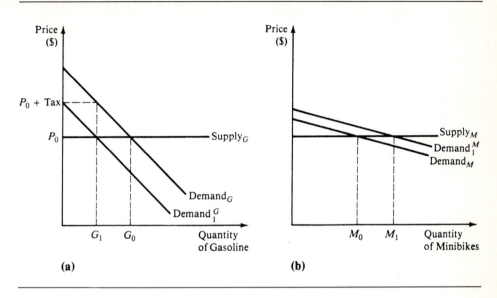

Because the price of gasoline has increased, consumers will act to reduce consumption, perhaps by substituting 60-mile-per-gallon minibikes for 20-mile-per-gallon cars. Thus, the demand for minibikes is expected to increase, shown by the rightward shift of demand in the minibike market. Given the assumption of perfectly elastic supply, the amount of minibikes purchased and produced rises, but the price remains the same in the long run. By consuming less gasoline, consumers have reduced the amount of gasoline tax they pay. [Consumers pay $(P_0 + t)G_1$ rather than $(P_0 + t)G_0$.]

The situation is only slightly more complex if constant costs do not prevail so that the supply curves in both markets are not perfectly elastic but are positively sloped, as depicted in Figure 6.6. In this instance, as previously discussed, the unit tax on gasoline causes both an increase in the consumers' price (but by less than the amount of the tax) and a decrease in the sellers' price. The increase in the consumers' price of gasoline causes an increase in the demand for minibikes that now brings about an increase in the price of minibikes due to the upward sloping supply. Because additional numbers of minibikes cost more to produce than do the previous ones, the price must rise to make that extra production worthwhile.

Because of this price increase, minibike consumers also are hurt by the gasoline tax; the higher minibike price is charged to all consumers, not just those who switch from cars due to the gasoline-price increase. Minibike consumers pay an increased amount equal to $(P_1 - P_0)M_0$. But this amount is not transferred revenue to the government, nor is it an efficiency cost lost to the economy. This extra amount consumers pay is transferred to the sellers through the higher price of minibikes.

FIGURE 6.6 *Multimarket Analysis of a Unit Excise Tax with Increasing Costs*

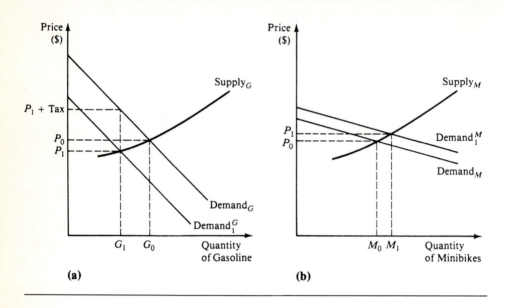

(a)

(b)

To complete this multimarket analysis, then, it is also necessary to expand the analysis to the factor markets behind these consumer-goods markets.

/ Effects in factor markets

Changes in consumption away from gasoline and cars and toward minibikes as a result of an excise tax on gasoline may also have implications for the factors of production used in the production of those goods. Some of those potential implications are shown in Figure 6.7. The decrease in the consumption of gasoline could lead to a decrease in the demand for the services of tanker trucks to carry gasoline to wholesale distributors and retail outlets. The immediate effect, given the number of trucks T_0, is a decrease in their value to P_1. If the long-run supply of tanker trucks is perfectly elastic, as depicted in Figure 6.7a, then the effect will be a reduction in the number of tanker trucks over time, so that the value of the trucks or the rental rate for tanker-truck services, returns to the previous level. Of course, the reduction in the number of tanker trucks or in the amount of tanker-truck service used may have implications for the drivers or producers of trucks.

Similarly, the increase in the demand for minibikes due to the tax on gasoline may increase the demand for plastic, assuming that minibikes primarily are constructed from plastic (and little plastic is used in producing cars). In this instance, we assume that the long-run supply of plastic is positively sloped, thus requiring a price increase to induce more production. The tax on gasoline therefore has the effect of increasing the revenue to producers of plastic, who *benefit* in effect from

FIGURE 6.7 Effects of an Excise Tax on Gasoline in Factor Markets

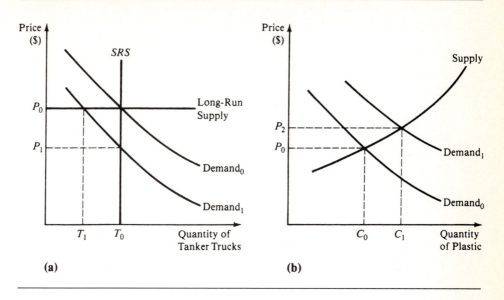

(a)

(b)

the gasoline tax. Recall that in Figure 6.6 we showed that minibike consumers pay an increased amount to minibike producers as a result of the gasoline tax. In the example, at least part of that gain to minibike producers becomes a gain to plastic producers. The excise tax on gasoline imposed a burden on gasoline consumers, but also caused a transfer from consumers to plastic producers.

Obviously, this story can continue, for instance, by asking whether the gain to plastic producers ultimately benefits workers in the industry or suppliers of chemicals used in plastic production. Indeed, one important aspect of multimarket tax analysis is deciding into how many different markets or how many different stages of production to carry the analysis. The appropriate answer depends on the case, including both the economic conditions in a market, which determines how large a price change is expected, and the importance of that market for the equity or efficiency result.

/ Application to state and local government issues

Multimarket analysis is essential when dealing with state-local government taxes because the focus is often on the effect of a tax levied by one state or locality when there is mobility among states or local jurisdictions. Examples abound. A consumer may go over a boundary to a store in a different location or order through a catalog to avoid sales tax. An individual may move his residential and work location to avoid an income tax, or an individual may change residential (but not job) location to reduce the residential property tax. Finally, a business may change its operating location to avoid a state business tax or local property tax. In all these cases, there might very well be economic effects in more than one market or location, both the one that imposes the tax and the one to which the economic activity moves. Multi-market tax analysis is required.

A simple relabeling of Figure 6.5 shows how the models in this chapter can be applied to these types of issues. Rather than thinking of one market for gasoline and one for minibikes, it is just as correct to let the Figure 6.5a represent the market for gasoline in jurisdiction G and the Figure 6.5b represent the market for gasoline in jurisdiction M. Before there are any taxes, gasoline sells for the same price in both locations. Now G imposes a $t unit tax on gasoline, so that consumers in jurisdiction G pay a price equal to $P_0 + t,$ which is greater than the price in *M*. Consumers in G now not only have the choice of switching to minibikes from cars but also of purchasing gasoline at a station in jurisdiction M. Obviously, some consumers from jurisdiction G decide to buy their gasoline from a station in M where the price is lower because there is no tax.[11]

Why don't *all* consumers switch their gasoline purchases to a station in M? They would unless switching is costly or unless they are not aware of the price difference. It could be costly to buy gasoline at a gas station in M rather than a station in G if one had to drive, say ten miles, from one's house to the nearest gasoline station in M. In that case, the cost (both in money and time) of the drive could outweigh the tax savings on gasoline. In contrast, someone who works in jurisdiction M but lives in jurisdiction G could switch gasoline purchases to M at little extra cost.

What is the gain to jurisdiction M from more gasoline sales? Possibly, there are now more retailers in M and fewer in G or at least more employment in M and less in G. The increased retail sales activity in jurisdiction M could also mean that property values in M increase. These changes would benefit workers in M (regardless of where they live) and property owners in M. The increased retail activity could (although it is not guaranteed) also increase the tax revenue to jurisdiction M from property taxes or from a local sales or income tax, if one exists.

If the price of gasoline is not determined in a national market (which is shown by the perfectly elastic supply) but rather determined in each local market, then the supply curves in each jurisdiction would be positively sloped, as in Figure 6.6. In that case, as consumers switch their gasoline purchases from jurisdiction G to M, the consumers' price of gasoline in jurisdiction G will fall and the price in M will rise. The market now creates a natural constraint on the movement of purchases from G to M; in the absence of costs of changing purchase location, consumers will reallocate their purchases until the consumers' prices in G and M are again equal.

This analysis of the interjurisdictional effects of taxes using a standard multi-market model is not limited to taxes on consumer goods but can just as easily be applied to taxes on factors of production such as labor, land, and capital. Of course, firms' payments for these factors become the wages, rent, and profits received by individuals, so these factor taxes are sometimes referred to as taxes on the sources

---

[11]It is just as correct to think that both G and M tax gasoline, but the tax in G is higher by $t.

(as opposed to uses) of income. One common application of this type is for sub-national government taxes on capital. The rate of return on capital investment is determined in a national (or world) market, so any one jurisdiction is a price taker; that is, the supply of capital to that jurisdiction is perfectly elastic (Figure 6.5). The suppliers of capital are individual investors, however, whereas the demanders are business firms. If one jurisdiction imposes a tax on capital, then the effect (just as with the gasoline tax in Figure 6.5) is expected to be a decrease in the amount of capital in the taxing jurisdiction and an increase in the other jurisdiction. These changes in the amount of capital are expected to have implications for consumers, workers, and landowners in both jurisdictions, implications that are considered in detail in Chapter 8.

/ Summary

Tax incidence is the analysis of which individuals bear the ultimate burden of taxes, that is, the burden after the economy has adjusted to any changes caused by the taxes. Incidence is defined as the change in private real incomes and wealth because of an adoption or change of a tax. This is different than statutory incidence, the actual payments made by taxpayers from whom the tax is collected.

The general rule of tax analysis is that the only way to (legally) avoid a tax is to change your behavior. Consumers or sellers who are less willing to change their behavior will bear the larger share of the burden.

The efficiency cost of a tax change arises because consumers or producers change their production or consumption so that marginal social cost no longer equals marginal social benefit.

Tax incidence and tax efficiency are inherently connected. If individuals and businesses do not change their behavior in response to a tax change, then no efficiency cost is created and the tax change is a burden only for those directly taxed. If individuals and businesses do change their behavior, then the tax change will have an efficiency cost, and determination of tax incidence will be more complicated.

Multimarket analysis is essential when dealing with state and local government taxes because the focus is often on the effect of a tax levied by one state or locality when there is mobility among states or local jurisdictions.

Perfectly elastic supply means that any amount of the product can be supplied at the market price but that none will be supplied if the price falls below that market equilibrium. This situation is common in state–local government finance, with individual states or localities being small enough that they are price takers for goods sold in national (or world) markets.

Discussion Questions

1. Suppose that the local legislative body in Your College Town (YCT) decides to levy a tax of $.50 for each 12 ounces of beer sold in the city (both by-the-drink and packages). The city sees the tax as a way to have students pay more for the city services they receive. Suppose that the beer market in YCT is competitive, the long-run industry supply in YCT is perfectly elastic, and the demand for beer in YCT is very price-elastic.

    a. What will the effects of the tax be on the price of beer in YCT, the amount of beer sold, and the number of beer stores in bars in YCT?

    b. Why might the demand for beer in YCT be so price elastic, given that it is known that overall demand for beer is rather inelastic? In view of that, what do you expect the effect of the tax will be on beer sales and the number of stores and bars in surrounding cities?

2. "If supply of a good is perfectly inelastic, then the sellers of that good are expected to bear the full revenue burden of an excise tax on the sale or consumption of that good." Evaluate this statement. Can you think of any examples of goods whose supply is (at least almost) perfectly inelastic?

3. If a unit tax is increased from $1 per unit sold to $2, the efficiency cost of the tax more than doubles. Explain.

4. Under what conditions would it be possible for an excise tax to have no efficiency cost and, in fact, increase economic efficiency? Give an example.

Selected Readings

Oates, Wallace E. *Fiscal Federalism.* New York: Harcourt Brace Jovanovich, 1972. See Chapter 4.

Rosen, Harvey S. *Public Finance,* 2d ed. Homewood, Ill.: Richard D. Irwin, 1988. See Chapters 13 and 14.

Appendix   *Indifference-Curve Analysis of Tax Efficiency*

Exposition of the consumer-demand model using indifference curves and budget lines was presented in the appendix to Chapter 3. Those tools can be used to more carefully describe the consumption changes and resulting efficiency cost from taxation than is possible with basic supply-and-demand analysis. Therefore, the consumer-theory model is used in this appendix to compare excise taxes on specific commodities with a general lump-sum tax.

    Suppose that consumers, who are price takers and have fixed amounts of resources (income), choose between gasoline and other goods. The consumer's budget before any taxes is shown by line YX in Figure 6A.1. This consumer can consume $\$Y$ of other goods by purchasing no gasoline or can consume a maximum of X gallons of gasoline by consuming no other goods. For this consumer, the consumption choice that gives highest utility is bundle B_0, implying that both gasoline and other goods are consumed.

    If an excise tax is levied on the consumption or sale of gasoline and thus the price of gasoline rises, the maximum amount of gasoline this consumer could afford,

FIGURE 6A.1   *Indifference-Curve Analysis of a Unit Excise Tax*

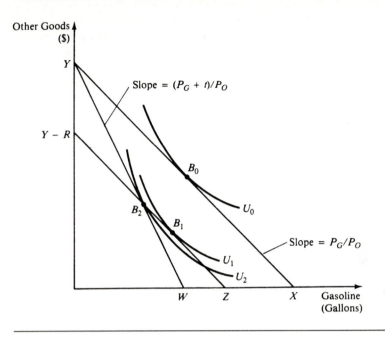

given a fixed income, decreases to W gallons. Now the consumer's budget limits choices to those on line YW. Because the slope of the budget line represents the ratio of the price of gasoline to the price of other goods and because the tax causes an increase in the price of gasoline, the budget line becomes steeper reflecting the fact that gasoline is now relatively more expensive compared to other goods than before the tax. Given the new budget, the consumption bundle that gives this consumer highest utility is B_2; in this case, the consumer purchases less gasoline and spends less on other goods due to the tax. The amount of tax paid by the consumer is shown as the vertical distance between the two budget lines, which is the difference between income that would be available to be spent on other goods if there were no tax and that actually spent.

The same amount of tax revenue could have been collected by a lump-sum tax equal to amount R, which would create budget line $(Y - R)Z$. Given those consumption choices, this consumer would receive highest utility at bundle B_1. The lump-sum tax also induces this consumer to reduce consumption of gasoline and other goods, but the decrease in gasoline consumption is less than occurs with the gasoline tax because the price of gasoline has not increased. With a lump-sum tax, the change in consumption occurs solely from the reduced available income.

Both taxes reduce this consumer's utility from private consumption (ignoring the utility received from the public services financed by the tax revenue), but the excise tax on gasoline reduces utility more than does the lump-sum tax, even though both taxes raise the same amount of revenue. Although both taxes have the same revenue burden, the excise tax has an *efficiency cost,* or *excess burden.* That efficiency cost can be measured by the difference between utility level U_1 and utility level U_2. The efficiency cost of the excise tax arises because the tax alters relative prices and thus causes an extra change in the consumption pattern beyond that caused by the tax revenue.[12] This efficiency cost will exist regardless of which bundle on budget line YW is selected, because budget line YW is always steeper than line $(Y - R)Z$. In particular, even if the consumption of gasoline is unchanged with the excise tax, an equal-yield lump-sum tax would provide this consumer higher utility than would a gasoline tax.

---

[12]The revenue burden of the tax is the difference between U_0 and U_1.

7 The Property Tax: Institutions and Structure

. . . No major fiscal institution . . . has been criticized at such length and with such vigor; yet no major fiscal institution has changed so little. . . .[1]

Dick Netzer

/ Property Tax Reliance and Trends

In 1986 state–local government property taxes generated nearly $112 billion of revenue, representing about 30 percent of total state and local government taxes and more than 17 percent of the total general revenue of state–local governments. This is about the same fraction as provided by federal aid. Property taxes amounted to about $463 per person and 3.4 percent of personal income in the United States.

The property tax has been and remains, however, primarily a source of revenue to local governments, with 96 percent of all property tax revenue going to local governments. Independent school districts collect the largest share of property taxes, nearly 42 percent. Not only do most property taxes go to local governments, but local governments are also very reliant on that tax. In 1986 property taxes provided more than 28 percent of the general revenue of local governments, second only to state aid in importance (Table 7.1). And despite the adoption of local sales and income taxes by some local governments, property taxes still provide about 74 percent of total local government taxes, as shown in Table 7.2. For all practical purposes, property taxes are just about the only tax used by school districts (97 percent of tax revenue) and townships (93 percent).

Local government reliance on the property tax has generally declined over the past twenty-five years, however. Property taxes provided 48 percent of aggregate local government general revenue in 1962 and the property tax share of local government taxes also declined for all types of local governments since 1962. The decline in property tax reliance has been most pronounced for municipalities, for whom property tax reliance fell by more than half since 1962. This decrease in property tax reliance resulted from larger increases in state and federal aid than property taxes over the period and from increased use of local government sales and income taxes and user charges.

---

[1]*Economics of the Property Tax*. Washington, D.C.: The Brookings Institution, 1966, 1.

TABLE 7.1

Property Taxes as a Percentage of General Revenue, by Level of Government, Various Years

		Local Governments					
Year	States	All	Counties	Municipalities	Townships	School Districts	Special Districts
1962	2.1	48.0	45.7	44.2	65.3	51.0	25.0
1967	1.7	43.2	42.1	38.1	61.8	46.9	21.5
1972	1.3	39.5	36.5	31.3	64.9	47.3	17.3
1977	1.3	33.7	31.0	25.8	56.8	42.1	14.0
1982	1.1	28.1	26.6	21.4	52.1	35.8	9.5
1986	1.1	28.2	27.3	20.5	52.1	36.2	10.4

Sources: U.S. Department of Commerce (1962, 1967, 1972, 1977, 1982; table entitled "General Revenue by Source, by Type of Government").

For 1986 data, U.S. Department of Commerce, Bureau of the Census. Governmental Finances, 1986.

/ The Property Tax Process

The property tax is different from other state–local government taxes in at least two important ways. First, both the tax rate and the tax base are determined by government. Unlike an income or sales tax, for which the value of the base (income or sales) is usually identified by private economic activity, the property tax base, which is property value, often must be estimated when market transactions are unavailable. This arises because the property tax is based on wealth, a stock, rather than an annual economic flow. Therefore, methods and procedures for **assessing** property value for tax purposes must be part of the property tax structure. Second, different government agencies, and sometimes even different levels of subnational government, are responsible for different aspects of the property tax process. Both of these factors have contributed to a general confusion about property taxes, which in turn has contributed to the tax payers' relative dislike of property taxes.

The typical procedure for assessing, levying, and collecting property taxes is outlined in Figure 7.1. First, the **assessed value** (taxable value) of each piece of

TABLE 7.2

Property Taxes as a Percentage of Taxes, by Level of Government, Various Years

		Local Governments					
Year	States	All	Counties	Municipalities	Townships	School Districts	Special Districts
1962	3.1	87.7	93.5	93.5	93.3	98.6	100.0
1967	2.7	88.6	92.1	70.0	92.8	98.4	100.0
1972	2.1	83.7	85.6	64.3	93.5	98.1	94.9
1977	2.2	80.5	81.2	60.0	91.7	97.5	91.2
1982	1.9	76.1	77.2	52.6	93.7	96.8	79.6
1986	1.9	74.0	74.5	49.3	92.7	97.4	79.8

Sources: See sources to Table 7.1.

property is computed by an **assessor** from an estimate of the market value of the property made according to a specific set of procedures, usually established by state law. Given that estimate of market value, the assessed value is specified by law or common practice as some specific percentage of market value, called the **assessment ratio rule.** It at least must be within some specified range of percentage of market value. Tax assessors are now most often professional employees of general-purpose local governments such as cities and townships, although in some areas assessors continue to be elected local government officials. In most states, local assessors are constrained by state laws and procedures, and their assessments may be reviewed by county and/or state officials. Assessment practices and procedures are discussed in greater detail subsequently in this chapter.

If different types or classes of property are assessed according to different assessment ratio rules, the tax is called a **classified property tax.** For instance, residential property might be assessed at 50 percent of market value and commercial and industrial property at 75 percent of market value. Classification provides a way to alter the distribution of property tax burden among different types of property. In addition, some types of property may be exempt from property tax. The assessed value of these properties is implicitly set equal to zero, although in practice exempt properties are often not considered or evaluated by assessors.

FIGURE 7.1   Property Tax Process

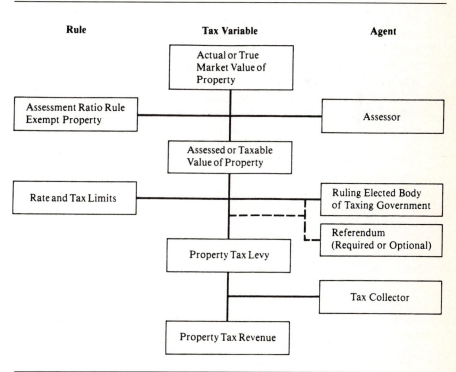

The revenue from any tax is computed by multiplying the tax base by a tax rate. Given the total assessed value of all properties in a taxing jurisdiction, therefore, the governing body of each local government—such as the city council, town commission, or school district board—sets a tax rate sufficient to generate the desired property tax revenue. In every state, the local governments are constrained in setting the property tax rate by state laws limiting the tax rate, property tax revenue, or both. There is great diversity among the states in both the types and magnitudes of these limits, as described in Chapter 20. In some cases, a referendum (popular vote) is required to approve or select the property tax rate or revenue.

Property tax rates have historically been specified in *mills,* with the property tax rate referred to as the *millage.* One mill is one-tenth of 1 percent, or $1 of tax per each $1000 of taxable value. There has been some tendency to reduce the use of the term *mills* in recent years in favor of characterizing the property tax rate as a percentage (similar to other tax rates) or by dollars per unit of taxable value. Either serves to reduce misunderstanding of and confusion about the property tax.

The **property tax levy,** or **bill,** for each property is determined from the tax rate and the assessed value for each property. The property taxes are then collected by a **tax collector,** often the municipal or county treasurer. It is common for the total property tax bill on a given piece of property to be collected by a single local government, even though that tax liability reflects rates imposed by several overlapping local governments. The property tax collections are then divided among the taxing jurisdictions proportional to their rates. In most states, property taxes are collected annually or semiannually. Many individual homeowners with mortgages pay a monthly amount to the mortgage lender (with their mortgage interest and principal payment) to cover property taxes; the government then collects the property tax from the financial institution according to the property tax collection schedule.

The following sample property tax computations illustrate the operation of the process. Suppose that state law requires that all properties be assessed at 50 percent of market value and that the tax rate (the sum of tax rates for all the taxing local governments) in the jurisdiction where the single-family house is located is $50 per $1000 of assessed value, while the tax rate in the jurisdiction where the commercial office building is located is $40 per $1000 of assessed value. Once the market values of these properties are estimated, the tax can be computed:

Tax Variable	Single-Family House	Commercial Office Building
Market value	$80,000	$5,000,000
Assessed value (AV)	$40,000	$2,500,000
Tax rate	$50 per $1000 of AV	$40 per $1000 of AV
Tax	$2000 ($50 × $40)	$100,000 ($40 × $2500)
Effective rate (tax as a percentage of market value)	2.5% ($2000/$80,000)	2.0% ($100,000/$5,000,000)

The **effective rate** of tax, the **ratio of tax to market value,** is a useful way to characterize property tax levels on different properties or in different jurisdictions. Because tax is compared to market value, the effective rate corrects for any difference in assessment ratio. Stating that the property tax is 2.5 percent of value, as with the single-family house in the example, is much clearer than explaining the tax rate in mills and the assessment ratio.

Although property taxes are primarily local government taxes, the state government also plays a role in the property tax process to a varying degree in different states. The state government plays a leading role in two states, Maryland and Montana, where all property assessment is done by a state agency. The more common model is for initial property assessment to be done locally, although subject to procedures specified by the state, with subsequent review of assessment by the state government. In most cases, the essence of the review is to ensure that each local government applies the assessment ratio rule in aggregate for all property in the jurisdiction, if not for each property. The approach is to *equalize* the aggregate assessment ratio for all local governments at the state standard. To accomplish this, the state specifies a proportion by which all property values in a community are multiplied, which increases the assessment ratio to the standard. For instance, if a local government assesses property at a ratio of 40 percent of the market value when the state standard is 50 percent, the state could impose an equalization factor of 1.25; a 25-percent increase in assessments brings the locality up to the state standard.

State governments have adopted uniform assessment ratio standards primarily for two reasons. First, taxable property value per capita or per student may be used to allocate state aid, with more aid going to less wealthy communities, that is, those with lower per-capita assessed values. This creates an obvious incentive for local governments to underassess to be eligible for more state aid. Assessment equalization is an attempt to avoid this problem by ensuring that assessed values are consistent measures across different localities. Second, uniform assessment ratio rules may also serve to improve the equity of assessment within localities, thus moving toward the objective that all taxpayers in a given community with property of equal market value pay the same tax. For these purposes, it does not matter *what* assessment ratio is selected, just that it be consistent across properties and communities.

/ Who is responsible for property tax increases?

The separation of responsibility for assessing property and setting tax rates can contribute to taxpayer confusion about the source of property tax increases. If property is required to be assessed at a given percentage of market value, then increases in the market value of property (even increases consistent with a general rise in prices) *should* lead to increases in assessed values. But if assessed values increase and tax rates remain constant, property tax revenues will increase. In other words, a general rise in property values allows local governments to increase property tax collections without increasing tax rates. Not surprisingly, some individuals are led to conclude that the assessment increase *caused* the tax increase.[2]

This view is not correct because each local government with property tax authority controls and selects, either explicitly or implicitly, the amount of property tax revenue to levy. Typically, the assessed values for a community are determined and known before the local governments adopt their budgets for the coming fiscal year. Given those tax bases, the governing bodies can adjust the amount of property tax revenue by adjusting tax rates. A decision to keep tax rates constant when it is known that assessed values have increased is a decision to increase property tax revenue. The announcement by a local government that "taxes will not be increased this year" must be scrutinized; is it the tax rate or tax revenue that is being held constant. It may be that it is politically easier to increase tax collections by keeping rates constant (with increased assessed values) rather than by increasing rates (when assessed values do not increase), but fiscally there is no difference.

The possibility for the political responsibility for property tax increases to be borne by assessors rather than the elected local government officials has induced thirteen states to adopt what have come to be called "truth-in taxation" procedures. Typically, these procedures require local governments to establish the property tax rate that will generate the same amount of *revenue* in the next fiscal year as was collected in the previous year, given the known change in assessed values. If the local government wishes to set a tax rate greater than this "equal revenue" rate, special procedures are required, usually including advertising of the proposed tax increase, public hearings, and a specific vote of the local governing body on the property tax rate. A sample newspaper advertisement of the proposed increase and hearings required by the Michigan law is shown in Figure 7.2. The purpose of these truth-in-taxation laws is to ensure the appropriate political accountability for property tax decisions.

FIGURE 7.2   Truth in Taxation Notice

INSTRUCTIONS TO NEWSPAPERS

The following notice is required by Act 5, P.A. 1982, which provides:

1. The body of the notice must be set in 12 point type or larger.
2. The headline "Notice of Public Hearing on Increasing Property Taxes" must be set in 18 point type or larger.
3. The notice cannot be smaller than 8 vertical column inches by 4 horizontal inches.
4. The notice cannot be placed in the portion of the newspaper reserved for legal notices or classified advertising.

(Continued)

---

[2]The same process happens with any other tax, that is, income tax revenues increase as incomes increase. However, with property taxes, unlike the others, the base is set by a government official.

Notice of Public Hearing on Increasing Property Taxes

The _____
name of governing body

of the _____
name of taxing unit

will hold a public hearing on a proposed

increase of _____ mills in the operating tax
rate

millage rate to be levied in _____ .
year

The hearing will be held on _____ ,
day

_____ at _____
date   time

o'clock in the ☐ a.m. ☐ p.m. at

_____ .
place—address

If adopted, the proposed additional millage will increase operating revenues from ad valorem property taxes _____ % over such revenues generated by levies permitted without holding a hearing.

The taxing unit publishing this notice, and identified below, has complete authority to establish the number of mills to be levied from within its authorized millage rate.

This notice is published by:

_____
name of taxing unit

_____
address

_____
address

_____
telephone no.

Source: Michigan Department of Treasury.

TABLE 7.3

Assessed Property Values, by Type, 1981

Type of Property	Amount[a]	Percentages of Gross Assessed Value
Gross assessed value	2958.2	100.0
State assessed	159.2	5.4
Locally assessed	2799.0	94.6
Real property	2514.9	85.0
Residential (nonfarm)	1520.0	51.4
Single-family houses	1328.7	44.9
Commercial	353.5	11.9
Industrial	195.8	6.6
Farm acreage	247.8	8.4
Vacant platted lots	109.4	3.7
Other	88.3	3.0
Personal property	284.2	9.6
Net assessed value	2837.5	100.0[b]
State assessed	159.0	5.6[b]
Locally assessed	2678.4	94.4[b]
Real property	2406.7	84.4[b]
Personal property	271.7	9.6[b]

Source: U.S. Department of Commerce, (February 1984, Tables A and C).

[a]In billions of dollars.
[b]Percentage of net value.

/ Property Assessment

/ Taxable property: Types, numbers, values

In 1981 there were more than 98,000,000 different parcels of property to be assessed for taxes with a total assessed value approaching $3 trillion, as shown in Table 7.3. Single-family homes constitute, both in value and number, the largest single class of property subject to property taxes, representing in 1981 nearly 45 percent of the total assessed value for property taxes and 56 percent of the number of parcels of assessed property. In contrast, the next largest classes were commercial property, representing about 12 percent of assessed value, and vacant platted lots, comprising about 20 percent of the number of parcels.[3]

The Census Bureau first characterizes property by whether it is initially assessed by local governments, which includes nearly 95 percent of total assessed value, or by state governments, which is the other 5 percent of value and mostly comprises railroads, telephone companies, and other utility property. The locally assessed property is then divided into **real property**—that is, land and buildings, which represents 85 percent of total assessed value—and **personal property** such as equipment, inventories, motor vehicles, and household property, which represents

---

[3]A vacant platted lot is land that has been surveyed and subdivided in preparation for development, but without any structure.

a little less than 10 percent of total assessed value (state-assessed is the other 5 percent). Real property is then further subdivided into residential (single- and multi-family dwellings—51 percent of assessed value), commercial (office buildings, stores, warehouses—12 percent), industrial (manufacturing plants—7 percent), farm acreage (8 percent), vacant platted lots (4 percent), and all other property (3 percent).

In most states, all real property is subject to property taxation with the exception of real property owned by governments and religious and charitable organizations, although as noted the degree of taxation may vary by type of real property. There is, however, much less uniformity in the property tax treatment of tangible personal property. Commercial and industrial personal property, which generally means business equipment and fixtures that are not permanently attached to buildings, is taxed in forty-three states and by local government option in two others. Business inventories, on the other hand, are included in personal property and taxed in only twenty-eight states. Motor vehicles are taxed as personal property in nineteen states, but household personal property such as furniture, appliances, clothes, and the like are broadly taxed in only seven states (nine others tax household personal property used in the production of income). When personal property is broadly taxed, it is usually not specifically and separately assessed, but rather a value is imputed as a percentage of the house value.

The 58 million residential parcels represent 59 percent of the total number of property parcels to be assessed. Not surprisingly, the average value of a residential parcel is substantially less than the average value of a commercial or industrial property, so the relative importance of residential property is lessened when measured by value. Although commercial properties represent only 3.6 percent of the number of parcels, they comprise 12 percent of the assessed value of properties; similarly, industrial properties are only 0.6 percent of the number of parcels but 6.6 percent of total value.

As always, these averages obscure substantial differences among the states. The distribution of locally assessed values for different types of real property for selected states in 1981 is shown in Table 7.4. The residential share of locally assessed real property varies from 75.2 percent in Massachusetts to 30.4 percent in North Dakota. Note that a large residential property share does not automatically translate into a large single-family value share as illustrated by New York, where 55.7 percent of assessed value is residential property although single-family houses represent only 35.6 percent. In general, there is somewhat less variation in the share of value from commercial and industrial property, although the range is still large—from 10.9 percent in South Dakota to 37.7 percent in New York. Texas represents another special case—the category ''other'' real property (which is not shown in the table) comprises 30.1 percent of the assessed value, mostly from oil and natural-gas property.

It is important to remember that these interstate comparisons reflect both differences in the state economies and differences in state rules regarding what types of property are subject to tax and how they are assessed. For instance, two states may in fact have the same amount of all types of property, but one state chooses to assess commercial and industrial property at a smaller fraction of value than

TABLE 7.4

Locally Assessed Taxable Real Property, Percentage Distribution by Type, Selected States, 1981

Jurisdiction	Total Residential	Single Family	Commercial and Industrial	Acreage
All states	60.4	52.8	21.8	9.9
California	66.1	54.9	22.9	4.4
Connecticut	74.3	69.2H	21.0	1.8
Massachusetts	75.2H[a]	64.6	20.5	1.5
Michigan	65.2	60.5	20.8	11.5
New York	55.7	35.6	37.7H	3.9
N. Dakota	30.4L	27.1L	13.9	53.8H
Rhode Island	73.1	59.2	21.3	1.1L
S. Dakota	34.3	31.1	10.9L	53.2
Texas	34.0	30.6	22.0	10.3
Washington	65.3	58.9	20.1	9.5

Source: U.S. Department of Commerce (February 1984, Table 6).

[a]H denotes highest value and L lowest value among the states.

residential property and the other assesses both at the same ratio. As a result, the commercial and industrial share of assessed value will be greater in the second state than in the first and the residential share correspondingly greater in the first.

/ Assessment methods

Property assessors use three basic methods to estimate market values of properties from which assessed values can be determined. The three approaches, which differ in the data used to estimate value, are (a) the comparative sales approach, which uses data from actual sales and property characteristics to estimate the values for properties which are not sold; (b) the cost approach, which bases the value on historic cost adjusted for depreciation; and (c) the income approach, which measures value by the present value (sometimes called capitalized value) of the future net income expected to be generated by the property. In most instances, the comparative sales approach is used for assessing single-family homes and land for which there are often numerous sales, while the cost and income approaches are usually used for commercial and industrial properties, which may be unique and for which comparative sales data are not available.

To implement the comparative sales approach, it is first necessary to prepare a listing of all properties including their location and physical characteristics, what is often called a tax roll. Sale prices for some of those properties can be used to statistically estimate implicit values (what are sometimes called shadow prices) for property characteristics. Using standard appraisal techniques, the value of each characteristic combined with the quantity of those characteristics in a property lead to an estimate of the total value of the whole property. As an illustration, suppose that a statistical analysis of sales prices and property characteristics of single-family homes yields the following regression:

$$V = 10,000 + 37.5 \cdot FT + 9000 \cdot BATH + 1750 \cdot BR + 2200 \cdot GAR$$

where V = value of the house (observed for sales)
     FT = square footage of the house
     $BATH$ = number of bathrooms
     BR = number of bedrooms
     GAR = number of stalls in the garage

The interpretation of the results is that an additional square foot of space adds $37.50 to the value, an additional bathroom $9000, an additional bedroom $1750, and so forth. These results for houses that actually sold can be used to estimate value for those that do not sell in a particular period if the characteristics of all houses are known. A 2000-square-foot house with two baths, three bedrooms, and a two-car garage would have an estimated market value of $112,650, whereas a 1600-square-foot house with one bath, three bedrooms, and a one-car garage would be expected to have a value of $86,450.[4]

While it is theoretically possible to reassess properties each year, in most cases assessment of properties based on their specific characteristics is done at selected intervals, for instance, every ten years. This may be because the characteristics of properties are not updated each year or because the statistical analysis is not done each year. In that case, some method for estimating changes in values in the intervening period is required. One common method is to subdivide an assessing jurisdiction into areas or neighborhoods, measure the percentage change in values each year in that neighborhood based on sales data, and apply that percentage to all properties in the neighborhood. This method will be more accurate the greater the homogeneity of the properties and the less the characteristics of the properties are altered. Some states do reassess annually, however, with the help of computers. If the assessment roll is computerized, changes in characteristics can be entered as they occur (using data from building permits, for instance) and used with annual estimates of shadow prices to estimate annual values.

The cost approach to assessment is based on the principle that the market value of a property cannot be greater than the cost of constructing that property. If an identical duplicate of an existing structure can be constructed for say $100,000, then no informed buyer would pay more than that $100,000 for the existing structure. (This refers to the value of the structure only; the land on which the structure sits has a value of its own.) On the other hand, the market value of an existing structure, which depends on the demand for structures of that type, can be less than the construction cost. Of course, one usually doesn't talk about constructing an identical duplicate of an existing structure, but rather a replacement for that structure (one cannot construct a fifteen-year-old factory). Accordingly, the historic cost of a

---

[4]For the 2000-square-foot house, the computation is $10,000 + $37.5 \cdot 2000 + $9000 \cdot 2 + $1750 \cdot 3 + $2200 \cdot 2$. The computation for the smaller house is similar.

structure must be adjusted for economic depreciation and any change in construction costs to get an estimate of the maximum potential market value of the existing property. To make these adjustments, assessors use factors specific to location and property type that are provided by state governments or appraisal firms to adjust historic cost. For instance, a factor of .5 for retail stores after ten years implies a 50-percent reduction from cost for that type of property with that age. To implement the cost approach, assessors require up-to-date adjustment factors and detailed data on historic cost for different components of all properties to be assessed.

The income approach to assessment is based on the notion that the value of an asset depends on the demand for that asset, and that demand depends on the net income or profit that that asset will generate. The following example illustrates the principle.

Suppose that there is an apartment building with twenty apartments, each renting for $400 per month, thus generating revenue of $96,000 per year ($400 × 12 × 20). The annual cost of owning and operating the apartment building, including all opportunity costs, is $80,000, so that the annual net income or profit is $16,000. Suppose further that this building is expected to continue to operate in exactly the same way for the next twenty years (although this is unrealistic because costs may rise or rents fall as the building becomes older), and that the building is worth zero at the end of that period. A potential buyer can therefore expect to receive net income of $16,000 per year for the next twenty years from the building. What is the maximum amount a buyer would be willing to pay now for that stream of future profits? The answer is the present value of the stream, which depends on the buyer's discount rate—that is, the rate that could be earned on alternative investments. If that rate is 8 percent, the present value of $16,000 per year for twenty years is $157,090. That is, $157,090 invested now at 8 percent will generate the same income as receiving $16,000 a year for twenty years. Therefore, the value of the apartment building is the value of the net income the building will generate, or $157,090. (In addition, the land on which the building sits must be valued.)[5]

Implementing the income method requires data on current profits of the business or operation, an assumption about future conditions in the market of this business, the expected future life of the asset, and an appropriate discount rate. Firms may be unwilling to divulge detailed profit information, and the other required factors are issues about which there is likely to be substantial uncertainty. Not surprisingly, different applications of the income method can lead to substantially different value assessments.

Perhaps the preferred method of assessing commercial and industrial properties is to use both the cost and income approaches when feasible and to use a weighted average of the two estimates to determine assessed value. In many cases, however, the absence of solid current- and future-income data prevents use of the income

---

[5]The formula for the present value of $1 to be received or paid t years in the future is $PV = 1/(1 + i)^t$, where i = discount rate, usually the interest rate available on alternative investments or projects. The present value of the twenty-year stream of profits is $\sum_{t=1}^{20} \$16,000/(1.08)^t$.

approach, so assessment based on cost plus depreciation is still the most common approach for business properties.

This basic discussion of property assessment methods does not do service to the many difficult economic, procedural, and legal problems that can arise in applying these basic ideas and approaches. Problems can arise in defining types of property, in interpreting tax implications of various contractural conditions, in acquiring and interpreting economic data, in defining the relevant market for a property, and in many other areas. One of these problems, one that shows the interaction of legal and economic principles, is discussed in Application 7.1. Partly for these reasons, property assessment has become a specific profession, regulated by many state governments and with its own professional association, the International Association of Assessing Officers (IAAO). These problems should be kept in mind in attempting to measure good assessment, as discussed in a following section.

/ APPLICATION 7.1
Opportunity Cost and the Value of Leased Commercial Properties

Suppose that a business signs a long-term (say, ten year) lease for commercial office or retail space at a monthly rent of $5 per square foot. Five years after this lease is signed, however, rents on similar properties have risen to $6 per square foot per month. This tenant continues to pay $5 because the owner is prevented from raising the rent by the contract. Has the value of this property increased, should the assessed value rise, and if so, who should be liable for any increased tax, the tenant or the owner?

Several institutional details are relevant. In most states, both the real and personal property involved will be taxed. It is common in some commercial rentals for the building owner to provide a shell, with the tenant adding and owning the interior including walls, floors, fixtures, and display materials. Therefore, some of the real property (that permanently attached to the building) may be owned by the building owner and some by the tenant, while the personal property is generally owned by the tenant. Moreover, many commercial lease contracts specify that the tenant will pay all property taxes, not just the personal property component.

Economically, this tenant has enjoyed a gain due to the rise in market rents for similar properties. The opportunity cost of the asset, the leased property, has increased, but the actual cost to the tenant remains constant. This business enjoys lower costs for the remaining length of the contract than for competitors who must pay the current market rent of $6. Indeed, this tenant could sublease the property for the $6 market rent and realize the gain. Economic principles imply therefore that the assessed value of the leased property based on the income approach to assessing should increase (if it is to be kept at a percentage of market value) and that the tenant should be liable for the tax increase (because the gain is to the tenant).

/ APPLICATION 7.1 Continued
Opportunity Cost and Value of Leased Commercial Properties

There are several legal complications, however. Suppose that the tenant's contract specifically prohibits subleasing. A basic legal principle holds that one cannot sell what one does not own; this suggests that because the tenant's gain is not marketable, there can be no gain in market value. Suppose that subleasing is not prohibited but that the tenant still does not do so. The tenant has a property right but no explicit gain, so some would argue that this property is "intangible" and thus not taxed under most property taxes (which usually apply only to "tangible" property). Finally, suppose that the lease contract requires the building owner to pay real property taxes and the tenant to pay the tax on any personal property. The increase in market rents has increased the value of the rental space, the building, but the implicit gain goes to the tenant, not the building owner. Indeed, the building owner is prevented from capturing the gain by the contracturally specified rent. It would therefore be inappropriate to increase the assessed value of the building and increase the owner's tax. An alternative is to define a new type of personal property, called "leasehold interests," equal to the difference between market and contracted rent, and to assess that interest to the personal property of the tenant.

While this specific issue is interesting and important, the purpose of this application is to illustrate the nature of problems that can arise in determining market and assessed values in actual, complicated situations. Even when market prices or values are observable, it is not always straightforward to apply the assessment approaches in determining an accepted value.

/ Evaluating assessment results

Given that property assessment is a difficult task, how can assessment quality be measured, how good of a job are assessors actually doing, and what accounts for less than perfect assessment (leaving to Chapter 8 the issue of whether nonuniform assessment matters)? Assessment quality has traditionally been measured by the variation in assessment ratios for different properties within the same assessing jurisdiction, assuming that good assessment involves uniform assessment ratios rather than achieving any specific assessment ratio. The statistic commonly used to measure the variation in assessment ratios within a community is the **coefficient of dispersion**, which is the average percentage deviation from the median assessment ratio. Computation of a sample coefficient of dispersion is shown in Table 7.5.

In the table, the actual sales prices of three properties are compared to their assessed values at the time of sale (so the assessor did not have the sales information in making the assessment). Property B is assessed at 50 percent of market value, which is assumed to be the statutory assessment ratio, while property A is over-assessed at 62.5 percent of value and property C is underassessed at 40 percent of the market price. Therefore, the median (middle) assessment ratio is .50, and the

TABLE 7.5

Sample Coefficient of Dispersion for Assessment Ratios, Single-Family Houses, One City

Amount or Calculation	Property		
	A	B	C
Market value	$ 40,000	$ 60,000	$100,000
Assessed value	$ 25,000	$ 30,000	$ 40,000
Assessment ratio	.625	.50	.40
Median assessment ratio		.50	
Difference from median ratio	.125	0	.10
Average difference		.075	
		(.125 + .10)/3	
Average percentage difference or coefficient of dispersion		.15	
		(.075/.50)	

coefficient of dispersion (the average percentage difference from the median) is .15, which means that on average assessment ratios vary 15 percent from the median.

Actual coefficients of intra-area dispersion of assessment ratios for single-family houses are computed by the Census Bureau for individual assessing districts based on sales data and prior assessed values, with the distribution and median reported for each state. These are shown for selected states in Table 7.6. For all states in 1981, the median coefficient of dispersion was .213, or 21.3-percent variation of

TABLE 7.6

Property Assessment Results for Single-Family Homes, Selected States, 1981

Jurisdiction	Median Assessment–Sales Ratio (%)	Median Coefficient of Intra-area Dispersion (%)
All states	36.9	21.3
Alabama	7.1	52.0H
California	65.1	28.2
Florida	69.2	18.5
Idaho	86.8H[a]	16.4
Massachusetts	59.6	14.8
Michigan	44.3	15.3
Montana	3.7L	35.4
New York	14.6	23.1
Pennsylvania	13.7	34.3
Ohio	30.2	22.3
Virginia	84.7	11.4L

Source: U.S. Department of Commerce (February 1984, Tables 17 and 18).

[a]H denotes highest value and L lowest value among the states.

assessment ratios within assessing jurisdictions. Table 7.5, then, represents a more uniform assessment result than was "typical" in 1981. State coefficients of dispersion for 1981 varied from a low of 11.4 percent to a high of 52.0 percent, with only eight states showing a median coefficient of 15 or lower. Accordingly, it appears that the illustration shown in Table 7.5 represents very good assessment compared to actual practice.

Why isn't assessment uniformity, at least as measured by the coefficient of dispersion, better? One possibility is that property is purposely misassessed for political reasons or outright dishonesty. A potential economic answer is that property assessment is costly and therefore competes with all other government services for a share of the available budget resources. For instance, assessment results can be improved by reducing the time between complete reexamination and reevaluation of all properties, but to do so requires more assessing and appraisal personnel. Similarly, assessment results may be improved by increasing the use of computers for storing characteristics data about properties and analyzing and applying sales data, but to do so requires not only more computers but also assessing officials who are appropriately trained. The cost of assessing is also influenced by the nature of the community. Assessing is likely to be more costly in communities with a very heterogeneous property mix than in those with a homogeneous one, assessing of some types of large commercial and industrial properties is more difficult than for houses or land, and maintaining uniformity in assessment will be more difficult in communities with rapid growth and changes than in more stable ones.

The wide variation in assessment quality reflected by the data in Table 7.6 undoubtedly partly reflect the fact that some communities are willing to spend more for "good" assessment than others, although that does not necessarily imply that every community and state are actually doing the best possible with the available resources. From that view, one might expect that "good" assessment would be less in demand in lower-income states and states that make relatively low use of property taxes. Indeed, of the nine states with the highest coefficients of dispersion of assessment ratios within communities in 1981, all at 33 percent or greater, eight had per-capita incomes below the national average, eight had property taxes as a lower percentage of personal income than the national average, and seven had property taxes that were a smaller fraction of total taxes than nationally.[6]

/ Property Tax–Relief Measures

States use a variety of measures in an attempt to reduce property taxes for specific classes of property or specific types of taxpayers. Five such methods of tax relief are considered here, including state government credits or rebates for local residential property taxes, state individual income tax deductions for property taxes, exemptions

---

[6]These nine states, in order from the highest coefficient of dispersion, are Alabama (52.0), Missouri (47.3), North Dakota (44.0), Kansas (39.9), South Carolina (38.9), Pennsylvania (34.3), New Mexico (33.6), Arkansas (33.5), and Indiana (33.0).

/ APPLICATION 7.2
Assessment in California After Proposition 13[7]

As a means of maintaining or achieving good assessment, why not just reassess properties as they are sold? At that time, the market value is obviously known, and assessed value can be set using the appropriate assessment ratio rule. But selectively reassessing properties at the time of sale may, in fact, lead to less uniform assessment because different properties sell at different rates. A single-family house that sells three times in ten years would have an assessed value closer to the nominal assessment ratio than one that is owned and occupied by one family for a longer period, say 30 years. The experience of California since the adoption of Proposition 13 in 1978 illustrates that problem.

The state constitutional amendment, which came to be called Proposition 13, was primarily intended to reduce and limit the growth of property taxes. To achieve these objectives, the amendment set assessed values of each property equal to market value in 1976 and limited the annual growth from that value to no more than 2 percent, except when a property is sold or added to by new construction. When a property is sold, it is reassessed at the current market value, and any newly constructed portions of a property are similarly assessed at current value. Because the assessed value of any property that is not sold or altered by new construction cannot increase by more than 2 percent per year regardless of the actual rate of increase in market values, the assessment ratio for these properties will continually decline as long as market prices are rising more than 2 percent. For properties that do turnover in the market, the assessed value will reflect the actual market value. As a result, identical properties may be assessed at different amounts and therefore have different effective tax rates even if located in the same jurisdiction.

A recent study by Michael Wiseman of the University of California of effective property tax rates in San Francisco confirms this expectation. Wiseman reports a coefficient of dispersion for single-family houses for 1984 of 0.58, consistent with the 0.53 coefficient reported by the Census for San Francisco for 1982. In contrast, four different studies for years between 1971 and 1978, the last year before Proposition 13 took effect, found coefficients of dispersion in the city of between 0.09 and 0.16. There is substantially less uniformity of assessment ratios of single-family houses since Proposition 13 than before. Wiseman concludes that "in 1978 a majority of California voters chose to sacrifice equity in property taxation for certainty regarding year-to-year changes in tax liability" (Wiseman 1986, 31).

---

[7]This application is based on Wiseman (February 1986).

of assessed value for homesteads, special assessment methods for farmland, and differential assessment ratios by class of property. Broad property tax relief may also be provided by intergovernmental grants (discussed in Chapter 17) and property tax limits (discussed in Chapter 20), while targeted property tax relief for businesses may be used as an economic development tool (discussed in Chapter 21). The discussion here focuses on those methods intended to specifically reduce residential and agricultural property tax burdens as shown in Table 7.7.

/ Homestead exemptions

The simplest and most widely used tax-relief method for houses is exemption from taxation of a specific amount of homestead value, similar to personal exemptions that are commonly used with income taxes. Homestead exemptions are used in forty-one states, with twenty allowing the exemption broadly for taxpayers of all ages, ten limiting the exemption to senior citizens only, and another eleven states limiting homestead exemptions to specific groups of taxpayers such as veterans or disabled homeowners. As shown in Table 7.7, broadly applied homestead exemptions tend to be most common in the south and west. In some cases, the exemption is a fixed amount for all eligible taxpayers; in others, the exemption varies by income or some other taxpayer characteristic. These types of homestead exemptions are illustrated by those used in Kentucky, Idaho, and Nebraska.

In Kentucky an exemption of $16,100 of assessed value (in 1985) was available for all elderly and disabled homeowners, with the value of the exemption adjusted for inflation every two years. In Idaho the exemption similarly applies to homeowners who have low income, are elderly, disabled, or have other special circumstances, but the exemption is 50 percent of assessed value, up to a maximum exemption of $50,000. In Nebraska all homeowners are eligible for a $3000 exemption of *actual value* (the assessment ratio is 70 percent), whereas elderly and disabled homeowners receive exemptions of between $7000 and $35,000 depending on income.

The operation of a simple exemption equal to $10,000 of assessed value is shown by the following example:

	Without Exemption	*With Exemption*[8]
Market value	$60,000	$60,000
Assessed value	$30,000	$30,000
Exemption	0	$10,000
Taxable value	$30,000	$20,000
Tax rate	$40 per $1000 of taxable value	
Tax	$1200	$800
New tax rate	$60 per $1000 of taxable value	
New tax	$1800	$1200
Percentage change in tax	50%	50%

---

[8]This assumes that the exemption does not affect market values, correct at least in the very short run.

TABLE 7.7

State Property Tax–Relief Methods

State	Property Tax Credit	Homestead Exemption	Deduction from State Income Tax	Special Farmland Assessment	Classified System
New England					
Connecticut	S[a]	L	Limited tax	R	
Maine	S	L	X	R	
Massachusetts		A		R	X
New Hampshire		S[b]	Limited tax	R	
Rhode Island	S	L	X	R	
Vermont	A	L	X	R, contract	
Mideast					
Delaware		S[b]	X	R	
Maryland	A	L		R	
New Jersey		A		R	
New York	A		X	R	
Pennsylvania	S	L		R	
Great Lakes					
Illinois	S	A	X	R	Cook County
Indiana		A	X	U	
Michigan	A	L		Contract	
Ohio	S			R	
Wisconsin	A		X	Credit	
Plains					
Iowa	S	A	X	U	X
Kansas	S		X	R	
Minnesota	A	A	X	U	X
Missouri	S		X	U	
Nebraska		A	X	R	
N. Dakota	S	S[b]	X	U	X
S. Dakota	S		No tax	U	
Southeast					
Alabama		A	X	R	X
Arkansas	S	L	No tax	U	
Florida		A	No tax	U	
Georgia		A	X	Contract	
Kentucky		S	X	R	
Louisiana		A	X	U	X
Mississippi		A	X	U	X
N. Carolina		S[b]	X	R	
S. Carolina		S	X	R	X
Tennessee	S		Limited tax	R	X
Virginia		S[b]	X	R	
W. Virginia	S	S	X	U	X
Southwest					
Arizona	S		X	U	X
New Mexico	S	A		U	
Oklahoma	S	A	X	U	
Texas		A	No tax	R	

continued

TABLE 7.7

Continued

State	Property Tax Credit	Homestead Exemption	Deduction from State Income Tax	Special Farmland Assessment	Classified System
Rocky Mountain					
Colorado	S	S[b]	X	U	X
Idaho	S	A	X	U	
Montana	S	L[b]	X	U	X
Utah	S	L	X	R	X
Wyoming	S	A[b]	No tax	U	
Far West					
Alaska		A	X	R	
California	S	A	X	Contract	
Hawaii	A[c]	A	X	R, contract	
Nevada	S		No tax	R	
Oregon	A	L	X	R	X
Washington		S[b]	No tax	R, contract	
Total number	8A	20A	33X	18U	15X
	24S	10S		28R	
		11L		4 other	

Source: ACIR, (1986c, Tables 71 and 72); U.S. Department of Commerce (February 1984, Appendices A and C).

[a]Legend: A = all ages, S = seniors only, L = other specific group only, X = has deduction, U = use value, R = use value with recapture.
[b]Low income only.
[c]Renters only.

The exemption reduces the tax by the amount of the exemption times the tax rate ($10,000 × $40/$1000 = $400). It follows, therefore, that a given exemption will be more valuable the greater is the property tax rate. Also, an important point of this example is that if assessed value is greater than the exemption, the exemption does not affect tax increases. Both with and without the exemption, a 50-percent increase in the tax rate causes a 50-percent increase in tax (although from a smaller base). This last observation is an important difference between homestead exemptions and property tax credits.

/ Property tax credits or rebates

A second major property tax–relief mechanism, now used in thirty-two states, is a state government financed credit or rebate for property taxes paid to local governments. Property tax relief of this type usually takes the form of a rebate paid to the taxpayer or a (refundable) credit against the state income tax, the relief is generally targeted to specific groups of taxpayers, and the credit/rebate usually applies to property taxes that exceed some specified percentage of a taxpayer's income. For the last reason, these credits have come to be called "circuit breakers," analogous to use of the term in electrical engineering; because the relief applies only when a taxpayer's income is "overloaded" by property taxes. Indeed, property tax credits, or circuit breakers were devised as a way of preventing senior citizens with high-valued houses relative to their retirement income from having to sell houses because of the property tax.

Of the thirty-two state property tax credit/rebate programs, twenty-four are limited to elderly taxpayers (or sometimes elderly and disabled taxpayers) with eighteen of the twenty-four applying to renters as well as homeowners. Taxpayers of all ages are eligible for the credits or rebates in the other eight states, seven of which allow both renters and homeowners to benefit while only renters are targeted in Hawaii. All but two of the states with these programs impose an income ceiling on eligibility, although that ceiling varies widely (from $3750 in Arizona to $79,950 in Michigan for single taxpayers in 1985). The two states with no income limit are Maryland and Montana, although Maryland does impose a $200,000 net-worth limit. The six states with the broadest and therefore largest programs, listed in order by per-capita tax relief from the program, are Michigan, Minnesota, Wisconsin, Vermont, Oregon, and Maryland. The credit programs in Michigan and Vermont illustrate how the general circuit-breaker idea can be applied.

/ *Michigan*.   The state government program in Michigan, begun in 1974, provides property tax relief to homeowners, renters, and farmers in the form of a refundable credit against the state income tax. For most taxpayers, the credit equals 60 percent of homestead property taxes that are greater than 3.5 percent of the household's income, up to a maximum credit of $1200. Senior citizens are eligible for credits equal to 100 percent of property taxes greater than a specified percentage of income, which varies from 0 percent for incomes less than $3000 to 3.5 percent for incomes of more than $6000. Renters use 17 percent of rent paid as a proxy for property tax in computing the credit. In 1985 the credit was reduced by 10 percent for each $1000 of income above $70,950, so that households with 1985 income of $79,950 or more can receive no credit (with the income limits indexed to the Detroit CPI). Taxpayers must have been a Michigan resident for at least six months in the tax year and may claim the credit for tax on one principal residence only. In many cases, farmers are eligible to claim the credit for taxes on their homestead and all farmland. Mathematically, the credit formula is

General Taxpayers	Senior Taxpayers
Credit = 60% (Tax − 3.5% Income) up to a maximum credit of $1200 or less	Credit = (Tax − 3.5%[9] Income)

In 1984 1.4 million Michigan taxpayers received credits from this program totaling nearly $561.5 million, an amount equal to about 19 percent of the residential and agricultural property taxes collected by local governments in the state. The average credit among recipients was about $400. Senior citizen credits equaled about $233 million (about 41 percent of the total) and went to 423,000 taxpayers.

---

[9]or less.

/ *Vermont.*   The Vermont program, adopted in 1969, provides property tax refunds to homeowners and renters who are full-year residents equal to all property taxes greater than a specified percentage of income, varying from 3.5 percent for incomes less than $4000 to 7 percent for incomes up to $31,999. Taxpayers with incomes of $32,000 or greater are not eligible. The maximum rebate is $750, and renters use 20 percent of rent as the proxy for property tax paid. Mathematically, the formula is Rebate = (Tax − 3.5%[10] Income), up to a maximum rebate of $750.

In 1985 the Vermont program provided total property tax rebates of $5.6 million to 21,622 taxpayers, for an average rebate of about $259. The program offset about 3 percent of residential property taxes in Vermont.

/ *Differences and characteristics of tax credit plans.*   These two programs illustrate two important differences and two common characteristics of the various state property tax–credit plans. First, some of the state plans, such as the Michigan plan for senior taxpayers and the Vermont program, provide relief for *all* property taxes above the income threshhold, whereas others such as the Michigan credit for general taxpayers provide relief for only a portion of taxes above the threshhold. Second, some states follow the Michigan example in setting the eligibility threshhold and ceiling so that a substantial fraction of taxpayers will receive some benefit, whereas other states limit eligibility to small groups, either explicitly or by the threshhold and ceiling amounts (as in Vermont). There may be something of a trade-off here between providing some relief to many taxpayers as opposed to providing a larger amount of relief to smaller targeted groups of taxpayers.

One common characteristic of these credits is that they reduce the marginal cost of property taxes for eligible taxpayers who receive less than the maximum credit or rebate. For the Vermont and Michigan senior-citizen programs, the marginal cost to a relief recipient of a property tax increase is zero because the credit covers *all* property taxes over the income threshhold. With the Michigan general property tax–credit program, the marginal cost of a $1 increase in property tax is $.40 because the credit covers 60 percent of the tax over the threshhold. This reduction of marginal property tax cost raises the question of whether these credits induce taxpayers to support higher property taxes, an issue considered in Chapter 8. The second common characteristic of these state programs is that they introduce some progressivity into state tax structures because they are structured to favor lower-income taxpayers. This is done either explicitly by limiting the program to lower-income residents or implicitly by applying a higher-income threshhold in the relief formula for higher-income taxpayers.

/ State income tax deductions for property taxes

Of the forty states with a broad-based individual income tax, thirty-three provide for itemized deductions from taxable income, which include deductions for local government residential property taxes (similar to the federal income tax itemized

---

[10]For income less than $4000; larger percentages for higher incomes.

deductions for state–local income and property taxes). Of course, the degree to which taxpayers with the option of itemizing deductions actually do so (rather than taking a standard deduction if available) will depend on the unique characteristics of each state's situation and thus is expected to vary substantially among the states. Because the income tax reduction that occurs from a deduction equals the amount deducted times the income tax rate, the value of a state income tax deduction of local property taxes depends directly on the magnitude of that state income tax rate. And if the state income tax has a progressive rate structure, the value of the deduction will be greater for higher-income taxpayers.

From the numbers of states with homestead exemptions, state property tax credits, and state income tax deductions for property taxes, it is apparent that many states use more than one of these programs, either for the same taxpayers or for different groups of taxpayers. In fact, every state uses at least one of these methods, and seventeen states use all three of these residential property tax-relief mechanisms to some degree. Another eleven states use homestead exemptions and allow state income tax deductions, five use homestead exemptions and state credits, and another four states use state credits and income tax deductions.

/ Special assessment of farmland

Every state uses some method of limiting property taxes on agricultural land, usually by using a different procedure for assessing farmland than other properties. The traditional approach, used by eighteen states, is to assess the value of farmland in its current use, which may be less than the full market value of the land. For instance, the income approach can be used to estimate the value of farmland by capitalizing the profits generated by farming activity on the land. But there may be alternative uses for the land that would generate a greater stream of profits and thus a higher value; these alternative uses are referred to as the "highest and best use" of the property.

For instance, farmland on the edge of an urban area might be more valuable if used for residential property, and rural farmland might be converted into recreational use. Use–value assessment of farmland, as it is called, serves to prevent increases in property taxes on farmland as these alternative uses become more attractive. The traditional reason for adopting use–value assessment is to reduce the conversion of farmland into these other uses, particularly where urban areas are expanding.

Another variation of use–value assessment, now used by twenty-eight states, allows assessment of farmland according to current use but imposes a deferred tax on the full value for some fixed number of past years if the property is actually converted to a nonfarm use. In this way, the tax advantage conferred by use–value assessment, at least for some number of years, is recaptured by the taxing governments if the tax advantage does not succeed in preventing conversion.

Several states require a contract between the government and farmland owners in order for the farmland to receive preferential assessment. The contract specifies that the owner will not convert the farmland into other uses for a specific period of years, usually ten, in exchange for use–value assessment or some other tax reduction. If the owner wishes to convert the land to other uses before the contract expires, back taxes at the full value of the property are levied, and sometimes a penalty is also added.

/ Property classification

A classified property tax is one in which the effective tax rate varies for different classes of property, usually accomplished by assessing these different property classes using different assessment ratios. Classified property taxes exist in fifteen states, usually applying a lower assessment ratio to residential property than commercial and industrial property. For instance, in Alabama utilities are assessed at 30 percent of fair and reasonable market value; agricultural, forest, historic, and single-family residential property at 10 percent; and all other property at 20 percent. Similarly, in Tennessee utilities are assessed at 55 percent of actual value, industrial and commercial property at 40 percent of actual value, and farm and residential property at 25 percent. A slight variation is used in North Dakota. All property is assessed at 50 percent of true and full value, but taxable value is 9 percent of assessed value for residential property; 10 percent of assessed value for commercial, agricultural, and railroad property; and varying percentages for other types. In effect, then, residential property is taxed on 4.5 percent ($.09 \times .50$) of true and full value.

/ Summary

The property tax is different from most other taxes, partly because methods and procedures for assessing the value of property for tax purposes must be part of the property tax structure.

In the typical procedure for assessing, levying, and collecting property taxes, the assessed value (taxable value) of each piece of property is first computed by an assessor from an estimate of the market value of the property. The assessed value is specified by law as some specific percentage of market value, called the assessment ratio rule. The governing body of each local government sets a tax rate sufficient to generate the desired property tax revenue. Property tax rates have historically been specified in mills, equal to $1 of tax per each $1000 of taxable value. The property tax levy, or bill, for each property is determined from the tax rate and the assessed value for each property.

Single-family homes constitute, both in value and number, the largest single class of property subject to property taxes, representing in 1981 nearly 45 percent of the total assessed value for property taxes and 56 percent of the number of parcels. Real property–that is, land and buildings—represents 85 percent of total assessed value and is further subdivided into residential (single- and multifamily dwellings—51 percent of assessed value), commercial (office buildings, stores, warehouses—12 percent), industrial (manufacturing plants—7 percent), farm acreage (8 percent), vacant platted lots (4 percent), and all other property (3 percent).

Property assessors use three basic methods to estimate market and assessed values of properties: (a) the comparative sales approach, which uses data from actual sales and property characteristics to estimate the values for properties that are not sold; (b) the cost approach, which bases the value on historic cost adjusted for depreciation; and (c) the income approach, which measures value by the present value (sometimes called capitalized value) of the future net income expected to be generated by the property.

The simplest and most widely used tax-relief method for houses is exemption from taxation of a specific amount of homestead value. A second major property tax–relief mechanism used in thirty-two states is a state government–financed credit or rebate for property taxes. Of the forty states with a broad-based individual income tax, thirty-three also provide for itemized deductions from taxable income, which include deductions for local government residential property taxes.

Every state uses some method of limiting property taxes on agricultural land, usually by using a different procedure for assessing farmland than other properties.

A classified property tax is one in which the effective tax rate varies for different classes of property, usually accomplished by assessing these different property classes using different assessment ratios. Classified property taxes exist in fifteen states, usually applying a lower assessment ratio to residential property than to commercial and industrial property.

Discussion Questions

1. In an annual budget message, one city's mayor remarked that "I am particularly pleased that due to our sound financial planning and careful budgeting, no property tax increase is needed this year." Yet a careful examination of the detailed budget submitted by the mayor showed expected property tax revenue in the coming year to be 10 percent greater than in the previous year. How can you explain the apparent contradiction in the mayor's statement and proposed budget?

2. Suppose that you live in a house with a market and taxable value of $50,000 in a community with a property tax rate of $40 per $1000 of taxable value.
   a. What is your property tax amount?
   b. What happens to your property tax bill if the market value of your property rises by 10 percent and the assessment ratio is kept constant? What if the tax rate were increased by 10 percent along with the value?
   c. Now suppose your community allows an exemption of the first $10,000 of taxable value. How much would the exemption reduce your property tax bill? What happens to your tax savings from the exemption as value increases? As the tax rate increases?

d. Suppose instead of the exemption that you are allowed a credit equal to one-half the amount of property tax that is greater than 5 percent of your income. If your annual income is $30,000, how much does the credit reduce your property tax? What happens to your tax savings from the credit as value increases? As the tax rate increases?

3. Suppose you are assigned to assess a 50,000-square-foot office building that currently is fully leased at $5 per square foot. The owner's annual costs of operation for the building (interest, maintenance, insurance) are $200,000. The building is ten years old and is expected to have an additional twenty years of useful life. Assuming these market conditions will continue, estimate the current market value of the building under the income approach if the discount rate is 10 percent. How does the estimate differ if the discount rate is 5 percent?

4. One thing that makes the property tax different from other taxes is that the government must estimate each taxpayer's tax base, that is, the value of the property. This assessment process is handled differently in various states. Find out how property assessment is handled in your jurisdiction. Consider which level of government does assessing, how assessors are selected, what assessment ratio(s) is used, how often assessments are redone or how annual adjustments are made, whether local assessment is subject to state review or correction, and the procedure for taxpayers to appeal a property assessment.

Selected Reading

Raphaelson, Arnold H. "The Property Tax." In *Management Policies in Local Government Finance,* edited by J. R. Aronson and E. Schwartz. Washington, D.C.: International City Management Association, 1987, 161–228.

8 Property Tax: Economic Analysis and Effects

> . . . The property tax system for the nation as a whole depresses the return on capital and changes the cost of capital to higher-tax communities and decreases the cost of capital to low-tax communities.[1]
>
> *Peter Mieszkowski*

With an understanding of microeconomic analysis of taxes and the specific property tax institutions used by state–local governments, attention now turns to analyzing the economic effects of property taxes. As always, those effects include equity issues—that is, the effect on the distribution of the tax burden—and efficiency questions such as the effects of the tax on the amount, type, and location of property selected. The analysis has a number of important policy implications, particularly regarding proposals to provide property tax relief either to specific types of taxpayers or specific types of communities.

/ Property Taxes as Capital Taxes

The modern economic analysis of property taxes considers them as one of several taxes levied on the income from or value of capital, which is one of the major inputs (with labor and materials) into the production of goods and services. Other capital taxes include the federal corporate income tax and state–local government corporate income or general business taxes. This characterization is important because it suggests thinking about property taxes as taxes on production, or specifically on a factor of production, rather than as a tax on consumption or consumer goods.

The characterization seems straightforward enough when thinking about commercial and industrial property—the tax is on the plant, land, and equipment, not the value of the product—but sometimes seems unusual when applied to housing, for people tend to think of a house as a consumer good. But the physical residential housing unit is only one input into the production of the consumer good "housing services," a fact most clearly seen for rental housing. The producer (the owner and landlord) combines land, labor, and a housing unit to provide housing service to

---

[1]"The Property Tax: An Excise Tax or Profits Tax?" *Journal of Public Economics* 1 (1972): 94.

the tenant or consumer. The only difference in the case of owner-occupied housing is that the producer and consumer are the same person. Therefore, the approach followed in this chapter is to first consider the effect of various property tax features on the price and amount of capital and then to consider the effect of the change in the price and amount of capital on the prices and quantities of other inputs (such as labor) and consumer goods (particularly, housing services).

/ A uniform national property tax

The first implication of this approach is that a uniform national tax on all property at a single rate would impose a burden that cannot be shifted, at least in the short run, on all property owners. Remember the simple rule of tax analysis from Chapter 6: The only way to avoid or shift a tax is to change behavior. But if all property is taxed at the same rate in all jurisdictions, changes in the type of property owned by an investor or the location of the property will not reduce the tax liability. The only option to avoid the tax is to reduce the amount of property owned, that is, to reduce investment. Note that a property owner would not be able to avoid the tax by selling the property to another investor. Once the tax is imposed and known, any potential buyer would be willing to offer less for the property because the future after-tax return is lower than in the absence of a tax.

This situation is depicted in Figure 8.1, which shows a perfectly inelastic supply of capital at quantity C_0, which would be the case if the amount of capital investment is fixed in the long run. The property tax is represented by a shift down in the demand curve, and the net or after-tax return on capital falls from P_0 to P_0 $(1 - t)$, where t is the property tax rate. The rate of return earned by property

FIGURE 8.1 Incidence with Perfectly Inelastic Supply

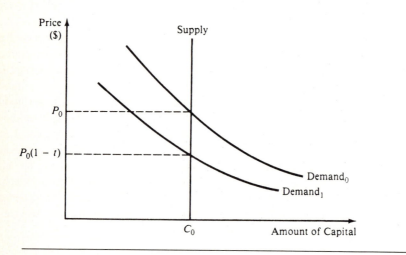

owners falls by the full amount of the tax simply because those owners *at the time the tax is levied* have no options to change behavior in ways to avoid the tax.

/ Differential taxation of different types of property

Obviously, the example of a uniform national property tax is not realistic, so adjustments to that case are necessary. Suppose, instead, that some types of property are exempt from taxation (or taxed at a zero rate) with all other property taxed everywhere at a uniform rate. In that instance, investors can avoid the tax by decreasing their investment in taxable property and increasing investment in exempt property. But that investor reaction itself will cause additional changes to the prices (and rate of return) of property. As investors reduce the amount (supply) of taxable property, the price of and investor return from that which remains will increase, offsetting the tax burden, while increases in the supply of exempt property would reduce the price and rate of return for those investments, mitigating the incentive to switch to nontaxable property. An equilibrium would be reached when the net-of-tax rates of return available from both types of property are equal.

This case is represented in Figure 8.2, showing an initial equilibrium at rate of return R_0 for two types of property (A and B) when there are no taxes (or both are taxed equally). Investors are presumably indifferent between the two types of investments because the (risk-adjusted) returns available from each are equal. If a property tax is imposed on type A only, the immediate effect is a reduction in the rate of return from type A to R_1, as reflected by Demand $_1^A$, which includes the tax. An investor in type A property earns a return of R_0, pays tax of $(R_0 - R_1)$, and retains a return of R_1. Because the tax has reduced the rate of return from type A

FIGURE 8.2 Effect of a Property Tax Differential in the Allocation of Capital

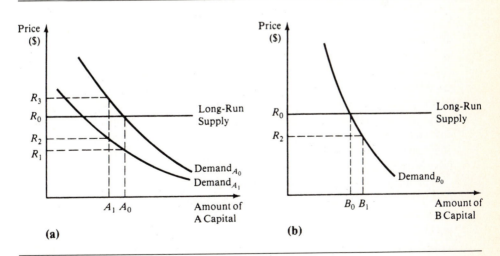

(a)

(b)

property compared to that available from investing in type B property, investors are expected to switch from A to B, as noted above.

As the amount of type A property falls below A_0, the rates of return from type A property rise, and as the supply of type B property rises, the price of or rate of return from that property falls. From another perspective, potential investors in type B property need not be offered as high a return as previously, because the property tax on type A has made investment in B relatively more attractive. In Figure 8.2, equilibrium is reached at quantities A_1 and B_1, with a net-of-tax rate of return in both markets equal to R_2. Of course, owners of type A property still have to pay the tax; so to earn a net rate of return equal to R_2, they must receive a gross return of R_3. For instance, the income from investing in A property might provide a 10-percent return before taxes are considered but only, say, 7 percent after taxes are paid. In that case, an investor in type B property would receive a 7-percent return and pay no tax. In contrast, when there were no taxes, all investors received return R_0, perhaps 9 percent to continue the numerical example.

Another way to view this case is to consider the prices for each property type as those charged to rent those properties. Once the tax is imposed, the price to the consumer to rent property A is higher than the price to rent property B (R_3 compared to R_2), so that the owners of both properties earn equal net-of-tax rent of R_2, which is, however, less than the rent received by the owners before taxes were imposed (R_0).

An important implication of this analysis is that owners of both taxable and exempt property will bear an ultimate tax burden, even though taxes are nominally collected only from owners of type A (taxable) property. Part of the tax levied on type A property is shifted to type B property through the market effects caused by the behaviorial change of investors. Remember, the reason to change behavior (in this case, switch from investing in A to B property) is to avoid or shift the tax, in this instance to owners of exempt property.

The analysis in Figure 8.2 also shows that the differential taxation of types of property creates economic inefficiency. The inefficiency arises because the tax differential creates an incentive for more of the untaxed property that is unrelated to its productivity. If the initial long-run supply R_0 represents the marginal social cost for both types of capital and initial demand the marginal social benefit, the tax differential induces an increase in the amount of type B capital so that marginal cost is greater than benefit. Similarly, the reduction in the amount of type A capital causes its marginal benefit to be greater than marginal cost. Because marginal social cost no longer equals marginal social benefit in each market, the change has reduced economic welfare or created an efficiency cost. The economy is supplying too much type B capital and too little type A.

Implicit in this discussion is an assumption that capital is perfectly mobile, that profit maximizing investors will always attempt to earn the highest possible return or profit, whereas consumers of these capital services are immobile, that is, unable to shift between the two types of properties. What happens if these assumptions are incorrect? If investors do not or are prevented from altering their investment types in response to the tax, then all of the tax burden falls on owners of taxed property. Essentially, the situation is again that represented in Figure 8.1.

If consumers of these types of capital can switch from one to the other, then the ''equilibrium'' we have identified is temporary. Because the consumer's price for type A property is now greater than that for type B property, the demand for type A property is expected to decrease and the demand for type B property to increase. As a result, the price charged for type A property will decline and the price charged for type B property will increase until the prices are equal again, meaning that investors in type A property will earn lower net returns than investors in type B property. Because of the differential tax on type A property, it is impossible both for investors in both types of property to earn equal net returns *and* for consumers of both types to be charged the same price. Typically, economists believe that investors' capital is more mobile than are consumers. For instance, if capital owned by profit-making businesses is taxed while capital used by nonprofit entities is exempt, the tax treatment of the property depends on its use, not any inherent characteristic of the property. To avoid the higher prices, profit-making firms would have to become nonprofit entities to consume type B property.

/ Differential tax rates by location

In the above example, all taxed property was taxed at a uniform rate, which is also unrealistic. The next step, then, is to extend the analysis by considering taxation of identical property at different tax rates by different jurisdictions. This extension is easy, however, because it is analytically identical to the case just considered and represented in Figure 8.2, with type A capital now representing property in jurisdiction A and type B capital representing property in lower-tax jurisdiction B. Although the example reflects some tax in A and no tax in B, it is just as applicable to a situation where there is some tax in B, say $30 per thousand of assessed value, and a higher tax in A, perhaps $35 per thousand. Only the *differential* in tax rates will influence movement between the localities.

The initial effect of the higher tax in A is to lower the rate of return received by owners/investors in A compared to that available in B. If capital is mobile, investors are therefore expected to shift their investments from jurisdiction A to jurisdiction B. The resulting reduction in the supply of property in A raises the value of or return from that which remains, while the increase in supply of property in B reduces the return from that property. Again, an equilibrium is reached when the net-of-tax returns available to investors in both jursidictions are equal. For that to happen, the consumer's cost of capital must be greater in jurisdiction A than in B; users of capital face higher costs in A, the higher-tax jurisdiction. The effect of the differential in tax rates between the jurisdictions is therefore to reduce the amount of property and increase the consumer's price for property in the higher-tax jurisdiction, with just the opposite effects in lower-tax jurisdiction B.

As before, some of the tax burden from the higher-tax jurisdiction is shifted to property owners in the lower-tax jurisdiction through the decrease in the rate of return, which is caused by the increased supply. If consumers of capital are also mobile, the story continues. Because the price (rental charge) for capital is greater in A than in B, some consumers of capital might move their operations to B in an attempt to enjoy those lower prices. That shift of demand would reduce prices in A, the higher-tax jurisdiction, and raise them in B. The outcome of this chase depends on the relative mobility of suppliers compared to demanders. Remember that capital or property in this discussion is considered an input into production, so the consumers of capital are firms that produce goods and services and households who own their residences and are thus "producers" of their housing services. Therefore, one additional step is necessary to determine the effect of the differential capital (property) tax on prices of other goods and services. This step is to consider what happens to the return to suppliers of other factors of production and to the prices of consumer goods.

/ *Labor.*

If capital is mobile, the higher tax rate in jurisdiction A causes less capital to be invested in that jurisdiction, which is expected to affect the demand for labor in jurisdiction A as well. If labor and capital are complementary, then the reduced amount of capital investment will also reduce the demand for labor, causing wages in jurisdiction A to fall. Just the opposite happens in jurisdiction B, where increased capital investment causes an increase in demand for labor and an increase in wages. If workers do not or cannot change jobs in response to these wage changes, the story stops; part of the differential property tax burden in A has been shifted to workers in A. But if workers are mobile and do respond to the change in relative wages, the supply of labor will fall in A (driving wages back up), and the supply in B will rise (driving wages down). In that case, the effect of the property tax differential in A is a reduction in employment rather than a change in wages.[2]

/ *Local Consumer Goods (Housing).*

The changes in the consumer prices of capital in jurisdictions A and B, caused by the difference in property taxes, are also expected to affect the prices of those goods produced and consumed locally that use capital in the production process. Because the consumer's price of capital (the rental rate) has increased in jurisdiction A, one expects that the prices of local goods that are capital intensive will also rise. Chief among these goods is housing. One expects that the price of housing service in A—that is, the consumer's cost of living in a house or apartment—will rise. In contrast, the decrease in the consumer's price of capital in jurisdiction B is expected to reduce the price of housing services in B.[3]

---

[2] If labor and capital are substitutes, then the story is reversed. The decreased capital investment increases the demand for labor.

[3] This analysis applies to locally produced and consumed goods. Goods that are sold on a national market presumably trade at a uniform price everywhere, except for differences caused by transportation cost and the consumer's cost of discovering any arbitrage opportunities. Even for local goods, the analysis is somewhat more complicated. For instance, the price of some labor intensive local goods could even fall if the price of labor falls.

The changes in jurisdiction A are depicted in Figure 8.3, with the shift of the supply curve resulting from the increased cost of producing housing services due to the higher property tax. The tax differential causes the cost of living in a housing unit in jurisdiction A to rise from P_0 to P_1. Note also that if there is some elasticity in demand, the net return to the owner of the housing unit also falls, from P_0 to P_2, implying that this unit will now command a lower selling price. How can the cost of living in a house go up at the same time that its market price falls? Market price falls by less than the amount of the tax, so the total cost of the house plus tax rises. Of course, if this is an owner-occupied house the distinction is irrelevant because the owner and consumer are the same person.

Just as with labor, whether the story stops or continues depends on whether housing consumers respond to the change in the relative price of housing services between the two jurisdictions. If consumers are aware of the differences and are mobile, then more consumers are expected to seek housing in B, where the price has decreased, and less in A. But the increase in housing demand in B will increase housing prices again, while the decrease in housing demand in jurisdiction A will bring housing prices down. If consumers are perfectly mobile, the resulting effect of the property tax differential, then, is a decrease in the amount of housing in A and an increase in the amount in B, but no change in the relative prices.

/ Land. Because of the positive property tax rate differential in jurisdiction A, the amount of capital investment in A is expected to fall, with the effect of decreasing the demand for the complementary input land. Further, if housing consumers react to the increased housing service price by leaving for other jurisdictions, the demand for land will further decline. These decreases in the demand for land will reduce

FIGURE 8.3 *Effect of a Capital Tax on Housing Prices*

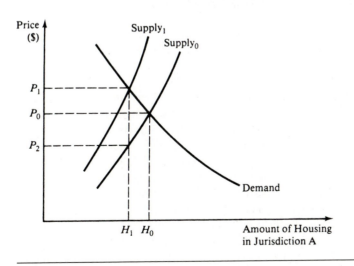

the price (value) of land in A. But landowners do not have the option, available to owners of other types of capital, of moving their investment (land) to a lower-tax jurisdiction; the supply of land in jurisdiction A is fixed, as represented in Figure 8.1. If all other capital, other inputs, and consumers are all mobile, then the burden of the tax differential that remains is reflected in a decreased value of land. If land is the only immobile commodity or agent, then all of the burden of the tax differential is capitalized into land values in the higher-tax jurisdiction, A in the example. Those hurt by the tax differential are landowners in jurisdiction A (while landowners in B benefit).

/ Putting the analysis together

The actual property tax environment, with effective tax rates differing by location and sometimes by type of property, can be analyzed by combining the three different theoretical scenarios presented above. For instance, suppose that a third of all jurisdictions tax property at an effective rate of 2 percent, another third at 3 percent, and the final third at 4 percent (and all have equal amounts of property), so that the average effective rate is 3 percent. This is equivalent to a national tax at that 3-percent rate coupled with an additional 1-percent tax levied by one-third of the subnational jurisdictions and a 1-percent subsidy (a negative tax) provided by another third. Analysis of the actual situation is equivalent to analysis of a national 3-percent tax coupled with analysis of the effects of the one percentage point differential from that average existing in some of the jurisdictions.

The effect of the average property tax rate, which can be thought of as a national tax at that rate, is a reduction in the return (income) from capital ownership and is thus a burden imposed on all owners of capital or property, as discussed above and depicted in Figure 8.1. Recall that this burden falls on owners of all types of property if capital is mobile, regardless of whether a particular type of property is taxed directly, and if taxed, whether at a high or low rate. This conclusion changes somewhat if the overall amount of capital in the society (that is, from savings and investment) is reduced by the fall in the rate of return from capital, which could raise goods prices or lower labor prices in the future. In that case, the average property tax rate imposes a burden on consumers and workers as well as capital owners in the long run.

The one percentage point property tax rate differential may cause changes in the prices of some consumer goods, of labor, and of land in the different jurisdictions. The nature and magnitude of these **excise effects** depends on the relative mobility of capital, labor, and consumers, as described above.

Consider one extreme set of assumptions first: Capital is perfectly mobile, whereas workers and consumers are perfectly immobile (workers and consumers do not move their economic activity across jurisdiction boundaries because of tax-induced price differences). Under these assumptions, the effect of the tax rate differential is to cause lower wages and land values and higher prices for locally produced consumer goods (housing) in the higher-tax jurisdictions compared to the lower-tax ones. This set of assumptions, although precisely unrealistic, may in fact be an adequate approximation (or at least a good starting point) for analyzing *interstate tax differentials*. It is costly for individuals to become aware of price differences available in other states, and individuals sometimes face substantial costs to take advantage of those price differences. In many, though not all cases, individuals have to change both their work and consumer location if they want to change either.

The opposite set of extreme assumptions, that workers and consumers as well as capital are perfectly mobile, leads to very different results. Because price differences cause and are ultimately removed by economic mobility, the remaining effect of the tax rate differential is to lower the value of land in the higher-tax jurisdictions compared to that in the lower-tax jurisdictions. This set of assumptions, although also unrealistic, is often applied to analyzing *tax differentials within states* or metropolitan areas. Because individuals are often aware of price differences within their area and because they can often change their job or residential location without changing both, the costs of mobility are less than for interstate differences. In this case, the burden of any tax differential is likely to fall on landowners of the higher-tax jurisdictions (who may or may not be residents of those jurisdictions).

One important policy implication of this view is that who will benefit from a property tax reduction depends on how that reduction is carried out. If some national program were used to reduce property taxes in all states and localities, the principal effect is a reduction in the average rate of tax, with little or no change in the tax differential between jurisdictions. A reduction in the national average rate of tax would increase the return to all capital owners and provide a benefit proportional to the amount of capital owned. On the other hand, if one (relatively small) state acted to reduce property taxes uniformly within that state, the effect on the national average rate of tax would be insignificant, and there would be no change in the tax differentials among localities within the state. But the relative position of that state compared to all the others would be altered, with the expected theoretical effect of raising wages and land values and lowering housing prices in that state.

Similarly, suppose that only one city were to lower property taxes (holding services constant). Now the changes to both the national and state average rates of tax would be insignificant, with only the differential between this city and others in its area being altered. If the extreme set of assumptions are applied as above, the expected result is an increase in land values in the city that lowered taxes. The new, more advantageous tax differential of this city is capitalized into higher land values, benefiting owners of land in the city at the time the tax is reduced. Accordingly, from this viewpoint it is not wise to attempt to state *the* effect from lowering (or raising) property taxes, as the expected result depends both on what all jurisdictions are doing simultaneously and on how individuals respond.

/ Is the Property Tax Regressive?

In his classic analysis of the property tax, published in 1966, Dick Netzer (1966, 32, 40) wrote:

In the past forty years, there has been little theoretical controversy over the incidence of the American property tax. By and large, the "conventional wisdom" is accepted. . . . In general, the results [of Netzer's analysis with 1957 data] conform with the conventional wisdom: the property tax is on balance somewhat regressive when compared to current money income.

Writing just nine years later, Henry Aaron (1975, 19) offered a very different view:

Economic analysis of differential tax incidence has undergone massive revision in the last decade. As a result, opinions among economists engaged in the study of tax incidence bear little resemblance to views generally held even a few years ago. The main contribution of recent research has been to show that the patterns of gains and losses generated when a single state or locality changes property taxes will differ markedly from that appearing after a change in the nationwide use of property taxes, and that none of these patterns resembles the profile of burdens from property taxes that economists formerly described.

The analysis to which Aaron refers is that which you have read in the previous part of this chapter. And although the viewpoint articulated by Netzer was held by economists and policymakers for more than fifty years, the analysis in this chapter is now certainly the "new conventional wisdom" among economists and increasingly among policymakers as well.

The long-standing notion that property taxes are regressive (that is, impose a more than proportionate burden on lower-income families and individuals) arose from a simple theoretical proposition and two statistical observations. It was assumed that property taxes operated as excise taxes on commodities and increased the price of the taxed goods. Residential property taxes were therefore assumed to increase the price of housing services and thus impose a burden in proportion to the amount spent on housing consumption. Nonresidential property taxes were assumed to increase the prices of goods produced with that property, thereby imposing a burden in proportion to the amount spent on consumption of goods, excluding housing. Because it is known that both annual consumption and housing expenditures are a greater proportion of annual income for lower- as opposed to higher-income individuals, the conclusion clearly followed that property tax burdens were a greater proportion of income for lower-income taxpayers than for higher-income ones. The property tax was perceived to be regressive.

By thinking of the property tax as a tax on capital rather than consumer goods, it became clearer that property tax burdens could be imposed on profits, wages, or land rents in addition to consumption, making the incidence conclusions more ambiguous. One conclusion was that the burden that arises from the average rate of property tax in the nation is imposed on owners of capital in proportion to the amount owned, at least in the short run. Because capital is more than proportionally owned by higher-income families and individuals, the burden of this part of the property tax is expected to be progressive (more than proportionally borne by higher-income taxpayers).

What of the tax burden that arises from the differences in property tax rates around that national average? The theory suggests that these burdens will fall on workers, landowners, and consumers in the higher–tax rate jurisdictions, with the division of the burden among these groups depending on relative mobility. One must know something about which jurisdictions have above-average tax rates in order to evaluate these burdens. If the high–tax rate jurisdictions are high-income jurisdictions, on average, then the decreased wages and land values and increased housing prices that result from the tax differential are felt mostly by those high-income taxpayers. The relationship between effective property tax rates and income is crucial to this evaluation.

Aaron (1975) reports that among the states there is a positive correlation between per-capita income and effective property tax rates; the high–tax rate states tend also to be the high-income states. Because the effect of the property tax rate differentials among the states is to hurt those with the higher rates, these burdens seem to be progressive. Aaron also reports a positive relationship between income and property tax rates among counties within states, although that relationship is not as strong as that among the states. In contrast, Aaron found a negative relationship between property tax rates and income among localities within counties in New Jersey, suggesting that the tax burdens that arise from property tax rate differentials within counties or metropolitan areas may in fact be regressive. Of course, this conclusion can vary by state or even for different areas within a state, so the facts must be examined for specific cases. Aaron suggests that when these factors are combined, a conclusion of general property tax regressivity is certainly not supported. In fact, increases in the average use of property taxes nationwide, at least, seem to introduce more progressivity into the state and local government tax structure.

The range of possible incidence conclusions about property taxes are reflected by the results reported by Joseph Pechman (1985), who calculates effective rates by annual income class for various taxes under alternative theoretical assumptions about the economic effects of those taxes. For property taxes, the assumption at one end of the spectrum is that all property tax burdens fall on owners of capital, which would result from a national uniform property tax. The opposite possibility is that property tax burdens fall on consumption due to higher prices of goods. This could occur if property tax rate differentials are large and consumers do not change behavior to avoid the resulting price differentials. Pechman's results for 1980, reported in Table 8.1, are not surprising. If all property tax burdens fall on owners of capital in proportion to the amount of capital, the property tax is roughly proportional for families with annual incomes below $25,000 and very progressive among families with higher annual incomes. If the property tax is assumed to increase consumer good prices, the property tax burden is regressive among families with annual incomes below $15,000 and proportional or slightly progressive among families with incomes above $15,000.

One potential problem with this measure of property tax incidence, regardless of the theoretical assumption adopted, is that property tax burdens are compared to annual incomes. But family or individual choices about the value of residence to purchase or own are long-run decisions, depending not just on current income but also on expected future income. Most individuals do not buy more valuable houses annually as their income rises, but buy a residence for a number of years

TABLE 8.1

Pechman's Analysis of Effective Property Tax Rates, 1980

Family Income (Thousands of Dollars)	Property Tax Burdens on Capital Ownership (%)	Property Tax Burdens on Consumption (%)
0–5	1.0	7.9
5–10	0.6	3.0
10–15	0.9	2.4
15–20	0.9	2.1
20–25	1.0	2.1
25–30	1.2	2.1
30–50	1.4	2.2
50–100	2.2	2.3
100–500	3.9	2.2
500–1000	5.2	2.2
1000 and up	5.8	2.3

Source: Pechman (1985,56).

based on their expected lifetime income, or at least income over some period. Current incomes are often poorly correlated with average lifetime incomes, particularly at the bottom and top of the income distribution. For instance, the typical low income of someone in medical school or just beginning a medical residency training program greatly understates that individual's expected economic welfare. If housing choices are based on average long-run incomes, then comparing property tax burdens to that same long-run income gives a more accurate picture of the true income distribution of the burden. If property tax burdens are compared to average lifetime income rather than annual or current income, the distribution is less regressive or more progressive.

Finally, one should recall from Chapter 4 that property taxes can serve as benefit taxes. If consumers choose residential locations based on the property tax and service package offered by the local government and if some mechanism arises to maintain the equilibrium, consumers who desire the same fiscal package are grouped together. The property tax is the "price" for consuming local services, with all consumers paying the costs that their consumption imposes on the government. In that case, it does not make sense to separately discuss the incidence of the tax separate from the provision of public services because the tax simply reflects the demand for the services.

/ Voting on Property Taxes

One relatively unique aspect of property taxes compared to other taxes is that taxpayers often have the opportunity to directly select, or at least influence, the tax rate through a referendum. In some cases, such a referendum is mandatory; in others, referendum is optional or required only under certain circumstances. These fiscal referenda are most common among independent school districts but are sometimes used by general-purpose local governments. The vote may be on the property tax rate directly or on the budget, which implicitly determines the tax rate.

Data from these local fiscal elections are often used to estimate the demand for local government services, especially education, as described in greater detail in Chapter 14. These demand studies show how various economic and social factors influence the amount of services selected and thus the amount of property tax levied. Not surprisingly, the two principal economic variables influencing demand are the tax price for additional services faced by the voters and the resources available to the voters, including income and intergovernmental grants. Three important features of the property tax environment—the amount of nonresidential property in a jurisdiction, federal and state income tax deductibility of property taxes, and state property tax credits—have the potential to affect the choice of the amount of property taxes or expenditures by altering voters' perceived tax prices for additional services.

/ Property tax prices

The property tax price for additional service facing any taxpayer is the net share of property taxes paid by that taxpayer. This price depends on that taxpayer's property value compared to the total taxable value in the jurisdiction and on any deductions or credits available to that taxpayer. This property tax price for any individual i, h_i, can be represented as follows:

$$h_i = \frac{V_i(1 - S)}{V}$$

where V_i = property value owned by taxpayer i
  V = total property value in the jurisdiction
  S = portion of taxpayer i's tax that is shifted through deductions or credits

The total property value in the jurisdiction comprises both residential and nonresidential property—that is, $V = R + NR$, with R representing the value of residential property and NR the nonresidential value. With a formulation that implicitly assumes that individuals do not perceive or bear any burden from property taxes on nonresidential property in their jurisdiction, increases in nonresidential value will reduce an individual's property tax price. Given this assumption, the expression for the property tax price can be written

$$h_i = \frac{V_i}{R} \times (1 - S) \times \frac{R}{V}$$

An individual's property tax price or share depends on that individual's residential property value relative to the average residential value in the jurisdiction, on the portion of that individual's tax that can be eliminated by deductions or credits, and on the share of total property value in the jurisdiction that is residential (because the nonresidential property tax is assumed to impose no burden on resident individuals). We now consider research about those factors that influence $(1 - S)$ and R/V and how those reductions in tax price affect property tax votes.

/ Composition of the property tax base

If individual voters believe there is no burden from imposing property taxes on "business" property in the jurisdiction—that is, industrial, commercial, and agricultural property—then the more of that property there is, the lower the cost to any individual of increasing per-capita government spending by $1. One should observe higher property tax rates being selected by voters in jurisdictions for which residential property is a smaller fraction of total property value, all other factors equal. Indeed, when the residential share of property value is included as a variable in statistical studies explaining per-capita taxes or spending among local governments, it commonly does have a significant, negative effect.

But the notion that higher and higher property tax rates can be imposed on industrial and commercial property with no cost to local residents is surely naive because capital is mobile at least to some degree. At some point, competition from other jurisdictions with lower tax rates will mean that some of the industrial and commercial tax base will be lost to a jurisdiction as tax rates are increased. Such a loss would increase the tax prices for government spending faced by individuals in that jurisdiction. If this effect is perceived by voters, then the existence of nonresidential property would be expected to have less of an effect on the choice of property tax rates. Moreover, if individuals believe that industrial and commercial property are not equally sensitive to property tax rates, then jurisdictions with substantial amounts of industrial property are expected to behave differently than those with substantial commercial property.

The possibility that the composition of the local property tax base will influence the choice of local per-capita taxes and spending was examined by Helen Ladd (1975) in a study of school expenditures in the Boston metropolitan area for 1970. Ladd's adjusted measure of the perceived residential share of the tax base is $1 - aC - bI$, where C represents commercial value, I is industrial value, and a and b are parameters representing the shares of the commercial and industrial bases that are perceived not to burden local residents. If a and $b = 1$, none of the business property tax burden falls on residents (as in the above formulation). If a and $b = 0$, voters treat business property the same as residential property, believing that all of the property tax is a local burden.

In Ladd's analysis, a was estimated to be 0.79 while b was estimated to be 0.45. This means that the voters did not act as if commercial and industrial property taxes had no local burden. Rather, it appears these voters believed that about 20 percent of commercial property taxes and a little more than half of industrial taxes did create local tax burdens. The voters apparently believed that the industrial tax base was substantially more sensitive to tax rates than was the commercial base, so that communities with relatively larger amounts of commercial property were more likely to select higher tax rates than were communities with relatively larger amounts of industrial property, all other factors equal, because of a fear of driving out that industrial property. These results are in accordance with the general notion that commercial location decisions are tied to the local market, whereas industrial property is more footloose and thus more sensitive to local fiscal conditions. The conclusion is that the existence of commercial and industrial property does reduce individual's perceived tax prices and contribute to higher selected tax rates and expenditures but that voters do not perceive commercial and industrial property taxes as completely "free."

/ Income tax deductions for property taxes

Another tax feature that can reduce individual's property tax prices is the income tax deduction for residential property taxes available to federal income taxpayers who itemize deductions and to taxpayers who itemize on state income taxes in thirty-three states. A deduction reduces taxes paid by the amount of the deduction multiplied by the taxpayer's marginal tax rate (the income tax rate applying to the last dollar of income). For instance, if the income tax rate is 30 percent, the taxpayer bears only 70 percent of the cost of the deductible item. If the taxpayer's property tax bill rises by $1, the deduction offsets $.30 of that increase so that the taxpayer bears only $.70.[4]

Analysis of the deductibility of property taxes is made more complicated because the deduction may be available for both federal and state income taxes and because state income taxes are also deductible by itemizers against federal income taxes and federal income taxes are deductible against state taxes in sixteen states. If a property taxpayer deducts property taxes only on the federal income tax, the net cost per dollar of property tax is $(1 - f)$, where f represents the taxpayer's federal marginal income tax rate. If a taxpayer deducts property taxes against the state income tax and both property and state income taxes against the federal income tax, the net cost is $(1 - f)(1 - s)$, where s represents the taxpayer's marginal state income tax rate.[5] The expression for the net property tax price in the case of reciprocal deductibility of state and federal income taxes is still more complicated.[6] Regardless of the institutional structure, the federal and state income tax deductions for residential property taxes do reduce the property tax price for taxpayers who itemize deductions.

The major federal income tax reform bill adopted in 1986 and the proposals and discussions leading up to that bill focused attention on this issue. Many of the proposals would have ended the federal income tax deductibility of property taxes altogether. In the tax bill that was adopted, deductibility for property taxes was retained, although increases in the standard deduction and changes in other deductions will reduce the number of taxpayers who itemize deductions and thus who deduct property taxes in practice. Moreover, the value of the property tax deduction

---

[4]This assumes that none of the foregone income tax revenue is made up by higher income tax rates, which is a reasonable assumption for any single taxpayer to make because the increase to offset only that taxpayer's deduction would be insignificant.

[5]f percent of the property tax is offset by the federal deduction and s percent by the state deduction. But the reduction of state income taxes equal to s reduces the federal deduction also by s, which *increases* federal tax by fs. The net cost is therefore $1 - f - s + fs$, which equals $(1 - f)(1 - s)$.

[6]See Fisher (1978, 399).

is reduced for those who continue to itemize because of the decrease in marginal income tax rates. (In the new structure there are only two nominal rates, 15 and 28 percent for joint filers, compared to a maximum rate of 50 percent in the previous structure.) By altering property tax prices, these federal income tax changes may have several effects on local government fiscal policy.

The primary concern among local government officials is that by increasing property tax prices for some taxpayers, federal tax reform may induce voters to select lower property tax rates or amounts of government expenditure. Edward Gramlich (1985a) examined this possibility, based on survey data of individual taxpayers in several Michigan cities. The survey included information on whether a taxpayer itemized federal income tax deductions, on taxpayer income (which allows calculation of marginal federal tax rate), on residential location, on whether the taxpayer votes, and on the taxpayer's desired simultaneous percentage change in local government taxes and expenditures. Gramlich uses the survey data to compute the desired tax/expenditure change—based on the tax price with property tax deductibility and what the tax price would be if deductibility were ended and tax rates lowered, assuming that the price elasticity of demand is .5—for each taxpayer. Assuming that the local fiscal choice process can be represented by the median voter model, Gramlich identifies the median desired tax/expenditure change in each locality when taxes are and are not deductible.

Under the tax structure existing at the time of the survey (property taxes deductible), Gramlich reports that the median position in each locality is "no change in taxes/expenditures." That is, the local governments had selected the tax/expenditure package desired by the median voters in each community. When property tax deductibility is ended, the property tax price rises for taxpayers who itemize deductions, but the effect of those price increases on desired spending varies by community. There is no change in desired taxes/expenditures in the two large central cities in the sample (Detroit and Lansing) because the median voter in those cities is not an itemizer and changes in other voters' desired taxes do not alter the median. Among the other communities in the sample (including city suburbs and rural areas), desired taxes/expenditures decrease from 1 to 10 percent, averaging about a 5-percent decrease.

These results from Gramlich's simulations with an assumed price elasticity of .5 are supported by other studies (notably, Inman 1985 and Holtz-Eakin and Rosen 1988) examining the actual taxing behavior of localities. For instance, Douglas Holtz-Eakin and Harvey Rosen related changes in taxes and expenditures from 1978–80 for 172 localities to changes in tax prices caused by federal income tax deductibility. Their results showed that if deductibility of all local taxes were removed completely, collections of all deductible taxes (property, income, and sales taxes together) by localities would fall by about 13 percent on average. So these studies provide support for the idea that the level of taxes adopted by taxpayers responds to changes in tax prices, although the magnitude of the effect due to federal deductibility is not huge.

A second concern arises from a change in the distribution of desired taxes. Not surprisingly, desired taxes/expenditures decrease more for higher-income taxpayers (and communities) because many of those taxpayers itemize and because their relatively high income tax rates make the property tax deduction more valuable. If these higher-income taxpayers are not the median voters in their communities, their decreases in desired taxes/expenditures will not be accommodated by actual decreases in taxes, which may be of particular concern in the large central cities. Gramlich (1985a, 458) notes that "this is likely to lead to a subtle form of intra-community fiscal tension, to changes in the character of public spending (increasing the bribe for the rich to stay put), or to emigration of the rich."

/ *State property tax credits*

State property tax credits are an additional intergovernmental tax incentive that reduce property tax prices, and thus may affect the choice of property tax rates and local government expenditures. These credits operate similarly to tax deductions, except that the net cost of a $1 increase in property taxes is reduced by the credit rate rather than the taxpayer's marginal income tax rate. The Michigan property tax credit is illustrative. The formulas for the Michigan property tax credit are as follows:

General Taxpayers	Senior Citizens
$C = .60 \, (PT - .035Y)$, up to $1200	$C = PT - aY$, up to $1200 with $0 \le a \le .035$, by income

where C = property tax credit
  PT = homestead property tax
  Y = household income
The credit was reduced 10 percent for each $1000 of income above $70,950 (1985), so no credit was available to households with income above $79,950 in 1985.

As a result of this program, Michigan taxpayers fall into one of four main categories with respect to the net cost of property tax increases. General taxpayers who received a property tax credit less than the maximum $1200 and with household income less than $70,950 in 1985 had a net cost of $.40 for each $1 increase in property tax (because the credit increases by $.60 if property tax rises by $1). Similarly, senior citizen taxpayers who received a credit less than the maximum with household income less than $70,950 faced a net cost per dollar of property tax increase equal to zero (the credit increases $1 for each $1 increase in tax). Credit recipients with income between $70,950 and $79,950 in 1985 faced marginal property tax prices between $.40 (zero for seniors) and $1. Those taxpayers who received no property tax credit or who were at the $1200 maximum faced a $1 net property tax price for each $1 increase in property tax. Therefore, most Michigan taxpayers paid either 0 percent, 40 percent, or 100 percent of marginal property tax increases.

The distribution of marginal property tax prices as a result of the credit in 1977 (before the income-based phaseout was in effect) was as follows:

Marginal Property Tax Price	*Percentage of Tax Returns*
1.00	67.0
0.40	22.0
0.00	11.0

Overall, then, one-third of taxpayers filing Michigan state individual income tax returns had their property tax price reduced by the state property tax credit. Relatively more homeowners than renters receive credits, with one estimate showing that between 50 and 60 percent of single-family homeowners receive credits and thus have their property tax prices reduced by the credit. If homeowners are more likely than renters to vote in local property tax rate elections, then the potential for the property tax credit to affect those votes is greater than that reflected by the overall distribution of prices shown above. Some analysts have suggested, however, that individual voters may not be aware of how the property tax credit reduces property tax prices, and thus that the credit will not influence property tax votes. For instance, R. Hamilton Lankford (1985) reports the results of a survey of taxpayers in Marshall, Michigan, showing that the differences between *perceived* and actual property tax costs, net of federal and state tax incentives, "are consistent with the expectation that such individuals do not consider the potential credit when formulating perceptions of net property tax costs. Even many of those who claim the credit apparently do not understand the effect of the credit on costs" (Lankford 1985, 84–85). Yet Lankford's results also show that voters are much more likely to correctly perceive property tax costs than are nonvoters.

The issue of whether the Michigan state property tax credit program affected property tax amounts has been examined (Fisher 1988) by comparing local government property tax changes from 1974–76, the two years immediately after introduction of the credits, to property tax changes in the 1972–74 period, when no property tax credit existed. The results show that, after adjusting for other factors that affect property tax changes, property taxes increased more from 1974–76 in those counties for which the credit reduced property tax prices the most. No similar effect of the property tax credit parameters was found for the 1972–74 period. Fisher (1988, 17) concludes that "the level of property tax in 1976 was between 5 and 12 percent greater than it would have been without the property tax credit. Given the mean price decrease of about 22 percent due to the credit, these results suggest that the elasticity of the level of taxes with respect to the price is between −.25 and −.5".

Michael Bell and John Bowman (1987) have similarly examined the effect of the state property tax credit in Minnesota on local government property taxes. They report that the state credit, which provides a 54-percent marginal subsidy of property taxes up to a maximum credit of $650, induces statistically significant increases in local property taxes net of credits. They conclude that because "local officials can increase local services by $1 without having to raise local taxes by $1, . . . a bloating of the public sector results from divorcing the pain of taxing from the pleasure of spending" (Bell and Bowman 1987, 293).

/ Summary

The modern economic analysis of property taxes considers them as one of several taxes levied on the income from or value of capital, which is one of the major inputs (with labor and materials) into the production of goods and services.

The first implication of this approach is that a uniform national tax on all property at a single rate would impose a burden—which cannot be shifted, at least in the short run— on all property owners. A second implication is that owners of both taxable and exempt property will bear an ultimate tax burden. The third implication is that any differential in tax rates between jurisdictions will reduce the amount of property and increase the consumer's price for property in the higher-tax jurisdictions, with just the opposite effects in the lower-tax jurisdictions.

Property tax burdens can be imposed on profits, wages, or land rents in addition to consumption. The effect of the average national property tax rate is a reduction in the return (income) from capital ownership and is thus a burden imposed on all owners of capital or property. If capital is perfectly mobile while workers and consumers are perfectly immobile, the effect of the tax-rate differential is to cause lower wages and land values and higher prices for locally produced consumer goods (housing) in the higher-tax jurisdictions as compared to the lower-tax ones. If workers, consumers, and capital are perfectly mobile, the effect of any tax-rate differential is to lower the value of land in the higher-tax jurisdictions as compared to that in the lower-tax rate jurisdictions.

When these factors are combined, a conclusion of general property tax regressivity is not supported. Increases in the average use of property taxes nationwide particularly will introduce more progressivity into the state—local government tax structure.

Taxpayers often have the opportunity to directly select, or at least influence, the property tax rate through a referendum. Three important features of the property tax environment—the amount of nonresidential property in a jurisdiction, federal and state income tax deductibility of property taxes, and state property tax credits—have the potential to affect the choice of the amount of property taxes or expenditures by altering voters' perceived tax prices for additional services.

Discussion Questions

1. "If one city lowers property taxes, then most of the benefits will go to land-owners in that city when taxes were reduced." Evaluate this statement.

2. Suppose that the national government creates a grant program to provide funds to all local governments and, as a result, that all local governments reduce property taxes proportionally. Discuss the economic effects of this property tax change. Which types of individuals are expected to benefit? Will the property tax change lead to a more or less progressive tax structure?

3. Suppose that all types of property are assessed equally in a given state with taxable value equal to market value. Now suppose that a change is made to

assess industrial property at 0 percent of market value, so that effectively no property tax is levied on industrial properties in the state.

    a. If the other types of property are commercial and residential, analyze the expected effect of this change on the amount, prices, and rate of return of industrial and other property in the state. Does it make any difference whether this tax change attracts any new investment from outside the state?

    b. How would the analysis and results be different if the state reduced industrial property taxes but required that total property tax revenue remain the same?

4. Suppose one state introduces a new property tax relief program that provides state-financed property tax credits equal to 20 percent of taxes up to a maximum of $500 for all homeowners with incomes no greater than $30,000. In one school district, homeowners pay $1500 in property taxes to finance per-pupil expenditures of $1500. You believe that the elasticity of property taxes with respect to the taxpayer's property tax price is 1.5.

    a. What is the effect of the credit on the marginal property tax price for taxpayers in this district with income less than $30,000? For taxpayers with income above $30,000?

    b. The school district proposes to increase homeowner property taxes by $400 to $1900 to provide education services of $1900 worth per pupil. Would district taxpayers with income less than $30,000 support such a change? Explain. (HINT: Compare the gain in benefits to the gain in taxes net of the credit.)

Selected Readings

Aaron, Henry J. *Who Pays the Property Tax*. Washington, D.C.: The Brookings Institution, 1975.

McLure, Charles E., Jr. "The 'New View' of the Property Tax: A Caveat." *National Tax Journal* 30 (March 1977): 69–75.

9 / Sales and Excise Taxes

The most extensive use of retail sales taxation in any country is to be found in the states of the United States.[1]

John F. Due

State–local governments use three major types of taxes to tax consumption by residents: so-called general sales taxes levied on retail sales, companion use taxes on resident purchases made in other jurisdictions, and excise taxes on specific goods or services. Examples of the latter are tobacco products, motor fuels, alcoholic beverages, transient accommodations, some utility services, and others. After reviewing recent trends in the use of these taxes and some important institutional details about their structure, the principal economic issues about the incidence and efficiency implications of these taxes are considered.

/ Reliance on Consumption Taxes

Just as property taxes are the major source of tax revenue for local governments, sales or consumption taxes remain the largest single source of revenue to state governments, providing about 29 percent of aggregate state government general revenue in 1986. State general sales, use, and gross receipts taxes alone accounted for 19 percent of state general revenue, second in magnitude only to federal aid, as shown in Table 9.1. State government reliance on general sales taxes has increased slightly since 1962, rising from 16.4 percent of revenue in that year, largely because of rate increases. State and local general sales taxes generated nearly $91 billion of revenue in 1986, representing 2.74 percent of personal income and a per-capita payment of about $376. General sales taxes are (and have been since 1969) used by forty-five states, with current rates varying from a low of 3 percent (in five states) to a median of 5.0 percent (in Utah) to a high of 7.5 percent (in Connecticut).[2] The interstate variation in tax rates can be somewhat misleading, however, because there is also substantial interstate variation in sales tax bases (described in the next section).

---

[1]*Sales Taxation*. Urbana: University of Illinois Press, 1957, 290.

[2]The states without a general sales tax are Alaska, Delaware, Montana, New Hampshire, and Oregon. The most recent sales tax adoption was by Vermont in 1969.

TABLE 9.1

General and Selective Sales Taxes as a Percentage of General Revenue, by Level of Government, Various Years

		Local Governments				School	Special
Year	States	All	Counties	Municipalities	Townships	Districts	Districts
1962							
General[b]	16.4	2.5	1.1	6.6	a	a	a
All[c]	38.6	3.8	1.5	9.9	1.5	a	a
1967							
General	17.1	2.1	1.6	5.1	0.1	0.1	a
All	35.7	3.4	2.1	8.5	1.5	0.1	a
1972							
General	17.9	2.6	3.2	5.4	a	0.2	0.8
All	33.7	4.1	3.8	9.1	1.6	0.2	0.9
1977							
General	18.3	3.1	3.9	5.8	a	0.3	1.2
All	31.0	4.6	4.7	9.6	2.1	0.3	1.2
1982							
General	18.3	3.6	4.4	6.9	a	0.4	2.2
All	28.6	5.3	5.5	11.1	0.1	0.4	2.2
1986							
General	19.0	4.2	5.6	7.4	a	0.3	3.9
All	28.6	5.9	6.7	12.0	a	0.4	3.9

Sources: U.S. Department of Commerce, (1962, 1967, 1972, 1977, 1982; table entitled "General Revenue by Source, by Type of Government"). For 1986 data, U.S. Department of Commerce, Bureau of the Census. *Governmental Finances 1986*, 1988.

[a]Less than 0.1 percent.
[b]*General* includes state and local government general sales and gross receipts taxes.
[c]*All* includes state and local government selective excise taxes and general sales and gross receipts taxes.

Although about 82 percent of total general sales tax revenue went to state governments in 1986, local government general sales taxes were also used by about 6500 local jurisdictions spread among thirty states. As reflected by the data in Table 9.1, these local sales taxes were mostly used by counties, where they accounted for 5.6 percent of revenue in aggregate, and by municipalities, where they provided 7.4 percent of general revenue. The importance of local government sales taxes has generally risen in the past twenty-five years as more localities were given authority to, and then adopted, local sales taxes. In one special case, sales taxes are used by many boroughs (counties) and municipalities in Alaska even though the state government does not use a general sales tax.

State–local governments also impose a number of "selective" sales taxes, which accounted for about 10 percent of state government general revenue and 1.8 percent of aggregate local government general revenue in 1986. Unlike general sales taxes, the share of state and local government revenue provided by these selective excise taxes has declined over the past twenty-five years. These selective sales taxes amounted to slightly more than $44 billion in 1986, or about $184 per capita. These selective sales taxes may be unit taxes, as with gasoline and cigarettes, or *ad valorem* (percentage) taxes, as are commonly used for hotel accommodations or telephone services. In many cases, these selective sales taxes are imposed in addition to the general sales tax on the sale of these goods or services.

/ Consumption Tax Structure Issues

/ General sales and use taxes

In principle, general sales taxes are intended to be taxes on the total final personal consumption of the residents of jurisdictions levying the tax. In practice, state general sales taxes fall short of this principle because (a) a substantial amount of personal consumption is statutorily exempt from taxation, making these taxes somewhat less than "general"; (b) final (retail) as opposed to intermediate consumption is difficult to define, so the taxes end up applying to sales of some intermediate goods (goods used in production of final consumer goods) in addition to consumer goods; and (c) states face inherent administrative difficulties in collecting taxes on purchases of final consumer goods made by residents in other jurisdictions. These deviations from the principle correspond to the three traditional features that characterize a sales tax structure, the *base* on which the tax is to be applied, the *stage(s) of production* at which the tax is to be collected, and the *location* at which the activity is to be taxed.

/ Tax Base.

If sales taxes were to be truly general consumption taxes, they would apply to total personal consumption—that is, all uses of income except for investment (saving by individuals) and purchase of government services.[3] In fact, no state's sales tax base approaches total personal consumption; all states exempt major categories of consumption from sales taxation, although the use of these exemptions also varies greatly among the forty-five sales tax states, as shown in Table 9.2. First, state sales taxes typically apply more commonly to consumption of goods than services. Sale of housing services for instance, whether from owner-occupied houses or rental housing, is exempt from direct sales taxation in all states. Generally, professional services (medical, legal, financial) are not taxed, while personal services (laundry, grooming) and repair services are partially taxed in only some states. Medical services, for example, are included in the general sales tax base in only Hawaii and Florida. Florida changed its sales tax base in 1987 to include many services, the only state other than Hawaii to have gone that far in taxing services. Florida's attempt to tax services generated substantial controversy (particularly because advertising in Florida periodicals and on Florida radio and television stations

---

[3]In simple macroeconomic models, national income comprises personal consumption, investment, and purchases of government goods and services, that is, $Y = C + I + G$.

TABLE 9.2

State and Local Government General Sales Taxes, by State, 1987

Jurisdiction	Tax Rate (%)	Food	Prescription Drugs	Consumer Electric and Gas	Local Tax	Government Types[a]	Rates (%)
New England							
Connecticut	7.5	X	X	X			
Maine	5.0	X	X	X			
Massachusetts	5.0	X	X	X			
New Hampshire				No Sales Tax			
Rhode Island	6.0	X	X	X			
Vermont	4.0	X	X	X			
Mideast							
Delaware				No Sales Tax			
Maryland	5.0	X	X	X			
New Jersey	6.0	X	X	X			
New York	4.0	X	X	X	X	C, M	1.0–4.5
Pennsylvania	6.0	X	X	X			
Great Lakes							
Illinois	5.0	X	X		X	C, M, T	.25–1.0
Indiana	5.0	X	X				
Michigan	4.0	X	X				
Ohio	5.0	X	X	X	X	C, T	.5–1.0
Wisconsin	5.0	X	X	X	·X	C	
Plains							
Iowa	4.0	X	X		X	M	1.0
Kansas	3.0		X	X	X	C, M	.5–1.0
Minnesota	6.0	X	X	X	X	M	1.0
Missouri	4.225		X	X	X	C, M	.375–1.0
Nebraska	4.0	X	X		X	M	1.0–1.5
N. Dakota	5.5	X	X	X	X	M	1.0
S. Dakota	5.0[b]		X		X	M	1.0–2.0
Southeast							
Alabama	4.0		X		X	C, M	.5–3.0
Arkansas	4.0		X	X	X	C, M	1.0–2.0
Florida	5.0	X	X	X	X	C	.25–1.0
Georgia	3.0		X		X	C, T	1.0–2.0
Kentucky	5.0	X	X	X			
Louisiana	4.0	X	X	X	X	P, M Sc, Sp	.125–5.0
Mississippi	6.0		X				
N. Carolina	3.0		X	X	X	C	1.0–1.5
S. Carolina	5.0		X	X			
Tennessee	5.5		X	X	X	C, M	.25–2.25
Virginia	3.5		X	X	X	C, M	1.0
W. Virginia	5.0	X	X	X			

continued

TABLE 9.2

Continued

Jurisdiction	Tax Rate (%)	Exemptions for — Food	Exemptions for — Prescription Drugs	Exemptions for — Consumer Electric and Gas	Local Tax	Government Types[a]	Rates (%)
Southwest							
Arizona	5.0	X	X		X	C, M	.5–2.0
New Mexico	4.75				X	C, M	.125–
Oklahoma	3.25		X	X	X	C, M	1.125
Texas	6.0	X	X	X	X	M, T	1.0–4.0
							.25–1.0
Rocky Mountain							
Colorado	3.0	X	X	X	X	C, M, T	.25–4.0
Idaho	5.0		X	X			
Montana				No Sales Tax			
Utah	5.0938		X	X	X	C, M	.75–1.125
Wyoming	3.0		X		X	C	1.0
Far West							
Alaska		No State Sales Tax			X	B, M	1.0–5.0
California	4.75		X	X	X	C, M, T	.5–1.25
Hawaii	4.0		X				
Nevada	5.75[c]	X	X	X	X		.25
Oregon				No Sales Tax			
Washington	6.5	X	X	X	X	C, M	.5–1.0
All states	5.0 (median)	28	45	32	30		

Source: ACIR (1986c, 92–98); ACIR (1988c, 54–61).

[a]C = Counties, P = Parishes, B = Boroughs, M = Municipalities, T = Transit Districts, Sc = School Districts, Sp = Special Districts.
[b]Rate reduced to 4.0 percent on May 1, 1988.
[c]Includes mandatory county sales tax at 3.75-percent rate.

was to be taxed) and was repealed in early 1988 (Hellerstein, 1988). In addition, sales of food for home consumption (groceries) are exempt in twenty-eight states, sales of prescription drugs are exempt in forty-five states, and sales of electricity and natural gas to residential consumers are exempt in thirty-two states.

The net effect of these exemptions is that state general sales taxes apply to perhaps only 50 to 60 percent of personal consumption in aggregate with obvious substantial variation among the states, depending on the degree of exemptions used.[4] The data in Table 9.3 illustrate how much the sales tax base can be eroded by even a few exemptions. In 1985 food purchases accounted for 18 percent of personal consumption, expenditures for housing services for 15.5 percent, and medical care

---

[4]In 1986 state government general sales tax revenue was about $74.8 billion, while total personal consumption was $2762.4 billion. At the median state sales tax rate of 5 percent, this implies a sales tax base equal to about 54 percent of personal consumption.

TABLE 9.3

Potential Sales Tax Bases, 1985

Category	Amount (Billions of Dollars)	Percentage of Personal Consumption
Personal income	3314.5	127.5
Disposable personal income	2828.0	108.7
Personal consumption	2600.5	100.0
Consumption expenditures on		
Food	469.3	18.0
Clothing	155.2	6.0
All services	1139.0	43.8
Housing	403.9	15.5
Medical care	290.1	11.2
Household gas and electric	89.9	3.5
Consumption less expenditures on food and all services	992.2	38.2
Consumption less expenditures on food, housing, medical care, and household gas and electric	1347.3	51.8
Consumption less expenditures on housing and medical care	1906.5	73.3

Source: U.S. Department of Commerce. *Survey of Current Business* (July 1986, 36–39).

services for another 11.2 percent. For illustration, if purchases of all services and food are excluded from the sales tax, the remaining base is only about 38 percent of total personal consumption. If only purchases of food, electricity and natural gas, and housing and medical care services are exempt, the remaining base represents about 52 percent of personal consumption. Even if only housing and medical care services are exempt from the sales tax, the sales tax base would represent only about 73 percent of personal consumption.

This suggests that in some ways distinguishing between "general" and "selective" sales taxes is an illusion; both apply only to some consumer purchases of goods and services, although the general sales tax base is still broader than even the sum of purchases to which selective sales taxes are applied. One interesting economic implication of the general sales tax exemptions is that they provide consumers a way to avoid sales taxes by shifting consumption toward goods and services that are not directly taxed. Of course, such a change in behavior would entail efficiency costs for the economy. In that sense, analysis of general and selective sales taxes is similar.

/ Stage of Production. Sales taxes can be levied at any and all stages of production of goods and services, although three options are generally considered. At one end of the spectrum, the tax is levied only on the final sale of goods and services for private consumption, at the so-called retail level. In this case, sale of intermediate goods—that is, goods to be subsequently used in the production of other consumer goods and services—is not subject to the tax. Because the tax is levied only at the last or final stage of production, it is clear that the effective tax rate is the nominal rate.

At the opposite end of the spectrum, a sales tax could be levied on *all* sales or transactions, that is, at all stages of production. Such a tax is often called a **multistage gross receipts tax**, as it applies to the gross receipts or sales of all firms. For instance, if a 1-percent gross receipts tax were applied to the production of bread, 1 percent would be levied on the sale of wheat by farmers to millers, 1 percent would be levied on the sale of flour by millers to bakers, 1 percent would be levied on the sale of equipment by manufacturers to bakers, 1 percent would be levied on the sale of bread by bakers to retailers, and, finally, 1 percent would be imposed on the sale of bread by retailers to consumers. The taxes levied at the stages of production before final retail sale become part of the costs of production and are therefore imbedded in the retail price charged to the consumer. The gross receipts tax is said to **cascade** or **pyramid**, through the various stages of production, and therefore the effective rate of tax paid by the consumer is greater than the nominal rate levied on the retail sale.

Multistage taxes of this type generate a number of equity and efficiency problems. Part of the tax burden is implicit or hidden, and because that implicit tax burden will vary for different types of goods, the effective tax rate will also vary among different goods. Because intrafirm transactions are not taxed, there is an incentive for firms to vertically integrate to reduce taxes. If only some producer inputs are subject to sales tax, the change in the relative cost of inputs creates an incentive for firms to alter production techniques. These issues are discussed in detail in Chapter 11 (because gross receipts taxes have been used by some states as general business taxes).

A sales tax can also be levied at one stage of production but before final retail sale. For instance, the tax might be levied on the sale of goods from wholesalers to retailers, with no additional tax then collected on the sale from the retailer to the consumer. Or a sales tax might be imposed only on the sale of a product by the manufacturer to a distributor, wholesaler, or retailer, a so-called manufacturer's sales tax. This tax structure avoids some but not all of the problems created by multistage sales taxes. There is no cascading of the tax—that is, no tax imposed upon prior tax—because the tax is levied only at one stage of production. But the effective tax rate paid by consumers will vary by product and producer, depending on the relative importance of the taxed stage in the final cost of the product. For instance, a wholesale sales tax would apply only to the cost of goods purchased by retailers to resell. But the retailer's business costs also include the labor and capital costs of the retail business. The wholesale sales tax would be a larger fraction of total retailer cost for retailers with *lower* labor and capital costs. Similarly, the larger the manufacturing costs of a good are (compared to distribution, marketing, and sales costs), the greater the effective rate to the consumer of a sales tax imposed only at the manufacturing stage.

If state sales taxes are intended to be retail taxes on the final sale of consumer goods (and some services), then sales of all goods used in production would have to be exempt, but no state goes that far. Nearly all states exempt from sales tax sales of goods that are to be resold and then taxed and sales of materials used in production that become a *physical ingredient of the final product*. States diverge in their sales tax treatment of equipment and machinery, of materials that are used in production but that do not become an ingredient of the product (fuels, for example), and of materials and supplies used in business but not in production (typewriters, for example). Regarding equipment and machinery, the Sales and Use Taxation Committee of the National Tax Association (Deasy 1987) reports that thirty-six of the forty-five sales tax states have a broad-based exemption for capital assets used in production, with the most common rule (twenty-eight states) being that the machinery and equipment must be *directly used in production*. In their classic treatise on sales taxes, John Due and John Mikesell (1983, 59) report that "West Virginia is the only state to exclude from tax virtually all producers goods used in manufacturing, retailing, and agriculture." Accordingly, state sales taxes are not exclusively retail taxes but apply to at least some purchases of intermediate goods by businesses.

State sales tax treatment of business purchases often also varies depending on whether the sale of the business's product is taxed. It is fairly common sales tax practice that firms that produce or sell nontaxable goods or services are treated as the final consumers of taxable goods or services used in business and thus must pay sales tax on those purchases. For instance, if the sale of a house is not taxed, the builder may have to pay sales tax on purchases of materials and supplies used in constructing the house. The economic effect of this treatment is equivalent to that from a direct sales tax on the goods or services produced by such firms, although at a lower rate than the general rate. If a firm providing a tax-exempt service spends 20 percent of its total costs on purchases of taxable materials and supplies (the other 80 percent being purchases of labor, real property, and utilities that are not taxed) at a sales tax rate of 5 percent, the tax raises the firm's costs by 1 percent and, if fully passed on to consumers, is economically equivalent to a 1-percent tax on the sale of the firm's service. Consumers of goods or services that are not taxed at the retail sale may still bear a sales tax burden therefore if sales tax is paid by the businesses producing those goods or services.

States often accomplish exemption of business purchases by issuing exemption certificates or exemption numbers to businesses that regularly purchase otherwise taxable goods or services that are to be used for production rather than for consumption. It is sometimes difficult to distinguish at the time of sale whether the good will be consumed or used in the production of other goods, which depends on the nature of the buyer rather than on the nature of the good. For instance, a truck purchased by an individual for private use is private consumption and the sale should be taxed under a retail sales tax; but a truck purchased by a manufacturer and used in production (to transport parts, perhaps) is an intermediate good, with that sale ideally not to be taxed under a retail sales tax. With the presentation of the certificate or number, a seller does not collect sales tax on sales of otherwise taxable goods or services to these businesses. The use of exemption certificates and numbers does create some administrative problems and the potential for fraud, however; a business owner may purchase items for personal use but represent them as for use in the business, or counterfeit exemption certificates may be used.

/ *Tax Location and Use Taxes*.   Consumption taxes may be based either on the **origin principle,** with tax based on the location of the sale, or on the **destination principle**, with tax based on the location of consumption or the consumer. Again in theory, state sales taxes are intended to be destination-based taxes, taxing consumption where it occurs. Accordingly, state sales taxes are not collected on purchases of otherwise taxable goods if those goods are to be delivered to a consumer in another state. For this reason, consumers are not charged sales tax on mail-order purchases if the mail-order company is located in a different state from the purchaser. On the other hand, sales tax is charged on purchases by nonresidents if the buyer takes possession of the good in the state where the purchase occurred. The presumption is that consumption occurs where the buyer receives the good.

To implement the destination principle, it is necessary, however, for a state's residents to be taxed on *all* taxable consumption, regardless of the location of purchase. But buyers pay *no* sales tax on purchases that are delivered to the state of residence from other states. The resident's state cannot impose a sales tax because no sale occurred in that state. To correct this difficulty, all states with general sales taxes also impose a companion **use tax** on the use of taxable goods and services at the same rate as the sales tax, which is collected only if the sales tax is not. An individual who avoids sales tax by purchasing a good in another state, therefore, owes use tax to his state of residence instead, equal to what the sales tax would have been. As one can imagine, the collection of use taxes is fraught with serious administrative difficulty that limits the degree to which the destination principle is achieved. Simply put, the collection of use taxes is often prohibitively expensive. In practice, retail businesses can be required to collect use tax for other states on sales to residents of those other states if that firm also has establishments (*nexus* is the legal term) in those other states. Otherwise, the collection of use taxes is generally limited to large purchases (such as taxable business equipment) and those that can be tracked through a state government's regulatory authority (such as automobiles, boats, airplanes).

/ Selective sales taxes

State–local governments also impose sales taxes on a number of specific commodities, usually including tobacco products, motor fuels, alcoholic beverages (in the bottle and/or by the glass), hotel and motel accommodations, restaurant meals, and some utility services (often telephone service). Unlike general sales taxes, for which often both the tax rate and tax base differ among the states, excise tax bases vary little among the states although tax rates vary substantially. The rates for two common state excise taxes, on cigarettes and gasoline, are shown in Table 9.4. Cigarette excise taxes vary from $.02 per pack of twenty (in North Carolina) to a median of $.18 per pack to a high of $.38 per pack (in Minnesota). State gasoline

TABLE 9.4

Selected State Excise Taxes, 1987

	Cigarettes		Gasoline	
Jurisdiction	*Excise Tax (Cents/Pack)*	*State Sales Tax Applied*	*Excise Tax (Cents/Gallon)*	*State Sales Tax Applied*
New England				
Connecticut	26	X	19	
Maine	28	X	14	
Massachusetts	26		11	
New Hampshire	17		14	
Rhode Island	25		13	
Vermont	17	X	13	
Mideast				
Delaware	14		16	
Maryland	13		18.5	
New Jersey	27		8	
New York	21	X	8	X
Pennsylvania	18	X	12	
Great Lakes				
Illinois	20	X	13	X
Indiana	15.5	X	14	X
Michigan	21	X	15	X
Ohio	14	X	14.7	
Wisconsin	30	X	20	
Plains				
Iowa	26	X	16	
Kansas	24	X	11	
Minnesota	38	X	17	
Missouri	13	X	11	
Nebraska	27	X	17.6	
N. Dakota	27	X	17	
S. Dakota	23		13	
Southeast				
Alabama	16.5	X	11	
Arkansas	21		13.5	
Florida	24	X	4	
Georgia	12	X	7.5	X
Kentucky	3	X	15	
Louisiana	16	X	16	
Mississippi	18	X	15	X
N. Carolina	2	X	15.5	
S. Carolina	7	X	15	
Tennessee	13	X	17	
Virginia	2.5	X	17.5	
W. Virginia	18	X	10.5	
Southwest				
Arizona	15	X	16	
New Mexico	15	X	14	
Oklahoma	25	X	16	
Texas	20.5	X	15	

continued

TABLE 9.4

Continued

	Cigarettes		Gasoline	
Jurisdiction	*Excise Tax (Cents/Pack)*	*State Sales Tax Applied*	*Excise Tax (Cents/Gallon)*	*State Sales Tax Applied*
Rocky Mountain				
Colorado	20		18	
Idaho	18	X	14.5	
Montana	16		20	
Utah	23	X	19	
Wyoming	8		8	
Far West				
Alaska	16		8	
California	10	X	9	X
Hawaii	29	X	11	X
Nevada	20	X	14.25	
Oregon	27		12	
Washington	31	X	18	
All states	18 (median)	37	14.5 (median)	8

Source: ACIR, (1986c, 101–102); ACIR (1987c, 62–63).

excise taxes vary from $.04 per gallon (in New Mexico) to a median of $.145 per gallon to a high of $.20 per gallon (in Wisconsin).[5] Perhaps surprisingly, there is more interstate variation in tax rates on cigarettes than gasoline, an issue we turn to later in considering the incentive for changes in the location of purchases caused by sales taxes.

As with general sales taxes, excise taxes may also be levied at either the manufacturing, wholesale, or retail stage of production. Commonly, state gasoline and local hotel taxes are levied at the retail stage, whereas state cigarette taxes are levied at the wholesale or distributor stage, for instance. And these excise taxes are not necessarily substitutes for state sales taxes. As shown in Table 9.4, cigarette sales are subject to the general state sales tax in thirty-seven states, while gasoline is also subject to the sales tax in eight states.

Besides generating revenue, excise taxes can serve two other purposes. One is to change consumer behavior, reducing consumption of goods that create consumption externalities or those that are otherwise determined to be socially undesirable. Excise taxes with this purpose are sometimes called **sumptuary taxes** and are intended to increase economic efficiency by offsetting negative externalities. Excise taxes can also be used for equity reasons, to alter the distribution of tax burden. For instance, excise taxes on goods consumed relatively more by higher-income individuals will increase the progressivity or reduce the regressivity of the state and local tax structure.

---

[5]The federal government also imposes excise taxes of $.16 per pack of cigarettes and $.09 per gallon of gasoline (in 1987).

/ Economic Analysis: Efficiency

Sales taxes can influence economic decisions in three major ways. The tax reduces consumers' disposable incomes and thus induces changes in the quantities of all goods consumed. This **income effect** arises because the tax transfers resources from private consumption to government and thus would be present with any revenue source used to generate equal collections. If the sales tax is at least partly paid by consumers, it also raises the relative price of taxed compared to untaxed goods, which may induce some consumers to substitute exempt commodities for taxable ones. In addition, if some states or localities do not tax a commodity as heavily as other jurisdictions and if use taxes cannot be effectively collected, consumers may be induced to substitute purchases in other jurisdictions for purchases in their own. These latter two **substitution** or **price effects** arise because of the nature of sales taxes and are therefore the sources of the potential efficiency costs of sales and excise taxes. Each is considered separately.

/ Optimal sales tax structure

Because sales and excise taxes alter the relative prices of some goods, creating incentives for consumers and producers (to the extent sales of intermediate goods are taxed) to change their behavior, the tax can result in a loss of economic efficiency or creation of an excess burden. It is natural therefore to consider what sales tax structure will minimize this efficiency loss for any given revenue yield—that is, what sales tax structure is optimal, where structure refers to the effective tax rate levied on consumption of various goods and services. As a policy matter, the question is usually phrased in terms of whether it is preferable to apply the sales tax to the broadest possible base of consumer goods and services all taxed at one rate as opposed to allowing numerous exemptions, effectively taxing some goods at lower or even zero rates.

The general theoretical rule for optimal commodity taxation, usually attributed to Frank Ramsey (1927), is disceptively simple: *The optimal set of sales taxes should cause an equal proportionate decrease in the compensated quantity demanded of all commodities* (the compensated demand is the demand after the consumer is compensated for the income effect of the tax).[6] If all consumer goods, including leisure, can be taxed, then the rule implies that an equal proportionate tax is best. With an equal percentage tax on all commodities, the *relative* prices of all goods are not changed, and consequently there are no substitution effects. The tax has only an income effect and is equivalent to a lump-sum tax. But what if, in practice, it is impossible to impose a sales tax on all commodities, especially leisure (inherently, time)? In that case, the rule becomes more complicated, and it is no longer the case that a uniform proportionate tax is most efficient.

---

[6]The reason for looking at compensated demand curves is that the issue is the structure of the tax, not the level; presumably, the same income is to be collected from consumers whatever tax structure is utilized.

FIGURE 9.1 *Efficiency Cost of Alternative Sales Tax Rates*

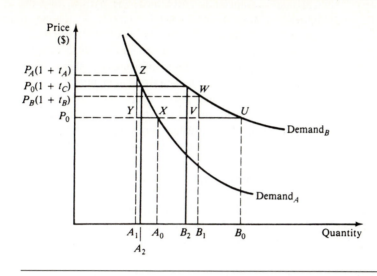

The intuition behind this notion is illustrated in Figure 9.1. Demand$_A$ and Demand$_B$ are the compensated demand curves for the only two taxable commodities, A and B (assume leisure is the other good). Before there are any taxes, the prices of both are equal to P_0, which reflects the social marginal cost of each, with consumption equal to A_0 and B_0. Suppose a tax rate of t_A is levied on consumption of A and a lower rate of t_B is levied on B. These rates were selected so that the consumption of both goods decreases by 20 percent, to A_1 and B_1. The efficiency cost of these taxes is represented by the loss of consumer surplus in both markets, equal to the sum of areas *ZYX* and *WVU* in Figure 9.1. If, instead, an equal tax rate sufficient to generate the same revenue, shown as t_C in the figure, was levied on consumption of both goods, the resulting efficiency loss would be greater. In essence, the somewhat smaller efficiency cost in consumption of A (because of the lower tax rate) is more than offset by the much larger efficiency cost in consumption of B (from tax rate t_C compared to t_B). Given the conditions of the illustration, the differential rates t_A, t_B generate a given amount of revenue with less excess burden than the single rate t_C.[7]

On pure economic efficiency grounds, then, this result contradicts what has often been the conventional policy wisdom favoring broad coverage. For instance, in their treatise on sales taxes Due and Mikesell (1983, 68) state that "any deviation from uniform coverage of a tax is inherently objectionable on grounds of . . . possible

---

[7]In this illustration, the demand for these two goods is independent; changes in the price of one do not affect the demand for the other. The price changes caused by the taxes may, however, affect the demand for the other commodity, leisure. The Ramsey rule applies as well if commodities are substitutes or complements.

`consumer excess burden´.'' But the above illustration shows that differential rates may be more efficient than a single rate. Moreover, the optimal rate on some commodities could be zero—that is, having sales tax exemptions could be optimal.

In general the optimal sales tax rule depends on whether it is feasible to set tax rates based on the price elasticity of demand and supply for those goods and on the cross-price effects among commodities. Unfortunately, this economic research has often been more successful at characterizing nonoptimal tax structures than in identifying feasible rules to guide policy decisions. David Bradford and Harvey Rosen (1976, 96) have stated that ''the extensive . . . work [on optimal taxation] has shown how difficult it is to sustain *any* simple rules for commodity taxation. . . . '' Nevertheless, the optimal tax rules for some conditions can be a guide to policy.

First, if the demands for different commodities are not related—that is, if they are neither substitutes nor complements—then the Ramsey optimal tax rule implies that commodities should be taxed inversely proportional to their price elasticity of demand; higher tax rates should apply to commodities with relatively less elastic demand. The intuition behind such a rule is simple. Because inefficiency results from consumers changing their behavior in response to the tax-induced price increase, inefficiency is minimized by imposing relatively higher taxes on consumers who will change behavior relatively little. In fact, this is exactly the case shown in Figure 9.1 because the demand for both A and B is not affected by changes in the price of the other good. The efficient tax structure required a higher tax rate on commodity A, the one with the less price-elastic demand.

Second, if it is not feasible to directly tax leisure with sales taxes, efficiency may be increased by imposing relatively high tax rates on commodities that are complementary to or jointly consumed with leisure. Certainly, these commodities should not be exempt from tax. By imposing taxes on those commodities consumed with leisure, one effectively imposes an indirect tax on the consumption of leisure. This argument can be used to support sales taxation of admissions to sporting events and other types of entertainment and of club dues, as well as selective excise taxes on leisure-time goods such as boats or other recreational equipment.

Although there has been no research attempting to directly measure the efficiency consequences of state sales tax exemptions in the United States, Charles Ballard and John Shoven (1985) have estimated efficiency effects of a uniform value-added tax (VAT) imposed by the national government in the U.S. compared to a VAT with exemptions and differential rates. A VAT of the type they consider is a type of national sales tax (although collected through businesses at each stage of production). They compare a tax at a flat rate on all personal consumption to one that exempts housing and services and imposes a lower rate on food, which, of course, is very similar to the typical state sales tax base. Ballard and Shoven (1985, 17) base their estimates on a simulation model of the U.S. economy and conclude that ''the rate differentiation reduces the efficiency gain offered by a consumption-type VAT [compared to the U.S. income tax] by an enormous amount. . . . The welfare sacrifice caused by rate differentiation is 17 percent of

GNP [in 1973 dollars], and about .46 percent of the present value of future welfare (including leisure).''

If these results are accurate, they suggest that the current exemptions from state sales taxes do reduce economic efficiency compared to more complete coverage, but that does not mean that some other sales tax structure of exemptions and differential rates might not be more efficient than a uniform tax. In many cases, however, policy evaluation of sales tax exemptions and the use of differential tax rates depends on more easily quantifiable factors such as the border effects from sales taxes and administrative cost considerations. Each of those issues is now considered.

/ Border effects

Individuals may also be able to avoid or reduce sales taxes by changing the location of their purchases, generally by making purchases in jurisdictions different from the one in which they reside. Two different opportunities for avoiding the tax are available. First, individuals may purchase goods in one state or locality for delivery to a different location, presumably the state or locality where the individual lives. The individual is not subject to sales tax in the jurisdiction of the purchase, but is subject to any use tax levied by the jurisdiction of residence. If that use tax is not or cannot be collected, no state or local consumption tax is levied on the purchase. Second, if purchases of goods or services are taxed at a lower rate in one jurisdiction than in another, an individual may make purchases and take possession in the lower-tax jurisdiction and thus pay the lower sales tax rate. Again, this individual may be liable for a use tax equal to the difference between the tax rates, but that tax may not be feasible to collect.

Both of these opportunities are concerns particularly along borders between states or between localities where local sales taxes are used, although they are not limited to border areas as the illustration about mail-order sales presented in Application 9.2 makes clear. Only the second of these sales tax avoidance methods arises from a difference in tax rates or sales tax bases; the first arises solely because of the difficulty in collecting use taxes. The magnitude of both effects depends on the size of transportation costs (of goods and/or consumers) compared to the potential tax savings, the variety of different goods or shops available in different locations, consumer awareness of tax differences and goods availability, and on the effectiveness of administrative arrangements to collect use taxes.

If one assumes that the net-of-tax prices of commodities sold in national markets will be equal at all locations (implying horizontal supply curves at each location equal to the national price), then the economic effects of a sales tax rate differential between jurisdictions are straightforward. The consumer's price for any given commodity will vary between high- and low-tax jurisdictions by the full amount of the tax-rate difference. This difference in prices, which is assumed to persist, induces consumers to substitute purchases in the lower-rate jurisdiction for those in the higher-rate jurisdiction. Accordingly, retail sales increase in the lower-tax jurisdiction while decreasing in the higher-tax one. With these assumptions, the tax-rate differential can never be eliminated by changes in demand until *all* purchases occur in the lower-tax jurisdiction.

For many practical tax-rate differential cases, it may be more reasonable to assume that the retail sector is characterized by increasing costs (upward-sloping, long-run supply curves), as shown in Figure 9.2. The positively sloped supply curves would result, for instance, if expansion of the retail sector in any area or state caused an increase in factor prices, perhaps an increase in land values or higher wages required to attract additional employees. In the figure, good X is sold at price P_0 in both locations without any tax differential (either no tax or equal taxes in both locations). Any tax-rate differential that arises (either because one taxes while the other does not or because one taxes at a higher rate) can be reflected by an upward shift in the supply curve equal to the amount of tax differential. As a result of that tax differential, the quantity of good X sold in the higher-tax jurisdiction falls (to X_1) because the price rises, while the demand for good X in the lower-tax jurisdiction rises. As a result of that increase in demand, the *amount* of good X sold in the lower-tax jurisdiction rises (to X_1) and the *price* of good X in the lower-tax jurisdiction also rises (to P_2). A price differential between the two jurisdictions may remain due to transportation or information costs (for instance, P_1 compared to P_2), although that price differential is less than the tax-rate differential. Although the lower-tax jurisdiction has gained additional sales of good X, consumers who always made purchases in that jurisdiction now face higher prices.

FIGURE 9.2   Effect of a Sales Tax Rate Differential

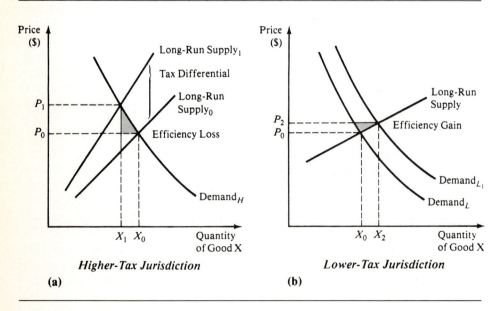

Higher-Tax Jurisdiction

(a)

Lower-Tax Jurisdiction

(b)

The efficiency cost of the additional tax in the one jurisdiction is also shown in Figure 9.2. The efficiency loss from reduced consumption of X in the higher-tax jurisdiction is the difference between the marginal value of the good to consumers and the marginal social cost of production, shown as the shaded triangular-shaped area in Figure 9.2a. This loss is partially but not completely offset by an efficiency gain (shown in Figure 9.2b) due to the increased sale of X in the lower-tax juris-diction (the price paid by consumers, which reflects their value, is greater than marginal cost). The tax-rate differential results in a net efficiency cost even if total consumption of X remains the same because consumers incur extra costs or incon-venience to purchase the commodity in the different location.

The effects of a tax-rate differential on consumption are not expected to be the same for all commodities. Tax savings per purchase is directly related to the price of the product and the quantity to be purchased, that is, proposed expenditure per trip. But any transportation cost incurred in making a purchase in a different location is usually related to distance and travel time rather than the amount spent. One expects therefore that the tax differential effect will be more important for com-modities purchased with a relatively large expenditure at one time. One exception to this generalization is if use tax can be collected on purchases such as automobiles or commodities sold by firms with establishments in both locations. Another ex-ception is if consumers can change the location of purchases without incurring any extra transportation cost. In addition to mail-order purchases, that may be easy for individuals who work and reside in different locations with different sales tax rates. Those individuals can often transfer purchases from their residential to their work location without additional cost.

There have been quite a number of studies examining the degree to which sales tax rate differentials actually do induce consumers to change the location of pur-chases, most of which examine the experience in specific geographic areas, although one is a general cross-section analysis of all large metropolitan areas in the United States.[8] These studies are quite consistent in finding that a disadvantageous sales tax rate differential leads to a statistically significant but relatively small reduction in sales in the higher-tax jurisdictions.

For instance, this author examined the effect of sales tax differentials between the District of Columbia and the surrounding Maryland and Virginia suburbs on retail sales in the District over the period from 1962–76 (Fisher, 1980b). Generally the District had a higher general tax rate than in the suburbs, including a higher tax rate on food than in Maryland but a lower rate on food than in Virginia. The study found no significant effect of the tax-rate differential on aggregate sales in the District but a significant negative effect on food sales. With respect to food, the analysis showed that one percentage point rise in the tax-rate differential (holding the District's rate constant) led to a 7-percent decrease in District sales tax revenue from food. The effect on food sales but not on sales of other commodities apparently arose because the food tax rate differences were greater than the differences in the

---

[8]For a general review, see Fisher (1980b). More recent analyses are Mikesell and Zorn (1985), Fox (1986), and Walsh (1986).

/ APPLICATION 9.1
Cigarette Taxes and Cigarette Bootlegging[9]

States levy widely differing excise taxes on the sale of cigarettes, as shown in Table 9.4. Because cigarettes are an easily transportable commodity, these tax differences create a possibility for individuals to purchase cigarettes in low-tax states for use or resale in higher-tax states, avoiding the state tax in the latter. This problem became particularly acute in the mid-1970s, leading to adoption of a federal law restricting this possibility. In addition, federal law prohibits state governments from levying cigarette excise taxes on sales of cigarettes on military bases, and various federal agreements and treaties similarly prevent state taxation of cigarette sales on Indian reservations. These two exemptions not only mean that cigarette consumption by military personnel and residents of Indian reservations escape state taxation but also create another opportunity for evading tax on sales to other state residents. Presumably, the higher the state cigarette tax, the greater the incentive for illegal sales from these sources to avoid the tax.

While there has always been some variation in state cigarette taxes, those differences increased greatly in the 1960s and 1970s along with a general rise in the level of those taxes. State cigarette excise taxes varied from 0 to $.08 in 1960 but from $.02 to $.18 by 1970 and from $.02 to $.21 in 1980. The U.S. Advisory Commission on Intergovernmental Relations estimated that, as a result, states were losing about 10 percent of potential cigarette excise tax revenue in 1975 due to cigarette smuggling across state boundaries and from sales on military bases and reservations, with the losses being particularly large in fourteen states. Although state laws made such transport and sale of cigarettes illegal, states were not very effective in enforcing those laws at least partly due to the inherent interstate nature of the activity.

As a result of requests by the states and a recommendation by ACIR, the federal government adopted the Contraband Cigarette Act in 1978, which made it a federal crime to transport, receive, ship, possess, distribute, or purchase more than 60,000 cigarettes (3000 packs) without paying the state tax of the state in which the cigarettes are located. This law was then vigorously enforced by the Bureau of Alcohol, Tobacco, and Firearms, a branch of the U.S. Department of the Treasury. By all accounts, this federal intervention, coupled with expanded state enforcement activity, greatly curtailed interstate cigarette sales to avoid state taxes. A subsequent study by ACIR showed that state revenue losses from illegal and exempt sales of cigarettes had declined to about 5 percent of cigarette excise tax revenue by 1983 and remained a serious problem in only two states (Connecticut and West Virginia), despite a continuing increase in the median level and variance of cigarette tax rates. Moreover, ACIR estimated that 70 percent of the 1983 revenue loss resulted from the exemption of sales on military bases and Indian reservations rather than interstate smuggling.

In essence, the differences in state excise taxes on cigarettes were able to be maintained, and even increased, largely because of the assistance of the

---

[9]This illustration is based on ACIR (1985a).

/ APPLICATION 9.1 Continued
Cigarette Taxes and Cigarette Bootlegging

federal government in preventing evasion of those state tax laws. The experience in the 1970s suggests that it is unlikely that states would have maintained as large a difference in cigarette tax rates as currently exists without that assistance. If tax-rate differences of the current magnitude were attempted, the high–tax rate states would have collected substantially less revenue than they currently do with the federal law and enforcement.

Cigarette bootlegging to avoid state taxes is not confined to the United States, but also occurs in Australia where all the continental state governments—except Queensland, which has no such tax—levy a "license fee" on tobacco products of between 25 and 35 percent. In 1986 a High Court reinterpretation of a constitutional provision allowed states to levy the fees on interstate trade as long as trade within the state was treated equally. As a result, the government of New South Wales began collecting its 30-percent fee on shipments from other states. The *Financial Review* (Jay 1987) reported that the New South Wales government had seized three shipments of cigarettes worth a total of $1 million (Aus.) from Queensland where the fee was evaded. As further evidence of the potential effects of smuggling, the state of Tasmania, which is an island and thus more likely to be able to control smuggling, is able to collect a fee of 50 percent.

States in the United States also seek federal assistance in reducing the loss of revenue from cigarette sales on military bases and Indian reservations. ACIR estimated that states did not collect $176 million in 1983 cigarette tax revenue due to military base sales, about 31 percent of which arose from sales to unauthorized personnel (smuggling off the bases). Foregone revenue from Indian reservation sales was estimated to be about $43 million.

The exemption for sales on military bases raises two issues: Should military personnel be exempt from these state taxes, and to what extent does this exemption allow nonmilitary personnel to evade state taxes? On the first issue, state governments argue that cigarette sales to military personnel should be taxed because (a) the exemption effectively means that residents of states with military bases pay for a fringe benefit to United States government military personnel through the foregone revenue (and thus higher tax rates), (b) the federal $.16 cigarette excise tax is levied on base sales, and (c) cigarette consumption can hardly be called a "necessity." The exemption may become less important over time, as several branches of the military in 1986 adopted restrictive rules on cigarette smoking, which are intended to reduce consumption, by personnel. Improved cooperation between military officials and state tax administrators is one option, short of removing the exemption, to reduce state tax evasion as a result of cigarette bootlegging from military bases.

/ APPLICATION 9.2
Mail-Order Sales and State Use Taxes[10]

Out-of-state mail-order sales, although creating somewhat different administrative problems than do state cigarette taxes, involve a similar issue of federalism. Because of the destination principle, states do not levy sales tax on mail-order purchases for delivery to other states. The buyers owe use tax on those purchases in their state of residence (if the state has a sales/use tax that taxes the commodity), but as a result of a series of court decisions states cannot force the mail-order firms to collect those use taxes if the firm has no business presence in the state. The question, as with cigarette taxes, is whether the federal government should intervene in some way to assist states in collecting use taxes on those mail-order sales.

In a 1967 decision (*National Bellas Hess* v. *Illinois Department of Revenue*) the U.S. Supreme Court held, largely on the basis of the Interstate Commerce Clause of the Constitution, that states could not require out-of-state mail-order firms to collect state use taxes if the firm's business in the state is limited to the sending of catalogs and similar advertising. However, if a mail-order firm also has a "business presence" in a state, such as retail outlets, then that state can require the mail-order firm to collect sales or use tax on mail-order purchases for delivery in that state. For instance, states (other than Maine, where the firm is located) cannot require L. L. Bean, Inc., to collect use taxes on sales, while most, if not all, states can require Sears, Roebuck and Co. to collect use taxes on orders, given that Sears has retail outlets in most states.

The ACIR estimates that state and local government sales and use taxes would have generated an additional $1.4 to $1.5 billion in 1985 if sales and use taxes had been collected on mail-order sales of taxable commodities. Accordingly, the magnitude of this tax enforcement issue is substantially larger than that for cigarette taxes. Mail-order firms are of two general types, those whose primary business is mail-order sales and those whose primary business

---

[10]*This illustration is based on ACIR (1986b).*

general rates and because the District had effective agreements with many retail firms with both suburban and District locations to collect District use taxes, at least for purchases of durable goods delivered to a District location.

More recently, John Mikesell and Kurt Zorn (1985) examined the effect of a temporary (three and one-half years) one-half percentage point sales tax differential in the small (population 7891) city of Bay St. Louis, Mississippi. Over the period 1979–82, the sales tax rate was 5.5 percent in Bay St. Louis and 5.0 percent in surrounding areas. Their analysis showed that the rate difference did reduce retail sales in the city (a one percentage point rate differential lowers sales by about 2.3 percent) primarily from lower sales per seller on average rather than a decrease in the number of sellers. This rate difference was planned and announced to be temporary, so city retail sales returned to the prior level after the rate difference was ended.

/ APPLICATION 9.2 Continued
Mail-Order Sales and State Use Taxes

---

is in some other line (often retail sales) but which also engage in mail-order sales. In 1985 it is estimated that there were about 5400 firms in the first category and 1700 in the second. Of these, it is estimated that only about 270 have annual sales greater than $10 million, although this 4 percent of mail-order firms accounts for as much as 70 percent of total sales.

Requiring mail-order firms to collect state–local government use taxes on mail-order sales could create substantial administrative costs for those firms. In addition to the forty-five states with sales and use taxes, they are also levied by about 6500 local governments. Moreover, there are wide differences in the tax bases and rates of those governments—a commodity sent to one city in state X might be taxed at a different rate than the same commodity sent to a different city in the same state, or a commodity might be taxed in one state but exempt in another. It could therefore be rather difficult and expensive for a mail-order firm to determine the appropriate tax on all sales.

In view of all these considerations, several options have been suggested. The federal government could require mail-order firms to collect a federal sales tax at a single rate on all sales with the revenue distributed to states based on sales tax collections, income, or population. Or the federal government might adopt a law allowing states to require mail-order firms to collect state (but not local) taxes, to reduce the compliance costs for firms. In essence, this second option is the recommendation of ACIR (1986b). Or the federal government might give the states authority to enter into cooperative agreements among themselves to have states collect the tax for each other from mail-order firms in their jurisdiction. This is essentially the dissenting recommendation of a minority of the ACIR (including the Attorney General and the Secretary of Labor). One possible option not requiring federal legislative action is for states to pursue in federal courts a change in the definition of business presence, which would broaden their tax-collection authority.

It is important to understand that results of this magnitude imply that increases in sales tax rates in individual cities are expected to increase revenue even with the small reduction in city sales. The increase in the tax rate more than offsets the small reduction in the sales tax base. In the District of Columbia case, an increase in the District's food rate from 2 to 3 percent (a 50-percent increase in tax rate) was estimated to increase sales tax revenue from food purchases by about 35 percent. In the Bay St. Louis case, an increase in the tax rate from 5.0 percent to 5.5 percent (a 10-percent increase) was estimated to increase sales tax revenue by about 8.8 percent.

These economic effects of sales tax rate differentials and the resulting attempts by state tax administrators to enforce use taxes raise several difficult issues inherent to a fiscal federalism. States (and the local governments they create) have autonomy in the selection of tax structures, including sales tax bases and rates. But because state and local governments encompass substantially open economies, tax decisions by individual states can influence interstate economic activity, regulation of which is reserved for the federal government by the Constitution. For states to levy taxes indirectly on that interstate activity requires either the cooperation of other states or intervention by the federal government, which may impinge on the autonomy of the states. Applications 9.1 and 9.2, concerning state cigarette taxes and mail-order sales, show some of the options available for resolving this issue and how the federal government decided to take opposite positions in the two cases. The federal government adopted a law and increased enforcement in the 1970s to assist states in collecting cigarette taxes but has declined to intervene in any way in the 1980s to assist states in collecting use taxes on mail-order sales.

/ Economic Analysis: Equity

/ Tax incidence

A truly general sales tax on all personal consumption would impose burdens on consumers in proportion to their amount of consumption. Consumers would be very limited in their ability to shift the tax because the tax would apply to nearly all consumer goods and services, although one remaining option for consumers would be to increase consumption of leisure, which is presumably untaxed. An increase in consumption of leisure is equivalent to a decrease in the supply of labor; individuals may be able to shift a general consumption tax, then, by working less, earning less income, and consuming fewer taxable goods and services in aggregate. These possible long-run effects may be minor, however, if the aggregate supply of labor is relatively price inelastic, as is usually assumed.

The typical incidence assumption about a general sales tax, then, is that it imposes tax burdens in proportion to the amount of consumption. Because the share of income represented by personal consumption tends to be smaller for higher-income as opposed to lower-income individuals (higher-income individuals do more saving), the conclusion is drawn that general sales taxes are regressive; that is, sales tax burdens as a proportion of income decline as one moves up the income distribution. For instance, if a family with a $50,000 income spends $40,000 on consumption, a 1-percent tax equals $400, or .8 percent of income; but if a family with a $10,000 income spends $9500 on consumption, the tax is $95, which represents .95 percent of income.

/ Exemptions

This perception of sales tax regressivity is the primary reason for most sales tax exemptions of consumer goods and services. Exemptions of goods and services that are relatively more important in the budgets of lower-income individuals, so-called necessities, are used to alter this distributional pattern. This is the rationale usually used to support such exemptions as food consumed at home, prescription drugs, housing, residential electric and gas utilities, clothing, and medical services.

Consumer spending on various categories of personal consumption as a fraction of income are reported in Table 9.5. As suggested, expenditures on food at home, residential electric and gas services, housing, and medical care do decline as a fraction of income as income rises. Note, also, that total consumption decreases as a fraction of income as income rises, with consumption being greater than income at the lower-income classes. Following the reasoning above, then, exempting food and residential electric and gas sales from the sales tax should tend to reduce any regressivity of the tax.

These effects are confirmed by many empirical studies of sales tax incidence. For instance, Donald Phares (1980) estimated the distribution of tax burden for each tax in each state and concluded that "there is little question about [the general sales tax's] regressive incidence," although "state-by-state data on general sales effective rates do suggest a less regressive pattern in states that exempt food" (p. 96). Although this analysis shows the sales tax to be regressive over the entire income distribution, it also shows that the tax is nearly proportional in the middle-income range between $6000 and $25,000 (measured in 1976 dollars). Pechman (1985) has estimated effective rates for federal, state, and local taxes for selected years between 1966–85, arranged both by income class and population decile. Assuming that sales and excise taxes impose burdens proportional to consumption, the results for federal, state, and local sales and excise taxes together for 1980, shown in Table 9.6, confirm the expected regressive pattern. However, for the upper middle half of the population in the fourth through eighth deciles, the burden is nearly proportional, falling between 4.5 to 5.5 percent of income.

There are at least three ways in which this conventional wisdom about sales tax incidence can be reconsidered. First, as previously noted, the general sales taxes used by states are really not very general, typically exempting about half of private

TABLE 9.5

Personal Consumption Expenditures as a Percentage of Income, 1984

Income Class[a]	Total Personal Consumption (%)	Food at Home (%)	Utilities and Fuel (%)	Housing (%)	Medical Care (%)
5–9.999[b]	159.4	23.4	17.1	29.8	10.6
10–14.999	118.3	15.0	11.0	21.0	6.6
15–19.999	102.0	12.1	8.9	17.8	5.4
20–29.999	91.3	10.0	7.1	15.3	3.6
30–39.999	80.7	8.3	5.6	12.9	2.7
40 and over	69.9	5.5	4.1	11.1	2.2
All consumers	90.1	9.5	6.8	15.2	3.7

Source: U.S. Department of Labor (1984).

[a]In thousands of dollars.

[b]Data for consumer units with income less than $5000 are not meaningful, as they often reflect a temporary situation.

TABLE 9.6

Pechman's Estimates of Sales and Excise Tax Incidence, 1980 (Effective Rates: Tax Burden as Percentage of Family Income)

Family Income[a]	Effective Rate (%)	Population Decile[b]	Effective Rate (%)
0–5	17.9	First	8.4
5–10	7.7	Second	7.0
10–15	6.2	Third	5.9
15–20	5.6	Fourth	5.5
20–25	5.2	Fifth	5.1
25–30	4.9	Sixth	4.9
30–50	4.5	Seventh	4.6
50–100	3.3	Eighth	4.5
100–500	1.6	Ninth	3.9
500–1000	0.7	Tenth	2.1
1000 and over	0.6		
All classes	4.0	All Deciles	4.0

Source: Pechman (1985, Tables 4.9 and 4.10).

[a]Thousand of dollars.
[b]Percentages of the population grouped by income from lowest to highest. The income classes and population deciles do *not* correspond.

consumption. As a result, consumers may be induced to shift consumption from taxed to untaxed goods as depicted in Figure 9.2. As a result of those consumption shifts, the sales tax may impose burdens on suppliers of factors of production; in essence, there may be a decrease in demand for factors used to produce taxable goods and services and a corresponding increase in demand for factors used to produce nontaxable commodities. Although these burdens could theoretically alter the overall distribution of sales tax burdens by income, they are typically ignored on the grounds that there is no reason to expect that taxable goods are produced by any higher- or lower-income individuals than are nontaxable goods.

Second, even if consumers do not shift consumption between taxed and untaxed commodities, it is generally not correct to assume that the effective tax rate on untaxed commodities is zero. In many cases, purchasers of exempt commodities bear an indirect sales tax burden because the producers of exempt commodities may have paid sales taxes on purchases of materials, supplies, or services used in their business. As previously noted, no state exempts all purchases of intermediate goods from sales tax. For example, although twenty-eight states exempt the retail sale of food from sales tax, many of those states levy sales tax on purchases of display equipment by food retailers, on the purchase of trucks and gasoline used to transport food, or sometimes on the equipment and supplies used in agriculture. These sales tax burdens are part of the cost of producing food commodities and are imbedded in the retail price of those food commodities. Similarly, all states (except Hawaii) exempt medical care services from the retail sales tax, but many do levy sales tax on the purchase of medical equipment and supplies by medical care providers. It is more correct to state therefore that purchasers of exempt commodities bear a sales tax burden, but at a rate less than the nominal general sales tax on taxed commodities.

These indirect sales tax burdens that arise from taxation of intermediate goods purchases also have an important implication for interstate comparison of sales tax burdens. Among states with the same nominal rate and identical sets of exempt consumer goods, the effective rate is expected to be greater in those states that levy the tax on a broader set of intermediate goods purchases. Similarly, it is entirely possible that the effective rate could be lower in a state with a 5-percent nominal rate and little taxation of intermediate goods (such as West Virginia) than in another state with a 4-percent rate but broad taxation of intermediate goods.

Finally, annual income may not be the best measure of a taxpayer's ability to pay taxes and may lead to inaccurate perceptions about tax incidence. Alternatively, some measure of lifetime or permanent income may give a more accurate, or at least different, picture of tax incidence. Over an individual's lifetime, all income is either consumed or transferred to subsequent generations for consumption. Given the assumption that sales tax burdens are proportional to total consumption and from the view that all income is eventually consumed, sales taxes can be thought of as proportional taxes. An intermediate approach between these two views is to measure sales tax incidence by consumption of taxed commodities only relative to some estimate of permanent or lifetime income. Such an analysis by Daniel Davies (1969) shows that sales taxes are indeed less regressive with respect to lifetime income than annual income and confirms that exemption of food for home consumption and utility services from the sales tax base makes the sales tax burden even less regressive.

/ Sales tax credits compared to exemptions

The major alternative to exemptions to reduce the expected regressivity of sales tax burdens is a tax credit, usually taken against the state income tax, to offset sales tax liability on some commodities for at least some taxpayers. In practice these credits are most often used as an alternative to an exemption for sales of food. According to ACIR, eight states used income tax credits to offset sales tax liability in 1985, seven of which do not provide a food exemption (the exception is Vermont, which exempts food and provides a credit). In many cases, these credits apply only to lower-income taxpayers or to senior citizens. If the tax credits apply only to a subset of taxpayers, they can achieve the desired increase in progressivity at lower revenue cost than through general exemptions applying to all taxpayers.

Although both sales tax exemptions and income tax credits can serve to alter the distribution of tax burden, they are not expected to influence consumer behavior in the same way. An exemption eliminates the tax on all purchases of an exempt commodity and thus effectively reduces the price of that commodity relative to those that are taxed. Therefore, besides reducing the regressivity of the sales tax, exemptions also create an incentive for consumers to increase purchases of exempt commodities. When income tax credits are used to offset sales tax liability on some commodities, however, the credit is usually set as a flat amount per person or per household, sometimes declining as income increases. The amount of the credit for any individual is usually not related to the actual amount spent on the taxed item. Therefore, the credit does not reduce the price of the taxed commodity but changes the overall tax burden and distribution. The effect of a credit program is to make the state's overall tax structure more progressive (or less regressive).

Contrary to what some analysts have suggested, it therefore is not necessarily poor policy for a state to use both sales tax exemptions and an income tax credit. If a state has two policy objectives, both to make food less expensive and to increase the overall progressivity of the state's tax structure, both tools may be used simultaneously (although the reason why a state would want to decrease food prices may be problematical). In other words, tax credits may be used to offset any regressive elements of the tax structure, not just those that arise from the sales tax. Note that income tax credits are typically restricted to state residents, whereas sales tax exemptions apply to all purchasers regardless of residence. Of course, those exemptions may induce nonresidents to make additional purchases in the state or may induce residents not to make purchases in other states.

Sales tax exemptions and income tax credits also may differ in their administration and compliance costs. Exemptions increase collection costs for sellers, particularly those who sell both taxable and exempt commodities, and audit costs for the state. On the other hand, tax credits require that taxpayers be informed about the credit and take the effort to file the required forms. State experience with these credits usually suggests that these compliance costs prevent some taxpayers, often those with lowest incomes or those who do not have a state income tax liability, from receiving the intended benefit.

/ Summary

State–local governments use general sales taxes levied on retail sales, companion use taxes to tax resident purchases made in other jurisdictions, and excise taxes on specific goods or services. Sales or consumption taxes remain the largest single source of revenue to state governments. Although about 83 percent of total general sales tax revenue went to state governments in 1984, local government general sales taxes were also used by about 6500 local jurisdictions spread among thirty states.

General sales taxes are intended to be taxes on the total final personal consumption of the residents of jurisdictions levying the tax. In practice, state general sales taxes fall short of this principle because (a) a substantial amount of personal consumption is statutorily exempt from taxation, (b) the taxes end up applying to sales of some intermediate goods in addition to consumer goods, and (c) states face inherent administrative difficulties in collecting use taxes.

The net effect of exemptions is that state general sales taxes apply to perhaps only 50 to 60 percent of personal consumption in aggregate, with obvious substantial variation among the states.

Because sales and excise taxes alter the relative prices of some goods, creating incentives for consumers and producers (to the extent sales of intermediate goods are taxed) to change their behavior, the tax can result in a loss of economic efficiency. The general theoretical rule for optimal commodity taxation is disceptively simple: The optimal set of sales taxes should cause an equal proportionate decrease in the compensated quantity demanded of all commodities.

Individuals may also be able to avoid or reduce sales taxes by making purchases in jurisdictions different from the one in which they reside. Individuals may purchase goods in one state or locality for delivery to a different location, or individuals may make purchases and take possession in a lower-tax jurisdiction and thus pay the lower sales tax rate. A number of studies are consistent in finding that a disadvantageous sales tax rate differential leads to a statistically significant but relatively small reduction in sales in the higher-tax jurisdictions.

The typical incidence assumption about a general sales tax is that it is regressive. Exemptions of goods and services that are relatively more important in the budgets of lower-income individuals are commonly used to alter this distributional pattern. The major alternative to exemptions to reduce the expected regressivity of sales tax burdens is a tax credit. Exemptions effectively reduce the price of that commodity relative to those that are taxed and create an incentive for consumers to increase purchases of exempt commodities. Credits do not reduce prices but make the state's overall tax structure more progressive (or less regressive).

Discussion Questions

1. Suppose that a state government levies an *ad valorem* sales tax on the purchase of all goods at retail but not on the purchases of services. The tax is levied only on final sales of goods and not on sales of any intermediate goods. The state has a companion use tax but makes little effort to collect that tax for consumer purchases except for automobiles. Discuss the various ways (there are at least four) an individual consumer could change behavior to avoid or reduce liability for the state sales tax. What economic costs could arise from each type of action?

2. ''It would be unfair to tax the sale of medical or legal services because effectively that would be taxing peoples' misfortune.'' Discuss this viewpoint. Would the same principle apply to the sale of car repairs? What about the purchase of a fire extinguisher or a child's car seat?

3. ''Sales taxes are fairer than income taxes because sales taxes cannot be avoided by the rich.'' Evaluate this idea. Describe the evidence about the distribution of sales tax burdens among different income taxpayers. Would it be possible to design a sales tax that is more progressive than an income tax?

4. The sales tax treatment of mail-order purchases is somewhat controversial, as discussed in the chapter. Think about the products you have purchased by mail order in the recent past and roughly how much you spent. Does your state have a use tax? Did you pay the use tax on taxable items? Why or why not? How much did the opportunity to avoid sales tax influence your decision to purchase by mail order? Do you think mail-order companies should be required to collect

state sales or use taxes on purchases? If not, then what other methods might states use to collect these taxes?

Selected Reading

Due, John F. and John L. Mikesell. *Sales Taxation, State and Local Structure and Administration*. Baltimore: Johns Hopkins University Press, 1983.

10 / Income Taxes

A federal fiscal system faces two kinds of tax coordination problems. The first arises when two or more different levels of government use the same tax base, as when the federal government and a state government tax the same income; . . . the second appears when . . . mobile individuals carry out economic activities in many different taxing jurisdictions at the same level of government. . . .[1]

George F. Break

/ Reliance on Income Taxes

Individual income taxes have become an increasingly important source of revenue for state–local governments in the last twenty-five years. In 1986 income taxes provided more than 17 percent of state government revenue on average, double the share provided by that tax in 1962, as shown in Table 10.1. Similarly, county governments in aggregate received 1 percent of their revenue from income taxes in 1986 compared to only .1 percent in 1962, whereas the income tax share of revenue for municipalities rose from 2.0 to 4.5 percent over that period. In 1986 state individual income taxes generated $67.5 billion, with local income taxes providing an additional $6.9 billion. Together these represent a payment of about $309 per person, or 2.2 percent of personal income.

Currently, forty state governments collect broad-based individual income taxes, and three states (Connecticut, New Hampshire, and Tennessee) collect income tax on a narrow base of capital income only (Table 10.2). Individual income taxes are also used by about 3500 local governments spread over eleven states and the District of Columbia, although 2700 of these local governments are in the state of Pennsylvania alone.[2]

In 1962 only thirty-two states used broad-based income taxes but a number of new adoptions occurred in the late 1960s and early 1970s; Michigan and Nebraska

---

[1] *Intergovernmental Fiscal Relations in the United States.* Washington, D.C.: The Brookings Institution, 1967, 28.

[2] Local income taxes are also authorized but not currently used in two other states, Arkansas and Georgia.

TABLE 10.1

Individual Income Taxes as a Percentage of General Revenue, by Level of Government, Various Years

Year	States	All	Counties	Municipalities	Townships	School Districts	Special Districts
				Local Governments			
1962	8.8	0.8	0.1	2.0	0.2	0.3	—
1967	9.4	1.6	0.1	4.2	0.4	0.3	—
1972	13.2	2.1	0.8	5.4	0.7	0.3	—
1977	15.1	2.1	0.9	5.1	1.1	0.3	—
1982	16.6	1.8	1.0	4.3	1.4	0.3	—
1986	17.1	1.8	1.0	4.5	1.3	0.3	—

Sources: U.S. Department of Commerce (1962, 1967, 1972, 1977, 1982; Census of Governments, *Compendium of Government Finances*, table entitled "General Revenue by Source, by Type of Government"). For 1986 data, U.S. Department of Commerce, *Governmental Finances, 1986* (1988).

TABLE 10.2

Income Tax Characteristics, by State, 1987

State	Base Conformance with Federal[a]	Taxable Income Rates (%)	Taxable Income Brackets Low	Taxable Income Brackets High	Local Tax Used	Local Tax Type of Government[b]
New England						
Connecticut		Limited Income Tax				
Maine	AGI	1.0–10.0	2000–25,000			
Massachusetts	AGI	5.0	Flat			
New Hampshire		Limited State Income Tax				
Rhode Island	TAX	23.46				
Vermont	TAX	25.8				
Mideast						
Delaware	AGI	1.0–7.7[c]	1000–40,000		X	CI
Maryland	AGI	2.0–5.0	1000–3000		X	C
New Jersey	None	2.0–3.5	20,000–50,000			
New York	AGI	2.0–8.5	1000–26,000		X	CI
Pennsylvania	None	2.1	Flat		X	M,S
Great Lakes						
Illinois	AGI	2.5	Flat			
Indiana	AGI	3.4	Flat		X	C
Michigan	AGI	4.6	Flat		X	CI
Ohio	AGI	.751–6.9	5000–100,000		X	CI,S
Wisconsin	AGI	4.9–6.93	7500–30,000			
Plains						
Iowa	AGI	0.4–9.98	1023–76,725		X	S
Kansas	AGI	2.0–9.0	2000–25,000			

continued

TABLE 10.2

Continued

State	Base Conformance with Federal[a]	Taxable Income Rates (%)	Taxable Income Brackets		Local Tax	
			Low	High	Used	Type of Government[b]
Minnesota	AGI	5.0–8.0[c]	13,000			
Missouri	AGI	1.5–6.0	1000–9000		X	CI
Nebraska	AGI	2.0–5.9	1800–27,000			
N. Dakota	TI	6.7–12.0	3000–50,000			
		or 14% of Tax				
S. Dakota		No State Income Tax				
Southeast						
Alabama	None	2.0–5.0	500–3000		X	CI
Arkansas	None	1.0–7.0	2999–25,000		Allowed	M
Florida		No State Income Tax				
Georgia	AGI	1.0–6.0	750–7000		Allowed	C,M
Kentucky	AGI	2.0–6.0	3000–8000		X	C,CI
Louisiana	AGI	2.0–6.0	10,000–50,000			
Mississippi	None	3.0–5.0	5000–10,000			
N. Carolina	None	3.0–7.0	2000–10,000			
S. Carolina	TI	3.0–7.0	4000–10,000			
Tennessee		Limited State Income Tax				
Virginia	AGI	2.0–5.75	3000–14,000			
W. Virginia	AGI	3.0–6.5	10,000–60,000			
Southwest						
Arizona	AGI	2.0–8.0	1155–6930			
New Mexico	TI	1.8–8.5	5200–41,600			
Oklahoma	TI	.751–6.9	1000–7500			
Texas		No State Income Tax				
Rocky Mountain						
Colorado	TI	5.0				
Idaho	TI	2.0–8.2	1000–20,000			
Montana	AGI	2.0–11.0	1300–6400			
Utah	TI	2.75–7.75	750–3750			
Wyoming		No State Income Tax				
Far West						
Alaska		No State Income Tax				
California	AGI	1.0–9.3	1650–3950			
Hawaii	TI	2.25–10.0	1000–20,000			
Nevada		No State Income Tax				
Oregon	TI	5.0–9.0	2000–5000			
Washington		No State Income Tax				

Source: ACIR (1986c, 1987c).

[a]The state income tax base may be determined starting from either federal adjusted gross income (AGI) or federal taxable income (TI). In a few cases, the state tax is a percentage of the federal tax (TAX), while in the remainder there is no direct relationship between the state and federal taxes (None).

[b]C = counties, CI = cities, M = all municipalities, and S = school districts.

[c]Effective in 1988.

in 1967; Illinois and Maine in 1969; Ohio, Pennsylvania, and Rhode Island in 1971. The most recent adoption of a state income tax was by New Jersey in 1976, whereas Alaska repealed its state income tax in 1980.

/ Income Tax Structure

/ Tax base

Although states consider a number of different factors in selecting an appropriate income tax base, the two principal issues are the degree of coordination between the federal and state income tax definitions and the treatment of income that crosses jurisdiction boundaries. In the first case, states can parallel the federal government to varying degrees in determining what income base is to be taxed or they can adopt an entirely different definition of taxable income. In the second, states must determine how to treat both income earned in other states by residents and income earned in this state by nonresidents (including the treatment of taxes paid to other states).

/ Federal–State Tax Base Coordination. Similar state and federal definitions of the individual income tax base provide advantages both to taxpayers, by reducing record keeping and making it easier to compute the tax, and to state tax administrators, by making it easier to check for income tax compliance. But if states substantially adopt the same income tax rules as the federal government, changes in those rules and definitions by the federal government may generate automatic changes in the states' taxes, unless the state governments explicitly act to offset the federal action.

State income taxes can be grouped into four general categories of tax base conformance with the federal individual income tax, as shown in Table 10.2. In four states (Colorado, Rhode Island, Vermont, and as an option in North Dakota), a taxpayer's state income tax liability is a percentage of the federal income tax, with only minor adjustments for any itemized deduction of the state income tax (included in the base), for interest earned on federal government securities (excluded from tax) or interest from other states' securities (included in the base). In essence these states adopt the income exclusions, deductions, exemptions, credits, and overall tax rate progressivity used by the federal government. This is illustrated by the Group 1 category in Table 10.3. Of course, there is no reason why additional state income tax credits cannot be applied as well. Discretionary changes in state income tax revenue are accomplished by adjusting the state percentage rate that is applied to federal liability.

The next closest conformance to the federal tax occurs if the state tax base equals federal taxable income, again with some minor adjustments. The eight states taking this approach effectively accept federal income exclusions, personal exemptions, and deductions but apply their own tax-rate structure and tax credits, as illustrated by Group 2 in Table 10.3. In this case, state income taxes are sensitive to changes in the definition of the federal tax base but not to changes in federal tax

TABLE 10.3

Alternative State Income Tax Base Conformance with the Federal Income Tax

$$\text{Federal Base} = I - X - N \times E - D$$

where
I = income
X = income excluded from tax
N = number of personal exemptions
E = value per exemption
D = deductions, standard or itemized

Federal Tax = Federal Base (Federal Rate Structure) − Federal Credits

Group 1: *State Tax Is a Percentage of Federal Tax*

State Tax = State Rate (Federal Tax)

Group 2: *State Tax Base Equals Federal Taxable Income*

State Tax = Federal Base (State Rate Structure) − State Credits
State Tax = $(I - X - N \times E - D)$(State Rate Structure) − State Credits

Group 3: *State Tax Base Equals Federal Adjusted Gross Income*

State Tax = $(I - X - \text{State Exemptions and Deductions})$ (State Rate Structure) − State Credits

Group 4: *State Tax Base Is Unrelated to the Federal Tax*

State Tax = (State Defined Base)(State Rate Structure) − State Credits

rates. Moreover, taxpayers and tax officials enjoy essentially the same compliance and administrative advantages with this system as when the state tax is a percentage of federal tax.

The most common approach in determining the state income tax base, used by twenty-six states, is to start with federal adjusted gross income, that is gross income less exclusions, and then apply state-defined personal exemptions and deductions. The state tax is then computed from this base using a state rate structure and any state income tax credits. This approach is particularly common in the Midwest because it is used by ten of the eleven Great Lakes and Plains states with income taxes. States using this method may then allow taxpayers the same number of exemptions as the federal tax but apply a different value to the exemptions or follow both different exemption number and value rules. These states may also allow deductions, either choosing which of the various federal deductions they wish to allow or adopting specific state deduction definitions or both (see Group 3 in Table 10.3). There will still be substantial compliance and administrative advantages if states taking this approach follow federal rules determining the *number* of exemptions and the federal definitions for deductions the states wish to have. Computation of the state tax then requires similar record keeping and follows the same pattern as the federal, with different values for the exemption and tax-rate parameters.

Six states make no specific attempt to relate the state income tax to the federal tax, opting instead for specific state definitions and rules regarding income exclusions, personal exemptions, deductions, credits, and rate structure. Four of the six states using this approach are in the Southeast (Alabama, Arkansas, Mississippi, and North Carolina). This use of an essentially dual income tax system potentially complicates matters for both taxpayers and tax administrators, although it leaves state government fully insulated from any direct effects of changes to the federal income tax (see Group 4 in Table 10.3).

/ *Deductions for State or Federal Income Taxes.* Besides some commonality in the definition of income for tax purposes, state and federal income taxes are also related by deductions for income taxes paid to the other type of government. In computing itemized deductions for the federal individual income tax, taxpayers are allowed to include deductions for state and local government income taxes.[3] If the total value of all itemized deductions for a taxpayer exceeds the standard deduction for that filing class ($5000 for married taxpayers filing jointly and $3000 for single taxpayers in 1988), the itemized deductions are claimed. In that case, the federal individual income tax base is income net of state and local taxes (and other itemized deductions) so that part of the taxpayer's state and local government income taxes are offset by a lower federal income tax liability. In 1986 about 39 percent of federal income taxpayers itemized deductions, although that percentage is expected to fall substantially as the larger standard deductions and curtailed allowed itemized deductions, which are part of the 1986 federal income tax reform, take effect.

In addition to these federal deductions for state and local taxes, twelve states allow a deduction for federal individual income taxes in computing the state tax. This **reciprocal deductibility** means not only that the federal tax base is income net of state and local income taxes but also that the state income tax base is income net of federal tax. This substantial narrowing of the state tax base may therefore necessitate higher tax rates.

Typically, the rationale for providing income tax deductions for income taxes levied by another level of government is to prevent tax rates from becoming too high through their cumulative effect. Theoretically at least, it is possible for the sum of federal, state, and local income tax rates to approach or even exceed 100 percent if those various governments set rates independently and without regard for the others. But such confiscatory rates would be counterproductive for all those taxing governments. Deductibility softens this effect.[4]

It is also sometimes suggested that income net of other governments' taxes is theoretically a better measure of "ability-to-pay," on the assumption that those other governments' taxes are not direct charges for service, and thus equivalent to expenditures on any consumer good. But this argument seems tenuous, at best, because individuals select their state and local government tax/service package

---

[3]Other allowed itemized deductions include home-mortgage interest, property taxes, and some charitable contributions, work-related costs, and medical expenses.

[4]Prior to 1981, the top federal marginal income tax rate was 70 percent. This, combined with a 10 to 15 percent state rate and any additional local income tax, could have approached this situation. With the current top nominal federal tax rate at 28 percent, this concern seems less important.

through voting or their choice of residential location. The economic effects of income tax deductibility are considered in the next section of this chapter.

/ *Coordination Among Different States.*

The final intergovernmental tax-base issue, which applies to local as well as state taxes, concerns the treatment of income that crosses jurisdiction boundaries, including income earned by the residents of a taxing jurisdiction for services performed in another jurisdiction (residents' income earned in other states) and income earned in a given taxing jurisdiction by residents of another jurisdiction (nonresidents' income earned in the state). Four possibilities exist: Income could be taxed only in the jurisdiction where it is earned, income could be taxed only by the jurisdiction where the earner resides, income could be taxed in both places, or in neither.

In practice, most states tax all the income of residents, regardless of where it is earned, and all income earned in that state by nonresidents. Residents are allowed a credit, however, for taxes paid to other states. If this practice were followed by all states, the effect is basically to tax income where it is earned, with two exceptions. Income earned in a state that does not have an income tax would be taxed in the earner's state of residence. Second, if the income tax rate is greater in an individual's state of residence than in the state where the income is earned, the state of residence would collect tax on that income proportional to the difference in rates. These rules typically apply among states that enter into agreements with each other to ensure consistent treatment of each others' residents. In the absence of these agreements, individuals may be subject to tax on such income by more than one state or by neither state.

The practice regarding local government income taxes is somewhat more confusing, if only because there is more variability as to which rules are applied. First, many local "income" taxes exclude property income and apply only to so-called earned income. These are often referred to as wage taxes. James Rodgers (1981) reports that local income taxes are generally residence-based in Maryland (where the tax applies only to residents), Michigan, and Pennsylvania, (except Philadelphia where taxpayers receive a credit for tax paid to the jurisdiction of residence against any tax due the jurisdiction where the income is earned). In contrast, the tax of the jurisdiction where the income is earned has preference in Alabama, California, Kentucky (where the base is income earned in the jurisdiction only), Ohio, and Philadelphia (where taxpayers receive a credit for tax paid to the jurisdiction where the income is earned against any tax levied by the jurisdiction of residence).

The practice in Pennsylvania is particularly confusing because different rules apply to Philadelphia as opposed to other jurisdictions in the state. Philadelphia has first claim to tax the income earned by nonresidents in the city. And because the tax rate in Philadelphia is greater than that allowed in the surrounding jurisdictions, these jurisdictions can effectively collect no tax on income earned by their residents in Philadelphia. Therefore, as Rodgers notes, many of those surrounding jurisdictions have not adopted income taxes. In other parts of the state, the jurisdiction of residence has first claim to residents' income earned in other jurisdictions. Consequently, Rodgers reports that after Pittsburgh adopted a local income tax, most

/ APPLICATION 10.1
Federal Collection of State Taxes

The Federal–State Tax Collection Act of 1972 authorized the U.S. Department of the Treasury to enter into agreements with states to administer and collect state income taxes along with the federal tax at no cost to the state governments. To be eligible, the state tax on residents would have to take one of two possible forms:

1. The state tax applying to residents has a base that equals federal taxable income (federal AGI less federal exemptions and deductions) minus interest on federal securities plus federal deductions for state and local income taxes and interest on bonds issued by other states or localities (thus states would not tax the interest income from federal bonds but would tax the interest from other states' bonds). A state rate structure would be applied to this base, with the possibility of a credit for income taxes paid to other states.
2. The state tax on residents equals a percentage of federal tax liability, after adjustments to remove any interest income from federal government bonds. States may also make other adjustments or use credits as noted above.

The state tax on nonresidents would have to be as follows: States can add a supplement to the federal tax of any nonresident who earns at least 25 percent of labor income in that taxing state, with nonresidents to be taxed no more heavily than residents. This allows states to tax nonresident income earned in that state based on the federal definition of taxable income and federal rates, but only if 25 percent of the taxpayer's labor income arises in that state.

    To date, no state has accepted this offer and entered into a tax collection agreement with the federal government. Such agreements would impose substantial conformance between state and federal income taxes and would

of the surrounding jurisdictions followed immediately in order to retain that income tax base for themselves.

George Break (1980) has suggested that the sensible treatment of nonresident income by local government income taxes depends on the nature of the service to be financed with the revenue. If the benefits of a service primarily accrue to residents of a jurisdiction, then a residence base rule seems most appropriate. Break argues that this situation applies if the income tax is used to finance local schools (given that state government revenue is also provided to schools to account for the external or social benefits of education). On the other hand, if the tax is to finance general city or county services, then Break argues that at least part of the tax should be origin-based to offset the service benefits received by nonresidents who work in the jurisdiction (such as local police protection, traffic control, or local parks). In

/ **APPLICATION 10.1** Continued
Federal Collection of State Taxes

subject the states to automatic revenue changes from nearly any and all revisions to the federal tax code. With the first possible structure above, states would effectively adopt the federal exclusions, exemptions, and deductions; whereas with the second possibility, states effectively adopt the entire federal structure. Although states could offset those revenue effects through rate changes, they are apparently unwilling to give up their autonomy in designing income tax structures. The rule for taxing nonresidents would restrict states' abilities to tax nonresidents compared to correct practice. In addition, states would give up their independent tax-auditing and -collection operations. The advantages from federal collection of state income taxes would be easier tax compliance for taxpayers, lower administrative costs for states, and perhaps lower administrative costs overall, if there are economies of scale in tax collection.

A less ambitious form of federal collection of state taxes has recently been proposed by tax lawyer George Guttman (1986). Guttman suggests that substantial savings of compliance and administrative costs are possible simply by filing federal–state forms together with the IRS without requiring states to automatically adopt the federal tax structure. Under Guttman's "one-stop filing," a state tax schedule would be attached to the federal return, with the state allowed to use their own exemptions, deductions, and credits. He argues that simply ending state *processing* of returns would save about half of state tax administration costs. Obviously, however, such a system would work best for those state taxes that do currently conform most closely to the federal tax, although states would not be required to automatically adopt all future federal tax changes. Guttman notes that a similar system is already used in Indiana, Maryland, and New York, where local income taxes can be collected by the state along with the state tax, and in Canada, where nine of the ten provincial income taxes are collected along with the national government tax.

the absence of user charges for such services, the local income tax may be the most effective way of reaching those nonresident commuters.

/ Tax rates

Not only do state income taxes differ widely in the definition of the tax base and somewhat in the treatment of nonresident income, but they also involve a wide variety of rate structures, as shown in Table 10.2. Only five of the forty states with broad-based taxes (Illinois, Indiana, Massachusetts, Michigan, and Pennsylvania) used flat rates in 1987. In the other states, the rate structure is progressive, although again to widely differing degrees. For example, in Utah the tax rates vary from 2.75 to 7.75 percent, but the highest rate applies to all taxable income above $3750;

consequently, this is nearly a flat rate tax for many, if not most, taxpayers. In contrast, 1987 tax rates in Hawaii varied from 2.5 to 11.0 percent, with the highest rate applying to taxable income above $20,000, so that the progression in the rate structure affected a substantial number of taxpayers in Hawaii. It is worth repeating that comparison of states based on tax rates is often very misleading because of differences in tax bases. For income taxes, this includes differences in the starting point for computing the base and in the allowed exemptions, deductions, and credits.

/ Economic Analysis

/ Incentive effects of state and federal income taxes combined

A crucial element of any income tax is that it creates incentives for individuals to change their behavior. Individuals may react to income taxes by changing the amount that they work (and thus the amount of income earned), by changing the amount of income they save, or by changing how they spend their income in response to various tax deductions. The income tax characteristic that determines the magnitude of these incentives is the **marginal tax rate,** that is, the *tax rate that applies to the last dollar earned.* It is this marginal tax rate that determines how much the tax can be reduced by working one less hour or by making a charitable contribution and taking that amount as a deduction. For instance, if a taxpayer faces a marginal tax rate of 50 percent, then an extra hour's work at $10 per hour would increase after-tax or take-home pay by only $5, while an extra $20 charitable contribution would reduce taxes by $10.

The marginal tax rate facing any taxpayer depends on the combined effect of all income taxes—federal, state, and local—paid by that taxpayer. Therefore, the relevant item is the aggregate marginal tax rate from all income taxes that applies to a given income or deductible expenditure amount. But the marginal tax rate that results from a set of income taxes depends not only on the separate tax rates but also on any deductibility of one tax against the other, as noted previously.

The effect of intergovernmental income tax deductibility on marginal tax rates is demonstrated in Table 10.4. The illustration assumes that a taxpayer faces a federal marginal tax rate of 28 percent and a state tax with a marginal tax rate of either 5 or 10 percent. With no deductibility of one tax against the other, the combined marginal tax rate is simply the sum of the two individual rates, either 33 percent or 38 percent depending on the state tax. Deductibility of the state tax against the federal tax reduces the combined marginal tax rate. If f represents the federal rate and s the state rate, the combined rate is $f + s - sf$ because the increase in state tax of s per dollar of income becomes a federal deduction equal to s, which reduces federal tax by sf. In the numerical example, the combined marginal rate is 32 percent if the state rate is 5 percent (compared to 33 percent with no deductibility) and 35 percent if the state rate is 10 percent (compared to 38 percent without deductibility). Thus, federal deductibility of the state tax not only reduces marginal tax rates but also narrows the difference in marginal rates between low-rate and high-rate state taxes.

TABLE 10.4

Combined Marginal Tax Rates from Federal and State Income Taxation

Tax Structure Characteristic	General Case	Example One	Example Two
Federal marginal tax rate	f	.28	.28
State marginal tax rate	s	.05	.10
Combined marginal tax rate if no deductibility	$f + s$	.33	.38
Combined marginal tax rate if state tax deducted against federal only	$f + s(1 - f)$	.32	.35
Combined marginal tax rate with reciprocal deductibility	$\dfrac{[f + s(1 - 2f)]}{1 - fs}$	.31	.33

Reciprocal deductibility—that is, simultaneous federal deductibility of the state tax and state deductibility of the federal tax—has much the same effect on marginal rates, although to a greater magnitude. In this case, the combined rate of $f + s$ is reduced by sf due to the federal deduction for the state tax and by fs due to the state deduction for the federal tax. However, it is then *increased* by f^2s due to a smaller state tax deduction against the federal and by s^2f due to a smaller federal deduction against the state tax, and so on. In Table 10.4, the combined marginal rates are 31 percent when the state rate is 5 percent and 33 percent when the state rate is 10 percent. Again, the marginal tax rate is lowered and the difference between the states is narrowed by reciprocal deductibility, both compared to no deductibility and federal deductibility of the state tax alone.

This table is a bit misleading because although showing the effect of deductibility on a given rate structure, it ignores changes in the rates that may be required if deductibility is allowed. Because state deductibility of the federal tax reduces the state tax base, higher average state tax rates are required to generate the same revenue as would be collected without that deductibility. Thus, those states that now allow deductibility of the federal tax may have adopted higher income tax rates than otherwise, but given those rates, the difference in rates between that state and others is less than nominally appears. In terms of this example, the choice for a state may be between a 5-percent rate with no deduction for the federal tax or the 10-percent rate with the deduction. The difference in combined marginal rates is 33 percent compared to 35 percent, less than the difference in the state rates alone.

An example of the effect of a charitable contribution on taxes based on Table 10.4 shows the importance and usefulness of these combined marginal tax rates. Suppose an individual who itemizes deductions for federal taxes and whose state income tax has a 10-percent rate and also allows a deduction for a charitable contribution makes a new $100 contribution to an eligible charity. The after-tax "price" or "cost" of the contribution to the taxpayer per dollar is $1 -$ marginal tax rate. If there is no reciprocal deductibility (only the state tax is deductible against the federal and not the converse), then the contribution reduces total taxes by $35 and "costs" the taxpayer $65 [$100 · (1 − f − s + fs)]. With reciprocal deductibility, the contribution costs the taxpayer $67 (the marginal rate is 33 percent). In both cases, the contribution costs more than the $62, which appears to be the cost from analyzing the state and federal taxes separately and ignoring intergovernmental tax deductibility.

/ State tax amounts and progressivity

Intergovernmental income tax deductibility also reduces the progressivity of the tax structure, with implications both for the choice of a tax structure within a subnational government and for intergovernmental tax competition. The general effect of income tax deductibility on tax liabilities is shown in Table 10.5. For the example, the federal tax has a 28-percent tax rate, a $2000 personal exemption, and no deductions except the state tax; the state tax has a $1000 personal exemption, no deductions except the federal tax (for the reciprocal deductibility case) and either a 5- or 10-percent rate. Taxes are computed for a family with three exemptions and income equal to $30,000.

As expected, total tax liability and thus the effective tax rate is decreased by deductibility with either state tax rate. But more importantly, the *difference* in tax

Table 10.5

The Effects of Income Tax Deductibility on Tax Liability

Assumptions: Family with $30,000 income and three exemptions
Federal personal exemption is $2000
State personal exemption is $1000

Tax Structure	Federal Tax ($)	State Tax($)	Total Tax($)	Effective Rate
Case A: *Federal tax rate = .28; state tax rate = .05*				
No deductibility	6720	1350	8070	.269
State tax deducted				
from federal	6342	1350	7692	.256
Reciprocal deductibility	6432	1028	7460	.249
Case B: *Federal tax rate = .28; state tax rate = .10*				
No deductibility	6720	2700	9420	.314
State tax deducted				
from federal	5964	2700	8664	.289
Reciprocal deductibility	6136	2086	8222	.274

Implications

Tax Structure	Total Tax in Case B Total Tax in Case A
No deductibility	1.167
State tax deducted	
from federal	1.126
Reciprocal deductibility	1.102

liability between the 5- and 10-percent tax rates is also reduced by deductibility. Taxes are 16.7 percent higher with the 10-percent rate rather than the 5-percent rate given no deductibility, but only 12.6 percent higher when the state tax is deducted against the federal tax and 10.2 percent higher with reciprocal deductibility. Put another way, although the state income tax is $1350 greater with the 10-percent than 5-percent rate, the deduction of that additional state tax against the federal reduces the federal tax by $378. As a result, the total tax liability is only greater by $972. With reciprocal deductibility, the difference in total tax liability between a 5- and 10-percent state tax rate is only $762. Thus, intergovernmental income tax deductibility mitigates the effect of a higher state–local income tax rate.

One implication of this effect is that states may choose more progressive income tax–rate structures due to federal deductibility of their tax than they would without those deductions. Higher-income taxpayers who could be affected by a more progressive state income tax structure are likely to itemize deductions for their federal tax and thus deduct the state tax. Therefore, part of those taxpayers' state income tax liability is offset by a lower federal liability; in essence, part of those taxpayers' state tax is paid by all taxpayers in the United States, perhaps in the form of higher federal rates necessitated by the lower federal tax collections. In a report prepared for the Minnesota Tax Study Commission, Joel Slemrod (1986, 130–31) argues that

> Because the proportion of itemizing-households increases with income, in general the more progressive is the state income tax, the greater will be the degree of tax exporting. In a sense, by loading the tax burden onto those high-income taxpayers who tend to be itemizers and also have high marginal federal income tax rates, the total net tax burden borne by Minnesotans declines.

A second implication of deductibility is that states may be able to collect more revenue (that is, have higher average tax rates) and thus spend more than without deductibility. Again from Table 10.5, if a state increases its tax rate from 5 to 10 percent, the state government's revenue from this $30,000 income family rises by $1350 (from $1350 to $2700), but the family's *total tax bill* (federal plus state) rises by only $972. In essence this family can "buy" another $1350 worth of state government services by paying only $972. Deductibility may therefore induce some voters to support higher state taxes and expenditures than otherwise. For taxpayers who itemize deductions, the incentive will be of greater importance the greater the federal marginal tax rate; so the incentive is expected to be more significant for higher-income taxpayers. Whether the change in the voters' positions will translate into a change in state behavior depends on the political system. In the median-voter framework, for instance, the issue is whether deductibility influences the median voter or changes the median voter's identity.

A third implication of the effect of deductibility is that interstate differences in taxes are less than is suggested by differences in income tax rates. Returning to the example in Table 10.5, if one state has a 5-percent tax rate and another a 10-percent rate, the difference in tax for a $30,000 family is $972 rather than $1350, if the state tax is deducted against the federal income tax. Deductibility therefore reduces the incentive for taxpayers who itemize federal deductions to move to lower-tax states or localities. Moreover, because the effect of deductibility is proportional to the federal income tax rate, this mitigating effect of deductibility on state taxes becomes stronger as the taxpayer's income increases.

The combined result of these implications is likely to be higher state–local expenditures and more progressive state–local tax structures in at least some states due to the federal deductibility of state income taxes. Again, this result is expected to be most prevalent in those states where a relatively large fraction of taxpayers itemize federal deductions and have higher incomes (thus facing the higher marginal federal tax rates). Prior to the federal income tax changes in 1987, 30 to 40 percent of federal taxpayers itemized deductions in a structure with federal marginal tax rates as high as 70 percent before 1981 and up to 50 percent in 1986. With such a federal tax structure, state income tax deductibility was particularly valuable. For a taxpayer with a 50-percent federal marginal tax rate, half of the individual's state income tax was offset by the deduction. Not surprisingly therefore, the effect of changes in the federal tax on the value of deductibility and the resulting possible

/ APPLICATION 10.2
Effect of Federal Tax Reform on State Income Tax Revenue

One obvious way to approach the issue of the effect of federal tax reform because of common tax definitions is to ask what the change in state individual income tax liabilities would be if states continue the use of the common definitions, effectively adopting those federal changes. This issue has been explored by the ACIR, whose preliminary estimates are shown in Table 10.6. These computations assume that states that base their state individual income tax on some component of federal income tax law will continue to do so and that the component will be as defined in the new 1986 federal tax act. Accordingly, these are estimates of the income tax–revenue changes states can expect if they adopt, either explicitly or implicitly, all of the federal tax changes.[5]

Although there are many federal changes that potentially might affect state taxes, five that seem particularly important are (a) increases in the personal exemption, standard deduction, and earned income credit (all of which act to *lower* federal and conforming state taxes); (b) full taxation of all capital gains; (c) restrictions on the use of tax shelters to offset income; (d) ending of the deduction for Individual Retirement Accounts (IRA) for many taxpayers; and (e) repeal of the deduction for two-earner families. The latter four elements increase the federal, and potentially state, tax bases. In addition the change in the federal tax rates is very important for those four states whose state tax is a percentage of the federal tax.

It is expected that taxpayers, if not state governments, will respond to the changes in federal tax law by altering their economic behavior. The ACIR

[5]Some states adopt the federal tax definitions of a specific year, rather than the current federal tax code, whatever that might be. If a state's tax is based on the federal code before 1987, most of the new changes will not affect that state until the state law adjusts to the new federal tax code.

responses of the states figured prominently in the debate about federal tax reform, as noted in Application 10.2 and 10.3.

/ APPLICATION 10.2 Continued
State Responses Income to Federal Income Tax Reform

estimates assume, for instance, that many taxpayers who previously made IRA contributions annually will no longer do so, that taxpayers will sell fewer assets and thus realize fewer capital gains annually because of the higher tax rate on those gains, and that taxpayers will slightly reduce the amount of their charitable contributions because the lower tax rates reduce the value of the deduction for contributions.

The ACIR estimates reported in Table 10.6 show that adoption of the federal tax changes would have increased state income taxes by at least 10 percent in seventeen states and the District of Columbia, increased state income taxes by less than 10 percent in about sixteen states (precise estimates were not available for four of these states), decreased state income taxes in ten states, and had no effect in the seven states with no type of income tax. The largest effect is an estimated 28-percent increase in Louisiana, a state that bases its income tax on federal adjusted gross income and uses most federal itemized deductions. Of the ten states where income tax revenue is estimated to decrease as a result of federal reform, the four states where the effect is large (Nebraska, North Dakota, Rhode Island, and Vermont) all based their state tax on federal tax liability before federal reform. Because the effect of the federal tax reform act of 1986 is an overall decrease in federal individual income tax liability (the rate reduction offsets the base broadening), these state income taxes also would have decreased by an amount depending on the expected magnitude of the federal decrease for residents of that state. The others in that group, Arkansas, New Jersey, North Carolina, and Pennsylvania, generally do not base their state tax on federal definitions, while New Hampshire and Tennessee have narrow income taxes on some property income only.

State Responses to Automatic Revenue Changes

In practice, states are expected to respond to the potential automatic change in state income tax revenue, either to eliminate the "windfall" revenue gains or prevent revenue decreases. In other words, the estimates in Table 10.6 are not expected to be actually realized. According to ACIR (1986c), ten states acted in 1987 to fully avoid any tax windfall that they would have received as a result of federal tax reform, and another seven states acted to avoid at least a portion of the potential windfall. In contrast, ACIR reports that twelve states retained the revenue windfall by deciding not to alter their personal income taxes. Of the four states whose income tax was a percentage of the federal tax, Nebraska converted to a conventional income tax, North Dakota increased its rate to increase revenue, while Rhode Island and Vermont effectively decreased state income taxes by not increasing their rates. Other states have not yet acted or had no windfall to react to.

TABLE 10.6

The Potential Effect of the Tax Reform Act of 1986 on State Personal Income Tax Liabilities[a]

Large (%)		Moderate to Small (%)		Negative (%)		No Effect
Louisiana	28	Michigan	6	Rhode Island	−11	Alaska
Colorado	22	Indiana	4	Vermont	−11	Florida
Montana	19	Wisconsin	4	Nebraska	−9	Nevada
Oregon	19	Arizona	[b]	N. Dakota	−10	S. Dakota
Utah	19	Mississippi	4	New Jersey	−1	Texas
Iowa	18	Idaho	[b]	New Hampshire	−1	Washington
Kansas	18	New Mexico	[b]	N. Carolina	−1	Wyoming
Missouri	18	S. Carolina	[b]	Pennsylvania	−1	
Oklahoma	18	Alabama	1	Tennessee	−1	
Hawaii	15	Massachusetts	1	Arkansas	Less than −1	
Minnesota	15					
Kentucky	14					
Maine	12					
Connecticut	11					
W. Virginia	11					
Delaware	10					
District of Columbia	10					
Georgia	10					
California	9					
New York	9					
Virginia	9					
Maryland	8					
Ohio	7					
Illinois	7					

Source: ACIR staff compilation based on Policy Economics Group (PEG), "A Description of the Linkage Between the Federal and State Personal Income Tax Codes," August 5, 1985 and data supplied by Policy Economics Group. This research was funded in part by the Ford Foundation. These estimates are based on microsimulation modeling of federal and state income tax codes. The data base is conceptually the same as that used by the U.S. Department of the Treasury and the Joint Committee on Taxation for analysis and revenue estimates of federal individual income tax changes. The number of records in the PEG data base, however, is substantially larger and, therefore, permits the calculation of meaningful results at the state level. The data file was extrapolated based on the Administration's February, 1985 economic forecasts of the national economy. All estimates are based on 1986 projected levels of income and are designed to represent the fully phased-in effects of all provisions in the tax reform plan. All features of current federal and state tax law for 1986, as of June 15, 1985, were simulated by the model. Adapted from ACIR (1986c).

[a]These are preliminary estimates of the percentage changes in 1986 total state individual income taxes due to conformity to federal tax law under assumption two. These numbers are preliminary and subject to change.

This analysis is based on the assumption that states coupled to federal law choose to update their references to the federal code and adopt the same conformity structure to provisions in the new tax law. (Since the District of Columbia and Utah couple to the personal exemption as of 7/75 and 1/74, respectively, it was assumed that these jurisdictions do not update their reference to this provision.) States that automatically conform to federal law are assumed to retain all features of current state law. In reality, however, state legislatures are likely to respond to either increases or decreases in state personal income taxes by adjusting their income tax structures. The percentage changes are based on estimates of 1986 state personal income tax liabilities that would be generated under prereform federal law and under the 1986 Tax Reform Act.

[b]Data are not yet available for these states.

As discussed, federal income tax reform can affect state income taxes in two ways. First, changes in federal definitions of income, exemptions, and deductions alter the base of state taxes that use those definitions, leading to changes in state income tax revenue if the state adopts the federal changes. This occurs automatically in many states if the state legislature takes no action. Second, changes in itemized deductions and tax rates alter the value of the federal deduction for state taxes, which raises the net cost of state income taxes for itemizers. This, in turn, may induce those taxpayers to encourage their state government to alter either the nature or mix of state taxes. Because the new federal income tax code has just taken effect at the time of this writing, the final state responses to the changes are not known. But the changes in state taxes in 1987 suggest the pattern of response, however. In addition a number of statistical analyses have been done to estimate what the effects would have been if states did not respond. These possibilities are discussed next.

/ APPLICATION 10.3
State Responses to Federal Tax Structure Changes

Federal tax reform, although planned to be "revenue neutral" in aggregate, substantially alters the distribution of federal–state income tax among taxpayers. Even if states respond to eliminate any windfall gains or losses, changes in the distribution of state income taxes will remain. Individual taxpayers will experience increases or decreases in their state income tax burden even if overall state income revenue is held constant.

The change in the federal income tax itemized deduction for state–local taxes is one of the most significant factors altering the distribution of state tax burdens. As a result of the federal Tax Reform Act of 1986, the federal itemized deduction for state–local sales taxes is eliminated. Also, fewer taxpayers will choose to deduct income and property taxes because of the larger standard deduction, while the much lower federal marginal tax rates for many taxpayers will reduce the value of that deduction for those taxpayers who still use it. The result is likely to be an increase in the net burden of state income taxes—that is, the burden after the federal deduction—for many taxpayers who have used the deduction, particularly higher-income taxpayers for whom the decrease in the value of the deduction is greatest. Even among taxpayers who do not experience a net increase in state taxes, the *relative attractiveness* of state income taxes may decrease compared to other state taxes, perhaps because a larger fraction of those other taxes can now be exported to other states' residents than can the state income tax.

/ **APPLICATION 10.3** Continued
State Responses to Federal Tax Structure Changes

As a response to these changes, a number of studies suggest that state governments are likely to reduce reliance on individual income taxes compared to other revenue sources and/or reduce the progressivity of their state tax structures. In one such study, Daphne Kenyon (1986) examined the determinants of the mix of state taxes using fiscal year 1981 data, paying particular attention to whether differences among states in the average federal marginal income tax rate and the percentage of a state's taxpayers who itemize federal deductions influence a state's use of different taxes. The federal tax influences are captured by the **burden price** of the state income tax, which is defined as the cost of a $1 increase in state income tax after subtracting the amount offset by the federal deduction. Kenyon reports that a 1-percent increase in the net burden of state income taxes (for instance, from a lower-value federal deduction) leads to an 11-percent decrease in per-capita state income taxes.

In another recent study of these issues, Mary Gade (1986) also examines the influence of tax exporting on the choice of state tax mix. In Gade's model, state officials choose a state tax structure to minimize the net burden on residents (thus, maximize exporting), and given that structure, the state's median voter determines the level of state taxes and spending. Gade finds that a 1-percent increase in the burden price of the income tax leads to a 3.4-percent decrease in the fraction of total state taxes raised from the individual income tax. Using these results to simulate the effects of the 1986 federal tax changes, Gade estimates that state per-capita individual income taxes will decrease by about 40 percent (with a corresponding increase in state use of selective sales and direct business taxes). Commenting on these and other studies, Kenyon (1986, 31) concludes

> The studies reviewed . . . provide consistent evidence that Federal tax deductibility has an impact on the extent of state reliance on individual income taxes. Together they predict that per capita individual income taxes would be approximately cut in half if that tax were no longer deductible.

/ Summary

Currently, forty state governments collect broad-based individual income taxes, and three states (Connecticut, New Hampshire, and Tennessee) collect income tax on a narrow base of capital income only. Individual income taxes are also used by about 3500 local governments spread over eleven states and the District of Columbia. In 1986 income taxes provided more than 17 percent of state government revenue on average, double the share provided by that tax in 1968.

The two principal issues in selecting an appropriate state income tax base are the degree of coordination between the federal and state income tax definitions and

| APPLICATION 10.3 Continued
State Responses to Federal Tax Structure Changes

Although state–local government income taxes are still deductible, the value of the deduction has been reduced by the other federal tax changes, as discussed previously. One way that states might respond to the change in the value of federal tax deductibility is to reduce the progressivity of state income tax rates. The change in the value of the federal deduction is largest and most important for higher-income taxpayers. Some states in the past were able to use steeply progressive income tax–rate structures without fear of driving away higher-income taxpayers to whom those rates applied because the federal deduction effectively reduced the impact of those state rates, as shown in Tables 10.4 and 10.5. Indeed, less progressive state income tax–rate structures have resulted. On the basis of the ACIR (1986c) analysis and one by Robert Tannenwald (1988), it appears that fourteen states acted in 1987 to lower marginal income tax rates. For instance, New York reduced its top income tax rate from nearly 14 percent to 8.5 percent, and West Virginia reduced its top rate from 13 to 6.5 percent.

Another major effect of the federal tax reform act of 1986 is that many low-income taxpayers, perhaps 6 million, will no longer have any federal income tax liability because of the increases in the personal exemption and standard deduction. If state income taxes have smaller exemptions and deductions, some low-income taxpayers will still have state tax liabilities even if they do not owe federal taxes. Thus, many states face an incentive to similarly exempt low-income taxpayers from income taxes altogether. Apparently, that is happening; Steven Gold (1988, 440) has noted that "states are emulating the federal government's behavior by increasing standard deductions and personal exemptions."

States began the process of revamping their tax structures in 1987 in response to the incentives created by the federal tax changes. It is too early, however, to know the final result of those deliberations. As the president of the National Center for Policy Alternatives was quoted in the *New York Times*, "For two years Congress wrestled with fundamental questions of tax reform. . . . In the next . . . days it will be the states' turn and the questions will be repeated 50 times over" (Herbers 1987, 18).

the treatment of income that crosses jurisdiction boundaries. State and federal income taxes are also related by deductions for income taxes paid to the other types of government.

State income taxes differ widely in the definition of the tax base and in rate structures. Only five of the forty states with broad-based taxes (Illinois, Indiana, Massachusetts, Michigan, and Pennsylvania) used flat rates in 1985. In the other states, the rate structure is progressive, although again to widely differing degrees.

The marginal tax rate, that is, the tax rate that applies to the last dollar earned, determines the magnitude of the incentive effects of income taxes. Federal deductibility of the state tax reduces marginal tax rates and also narrows the difference in marginal rates between low-rate and high-rate states. Reciprocal deductibility—

that is, simultaneous federal deductibility of the state tax and state deductibility of the federal tax—has much the same effect, although to a greater magnitude.

Intergovernmental income tax deductibility reduces the progressivity of the tax structure. As a result, states may choose more progressive income tax–rate structures than they would without those deductions, states may be able to collect more revenue and thus spend more than without deductibility, and interstate differences in taxes are less than are suggested by differences in income tax rates.

One potential effect of federal tax reform is change in state income tax revenue because of common income tax definitions. Estimates by ACIR show that adoption of the recent federal tax changes by the states would have increased state income taxes by at least 10 percent in seventeen states and the District of Columbia, increased state income taxes by less than 10 percent in about sixteen states, decreased state income taxes in ten states, and had no effect in the seven states with no type of income tax.

Another important effect of federal tax reform is likely to be an increase in the net burden of state income taxes—for taxpayers who have used the itemized deduction for state income taxes. As a response to this effect, a number of studies suggest that state governments over the long run may reduce reliance on individual income taxes compared to other revenue sources and/or alter the progressivity of their state tax–rate structures.

Discussion Questions

1. Suppose that a taxpayer is in the 15-percent tax-rate bracket for the federal individual income tax and faces a 5-percent state income tax rate.
   a. If the taxpayer cannot deduct either tax against the other, what is the taxpayer's combined marginal tax rate? What is the marginal rate if the taxpayer itemizes federal deductions and deducts the state tax? What if there were reciprocal deductibility?
   b. Now recalculate all three combined marginal tax rates assuming that the state tax rate is 10 percent. How do they change?
   c. Compute your combined marginal income tax rate (federal, state, and local, if appropriate) using your income last year or that expected this year.

2. Suppose a taxpayer faces a federal marginal income tax rate of 15 percent and pays local property taxes of $2000 per year.
   a. Although the taxpayer itemizes federal deductions and thus deducts the local property tax in calculating federal income tax, suppose that no state income tax deduction for local taxes exists. What is the net, after-tax cost of property taxes to this taxpayer?
   b. Now suppose the state introduces an income tax *credit* for 25 percent of property taxes up to a maximum of $600. What is the taxpayer's net property tax cost now? (Remember that the state income tax is also deducted against the federal tax.) How much does the net cost fall because of the credit? How

much more would this taxpayer pay (net) if property taxes were increased to $2100?

3. The two most important state taxes are income and general sales taxes. Compose the relative desirability of the two both before and after adoption of the federal Tax Reform Act of 1986.

4. Does your state have an individual income tax? If so, how closely does it conform to the federal tax? Can one deduct the federal tax in computing the state income tax? List some specific ways that the federal and state tax bases differ. What problems, if any, do these differences create in computing your taxes?

Selected Readings

Advisory Commission on Intergovernmental Relations. ''Federal Income Tax Deductibility of State and Local Taxes: What Are Its Effects? Should It Be Modified or Eliminated?'' In *Strengthening the Federal Revenue System: Implications for State and Local Taxing and Borrowing,* Report A–97. Washington, D.C.: Author, 1984, 37–66.

Break, George F. *Financing Government in a Federal System.* Washington, D.C.: The Brookings Institution, 1980. See Chapter 2, ''Tax Coordination.''

11 / *Business Taxes*

The state corporation income tax does not do what many seem to intend it to do, and it works only very clumsily and possibly at considerable cost. . . . Any single state would seem to be well-advised at least to replace the corporation income tax with a tax levied directly on corporate sales, payrolls, and property. . . .[1]

Charles E. McLure, Jr.

/ Reliance on Business Taxes

All states have at least one major tax directly collected from businesses; indeed, most states use more than one. Among taxes generally applicable to most businesses, corporate income taxes are the most common, being used by forty-five state governments and the District of Columbia, whereas general gross receipts taxes are used by four states (Hawaii, Indiana, Washington, and West Virginia, although Hawaii and West Virginia use both, and Indiana is phasing out its gross receipts tax in favor of its corporate income tax). A value-added tax (VAT) is used only by Michigan. Other types of general business taxes are used by Nevada, Texas, and Wyoming.

State (and sometimes local) governments also commonly levy a set of different taxes on specific businesses, defined either by type or industry. Among the most important of these taxes are corporation license fees (used by forty-nine states), severance taxes—that is, excise taxes on the value of minerals extracted in the state—(used by thirty-three states), and special excise taxes on such industries as utilities, telephone, and insurance. Severance taxes are the primary business tax in Texas and Wyoming and have provided such a substantial amount of revenue that the more general business tax types have not been required. Nevada, too, relies on a specialized source of revenue collected from business, excise taxes and license fees on gambling activities. A summary of the use of these business taxes is given in Table 11.1.

In 1986 state government corporate income taxes and the one VAT generated about $18.4 billion, or 4.7 percent of state government general revenue, a share that has been relatively stable between 4 and 5 percent over the past twenty-five years. Gross receipts taxes collected from business generated another $1.7 billion,

---

[1]"The State Corporate Income Tax: Lambs in Wolves' Clothing." In *The Economics of Taxation,* edited by H. Aaron and M. Boskin. Washington, D.C.: The Brookings Institution, 1980, 342.

TABLE 11.1

State Business Tax Use, 1986

Type of Tax	Number of States	1985 Revenue (Billions of Dollars)	Percent of State General Revenue
Corporation income	45	16.915	4.3
Gross receipts	4	1.670	0.4
Value-added	1	1.448	0.4
Corporation license	49	3.065	0.8
Severance	33	6.125	1.6
Insurance premiums	50	5.489	1.4

Source: U.S. Department of Commerce (1987a).

while severance taxes provided about $6.1 billion and corporation license fees about $3.1 billion, as shown in Table 11.1.

Corporate income taxes easily represent the largest state-local business tax in aggregate. Of the forty-five states with corporate income taxes, twenty-nine have a single flat tax rate with the other sixteen using graduated rates. Although most state corporate income taxes share a number of common tax definitions with the federal corporate income tax, the degree of similarity has decreased substantially since 1981 when liberalized federal depreciation rules were not adopted by many states. Richard Aronson and John Hilley (1986) report that while thirty-three states generally followed the federal corporate tax base in 1973, by 1985 only six did. For the states using a corporate income tax, it provides between 1.8 percent (in South Dakota) and 8.9 percent (in New Hampshire) of state government general revenue and between 3.5 percent (in Oklahoma) and 22 percent (in New Hampshire) of state taxes.

/ Business Tax Structure Issues

The two principal issues facing state–local governments in designing taxes to be collected directly from businesses are the choice of the tax base—that is, the type of tax—and the method for apportioning that base among the various subnational governments in which a firm does business. Both choices have important implications for the incidence and economic efficiency of the state–local tax structure.

/ Alternative business tax bases[2]

The three primary potential business tax bases are gross income or gross receipts, value-added—the increase in the value of goods caused by one stage in the production process—and net income or profits. A description of these bases (and several variations) is shown in Table 11.2 and discussed next.

---

[2]This section is drawn from material prepared for the U.S. Department of the Treasury and reported in *Economic Analysis of Gross Income Taxes,* 1986.

TABLE 11.2

Alternative Business Tax Bases

Type	Subtraction Base	Additive Base	Tax Base
Gross receipts	Revenue	Purchases + wages + depreciation + interest + rent + profits	$a \cdot$ GNP, $a > 1$
Value added, gross income	Revenue − purchases of materials	Wages + depreciation + interest + rent + profits	GNP
Value added, net income	Revenue − purchases of materials − depreciation	Wages + interest + rent + profits	National income
Value added, consumption	Revenue − purchases of materials − capital purchases	Wages + interest + rent + profits − net investment	Consumption
Net income or profits	Revenue − purchases of materials − wages − interest − rent − depreciation	Profits	Profits or return on investment

/ *Gross Receipts Tax.* A gross receipts tax collected from business is a tax on the total receipts or total revenue of a firm, with no deductions for any type of expenses allowed. Because revenue is, by definition, equal to costs plus profits, a gross receipts tax is the same as a tax on both profits and all types of costs (materials and supplies, labor, interest, rent, depreciation). If this type of gross receipts tax is applied to all firms, the total tax base for the economy would be a multiple of GNP because the tax applies to all business sales, including interbusiness sales, and those taxes are then added to the base for sales at later stages of production and distribution.

It is common, however, for sales of some commodities or sales by some types of firms to be exempt from gross receipts taxes. For example, government and nonprofit entities are almost always tax-exempt. In that case, the aggregate base of a gross receipts tax would be smaller and could even be less than GNP.

/ *Value-Added Taxes.* Value added by a business is, in general, the difference between the sales of a firm and the cost of goods or services purchased from other firms that are used in production. The simple example outlined below illustrates the value-added concept.

Business:	Bakery	
Costs:	Labor	—Baker, salesclerk
	Materials	—Flour, sugar, spices, utilities
	Capital	—Mixer, utensils, oven
	Space	—Building rent
	Credit	—Interest paid on loans

Revenue = Wages + Purchases of Materials + Depreciation + Interest + Rent + Profit

Value Added = Revenue − Purchases of Materials
= Wages + Depreciation + Interest + Rent + Profit

The value added by the bakery is the difference between the sales value of the bakery's products and the value of the materials purchased in producing those products. There are two alternative but equivalent ways of calculating value added. One method is simply to subtract materials costs from sales. The alternative is to add labor costs plus depreciation plus interest paid plus rent plus profit.

Three variants of the VAT concept arise from different methods of treating capital-goods purchases. If no subtraction or deduction is allowed for capital expenditures or capital depreciation, then the tax is a **gross income-type VAT,** which is equivalent to a tax on the sum of wages plus interest plus rent plus depreciation plus profit. If all business entities were taxed, the aggregate base of the tax would be GNP.

If depreciation deductions are allowed, then the tax is a **net income-type VAT,** with the base for the firm equal to wages plus interest plus rent plus profit and the aggregate base equal to national income (consumption plus net investment). In this case, deductions are allowed not only for the materials used in production but also for the capital goods "used-up" in production, that is, for the depreciation of capital goods during the production period. Because the aggregate base of this type of tax is national income if applied to all firms in the nation, the base is equivalent to that of a national personal income tax.

The final VAT variant is a **consumption-type VAT.** In this case, all capital expenditures are subtracted from revenue in addition to materials purchases. The base of this tax is wages plus interest plus rent plus profit less net investment, which is equal to total consumption in a national accounting sense. In essence, capital income to individuals is not taxed unless consumed. This is now the predominant form of business taxation in Europe. The aggregate base of this tax is national consumption if levied on all firms in a nation and is thus equivalent to a national retail sales tax or a personal consumption tax.

/ *Net Income Tax.* For the traditional net income or profits tax, a business may deduct most all business expenses, including costs for materials, labor, interest, rent, as well as depreciation of capital equipment, from gross income. The resulting tax base equals the return on investment to the business, that is, profit. No deductions are allowed for dividend payments out of profits to shareholders, so the business net income tax is independent of whether profits are distributed.

/ *Illustration of Alternative Business Tax Bases.* A numerical example of the bakery case, outlined in Table 11.3, illustrates how these alternative tax bases compare. A bakery purchases flour from a miller, who has purchased grain from a farmer. The bakery also purchases an oven from the oven manufacturer, who has purchased steel from a separate steel producer. Other capital goods or material inputs that might realistically be required have been surpressed to avoid cluttering the example.

The baker's revenue or retail sales are $2000, which equals total consumption in this simple economy. The oven producer's sales are $500, which represents production of one oven, the only capital good (or investment) in this economy. GNP in this economy (consumption plus investment) therefore equals $2500. In

TABLE 11.3

Tax Bases and Production Stages

	Farmer	Miller	Baker	Oven Producer	Steel Producer	Total
Sales	$100	$500	$2000	$500	$200	$3300
Purchases of materials	0	100	500	200	0	800
Purchases of capital goods	0	0	500	0	0	500
Gross receipts tax at 10%	10	50	200	50	20	330
Value-added, gross income[a]	100	400	1500	300	200	2500
Gross income VAT at 10%	10	40	150	30	20	250
Depreciation	0	0	100	0	0	100
Value-added, net income[b]	100	400	1400	300	200	2400
Net income VAT at 10%	10	40	140	30	20	240
Value-added, consumption[c]	100	400	1000	300	200	2000
Consumption VAT at 10%	10	40	100	30	20	200
Profit[d]	8	40	160	40	16	264

[a]Value-Added, Gross Income = Sales − Material Purchases
[b]Value-Added, Net Income = Sales − Material Purchases − Depreciation
[c]Value-Added, Consumption = Sales − Material Purchases − Capital Purchases
[d]Profit = Sales − Material Purchases − Depreciation − Labor and Other Costs

addition, the farmer makes $100 of sales to the miller, who makes $500 of sales to the baker, while a steel producer makes $200 of sales to the oven manufacturer.

The base of a gross receipts tax is the total sales of all firms, which equals $3300 in the example, so that a 10-percent gross receipts tax generates $330 of revenue. In this case, the base of the gross receipts tax is 132 percent of GNP ([$3300/$2500] · 100). The base of a gross income VAT is total sales minus purchases of materials from other firms, which equals GNP, or $2500 in the example. A 10-percent gross income VAT generates $250 of revenue, while a rate of 13.2 percent would be required to equal the gross receipts tax revenue. The net income VAT is based on sales minus purchases of materials and depreciation and generates $240 of revenue at a 10-percent rate. (The example uses straight-line depreciation over a five-year life for the oven so the depreciation deduction is ⅕ of the price). The consumption-type VAT is based on sales minus purchases of materials and capital goods and provides $200 of revenue at 10 percent. Note that the consumption-type VAT generates revenue equal to a retail sales tax levied at the same 10-percent rate. The only retail sales in the example are by the bakery, equal to $2000.

The base of a traditional net income or profits tax would be sales minus purchases of materials and depreciation minus other costs such as those for labor, interest, and rent. The profits tax base would equal the net income value-added base minus those other costs. Without specifying those other costs, sample profit figures, which are consistent with the ratio of corporate profits to net national income (GNP less depreciation) for the United States, are presented in the bottom row of Table 11.3. Total profits from these operations amount to $264. Therefore, a 10-percent profit tax rate would generate only $26.40. A much higher rate is required to match the revenue from a 10-percent rate applied to the other tax bases.

/ Allocating tax bases among jurisdictions

If firms do business in more than one taxing jurisdiction, an additional issue is how to allocate that firm's tax base, whatever type of tax is used, among those jurisdictions. Using the bakery example, what if the bakery sells its products in more than one state, or what if the bakery produces its products at two plants located in different states and sells those products in all states? And what if the bakery does business in another nation? There are two issues to be resolved here: Under what conditions should a business be taxed by a specific jurisdiction, and if the business is taxable, what share of the firm's business can reasonably be allocated to that jurisdiction?

The current practice is that a business is taxable in a state only if it has a "business nexus or presence" in the state such that the business benefits from state activities. After a 1959 Supreme Court decision, Congress "prohibited a state's taxing of income derived from sales within its borders when the only business activity in the state was the solicitation for orders to be sent outside the state for approval and shipment" (Break 1980, 61). This is the rule regarding mail-order sales discussed in Chapter 9. In practice, therefore, interstate businesses generally are taxable in a state only if they maintain employees or property in the state.

If a business is to be taxed by a jurisdiction, three general methods may be used to apportion that firm's tax base among all taxing jurisdictions. One method requires **separate accounting** for some specific component of the business. Under this method, the firms' operations in different states or jurisdictions must be treated as separate firms with calculation of the tax base separately for each one. It is often economically inappropriate and practically very difficult to do separate accounting in any convincing way for entire business entities. If an automobile manufacturer produces engines in one state, transmissions in another, and assembles the cars in still a third state, how can the profit made from selling a car be separately allocated to the engine, transmission production, and assembly? The car as a final consumer product would have very different value without any one of the three. The value of final product also includes the influence of nonmanufacturing operations of the firm, such as advertising and distribution. **Specific allocation** is a second apportionment method that is sometimes effective for various kinds of subsidiary income of a firm. For instance, interest, or dividend income for a manufacturer can be separated from the income for the whole entity and that income may be *specifically allocated* to the state where the business is headquartered.

The third allocation method, the one used most commonly, is to apportion tax base by some arbitrary **formula**. The most commonly used formula (now used by forty-five states) includes three factors: the firm's share of its payroll, property, and sales in the state. If all are equally weighted, the firm's allocation factor is the average of the payroll, property, and sales shares. Mathematically the formula is

$$A_i = \frac{\dfrac{W_i}{W} + \dfrac{P_i}{P} + \dfrac{S_i}{S}}{3}$$

where A_i = apportionment factor to state i for a firm
W_i = wages paid by the firm to employees in state i
W = total wages paid by the firm
P_i = value of property owned by the firm in state i
P = value of all property owned by the firm
S_i = dollar amount of sales by the firm in state i
S = total sales by the firm

The operation of this formula is illustrated by two examples shown in Table 11.4. Firm I does all of its production in state A, and thus all of its employees and property are located there. Only 10 percent of firm I's sales take place in state A, however, with the rest of its production sold to residents of other states (perhaps by mail order or through independent manufacturers' representatives in those states). Because this firm has no property or employees in those other states, it is unlikely that those other states would attempt to levy tax on this firm. In that case, only $87,000 of the firm's total profit of $125,000, or 70 percent, would be taxed by state A. Because some part of this firm's net income goes untaxed by any state, some states have adopted rules that require that such untaxed sales be thrownback

TABLE 11.4

Tax-Base Apportionment Example

	Firm I		Firm II	
Tax Component	State A	All States	State A	All States
Wages	$500,000	$500,000	$2,000,000	$5,000,000
Property	$1,200,000	$1,200,000	$5,000,000	$12,500,000
Sales	$250,000	$2,500,000	$250,000	$25,000,000
Profit	—	$125,000	—	$1,250,000
Wage factor	1.00	—	0.40	—
Property factor	1.00	—	0.40	—
Sales factor	0.10	—	0.01	—
Three-factor	0.70	—	0.27	—
apportionment	[(1+1+.1)/3]		[(.4+.4+.01)/3]	
Taxable profit	$87,500 if other states tax remainder $125,000 if sales in other states are "thrown back" to state A			$341,250

into calculation of the apportionment formula for the state (or states) where production occurs. If state A had such a **throwback provision,** then the entire $125,000 of the firm's profit would be taxable by state A.

Firm II is an example of a firm that both produces and sells in more than one state. In this example, 40 percent of both the firm's payroll and property are located in state A, although only 1 percent of the firm's sales volume arises in that state. Assuming that the other 99 percent of sales are included in the allocation formulas for other states (no throwback), then 27 percent of the firm's total profits would be subject to tax in state A.

One of the most controversial aspects of the three-factor apportionment formula is the inclusion of sales shares. Under current general practice, sales location is defined on a *destination basis;* the sale location is the location of the consumer. As a result, a business such as firm I in Table 11.4 may avoid state taxation on some part of its total net income or sales, even though all of its production and facilities are located in one state. If the allocation formula is to apportion a firm's tax base proportionate to the benefits received from state services, then the theoretical issue is whether those benefits better correspond to the location of production or the location of the consumers of the product. Because many economists believe that the benefits from "the privilege of doing business in a state" arise from the location of production, a common suggestion is that a two-factor formula based on payroll and property is more appropriate for apportioning profits among states, if separate accounting or allocation is not feasible.

Another important aspect of formula apportionment arises from the degree of uniformity among states. If all states use the same formula such as the equally weighted three-factor formula then the sum of a firm's tax bases in all states exactly equals the total tax base for the firm. That is, the sum of all states' apportionment factors for the firm equals 1, as shown below:

$$\sum_i \frac{(W_i/W + P_i/P + S_i/S)}{3} = 1/3 \left[\sum_i (W_i/W) + \sum_i (P_i/P) + \sum_i (S_i/S) \right]$$

$$= 1/3 \left(\frac{\sum_i W_i}{W} + \frac{\sum_i P_i}{P} + \frac{\sum_i S_i}{S} \right)$$

$$= 1/3(1 + 1 + 1) = 1$$

If states use different formulas, however, involving different factors or different weights or if some states do not use formula apportionment in favor of some type of separate accounting, then the sum of a firm's tax bases in all states may be either greater than or less than the total base for the whole firm. Either some of the firm's profit may be taxed by more than one state or some part is taxed by no state.

The use of sales shares in the apportionment formula and the choice of the destination principle for defining sales is a major factor contributing to this possible inconsistency in apportionment. The sales-factor issue is also a major difficulty in getting states to agree on apportionment methods. Those states with the larger shares of payroll and property of multistate firms could increase their share of the

---

/ APPLICATION 11.1
Worldwide Unitary Taxation

The treatment of multinational (as opposed to multistate) firms is also controversial for states following the unitary formula apportionment method. As recently as 1983, thirteen states used the worldwide unitary method of taxation under which formula apportionment was applied to the profits of a multinational firm from its operations worldwide. These states took the position that the whole firm including all subsidiaries was the business unit to be taxed. If a two-factor apportionment formula (based on payroll and property) is used by the state, the shares of each would be relative to the entire multinational firm, but the profits from the entire entity would be subject to state taxation. The United States Supreme Court upheld the constitutionality of state worldwide unitary taxation in a 1983 decision, which arose from California's application of the rule.[4]

For many multinational firms, the worldwide unitary method increases the amount of state tax owed comparable to formula apportionment that considers U.S. operations only or compared to separate accounting. A Japanese automobile manufacturer, for instance, might set up a U.S. subsidiary to operate one manufacturing facility in one state, with all of those cars sold in the United States. If the state where the facility is located followed the worldwide unitary method, that firm's profits from its worldwide production and sale of cars would be taxed by that state, although the firm's allocation factor would be small because only a small fraction of the firm's worldwide payroll and property are in that state. The method also applies to U.S. firms with international operations. Suppose, for example, that a U.S. computer manufacturer, which does the majority of its manufacturing in the United States, makes substantial sales (and thus profits) through its foreign subsidiaries. Applying the worldwide unitary method might have little effect on its apportionment factor for a state (because the bulk of its payroll and property are in the U.S.) but would greatly increase the total profit amount to which that apportionment factor is applied.

Economically, there is much to recommend the worldwide unitary apportionment method. In following this approach, states treat multistate and

---

tax base by excluding sales from the formula or by defining sales by the origin principle. States with a substantial share of consumption but less of production obviously receive larger tax bases with destination-based sales in the formula. For instance, Iowa uses only a sales factor in its formula, and some other states give the sales factor double weight in their formulas. If tax rates differ among states as well, then the firms may also have a preference for one formula over another as a way of minimizing total state tax burdens.[3]

---

[3]The use of formula apportionment creates a number of other incentives for firms to alter behavior. For a discussion, see Gordon and Wilson (1986).

/ APPLICATION 11.1 Continued
Worldwide Unitary Taxation

multinational firms equivalently. Some costs such as those for central management or product design benefit the entire firm and cannot be feasibly allocated to any one location. Any economies of scale that may arise in management or from advertising may apply to U.S. as well as foreign operations. And allowing separate accounting for foreign operations opens another avenue for tax avoidance if tax rates differ in the United States and foreign nations. On the other hand, worldwide unitary apportionment also suffers from some difficulties, not the least of which is the fact that separate accounting is the conventional method for taxing multinational firms by most other nations and has been incorporated in many tax treaties between other nations and the United States.

States using the worldwide unitary apportionment method found themselves under pressure from both the federal government in the United States (reflecting the concern of foreign nations) and multinational businesses (some threatening the relocation of some facilities from worldwide unitary states) to elect a different approach to taxing multinational firms. President Reagan appointed a Worldwide Unitary Taxation Working Group with representatives from the federal government, state governments, and businesses to consider and recommend a resolution of the issue. Given assurances from the U.S. Department of the Treasury that the federal government would assist states in enforcing separate accounting rules through federal auditing and sharing of tax-return data and given the competitive forces operating among the states, a number of states stopped using the worldwide unitary approach. Instead, formula apportionment was based on and applied to a multinational firm's operations only in the United States, what has been called the "water's edge" approach. At present, only a few states (Alaska, California, Montana, New Hampshire, and North Dakota) continue to use the worldwide unitary apportionment method in some form.

---

[4]*Container Corporation of America v. Franchise Tax Board, 463 U.S. 159 (1983).*

/ Economic Analysis

/ Incidence and efficiency implications of gross receipts taxes

The use of gross receipts or gross income as the base of a general state tax collected from business creates a fundamental structural difficulty. Sales of all intermediate goods are taxed under a gross receipts tax, while sales of intermediate capital goods are taxed under a gross income VAT. Tax is levied on each of those transactions, and that tax "cascades" down into the price charged at the next production stage, on which tax is also levied. In that way, the tax is said to "pyramid" through the various stages of production, ending up larger than the single nominal rate might suggest.[5]

This factor underlies the three most fundamental criticisms of general gross income and gross receipts taxes:

1. The effective tax rate will be greater than the nominal tax rate, the difference depending on the number of stages of production.
2. The effective rate will arbitrarily vary between economic sectors, depending on the number of stages of production.
3. The tax creates an incentive for vertical integration to reduce taxes.

Returning to the numerical illustration in Table 11.3, recall that total consumption is $2000 although the gross receipts tax base is $3300 and the gross income VAT base is $2500. Therefore, the 10-percent nominal gross receipts tax has an effective tax rate of 16.5 percent of consumption; it generates the same amount of revenue as would a 16.5-percent retail sales tax. Similarly, the gross income VAT nominally levied at a 10-percent rate has an effective rate of 12.5 percent on consumption. As noted above, effective rates exceed the nominal rates.

Also as noted above, the baker can reduce gross receipts tax by integrating with any of the other firms in the production chain, while the baker can reduce gross income VAT by combining with the capital good supplier, the oven producer. If the baker integrates with the miller or the oven producer, gross receipts for the combined firm are $2000 rather than $2500 from the sum of the independent firms. If the baker integrates with the oven producer, aggregate gross income value added for the two is $1300 rather than the $1800 with separate firms. If this type of integration occurred in some sectors of the economy but not others, then the tax burden would vary among those sectors even if they are the same size economically.

Because gross receipts taxes are effectively taxes on consumption, they tend to be regressive with respect to current income, as described in Chapter 9. To alleviate both the potential regressivity and any differences in effective rates among industries that arise, exemptions from tax or differential rates for specific types of goods or industries are common.

/ *Current State Gross Receipts Tax Use.* Three states—Hawaii, Washington, and West Virginia—currently use a gross receipts tax as a broad general tax collected from businesses. Their experience with those taxes illustrates the difficulties noted above. In addition, many states apply gross receipts taxes to specific industries.[6]

---

[5]Such taxes are sometimes called "turnover" taxes because tax is collected at each stage of production.

[6]Gross income taxes have also been used by several other states on a more limited basis. Indiana has a business gross income tax that is an alternative for taxpayers to a 2-percent corporate profits tax, with firms required to pay whichever is greater, according to Due and Mikesell (1983). Since 1977 the gross income tax rate has been scheduled to decrease each year by .05 percentage point. Also, a gross receipts tax was repealed by Alaska for all businesses but banks in 1979, with the tax on banks repealed in 1983.

/ *The Hawaii General Excise Tax.*   Hawaii's General Excise Tax (GET) is a combination gross receipts tax on all businesses and retail sales tax collected at a rate of 4 percent on all "final" sales, including retail sales of goods and services (including medical and professional services) and intermediate sales of goods and services purchased by a business but not used directly in production. A rate of 0.5 percent is collected on nonretail sales of goods. Economically, this is equivalent to a 0.5-percent gross receipts tax on all businesses (including retail) and a very broad-based 3.5-percent general sales tax. The nonretail component of the GET provided slightly more than 25 percent of state taxes in Hawaii in 1984.

In a report to the Hawaii Tax Review Commission, Bruce Billings (1984) estimates that pyramiding and taxation of intermediate sales increase the effective tax rate on sales from the nominal 4-percent rate to an effective rate between 4.79 percent and 5.42 percent, an increase of about 25 percent. The Commission Report stated that "the 4% retail rate is actually about a 5% rate, on average, when the pre-retail general excise tax imbedded in the price is considered" (*Report of the First Tax Review Commission* 1984, 8). It also appears that the gross excise tax may have contributed to vertical integration in the state. Billings (1984) found significantly higher levels of integration in manufacturing industries in Hawaii compared to all other states for 1972 and 1977 and compared to fifteen selected states relatively similar to Hawaii for 1967, 1972, and 1977. With respect to manufacturing, Billings (1984, 37) concludes that "it appears that Hawaiian industry is somewhat more vertically integrated than the U.S. norm."

Even so, the Tax Review Commission recommended retention of the GET for three reasons: A single replacement tax on a narrower base would require a substantially higher rate; changeover to a different tax would alter the distribution of taxes among businesses; the potential substitute taxes appeared to be administratively more complex. This illustrates an important feature of tax reform as opposed to tax design. Once a tax has been in place for several years, the economic and business structure will have reacted to that structure so that any change to generate benefits in the long run must accommodate the short-run disruptions that result.[7]

/ *The West Virginia Business and Occupation Tax.*   A general gross receipts tax, called the Business and Occupation Tax (B&O Tax), is also used by West Virginia. The tax is used in addition to a corporation and transportation net income tax, a personal income tax, and a 4-percent retail sales tax, although the B&O Tax is the single largest state revenue source, providing about 31 percent of total state taxes. The B&O Tax had twenty-six classes of different types of economic activity involving eighteen different tax rates in 1984. In addition, some economic activities (such as insurance companies, which are subject to a premiums tax, religious or

---

[7]The State of Washington also levies a multistage gross receipts tax, called the Business and Occupation Tax (B&O Tax). The general rate is 0.484 percent. In concept the combination of Washington's B&O and 6.5-percent retail sales taxes is very similar to Hawaii's GET; therefore, the Washington B&O Tax suffers from the same problems as Hawaii's GET.

charitable organizations, many nonprofit associations, and businesses engaged in agriculture or selling stocks and bonds) are tax-exempt.

Effective business tax rates in West Virginia in 1982 for businesses subject to the tax were 1.162 percent for services, 1.833 percent for durable manufacturing but only 0.385 percent for nondurable manufacturing, 2.890 percent for retailing, 3.265 percent for wholesaling, and 4.262 percent for construction. The relatively high effective rates for retailing and wholesaling, despite very low nominal rates, primarily reflect the B&O taxes levied on sales at prior stages of production and distribution, the pyramiding or cascading effect of the tax (Strauss 1983, Table 5.16). When the West Virginia Tax Study Commission (1984, 52) recommended abolition of the B&O tax in 1984, it concluded

> Because it [the B&O Tax] taxes activities at many different rates, and taxes transactions many times below the retail level, it distorts economic decisions and creates artificial incentives to reorganize activities so they fall into lower tax rate classifications. There does not appear to be any rationale for the current structure of tax rates and classifications under the B&O tax, and, therefore, the elimination of the B&O tax should be a high priority for the Legislature.

/ Incidence and efficiency effects of state corporate profit taxes

Understanding of the incidence and long-run economic effects of corporate income taxes is one of the most unresolved and controversial topics of public finance. And the special aspects of state government use of corporate income taxes, especially formula allocation of the tax base, complicate matters still further. All the issues obviously cannot be resolved or even discussed carefully here. The approach therefore is to describe the potential effects of a national corporate income tax and then to consider how the special features of state use of the tax alter the story. The specific focus on state corporate income taxes also separately considers the aggregate effect of all state taxes together as opposed to the effect of a single state's tax from the viewpoint of that state.

/ A National Corporate Income Tax.

The economic analysis of a national corporate income tax is essentially similar to the analysis of a national property tax discussed in Chapter 8. In the short run, a uniform national tax on the net income or profits of corporations attempting to maximize profits is expected to reduce the return to corporate capital owners. This is based on the notion that firms are unlikely to be able to shift the tax to consumers or workers in the short run, either because of competitive pressures or because it would not be profit maximizing for them to do so (given that capital costs are fixed costs in the short run). Even this result is not guaranteed. Firms that have some objective other than maximizing profits, especially those operating in oligopolistic markets, may shift the corporate tax through higher prices or lower wages even in the short run.

If the tax is not shifted in the short run, there are (at least) two means for corporate capital owners to avoid or shift the burden of the tax in the long run.

First, by shifting capital from the corporate to noncorporate sector of the economy, tax burdens may be reduced because only corporations are subject to the corporate tax. The increase in supply of noncorporate capital reduces the return to owners of noncorporate capital as well. The tax on corporate capital is therefore shared by the owners of all types of capital. Second, if the tax reduces the return to capital ownership generally, capital suppliers may respond by reducing the amount of capital accumulation in society. Over time, this means there will be a lower stock of capital in society than there would be without the tax, which causes labor productivity and thus real wages to be lower than they otherwise would be. In that case, part of the tax on corporate capital is shifted to labor in the long run.

/ State Corporate Taxation: Aggregate View.

Two important features of state government corporate income taxation require alteration of this conventional analysis. First, not all states use a corporate income tax, and among those that do there is substantial variation in tax rates. This creates an additional opportunity for shifting the corporate income tax by moving capital investment from high- to low- (or no-) tax states. Second, corporate net income of multistate firms is generally apportioned among the taxing states by formula, most commonly the three-factor formula described previously. Charles McLure (1980, 1981) has carefully explained how this type of formula allocation effectively converts a state corporate income tax into a set of taxes on the formula's factors, that is, wages, sales, and property.

Following the discussion by McLure (1981), suppose that a state levies a tax at rate t on the national profits, denoted Y, of corporations. For multistate firms, the tax base is allocated among states according to the average of the share of the firm's wages W, sales S, and property P in that state. The corporate income tax can be represented mathematically as

$$T = 1/3(S_i/S + W_i/W + P_i/P)tY$$

or

$$T = \frac{tY}{3S} S_i + \frac{tY}{3W} W_i + \frac{tY}{3P} P_i$$

where i represents sales, wages, or property in state i.

From this view, the tax is seen to be a set of three taxes on sales, wages, and property in state i, with the tax rate for each equal to one-third the nominal rate multiplied times the firm's profit rate on sales, wages, and property, respectively. Therefore, not only might tax rates differ among states, but the effective rate imposed by a single state on activity in that state may differ by firm, depending on that firm's national profit rate.

Just as with the analysis of property taxes, state corporate income taxes involve two effects—the effect of the average rate of tax in the nation and the effect of the differentials from that average. As with a national corporate tax, the average burden of state corporate income taxes represents a decrease in the return to owners of corporate capital, as demonstrated by Peter Mieszkowski and George Zodrow (1985). In the long run, that burden may be shifted to owners of all capital if activity is shifted from the corporate to the noncorporate sector, and the burden may also be partly shifted to labor in the long run if savings and capital investment are affected.

The effect from state tax-rate differentials around the national average is best seen in the context of the three separate taxes that arise from formula apportionment of the corporate income tax base. Transfer of sales, employment, or property from one state to another state with a lower-tax rate will reduce a firm's overall tax liability. In effect it is as if states are imposing taxes on sales, payrolls, and property values in the state at differential rates. There is therefore an incentive from each component of the formula for firms to move their economic activity to lower–tax rate states.

For instance, the effect of the property component of the allocation formula is expected to be the same as the excise effects that result from a statewide property tax. If property owners move investment from higher– to lower–tax rate states, decreases in the prices of immobile capital, labor, and land are expected in the higher-tax states. Corresponding increases in the prices for those immobile factors are expected in the lower–tax rate states. Similarly, the sales component of the tax is expected to increase prices for consumers in the higher-tax states and lower prices in the lower-tax states, while the payroll tax component is expected to lower wages in the higher-tax states and raise wages in the lower-tax states if workers are largely immobile among states. In short the excise effects from differentials in state corporate income tax rates are expected to impose relative burdens on immobile workers, consumers, and owners of land and immobile capital in the higher-tax states.

Mieszkowski and Zodrow (1985) have noted that the increased consumer prices and decreased wages and prices of immobile capital and land in the higher-tax states will be matched by decreased consumer prices and increased wages and prices of immobile capital and land in the lower-tax states. But it is not at all clear that these excise effects cancel out in any meaningful economic sense. If individuals' incomes are different in the higher– and lower–tax rate states, then these excise effects can have substantial effects on the distribution of tax burdens across income classes and can have macroeconomic effects if marginal propensities to consume differ by income.

/ State Corporate Taxation: Single-State View.

From the viewpoint of a single state, the effect of an increase in that state's corporate income tax is best represented by the effects from the implicit taxes on sales, payrolls, and property in the state. The national burden on all capital from the change in the average rate of tax is diffused among all states, and the gains to workers, consumers, and capital owners in the other states are of no concern to the state in question. Therefore, from the viewpoint of a single state, an increase in the state corporate income tax rate is expected to impose burdens on workers, consumers, and owners of immobile capital and land in that state. In other words, this tax increase is not generally exported to nonresidents in the sense that changes in real income of residents do not occur.

/ State value-added taxes: The Michigan experience[8]

The Michigan state government's general business tax is a consumption-type VAT, called the Single Business Tax (SBT), which was adopted in 1975 and provides about 15 percent of the state's tax revenue. Michigan is the only state to use the VAT approach, which it also used from 1953–67 in the form of Michigan's Business Activity Tax (BAT). Michigan experimented with a state corporate profits tax during the intervening years. Recall that the base of a consumption-type VAT is revenue minus purchases of all intermediate goods and services, including capital goods. Therefore, the equity and efficiency problems caused by pyramiding of gross income taxes do not occur with a consumption-type VAT. For the SBT, the tax base is computed by the equivalent approach of adding up wages plus interest plus rent plus profit and subtracting net investment (although the subtraction approach was used for the older BAT).

The Michigan SBT has a single rate (2.35 percent) and is applied to a relatively broad spectrum of economic activities, with only government, nonprofit organizations, and agricultural firms exempt. The tax does include several exemptions, deductions, and credits, although a recent analysis by the Michigan Department of Treasury shows that when comparing firms of equal size (value-added), effective tax rates vary little between different business sectors. That analysis showed that the average effective rate after deductions and credits was 1.39 percent with only about 17-percent average variation among different types of businesses. For instance, the average effective rate for retail businesses was 1.43 percent, compared to 1.27 percent for service businesses and about 1.6 percent for manufacturing. As a result of the tax adjustments, the effective rate rises with the size of the business so that firms with less than $500,000 of value added have, on average, an effective rate less than the state average.

In effect, then, Michigan's tax structure has the advantages usually attributed to gross income taxes—broad-base, low-rate, and relatively stable revenue stream—without the efficiency and equity problems of gross income taxes. Because VATs are not common in the United States (although that is the standard business tax form in Europe), there is some confusion and many misconceptions about the SBT among the state's taxpayers, however.

One potential economic advantage of a consumption-type VAT compared to a profits tax is a lower effective tax on capital income because capital expenditures are deducted. If capital is mobile among states, then the substitution of a consumption-type VAT for a state profits tax is expected to increase the rate of return to capital in that state, thus stimulating an increase in investment in that state. Nationally, such a tax would have the same base as any national consumption tax, such as a retail sales tax or personal expenditure tax. In contrast, the equivalence between a consumption-type VAT and retail sales tax may not exactly hold for a state if the sales tax is levied on consumption in the state while the VAT is levied on goods produced in the state for consumption anywhere.

---

[8]This section is based on Michigan Department of Treasury (1985).

/ APPLICATION 11.2
Discriminatory Business Taxes: The Insurance Case[9]

The fundamental legal issue regarding taxation of business in a federal system is the degree to and manner in which subnational governments may tax economic activities that cross jurisdiction boundaries, what is usually called interstate commerce in the United States. The Commerce Clause of the United States Constitution prohibits states from enacting laws designed to restrict interstate commerce, while the Fourteenth Amendment's Equal Protection Clause prohibits states from enacting laws that do not give all individuals equal protection (treatment). In general, states have been prohibited from applying taxes that discriminate against out-of-state firms. We have already seen these issues arise in the application of state sales and use taxes and in the apportionment of business income among states.

Still another example of the complex interaction of the relevant economic and legal principles arises concerning state taxation of insurance companies. All fifty states levy specific sales taxes on insurance companies equal to some percentage tax rate multiplied times the amount of insurance premiums on contracts sold in the state. As of 1981, thirty-four of these state insurance premiums taxes provided lower taxes (usually through lower rates) for insurance companies headquartered in the state (so-called domestic companies) than for insurance companies from other states (foreign companies). Typically, rates for domestic companies are 2 percent or less and rates for foreign companies one- or two-percentage points higher. This discriminatory taxation has been defended by the states on grounds of encouraging expansion of the domestic insurance industry to ensure insurance for residents at the lowest cost and as a means of increasing investment in the state (because insurance companies use their cash flow to invest in many industrial and commercial projects).

The McCarran–Ferguson Act (1945) specifically gives states the authority to regulate and tax insurance activities, effectively limiting the Commerce Clause's application to the insurance industry. The insurance industry has challenged these state domestic preference taxes on grounds that they violate the Equal Protection Clause, however, and in a 1985 decision (*Metropolitan Life Insurance Co. v. Ward*) the United States Supreme Court supported that view. The court rejected Alabama's domestic preference tax for insurance companies, arguing that the two reasons offered in support of the tax—to encourage the formation

---
[9]*For additional information on this topic, see Baldwin (1986).*

/ Summary

The two principal issues facing state–local governments in designing taxes to be collected directly from businesses are the choice of the tax base and the method for apportioning that base among the various subnational governments in which a firm does business.

/ APPLICATION 11.2 Continued
Discriminatory Business Taxes: The Insurance Case

of insurance companies in the state and to encourage foreign insurancecompanies to increase investment in the state—were not legitimate constitutional reasons for state discriminatory taxation.

Subsequent to this Supreme Court decision, nine states that previously had domestic preference taxes have substituted premiums taxes with equal rates for domestic and foreign companies. Another six states revised their insurance premiums taxes to levy equal tax rates on domestic and foreign insurers but provide tax credits based on some other measure of the firm's activity in the state (such as investment, property value, or location of corporate headquarters). It is problematic whether this tax-credit approach will survive judicial scrutiny. Judicial or legislative action on the issue of discriminatory insurance taxes is pending in most of the states with domestic preference taxes still in place.

Economically, there is some question as to whether these domestic preference taxes could, in practice, accomplish the basic objective of expanding the insurance industry within a state. The largest insurance companies that market nationally sell insurance in many or nearly all states. The lower premiums tax rate in such a company's home state applies only to insurance purchased by residents of that state, which typically would be a small fraction of the total insurance sold by a national firm. Thus, the differential rate for domestic and foreign insurers cannot advantage an insurance company that desires to be national in scope (to lower taxes, it would have to do most of its sales in its home state or move its headquarters to the state where it does most of its business).

The domestic preference is, therefore, likely to be an advantage only for smaller regional or state firms that sell a substantial part of their insurance in their home state. But for the domestic industry in a state to expand at the expense of the national companies, the domestic companies would have to offer insurance at lower prices than the national firms; that is, the lower state taxes would have to be at least partially passed on to consumers in the home state. But if entry of new insurance companies into a state can be limited by other means such as regulation or advertising, it seems more likely that the domestic preference tax would simply lead to higher profits for the domestic firms rather than lower prices.

A gross income tax collected from business is a tax on the total receipts or total revenue of a firm, with no deductions for any type of expenses allowed. A VAT tax is a tax on the difference between the sales of a firm and the cost of goods or services purchased from other firms, which are used in production. The base for the traditional net income or profits tax is revenue minus most all business expenses, including costs for materials, labor, interest, rent and depreciation of capital equipment, from gross income.

The most often used method to apportion a multistate firm's tax base among all taxing jurisdictions is formula allocation, usually involving the firm's share of its payroll, property, and sales in the state. If all are equally weighted, the firms allocation factor is the average of the payroll, property, and sales shares.

As recently as 1983, thirteen states used the worldwide unitary method of taxation for multinational firms under which formula apportionment was applied to the profits of a multinational firm from its operations worldwide. As a result of assurances from the U.S. Department of the Treasury that the federal government would assist states in enforcing separate accounting rules and the competitive forces operating among the states, a number of states have substituted formula apportionment based on a multinational firm's operations only in the United States, what has been called the "water's edge" approach.

The three most fundamental criticisms of gross receipts taxes are that the effective tax rate will be greater than the nominal tax rate, depending on the number of stages of production; the effective rate will arbitrarily vary between economic sectors; and the tax creates an incentive for vertical integration to reduce taxes.

The average burden of state corporate income taxes represents a decrease in the return to owners of capital just as with a national corporate tax. Differences in state corporate income tax rates among states are expected to impose relative burdens on immobile workers, consumers, and owners of land and immobile capital in the higher-tax states. From the viewpoint of a single state, an increase in the state corporate income tax rate is therefore expected to impose burdens on workers, consumers, and owners of immobile capital and land in that state.

Michigan is the only jurisdiction in the United States to use a VAT, although that is a common business tax in other parts of the world. VATs have many of the advantages of gross income taxes—broad-base, low-rate, and relatively stable revenue stream—without the efficiency and equity problems of gross income taxes. One additional economic advantage of a consumption-type VAT compared to a profits tax is a lower effective tax on new investment because capital expenditures are deducted.

Discussion Questions

1. According to the "benefit principle" of taxation, a business's tax in a state should be related to the benefits to the business from services provided by the state and local governments. Practically, a firm's business activity or tax base is usually divided among states based on the state's share of the firm's capital, employment, and/or sales. Discuss how well each of those components of the allocation formula might correspond to service benefits. Does a firm with sales (through mail-order, perhaps) but no employees or capital in a state benefit from any state or local government services?

2. Gross receipts, value-added, and net income are three different potential business tax bases. For each of three firms—an automobile manufacturer (assembly plant), a food retailer, and a private-practice physician—list the components of each

potential tax base and describe how the bases differ among each other for one tax and among the three taxes.

3. It can be shown that a national consumption-type VAT has the same base as a national retail sales tax (assuming no exemptions or the same exemptions for each). If one state has a consumption-type VAT (similar to Michigan's SBT), is that tax on the same base as a state sales tax? Suppose that every state adopted a consumption-type VAT. Would the cumulative effect of those taxes be the same as a national sales tax? How does the answer depend on how the tax base is allocated among states?

4. "If our state has to raise taxes, it should increase the corporate income tax. That way a good part of the tax will be paid by consumers in other states, not just taxpayers in this state." Evaluate this position.

Selected Readings

McLure, Charles E., Jr. "The Elusive Incidence of the Corporate Income Tax: The State Case." *Public Finance Quarterly* 9 (Oct. 1981): 395–413.

Michigan Department of Treasury, Taxation and Economic Policy Office. *Analysis of The Michigan Single Business Tax*. Lansing, January 1985.

Mieszkowski, Peter and George R. Zodrow. "The Incidence of a Partial State Corporate Income Tax." *National Tax Journal* 38 (Dec. 1985): 489–96.

12 / *Debt*

A subsidy geared to the volume of borrowing by a governmental unit is objectionably stimulative of borrowing.[1]

James A. Maxwell

/ Types of and Uses for Debt

In 1986 state–local governments in aggregate had total outstanding debt of nearly $659 billion, which amounts to more than $2700 per person in the United States. And, as shown in Table 12.1, the magnitude of that debt has grown substantially in the past twenty years and increased particularly quickly in the 1970s. The magnitude of state–local government debt has, however, remained relatively stable compared to the size of the economy as measured by GNP and compared to the annual total revenue of subnational governments. As shown, the value of the subnational government debt has stayed at about 14 percent of GNP over these years. Over these past twenty years, there has been some centralization of subnational government borrowing, with the state government debt now representing about 37 percent of the total subnational government debt, up from about 27 percent in 1964.

/ Why do state and local governments borrow?

State–local governments borrow money for three primary purposes: to finance capital projects such as schools, roads, water and sewer systems; to support and subsidize capital investment by private individuals and businesses; and to provide cash flow for short-term spending or for special projects. In contrast to the Federal government, it is not common and indeed often prohibited by state constitutions or laws for state–local governments to borrow to finance deficits in operating budgets. Each of the three major reasons for borrowing is considered separately next.

Capital spending has traditionally represented the major reason for state–local government borrowing. In 1986 state–local governments spent more than $90 billion on capital goods, which amounts to about $375 per person, as shown in Table 12.2. The largest share of that amount, nearly 30 percent, went for highway expenditures, with another 17.1 percent for educational facilities, 12.8 percent for water and

---

[1]*Financing State and Local Governments*. Washington, D.C.: The Brookings Institution, 1965, 236.

TABLE 12.1

State–Local Government Debt Outstanding

Year	Total Debt (Billions of Dollars)	Per-Capita Debt ($)	Debt as Percentage of GNP	Debt as Percentage of Annual Receipts[a]	State Share of Debt (%)	Local Share of Debt (%)
1964	92.2	480	14.5	133	27.1	72.9
1967	114.6	579	14.0	122	28.3	71.7
1972	174.5	838	14.4	97	31.2	68.8
1977	257.5	1190	12.9	86	35.0	65.0
1980	335.6	1474	12.8	87	36.3	63.6
1982	399.3	1719	13.0	90	36.9	63.1
1984	505.0	2134	13.8	96	36.9	63.1
1986	658.9	2733	15.6	106	37.6	62.4

Source: U.S. Department of Commerce, Bureau of the Census. *Governmental Finances,* various years.

[a]Total receipts as defined in the national income and product accounts.

sewer systems, and 11.3 percent for other state–local utilities including electric, natural gas, and public transit. Thus, these four categories account for more than 70 percent of state–local capital outlays. The pattern of state–local government capital spending has changed over the past 20 years with the share of spending for both education facilities and highways having declined substantially. That decline reflects both demographic changes reducing the demand for further increases in the number of schools and the substantial completion of the interstate highway system. In contrast, the percentage of spending on utilities has increased substantially.

The key economic characteristic of capital goods is that a relatively large initial expenditure is required to purchase facilities that then generate benefits over a number of years. There are two alternative ways for state–local governments to finance such capital purchases, either by building up a reserve of funds from taxes over several years or by borrowing the funds to be repaid with interest from taxes

TABLE 12.2

State–Local Government Capital Expenditure

Year	Total Expenditure (Billions of Dollars)	Per-Capita Expenditure($)	Percentage for			
			Education	Highways	Water and Sewerage	Other Utilities
1986	90.5	375	17.1	29.6	12.8	11.3
1984	70.7	300	16.4	28.8	12.9	13.0
1982	66.4	285	16.5	27.4	14.5	13.1
1980	62.9	278	17.1	30.4	15.3	10.5
1977	44.9	208	20.6	27.8	14.5	8.5
1972	34.2	164	23.5	36.0	10.0	4.7
1967	24.5	124	27.3	38.9	8.8	4.0

Source: U.S. Department of Commerce, Bureau of the Census. *Governmental Finances,* various years.

in future years. The latter method, sometimes referred to as "pay-as-you-use" finance, recognizes both the irregular nature of capital expenditures and the fact those who will benefit from the capital facility are the future residents of the jurisdiction. By borrowing the cash for the facility now but effectively paying for the facility with future taxes, those who receive the services from the facility will be paying for it. But pay-as-you-use finance is also sometimes criticized as creating an incentive for overcapitalization by subnational governments if the individual voters who approve projects do not perceive their future costs. Such an incentive may be larger in jurisdictions where a greater fraction of the voters are temporary residents.

Traditionally, state–local governments have financed about half of their capital expenditures, on average, with borrowed funds and the other portion with current funds. Although expenditures for individual capital projects are clearly "lumpy," many governments do tend to make some capital expenditures annually, if only for maintaining the existing capital stock. Therefore, some fraction of the annual revenues can be spent on capital goods each year.

Increasingly, in recent years state–local governments have used borrowing as an economic development tool, using borrowed funds to subsidize investment by private individuals and firms. State–local governments face lower interest rates on borrowed funds than do private individuals and businesses (because the interest income to investors in state–local bonds is not taxed by the national government, as discussed in the next section). Therefore, state–local governments can acquire funds by borrowing at relatively low interest rates and then reloan those funds to businesses and individuals at the same or slightly higher interest rates, but still lower rates than those private investors face alone. Such activity is justified as a way of attracting jobs and a tax base to the jurisdiction. This type of borrowing has been facilitated by the proliferation of various state government financing authorities and local economic development corporations, agencies that often carry out this private purpose state–local borrowing. In essence, state–local governments themselves or through their agencies transfer their authority to borrow at tax-exempt interest rates to private investors who would otherwise face higher borrowing costs.

The third primary reason for state–local government borrowing is to even out cash flow between the periods when these governments receive revenue. Typically, state–local governments do not receive revenue uniformly over the fiscal year; rather, receipts tend to be concentrated at particular times of the year. Local governments usually collect property taxes only once or twice a year, and those times may not correspond to the start of the localities' fiscal year when spending begins. And although most state government taxes are collected monthly or quarterly (through income withholding, for instance), that pattern of receipts may not match the pattern of state spending. Some states, for instance, make intergovernmental aid payments to localities at the beginning of the state's fiscal year.

Therefore, if a state or local government wishes to spend revenue in a fiscal year before that revenue is received, they may borrow for a short period against that revenue to be received later. Borrowing for cash-flow purposes is typically for only a three- or six-month period. It is important to understand that this type of

TABLE 12.3

State–Local Government Debt Outstanding, by Type

	Percentage for					
Type	*1986*	*1982*	*1980*	*1977*	*1972*	*1967*
Long-term	97.2	95.2	95.8	94.8	91.0	93.9
Full-faith and credit	28.8	37.9	44.5	53.5	54.9	54.8
Nonguaranteed	68.4	57.4	51.3	41.3	36.1	39.1
Short-term	2.8	4.8	3.9	5.2	9.0	6.1

Source: U.S. Department of Commerce, Bureau of the Census. *Governmental Finances,* various years.

borrowing is *not* to finance deficits; the fiscal year budget is balanced, and it is just that the revenue and spending do not occur at the same times in that year. A parallel in personal finance may be the use of bank credit cards to make purchases that are then fully paid at the end of the month when the individual receives a salary payment. The individual is not spending more than is earned but is borrowing to spend before the income is received.

/ How do state and local governments borrow?

State–local governments borrow money by selling bonds. A **bond** is a financial agreement or promise between a borrower and a lender (sometimes called an investor). The lender buys the bond from the borrower now, which provides funds to the borrower. In exchange the lender receives a promise from the borrower to pay a fixed amount of money (or interest rate) per year for a fixed period and to repay the original amount at a future date. For instance, a state or local government might sell a bond with a face value of $10,000 that carries with it annual payments of $500 for twenty years, at which time the loan is repaid. If a lender (investor) pays $10,000 for such a bond, then the lender earns a 5-percent return ($500/$10,000 = .05), and the state or local government pays a 5-percent interest cost on borrowing. If the bond sells for less than $10,000, then the investor earns a higher rate of return, and the borrowing government faces higher borrowing costs. For instance, if the bond sells for $9090.91, the effective interest rate is approximately 5.5 percent ($500/$9090.91 = .055).[2]

Different types of state–local government bonds correspond to the different reasons why state–local governments borrow. The great bulk of state–local government debt, and thus the great majority of bonds issued, is **long-term debt,** which carries a repayment period of more than one year, typically ten, twenty, or even thirty years. In 1985 nearly 97 percent of the total outstanding state–local debt was for long-term bonds, as shown in Table 12.3. Long-term debt has historically accounted for more than 90 percent of state–local debt, with that percentage some-

---

[2]The effective interest cost is slightly higher because the borrower must repay the lender $10,000 at maturity.

what higher in recent years than in the 1960s and 1970s. Long-term debt is used for nearly every purpose except cash-flow borrowing, which by nature is short-term debt. Long-term borrowing is particularly appropriate in financing capital projects on a pay-as-you-use plan because the term of the loan can be set to correspond to the expected life of the asset.

Long-term state–local government bonds are of two types. **General obligation (GO) bonds** pledge the **full-faith and credit** of the issuing government as security. This means that the issuing government must use funds from any available source to pay the interest and repay the principal to the investors. The government may use revenue from any tax or charges to repay the debt, and if existing revenue sources are not sufficient for that purpose, then the government pledges to raise taxes or charges to generate the necessary funds. If for some reason a state or local government is unable or unwilling to generate sufficient funds to repay the bond-holders, then the government is said to **default** on the bonds. In that case, the government is effectively in bankruptcy and the bondholders may go to court to seize the assets of the government or agency.

The second type of long-term bond is called a **revenue,** or **nonguaranteed, bond**. With revenue bonds, only the revenues from a particular source are pledged to pay the interest and repay the principal to the investors. If the revenues from that particular source are not sufficient to fully pay the interest or principal, then the bondholders suffer the loss. In general therefore, revenue bonds are more risky investments than GO bonds from the point of view of investors. As an example, a state or a state transportation agency might issue revenue bonds to finance the building of a bridge, pledging the revenues from bridge tolls to repay the investors. If the actual amount of bridge use is less than forecast and if the difference cannot be made up with higher tolls, the bondholders may suffer a loss. Or, as another example, a state university might issue revenue bonds to build dormitories, pledging the room charges of the students to repay the loan. The security or risk of those bonds depends on the success of the university in filling those dormitories. (Note that this may be one reason why some colleges and universities require students of particular ages or classes to live on campus.)

Revenue bonds are also used by state–local governments when the borrowed funds are to be used to support private investment, what have come to be called **private-purpose bonds.** For example, a local government economic development corporation (EDC) may sell revenue bonds and use the proceeds to assist in down-town commercial development. In essence the EDC uses the bond proceeds to make loans or grants to private developers of downtown office buildings, hotels, or stores. In that case, the bondholders will be repaid either from the payments made by the private developers to the EDC or perhaps from specific local (property) taxes generated by the new development. Obviously, the security of these bonds depends on the success of the private commercial development; if the offices or hotel remain largely vacant and the stores not patronized, then there may be insufficient profits to repay the EDC or no new local tax revenue generated. In essence the security of these private-purpose revenue bonds depends on the economic success of the private firms that are subsidized.

/ *Evidence.* In 1986 about 29 percent of state–local government debt was of the GO or full-faith and credit variety, whereas 68 percent was from revenue bonds of various types. This relative importance of revenue bonds reflects a substantial change in the borrowing behavior of state–local governments since the 1960s. As shown in Table 12.3, in the 1960s and 1970s and even as late as 1977, more than half of the debt was general-obligation. Still, the unmistakable trend since the early 1970s has been a decrease in the use of GO bonds in favor of revenue bonds. As discussed in a subsequent section, there are at least two reasons for this shift. State–local governments typically face more restrictions in issuing GO than revenue debt, including state debt limits and often a requirement of voter approval to issue new GO bonds. Second, state–local governments have simply changed the type of activity financed by borrowing.

Some idea of the uses for long-term debt by states and cities is given by the data in Tables 12.4 and 12.5. In 1986 15.3 percent of state long-term debt was used for educational facilities (including higher education), nearly 11 percent for hospitals, and about 7 percent for highways. These three together, then, accounted for about one-third of total outstanding state debt. In 1967, in contrast, the education and highway functions alone accounted for more than 60 percent of state long-term debt. Similar changes, although a bit less dramatic, are evident for city government debt. In 1967 water and sewer systems accounted for about one-fourth of city government long-term debt but only about 15 percent in 1986. Again, these changes reflect both the substantial completion of an educational, highway, and water and sewer infrastructure as well as the increasing use of private-purpose bonds. Note also the decrease in the relative magnitude of city debt for public-transit systems, which reflects the increased federal government role in financing transit systems.

It is also useful to understand a bit about the procedural details involved in selling state–local government bonds. First, the issuing government will employ the services of a number of intermediaries in the actual process of selling bonds. These include **bond counsel** (attorneys), who examine the legality of the issue, assure the prospective investors that the government has taken all required and

TABLE 12.4

State Government Long-Term Debt Outstanding, by Function

	Percentage for				
Year	Education	Highways	Hospitals	Housing and Community Development	Utilities
1986	15.3	6.6	10.7	2.7	4.0
1984	16.1	8.1	8.8	3.0	4.0
1982	16.7	10.2	6.5	na	3.8
1980	18.3	12.9	5.2	na	3.8
1977	22.2	19.1	3.7	na	na
1972	26.4	30.7	1.6	na	na
1967	27.2	36.1	1.1	na	na

Source: U.S. Department of Commerce, Bureau of the Census. *State Government Finances,* various years.

TABLE 12.5

City Government Long-Term Debt Outstanding, by Function[a]

			Percentage for		
Year	Water	Sewerage	Housing and Community Development	Electric	Transit
1986	9.1	6.2	6.9	10.8	2.4
1984	10.2	7.6	7.8	10.2	3.0
1982	11.1	8.9	11.5	11.7	3.8
1980	11.3	7.6	15.7	11.5	4.8
1977	10.3	7.3	10.8	9.6	6.6
1972	12.8	8.5	12.0	6.8	8.7
1967	15.2	9.2	12.9	5.4	12.2

Source: U.S. Department of Commerce, Bureau of the Census. *City Government Finances,* various years.

[a]For 1977–85, applies to the cities with population above 300,000. For 1972 and 1967, data are for the forty-eight largest cities.

appropriate legal steps in order to sell the bonds, and work to ensure that the interest will be exempt from federal income tax, and a **financial advisor and underwriter** (which may be the same or different firms), who advises on the structure of the bonds, prepares the necessary financial documents, and markets the bonds to investors. Second, state–local government bonds are usually given a **credit rating** by at least one of the two private rating firms, Moody's Investor Service or Standard and Poor's. The credit rating (denoted AAA, AA, A, BBB, and so forth) is intended to provide information to potential investors about the perceived risk of the bonds and thus depends both on the economic and fiscal health of the issuing government and the specific purpose or project for the borrowed funds.[3]

Finally, there is generally an active market for existing state–local tax-exempt bonds, through mutual funds if no other way. This means that some investors may be able to sell state–local government bonds to other investors, thereby receiving return of the principal before the term of the bond is up. Of course, the price for which owners may sell the bonds will depend on the annual interest payment, current market interest rates, and the remaining term of the bond. In fact, in some cases the bonds may be repurchased by the issuing government before the planned term. In that instance, it is said that the bonds have a **call provision,** or that they have been called, meaning that the seller may repurchase the bonds at a predetermined maximum price. An issuing government may wish to repurchase the bonds so that the debt may be refinanced if interest rates decline or to pay off the debt ahead of time to avoid future interest costs.

/ Tax Exemption for State and Local Bond Interest

The fundamental economic characteristic about state–local government bonds is that the interest income received by investors is not taxed by the federal government,

---

[3]For more detail on the practice of state and local government borrowing, see Kaufman and Fischer (1987, 287–317).

either by the individual or corporate income taxes. That interest income may be taxed by state income taxes, however. Typically, states exempt the interest income paid to residents from bonds issued by that state or its localities but not from bonds issued by other states. Similarly, state income taxes exempt interest income on federal government bonds. Accordingly, state–local government bonds are a type of tax shelter or tax-favored investment for lenders.

The federal tax exemption of state–local bond interest dates from the first federal Income Tax Act of 1913. There has always been controversy about the constitutional authority of the federal government to impose a tax on the income from state–local government securities in any case. Beginning with the case of *McCulloch v. Maryland* in 1819, the United States Supreme Court established the doctrine of "reciprocal immunity," holding that both the states and the federal government are immune from tax interference with the other. The Sixteenth Amendment to the Constitution established the right of the national government to collect direct taxes on income "from whatever source derived." Although with the initial and subsequent income tax acts Congress did not impose tax on state–local bond interest, the constitutional issue has been whether the Sixteenth Amendment gives Congress that authority. But in a 1988 decision, the Supreme Court ruled that the federal government does have the authority to tax state–local bond interest. In any case, Congress has acted in recent years to restrict the type of bonds for which the tax exemption applies.

Regardless of the rationale for the tax exemption, its primary economic effect is to allow lower interest rates for state–local bonds than similar taxable bonds. As a result, the tax exemption serves to subsidize both state–local governments, through lower borrowing costs, and investors in state–local bonds, through higher-net (after-tax) returns. These effects of the tax exemption are demonstrated in Table 12.6. In this example, a state–local bond with a face value of $10,000 that carries an interest rate (coupon rate) of 7 percent is compared to a corporate bond of the same risk and maturity but paying a 10-percent interest rate. An investor in the nontaxable state–local bond would receive a $700 interest payment annually on which no federal

TABLE 12.6

Effect of the Tax Exemption for State–Local Bonds on Different Investors, $10,000 Face-Value Bond

Marginal Tax Rate	Tax-Exempt State–Local Bond at 7%-Interest Rate			Taxable Corporate Bond 10%-Interest Rate		
	Annual Interest ($)	Tax	Net Return (%)	Annual Interest ($)	Tax ($)	Net Return (%)
.10	700	0	7	1000	100	9.0
.15	700	0	7	1000	150	8.5
.20	700	0	7	1000	200	8.0
.28	700	0	7	1000	280	7.2
.30	700	0	7	1000	300	7.0
.32	700	0	7	1000	320	6.8
.40	700	0	7	1000	400	6.0
.50	700	0	7	1000	500	5.0

income tax would be owed and no state income tax if the bond were issued in that state. Therefore, the net or after-tax return to any investor who pays $10,000 for the bond is 7 percent ($700/$10,000).

Continuing the illustration, an investor in the taxable corporate bond, in contrast, receives an annual interest payment of $1000 and must pay federal and state income tax on that amount. The amount of tax to be paid depends on the investor's **marginal income tax rate**, that is, the investor's tax bracket. A taxpayer with a 20-percent marginal tax rate therefore would owe $200 of tax on the $1000 of interest income. That taxpayer's net or after-tax return is thus $800, or 8 percent ($800/$10,000). With a 28-percent marginal tax rate, the net return is $720, or 7.2 percent. A taxpayer with a 30-percent tax rate, however, receives only a 7-percent net return from the tax-exempt bond (tax equals $300, so the net return is $700). If t = the marginal tax rate and r = the nominal interest rate on the taxable bond, then the net return to an investor in a taxable bond is equal to $(1 - t)r$. Thus, the investor with a 32-percent marginal tax rate earns a net after-tax return of 6.8 percent by investing in a 10-percent taxable bond, and a 50-percent marginal tax rate generates a 5-percent net return.

As shown in Table 12.6, taxpayers with marginal tax rates above 30 percent earn higher net returns by investing in the 7-percent tax-exempt state–local bond than in the 10-percent taxable corporate bond. On the other hand, taxpayers with a marginal tax rate of 30 percent get exactly the same net return—7 percent—from either investment, while those with marginal tax rates of less than 30 percent earn higher net returns by investing in the taxable bonds and paying the required income tax. *The marginal income tax rate at which an investor gets the same return from both a taxable and nontaxable bond is equal to the percentage difference between the interest rates on the taxable and tax-exempt bonds.* Mathematically, this relationship is

$$t^* = (r - s)/r$$

where t^* = tax rate at which an investor is indifferent
           between a taxable and tax-exempt bond
   r = taxable-bond interest rate
   s = tax-exempt bond interest rate

It follows therefore that state–local government bonds can carry lower interest rates than comparable private sector or U.S. government bonds because of the tax exemption. The annual yields on long-term state–local government bonds, twenty-year U.S. Treasury bonds, and AAA-rated corporate bonds from 1970–86 are shown in Table 12.7. The yields on the tax-exempt bonds are indeed lower than those on taxable bonds, although the yield differential varies over time with supply-and-demand conditions for the specific securities. During the 1970s, the yield differential between state–local and corporate bonds was generally between 20 and 30 percent, averaging about 26 percent. Similar yield differentials also held in the 1960s, although differences of 30 to 40 percent have prevailed in some previous periods. The yield differential between taxable and tax-exempt bonds has been

TABLE 12.7

Comparative Bond Yields, 1970–86

Year	Annual Yield Tax-Exempt State–Local Bonds[a]	Annual Yield 20-Year Treasury Bonds	Difference from State–Local Rate as Percentage of T-Bond Rate	Annual Yield AAA Corporate Bonds	Difference from State–Local Rate as Percentage of Corporate Rate
1987	7.65	8.49	7.59%	9.38	18.44%
1986	7.32	7.85	6.75%	9.02	18.85%
1985	9.11	10.97	16.96%	11.37	19.88%
1984	10.10	12.48	19.07%	12.71	20.54%
1983	9.51	11.34	16.14%	12.04	21.01%
1982	11.66	12.92	9.75%	13.79	15.45%
1981	11.33	13.72	17.42%	14.17	20.04%
1980	8.59	11.39	24.58%	11.94	28.06%
1979	6.52	9.33	30.12%	9.63	32.29%
1978	6.03	8.48	28.89%	8.73	30.93%
1977	5.68	7.67	25.95%	8.02	29.18%
1976	6.64	7.86	15.52%	8.43	21.23%
1975	7.05	8.19	13.92%	8.83	20.16%
1974	6.17	8.05	23.35%	8.57	28.00%
1973	5.22	6.30	17.14%	7.44	29.84%
1972	5.30	5.63	5.86%	7.21	26.49%
1971	5.62	5.74	2.09%	7.39	23.95%
1970	6.42	6.59	2.58%	8.04	20.15%

Source: Board of Governors of the Federal Reserve System. *Federal Reserve Bulletin,* various issues.

[a]*Bond Buyer* series, GO bonds with twenty years to maturity.

substantially smaller in recent years, however, averaging less than 20 percent between state–local and corporate bonds in the 1980s. This charge resulted partly from the reduction in federal marginal income tax rates in the 1980s.

The yield differential between tax-exempt state–local bonds and taxable U.S. Treasury bonds is generally smaller than that between state–local and corporate bonds, reflecting the perceived lower risk of the U.S. government bonds compared to corporate securities. And the yield differential between state–local and Treasury bonds is substantially more variable than that between the state–local and corporate bonds, reflecting the related operation of supply-and-demand factors in the markets for those two types of bonds.

The perceived default risk of these various bonds also influences their relative yields. Treasury bonds are believed to be the least risky in this regard, but the relative risk of state–local as compared to corporate bonds as a group is not clear. Defaults occasionally do occur with state–local bonds, as recently happened in the case of the Washington (state) Public Power System. Of course, corporate defaults and bankruptcies also occur. Perhaps the most accurate characterization is that among both state–local and corporate bonds the degree of default risk varies greatly and is reflected by yield differentials within each category of bond.

The tax exemption for state–local government bonds and the resulting differential in interest rates between these and other types of securities is the fundamental factor underlying most economic issues about state–local government borrowing. Therefore, we turn now to those economic implications of the tax exemption.

/ Implications and Analysis of the Tax Exemption

/ Nature and behavior of investors

Fundamentally, investors in stocks, bonds, and other instruments will find tax-exempt state–local government bonds attractive financially if the investors' marginal income tax rate is greater than the percentage difference in the effective interest rate on the tax-exempt bonds compared to that on alternative taxable securities. But this general rule can apply to different types of investors, both individuals and firms. Historically, state–local government bonds have been purchased almost entirely by three distinct groups—individuals, commercial banks, and property and casualty insurance companies—as demonstrated in Table 12.8. These three groups have held about 90 percent of the outstanding state–local government bonds during the 1980s. Banks and insurance companies (but commonly not other types of corporations) are large holders because their business is essentially investment of cash.

There have been substantial changes in the distribution of ownership among these three groups over the years, however. While individuals owned more than 40 percent of state–local debt in the 1950s, that share gradually declined to about 25 percent in 1980 but increased to about 37 percent by 1985. In contrast, the share owned by commercial banks rose substantially throughout the 1960s and early 1970s and subsequently declined, so that by 1985 individuals and banks owned roughly equal shares of the outstanding state–local debt.

It is important to understand that these ownership data reflect the aggregate or average ownership of state–local bonds, not only the demand for new issues of bonds. There is no presumption that new issues of bonds will be purchased by these groups in these ratios. In many cases, it is more useful for economic analysis to consider which of the groups represent the **marginal investors,** that is, those whose tax rates make tax-exempt bonds just marginally financially attractive. Suppose,

TABLE 12.8

Demanders of State–Local Government Bonds

Year	Percentage of Outstanding Bonds Owned by		
	Individuals	Commercial Banks	Insurance Companies[a]
1985	37.0	34.3	12.9
1982	30.4	37.4	20.5
1980	25.1	42.4	22.9
1972	27.4	51.0	14.1
1962	38.8	31.3	12.2

Source: Board of Governors of the Federal Reserve System. Flow of Funds Accounts, various years.

[a]Property and casualty insurance companies only.

tax rates make tax-exempt bonds just marginally financially attractive. Suppose, for example, that there is a 25-percent difference between the yields on taxable and tax-exempt bonds. If the corporate tax rate were 48 percent, then presumably profitable banks and insurance companies would find tax-exempts very attractive and would have increased their holdings of them. A similar argument applies to individuals with tax rates well above 25 percent. If more bonds are to be sold, which requires more investors, the likely source of those investors is individuals with tax rates around or slightly below 25 percent. If the percentage difference in interest rates is narrowed, those individuals would then find tax-exempt bonds attractive. In that case, the marginal investment group is middle-income individuals, even though the bulk of outstanding bonds may be owned by banks and insurance companies.

/ *Individuals.* Historically, individual investors in state–local bonds have come mostly from higher-income households, for two reasons. First, these investors must have had relatively high marginal federal income tax rates, generally in the 30 to 40 percent range, in order for yields on tax-exempt bonds to be attractive. Given the graduated rate structure of the federal individual income tax, marginal tax rates of that magnitude required relatively high gross incomes. For instance, in 1984 a marginal tax rate of 33 percent was reached with a taxable income of $35,200 for a household filing a joint return. But because taxable income is net of exclusions, personal exemptions, and deductions, $35,200 of taxable income requires about $41,000 of gross income, at least, and more likely an income of $45,000 to $50,000 for a family of four persons. In contrast, median (middle) family income in 1984 was $26,433, while a family income of $45,000 was about at the 80th percentile (80 percent of families in the United States had incomes less than $45,000 in 1984).

Second, state–local bonds are sold in relatively large denominations (usually at least $10,000), which historically restricted the set of purchasers to individuals willing to invest at least those amounts. In recent years, this constraint has been eased by the proliferation of tax-exempt bond mutual funds, in which a financial intermediary buys the bonds and sells shares in a fund comprised of many different bonds for relatively small amounts, even as low as $500. In addition to opening up the tax-exempt bond market to more individual investors, this method also reduces the risk to individuals by effectively allowing them to own fractional shares of different bonds from many different issuing governments. Still, Eric Toder and Thomas Neubig (1985, 401) report that more than 80 percent of the value of tax-exempt bonds held by individuals in 1983 was owned by individuals with household income above $100,000.

/ *Corporations and Banks.* Analysis of the behavior of corporate investors in state–local bonds, particularly banks and insurance companies, is somewhat more uncertain than that of individuals for several institutional reasons. Commercial banks borrow funds at taxable interest rates, for instance, by taking deposits from individuals and selling certificates of deposit (CDs). Until 1987 commercial banks were allowed to deduct those interest costs against their federal corporate income tax even if the funds were used to buy tax-exempt state–local bonds. Accordingly, the borrowing cost for the banks was the nominal interest rate paid on deposits net of the corporate tax deduction. If that borrowing cost is less than the yield on tax-exempt bonds, banks could make profits by taking more deposits and buying more tax-exempts.

A numerical example is illustrative. Suppose that the interest rate on bank deposits is 10 percent and that the corporate tax rate is 50 percent. If a bank sells a $10,000 CD to an individual, the bank pays the depositor annual interest of $1000. But because that interest cost is tax deductible by the bank, the net cost to the bank is $500 [interest × (1 − tax rate) = $1000 × .50]. Now if the $10,000 deposit is used to buy a tax-exempt state–local bond with a 7-percent yield, the bank receives annual interest payments of $700. The bank is said to engage in **arbitrage,** effectively incurring a $500 cost to earn $700 and is therefore expected to continue these transactions as long as those gains are possible. But the process of selling additional CDs and buying more state–local bonds by all banks is expected to increase the nominal interest rate on CDs and reduce the rate on state–local bonds until all arbitrage opportunities are eliminated. For instance, if the CD rate is 11 percent but the tax-exempt bond yield is 5.5 percent, the bank's net borrowing cost of $550 is just matched by the potential tax-exempt bond earnings of $550—all arbitrage opportunities are eliminated.

Similar types of arbitrage opportunities may also be available to other corporations such as insurance companies to the extent that those firms can adjust their taxable income in different ways. One well-known theory (Miller 1977) is that firms adjust their mix of debt to equity so that the net cost of corporate debt (which is a deductible cost for the firm) equals the net cost of equity income to shareholders (which is taxed). The marginal investor in the corporation will then have a federal marginal income tax rate equal to the corporate tax rate. And if investors view corporate equity income and tax-exempt bond income as substitutes, then the yield differential between corporate and tax-exempt bonds will also be determined by the corporate tax rate.

The common result of all these arbitrage models is that the percentage differential between taxable and tax-exempt bonds will equal the corporate tax rate. This results because these models make the corporations the marginal investors, and thus the yield differential should make nontaxable bonds just attractive to corporations. But as the data in Table 12.7 illustrate, the yield differential has generally been less than the corporate tax rate (which was between 48 and 46 percent until 1987). Two alternative institutional explanations have been offered as to why bank and insurance company arbitrage has been less than complete. One possibility is that state–local government bonds are perceived to be more risky than comparable U.S. Treasury and corporate bonds. Although that notion of relative risk may be true regarding Treasury bonds, it does not seem likely that state–local bonds as a group are any more risky than corporate bonds in aggregate. A second possible explanation concerns the preferred maturity of bonds by different investors. If banks prefer short-term obligations (in order to maintain liquidity) and insurance companies prefer long-term obligations, then individuals may be the marginal investors in long-term state–local bonds. The arbitrage story would then be limited because each type of demander is restricted by the amount of bonds of a given maturity.

/ *Efficiency of the tax exemption*

If the objective of the tax exemption for interest on state–local government bonds is to subsidize subnational government borrowing costs, then the tax exemption can be shown to be an inefficient subsidy in the sense that the Federal government loses more than $1 of tax revenue for each $1 of interest cost saved by state–local governments. This inefficiency is demonstrated in Table 12.9, in which the interest-cost saving to the state or local government from tax-exempt as opposed to taxable bonds is compared to the federal income tax saving of investors. The latter is, of course, also the tax revenue loss to the federal government.

The example in Table 12.9 again concerns a $10,000 bond with a 7-percent interest rate for tax-exempt securities and a 10-percent rate for taxable ones. For each bond sold then, the issuing state or local government saves $300 of interest cost per year. The federal tax saving to an investor from the tax-exempt compared to the taxable bond depends on the investor's federal marginal income tax rate. The tax savings is $1000 (the interest payment) multiplied by the tax rate, or $300 for taxpayers in the 30-percent tax rate bracket, $320 for taxpayers with a 32-percent marginal tax rate, $400 for taxpayers with a 40-percent marginal tax rate, and $500 for those in the 50-percent tax rate bracket. All investors in tax-exempt state–local government bonds with marginal tax rates greater than t^*—the tax rate at which the after-tax return on both type of bonds is equal—save more in federal income taxes from buying the tax-exempt bond than the state or local government saves in interest cost. To put it another way, all tax-exempt bond investors with tax rates above t^* are receiving greater returns than necessary to induce them to buy the state or local bond. The difference between the amount of interest saving to subnational governments and the tax loss of the Federal government is a net gain to these investors with high tax rates.

As the demand and supply of bonds changes, thereby affecting the yield between taxable and tax-exempt bonds, the tax rate at which an investor is indifferent between taxable and tax-exempt bonds also changes. In essence that tax rate (and the relative

TABLE 12.9

Efficiency of the Tax Exemption for State–Local Bonds; $10,000 Face-Value Bond, 7%-Interest Rate on Tax-Exempt Bonds, 10%-Interest Rate on Taxable Bonds

Marginal Tax Rate	Interest-Cost Saving to State–Local Government due to Tax Exemption ($)	Federal Income Tax Saving to Investor in State–Local Bond Compared to Taxable Bond ($)
.10	Not a tax-exempt investor	
.20	Not a tax-exempt investor	
.28	Not a tax-exempt investor	
.30	300	300
.32	300	320
.40	300	400
.50	300	500

yields) adjusts so that just enough investors are willing to buy the supplied bonds. But whatever the identity of these marginal investors, those investors with higher tax rates earn economic benefits from the tax exemption.

In some cases, it is possible for the state or local government (and implicitly, their taxpayers) to benefit from the differential in yields on taxable and tax-exempt bonds. If a state or local government sells bonds at the tax-exempt rate and can invest those funds at the higher taxable rates, the government earns profits because it is not liable for any tax on the income from the taxable bonds. This is a type of arbitrage by the subnational governments—effectively playing on the difference in rates. Internal Revenue Service (IRS) rules restrict the opportunity for subnational governments to earn arbitrage profits in this manner but do not eliminate them. It is recognized that capital projects require some time to get started, so a government may sell bonds to finance a capital construction project but not face any bills for some subsequent period. If the funds are invested over that period, arbitrage profits may be earned. The Tax Reform Act of 1986 limits the period for such activity to six months, however. In other cases, subnational governments may sell bonds for a specific purpose (for example, student loans or cash flow) even though they have surplus funds on hand. Using the borrowed funds rather than the reserve funds for the projects allows the reserve funds to be invested at the higher taxable interest rates. This, too, is a type of arbitrage and is permitted by the IRS.

Besides being an inefficient way for the Federal government to subsidize state–local government borrowing, tax exemption also increases the amount of state–local government borrowing by lowering the borrowing cost. Similarly, tax exemption induces some investors who otherwise might not do so to buy state and local government bonds. If some of the investors in state–local bonds would buy corporate bonds instead, that could lower the borrowing costs of private firms. Therefore, in the absence of some imperfection in the capital markets that works against state–local bonds or some externality among subnational governments that leads to an inefficiently low amount of investment by those governments, any subsidy of state–local borrowing costs leads to an inefficient use of society's resources.

/ Growth of private-purpose bonds

The most dramatic change in the state–local bond market over the past fifteen years has been the tremendous growth in the use of tax-exempt state–local bonds for nontraditional private purposes. These **private-purpose tax-exempt bonds** effectively allow state–local governments to transfer their tax-exempt borrowing authority to private individuals and firms for activities that would otherwise be financed through taxable debt. These private entities are therefore able to borrow at the generally lower tax-exempt interest rates rather than taxable interest rates. The largest category of these bonds consists of **industrial development bonds,** which are bonds sold by subnational governments or their development authorities such as EDCs, with the funds transferred to private firms to finance investment in the subnational jurisdiction. Other categories of private-purpose bonds include those for pollution-control facilities installed by private firms, investment by private hospitals and educational institutions, higher-education student loans, construction of rental housing (particularly for lower-income individuals), and mortgage loans to individuals for owner-occupied housing.

Private-purpose tax-exempt bonds are revenue bonds, with the bondholders to be repaid from proceeds of the underlying private activity. In the case of industrial development bonds, for instance, the funds from the bond sale may be used to partly finance construction of a new shopping center or expansion by a manufacturer. The interest and principal on those bonds will effectively be paid by the shopping center developer and the manufacturing firm, although the funds may be paid through a development authority. Similarly, a state or locality may sell bonds and use the funds to make mortgage loans through private financial institutions. Those loans would carry interest charges below private mortgages and are typically restricted to households with income less than some percentage, perhaps 125 percent, of the area's median income. The security for the bondholders in this case comes from the mortgage payments by the borrowers and the market value of the mortgaged properties.

The increased use of tax-exempt bonds for private purposes is therefore reflected by the increase in share of long-term debt in the form of revenue bonds (see Table 12.3). Currently, nearly two-thirds of the outstanding long-term state–local debt is in the form of revenue bonds, as previously noted. Similarly, the growth of private-purpose tax-exempt bonds compared to all long-term tax-exempt bonds issued in various years is depicted in Figure 12.1. In 1984 64 percent of all long-term state–

FIGURE 12.1   *Long-Term Tax-Exempt Bond Volume, 1975–84*

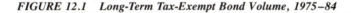

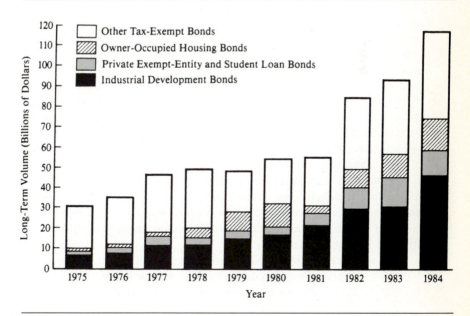

local bonds issued in that year ($74 billion out of about $116 billion) were for private purposes, as defined by the IRS. In 1975 by contrast only about one-third of new long-term tax-exempt bonds issued were for private purposes. It is also apparent from Figure 12.1 that use of all categories of private-purpose bonds increased greatly from 1981–84, a trend that by all reports will be continued as data for 1985 and 1986 become available.

I Costs of Private-Purpose Bonds. The use of state–local governments' tax-exempt borrowing authority for otherwise private purposes magnifies the economic problems arising from tax-exempt bonds discussed in the two prior sections. Substitution of tax-exempt bonds for taxable debt by individuals and firms reduces the revenue yield of the federal income taxes, necessitating higher federal income tax rates, lower federal government expenditures, or larger federal budget deficits. An estimate prepared for the 1986 Federal government budget showed that income tax exemption for interest on private-purpose state–local bonds were expected to reduce Federal revenue by more than $11 billion in 1986.[4] Moreover, this revenue cost to the federal government is greater than the interest-cost savings by the borrowers. Some recent research by the Office of Tax Analysis of the U.S. Department of the Treasury shows that substitution of $10 billion of tax-exempt debt for the same amount of taxable corporate debt increases the federal government budget deficit by $1.31 for each $1 of borrowing costs saved by the corporations.[5] The difference between the revenue cost to the Federal government and the cost savings to the borrowers goes to the buyers of the tax-exempt bonds. Extension of tax-exempt borrowing rights to private individuals and firms also exacerbates the allocational inefficiency resulting from the exemption—investment funds are transferred to those projects that are selected by state and local governments to receive the borrowing subsidy.

It is not hard to understand, however, why state–local governments find tax-exempt bonds an attractive way to attempt to subsidize investment and stimulate economic development. This tool appears to impose no cost on the state–local governments themselves (or their taxpayers) in contrast to direct expenditures or direct state–local tax breaks given to firms or individuals. In fact, if individual state–local governments believe that the cost of private-purpose bonds is imposed on all federal income taxpayers nationwide, then each government implicitly believes that they are exporting part of their economic development costs to residents of other states or localities by selling private-purpose bonds. Indeed, because a state's taxpayers bear costs from all states' private-purpose bonds in proportion to their federal taxable income, a state can "win" in the game only by issuing more and more tax-exempt bonds. Those states whose share of tax-exempt bond volume is greater than their share of federal taxable income are presumably the "winners" from the interest tax exemption.

But the perception by state–local governments that private-purpose tax-exempt bonds are costless to them may be faulty. The increase in funds to borrow required by state–local governments for these purposes is expected to increase the interest

[4]See U.S. Executive Office of the President (1985, Table G–2).
[5]Toder and Neubig (1985, 410).

FIGURE 12.2   The Market For State–Local Borrowing

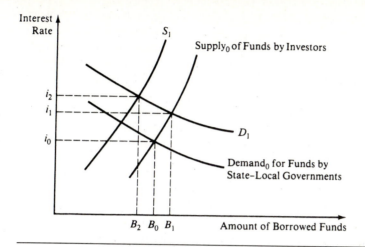

rate on all long-term state–local tax-exempt bonds. The relatively higher return on tax-exempt bonds is required to induce additional investors to supply the funds, that is, buy the bonds. Recent estimates suggest that each \$1 billion of additional tax-exempt bonds increases the tax-exempt interest rate between 1 and 7 basis points (a basis point is one one-hundredth of a percentage point).[6] In that case, use of tax-exempt bonds for private purposes increases the cost to state and local governments for borrowing for traditional public purposes (such as construction of roads, schools, and water and sewer systems).

This possibility is demonstrated in Figure 12.2, which shows a positively sloping supply curve for funds supplied by investors to state–local governments (a higher yield is required to induce more individuals and firms to loan money to subnational governments) and a negatively sloping demand curve for funds by the state–local governments (subnational governments are willing to borrow more when tax-exempt interest rates are lower). Given the initial market conditions, the interest rate on long-term tax-exempt bonds is i^0. If state–local governments desire to undertake additional borrowing for these private purposes, then the demand for borrowed funds by state–local governments increases to D_1. If there is no change in the underlying behavior of investors, then the interest rate rises to i_1. It should also be noted that if the tax-exempt debt substitutes for taxable bonds that would have been issued there is a corresponding decrease in funds by private borrowers that is expected to decrease interest rates on taxable bonds. The net effect is a narrowing of the differential in yields between taxable and tax-exempt bonds.[7]

---

[6]Clark (1986, 59).

[7]An exception to this analysis occurs if the supply of funds to the tax-exempt bond market is perfectly elastic, that is, a horizontal supply curve. Such a situation could occur if banks are the marginal investors and can simultaneously issue additional taxable debt and use the funds to buy additional tax-exempt debt. In that case, the differential between the taxable and tax-exempt interest rate will equal the corporate tax rate, a hypothesis not confirmed in practice.

/ *Limits on Private-Purpose Bonds.* Despite the effect that the growth of private-purpose bonds has had on tax-exempt bond interest rates, states and localities have shown no evidence of restricting their use of tax-exempt debt for new purposes. Rather, the federal government, reacting both to the perceived reductions in federal income tax revenue and to investment distortions caused by the borrowing subsidy, started in the late 1970s to restrict the uses of tax-exempt debt by subnational governments. The first restrictions applied to so-called small-issue industrial development bonds (IDBs), those sold to directly assist private firms mostly in manufacturing. In 1979 the limit for one issue (a bond sale by a jurisdiction for a firm) was raised from $5 to $10 million with a constraint that if the issue is more than $1 million, the total capital expenditure on the firm's facilities in that jurisdiction for the three years before and three years after the issue must be less than $10 million. In effect this restriction limited the use of IDBs for larger firms. Still, IDB use increased substantially in the early 1980s, as depicted in Figure 12.1.

The Deficit Reduction Act of 1984 further limited the use of tax-exempt private-purpose bonds by defining those bonds and by imposing an annual ceiling on the amount of those bonds for each state. The state limit was set equal to the larger of $150 per capita or $200 million per year, which applied to bonds for industrial development, student loans, and mortgage subsidies (bonds for private hospitals and educational institutions, multifamily residential rental housing, and such projects as airports and convention centers were not included). Although the limits took effect in 1984, bond issues that were approved (though not necessarily made) before June 19, 1984, were excluded so that the law did not apply retroactively. Thus, 1985 was the first year when the limits were fully effective.

The Tax Reform Act of 1986 substantially changed many aspects of the tax-exempt bond market, including imposition of tighter restrictions on the use of tax-exempt bonds for private purposes. First, the act specifies that unless 90 percent of the proceeds of a bond issue directly benefit a state or local government or its agency, the bonds will be considered private-purpose bonds (although bonds for private hospitals and educational institutions would generally continue to be excluded from this rule). Second, the annual issuing limits for these private-purpose bonds are reduced to the larger of $75 per capita or $250 million in 1987 and to $50 per capita or $150 million in 1988. Private-purpose bond issues in 1985 exceeded the less stringent 1987 limits in twenty-nine states.[8] Finally, the use of tax-exempt bonds for some types of projects—airports, convention centers, sports stadia—are prohibited or severely limited. The net effect of all these tax-law changes is expected to be a decrease in the amount of tax-exempt borrowing by state and local governments for these private purposes. And that reduction in the demand for borrowed funds by subnational governments will create market forces tending to reduce tax-exempt interest rates. Returning to Figure 12.2, as the demand for funds falls back from D_1, the interest rate on tax-exempt bonds can decline.

---

[8]Peers (1986).

/ *Effect of federal income tax changes*

Federal income tax changes also can have substantial effects on the supply of funds to the tax-exempt bond market, that is, on the behavior of buyers of bonds. First among these influences is changes in marginal tax rates. Recall that it is the investor's marginal tax rate compared to the percentage difference in yields on taxable and tax-exempt bonds that determines the attractiveness of tax-exempt bonds as an investment. For any given difference in yields therefore, a decrease in marginal tax rates will make tax-exempt bonds unattractive to some investors for whom they were previously a good deal. To retain or reattract those investors to tax-exempts requires relatively higher yields—that is, a smaller difference in yields between taxable bonds and tax-exempts. Returning again to Figure 12.2, a reduction in federal marginal income tax rates is expected to reduce the supply of funds for the tax-exempt market to S_1. This change alone is expected to cause an increase in interest rates for tax-exempts (and a narrowing of the differential).

Federal income tax–rate reductions have been the main tax story of the 1980s. The Tax Reduction Act of 1981 reduced federal marginal income tax rates across the board over a three-year period. Even more important, given the fact that tax-exempts are purchased by higher-income individuals, the maximum personal income tax rate was reduced from 70 to 50 percent.

A second category of tax changes influencing buyers of tax-exempt bonds concerns alternative tax-favored investments. The 1981 tax act expanded the opportunity for individual *tax-deferred* investment through Individual Retirement Accounts (IRAs), Keogh plans, and other tax-deferred savings options primarily intended for retirement saving. With respect to IRAs, individuals were allowed to invest up to $2000 annually without paying income tax on that amount or on the interest that accrued until the funds were subsequently withdrawn to be spent (presumably at retirement). Although the tax is simply deferred and not eliminated, such savings opportunities are expected to have reduced the relative attractiveness of tax-exempt bonds for some individual investors. To the extent which that occurred, the supply of funds to the tax-exempt market was further curtailed, creating additional pressure for an increase in tax-exempt interest rates.

The combined effect of the 1981 tax changes may go a long way therefore in explaining why the difference in yields on long-term taxable and tax-exempt bonds narrowed substantially in the 1980s. The expected effect of both the tax-rate reductions and the liberalized rules for individual tax-deferred saving is a decrease in the supply of funds to the tax-exempt bond market. On the other hand, the 1979 increase in the maximum size of IDBs and state–local expansion of borrowing for private purposes served to increase the demand for funds by the tax-exempt market. As shown in Figure 12.2, the combined effect of an increased demand and reduced supply of funds is an increase in the tax-exempt interest rate (or a narrowing of the differential between taxables and tax-exempts). It is important to note that this increase in the interest rate could be accomplished by either an increase, decrease, or no change in the total value of bonds issued. (In the figure, the quantity actually falls, but any change in quantity is possible depending on the relative size of changes in demand and supply).

Empirical support for the idea that changes in tax characteristics affect the interest rates on tax-exempt bonds is reported by James Poterba (1986), who statistically related the interest-rate differential between taxable and tax-exempt bonds to various tax-policy events from 1955–84. Poterba (p. 6) concluded that

> By examining data from four events that substantially altered tax rates—the 1964 Kennedy–Johnson tax cut, the Vietnam War tax surcharge, the 1969 Tax Reform Act, and the 1981 tax cut—this study provides new evidence that *both* personal and corporate tax changes affect the relative yields on taxable and tax-free bonds.

Poterba's results suggest that the 1981 tax changes explain one-quarter to one-half of the changes in interest-rate spread from 1980–82. And the evidence that personal tax rates matter suggests that corporations do not solely comprise the set of marginal investors.

The environment for tax-exempt bonds was changed substantially again by the Tax Reform Act of 1986, which involved several changes that make tax-exempt bonds less attractive investments. Most importantly, marginal income tax rates were further reduced—only two personal income tax–rate brackets of 15 and 28 percent remain (33 percent if the phaseout of the personal exemption for very high-income taxpayers is included), and the top corporate tax rate was reduced to 34 percent from the previous 46 percent. In addition, commercial banks are no longer allowed to deduct interest costs on deposits when the funds are used to purchase tax-exempt bonds, a change that may reduce banks' interest in buying tax-exempts. Both the individual and corporate income taxes include a minimum tax that is computed on a base that includes some types of tax-exempt income, especially interest earned on private-purpose tax-exempt bonds. This may induce investors to prefer public-purpose tax-exempt bonds and cause higher interest rates for revenue bonds.

Besides the more restrictive limits on private-purpose tax-exempt bonds, the 1986 Tax Reform Act also included several other important changes affecting the tax-exempt bond market. First, the expanded opportunity for tax-deferred saving through retirement accounts introduced in 1981 was cut back. Families with incomes above $50,000 with a member covered by a pension plan are no longer allowed a tax deduction for the amount of IRA saving, although the interest can still accrue on a tax-deferred basis. Other types of tax-deferred savings were also restricted. Second, the opportunity for individuals to shelter income with depreciation deductions or credits from passive investments (investments in businesses in which they do not work) was greatly cut back. These two changes together are expected to make tax-exempt bonds more attractive to some investors—in essence, tax-exempt bonds are one of the remaining allowed tax shelters.

The overall effect of the Tax Reform Act of 1986 on the market for tax-exempt bonds is uncertain. The demand for tax-exempt funds is expected to be reduced, which should allow for lower interest rates. But the overall effect on the supply of funds is unknown—with the lower tax rates, end of the bank deduction, and the minimum taxes implying a decrease in the supply of funds, but with the curtailment of tax shelters and tax-deferral opportunities suggesting an increase in the supply of funds. And even if the overall effect is a decrease in the supply of funds to the tax-exempt market and if the decrease in demand for funds is bigger, tax-exempt interest rates may decline (or, more correctly, the difference in taxable and tax-exempt yields may widen, so that the relative borrowing cost for state–local governments declines).

/ Taxable municipal bonds

Because of the problems created by the tax exemption of interest from state–local bonds, economists have long suggested that state–local governments issue taxable bonds with the federal government using a direct subsidy if it wished to reduce state–local borrowing costs. For instance, if a subnational government issued taxable bonds at a 10-percent rate when tax-exempt bonds had been yielding 7 percent, a federal subsidy equal to 30 percent of the state or local government's interest cost would reduce borrowing costs equally to the tax exemption. The prime advantage of this method is that it would cost the federal government $1 for each $1 saved by the subnational governments rather than more than $1, as is the case with the tax exemption. In other words, this direct payment would be a more efficient way for the federal government to subsidize state–local borrowing costs.

Historically, state–local governments have not been very interested in taxable debt with or without a direct federal subsidy. Subnational governments have been wary about substituting a subsidy payment for the tax exemption in part because a direct federal subsidy could be changed by the federal government in the future. If state–local governments no longer had a tax-exempt bond option, there is no guarantee that the Federal government would always offer a subsidy rate equal to that which was obtainable from the tax exemption. And state–local governments often continue to argue that the federal government has no constitutional authority to tax state–local bond interest.

The restrictions on the use of tax-exempt state and local government debt for private purposes included in the Tax Reform Act of 1986 may be sufficient incentive, however, to induce states and localities to begin using taxable debt to a greater degree than in the past. For example, Alexandra Peers (1986) reported that state–local governments sold about $3.1 billion of taxable bonds in the first ten months of 1986 compared to only $350 million worth in all of 1985. In this way, those governments were insulated from the tax-law changes, which were still uncertain at that time in 1986. Now that the new restrictions have taken effect, it is anticipated that many states and localities will use taxable debt at least for those private purposes no longer eligible for tax exempt financing. As Peers (1986) noted, "Taxable debt is more expensive for municipalities and other issuers, but it can be put to uses that Congress doesn't approve for tax-exempt bonds, such as aid to farmers, pollution control projects and loans to local businesses."

Some local governments have already been quite innovative in using taxable debt. As part of a plan to refinance some tax-exempt debt at lower interest rates in 1986, Los Angeles County issued both new tax-exempt and taxable bonds. The taxable bonds carried an interest rate about four percentage points higher than the new tax-exempt bonds, but the county was not bound by the IRS rules against arbitrage and thus could invest those funds at the highest interest rate they could find. It turned out that Los Angeles County was able to earn a higher return from investing those funds than the taxable bonds cost (Carlson 1986a).

Eugene Carlson also reported that Los Angeles County has explored selling taxable bonds in Japan, where the interest costs may be lower than in the United States. In that case, the County bonds to be sold in Japan would be denominated in yen, requiring that the interest payments also be specified in yen. With bonds denominated in a foreign currency, the borrower faces an additional problem— changes in the exchange rate. If a borrower sells yen-denominated bonds and the dollar's value subsequently declines against the yen, more dollars are required to make the interest payments that are equal to a certain amount of yen.[9] If state and local governments do expand their use of taxable debt, their financial experience will become similar to that of private firms who have always relied heavily on taxable bonds.

/ Summary

State–local governments borrow money for three primary purposes: to finance capital projects such as schools, roads, water and sewer systems, and power plants; to support and subsidize capital investment by private individuals and businesses; and to provide cash flow for short-term spending or for special projects. In 1985 state–local governments in aggregate had total outstanding debt of more than $659 billion, which amounts to about $2700 per person in the United States.

In 1985 state–local governments spent nearly $80 billion on capital goods, traditionally the major reason for borrowing. Capital purchases may be financed either by building up a reserve of funds from taxes over several years or by borrowing the funds to be repaid with interest from taxes in future years. In practice state–local governments finance about half of their capital expenditures with borrowed funds and the other portion with current funds.

State–local governments borrow money by selling bonds. The lender buys the bond from the borrower now and receives a promise from the borrower to pay a fixed amount of money (or interest rate) per year for a fixed period and to repay the original amount at a future date.

Long-term state–local government bonds are either GO, which pledge the full faith and credit of the issuing government as security, or revenue bonds, with only the revenues from a particular source pledged to repay the investors. In 1986 about 29 percent of state–local government debt was of the GO or full-faith and credit variety, whereas 68 percent was from revenue bonds of various types. This relative importance of revenue bonds has increased substantially since the 1960s.

The interest income received by investors in state–local government bonds is not taxed by the federal government, either by the individual or corporate income

---

[9]*The Wall Street Journal*, 28 October, 1986.

taxes. The primary economic effect of the exemption is to allow lower interest rates for state–local bonds than for similar taxable bonds.

The marginal income tax rate at which an investor gets the same return from both a taxable and nontaxable bond is equal to the percentage difference between the interest rates on the taxable and tax-exempt bonds. Consequently, individual investors in state–local bonds have come mostly from higher-income households because those investors have relatively high marginal federal income tax rates.

The tax exemption for interest on state–local government bonds is an inefficient way to subsidize subnational government borrowing costs because the Federal government loses more than $1 of tax revenue for each $1 of interest cost saved by state–local governments.

The most dramatic change in the state–local bond market over the past fifteen years has been the tremendous growth in private-purpose tax-exempt bonds, effectively allowing state–local governments to transfer their tax-exempt borrowing authority to private individuals and firms. This magnifies the economic problems arising from tax-exempt bonds and is expected to increase the interest rate on all long-term state–local tax exempt bonds.

Discussion Questions

1. Suppose that a city must substantially replace in the city system aging water pipes that is expected to cost $50 million. The new pipes are expected to last for about thirty years. The city has an annual budget of about $250 million and is trying to decide whether to finance the pipe replacement out of current revenues, through a one-year, temporary tax increase, or by borrowing the money by selling thirty-year bonds at an interest cost of 7 percent. Outline the advantages and disadvantages of each financing method. Which would you recommend? Might there be any reason to combine the methods?

2. "Exempting the interest on state–local government bonds from federal income taxation is the lowest cost way for the Federal government to subsidize state–local borrowing costs." Evaluate this statement.

3. Describe and explain the expected effect on state–local bond interest rates of each of the following federal changes:
   a. Lowering of the maximum federal personal income tax rate from 50 to 28 percent.
   b. A federal law restricting the use of IDBs by state–local governments.
   c. Elimination of IRAs, a form of tax-deferred personal savings.
   d. Increased use of tax-exempt bonds by cities to provide home mortgages.

4. State–local governments often use their borrowing authority to provide low-cost loans to the private sector through the sale of tax-exempt revenue bonds. What are the costs of this activity to a state that issues such bonds? To the nation? Do you believe that it would be in an individual state's interest to unilaterally cutback on the use of revenue bonds?

Selected Readings

Advisory Commission on Intergovernmental Relations. "Tax Exempt Bonds". In *Strengthening the Federal Revenue System: Implications for State and Local Taxing and Borrowing,* Report A–97. Washington, D.C.: Author, 1984, 115–32.

Kaufman, George C. and Philip Fischer. "Debt Management." In *Management Policies in Local Government Finance,* edited by J. Aronson and E. Schwartz, 287–317. Washington, D.C.: International City Management Association, 1987.

Poterba, James M. "Explaining the Yield Spread Between Taxable and Tax-Exempt Bonds: The Role of Expected Tax Policy. In *Studies in State and Local Public Finance,* edited by H. Rosen, 5–49. Chicago: University of Chicago Press, 1986.

13 / Revenue from Government Monopoly

> . . . Gambling is not a fiscal panacea, and we would be foolish,
> indeed, to expect it to provide much in the way of budgetary
> relief.[1]
>
> *Daniel B. Suits*

State–local governments may generate revenue by becoming the monopoly producer of a good or service and then charging prices for that good or service that are greater than costs. Three common examples of this behavior are considered in this chapter: operation of government-owned utilities, state government alcoholic beverage stores, and state lotteries. In all these cases, production by private firms is clearly an alternative and indeed is used in some jurisdictions. Therefore, one issue is why government as opposed to private production is desired, given that the government could also generate revenue from these activities by taxing the production or sale of the commodities by private producers. A separate but related issue is whether monopoly production is necessary, regardless of the choice between public and private production. As we will discover, if government production is selected to generate revenue, then the monopoly structure directly follows.

It is important to note that the issues considered in this chapter are different from the more general question of whether the characteristics of some goods and services lead the private market to an inefficient result, requiring government intervention (as discussed in Chapter 2). First, government can intervene in the market and even become a producer without taking a monopoly position—private schools typically coexist with public schools, for instance. Second, for the cases considered in this chapter, private production is not only feasible but is used in some states and localities. The issue therefore is really how government can best regulate and generate revenue from these certain economic activities.

/ Economics of Government Monopoly

/ Reasons for government monopoly

The existence of increasing returns to scale—that is, average cost decreasing as output rises—is the classic instance where monopoly production is most efficient. With those cost conditions, goods or services can obviously be produced at lower

---

[1]"Gambling Taxes, Regressivity, and Revenue Potential." *National Tax Journal* 30 (March 1977): 34.

unit cost by a single firm than by a set of smaller, competing firms. Because of the relatively large fixed-cost component involved in the production and distribution of such utility services as electricity, natural gas, water, and mass transit, increasing returns to scale may be expected. Thus, monopoly production may be desired; indeed, these industries are sometimes referred to as "natural monopolies." But the existence of increasing returns does not require government monopoly. Instead, government may grant monopoly rights to a private producer subject to government regulation or taxation. Among these utility services, government monopoly is most common for water–sewer and local mass transit, whereas private regulated monopoly is more common for electricity, natural gas, and intermetropolitan transit. Still, some electricity generation and distribution monopolies are owned and operated by state governments in seven states, by county governments in six states, and by city governments in forty-six states as well as being provided by special districts in some states.[2]

There is some evidence of economies of scale in the administration of lotteries as well. Larry DeBoer (1985) reports that the administrative costs of state lotteries per dollar of sales decline as sales increase. Indeed, DeBoer finds that this result apparently continues to be true even for those states with the largest lotteries, suggesting that production of lottery services is similar to that of the utilities. This tendency is even reflected in the aggregate data in Table 13.3, which show that administrative costs as a fraction of sales do tend to be lower in those states with a larger dollar volume of sales. But again, even with economies of scale, why should the monopoly be operated by government? Presumably, a state could grant the lottery monopoly to a private firm similar to a private utility and then regulate and tax that entity.

Using a monopoly for the distribution or sale of alcoholic beverages seems more problematic. Economies of scale are not expected to be important in this industry; indeed, (government) monopoly sale is used in only eighteen states. Rather, the argument usually made for government monopoly in providing lotteries and sale of alcoholic beverages concerns control of externalities associated with these types of consumption. Presumably, the idea is that because sales are made only through the government, regulations such as those regarding underage consumption can be enforced more easily.

/ Economic objectives

Whatever theoretical arguments might be offered to support government monopoly provision of these services, the political fact is that these monopolies often are effective ways for states and localities to generate revenue. Again, this is not to imply that government monopoly exists *only*, or *even* to produce revenue. Monopoly may serve to provide a service that would otherwise not exist, as in the case of

---

[2]These are monopolies only in their service areas. It is entirely possible to have private producers with exclusive rights to serve some areas of a state and government producers as the exclusive suppliers to other areas.

increasing returns, or monopoly provision may serve other objectives of government. Generating revenue is only one but the main focus of this chapter.

The economic options to a government monopoly in terms of pricing and sales, which determine revenue for the government, are no different than for private-sector monopolists. The standard economic analysis is shown in Figure 13.1. The monopolist faces a downward sloping demand for its product, which implies that additional sales can be achieved by reducing the price. Consequently, the **marginal revenue**—that is, the additional revenue from selling one more unit of the good or service—is always less than the price charged for that last unit. Selling more output entails reducing prices for all units of output sold. Graphically, this is reflected by the fact that the marginal revenue curve lies below the demand curve (for any given quantity, marginal revenue is less than the price determined from demand). In general, the equation for marginal revenue for any given output is

$$MR = P(1 - 1/E_d^P)$$

where P = price so that the output is demanded
E_d^P = the (absolute value) of the price elasticity of demand at that output

If the price elasticity of demand equals one, then marginal revenue equals zero—increases or decreases in price do not generate any additional revenue to the monopolist. An increase in price would cause fewer units to be sold, with both effects exactly offsetting. If demand is price-elastic (the price elasticity of demand is greater than one), then marginal revenue is positive but less than price. In that

FIGURE 13.1   Monopoly Pricing

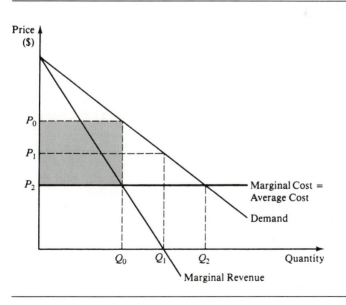

case, a decrease in price will cause an increase in sales revenue to the monopolist—the price decrease is more than offset by an increase in the number of units sold. Finally, if the price elasticity of demand is less than one (demand is price-inelastic), then marginal revenue is negative. Any increase in the number of units sold from lowering the price will not be sufficient to offset the lower price, so sales revenue would decline.[3]

To illustrate the monopolist's pricing options, the cost per unit of production is assumed constant in this case, so that marginal cost and average cost are equal. The price the monopolist should charge to get the highest possible profit is that which corresponds to the output where marginal cost and marginal revenue are equal, quantity Q_0 in Figure 13.1. Recall from microeconomics that as long as the extra revenue from selling one more unit (marginal revenue) is greater than the extra cost (marginal cost), more production will generate more profit. The maximum profit is attained when all those opportunities are taken, that is, when marginal revenue and marginal cost are equal. So a price of P_0 and the resulting quantity of Q_0 provide the highest possible profit to a monopolist with these demand and cost functions. That profit is the difference between sales revenue and cost, which is shown as the shaded area in the Figure 13.1

It is useful to note that maximizing profits by a monopolist is generally not the same as attempting to maximize the dollar volume of sales. Maximum sales revenue results when marginal revenue is zero, that is, at price P_1 and quantity Q_1 in Figure 13.1. Of course, the difference between the two is that sales revenue alone takes no account of production cost. Lowering price to increase quantity sold beyond Q_0 simply does not pay off in increased profits because the marginal revenue from those transactions is less than marginal cost. Finally, if this product were produced by a competitive industry or if the government provider was trying to maximize consumer surplus, the price would equal P_2, and the quantity sold would be Q_2. Competition serves to drive prices down to just cover costs (including the opportunity costs of the investors). At quantity Q_2, price equals marginal and average costs.

The economic opportunity for a monopolist should now be clear. By increasing prices above those that would be charged by a competitive industry, the monopolist sells fewer units of product but may earn returns above those available in other industries if prices are greater than average costs. There is a limit, however, to how high the price should be. If the monopolist sets the price too high, the amount sold may decline so drastically so as to miss some potential profit. The trick is to balance marginal revenue and marginal cost, which depends on how sensitive consumers are to price. For any given production cost, the price the monopolist should charge to maximize profits is higher, the less price elastic is demand.

The analysis is only slightly different if production exhibits increasing returns to scale, as shown in Figure 13.2. Because average cost decreases as quantity rises, marginal cost is always less than average cost. It follows that if price is set equal to marginal cost at any output, financial losses result because the price (revenue

---

[3] If you are confused by these uses of price elasticity, refer to the review in Chapter 14.

FIGURE 13.2 Monopoly Pricing with Increasing Returns to Scale

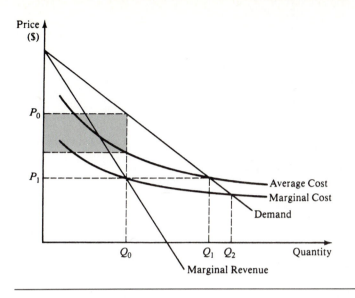

per unit) would be less than average cost (cost per unit). This is implicitly why these situations are called natural monopoly; competitive market prices always generate losses. If the price is set equal to average cost at price P_1 and quantity Q_1, profits are zero. Because all costs are covered, the monopolist could continue to operate at this position, but no revenue above costs would be generated either for the private or public (government) monopoly owners. As before, profit-maximizing output occurs when marginal revenue and marginal cost are equal, which occurs at price P_0 and quantity Q_0. Again, the profit earned by the monopolist is indicated by the shaded area of Figure 13.2

This analysis explains how a government monopoly can be used to generate revenue for the government for general purposes. As long as the government charges a price above average cost, economic profits result. In other words, the government monopoly would earn profits beyond the normal rate of return on its investment in the business. Those profits could be used as revenue for general purposes or some specific earmarked purpose.

Even if government uses a monopoly position to generate general revenue, it does not necessarily follow that the government will—or should—set prices so as to maximize profits, thus maximizing general revenue to the government. The monopoly profits are only one of many sources of revenue to state or local government and should be evaluated by the same economic criteria applied to all revenue sources—equity, efficiency, and administration cost. Just as state–local governments may choose to set less than revenue-maximizing tax rates on some activities because of equity or efficiency factors, so too might the government choose to set less than revenue-maximizing prices for goods produced by government monopoly. For instance, recall

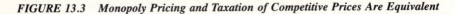

FIGURE 13.3   Monopoly Pricing and Taxation of Competitive Prices Are Equivalent

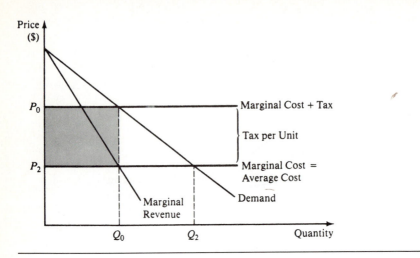

from Chapter 9 that many states exempt food sales from the sales tax in order to reduce regressivity of the state's tax structure; but a zero state tax rate on food is surely less than the revenue-maximizing rate. The appropriate price for goods produced by government monopoly must be evaluated in a similar manner, depending on whether the objective for having government monopoly is to generate revenue and the equity and efficiency implications of raising revenue in that way.[4]

/ Monopoly versus taxation

Any general government revenue generated through a government monopoly could also be obtained through taxation of private producers, regardless of whether the market is served by a monopoly or competitive firms. This point is illustrated by Figure 13.3, which compares a profit-maximizing government monopoly to a profit-maximizing private competitive industry that is taxed by the government. With the government monopoly, the profit-maximizing price of P_0 and quantity Q_0 generate economic profits or revenue to the government, represented by the shaded area. If this good or service was instead produced by a set of private competitive firms, the price would be P_2, equal to marginal cost. An excise tax levied on sales by those private firms would increase marginal cost; if the tax rate is t^*, the new marginal cost is $MC(1 + t^*)$. If t^* is chosen so that the new competitive market price is P_0, the quantity sold will equal Q_0, and the tax revenue generated will

---

[4]Jeff Biddle has pointed out to me that states can gain monopoly power through their sovereignty. For instance, states require all drivers to have licenses that are provided only by the state. Theoretically, states could charge relatively high fees for those licenses but do not.

again equal the shaded area. Obviously, both the monopoly profits and the excise tax revenue can be equal. If economic conditions call for monopoly production, whether by government or a private firm, taxes and government production can again be equivalent. If production is to be by a private monopoly, the government can just tax away all or part of the private firm's profits.[5]

From this viewpoint, it is clear that revenue generated from government monopoly prices above average cost is implicitly a tax. If the government monopoly sets prices above average cost, the same good or service could be provided by the government firm at lower prices. This is essentially equivalent to taxing the production or distribution of the service by a private firm. Although these two sources may be called and classified differently—one as revenue from government production and the other revenue from a tax—economically this is a distinction without a difference. In both cases, government has intervened in the economy to increase the price of a good or service in order to generate government revenue. There may be important political distinctions between a "tax" and "monopoly revenue," however. A monopoly may permit the government to gain revenue without anyone having to vote for higher taxes, the monopoly revenues may not be subject to constitutional or statutory revenue limitations, and monopoly revenue may be perceived as a type of user charge paid only by consumers of particular services.[6]

/ Operation of Government Monopoly

/ Utilities

Although government production of utility services is most common for water–sewer and urban mass transit, government monopolies also provide for the production and distribution of electricity and natural gas in a number of states, as noted previously. Municipalities are the most common form of government to own and operate these utilities, although special districts are also used in some states. Cities in forty-six different states operate electric utilities, and city-owned gas utilities operate in thirty-four states. In contrast there are county-owned electric utilities in six states and state-owned utilities in seven states. For natural gas, the comparable data are county-owned facilities in four states but no state-owned facilities. In those states where there are city-owned electric and gas utilities, they typically serve only a limited geographic area. For instance, in Ohio city electric utilities operate only in Cleveland, Columbus, and Hamilton; in Texas they operate in Austin, Brownsville, Bryan, Garland, Lubbock, and San Antonio. In most cases, city utilities can

---

[5]It is a standard microeconomic result that a proportional tax on true economic profits (excluding the normal return to capital) will have no effect on the monopolist's choice of price and output.

[6]However, it is not correct to state that the government monopoly is generating consumer surplus by producing a good or service that is valued by consumers. Such an argument presumes that this good or service would not be provided by private firms in the absence of the government production. But if the government monopoly was created by first prohibiting private production or sale, government has created the possibility of providing a demanded service to consumers. That demand can be satisfied either by allowing private firms to operate or by government production.

buy power from or sell power to the private electric firms as production and market conditions warrant. If a municipal utility does not own generating or production facilities, it would enter into a long-term contract with a private provider or another municipal utility. Thus, the city monopoly is more in distribution than production.

Some economic information about the operation of these government-owned utilities, at least in aggregate, is given in Table 13.1. Both net income (sales minus operating and debt expenses) and net income as a fraction of sales are shown for each of the four main types of utilities owned by states, counties, or cities. Several implications follow. First, net income of the transit utilities is negative in each instance, showing that the consumers of these services do not pay enough in prices to cover the costs of the service. Not only are transit monopolies not sources of other revenue for the operating governments, they in fact require subsidy from other sources, as discussed in more detail in Chapter 19. Second, city-owned electric, gas, and water utilities do provide positive net income—that is, revenue beyond operating costs and debt service. But the positive net income does not guarantee that the utility is generating economic profits because all the opportunity costs to the government of owning the utility are not measured. Specifically, the operating costs do not include any measure of depreciation. And because the government has a large investment in capital goods in the utility, part of the net income is simply the normal or average return on that investment, equivalent to what the city could have earned by investing those funds elsewhere.

The question of economic profits is better shown by the ratio of net income to sales, the ''profit'' rate on sales, if you will. For city utilities, the highest ratio of net income to sales is for water service, about 20 percent. This means that for every $1 of water sales, $.20 remain after operating costs and interest charges are paid, a substantially higher amount than for city electric and gas utilities. This suggests that the most likely city-owned utility to be generating economic profits or revenue for other purposes is the water company. Such a result would not be surprising economically because there are usually few private firms providing this service for

TABLE 13.1

Operation of Utilities Owned by Subnational Governments, 1986
(Net Income in Millions of Dollars)

	States		Counties		Cities	
Utility	Net Income[a]	Income/ Sales[b] (%)	Net Income	Income/ Sales (%)	Net Income	Income/ Sales (%)
Water	−3.0	−5.0	95.6	11.1	1850.0	20.1
Transit	−1037.7	−118.2	−305.6	−293.5	−1794.9	−113.8
Electric	359.1	18.2	−6.1	−10.1	1478.0	10.4
Nat. Gas	na	na	0.7	5.8	199.0	7.7

Sources: U.S. Department of Commerce, Bureau of the Census. *State Government Finances, County Government Finances,* and *City Government Finances,* 1985–86.

[a]Revenue minus expenditure excluding capital expenditure equals revenue minus operating expenses minus debt service, in millions of dollars.
[b]Net income as a percentage of revenue.

comparison. Thus, consumers may not be aware that a government water monopoly is earning economic profits through its pricing policies. On the other hand, if the city electric company attempted to generate large profits, it would be relatively easy to compare that firm's prices and rate of return to those of private utilities serving neighboring areas.

/ Alcoholic beverages

States follow one of two general methods for regulating the sale of alcoholic beverages. Under the so-called **control method** used by eighteen states, the state government has a monopoly on at least the wholesale distribution of distilled liquor. In some cases, the state wholesale monopoly also extends to beer and/or wine. Some states with a wholesale-distribution monopoly also impose one or more restrictions on retail sale, varying from retail sale of alcoholic beverages in state liquor stores (exclusively or in competition with private retailers) to establishment of minimum retail prices to limitations on the number and business hours of retail outlets to restrictions on advertising about the retail sale of alcoholic beverages. In the control states, the state government wholesale monopoly allows the state to set wholesale prices in order to generate revenue for the state government, although state taxes on the sale of alcoholic beverages may be levied also.

The alternative **open method** used by the other states involves wholesale and retail sale of alcoholic beverages by private firms, usually quite a number, so that the market is relatively competitive. In these states, the sellers are licensed by the state government (thus, the method is sometimes referred to as a **license system**), with the licensed private sellers also sometimes constrained by sales rules setting minimum prices or restricting business hours or advertising. These states also levy excise taxes on the sale of alcoholic beverages, typically collected at the wholesale level, with these taxes being the main source of revenue from alcohol in contrast to the control states. Examination of these state systems by Barbara Weinstein (1982) and others shows a great variety of regulation systems used by states of both general types.

These two systems of state involvement in the sale of alcoholic beverages clearly show that state taxation and regulation of private firms is an alternative to state monopoly production. The history of the two systems is that states adopted one or the other at the time of the repeal of prohibition in 1933, and no state has since switched from one general method to the other (although states have altered the rules and restrictions used within their system to bring about more or less economic competition).

Economic information about the operation of the state alcoholic beverage monopolies in seventeen states is reported in Table 13.2 (the Bureau of the Census does not report data for North Carolina, a control state, evidently because North Carolina contracts with a private firm to operate the state wholesale-distribution monopoly). The state monopolies in these seventeen states generated about $416 million of income above operating and debt expenses in 1986, which represents a return of about 15 percent of sales. In per-capita terms, state alcoholic beverage

TABLE 13.2

Operations of State Alcoholic Beverage Monopolies, 1986

State[a]	Sales (Millions of Dollars)	Net Income[b] (Millions of Dollars)	Net Income as Percentage of Sales	Per Capita Net Income ($)
Alabama	141.3	19.4	13.7	4.79
Idaho	37.1	8.3	22.4	8.28
Iowa	114.2	31.4	27.5	11.01
Maine	45.6	0.2	0.4	.17
Michigan	429.2	63.4	14.8	6.93
Mississippi	114.6	22.9	20.0	8.72
Montana	38.0	7.2	18.9	8.79
New Hampshire	164.0	32.1	19.6	31.26
Ohio	323.2	54.5	16.9	5.07
Oregon	139.2	47.8	34.3	17.72
Pennsylvania	605.3	40.4	6.7	3.40
Utah	68.7	18.3	26.6	10.99
Vermont	29.4	1.1	3.7	2.03
Virginia	255.7	37.8	14.8	6.53
Washington	213.1	18.6	8.7	4.17
W. Virginia	58.3	9.7	16.6	5.05
Wyoming	31.1	2.6	8.4	5.13
Total	2808.0	415.6	14.8	6.61

Source: U.S. Department of Commerce, Bureau of the Census. *State Government Finances, 1985–86.*

[a]North Carolina is also a controlled state, with the state government contracting with a private firm to operate the state wholesale distribution of liquor at prices set by the state. North Carolina is not included in the Census list of state liquor stores, however.

[b]Net income equals sales of state stores excluding taxes and discounts minus costs of goods sold minus operating expenses plus other income minus other expense.

monopoly net income equaled $6.61, on average. Remember, though, that depreciation, capital opportunity costs, and capital construction costs are not included.

There is wide variation among the monopoly states in the magnitude of per-capita net income generated. While most of these states fall in the $5 to $8 range, Maine ($.17) and Vermont ($2.03) generate substantially smaller amounts of net income per person while New Hampshire ($31.26), Oregon ($17.72), Iowa ($11.02), and Utah ($10.99) have substantially larger amounts of net income from alcoholic beverage sales than average. Such differences in per-capita net income from alcoholic beverages could arise from differences in the level of per-capita alcoholic beverage consumption by residents of these states, from differences in the costs of operating state liquor monopolies, from differences in the pricing policies, or from interstate transactions (residents of one state buying liquor from stores in a different, probably neighboring, state). Evidence and experience seem to suggest that the last of the three is the dominant explanation. The policy of the New Hampshire liquor monopoly to seek purchases from residents in the surrounding states is well known, as described in Application 13.1; indeed, New Hampshire generates the highest per-capita income from liquor sales while the neighboring states of Maine and Vermont have the lowest. Similarly, per-capita income from state liquor sales in

Oregon is high while per-capita net income from the state monopoly in Washington is lower than average (at $4.17).

/ *Control and Licensing Compared.*   The potential effects in a state from switching from one regulation system to another are uncertain because no states have changed systems. But research comparing the open and control states does suggest some potential economic differences between the two methods. First, state whole-sale-liquor monopolies not only control the sale of liquor in a state but also the purchase of liquor from the manufacturers. As the single buyer from the distillers for all the retail establishments in the state, the state monopoly may also have **monopsony power**. A monopsony, the parallel of monopoly but from the demand-ers' side of the market, is defined as a single buyer of a commodity. Just as monopolies can use their market power on the supply side to charge higher prices than would prevail in competition, so too monopsonies can use their market power on the demand side to pay lower prices for the product they are purchasing than they would in a competitive market. Weinstein (1982, 726) reports, for instance, that the Michigan Liquor Control Commission "is the world's largest single pur-chaser of distilled spirits. . . ." Although distillers are generally prohibited by state laws from explicit price discrimination among the states, some large state govern-ment buyers may still be able to pay lower prices in effect by altering their timing of purchases from and payments to the manufacturers. To the extent that the state monopoly distributors can exercise monopsony power over the distillers, the whole-sale cost of liquor would be lower in the control states.

Second, several different studies have shown that retail prices of liquor tend to be slightly lower in the control states compared to the open states, but not by any significant amount. Weinstein (1982) reports, for instance, that the retail price in 1980 for a fifth of Seagram's 7 averaged $6.12 in the eighteen control states and $6.37 in the other open states, while an average price for nine different brands was $7.36 in the control states and $7.57 in the others. There does appear to be more variation in prices, however, within open-system states than in the control states, which may reflect more direct restrictions on retail prices in the control states, more restrictions on advertising, or fewer retail outlets. Indeed, a third observation is that per-capita consumption of liquor tends to be greater in the open compared to the control states. Now the full price of consuming liquor to a consumer includes not only the retail price charged by the store or bar but also the time and out-of-pocket costs of going to the sales outlet. If there are few retail outlets or if they have limited hours, this second component of the cost of consuming liquor could be substantial. Even if retail prices are the same in two states, the full consumers' price will be higher in states that limit retail competition. If control states limit retail competition more than the open-system states, then the lower alcohol-consumption levels in the control states are consistent with economic expectations about demand. Of course, it is also pos-sible that a state's residents' attitude about alcohol simultaneously determines the level of consumption and the type of distribution system.

Data tabulated by the Distilled Spirits Council of the United States (DISCUS) for 1985 show that there are 1.25 retail outlets selling liquor (including both on-premise and off-premise consumption) per 1000 people in the open states, on

/ APPLICATION 13.1
New Hampshire Sells Liquor[7]

Although eighteen states generate revenue from the monopoly sale of liquor in their states, at least at the wholesale level, New Hampshire, a state with neither a personal income nor sales tax, relies on this revenue source more than any of the others. The state's liquor store sales of more than $164 million in 1986 accounted for more than 13 percent of the state government's general revenue, while even the net income from the stores amounted to about 2.6 percent of the state's general budget.

New Hampshire, a state with slightly more than 1 million residents, achieves such a high level of sales and net income by setting prices lower than in the surrounding states, aggressively advertising those bargains, and then locating state liquor outlets along major highways just over the state border. For instance, according to a survey conducted by DISCUS, the price for a 750-milliliter bottle of Seagram's 7 at the New Hampshire stores was $5.33 in 1984 compared to a price of $6.89 in Maine and $6.40 in Vermont (both monopoly states) and $7.32 in Massachusetts (an open state). According to *The Wall Street Journal,* about 80 percent of the advertising expenditures by the New Hampshire Liquor Commission go for ads in those other states. As a result, the state estimates that about 55 percent of its liquor sales are made to out-of-state residents, mostly from Connecticut, Maine, Massachusetts, New York, Rhode Island, and Vermont. In essence, the state government in New Hampshire is in the business of marketing and selling wine and liquor throughout the New England region.

Not surprisingly, this behavior by New Hampshire is not appreciated by the governments in the neighboring states, which receive less revenue from their own alcohol monopolies and taxes because residents of those states make purchases in New Hampshire. Indeed, most states have laws limiting the amount of wine and liquor individuals are allowed to transport from other states in an attempt to protect the state's monopoly and collect the state's taxes. Although those laws are difficult and expensive to enforce effectively, New Hampshire's neighboring states do sometimes identify their residents at New Hampshire stores and then stop them for inspection after they leave the state.

---

[7]See *The Wall Street Journal* (1985b).

average, compared to 1.05 outlets per 1000 population in the control states. This is equivalent to about 1 outlet for each 800 people in the open states and 1 outlet for 955 people in the control states. The difference between the two groups of states is most apparent for retail stores selling for off-premises consumption only: There is 1 store for every 3220 people in the open states, but only 1 store for every 8184 people in the control states (DISCUS, 1985).

The fourth observation from comparing control and open states is that per-capita state liquor revenue (from sales and taxes) tends to be greater in the monopoly-control states. That this results despite lower per-capita consumption suggests that

---

/ APPLICATION 13.1 Continued
New Hampshire Sells Liquor

This interstate purchase and transport of wine and liquor because of state government induced-price differentials is no different economically than interstate cigarette purchases to take advantage of state excise tax differences or interstate and mail-order purchases because of state sales tax differences, which were considered in Chapter 9. This emphasizes the point that state monopoly and state taxation can be equivalent ways of raising revenue through higher prices. The only possible political difference is that it is New Hampshire's policy to create and exploit liquor-price differences. Recall that the federal government intervened in the case of cigarettes, making interstate transmission a federal crime and assisting the states in enforcing their cigarette taxes. In the case of mail-order sales, however, the federal government has not acted to assist states in collecting use taxes nor has the federal government acted to assist states in enforcing liquor taxes.

Is there any economic reason why New Hampshire should be prohibited from undertaking this activity? Theoretically, a state could monopolize the sale of any good (say automobile tires) on grounds of ensuring public safety and use the advantages of government monopoly to undercut the prices of private sellers in other states. The result would be a redistribution of sales and resources from one state to another. Of course, if all states followed this strategy—for the same commodity or for different ones—there would not necessarily be any interstate redistribution. The exporting of state taxes in this way could lead to inefficient public-goods provision because the correct cost of financing government is not perceived by residents. Another potential problem is that the ability of a state to regulate sale and consumption of a commodity for safety or externality reasons is affected by other states' provision.[8] But restricting interstate competition reduces consumers' welfare with no corresponding increase in public welfare if such externality problems do not exist.

---

[8]*Liquor provides a clear example. One state may set a high legal drinking age for highway safety reasons and enforce it partly through state monopoly sale. If another nearby state makes liquor easily available to younger drivers, the state's ability to regulate public safety is diminished. Partly for this reason, the national government created incentives for all states to adopt a legal drinking age of twenty-one.*

the source is higher explicit taxes or higher implicit taxes through the state monopoly. But as previously explained, the revenue generated by the state monopoly includes both the normal return to investment and the true economic profits. Thus, the apparently higher state government revenue from the control system may partly be an illusion, given that the state also incurs a substantial capital and inventory cost from operating the state stores. Thus, after reviewing all the available information from several studies, Weinstein (1982, 738) could only conclude that "there is not enough evidence regarding the relative efficiency of public and private liquor distribution systems to shed much additional light on'' the economic advantages of one method over the other.

/ Gambling and lotteries

Although states have generated revenue from gambling activities for many years, mostly from taxes on betting at horse and dog races, states have increased their reliance on gambling revenue and changed the nature of state involvement substantially over the past twenty years with the growth of state lotteries. In 1986 twenty-two states and the District of Columbia operated lotteries, as shown in Table 13.3. The first state lottery was adopted by New Hampshire in 1963, and by 1975 thirteen states had begun lotteries. In the twenty-two states with lotteries operating through 1986, they generated an average of 1.9 percent of the states'

TABLE 13.3

Operation of State Lotteries, 1986

State	Sales[a] (Millions of Dollars)	Percentage of Sales to			Implicit Tax Rate[b]	Lottery Revenue as Percentage of State General Revenue
		Prizes	Administration	Revenue		
Arizona	113.6	48.5	14.3	37.2	59.1	0.9
California	1675.7	53.0	6.1	40.9	69.3	1.4
Colorado	102.4	60.2	14.3	25.5	34.2	0.5
Connecticut	406.6	53.6	5.7	40.7	68.7	2.6
Delaware	37.7	52.4	6.5	41.1	69.8	1.0
Illinois	1199.9	52.7	1.9	45.4	83.2	3.3
Iowa	77.2	50.9	15.0	34.1	51.7	0.6
Maine	36.2	55.5	6.7	37.9	60.9	0.7
Maryland	689.5	48.9	4.2	46.9	88.3	4.2
Massachusetts	910.9	59.1	5.9	35.0	53.8	2.6
Michigan	931.0	51.7	5.0	43.3	77.7	2.4
Missouri	196.5	49.0	10.3	40.7	68.6	1.3
New Hampshire	33.8	49.1	20.6	30.3	43.5	0.8
New Jersey	937.1	51.8	3.8	44.4	79.9	2.9
New York	1204.7	49.7	3.2	47.1	89.0	1.4
Ohio	888.3	52.2	5.0	42.9	75.0	2.4
Oregon	83.1	55.0	19.3	25.7	34.6	0.5
Pennsylvania	1234.2	53.6	2.7	43.7	57.1	3.0
Rhode Island	50.0	53.6	5.0	41.4	70.6	1.1
Vermont	11.8	52.8	24.7	22.5	29.0	0.3
Washington	181.5	49.4	14.8	35.8	55.8	0.8
W. Virginia	53.0	49.5	8.8	41.7	71.5	0.7
Total	11054.5	52.5	5.0	42.4	73.7	1.9

Source: U.S. Department of Commerce, Bureau of the Census. *State Government Finances, 1985–86.*

[a]Ticket sales excluding commissions paid to ticket sellers.
[b]Revenue as percentage of prizes plus administration costs.

general revenue. These state lotteries are operated as state government monopolies (with potential competing private lotteries made illegal by the states). This stands in contrast to the more traditional way states have generated revenue from gambling, that is, taxation of gambling provided by private firms on such activities as racing, casino games, and sporting events. Even though state governments have always closely regulated these private gambling activities, it was generally not until lotteries that the states directly operated, and indeed encouraged, the gambling activity.[9]

State lotteries are not homogeneous goods, with lottery bureaus or commissions typically operating several different types of games simultaneously. The most common types of games include instant lotteries, for which the player buys a ticket and scratches off a covering surface to reveal the prize, if any; number games or the daily lottery, for which the player chooses a three- or four-digit number and a fixed payoff is made daily on a randomly selected winning number; and lotto, involving parimutuel betting in which the player selects a six-digit number from a choice of forty to forty-nine possibilities. The winning number is selected randomly weekly or semiweekly, and if there is no winner in one period, the money pool rolls over into the next game period. According to John Mikesell and Kurt Zorn (1986), the numbers games currently provide the largest percentage of sales on average and in most states, with the lotto games second in significance, but growing in importance. States typically use a particular game only for a limited period and then switch to a "different" game, even though it may be of the same generic type. The state lottery bureaus or commissions usually contract with one of only a few private firms that design the different state games. And the state gambling industry even has its own trade magazine, *Public Gaming*.

Although the lottery games differ somewhat financially, an overall picture of the economics of state lottery operations is shown by the data in Table 13.3. For these twenty-two states, the lottery pays out $.52 in prizes for each $1 of sales, on average, with another $.05 going for administration costs. (This understates the size of operation costs because the Census reports lottery sales net of sales commissions. Lottery tickets are typically sold by private retailers who are allowed to retain a percentage, often 5 to 8 percent, as compensation. If commissions are included, then, operation costs are closer to $.10 per $1 of sales, with the shares for prizes and state revenue correspondingly lower.) Understanding this complication, the Census data show that about $.42 of every lottery-sale dollar ends up as revenue for the state government, on average.[10]

In the case of lotteries, state monopoly pricing of the service is economically equivalent to state taxation of the service. The implicit tax rate embodied in lottery prices is the ratio of the revenue share per $1 of sales to the sum of the prize and cost shares. For these twenty-two states, the average lottery tax rate is nearly 74

---

[9]One other example of a state-operated gambling monopoly is off-track betting.

[10]In contrast to the lottery, bettors at a thoroughbred race track get back $.80 to $.85 in winnings per $1 bet. The remainder goes to the track (usually private) and to state taxes. At a Las Vegas or Atlantic City casino, the "house cut" is perhaps only 5 to 10 percent.

percent. In other words, only $.57 of each sale dollar are used to operate the lottery and pay out prizes, but the price is $1, about 74 percent greater.[11]

There is substantial variation in revenue significance among these states with lotteries. Because the eight state lotteries with the largest sales—California, Pennsylvania, New York, Illinois, New Jersey, Michigan, Massachusetts, and Ohio— accounted for more than 81 percent of total lottery sales in 1986, the economic characteristics of their lotteries dominate the average. But as has been previously noted, the administrative cost share is substantially greater than average in several states with small or recently enacted lotteries. Largely as a result of these higher administration costs (and in some cases because of slightly higher than average shares for prizes), the implicit tax rates on lotteries also vary substantially among the states. The highest tax rates are the 89 percent in New York (only $.50 per $1 goes to prizes and $.03 to administration) and the 88 percent in Maryland ($.49 to prizes and $.04 to administration), while the lowest tax rates are 29 percent in Vermont ($.53 to prizes and $.25 to administration) and 34 percent in Colorado and Oregon ($.60 to prizes and $.14 to administration in Colorado and $.55 and $.19 in Oregon). Similarly, the lottery provides 3 percent or more of state governmental general revenue only in Maryland (4.2 percent), Illinois (3.3 percent), and Pennsylvania (3.6 percent), while the lottery provides 1 percent or less of state revenue in ten of these twenty-two states.

/ Economic Analysis.

What are the economic gains from lotteries and what are the economic reasons for government provision of lotteries? Although these two questions are often considered together, they are logically separate. The economic gain from the existence of lotteries is the same as the gain from the provision of any service, consumers get happiness or economic welfare from consuming the service, in this case either because of the potential for winning or because of the entertainment value or both. After all, why do consumers get pleasure from watching hockey games or going to the theater or anything else? Some do. And if individuals voluntarily choose to spend resources to consume those services, they must receive some pleasure. So the provision of lottery services does increase consumer welfare because consumers are willing to pay to have that service. But this is not a reason why the government must or should provide lotteries. They just as easily could be provided by private firms, as horse racing and casino gambling are, with government taxation if revenue collection from those activities is desired. Indeed, numbers games (the largest type of state lottery game) have in the past and continue, by all reports, to be provided by private firms as well as states. Of course, the states argue that these private firms are run by criminals, but that is partly circular logic given that it is the state that declared private numbers games illegal (although these firms may also be involved in other illegal activities).

Economic arguments for government as opposed to private lottery provision could be that the state revenue can be collected at lower administration cost with

---

[11]If a lottery ticket sold for $.57 and was taxed at a rate of 74 percent, the tax would be $.42, giving a total ticket cost of $.99.

government provision rather than taxation or that provision of lotteries either creates or generates opportunities for other effects that require regulation and that they can be more efficiently regulated by state provision. The case for the first argument seems weak; Mikesell and Zorn (1986) have noted that the administrative cost of broad-based state taxes is usually estimated to be less than 5 percent of tax revenue collected, which is less than half the corresponding cost ratio for lotteries. The common version of the second argument regarding lotteries is that gambling can be complementary with other types of criminal activity, as a source of cash, as a way of transfering funds gained illicitly to legal uses, or as a means of fraud or extortion. By having gambling provided by the government, these potential secondary activities can presumably be limited. This argument is problematic, at best, because it presumes that legal state-provided gambling reduces demand for illegal private gambling; but if state gambling and the attendant advertising increases the overall demand for gambling, the opposite is possible.

One economic fact about state government revenue generated by lotteries, whether from government production of lotteries or taxation of private lotteries, is that the revenue comes disproportionately from lower-income households. A number of studies based on data from different sources and states shows uniformly that low-income households spend a larger fraction of their income on lotteries than do high-income households, so that state lotteries are a regressive source of revenue. One analysis based on a nationwide survey of gambling behavior (Suits 1977) showed that in 1974 families with income less than $10,000 spent about .1 percent of income on lotteries while families with income above $30,000 spent only about .01 percent of income. As a result, about 25 percent of state lottery revenue came from families with incomes below $10,000, although those families represented only about 11 percent of total income in 1974. By some measures, lottery revenues appear to be twice as regressive as state sales taxes.

These results are supported by a more recent study. Charles Clotfelter and Phillip Cook (1987) collected data on lottery expenditures by players in California, Maryland, and Massachusetts for a variety of current games including instant games, numbers games, and lotto. The authors (1987, 544) conclude that "The evidence presented here demonstrates that the incidence of the implicit tax on lottery products in the 1980s is decidedly regressive, as it was in the 1970s." Clotfelter and Cook also report that purchase of lottery products tends to be concentrated in a relatively small sector of the population, even within income classes, and that lottery products tend to be consumed relatively more by blacks, males, and individuals with less education.

Increased state reliance on lotteries for revenue is equivalent, in an equity sense, to increased state taxation of any good that is consumed relatively more heavily by lower-income households. The curious difference about lotteries, of course, is that states promote and encourage consumption of this service so that additional revenue can be generated. Would the public be equally tolerant of state advertising to encourage cigarette smoking so that state tobacco taxes would generate more revenue? As Daniel Suits argued in 1975 regarding state-run gambling. "the government has become a pusher. And they're not pushing fire or police protection— only dreams" (*Business Week* 1975, 68).

/ APPLICATION 13.2
Beating the Odds: Betting Syndicates

In a common state lotto game, players pick a six-number sequence using the numbers between 1 and 40 once (for instance, 6–9–24–26–27–32) and buy a $1 ticket for that number. In such a game, there are about 3.5 million possibilities, so a player or group of players could guarantee winning by purchasing a ticket for each of the possible combinations costing about $3.5 million. Would this ever make sense? Interestingly, the answer may be yes, because lotto is a parimutuel game with the pot growing until there is a winner. If there was no winner in a state lotto game for several weeks, the prize pool might grow to $10 or $15 million. If someone or some group spent $3.5 million on all ticket combinations, a win is guaranteed. The possibility of winning less than $3.5 million arises only if there are a sufficient number of multiple winners. For instance, if the pot is $15 million, there would have to be more than four winners for the group betting all combinations to lose.

Gary Cohn (1986) recently described just such a bet on a series of jai alai games at a Miami, Florida, fronton. Four individuals spent $524,288 to bet every possible combination of winners in six jai alai games involving eight players each. Their guaranteed winning bets paid $752,778, so the four pocketed a total of more than $228,000 for a night's work and investment of over half a million dollars. The four were gambling because it was possible that another bettor could also have picked the winning combination, requiring that the winnings be split. But by betting all the combinations, the four had clearly substantially increased their odds of winning.

The same *Wall Street Journal* story reported that a number of private betting syndicates have been formed around the country to follow this betting strategy for horse and dog racing as well as jai alai. The syndicates typically bet exclusively on so-called exotic wagers, those requiring selection of a series of winners in order of finish, that often have very high payoff. For instance, in a "pick-six" bet, which is the one used by the jai alai syndicate noted above and is also widely used for racing, the object is to pick the winners of six consecutive events. Syndicate betting is even more attractive if the betting pool rolls over to the next game or day should there be no winner, like in lotto and many exotic race games. In that case, the players can know ahead of time the maximum amount to be won by covering the board.

There seems to be a mixed attitude toward betting syndicates by the firms selling gambling services. On the one hand, there is concern that smaller regular bettors may be discouraged by the large syndicates, which may be perceived as unfair competition. On the other hand, the large amounts of wagering required by syndicate bets may increase interest and excitement in the game and stimulate more small bets. It is interesting, however, that a number of state lotto games were changed in 1985 and 1986 to picking a series of six numbers from the set of 1 to 44 (rather than 40). That seemingly insignificant change increased the number of possible combinations from about 3.5 million to about 7 million, greatly reducing the opportunity for a winning syndicate bet on state lotto.

/ APPLICATION 13.3
METOO–1: Personalized License Plates

Although state–local governments are the exclusive providers of a number of services, they have generally used their monopoly power to set high prices to generate surplus revenue only in cases where the government can justify a strong regulatory role. One case is the sale of personalized license plates, an option sold by all states for an additional fee beyond that for regular automobile registration. A recent study by Neil Alper, Robert Archibald, and Eric Jensen (1987) shows that the initial fees vary from $10 to $100 with renewal charges from zero to $60, so that the average annual charge over a five-year period for personalized plates is about $22 (above that charged by the state for automobile registration generally). According to Alper and his colleagues, only about 2 percent of all automobile plates were personalized in 1984, although the share of personalized plates was substantially greater in three states—New Hampshire (10.1 percent), Connecticut (8.4 percent), and Virginia (7.4 percent) than in all the others (the next two highest are Rhode Island at 4.9 percent and Vermont at 4.2 percent).

Economic analysis can help explain just what factors influence people to buy personalized plates and thus why personalized-plate usage differs among different states' residents. The economic study by Alper and his colleagues and another by Jeff Biddle (1987) both show that use of personalized plates is negatively related to price and positively to income, as economists would tend to expect. Aggressive marketing also seems to increase demand. This research also shows that the demand for personalized plates is price elastic, at least in quite a number of states. When combined with information about the marginal cost of the plates (expected to be between $2 and $10, depending on whether it is an initial or renewal sale), the estimated demand curves suggest that many states are charging less than profit-maximizing prices for personalized plates. (Biddle suggests that the profit-maximizing price may average about $40 if fixed annual charges are used, although the figure will vary by state.)

But Biddle also reports that the demand for personalized plates differs in at least one important way from the standard economic concept of demand. He notes that there are typically substantial increases in the sale of personalized plates in the years immediately following the start of a program, which are not explained by changes in prices or income. Apparently, the purchase of personalized plates by some individuals causes an increase in demand by others. Biddle offers two possible explanations for this behavior: The use of the plates by some is a type of advertising, conveying information about the existence of the program to individuals who are not aware of it, or the use of personalized plates by some people makes them more attractive to others who also want to be part of the fad, what has come to be called the "bandwagon effect." Indeed, Biddle's research shows that sales of personalized plates in one year are positively related to sales in the prior year, after accounting for other demand factors. One important implication of Biddle's observation, regardless of which of the two possible explanations cause it, is that it may be attractive for states to maintain relatively low prices for personalized plates in the early years of the program if they wish to generate as much state revenue as possible. The initial lower prices are expected to attract consumers whose use of the plates would then attract even more consumers in subsequent years.

/ Summary

State–local governments may generate revenue by becoming the monopoly producer of a good or service and then charging prices that are greater than costs for that good or service. Three common examples of this behavior are operation of government-owned utilities, state government alcoholic beverage stores, and state lotteries.

The existence of increasing returns to scale—that is, average cost decreasing as output rises—is the classic instance where monopoly production is most efficient because goods or services can obviously be produced at lower unit cost by a single firm than by a set of smaller, competing firms. But the existence of increasing returns does not require government monopoly. Instead, government may grant monopoly rights to a private producer subject to government regulation or taxation.

The political fact is that monopoly often is an effective way for states and localities to generate revenue, although raising revenue is not the only reason for government monopoly. As long as the government charges a price above average cost, the economic profits beyond the normal rate of return on investment represent potential government revenue. The monopoly profits should be evaluated by the same economic criteria applied to all revenue sources—equity, efficiency, and administration cost.

Government revenue generated from government monopoly prices above average cost is implicitly a tax because the same good or service could be provided by the government at lower prices. Although these two sources may be classified differently—one as revenue from government production and the other revenue from a tax—and have different political implications, economically this is a distinction without a difference.

States follow one of two general methods for regulating the sale of alcoholic beverages. Under the so-called control method used by eighteen states, the state government has a monopoly on at least the wholesale distribution of distilled liquor. In some cases, the state monopoly also extends to beer and/or wine or to retail sales. The open method used by the other states involves wholesale and retail sale of alcoholic beverages by private firms, which are licensed by the state government and sometimes constrained by sales rules. These states levy excise taxes on the sale of alcoholic beverages, typically collected at the wholesale level.

In 1986, twenty-two states and the District of Columbia operated lotteries as state government monopolies (with potential competing private lotteries made illegal by the states). Those lotteries generated an average of 1.9 percent of the states' general revenue. Lotteries pay out, on average, $.52 in prizes for each $1 of sales, with another $.05 going for administration costs, so that about $.42 of every lottery-sale dollar ends up as revenue for the state government.

One economic fact about state government revenue generated by lotteries, whether from government production of lotteries or taxation of private lotteries, is that the revenue comes disproportionately from lower-income households. By some measures, lottery revenues appear to be twice as regressive as state sales taxes.

Discussion Questions

1. More than twenty-five states now operate or will soon introduce state lotteries. In most of those states, the lottery was approved by a majority vote of the residents in a statewide election. States operate lotteries as a revenue source to finance state services. It is also true that a number of studies show that the state revenue generated by lotteries comes disproportionately from lower-income people—it is a regressive revenue source. Do you think that concern about the incidence of lottery revenue is irrelevant because it was approved by the voters? If you were someone who never (or seldom) intends to buy lottery tickets (not because you are morally opposed to gambling but because you simply do not choose to gamble in this way), how would you have voted on the lottery? What would you consider in making that decision?

2. It is sometimes argued that state revenue generated by lotteries is different from tax revenue because people choose to buy lottery tickets. Compare three state-revenue sources—cigarette excise taxes, personal income taxes, and state lotteries—in terms of the usual economic criteria of economic efficiency, equity, and administrative cost. Do all three arise from voluntary acts of taxpayers and does that matter for the economic analysis?

3. States can generate revenue either by becoming the sole producer of a good or service and retaining the monopoly profits as revenue or by taxing goods or services provided by private competitive firms. One such case is the choice between a state monopoly for liquor sales and state taxation of private sellers. Another is the different treatment of lotteries and horse racing. Can you think of any reasons why states decided not to make lotteries legal and tax the private firms or why states generally decided against state-owned and -operated race tracks?

4. Suppose that the demand for personalized license plates and the marginal cost of production in a state is as shown in Figure 13.1 (pg. 261). If all the profits go to the government and the state wants to maximize revenue, what price should the state charge for the plates and how many will be sold? Suppose that the state actually sets a price 10 percent lower than is profit-maximizing. Show graphicly how much profits are reduced. Does the incorrect pricing cost the state very much? What might the state gain by setting the price a bit lower than the immediate profit-maximizing level?

Selected Readings

Clotfelter, Charles T. and Phillip J. Cook. "Implicit Taxation in Lottery Finance." *National Tax Journal* 40 (Dec. 1987): 533–46.

Suits, Daniel B. "Gambling Taxes: Regressivity and Revenue Potential." *National Tax Journal* 30 (March 1977): 19–35.

Weinstein, Barbara. "The Michigan Liquor Control Commission and the Taxation of Alcoholic Beverages." In *Michigan's Fiscal and Economic Structure,* edited by H. Brazer, 720–54. Ann Arbor: University of Michigan Press, 1982.

Provision of State and Local Goods and Services

Part 4 presents the economic theory and evidence about the demand for and supply of goods and services usually provided by state–local governments in the United States. The central issue is how the important economic factors that determine demand and supply—prices of those goods and services, incomes, prices of factors of production, and production technology—influence the amount of those goods and services desired and produced. Among the questions to be considered are these: How sensitive is consumption of, say education, to changes in the price of that service? Does desired consumption of state–local government services increase or decrease as consumers' incomes rise, and by how much? How important are labor costs for subnational governments, and how can those governments respond to wage increases?

The method of financing state–local government goods and services can obviously affect the amount of those goods and services produced, so the effects of user charges and intergovernmental grants are also considered in this section. The characteristics of services for which user-charge financing is most appropriate and the ways in which user-charge financing can improve the efficiency and fairness of subnational government provision are discussed. In addition, intergovernmental grants, which serve to affect the prices of goods or services and the resources available to a community, are evaluated as a method of influencing spending and taxing decisions of subnational governments. The potential purposes for grants are presented and matched to the expected effects of grants of different types.

Of course, no discussion about the supply and demand of any commodity can go forward without first specifying what the commodity is and how it is to be measured. This seemingly straightforward task, however, is fraught with difficulties for many of the services provided by government. What, for instance, is the appropriate measure of service provided by local schools or a city police department? While amounts of money spent on those functions—expenditures—are the most readily available and commonly used measure of the quantity of service, that measure is often not very informative. Additional expenditures that do not translate into more educated students or a safer environment may not represent more "service." Throughout this section of the book, and particularly in Chapters 14 and 15, the problems of appropriately measuring service and the limitations of using expenditures as that measure are emphasized.

14 / Demand for State and Local Goods and Services

Utility . . . maximization has already played a fundamental role in the development of such basic economic concepts as consumer demand functions. . . . It takes only a few extensions . . . to construct a theory of state and local behavior. . . .[1]

Edward M. Gramlich

The demand for the goods and services provided by state–local governments is the relationship between the amount of those goods and services desired by consumers and the tax prices, incomes, and social characteristics of those consumers. The task in this chapter is to consider how prices, income, and various characteristics influence demand for state and local goods. After reviewing the basics of price and income elasticity, the sources of data and statistical methods used by economists to measure demand are discussed. The results of those studies are then presented, showing, perhaps surprisingly, that the desired amount of state–local government goods generally *rises* with income.

/ Characterizing Demand

The standard measures of how price and income influence demand are the price and income elasticities of demand, the percentage change in quantity demanded that results from a given percentage change in those variables. Demand reflects how consumers behave, and the elasticities are simply measurements of that behavior. Although most readers of this book undoubtedly have been introduced to the concept of demand elasticities previously, they are reviewed next. (If you are comfortable with this information, skip the next two sections.)

/ Price elasticity

The price elasticity of demand is a measure of the responsiveness of consumption to changes in price, defined as the percentage change in quantity demanded from

---

[1]"Alternative Federal Policies for Stimulating State and Local Expenditures: A Comparison of Their Effects." *National Tax Journal* 21 (June 1968): 119.

TABLE 14.1

Price Elasticity Values and Terminology

Elasticity	Name	Effect
$E_D^p > 1$	Price elastic	$P \times Q$ falls as price increases
		$P \times Q$ rises as price decreases
$E_D^p < 1$	Price inelastic	$P \times Q$ rises as price increases
		$P \times Q$ falls as price decreases
$E_D^p = 1$	Unit elastic	$P \times Q$ constant as price increases
		and as price decreases
$E_D^p = 0$	Perfectly inelastic	Demand curve vertical
		Quantity constant
$E_D^p = \infty$	Perfectly elastic	Demand curve horizontal
		Price constant

a 1-percent change in price, assuming that *only* the price changes—incomes, tastes, and other characteristics are held constant. The definition is

$$\text{Price Elasticity of Demand} = \frac{\text{Percentage Change in Quantity}}{\text{Percentage Change in Price}}$$

If demand curves are negatively sloped, as is usually the case, then the price elasticity will be negative because price and quantity move in opposite directions; an increase in price will cause a decrease in quantity, and *vice versa*. For example, if the price elasticity of demand is -2.0 and price rises by 5 percent (the percentage change in price is $+5$), then the quantity demanded decreases by 10 percent (the percentage change in quantity is -10).[2]

In evaluating the price elasticity of demand, distinction is made as to whether the (absolute value of the) elasticity is greater or less than one, as outlined in Table 14.1. If the price elasticity is *greater than 1.0*, demand is said to be **price elastic,** and consumption is relatively responsive to changes in price. For example, a 1-percent decrease in price would lead to a more than 1-percent increase in consumption, perhaps 3 percent. If the price elasticity is *less than 1.0*, demand is said to be **price inelastic**. Consumption is not very responsive to changes in price because a 1-percent decrease in price would cause a less than 1-percent increase in quantity, perhaps only 0.5 percent. If the demand curve is vertical, implying that consumers demand the same quantity regardless of price, then the price elasticity of demand *equals 0.0* and demand is said to be **perfectly inelastic**. This represents a situation where consumers will pay any price for a product, a commodity that is truly priceless. At the other extreme, if the demand curve is horizontal, implying that any amount will be demanded at a given price but that none is demanded at a higher price, the price elasticity is *undefined* and demand is said to be **perfectly elastic**.

---

[2]For convenience, the price elasticity is often presented as the absolute value of the percentage change in quantity divided by the percentage change in price, so the number is positive.

FIGURE 14.1   Demand and Price Elasticity

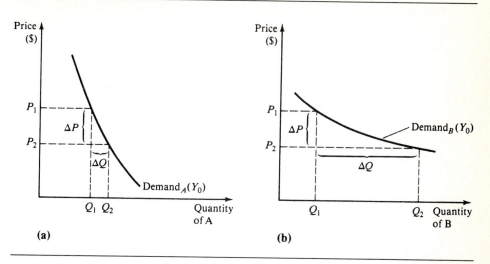

(a)

(b)

As shown in Table 14.1, whether demand is price elastic or inelastic has implications for what happens to total expenditure $(P \times Q)$ as price changes. If demand is price elastic, then an increase in price causes a relatively larger decrease in quantity purchased so that total expenditure on the product falls. In contrast, if demand is price inelastic, that same increase in price causes a relatively smaller decrease in quantity so that total expenditure rises. Whether total expenditure rises or falls from a given price change depends, then, on how much consumers react to the price change.

In some cases, the relative magnitude of the price elasticity in different markets is more important than the actual magnitude of those elasticities. For example, the price elasticity might be 0.5 in one market and 0.8 in another. While demand is price inelastic in both cases, it can be said to be relatively more inelastic in the first market or relatively more elastic in the second. This is represented in Figure 14.1, with demand curve A being more inelastic than demand curve B, because for the same decrease in price, quantity rises more in market B than in A. For the same reason it could be said that demand in B is relatively more elastic than demand in A.[3]

Remember that price elasticities are simply measurements of how consumers behave. If demand is price inelastic, consumers are unwilling or unable to alter their behavior much in response to price changes, perhaps because there are no good substitutes for a commodity or perhaps because consumers require some time to switch to substitute commodities or to change their behavior. Finally, the degree

---

[3]To compute an approximation of the price elasticity of demand, one can use the formula $E_D^p = [\Delta Q/(Q_1 + Q_2)]/[\Delta P/(P_1 + P_2)]$, where ΔQ equals $Q_1 - Q_2$ and ΔP equals $P_1 - P_2$.

to which consumers alter consumption in the face of price changes depends on how important the price change is to them and how much they value the product. A given price change has more impact the more one spends on a commodity and the lower one's income. Thus, demand may be more price-inelastic for higher-income consumers and for products that occupy a small fraction of consumers' budgets.

/ Income elasticity

The income elasticity of demand is a measure of the responsiveness of consumption to changes in income, defined as the percentage change in quantity demanded from a 1-percent change in income, assuming that *only* income changes. The definition is

$$Income\ Elasticity\ of\ Demand = \frac{Percentage\ Change\ in\ Quantity}{Percentage\ Change\ in\ Income}$$

For example, if the income elasticity of demand is 2.0 and income rises by 5 percent (the percentage change in income is $+5$), then the quantity demanded increases by 10 percent (the percentage change in quantity is $+10$).

Possible values for the income elasticity of demand and some effects of those values are shown in Table 14.2. If the income elasticity of demand is negative, then quantity demanded falls as income increases, and the good is said to be an inferior good. As consumers become richer, they consume less of this commodity and presumably substitute some others. In contrast, the income elasticity is positive if consumers demand more of a commodity as income increases. These commodities are said to be normal goods. If the income elasticity is *positive but less than 1.0,* reflecting a smaller percentage increase in consumption than income, demand is said to be **income inelastic**. Because an increase in income causes a relatively smaller increase in quantity, expenditure rises by a smaller percentage than income, and consumption of the commodity takes a smaller share of the consumer's income

TABLE 14.2

Income Elasticity Values and Terminology

Elasticity	Name	Effects
$E_D^Y < 0$	Inferior good	Q falls as income increases
		Q rises as income decreases
$E_D^Y = 0$	No income effect	Q constant as income changes
$0 < E_D^Y < 1$	Normal good	Q rises as income increases
	Income inelastic	Q falls as income decreases
		$(P \times Q)/Y$ falls as income increases
$E_D^Y = 1$	Normal good	Q rises as income increases
	Unit elastic	Q falls as income decreases
		$(P \times Q)/Y$ constant as income increases
$E_D^Y > 1$	Superior good	Q rises as income increases
	Income elastic	Q falls as income decreases
		$(P \times Q)/Y$ rises as income increases

FIGURE 14.2   Demand and Income Elasticity

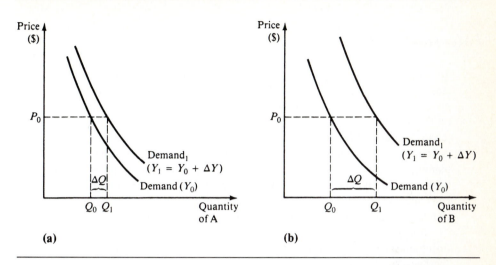

(a)

(b)

than before the income increase. If the income elasticity is *greater than 1.0*, then quantity rises by a larger percentage than income rises. In that case, the commodity is said to be superior and demand is **income elastic.**[4] Total expenditure on the product rises by a larger percentage than income so that consumption of this commodity takes a larger share of the consumer's income.

Two possibilities are shown in Figure 14.2. In both markets A and B demand rises as income increases; A and B are normal goods. In both the increase in income from Y_0 to Y_1 causes an increase in consumption from Q_0 to Q_1, assuming a constant price of P_0. But the increase in consumption is greater in market B than in market A. Although the income elasticity is positive in both markets, it is larger in B. Demand is relatively more income elastic in market B, or demand is more inelastic in market A. If the income elasticity for A is 0.5 while the income elasticity for B is 1.2, for instance, spending on A becomes a smaller fraction of this consumer's income whereas spending on B takes a larger share of the consumer's budget.[5]

Again, remember that the income elasticity is a measure of how consumers behave. It is usually argued that demand for basic commodities or necessities such as food will be income inelastic because all consumers choose a basic amount of those commodities regardless of income. Of course, even if the demand for food in aggregate is income inelastic, the demand for any one food, say caviar, can be income elastic. Commodities for which demand is income elastic are often referred

---

[4]Neither of the terms *inferior* or *superior* carry any pejorative connotations about quality. They merely describe consumer behavior.

[5]To compute the income elasticity of demand, one can use the following formula
$E_D^Y = [\Delta Q/(Q_0 + Q_1)] / [\Delta Y/(Y_0 + Y_1)]$, where $\Delta Q = Q_0 - Q_1$ and $\Delta Y = Y_0 - Y_1$.

to as luxuries simply because they tend to be consumed in relatively larger quantities by higher-income consumers.

/ Measuring Demand

To use demand in policy analysis, it is necessary to estimate the price and income elasticities of demand for the specific goods and services provided by state–local governments. Those computations can be made using statistical techniques if data on the amount of services consumed, prices, incomes, and other personal characteristics are available. Those data may come from census measurements of individual governments, such as the amount of government spending, personal income, population, and types of taxes for each state; they may come from the observed voting behavior in individual precincts; or they may be collected by surveying individual consumers. Variations in the selected amount of government service in the data can be related to the variations in price and income, providing estimates of the elasticities.

Suppose, for instance, that the actual selected amounts of expenditures for different categories of services are available for a group of subnational governments (perhaps for all states, cities with a population of more than 100,000, or all school districts in a given state). But many different individuals or voters comprised each of those jurisdictions. Each individual's demand for government services is influenced by that individual's budget. The budget is:

$$Y_i = C_i + t_i (T)$$

where Y_i = the income of person i

C_i = private consumption spending by person i

t_i = the state or local tax share of person i

T = total tax collected by person i's state or local government

The budget for the state or local government is:

$$E = T + G$$

where E = total spending by the state or local government

G = lump-sum grants received by the government

Solving for the jurisdiction's taxes T and substituting into the individual's budget yields:

$$Y_i = C_i + t_i (E) - t_i(G)$$

The tax share for person i depends on the jurisdiction's tax structure. If the only tax is a property tax, then recall from Chapter 8 that person i's tax share is:

$$t_i = \frac{V_i}{V} (1 - S)$$

where V_i = taxable property value of person i

V = total taxable property value in the jurisdiction

S = the portion of person i's tax which is offset by tax deductions and credits

If that tax share is substituted into the equation for the individual's budget, the result is

$$Y_i - C_i - \frac{V_i}{V}(1 - S)E + \frac{V_i}{V}(1 - S)G = 0$$

Given income, property values, and tax credits and deductions, the individual desires to consume whatever quantities of C_i and E give the highest happiness or utility from those that can be afforded. The demand for government spending E by this person depends, therefore, on this person's income, tax price (which is determined by the person's property value with a property tax), credits or deductions that reduce this person's tax cost, and the intergovernmental grants to the government.

For each jurisdiction, which individual's tax price and income should be used to characterize that jurisdiction in estimating the price and income elasticities? The answer depends on how the expenditure choice was made in that community. Given the choice or voting system, the issue is which voter in each jurisdiction is decisive in the choice; that is, which voter best "represents" that jurisdiction.

/ Median-voter models of demand

It was shown in Chapter 3 that if the choice of the amount of government expenditure is made through majority voting, the selected amount will be the median (middle) of the desired amounts of all the voters. Moreover, the demand by any other voter is irrelevant because only the median position can generate majority support. It is as if the median voter's demand *is* the demand of the entire community. If the individual who desires that median expenditure can be identified, then that individual's characteristics—tax price, income, social characteristics—can be used to "represent" the community in estimating the elasticities of demand. So the issue is finding a way to identify the median, or decisive, voter, assuming that the conditions required by the median-voter model apply in that community.

Will the median voter have median income? One solution to this issue has been offered by two economists, Theodore Bergstrom and Robert Goodman (1973), who show that under certain conditions the voter who has the median desired-expenditure amount in a community is the voter with median income. Because data for median income and other median social characteristics are generally available for individual subnational governments, this result allows easy computation of demand elasticities, assuming that those conditions exist.[6]

---

[6]Bergstrom and Goodman show that the following conditions are sufficient to ensure that the median voter will be the individual with median income:

1. Individuals' (or family) tax prices are constant elasticity functions of income ($h = wY^c$), where Y = income and w is a constant > 0.
2. All individuals (or families) have the same form of demand for public services, which depends only on that individual's tax price and income and which has constant price and income elasticities ($E = WY^ah^b$).
3. Given the elasticities a, b, and c, $(a + bc)$ must not equal zero.
4. All individuals vote in a majority vote based on their actual demand (no strategic voting).
5. The distribution of income for all population subgroups in any one community is proportional to the distribution of income for those subgroups in all other communities.

FIGURE 14.3   Desired Government Expenditure Is Determined by Demand and Tax Prices

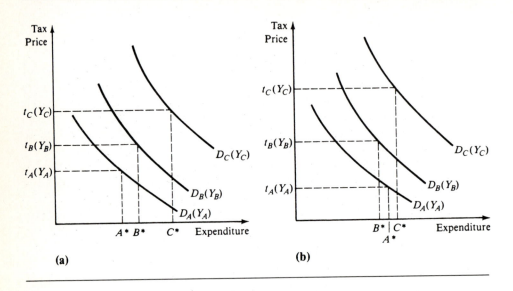

(a)   (b)

The intuition behind the Bergstrom–Goodman analysis can be demonstrated in Figures 14.3 and 14.4. Suppose, for example, that subnational goods are normal (demand rises with income, so the income elasticity is positive) and that tax prices also increase with income. This is different than traditional demand analysis in which different individuals face the same price. The price of a shirt at Your Favorite Store, say $20, is usually the same for both low-income and high-income customers. But because the prices for government goods are determined by the taxes one pays and because taxes are not the same for individuals with different incomes, tax prices for subnational government goods and services will also vary by income.[7] Given that $Y_c > Y_B > Y_A$, demand rises as income rises in both cases in Figure 14.3, and tax prices rise with income, although differently, in both cases. Given the demand and tax price for each individual in each case, the desired expenditure amounts for each individual are labeled A^*, B^*, and C^*.

In Figure 14.3a, although prices increase with income, demand increases more, so that desired expenditures rise as income rises. The lowest-income individual wants the least amount of government expenditure, the middle-income individual wants the middle amount of expenditure, and the highest-income individual wants the most expenditure. This is exactly one possibility envisioned by Bergstrom and Goodman. With a majority vote among the three, B^* would win, and individual B has middle or median income. As shown in Figure 14.4a, desired expenditure rises as income rises.

---

[7]This is true regardless of whether the jurisdiction uses an income tax. For instance, a tax on consumption or one on property value is also expected to vary with income because total consumption and the values of houses chosen by different consumers vary by income.

FIGURE 14.4   The Relationship Between Desired Expenditure and Income

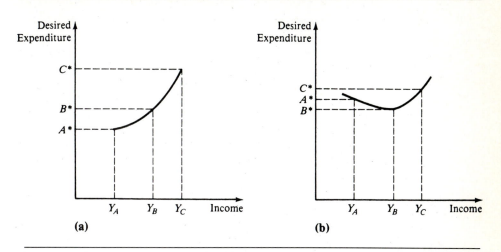

(a)   (b)

But this outcome is not guaranteed, as shown by the situation in Figures 14.3b and 14.4b. In that case, the individual with the median desired expenditure is A, the lowest-income individual. In a majority vote among the three desired amounts of expenditure, A^* is selected, so that the median voter is the low-income individual. In this case, Bergstrom and Goodman's conditions are not satisfied. As shown in Figure 14.4b, desired public expenditure is a U-shaped function of income—the high- and low-income voters join together to select a higher level of expenditure than desired by the middle-income voter.

The Bergstrom–Goodman result depends, then, on the relationship between desired expenditure and income. If desired expenditure rises with income as depicted in Figure 14.4a or if desired expenditure falls continuously with income, the median desired expenditure is held by the median-income voter. If desired expenditure initially falls with income and then rises with income (the U-shaped relationship) or if desired expenditure initially rises with income and then falls (an inverted U-shaped relationship), the median voter may not be the individual with median income.[8]

Therefore, if one is willing to assume that desired expenditure is either a continually increasing *or* decreasing function of income—that is, if one believes the Bergstrom–Goodman conditions are satisfied for the jurisdictions being considered—then the demand elasticities for the jurisdictions can be found by estimating demand for the median-income individuals. This assumption and method has, in fact, been the most used method during the past fifteen years for estimating the

---

[8]The result depends on the elasticities a, b, and c from footnote 6. Substituting the equation for tax price into that for demand gives $E = Ww^bY^{a + bc}$. If $(a + bc) > 0$, then E rises as income rises. If $(a + bc) < 0$, E falls with income.

price and income elasticities of demand for subnational government goods and services.

But is the method appropriate? Is the relationship between income and desired expenditure always a continuously increasing one? There is some evidence that the answer to both questions is no. Byron Brown and Daniel Saks (1983) examined the spending behavior of Michigan school districts for 1970–71, partly to test whether there was a continually increasing or U-shaped relationship between desired school spending and income. If the relationship is, in fact, U-shaped, then spending in a school district should depend on the variance, or "spread," of the income distribution as well as on median income because it is the voters at each end of the income distribution who form a coalition to select spending. Brown and Saks reported that school spending in these districts did depend on the variance of the income distribution in each district and concluded that "the correctly specified . . . curve . . . is U-shaped with a minimum at a family income of about $8300" (in 1970 dollars).[9]

Which view of the world is correct? At this point, no one can be completely sure; it remains an unresolved issue in state–local government finance. In fact, it may be possible for *both* views to be correct. For the U-shaped function in Figure 14.4b, desired expenditure decreases with income for incomes less than Y_B and increases with income for incomes above Y_B. Thus, in communities whose residents (mostly) have incomes either below or above Y_B, the relationship in that community is always rising or falling and the Bergstrom–Goodman conditions are satisfied. In communities where residents' income substantially fall across Y_B, the function is U-shaped. It may also be that the minimum occurs at a different income—that is, at a different Y_B—in different communities. Even in those cases, all is not lost because Brown and Saks and others have developed methods to estimate demand for government goods and services in those instances. The difference is that a single number cannot characterize the entire relationship between income and desired quantity in those cases; one must estimate how income and desired quantity are related at all income levels.

/ Demand and voter participation

Another potential difficulty in using voting models to analyze demand is that typically only a small fraction of eligible voters actually participates in state–local elections. This is particularly true of special fiscal elections or referenda such as those to select government spending or the property tax rate; voter turnout of only 10 to 20 percent is common in those cases. It is the characteristics of *voters* that determine local fiscal decisions, then, not the characteristics of the whole community. Moreover, the choice to vote is not random but influenced by the individual's stake in the outcome. Families with children in public schools, for instance, might be more likely to vote on the local school district budget than others, and they might also desire higher spending than other residents. Similarly, a larger percentage

[9]See Brown and Saks (1983, 37). Similar results for other cases have been reported by Jorge Martinez-Vazquez (1981) and John Beck (1984).

of higher- as compared to lower-income residents tends to vote in local elections; if desired spending increases with income, then the voter participation pattern leads to a higher level of government spending than desired by the entire community.

The importance of voter participation patterns for measuring demand is illustrated by a study of school-spending decisions in fifty-eight Long Island districts undertaken by Robert Inman (1978). On average about 20 percent of the voters in these districts participated in the school-budget election. By statistically analyzing the results of the elections and the characteristics of the communities and voters, Inman found that among districts with relatively few poor families increased voter participation led to lower selected spending levels. This is consistent with the idea that supporters of spending are most likely to vote, and if participation is unusually high it is because a group of ''no'' voters decided to vote. Consistent with the first result, Inman also reported that income apparently affects both the demand for service and the choice to vote. He concluded that ''the poor, who are low demanders but non-voters, appear to be underrepresented in the public choice process'' (p. 56).

/ Alternative models of demand

Of course, not all estimates of the demand for state and local government services have been based on the majority-voting/median-voter theory. One alternative theory assumes that spending decisions are made not by voting but by a government official acting on behalf of residents of a jurisdiction. This so-called dominant party model is intended to represent a situation where there is no credible political threat to the existing officials or party. The decision-making official is assumed to care about the per-capita (or average) taxes and expenditures in that community. In essence, studies of demand based on this theory statistically relate per-capita spending on government services to per-capita income of the residents, to some measure of per-capita tax burden (as a measure of price), and to other average characteristics of the community. (The study by Gramlich and Galper, 1983, reported on later in this chapter is an example of this type.)

Monopoly bureaucrat theories, previously discussed in Chapter 3, are also used as the foundation for studies of demand. In these theories, spending decisions are made by majority voting, but the bureaucrat controls the choices from which the voters may choose. As a result, some voter is decisive, but the selection will not be that voter's most preferred amount of spending but rather that voter's preferred amount *among those offered* by the bureaucrat. Using this theory, per-capita or median spending is related to per-capita or median-fiscal variables *plus* some political variables representing the limited choices voters face.

/ Evidence on Demand

Despite these alternative theories on which demand studies are based and very different data sources, two fundamental conclusions have consistently emerged: Consumption of most state–local government services is relatively insensitive to price, and demand for state–local services generally rises with income (holding price constant). The typical ranges for estimated income and price elasticities for various categories of state–local government services are listed in Table 14.3. For comparison, the demand elasticities for selected privately provided goods and services are also listed.

/ Price elasticity

When all services are aggregated, the price elasticity tends to fall in the range from − .25 to − .50, indicating very price inelastic demand. It further appears that among local government services demand for education is relatively more price inelastic than demand for other traditional local government services. The demand for state–local services has similar price elasticities to that for such goods as coffee, tobacco, and (at least in the short run) electricity and alcohol.

These services traditionally provided by state and local governments are viewed by consumers therefore as basic commodities, similar in character to basic food stuffs and maintenance services. Public safety and quality education are, after all, two of the most sought after characteristics of local communities. One should emphasize that it is the characteristics of these services that make demand price inelastic, not the fact that they tend to be provided by government. If these estimates are correct, demand for education would be very price inelastic even if education were entirely provided by private schools, just as the demand for coffee would still be price inelastic if suddenly all coffee sales were monopolized by governments.

The fact that demand for state–local government services tends to be price inelastic has many important policy implications. Because consumption is not very

TABLE 14.3

Representative Estimated Price and Income Elasticities

Good or Service	Price Elasticity	Income Elasticity
For Government Expenditures		
Total local	− .25 to − .50	.60 − .80
Education	− .15 to − .50	.40 − .65
Police and fire	− .20 to − .70	.50 − .70
Parks and recreation	− .20 to − .90	.90 − 1.30
Public works	− .40 to − .90	.40 − .80
For Selected Private Goods		
Coffee	− .25	0
Electricity (residential)	− .13 (−1.9LR)[a]	.20
Tobacco	− .51	.64
Alcohol	− .92 (−3.6LR)[a]	1.54
Gambling (horse races)	− 1.59	.86
Restaurant meals	− 1.63	1.40
Automobiles	− 1.35	2.46

Sources: For government expenditures: Inman (1979a, Table 9.1, 286–88). For private goods: Kohler (1982, Tables 4.2–4.4, 101–02); Suits (1979, Table II, 160).

[a]Long run

sensitive to price, attempts to alter the amount or type of government expenditure by reducing prices—with intergovernmental grants, for example—will be only moderately successful. And if the prices of state–local services rise, perhaps because of increases in the costs of providing them, consumers are not expected to reduce consumption much, requiring that increasing funds be allocated to those types of consumption. These implications are examined in Chapters 15 and 17.

/ Income elasticity

State–local government services are normal goods. That is, increases in income (holding prices constant) tend to cause demand to increase, although for most of these services, demand is income inelastic—demand changes less than proportionally to the income change. Demand appears to be income elastic for parks and recreation services—that is, demand increases more than proportionally to an increase in income. That parks and recreation services are superior goods seems reasonable, given the evidence that the demand for vacations and restaurant meals is also income elastic. These commodities are demanded in greater proportion by higher-income consumers.

Although the income elasticity of demand is a measure of the percentage change in government expenditure due to a percentage change in income, it is sometimes more useful to translate this into a measure of the dollar change in expenditure due to a $1 change in income. Given the actual magnitude of expenditures and incomes, the range of elasticities reported in Table 14.3 are consistent with between a $.01 to $.10 increase in state–local government expenditures for each $1 increase in consumers' incomes.[10]

As with the price elasticity, these income elasticity estimates have important implications for the expected effects of intergovernmental grants on subnational government expenditures (see Chapter 17) and for the prospects of controlling the growth of the state–local government sector through the use of tax and expenditure limits (see Chapter 20).

/ Two classic studies

Although it is intended that the general discussion in this chapter explain how economists go about measuring the demand for state–local government services, a better understanding may be obtained by examining exactly how specific analysts have proceeded. What follows is a review of two, now classic, studies of the expenditure behavior of state and local governments, one based on a majority-voting model of choice and the other on a theory of decision making by government officials.

---

[10]The income elasticity can be written as $E_Y^b = (\Delta E/\Delta Y)(Y/E)$, where E = expenditure, Y = income, and Δ means "change in." Given values for the elasticity, expenditure, and income, $\Delta E/\Delta Y$ can be computed.

/ Bergstrom–Goodman Study.   Bergstrom and Goodman (1973) examined the expenditure behavior of 826 municipalities located in ten states based on 1962 data for three different expenditure categories: total expenditures (excluding education and welfare because not all municipalities in the sample had responsibility for those functions), police expenditures, and parks and recreation expenditures. The analysis was based on the standard median-voter theory, so they assumed that selected expenditures were the desired expenditures of the median-income consumer in each municipality.

Accordingly, actual expenditures for each category in each municipality were statistically related to median income in that municipality, the share of property tax paid by the median voter, the population of the municipality, and a set of social characteristic variables designed to capture differences in costs (density, percentage of population change 1950–60, employment–resident ratio) or differences in demand not related to income (percentage of population sixty-five years and over, percentage of nonwhites, percentage of homes that are owner-occupied). Separate estimates were made for each state and with the full sample combined. Their results for that combined sample are reprinted in Table 14.4.

Before proceeding to those results, some discussion of the statistical concepts underlying these types of studies might be helpful in interpreting the results. Statistical analysis of data to clarify economic issues is called **econometrics**. The first step in doing econometrics is to postulate some relationship between the variables of interest. In this case, that relationship arises from the median-voter model. Government spending is influenced by median income, the tax price for the median voter, production costs, and the median voter's tastes. A simple mathematical statement of the relationship might be

$$E = a + b \cdot Y + c \cdot P + d \cdot N + e \cdot D + u$$

where E = spending
 Y = income
 P = tax price
 N = population
 D = population density
 u = random error, representing other potential effects on spending not captured by the included variables

Parameters a, b, c, d, e, which are to be estimated, represent the effect of a change in each of the variables on government spending. For instance, if $b = .10$, then spending increases by $.10 for each $1 increase in median income. Once data are available, various statistical techniques can be used to make these estimates. The most common technique used by economists is multiple regression analysis, which finds the set of estimates for all parameters that ''best'' characterizes the observed relationship among the variables.[11]

---

[11]For more information about econometrics, see Harry Kelejian and Wallace Oates (1981).

TABLE 14.4

Bergstrom–Goodman Results; Determinants of Municipal Expenditures, 1962, All Observations Pooled[a]

	General Expenditures	Police Expenditures	Parks and Recreation
Income elasticity ϵ	0.64[b]	0.71[b]	1.32[b]
	0.07	*0.13*	*0.22*
Tax share elasticity δ	−0.23[b]	−0.25[b]	−0.19[b]
	0.03	*0.05*	*0.08*
Population elasticity α	0.84[b]	0.80[b]	1.17[b]
	0.03	*0.06*	*0.11*
Crowding parameter $\gamma = [\alpha/(1 + \delta)]$	1.09[c]	1.07	1.44[c]
Percent population change (1950–60)	−0.04[b]	−0.04[b]	−0.08[b]
	0.01	*0.01*	*0.02*
Employment residential ratio	0.12[b]	0.01	0.24[b]
	0.02	*0.04*	*0.06*
Percent owner occupied	−0.77[b]	−1.12[b]	−0.78
	0.13	*0.25*	*0.42*
Percent nonwhites	0.84[b]	0.90[b]	−0.20
	0.19	*0.36*	*0.60*
Density	−0.07[b]	0.01	−0.02
	0.02	*0.04*	*0.06*
Percent population 65 +	1.75[b]	1.27	4.94[b]
	0.45	*0.85*	*1.43*
Percent living in same house (1955–60)	−0.65[b]	−0.77[b]	−1.99[b]
	0.17	*0.32*	*0.53*

Source: Bergstrom and Goodman (1973, Table 4, 290), reprinted with permission.

[a]Values in italics are the standard errors of the coefficients.
[b]Indicates a coefficient that is significant at the 95 percent confidence level.
[c]Indicates a value of γ that is significantly different from 1 at the 95 percent level.

Consistent with other studies, Bergstrom and Goodman reported that price elasticities (with price measured by tax shares) are negative and inelastic. Consumption of these services in these cities in 1962 was not very sensitive to changes in the share of taxes paid by middle-income consumers. The income elasticities are all positive, with the demand for parks and recreation being income elastic ($E_D^Y = 1.32$) while the demand for all other services in aggregate is income inelastic ($E_D^Y = .64$). Moreover, by the usual statistical tests, they could conclude that these estimates were significantly different from zero.

Among the other taste/cost variables, population is positively related to expenditures, but the percentage change in population over the previous decade is negatively related, suggesting perhaps that expenditures respond to a growing population only gradually. A larger percentage of the population over the age of sixty-five seems related to higher expenditures, suggesting that older consumers demand more services than younger consumers with the same income and tax share. In contrast, a larger percentage of consumers who live in their own house seems related to lower expenditures, perhaps because owner–occupiers are more sensitive to property taxes than are renters.

/ Gramlich–Galper Study.

Edward Gramlich and Harvey Galper (1973) actually undertook two analyses based on a budgetary model of behavior. A subnational government official had four objectives: to increase expenditures for current services, to increase private disposable incomes, to increase the stock of government capital, and to increase the amount of financial assets (or saving) held by the government. Obviously, all these objectives are competing, and the official is constrained in achieving them by the available resources, including the resources provided by intergovernmental grants.

Gramlich and Galper used this basic model to analyze both the aggregate annual expenditures for all state–local governments from 1954–72 and the expenditures of ten large cities over the period 1962–70. In the case of the cities, expenditures for education, public safety, social services, urban support, and general government were separated. Gramlich and Galper's analysis differed from Bergstrom and Goodman's, then, both in theory and data. Gramlich and Galper did not have a voting model but assumed that all decisions were made by some dictator, and Gramlich and Galper used data over a time period—what is called a time-series—rather than comparing different jurisdictions at a definite time—what is called a cross-section.

Although the primary focus of Gramlich and Galper's results was on the effects of different types of intergovernmental grants (see Chapter 17), the analysis also provided measures of the price and income elasticities. From the time-series analysis of total state–local expenditures, the price elasticity is $-.04$, and the income elasticity is 1.08. Here it appears that state–local expenditures *together* increase slightly more than proportionately with income—that state–local expenditures are superior. Of course, as previously noted, the state–local sector grew substantially during the period used for this study, 1954–72. Even so, this elasticity implies that state–local expenditures grow only by $.095 for each $1 increase in income. The results from the analysis of city expenditures are more similar to those of Bergstrom and Goodman. Here the price elasticities vary from $-.71$ to $-.92$, and the income elasticity is .86; demand is price and income inelastic.

/ Subsequent research

During the past fifteen years, there have been many such analyses of the expenditure behavior of state–local governments, a good number using the same theoretical approach as the two studies reviewed. But research involving both alternative theories and improved statistical methods gives the same fundamental results: The demand for state–local government services is, in most cases, price and income inelastic.

/ APPLICATION 14.1
Business Demand for Government Service

Although individuals ultimately benefit from and pay for state–local government services, the business sector often plays a role in the public-choice process about taxes and government spending. Taxes are a cost of doing business that may arise from the sale of a product (sales or excise tax) or from the use of a productive input such as labor (unemployment insurance tax) or capital (property taxes). On the other hand, many of the services provided by state–local government become inputs into the production of goods and services by private firms. For instance, businesses make use of highways and other transportation facilities, are protected from loss by government public-safety services, employ workers who have been educated or trained in public schools and colleges, and use public sanitation and utility services. To the extent that these services or facilities are provided by government, private firms do not have to provide them separately; in that way, government services reduce private business costs.

Voting models really do not characterize how business influences these fiscal decisions. *Individuals* vote in elections, not businesses. But businesses try to influence the outcomes of specific elections as well as the decisions of elected representatives by influencing public opinion and by lobbying public officials. As with individuals, businesses are expected to work to achieve fiscal-policy objectives that are in their self-interest.

Certainly, businesses can be expected to and often do argue for lower business taxes, but businesses can also be concerned about the level and quality of government services. *The Wall Street Journal* (1987b) recently reported about a survey of the factors chief executives said are "absolutely essential" in considering new office locations. The most often cited factor was "good public schools" (by 23 percent of the CEOs) followed by "a low crime rate" and "an efficient highway system" (both by 20 percent). "Reasonable state and local taxes" was also mentioned (by 17 percent).

The common perception that business groups always oppose taxes may be wrong, therefore. Interest in good state and local services can lead business groups to support higher taxes sometimes. David Shribman (1986) reported that twenty local chambers of commerce in Colorado had launched a campaign to *raise* state taxes to maintain and improve public facilities and services. Shribman quoted the chambers' position as the following: "Without additional revenues, Colorado will be left little choice but to woefully underfund areas such as higher education, elementary and secondary education, our state highways, water resources and vital capital construction and maintenance projects." The chambers took this position because an increase in the number of state residents had reduced the quality of services and because these services were seen as important for attracting and retaining businesses.

Indeed, Colorado did increase state taxes in 1986 and 1987. The gasoline tax, diesel-fuel tax, cigarette tax, and corporate income tax were all increased in 1986, and personal income taxes effectively increased in 1986 and 1987. In this case, business was an explicit and successful demander of more or better quality government service.

/ Summary

The price elasticity of demand is a measure of the responsiveness of consumption to changes in price.

$$Price\ Elasticity\ of\ Demand = \frac{Percentage\ Change\ in\ Quantity}{Percentage\ Change\ in\ Price}$$

If the absolute value of the price elasticity is greater than 1.0, demand is said to be price elastic, and consumption is very responsive to changes in price. If the price elasticity is less than 1.0, demand is said to be price inelastic, and consumption is not very responsive to changes in price.

The income elasticity of demand is a measure of the responsiveness of consumption to changes in income.

$$Income\ Elasticity\ of\ Demand = \frac{Percentage\ Change\ in\ Quantity}{Percentage\ Change\ in\ Income}$$

If the income elasticity of demand is negative, then quantity demanded falls as income increases, and the good is said to be inferior. If the income elasticity is positive but less than 1.0, demand is said to be income inelastic. If the income elasticity is greater than 1.0, the commodity is said to be superior and demand is income elastic.

Despite the alternative theories on which demand studies are based and very different data sources, two fundamental conclusions have consistently emerged: Consumption of most state–local government services is relatively insensitive to price, and demand for state–local services generally rises with income (holding price constant). When all services are aggregated, the price elasticity tends to fall in the range from $-.25$ to $-.50$, indicating very price inelastic demand.

Most state–local government services are normal goods. Increases in income (holding prices constant) tend to cause demand to increase, although for most services demand changes less than proportionally to the income change. The range of elasticities reported suggests between a $.01 to $.10 increase in state and local government expenditures for each $1 increase in consumers' incomes.

There is some evidence that the relationship between income and desired expenditure is not always a continuously increasing one: Brown and Saks (1983) reported that school spending in Michigan districts depended on the variance of the income distribution in each district in addition to median income and concluded that "the correctly specified . . . curve . . . is U-shaped with a minimum at a family income of about $8300" (in 1970 dollars).

Discussion Questions

1. Suppose you believe that the income elasticity of demand for state government services (measured by expenditures) is on the order of 0.80. If state per-capita income is expected to increase by 20 percent over the next three years, what is

the expected effect on desired state spending? If the increase in income were the only economic change expected in these years (no inflation, population growth, or change in consumer preferences), what might be expected to happen to state spending as a percentage of state personal income?

2. Suppose that in one community there are three groups of voters that differ by income, with P denoting the lowest, M the middle, and R the highest. The demand for local government services by these groups is shown below. Under what conditions would the desired amount of service be the same for all three groups? Is it clear whether the tax structure that generates such a result would be regressive, proportional, or progressive? Is it possible under other conditions that the low-income group would desire the most service, followed by the M group and then the R group?

3. There is some evidence that the relationship between desired local government services (spending) and income is U-shaped—that is, lower- and higher-income voters may form a coalition to support higher amounts of local spending than desired by middle-income voters. Using two services for illustration, police protection and education, discuss why this might be the case. Remember that, in general, demand depends on price, income, and tastes.

Selected Reading

Inman, Robert P. "The Fiscal Performance of Local Governments: An Interpretative Review." In *Current Issues in Urban Economics,* edited by P. Mieszkowski and M. Straszheim, 270–321, Baltimore: Johns Hopkins University Press, 1979.

15 / Costs and Supply of State and Local Goods and Services

> . . . Rising unit costs have been a major (probably the single most important) source of recent increases in local public budgets.[1]
>
> *David Bradford, R. A. Malt, and Wallace Oates*

In economics, analysis of supply is essentially an analysis of production cost. The cost of producing alternative amounts of output, combined with the structure of the market, determines how producers behave. Similarly, the costs of producing services provided by state–local governments and the factors that alter those costs are crucial for understanding and comparing the fiscal behavior of subnational governments.

Before discussing production technology and cost, it is necessary to define and be able to measure the good or service produced. This is not straightforward for many services, including those provided by state–local governments. Although education is the dominant subnational government service in the United States, is education output to be measured by dollars spent per pupil, by the number of graduating students, or by student test scores? The action required to increase each of these alternative measures of education may be different so that the cost of producing "more" of each may vary and even depend on different factors. The first task in this chapter, then, is to consider alternative ways to characterize the output of state and local government services so that "cost" may be properly defined and the factors that affect cost (and thus supply) investigated.

/ Measurement and Production of Government Services

/ Production functions[2]

To produce services, state–local governments purchase inputs such as labor services, capital goods, materials, and supplies and combine then in some way to provide public facilities, or what can be called **"directly produced" output** such as police patrols or classrooms with teachers and books. The ways in which inputs can be combined to produce this type of output are together referred to as **technology** and

---

[1]"The Rising Cost of Local Public Services: Some Evidence and Reflections." *National Tax Journal* 22 (June 1969): p. 201.

[2]The discussion in this section follows that in David Bradford, R. A. Malt, and Wallace Oates (1969).

can be represented mathematically by a **production function.** For instance, the directly produced education output is a function of the number of teachers and administrators, the number of buildings and classrooms, and the number of books, desks, and other equipment provided. Mathematically, one can write

$$Q = q(L, K, X)$$

where Q = directly produced output
L = labor input
K = capital input
X = the set of other inputs such as materials and supplies

The $q(\ )$ function represents production technology. It is important to understand that any given amount of directly produced output can usually be produced by different combinations of inputs—that is, there is usually more than one way to combine inputs to produce a service. In other words, the production function $q(\ )$ does not specify a unique input combination for each output but rather the possible input combinations to produce each level of output.

The **cost** of producing any amount of directly produced output depends both on this production technology and the prices of the required inputs. In defining production cost, economists usually assume that for each possible level of output, producers select the combination of inputs that will produce the chosen output at lowest cost.[3] For instance, if L_1, K_1, and X_1 are the amounts of inputs that will produce output Q_1 at lowest cost, then the

$$Cost\ of\ Q_1 = wL_1 + rK_1 + pX_1$$

where w = the price of labor
r = the price of capital
p = the set of prices for the other inputs

Of course, this cost of the directly produced output is also the **expenditure** of the government on this service.

These public facilities or directly produced outputs provided by state–local governments may not reflect the services desired by consumers, however. One can argue that citizens are more concerned about results than production; for instance, the education output of interest is knowledge and skills acquired rather than merely the number of classroom hours per year. The service result, which is what individuals consume, depends both on the directly produced output provided by the government and on the characteristics of the community and the population. An equal number of classroom hours, teachers, and books will not necessarily produce an equal amount of learning in districts with different numbers and types of students. It is useful, therefore, to distinguish "**consumer output,**" which means results, from the directly produced output or facilities. Mathematically,

---

[3]Of course, governments might not always select the minimum cost input mix. For instance, it has been argued that due to patronage considerations or public-employee unionism, state–local governments may choose to use more labor than is cost minimizing.

$$G = g(Q, N, E)$$

where G = consumer output
     N = population to be served
     E = environment, a set of community and population characteristics
     $g(\quad)$ = transformation function from output to results

It is now clear that the "cost" of producing more directly produced output Q is different from the "cost" of producing more consumer output G. The latter depends on community characteristics E and N, which are often outside the direct control of the state or local government. Changes in population or the environment may require a larger Q just to keep G constant. For instance, to reduce class size from twenty-five to twenty students requires 25 percent more teachers and classrooms (assuming teacher workload and school operating hours are to remain the same), but such a change may not provide a 25-percent increase in the desired result of "learning" per student; indeed, it may not increase "learning" at all!

This discussion suggests that there are at least three different, broad ways to measure the output of state–local governments. Output can be measured by the amount of money spent by a government on a service, what are referred to as expenditures. But expenditures are really a measure of the inputs used by the government in the production process. Alternatively, government service may be measured by the amount of directly produced output provided by the government. Finally, government service may be measured by results, by the level of consumption enjoyed by citizens.

Examples of how these three different measurement concepts can be applied to specific state–local government services are shown in Table 15.1. Fire protection services, for instance, may be measured by the amount of money spent on firefighters, stations, trucks and other inputs; by the number of hydrants and stations per square mile; or by some mix of the number of fires (prevention) and damage per fire (suppression). Similarly, police protection services may be measured by expenditures on officers, vehicles, jails, and other inputs; by the number of police patrols per square mile; or by the number of arrests and crimes solved. Similar measures can be devised for every service function or responsibility of state–local governments. But which measure is best? Or perhaps more appropriately, how do the measures differ in the information they provide?

/ Expenditures compared to produced output

Is it possible for directly produced output on a service to fall even though expenditures are constant or even increasing? Similarly, is it possible that two different subnational jurisdictions with equal per-capita expenditures on a particular function will provide different produced outputs for that service? The answer to both questions is yes!

Expenditures equal costs, and costs depend both on the amount of inputs used *and* the prices of those inputs. If the prices of inputs rise, then it will cost governments more to provide the same produced output. Of course, governments may select a different production technology if relative input prices change—using rel-

TABLE 15.1

Sample Output Measures for Selected State–Local Services

Service	Inputs	Direct Outputs	Consumption
Fire protection	Firefighters, inspectors, stations, trucks, equipment, water supply	Stations per square mile, firefighters per station, trucks per station, hydrants per square mile	Fire prevention and suppression: Number of fires per household or employees, damage ($) per fire, civilian fire deaths per fire, fire insurance rates
Police protection	Patrol officers, supervisory officers, stations, radios, vehicles, jails, weapons	Stations per square mile, number of patrols (or patrol officers) per square mile, number of intersections with traffic control, number of jail cells per capita	Crime prevention and punishment: Crimes per capita (perhaps by type), civilian deaths and/or injuries from crime, amount ($) of stolen merchandise, arrests per crime, crimes solved per reported crime
Education	Teachers, books, buildings, desks, classrooms, computers and other equipment	Teachers per student, books per student, classroom hours per year, class size, number of subjects taught	Knowledge and Skills: Average and/or variance of test scores, percentage graduating "on time," percentage attending college, percentage employed after x years, added earnings

atively less of those inputs whose prices increase the most—but even then, total cost for every amount of directly produced output will increase, although perhaps by less than if the government did not alter production methods. It follows that if input prices differ for different subnational jurisdictions, equal expenditures do not necessarily translate into equal produced output. Simply put, if teachers of the same quality cost more in one state than in another (and all other inputs cost the same), equal per-pupil expenditures in the two states translate into larger class sizes in the higher-cost state or less of some other input (books, for example) in the higher-cost state.

These implications are very important because expenditures are the most commonly used measure of subnational government output, at least for comparisons over time and among different jurisdictions. But over time, increases in input prices require increased expenditures unless directly produced output is to fall or unless new ways (technologies), which require fewer inputs, for producing those services can be found. As with consumer expenditures, one can attempt to allow for changing input prices over time by deflating government-expenditure data with a price index, usually the GNP implicit price deflator, which is separately available for federal and state–local government expenditures. For comparisons among different jurisdictions, no such general correction is available, although there is evidence of substantial variation of some input prices among different state–local governments. Particularly, land prices and labor prices appear to vary widely at different locations, and both inputs are purchased in substantial amounts by state–local governments.

/ Produced output compared to consumed output

Is it possible that the consumed output or result for a particular service could decline or worsen even though a government provides constant or even increasing direct output? And is it possible that even if two governments provide equal directly produced output that citizens in those jurisdictions may receive different amounts of consumed output—that is, get different results? Again, both answers are yes.

The consumer output, which results from a given amount of directly produced output, depends on the environmental characteristics of the community and population. Between two cities with identical fire departments, one might expect more fires and more serious fires in the city with older buildings or with more wooden (as opposed to metal or brick) buildings. Equal fire protection in both cities may require more directly produced output in such a city—perhaps fire stations closer together, more pumper trucks per-capita, or a more aggressive fire-inspection program. Similarly, as environmental conditions change over time, changes in directly produced outputs will be needed if consumer results are to remain the same. Of course, the environment can change in a positive way over time as well, requiring less produced output to maintain consumer results. For instance, if building materials and technology mean that newer buildings are at lesser risk from fire, then the amount of directly produced fire-protection output consistent with constant fire protection could decline.

This discussion suggests three reasons why government expenditures may not be very good measures of the results of government production enjoyed by consumers. Differences or changes in production technology, input prices, and community environmental characteristics all can intervene in that relationship. For instance, rising expenditures may be sufficient to maintain constant produced output, given rising input prices, while a deteriorating environment may require increased produced output to maintain results. Thus, rising expenditures may not be inconsistent with falling consumed output or declining service quality. The opposite may also be true. In some cases, decreasing expenditures can be consistent with rising service results or quality if input prices decrease and/or the production environment improves. Therefore, at the very least, these three factors must be controlled for when using government expenditures for comparison purposes.

/ Employment and labor costs

When expenditures are used as the measure of the amount of government service supplied, output is actually being measured by the government's costs, and the major component of state and local government costs is labor cost. As shown in

TABLE 15.2

Employee Compensation as a Percentage of Noncapital Direct Expenditure, by Type of Government, Selected Years

				Level of Government					
Year	Federal	State–Local	State	Total Local	County	Municipal	Township	School District	Special District
1967	27.5	54.5	42.7	60.5	48.0	56.2	52.4	74.1	41.7
1972	28.7	51.2	39.7	57.9	44.9	52.3	54.7	73.4	41.6
1977	20.3	45.2	31.5	54.5	47.5	47.5	54.6	68.8	38.4
1982	16.1	42.0	30.1	50.3	45.0	42.9	47.9	66.7	33.0
1986	13.7	40.9	29.5	49.0	43.4	41.5	46.4	66.2	30.7

Source: U.S. Department of Commerce. Table entitled "Governmental Expenditure by Character and Object," (1967, 1972, 1977, 1982). U.S. Department of Commerce. *Governmental Finances, 1986* (1987).

Table 15.2, about 41 percent of state–local government direct noncapital expenditures in 1986 went to cover compensation of employees. Labor costs represented 49 percent of those expenditures by local governments, on average, but more than 66 percent of direct expenditures in school districts. In comparison, labor costs were only about 16 percent of federal government noncapital direct expenditures in 1982. If comparison is limited to expenditures for current operations, labor costs are obviously an even larger share. In 1986 employee compensation was 50 percent of current operation expenditures for state–local governments together, more than 41 percent for states and 55 percent for all local governments.[4]

For the 20 years represented in Table 15.2, the labor-cost share of direct expenditures for all levels of government in the United States decreased substantially. From 1967–86, labor costs decreased from 42.7 to 29.5 percent of direct expenditures for states and from 60.5 percent to 49 percent for local governments. Similarly, the labor-cost share of direct expenditures for the federal government fell from 27.5 percent to 13.7 percent. This decline in the labor-cost share partly reflects some external factors (interest-cost shares are greater in 1986, partly because of higher interest rates), but also reflects changes in what state–local governments do and how they do it. As governments make relatively more transfer payments, for instance, the labor-cost share of spending falls because the government is spending the money on direct payments to the poor rather than to labor. Similarly, if government substitutes capital for labor in producing some services—automated trucks for sanitation workers, for example—the labor-cost share will also fall.

In 1986 state and local governments employed about 14 percent—that is, one in every seven—of all payroll employees in the United States, as shown in Table 15.3. The share of total employees working for state and local governments has declined since 1975, however, and the number of state–local government employees was about the same in 1986 as in 1980. Given the importance of labor costs to

---

[4]Direct expenditures are total expenditures excluding intergovernmental transfers. Expenditures for current operations are direct expenditures excluding expenditures for capital, assistance and subsidies, interest, and insurance benefits. Expenditures for current operations represent money spent for current goods and services.

TABLE 15.3

State–Local Government Employment and Earnings

Year	State–Local Employment (Thousands)	Percentage of Total Employment[a]	State–Local Average Annual Earnings per FTE[b] ($)	State–Local Earnings as Percentage of Average Annual Earnings per FTE in		
				Federal Government	All Industries	Manufacturing
1965	7,696	12.7	5,616	96.0	98.4	87.9
1970	9,823	13.9	7,818	95.7	103.3	95.9
1975	11,937	15.5	10,900	86.3	100.1	91.3
1980	13,375	14.8	15,142	85.6	95.9	84.3
1982	13,098	14.6	17,826	84.6	96.7	84.7
1984	13,216	14.0	19,927	85.7	98.8	85.7
1986	13,811	13.9	22,427	89.6	102.3	88.1

Sources: Employment: *Economic Report of the President.* (February 1988, 296–97). Earnings: U.S. Department of Commerce. *Survey of Current Business,* Income and Employment by Industry, various years.

[a]State–Local employment as a percentage of total nonagricultural payroll employment.
[b]Average annual compensation per full-time equivalent employee.

state and local governments, it is not surprising that this pattern mirrors the course of state–local government expenditures relative to GNP noted in Chapter 1—the state–local government sector grew compared to the rest of the economy until the mid-1970s, but the sector has grown at about the same rate as the rest of the economy since.

In 1986 state–local governments paid an average salary of about $22,400 to full-time employees. That annual income was just slightly above the average full-time employee earnings for all industries in the United States but was only about 88 percent of the average annual earnings for employees in manufacturing and 90 percent of that in the federal government. As shown in Table 15.3, state–local government employee earnings have taken a roller coaster ride compared to average earnings in all industries over the past twenty years. State–local government employee earnings were below the economy-wide average in the 1960s, rose to parity with average earnings in the first half of the 1970s, lost ground to economy-wide earnings in the last half of the 1970s, and have risen back to parity with average earnings in the 1980s. Although something of a cyclical pattern also applies in comparing state–local government earnings to those of federal government and manufacturing employees, state–local government employees have consistently earned less, on average, than employees in manufacturing and the federal government.

/ Productivity and Costs

Input price increases will lead to increased costs of providing state–local government services unless the input price increases are matched by increases in productivity. Further, because of the substantial importance of labor costs for state–local governments, changes in wages and worker productivity should be particularly important. But the market for state and local government workers is not isolated from the rest of the economy. Changes in the demand for and supply of labor throughout the economy can have important implications for the costs of providing state–local government services. This relationship among worker productivity, wages, and production costs between the state–local sector and the rest of the economy is the basis for one theory of state–local government costs that has proved valuable in understanding the growth of state–local government spending.

| The Baumol hypothesis

In a now well-known 1967 article, William Baumol argued that productivity increases in some sectors of the economy would force wage increases throughout the economy, increasing the production costs in those sectors where productivity improvements do not occur. Baumol further argued that the nature of some services, including many of those provided by state–local governments, effectively precludes productivity gains because the essence of the service is the labor itself. Higher wages simply can not be offset by substituting other inputs for labor. For those services, unit production costs would certainly increase, and the choice for consumers is either to substantially reduce consumption of the service or to spend ever increasing amounts to continue consuming current levels.

The first part of Baumol's argument is represented in Figure 15.1. The economy is divided, obviously somewhat artificially, into two sectors, one where productivity gains occur relatively easily and regularly (Figure 15.1a) and one where productivity

FIGURE 15.1 *Productivity Gains Cause Wage Increases*

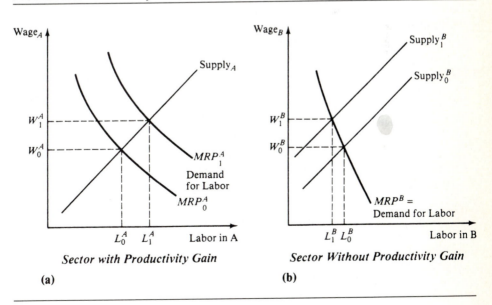

Sector with Productivity Gain

(a)

Sector Without Productivity Gain

(b)

gains are difficult to achieve (Figure 15.1b). For this second sector, Baumol has in mind labor-intensive services with little opportunity for capital/labor substitution. In his words (1967, 416),

> There are a number of services in which the labor is an end in itself, in which quality is judged directly in terms of amount of labor. Teaching is a clear-cut example. . . . Here, despite the invention of teaching machines and the use of closed circuit television and a variety of other innovations, there still seem to be fairly firm limits to class size. . . . An even more extreme example is one I have offered in another context: live performance. A half hour horn quintet calls for the expenditure of 2½ man hours in its performance, and any attempt to increase productivity here is likely to be viewed with concern by critics and audience alike.[5]

Obviously, one can debate for which services and to what degree this characterization applies. At this juncture, it is only necessary to accept that productivity gains for some state–local services are more difficult to achieve than in some other industries. Accordingly, the demand for labor in both sectors is shown in Figure 15.1, with demand less elastic in that sector where substitution for labor is more difficult. Note that the demand for labor is labeled the marginal revenue product of labor (*MRP*), which is defined to be the extra revenue a firm receives from hiring one additional unit of labor. The marginal revenue product is marginal revenue times the marginal product of labor and thus depends both on labor productivity and the value of the product produced. From microeconomic principles, a profit-maximizing firm will employ additional labor as long as the marginal revenue product is greater than the marginal cost of another worker, which is the wage in a competitive labor market. The demand for labor, then, represents the benefit to a firm from more labor, which must be compared to the cost of hiring another unit of labor.

An increase in labor productivity in sector A is represented by an increase (a shift up) in the demand curve for labor; marginal revenue product is greater for every amount of labor because workers now produce more. The increase in labor productivity brings forth an increase in wage, at least in a competitive labor market. Presumably, the same occurs in a controlled labor market as unions recognize the increased productivity of their members and bargain accordingly. The increase in wage in labor market A means that workers in sector A are now earning a relatively higher wage compared to those in market B than before the productivity improvement. The relatively higher wages in A will attract workers from market B, causing a reduction (a leftward shift) in the supply curve of workers to market B and thus an increase in wage of workers in B. In essence, employers in market B must match the wage increase in market A to retain employees.

But these wage increases have very different effects in these two sectors. For sector A, workers are earning *and* producing more so that cost per unit of output need not increase. For sector B, the higher wages have been forced by changes in the other market and are not matched by productivity gains; remember that the

---

[5]Perhaps Baumol did not foresee the advent of computer-based music synthesizers, so that one programmer–performer could produce the horn quintet. But one might suspect that Baumol, and others, would see this option as another good (or bad) completely.

premise of sector B is that substantial productivity gains are not possible. Therefore, the cost of producing a unit of sector B output rises. If B represents the position of state–local governments (and other industries as well), productivity gains in the industrial sector of the economy *cause* cost increases in the production of state–local government goods and services.

The effect of these cost increases on consumption of sector B's output is represented by Figure 15.2. If the demand for output B is price inelastic (Figure 15.2a), then the increased cost results in a higher price but only a small decrease in quantity. As a result, total expenditures on service B rise. If, on the other hand, demand for output B is price elastic (Figure 15.2b), then the cost increase causes only a small increase in price but a large decrease in consumption. As discussed in Chapter 14, the evidence suggests that the demand for the services provided by state–local governments is very price inelastic. Therefore, the implication of the Baumol hypothesis is that productivity gains in some sectors of the economy will force increasing amounts to be spent on state–local government services. This is consistent with state–local government expenditures representing a larger and larger share of GNP. Moreover, as long as private-sector productivity gains continue and public-sector productivity gains are difficult to achieve, this problem will remain.

This story, although simplified, seems applicable to many actual circumstances. As wages in manufacturing and the business-service sector rise, fewer students may be attracted to teaching, a phenomenon that can be particularly evident for science, math, or business teachers who may find an attractive private market for their general knowledge and skills. As improved technology becomes a more important factor in manufacturing and demand for engineers and computer specialists rises,

FIGURE 15.2 *How Increases in Costs of Government Services Affect Spending on Services*

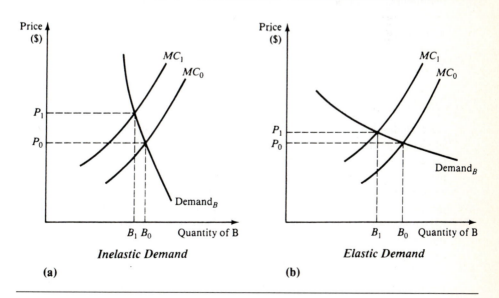

it becomes more and more difficult and expensive for universities to staff engineering schools. Of course, as noted by Baumol, the process applies to many other services such as the arts, restaurant meals, fine hand-crafted furniture, and clothes.

/ Evidence: Government productivity

It is difficult to directly measure productivity change in the production of government services precisely because it is difficult to measure the output being produced. One recent study (Hulten, 1984) attempted to measure productivity change in state and local governments indirectly, however, by utilizing the difference between directly produced output and consumed output. Households can be thought of as producing all final services by purchasing and combining different directly produced outputs, some provided by the private sector and some by government. (For instance, a household combines a privately produced recreational vehicle with a publicly pro-vided park to produce a service called camping.) In that case, the share of public to private expenditures depends on the relative prices of the products and relative change in productivity and environmental factors for the sectors. From observed data on the share of state–local expenditures in GNP and relative prices, the com-bined change in productivity and environmental factors for the state–local sector can be inferred.

Using quarterly data for the 1959–79 period, Charles Hulten estimated the annual rate of change of the combined productivity/environmental factor to be -0.50 percent, although the estimate was not significantly different from zero. Hulten reported that one ''cannot reject the hypothesis of zero productivity growth for the state–local sector'' (p. 261). Perhaps more accurately, if there had been productivity growth over this period, it was not sufficient to offset a deteriorating production environment. After noting that private-sector productivity had increased at an av-erage 1.45-percent annual rate over this period and that the state–local share in GNP had risen substantially in this time, Hulten concluded that ''the results of this paper are thus consistent with the Baumol hypothesis on unbalanced growth. . . .'' (p. 263).

/ Evidence: Government costs

Other studies have directly examined the costs of producing state–local government services and changes in those costs over time. In one such study, the changes in the prices of inputs and workloads from 1962–72 for different state–local govern-ment services were computed and compared to changes in expenditures for those services over the period (Sunley 1976, reporting work by Robert Reischauer). For instance, local school input prices include teacher salaries, book prices, and trans-portation costs, whereas workload is the number of school-age children. If expen-ditures increased more than required by increases in input prices and workloads, the remainder is assumed to represent increases in amount or quality of service.

The result of this study was that 52 percent of the increase in total state–local expenditures over this ten-year period was due to increases in input prices and that

13 percent resulted from increased workloads. Thus, only about 35 percent of the increase in state–local government spending in that decade represented increased quality or new service. There were, however, substantial variations for different types of service. Workload and price increases were particularly important for highways and parking, health and hospitals, and police and fire protection. The increase in input prices and workloads alone were sufficient to increase total state–local government expenditures from 11.4 percent of GNP in 1962 to 12.0 percent of GNP by 1972. As shown in Table 15.3, this was a period when state–local government wages were increasing rapidly in an attempt to catch up with private-sector wages. As suggested previously, state–local sector costs are influenced by changes in the rest of the economy, and increases in state–local expenditures do not necessarily represent increases in output or service.

Since the latter half of the 1970s, state–local government expenditures have not risen relative to GNP, however, suggesting that some aspect of the story changed. Possible explanations are that large productivity gains have, in fact, been made in producing state–local services or that the demand for state–local services has become more price elastic. But the evidence reported in Table 15.4 suggests that the inverse of the Baumol hypothesis was operating from the mid-1970s through the early 1980s—low productivity growth in private industry helped to hold down relative state–local sector costs.

From 1973–82, average annual earnings for full-time employees in all industries rose by 102.4 percent while business productivity, measured as output per unit of labor, rose by only 4.6 percent; consequently, unit labor costs for business rose by 109.1 percent. Over these years, increases in private-sector wages were *not* matched by productivity gains, so business labor costs rose substantially, presumably inducing business to demand *less* labor. Fewer private-sector jobs created some slack in the labor market, allowing state–local governments to hold down wages. Over these years, average annual full-time employee earnings in state–local government rose 89.1 percent, losing ground to private-sector earnings. As measured by the GNP implicit price deflator, the prices of consumer goods rose 96.1 percent over these years while the price of state–local services rose 109.2 percent. Although the price of state-local services rose slightly compared to private consumer goods, the difference was much smaller than in the other two periods, when private productivity

TABLE 15.4

Percentage Change in Private-Sector Productivity and State–Local Costs

	Earnings		Business		Implicit Price Deflator	
Period	All	State–Local	Productivity	Unit-Labor Cost	Consumption	State–Local Expenditures
1963–73	73.7	81.9	27.4	46.7	38.6	71.3
1973–82	102.4	89.1	4.6	109.1	96.1	109.2
1982–85	9.3	12.2	5.0	7.2	12.2	17.2

Sources: U.S. Department of Commerce. *Economic Report of the President.* (February, 1986, 302). *Survey of Current Business,* July issues, various years, and February 1986.

gains were large. Therefore, as one would expect, state–local government expenditures decreased from about 11.2 percent of GNP to 10.6 percent over these years.

So far, the period since 1982 is similar to the 1963–73 period when substantial business productivity gains allowed earnings to rise with only modest increases in labor costs. The increase in state–local earnings from 1982–85 is much greater than the increase in business unit-labor costs, and therefore the price of state–local services is again increasing much faster than the average price of private consumer goods. Thus, as expected, the share of GNP represented by state–local expenditures increased slightly between 1982 and 1985. If growth of private-sector productivity and the conditions for the Baumol hypothesis continue, one expects that the state–local expenditure share of GNP will also continue to increase.

/ Private Provision of Public Services

/ What is privatization?

One idea that has been proposed to increase the productivity of government and thus reduce costs is to transfer production of government services to private firms, what has come to be called **privatization.** The term privatization has been applied, however, to three different ways of increasing the activity of the private sector in providing public services; private-sector choice, financing, and production of a service; public-sector choice and financing with private-sector production of the service selected; and deregulation of private firms providing services. The first simply means that all responsibility for a service be transferred from the public sector to individual consumers who would select the amount of service they desire and purchase that service from private suppliers. The third version of the concept means that government reduce or eliminate its restrictions imposed on private firms providing individually selected services. As an example of the first, solid-waste collection is provided and produced by some local governments but left to private choice and private collection firms in other communities. The recent deregulation of the airline and trucking industries is an example of the latter. Thus, both essentially can be characterized as "let the private sector do it alone."

The second version of privatization refers, however, to joint activity of the public and private sectors in providing services. The notion is that consumers collectively select and pay for the amount and type of service desired through government, which would then contract with private firms to produce the desired quantity and type of service. As discussed in Chapter 5, some local governments often contract with other governments to produce services in order to take advantage of economies of scale. The idea here, too, is that contracting with private firms to produce goods and services may also reduce costs. For the example of solid-waste collection, the idea is that the community would select a level of collection service financed by taxes or government fees and that the government would contract then with a private firm to do the collection and disposal. *The government would provide for the service, although a private firm would produce it*. It is this concept of privatization that has been particularly at issue in recent years as some states and localities have experimented with it or at least considered using it for services usually both provided and produced by government in the past. This is the concept of privatization that we focus on in this chapter.

Private production of publicly selected and financed goods and services can be applied to intermediate goods used by government in producing services (such as cars and trucks, paper, machines, and materials), to services consumed by government in carrying out their responsibilities (such as maintenance and repair, construction, data processing, and management and financial services), and for the final services consumed directly by taxpayers (such as education, police and fire protection, and transportation). Indeed, in the first instance privatization is nearly universal. Few, if any, governments or government agencies produce their own furniture, forms, buses, or computers—all are purchased by government from private producers. Concerning the other possibilities, in a review of privatization experience Robert Poole and Philip Fixler (1987, 617) note that ''most privatization at state and local levels of government has been applied to either routine housekeeping services in which government itself is the customer (maintenance of public buildings, vehicles, and infrastructure) or public services with well-defined tangible outputs (garbage collection or recreation, for example).''

/ How might privatization reduce costs?

In its simplest form, the argument is that government producers have no incentive to hold down production costs, whereas private producers who contract with the government to provide service do. Suppose, for example, that a private firm contracts with a local government to pick up six bags of garbage per house per week in the community for a fee of $100 per house per year. Obviously, the lower the cost incurred by the firm in satisfying the contract, the greater profit it makes. Competition among potential private suppliers for this contract (for a limited period, after which government can change contractors) is expected to bring government the lowest possible cost for the specified level of service. As summarized by Janet Rothenberg Pack (1987, 527), ''*competitive* bidding by profit-maximizing firms for a well-specified output guarantees that the product will be produced at the lowest cost. The absence of competition and profit incentives in the public sector is not likely to result in cost minimization.''

The simple notion that government has no incentive to hold production costs down may be too strong, at least in the local government context, because local officials face competition from potential candidates and communities face competition from other communities both for residents and businesses. If government production costs for a service in one community are higher than they need be, then taxes in that community are also higher than they need to be. As a result, households or businesses might move, as in the Tiebout process (see Chapter 4), to those communities with lower production costs for a given level of service. Similarly, candidates for public office could make the production inefficiency an issue in the local election. Therefore, it may be more accurate to argue that the incentive to hold cost down is greater for a profit-maximizing firm than it is for a government but not completely lacking in the latter. Essentially, the contention is that economic competition is more effective than political competition.

The three potential sources of lower production costs for private firms most often cited are lower labor costs, better management, and more research and development and faster innovation of the results. Lower labor costs may arise either from lower wages (which means that the government was paying wages higher than necessary for a given skill) or from less labor input (which means that government was hiring unnecessary workers or that fewer workers are needed with an alternative production method). A private firm may more readily try out different production approaches, whereas government may tend to stick with the current approach, given that change often creates substantial political difficulties for local officials. Indeed, better management or experimentation and innovation with different production methods may be the reason why a given level of service can be produced with fewer workers. In addition, private firms may use retained earnings to finance research or to purchase new capital equipment, which lowers unit production costs, whereas government may not be able to allocate tax revenues to those purposes as easily, given the many competing demands for a share of the government's budget.

/ When might privatization not work well?

The three most often cited potential problems with private provision of government services arise from the bidding process, the precise specification of the contract, and monitoring and enforcement of the contract. First, competitive bidding may not provide the service at lowest cost to the contracting government if there are only a few (or even one) potential suppliers and the government has a limited idea about the level of costs. This might particularly be the case in rural areas or when the production technology is relatively new. In addition, there is concern that potential suppliers may initially offer a price to the government that is less than actual production costs to induce the government to adopt privatization or to win the contract. Subsequently, the contractor would then demand a higher price after the government has eliminated or dismantled its own production system. The chance of such "low-balling" in the bidding process may be reduced if the local government requires relatively long-term contracts.

The second potential difficulty with privatization concerns the specification of the service to be provided in the contract. Earlier in this chapter, you learned that the output of a government service can be characterized by the inputs used or by alternative measures of the produced output or final result, none of which are unique for a particular service. Characterizing output for some services is particularly difficult when the government has multiple objectives. If society and the government are not certain what "good" education is and how to measure it, for instance, how can government contract for it? In the discussion about producing education in Chapter 18, the distinction between the average student-test score and the variance of scores will be emphasized. Getting the highest average test score may require applying more educational resources to the better students with the effect of reducing the scores for the students at the bottom. As a result, the variation in test scores would increase, which might contradict the distributional objective of government provision of education. It is difficult to think about how one would begin to specify the contracted output for police protection (a specified percentage of different types of crimes must be "solved"?) or fire protection (fires must be responded to in x minutes with average damages limited to y?).

The third potential problem with private provision concerns monitoring the service quality provided by the private supplier and enforcing the contract when problems arise. Monitoring the performance of the private contractor itself creates costs, which may be substantial, for the government. In some cases, new data may have to be collected and analyzed. As one example, consider the costs of the U.S. Department of Defense in testing and evaluating weapons produced by private contractors to ensure they meet the contract standards. In addition, there must be a reasonable remedy if the supplier does not provide or stops the expected service. Suppose that the contractor underestimates the cost of production so that the price charged the government is not sufficient to cover all production costs, resulting in losses for the firm. If the firm simply stops providing the service, the implications could be serious in the case of many services such as police and fire protection.

David Sappington and Joseph Stiglitz (1987) have termed these contractual issues *the need for and costs of intervention in the private production process.* They suggest that government should consider both the probability that intervention will be necessary and the costs of intervening if necessary. They conclude that "two important elements of this calculation include the complexity of the task under consideration and the need for rapid adaptation to unforeseen contingencies. When the task is particularly novel and complex, unforeseen contingencies are likely to arise. If rapid adaptation to these events is crucial, . . . public provision is more likely to be the preferred mode of organization" (p. 581).

/ Experience with and prospects for privatization

The available evidence shows that while the number of state–local governments contracting with private firms to provide final services to consumers and intermediate services to the government remains relatively small, that number has increased substantially in the past decade. For instance, Poole and Fixler (1987) report that about 500 cities contracted with private firms for refuse collection in 1982, up from only about 340 in 1973, and that about 340 contracted for data processing in 1982 compared to only 9 in 1973. They also report that about 47 percent of the cities and counties with emergency medical service provided it through private sources, including use of volunteers and contracting with for-profit firms, and that 36 localities contract with private firms for municipal or airport fire protection. Other increasingly common examples include government contracting for protection of public schools, parks, libraries and the like; public and school bus transportation; and numerous public-health services. In addition, government continues to purchase most intermediate goods from private producers.

There is also substantial and increasing evidence that the use of private firms to produce services has resulted in lower costs, especially for the more typical types of privatization. Studies by E. S. Savas and Barbara Stevens (1977) and by James McDavid (1985) have found that public solid waste-collection services are 50 to 70 percent more expensive than equivalent private collection services. (This may not be too surprising because waste collection is entirely a private-sector activity in many communities, suggesting that where collection remains a public service there may be specialized reasons.) Poole and Fixler (1987) also report about several studies showing that private school bus services are less expensive than public school buses, and some studies show the same for municipal bus services (although it is not clear that the nature of bus routes—that is, service quality—is held constant in those studies). Still, a variety of statistical studies do show that government contracting with private firms can be less costly than public production.

Two areas where privatization has been tried remain very controversial. For many years, fire-protection service in Scottsdale, Arizona, has been provided by a private contract service. Although this case has received substantial attention and at least one study shows it to be less costly than public protection, private fire-protection service is mostly restricted to specialized cases such as airports. There are also at least five private adult prisons currently in operation. Here again these cases have received substantial attention, but numerous concerns have prevented widespread use of the idea. Poole and Fixler (1987, 619) also argue that "four other functions generally carried out by government today are likely candidates for privatization in the next decade: transit, highways and freeways, water supply, and education." Although private provision is already used in all four of these areas to some degree (including both the tunnel under and the bridge over the Detroit River between Detroit, Michigan, and Windsor, Ontario, which are privately owned and operated), education may be the most controversial.

As described in further detail in Chapter 18, there is already a mixture of public and private provision in education involving not only private elementary and secondary schools but also private day care, nursery schools, tutorial services, and extracurricular activities (for example, music, language, and sports). But the notion of additional privatization in education as usually envisioned by its proponents involves either private provision entirely or direct competition between private and public schools. Individuals could receive education vouchers from government that could be "spent" for any school desired. Thus, government would continue to finance a substantial portion of education through taxes, but the education service would be produced by private schools. Proponents argue that the resulting competition would reduce education costs and/or improve education results, partly because students would select schools most appropriate for them. Opponents of more privatization in education usually cite concerns about the distributional effects if students become more sorted by ability or other characteristics than they are with the current system. Indeed, some have argued that a diverse student mix is essential to the socialization objective of education and are concerned that there would be less diversity with private education than there is with the current public school structure. These are reasons why education may have important externalities, and thus should be provided publicly.

/ APPLICATION 15.1
Producing City Fire-Protection Services[6]

In 1975 Malcolm Getz surveyed 371 central-city fire departments about inputs and production methods, costs, city characteristics, and results. The survey resulted in usable data from 187 different cities covering forty-four states plus the District of Columbia. Many other state–local government services have also been studied (transportation and education are discussed in subsequent chapters), but this detailed examination of fire protection provides an interesting example of many of the issues discussed in this chapter.

Getz discovered great diversity among these city fire departments in the amount and types of inputs used to produce fire protection. On average, each fire station served an area covering three and one-half square miles, although the range was from one station for one square mile to one for nine square miles. Similarly, there were 6.8 firefighters per station on average, with a range from 3.3 to 11.6. Perhaps even more interesting, given their low cost, is the large variation in number of fire hydrants; on average, there were 85.6 hydrants per square mile, although the standard deviation was 50 and the range from 14 to 302! Input prices also varied substantially. Compensation cost per full-time employee (a weighted average of salaries and fringes for a first-class firefighter and a department captain) varied from $27,000 in Springdale, Arkansas, to $119,000 in Washington, D.C. An index of the cost of building and operating a fire station in these cities varied from 76 to 114, with an average of all the city values equal to 96.

Economists would suspect that the amount and type of inputs selected by these departments would be influenced by input prices. Indeed, Getz reported that the elasticity of labor per square mile with respect to the wage was $-.36$; cities with higher wages used fewer firefighters per square mile, although demand is relatively inelastic. Interestingly, cities with higher wages also used *fewer* stations and trucks per square mile. Apparently, these fire departments attempted to keep the amount of firefighters and trucks per station constant and responded to higher wages by decreasing use of all three. Getz also found that the amount and mix of inputs depended on city characteristics. Cities with older housing tended to use more of all inputs, cities with more manufacturing used relatively more aerial trucks compared to pumpers, while cities that had more business than residential activity also used more of all inputs.

Getz attempted to measure how variations in inputs influenced the effectiveness of the fire department but found very little statistical relationship between additional inputs and improved output. Fire-department output was measured by number of fires per 1000 houses and per 1000 commercial and residential employees, by the dollars of damage per fire, and by the number of civilian fire deaths per million population. Two results that did appear were that more fire-code inspectors decreased the number of multifamily house fires and that more stations per square mile decreased the amount of damage per

---

[6]*See Getz (1979).*

> ## / *APPLICATION 15.1* Continued
> ## Producing City Fire-Protection Services
>
> industrial fire. In the statistical work, both the number of and damage from fires was mostly related to the age of structures in the city—cities with older structures had more fires and more serious fires.The premise of the Baumol hypothesis is that productivity improvement is difficult to achieve for some services, state–local government services included. But Getz did find some major technological changes in the methods and equipment used in fire fighting. Among methods, upon arriving at a fire a department must choose whether to first run water-supply hoses from the nearest water supply or to immediately attack the fire using a relatively small amount of water carried in a pumper truck. The latter method, called a "booster attack," was introduced around 1922 and is now routinely used by slightly more than half of the departments. Technological changes involving equipment include use of breathing apparatus (first used in 1940, now used by all departments); power saws for quick access (1958, 95 percent); chemicals added to water for fighting flammable-liquid fires, called "light water" (1956, 50 percent); and a quick-connect hose coupling (1964, 10 percent). Although some productivity improvement has therefore occurred in producing fire protection, it is not clear that the gain has been sufficient to prevent cost increases.

/ *Summary*

There are at least three different, broad ways to measure the output of state–local governments. Output can be measured by the amount of money spent by a government on a service, referred to as expenditures; by the amount of directly produced output provided by the government; or by results—the level of consumption enjoyed by citizens.

State–local governments purchase inputs such as labor services, capital goods, and materials and supplies and combine them to provide public facilities or what can be called directly produced output. The cost of the directly produced output, which depends on the production technology and the prices of the inputs, is the expenditure of the government on this service.

The service result, what can be called the consumed output, depends both on the directly produced output provided by the government and on the characteristics of the community and the population.

If the prices of inputs rise, then it will cost governments more to provide the same produced output. And if input prices differ for different subnational jurisdictions, equal expenditures by different jurisdictions do not necessarily translate into equal produced output.

Expenditures for direct-labor services represent about half of the expenditures by state–local governments on average. State–local governments are also one of the largest employers in the economy, employing about one of every seven employees. On average, state–local government employee wages fall below those paid by manufacturing industry and the federal government.

Baumol argued that productivity increases in some sectors of the economy would force wage increases throughout the economy, increasing the costs in those sectors where productivity improvements do not occur. Productivity gains will be difficult for some state–local government services because the essence of the service is the labor itself. For those services, the choice for consumers is either to substantially reduce consumption of the service or to spend ever increasing amounts to continue consuming current levels.

Discussion Questions

1. "If one city spends more on police-protection services per capita than does another, one expects less crime in the first city than in the second." True, false, or uncertain? Explain.

2. At a public budget hearing, a citizen once argued, "Education expenditures have increased 5 percent in each of the past three years even though student enrollment has been declining. Where is the extra money going? It seems to me that if the number of students declines, expenditures should also decline." Is the citizen right or wrong?

3. "If the Baumol hypothesis is correct concerning local government finances and if the price elasticity of demand for local services is inelastic, then we are in trouble—eventually, spending for education, police and fire protection, and sanitation will require half of our incomes." Evaluate this concern. What changes could occur to prevent this from happening?

4. Competing with private-sector salaries is a common problem for some academic departments in universities, particularly in engineering, accounting, and other business fields. If universities do not match the salaries, they may be unable to hire professors, or at least the better candidates, and if they do match the salaries then the cost of operating those programs (and eventually tuition) will increase. How might universities change the production of engineering or business education to avoid this problem—that is, how could professors be substituted for or made more productive? Do you think those changes would affect the "quality" or nature of education in these fields? Does this problem apply to private as well as public universities?

Selected Readings

Baumol, William. "Macroeconomics of Unbalanced Growth: The Anatomy of the Urban Crisis." *American Economic Review* 62 (June 1967): 415–26.

Bradford, D and F., R. A. Malt, and Wallace E. Oates. "The Rising Cost of Local Public Services: Some Evidence and Reflections." *National Tax Journal* 22 (June 1969): 185–202.

Hirsch, Werner. "State and Local Government Production." In *The Economics of State and Local Government*. New York: McGraw-Hill, 1970, 147–65.

Pack, Janet Rothenberg. "Privatization of Public-Sector Services in Theory and Practice." *Journal of Policy Analysis and Management* 6 (Summer 1987): 523–40.

16 / Pricing of Government Goods— User Charges

> The economic case for the expansion and rationalization of pricing in the urban public sector rests essentially on the contribution it can make to allocative efficiency. Prices will provide correct signals to indicate the quantity and quality of things citizens desire. . . .[1]
>
> *Selma J. Mushkin and Richard M. Bird*

User charge refers, generally, to prices charged by state–local governments for specific services or privileges, used to pay for all or part of the cost of providing those services. They are to be distinguished from financing services through general taxes, with no direct relationship between tax payment and service received. In practice some financing methods other than direct charges, such as license fees and some earmarked taxes, can serve the purpose of user charges. Common examples of user-charge financing in the state–local government arena include water charges, tuition at public colleges and universities, public hospital charges, parking fees, and highway tolls.

/ Types and Use of Charges

The types of financing methods that can be considered as user charges include direct charges for use of a public facility or consumption of a service, license taxes or fees paid for the privilege of undertaking some activity (such as fishing license and driver license fees), and special assessments, a type of property tax levied for a specific service and based on some physical characteristic of the property, such as front footage (for example, assessments for sidewalk construction). More than $98 billion of these types of charges were collected by state–local governments in 1986, with traditional user charges accounting for nearly 82 percent of the total, as shown in Table 16.1. These charges and fees represented 15.3 percent of the general revenue of state–local governments, with traditional user charges alone representing about 12.5 percent of revenue.

Education and hospitals are the two budget categories from which most state–local user charges arise. As shown in Table 16.2, on average nearly 60 percent of

---

[1]"Public Prices: An Overview." In *Public Prices for Public Products,* edited by Selma Mushkin, 11. Washington, D.C.: The Urban Institute, 1972.

TABLE 16.1

Amounts of Charges and Fees, State–Local Governments, 1986

Type	Amount (Billions of Dollars)	Percent of General Revenue	Total
User charges	80.40	12.5	82.0
License and other taxes	15.49	2.4	15.8
Special assessments	2.22	0.3	2.2
Total	98.11	15.3	100.0

Source: U.S. Department of Commerce. Governmental Finances in 1985–86 (1987).

TABLE 16.2

State–Local User Charges and Expenditures, by Category, 1986

Category	Category User Charge as Percentage of All User Charges	Category User Charge as Percentage of Direct Expenditures in Category
Education	29.5	11.3
Hospitals	28.4	58.4
Sewers and sanitation	13.4	56.5
Air transportation	4.3	81.1[a]
Highways	3.6	5.9
Parks and recreation	2.7	21.7
Other	18.0	—

Source: U.S. Department of Commerce. Governmental Finances in 1985–86 (1987).

[a]Percent of airport expenditures.

all subnational government direct user charges are attributable to those categories. Of all other individual categories, only sewers and sanitation account for more then 10 percent of charges. For that reason, extreme caution must be used when comparing user-charge use among different states (or localities). Without large public higher-education and hospital systems, user charges may appear as a small fraction of revenue simply because those services are not provided. Interjurisdictional comparisons should be made by budget category.[2]

More than half of state–local expenditures on airports, hospitals, and sewer and sanitation systems are financed by user charges, whereas only about 11 percent of education expenditures are financed that way. Although tuition and other charges

---

[2]In fact, user charges as a percentage of general revenue are largest for states with relatively lower pre-capita revenue and smallest for high-revenue states. The five states with the largest fraction of revenue from user charges are Mississippi (20.7 percent), Alabama (18.9 percent), Georgia (18.8 percent), Nevada (18.5 percent), and Florida (18.1 percent), whereas the five with the smallest user-charge ratios are Alaska (6.6 percent), Connecticut (7.8 percent), New York (9.0 percent), Illinois (9.1 percent), and New Mexico (9.2 percent).

by public colleges and universities are a large fraction of total user charges, they represent a small fraction of total state–local education expenditures when the mostly tax-financed primary and secondary school expenditures are included. The opposite is true for airports, sewer and sanitation systems, and parks and recreation services, for which user charges are a small fraction of all charges but represent a large fraction of spending in those categories.

Changes in the pattern of user-charge reliance since 1962 for different types of subnational governments are depicted by the data in Table 16.3. Reliance on user charges, license fees, and special assessments together decreased for both state and local governments from 1962–77, while subsequently local government charge reliance has increased and state government reliance remained about the same. Among local governments, user-charge reliance by county governments has continually increased while use by municipalities and townships followed the general pattern of decreasing until the late 1970s and subsequently has been increasing. Charges provide a very small fraction of revenue for school districts and a relatively large fraction for special districts, although that percentage has declined over the

TABLE 16.3

User Charges and User-Associated Taxes as a Percentage of General Revenue, by Level of Government, Various Years

		Local Governments					
Year	*States*	*All*	*Counties*	*Municipalities*	*Townships*	*School Districts*	*Special Districts*
1962							
Charges	7.1	10.6					
All[a]	16.3	13.7	11.9	17.8	7.8	6.6	48.2
1967							
Charges	8.1	10.8					
All	15.7	13.3	12.3	16.7	8.6	6.9	44.9
1972							
Charges	7.9	10.5					
All	14.0	12.7	13.4	15.3	7.7	5.7	44.3
1977							
Charges	7.1	10.7					
All	11.8	12.6	14.0	14.6	6.6	4.7	39.0
1982							
Charges	6.4	11.4					
All	11.7	14.7	16.6	17.3	9.3	4.9	38.1
1986							
Charges	7.6	13.2					
All	11.9	15.5	17.0	19.0	10.5	4.6	38.5

Sources: U.S. Department of Commerce. Table entitled "General Revenue by Source, by Type of Government" (1962, 1967, 1972, 1977, 1982). For 1986 data, by U.S. Department of Commerce. *Governmental Finances in 1985–86 (1987).*

[a]Charges plus license and other unallocable taxes plus special assessments.

past twenty years (perhaps because of increased use of special districts for services traditionally financed at least partly by general taxes). A similar pattern applied to reliance on direct user charges alone. Clearly, total user charges of state–local governments, whether broadly or narrowly defined, have increased faster than other revenues since the late 1970s.

/ Theory of User Charges

In theory user charges should operate as benefit taxes (discussed in Chapter 2), with an individual's charge depending both on benefit (use) and cost of provision. In thinking about user charges, it is helpful to distinguish between the *amount* of a service or facility to provide—the long-run production decision—and the *use* of a given facility, which is a short-run decision. For instance, a local community faces a decision about the appropriate number and size of parks to provide, whereas a state government selects the number and size of public colleges. But once a given amount of those facilities are provided, each government also faces a choice about how much and by whom those facilities are to be used. Should park use be free or should there be an entrance charge? Should the charge be different for residents and nonresidents? Should the charge be different at different times? Similar questions apply to college tuition. User charges can have a role to play in the decisions both about amount and use.

The principal rule for economic efficiency requires that marginal benefit equal marginal cost. For services that primarily benefit the direct consumer, the price charged should equal marginal cost. But marginal cost of what? In essence the distinction between amount and use of public facilities translates into the difference between short-run and long-run cost, as shown in Figure 16.1.

In this example, long-run average costs (*LRAC*) are constant at C_0, reflecting constant returns to scale. This would be true, for instance, if twice as many trucks, gallons of gasoline, workers, and disposal sites would allow refuse to be collected from twice as many houses, so the average cost per house (*LRAC*) remains constant. The service can always be provided at a cost of C_0 dollars per unit simply by expanding the scale of the operation, that is, buying more of all inputs including capital. In Figure 16.1, $Q_2 = 2Q_1$, so operation size A entails half as many inputs as operation size B. Communities of different sizes can produce the service at the same cost, although larger communities will require more (or larger) facilities.

For each size facility selected, the amount of the service produced can vary. But, given a size of operation, average cost depends on use. It would be possible to collect refuse from Q_2 houses with a size A collection system, but the cost per house (*SRAC_A*) would be much greater than with a larger, size B system (*SRAC_B*). But for efficiency considerations, marginal cost is more important than average cost. If a community selects a size B refuse-collection system (many trucks, workers, a large landfill), the extra cost of serving another household, the short-run marginal cost (*SRMC_B*) is very small. Once the large capital stock is acquired, efficiency requires that it be used.

FIGURE 16.1   Costs for Small- and Large-Scale Operations

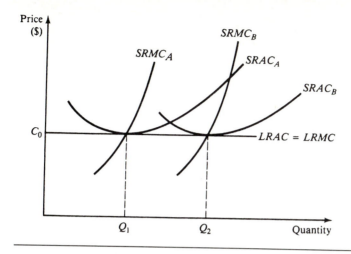

/ Efficient amounts

If consumers believe that public services and facilities are "free"—that is, that more can be produced at no cost to the consumer, when in fact additional amounts do entail a production cost—consumers will be induced to demand more than the efficient amount of those services or facilities. One function of user charges, therefore, is to make consumers face the true costs of their consumption decisions, thereby creating an incentive for efficient choice.[3]

The basic idea of that choice is illustrated by Figure 16.2, which depicts the marginal benefit schedules for both direct users (MB_U) of a service or facility and all of society (MB_S), who also benefit generally. Those marginal benefits are added together to determine the aggregate marginal benefit to the entire society or community from an additional unit of the service (ΣMB_i). Given a cost of producing one more unit equal to MC, the efficient amount of the service or facility is Q^*. The private marginal benefits to users and general marginal benefits to all at that quantity determine how the production costs should be divided among users (a user charge) and all of society (general taxes). In this case, user charges should account for MB_U^*/MC of the cost of the facility. Because direct users would face a marginal cost of MB_U^*, they would demand quantity Q^*, which is the efficient quantity.

In contrast, if users perceive the marginal cost to be zero, they would demand amount Q_2. This is not efficient because the marginal benefits to everyone—the sum of the marginal benefits to direct users and to society generally—are less than the cost of production for all the units of output between Q^* and Q_2. That difference

---

[3]You may wish to review the section on public goods and benefit taxation in Chapter 2.

FIGURE 16.2 *Allocation of Costs to Direct Users and Society in General*

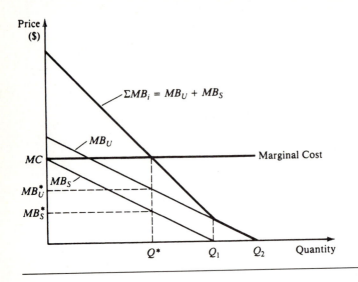

between marginal cost and aggregate marginal benefit represents the potential efficiency cost of not charging appropriate prices for this service.

Several general principles of efficient user charges follow from this analysis.

1. User-charge financing is more attractive, the greater is the share of marginal benefits that accrues to direct users.
2. User-charge financing requires that direct users can be easily identified and excluded (at reasonable cost) from consuming the service unless the charge is paid, assuming that most of the benefits of a service or facility go to direct users.
3. Marginal benefits, not total benefits, matter for determination of user charges. For instance, in Figure 16.2, quantities of the facility beyond Q_1 provide benefits only to direct users. Thus, despite the fact that all of society benefits some from this facility, production of amounts greater than Q_1 should be financed *entirely* by direct users.
4. The efficiency case for user-charge financing is stronger, the more price elastic is demand. In the special case of a perfectly inelastic (vertical) demand, price does not matter. No inefficiency would result if consumers underestimate cost. Obviously, the more price elastic is demand, the greater the potential for inefficiency if consumers do not face true costs.

One should understand that while direct users should pay all or part of the long-run production cost of public facilities, these charges should be independent of the amount of actual use of the facility. To be a user at all is to incur the charge for the provision of the facility. These charges therefore might be flat per-capita or

FIGURE 16.3 Efficient User Charges With and Without Congestion

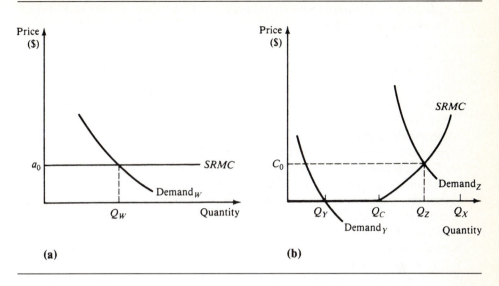

(a)   **(b)**

per-household charges, or perhaps charges based on property size if long-run capital costs vary by size. Examples include a fixed-service charge common in public water systems to cover the capital costs (pipes, pumps, storage) and special assessments for sidewalks, street lights, neighborhood parks.

/ Efficient use

Once a public facility—whether a park, road, water system, or college—has been provided, attention must turn to covering the variable or operating costs. How this is accomplished determines how much and by whom the facility is to be used. The general principle of efficiency, again, is that price should equal marginal cost, but now the relevant marginal cost is short-run marginal cost, the cost of accommodating an additional consumer or providing another unit given the capital input selected. At issue here is the appropriate charge for each gallon of water consumed or for each admittance to the park.[4]

Some possibilities are illustrated in Figure 16.3. In Figure 16.3a, short-run marginal cost is positive and constant; each additional unit of service imposes a constant additional variable cost of a_0. Demand for this service is represented by

---

[4]It may not be practical to separate long-run and short-run pricing decisions, however, because that might require prices to change substantially over time. If price is set equal to short-run marginal cost, higher prices are called for as demand rises. Because those prices will be greater than long-run average cost, funds will be provided to finance the desired capital expansion. But once the facility is enlarged, marginal costs, and thus prices, will fall again. Some type of average cost pricing would maintain more price stability, but would be inefficient. Price stability, in itself, might be desirable though.

Demand$_W$. The appropriate use charge (if users can be identified and excluded) is a_0 dollars *per unit* consumed—for example, $.01 per gallon of water or $2 per car for admittance to a park.

/ Congestion. The situation for some state–local government services is very different. If there is no additional cost to the government of providing a service to an additional consumer, the government does not need to collect more revenue for operating expenses. Parking spaces, tennis and golf courses, bridges, roads, and parks are all classic examples. No additional cost is imposed on the government if one additional car parks in a space or an additional couple uses a tennis court. Yet, governments often charge user fees for all of these services.

One reason is that for these services, an additional consumer may impose extra costs on other users, called **congestion costs.** As roads and bridges become more crowded, traffic slows and the (time) costs to all users increase; as parks become more crowded, there is less space for those in the park to enjoy activities; and when all the parking spaces and tennis courts are occupied, other potential users incur a waiting cost (or must forego the activity). The purpose of use fees in those situations is to allocate a scarce resource among competing demands.

This economic notion of congestion is formally represented in Figure 16.3b. For quantities of use or service less than Q_C, additional consumers can be accommodated without imposing any costs on other users. In essence the facility is not yet "crowded." Because marginal cost is therefore zero, the efficient price is also zero; no use fee is required. If demand for the service is Demand$_Y$, no use fee should be charged, with capital costs covered either out of general taxes or by some fixed charge as discussed above. For quantities of use or service above Q_C, the facility starts to become crowded; additional consumers do impose congestion costs on other users (at an increasing rate in Figure 16.3b). Therefore, if demand for this service is Demand$_Z$, the appropriate use fee is C_0, with a resulting amount of use equal to Q_Z. If no use fee were charged, then the amount of use would be Q_X and the facility would be overused, that is, "too crowded."[5] Obviously, efficient application of use charges could generate revenue, which is not necessary to cover extra operating expenses, for the government.

Pricing with user charges to correct for congestion costs may require charging different fees at different times. For the service represented in Figure 16.3, it may be that demand is sometimes Demand$_Y$, requiring an efficient use charge of zero, and sometimes Demand$_Z$, when the efficient use charge is C_0. For instance, parks may be crowded on weekends and not during the week, demand for bridge crossings may be great at the commuting hours and low at other times, or public-transit facilities may be used extensively at rush hour and little at other times. In other words, there may be a difference between demand at *peak times,* when higher use fees are appropriate, and demand at *offpeak times,* when lower or even zero use fees may be appropriate.[6]

---

[5]At Q_Z, the marginal benefit to the last user is C_0, equal to the marginal cost that user imposes on all other users.

[6]Examples of congestion pricing for roads and highways are discussed in Chapter 19.

/ APPLICATION 16.1
Pricing at Congested Tennis Courts

At one university, the school's policy was to not charge students and faculty members any fee for use of the tennis courts, the argument being that use of the university's facilities should be "free" to those who already paid tuition or worked for the school. Because this university is in a northern city and because the tennis courts are outside, this policy posed no problem for half of the academic year. But in the Fall and especially in the Spring, there was substantial excess demand for the tennis courts; waits of thirty to sixty minutes for a court were common. The courts were therefore not "free" but were allocated by having people wait. Presumably, those who had the lowest-valued time ended up using the tennis courts more. This university had no summer session and so made their tennis courts available to the general public during the summer months. The difference was that a use fee was charged in the summer to everyone—students who remained in the town, faculty, and the public. Not surprisingly, there were many vacant courts during the summer.

This situation is represented in Figure 16.4. The supply of tennis courts is fixed at Q_c, so marginal cost is zero for quantities less than Q_c (there is no extra cost if there are vacant courts); however, marginal cost becomes very high once all the courts are in use (the cost of accommodating another user is the cost of building another court). When demand is Demand$_y$, as during the summer in the story, there is excess capacity, and no fee should be charged. When demand is at the peak level of Demand$_z$, a use fee equal to C_z would generate efficient use—only those who are willing to pay C_z, that is, those who get C_z dollars worth of benefit from using the tennis court would play. With the fee, there is no excess demand for the facility. By charging a fee during the Summer when demand was low (when the university was not in session) in an attempt to generate revenue from the public, the university's facilities were wasted from society's viewpoint. By not charging a fee during the Spring when demand was high, the university made an implicit decision to allocate the scarce tennis courts by having people wait—what is often called "first come, first served." Queuing is a type of price because of the value of the time spent waiting and simply because waiting time may be particularly unpleasant. Although allocation either by fees or waiting gives some consumers an advantage over others, under the first come–first serve system potential tennis players do not know the charge (the required amount of time to wait) until they arrive at the courts.

One might believe that the proper policy for the university in this case is to build more tennis courts because the excess demand during the Spring and Fall suggests that more are "needed." But that analysis is faulty. There is excess demand only because tennis court use appears to be "free." And while the extra courts would be used during the peak times, they would enlarge the excess capacity that exists during the offpeak time. As the discussion about the efficient *amount* of public facilities showed, more tennis courts should be built only if those who demand the courts are willing to pay the full cost of constructing them (assuming that extra tennis courts benefit only direct users). Interestingly, use fees provide a test of that hypothesis. The efficient use fee C_z

in Figure 16.4 equals the marginal benefit of a tennis court to users. If the fee that equates supply and demand turns out to be large enough to finance another court—that is, if marginal benefit is greater than marginal cost—then another court should (and can) be built.

FIGURE 16.4   Efficient Pricing When Supply Is Fixed

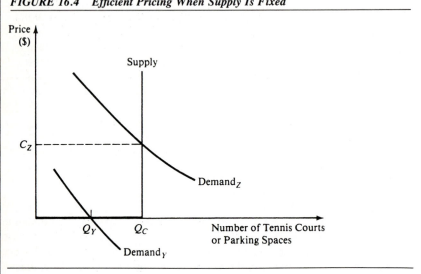

The analysis and diagram of Application 16.1 can be applied to the question of parking meters. Consider the following argument: *The streets have been paid for by and belong to the people. Therefore, parking meters should be abolished.* Analyze that position and prescription in light of the above discussion. If there were no parking meters or fees, how do you think the available parking spaces would be allocated? Would that allocation system be better? For whom? Without parking fees, do you think people would perceive that there is more or less of a "parking problem"? If parking fees are to be used, should they vary by location? Time of day? Time of year?

/ User charges with natural monopoly

A natural monopoly is said to exist if the production of a good or service exhibits increasing returns to scale, so that the long-run average cost continually decreases as output increases. This situation, depicted in Figure 16.5, leads naturally to monopoly because among several firms, the largest always has a cost advantage. Any given output can be produced at lower average cost by one large firm than by several smaller firms. Decreasing average cost arises when there are very large capital or fixed costs relative to variable costs. Average fixed cost decreases as the fixed cost is spread over a larger and larger output, and the decreasing average fixed cost (combined with relatively small marginal costs) causes average total cost to

FIGURE 16.5   Two-Part Pricing by a Natural Monopoly

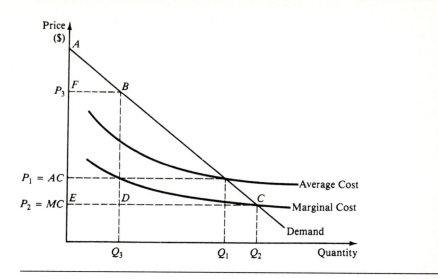

decrease as well. Average total cost always decreases as output rises, and marginal cost is always less than average cost.

This cost situation is usually said to characterize most utilities including electricity, natural gas, and perhaps water and sewer and public-transit services. Because a monopoly would naturally arise in a competitive market and because the service can be produced most efficiently by one firm, the usual approaches are either for the government to grant a private firm monopoly rights to a given market and then regulate the prices the firm may charge or for the government to become the producer directly. Both approaches are used in the United States. Although private regulated firms are the most common method for electricity production, some municipalities in the United States operate their own electric utilities; although government production of water and sewer services is most common, some localities contract with private water-supply firms and in some areas private water companies provide service without government involvement.

Setting an efficient price or charge in the case of natural monopoly faces an inherent conflict. If price is set equal to marginal cost (for instance, at P_2), then price is less than average cost, and the firm cannot cover all of its costs, that is, earn a normal profit. If price is set equal to average cost, at P_1, so that the firm will earn exactly an average rate of return on investment, then price is greater than marginal cost, causing the capital facility to be used less than is efficient. It is sometimes suggested that the government regulators should enforce a price equal to marginal cost, with the government using general tax revenues to compensate the firm for its resulting financial losses. But that, too, leads to inefficiency because of the inherent inefficiencies created by the taxes necessary to offset the utility's operating losses. In practice, utility regulation often settles on solutions that effectively set charges equal to average cost—for example, at P_1—allowing the regulated utility to earn average profits.

One possible and often practical solution to this difficulty is to set a **two-part price,** charging different prices for different quantities of the service. For example, in Figure 16.5, one could set a price of P_3 for quantities up to Q_3 and a price of P_2 for amounts greater than Q_3. Because the charge for marginal units of output is equal to marginal cost, total consumption will equal the efficient amount of Q_2. But the firms may be able to avoid operating losses because the price discrimination generates larger revenue than if a single price is charged. With the two-part price revenue is $P_3Q_3 + P_2(Q_2 - Q_3)$ or $(P_3 - P_2)Q_3 + P_2Q_2$, which is greater than the revenue from a single price, equal to P_2Q_2.

Two-part pricing takes advantage of the fact that some consumers are willing to pay prices higher than marginal cost for so-called inframarginal units (units other than the last one purchased). The two-part price captures some of that consumers' surplus for the producer, allowing the producer to charge a marginal cost price for marginal units and still cover all costs. With a single price of P_2, consumers enjoy a surplus represented by the area of triangle ACE. With the two-part price involving P_2 and P_3, consumers' surplus is smaller, represented by the areas of triangle ABF plus BCD. Rectangle $BDEF$ represents the added revenue to the producer. Of course, there is no reason why the inframarginal price needs to be set at P^3; that price must be selected to generate enough extra revenue to cover the producer's operating losses, if possible. In fact, the inframarginal price could apply only to the first unit consumed, effectively serving as a type of cover or access charge. In the case of Figure 16.5, that could entail charging a price of $\$A$ for the first unit and a price of P_2 for all subsequent units.

Two-part prices of this type are already in use for some services. Many public water systems charge a per-gallon use fee and a fixed monthly access charge. The latter is a second price effectively imposed on the first gallon of water consumed and serves to cover the fixed costs. Some public-transportation systems sell passes that allow riders to pay a lower fee for each ride than paid by consumers without the pass. Those who purchase the pass effectively pay a high price for the first ride in each period (the inframarginal ride) and a low price (usually zero) for all subsequent rides (the marginal ones). The Michigan Department of Natural Resources uses a similar system of admittance fees for Michigan state parks. Users may purchase an annual vehicle pass for $10, which entitles that vehicle to unlimited admittances without further charge to all state parks for that year. Those who purchase the pass therefore pay $10 for the first admittance in a year and a zero price for all others. Without such a pass, each vehicle admittance costs $2.50.[7]

/ Potential user-charge problems

The theoretical discussion suggests that user charges are most appropriate when most of the benefits of a government service go to identifiable direct consumers of a service

---

[7] Even with the pass, there is a daily charge for camping in the park, rather than just a visit.

whose demand shows some price elasticity. Even in such a case, two other potential issues must be considered. In some cases, objection is raised to user fees on the grounds that they are a disadvantage for consumers with lower incomes. That notion is often coupled with the statement that general taxes, in contrast, are based on "ability-to-pay." The presumption of such an argument is that it is not fair to base consumption of the government service in question on income or "willingness-to-pay," as is done when following the "benefit principle" of public finance.

It is certainly true that allocation of any good or service by money prices gives an advantage to those consumers with more money. But because that point is general, the relevant issue is why a particular government service that mostly benefits direct users should be treated differently than privately provided goods and services such as medical care or Mercedes automobiles. One possible explanation is that the service is a means of redistributing income, which is one of the economic roles of government. This is undoubtedly part of the reason why primary and secondary education is financed almost entirely from taxes. Education provides external benefits to all of society, one of which is a means of improving the economic conditions of the poor. Caution should be exercised in not carrying this argument too far, however. It is not clear that free use of public golf courses, for instance, is a very effective way of assisting the poor.

Avoiding user charges may also be an inefficient way of helping the poor. Some state–local government services are consumed much more by higher-income consumers than lower-income ones. Avoiding user-charge financing in those cases to assist lower-income consumers may actually benefit higher-income consumers to a greater degree. It could be more efficient for the government to charge everyone the user charge and give direct assistance of some type to the lower-income consumers affected by the charge.

A second potential problem with user charges is that the administration costs (to the government) and compliance costs (to the consumers) of collecting the charge are, in some cases, large enough to offset any expected efficiency gains from user-charge, as opposed to tax, financing. Typically, administration costs include costs of measuring use, billing users, and collecting the fee, whereas compliance costs include delay at road or bridge toll booths and the time and postage cost of making the required payments. Besides the other necessary conditions therefore, user-charge financing is attractive only if a means of collecting the charge at reasonable cost is available. (For instance, the advantages and disadvantages of alternative ways of administering highway user charges are discussed in Chapter 19.)

/ Application of User Charges

The application of user charges to three specific state–local government services—public higher education, water and sewer service, and refuse collection—is discussed in this section. Discussion of transportation-related user charges is presented in Chapter 19, and charges to offset the infrastructure costs associated with economic growth and development are covered in Chapter 21.

/ Financing public higher education[8]

For most readers of this book, and especially for those attending public colleges and universities, tuition is the best known of all subnational government user charges and the one with personal as well as academic implications. In the United States, tuition generally covers between 20 and 35 percent of the expenditures of public colleges and universities, with the remainder financed mostly from state (and for community colleges, sometimes local) taxes. There is substantial variation among states in the reliance on tuition, however; indeed for many years some states provide ''free'' college education to qualified residents. This naturally leads to a question of whether public college students should pay a larger (or smaller) fraction of the cost of their college education.

Those who argue that tuition (or other user charges) should be more important in financing public higher education usually suggest that most of the benefits of that education are captured directly by the students in the form of higher incomes, jobs with more prestige, and information that assists those individuals in all aspects of their lives. Moreover, those beneficiaries are directly identified, the charge can be collected at low cost (indeed at zero extra cost once any tuition is levied), and students can be easily prevented from consuming the service unless they pay the charge. With that viewpoint, higher education seems to meet all the tests for substantial user-charge financing. But there are at least four issues that suggest that this view is incomplete.

First, public institutions of higher education usually produce research and public service in addition to education of students, although those three outputs are clearly not independent. Even if one holds the position that all the benefits of the education component of output are captured by students, the research and public service components of output benefit all of society and are thus appropriately financed by the government. Indeed, pure scientific research is usually identified as a classic public good; discoveries, once made, can be used by anyone at zero marginal cost to society. Research and public service *should* therefore be financed by the general society and not directly by students.[9]

It remains to be determined what fraction of public higher-education output is research and public service compared to education, a fraction that undoubtedly differs by type of institution. In major state universities, research and public service usually represent at least half of a faculty member's job and similarly at least half of the university's output. The output of community colleges, in contrast, is usually almost entirely education. It follows therefore that the appropriate degree of user-charge (tuition) financing might be greater for institutions primarily producing education as opposed to those producing education and research. Indeed, public subsidies to four-year colleges are generally greater than to two-year colleges.

---

[8]For discussion and evidence concerning these issues for specific states, see Lee Hansen and Burton Weisbrod (1969) and John Goddeeris (1982).

[9]For that reason, it is often argued that research should be largely financed by the federal government. And the federal government, through such entities as the National Science Foundation, the National Institute for Education, and the National Institutes for Health, does substantially support university research.

Second, students already bear a larger fraction of the social cost of public higher education than it appears from comparing tuition and state appropriations. A hypothetical but illustrative computation of both the social and private cost of public higher education for one student is shown below:

Illustration: Per-Student Economic Costs of Higher Education

Category	Social Cost ($)	Student Cost ($)	Percentage
Instruction	6,000	2,000	33
Books, supplies, transportation	1,000	1,000	100
Foregone income	7,000	7,000	100
Total	14,000	10,000	71

The cost of instruction, which is essentially the college or university expenditures per student, is assumed to be $6000, of which one-third is covered by student tuition. The cost of books, supplies, and transportation represents expenditures on these items greater than would be made if the student did not attend college. These costs are therefore true opportunity costs of choosing to attend college. Similarly, foregone income represents the difference between the income the student could have earned if not attending college and actual income earned. In the example, $7000 is the approximate annual earnings for a full-time employee paid the minimum wage. This foregone income is a true social cost, in addition to a cost to the student, because society gives up the goods and services that this individual's work would have produced, the value of which can be estimated by the factor payment.[10] In the illustration, then, students bear more than 70 percent of the social cost of their public college education, not the 33 percent that appears from comparing tuition to college operating expenses.[11]

Third, even if, after consideration of these two issues, greater reliance on tuition for financing public higher education is desired in a given state, it may be difficult for individual states to act unilaterally. Potential college students can change their states of residence toward those states that make low reliance on tuition and away from those states that act to increase tuition reliance. Moreover, with an increasingly mobile society, what social benefits there may be from higher education are not likely to be confined to any given state.

Fourth, it may be that the cost to the university of adding another student—the marginal cost—is close to zero, at least for some limited number of additional students. If the university is not crowded—that is, if another student can be accommodated without reducing the education provided to other students—then it is inefficient to charge a positive price.

---

[10]This computation is different than the out-of-pocket budget students usually consider; for instance, costs of room and board are not included. Because some room and board costs are incurred regardless of whether the individual attends college, those costs would be included in the economic cost computation only to the extent that they are larger because of college attendance.

[11]The results in the illustration are very similar to the results reported by Hansen and Weisbrod (1969) for the California state college and university system.

The argument usually raised against increased reliance on tuition—that it would prevent many lower-income students from attending college—may also be faulty. The evidence shows that college students, including public college students, tend to be mostly from higher-income (above the median) families; at least, the fraction of students attending college increases with family income. To maintain low reliance on tuition for all students, then, provides substantial benefits to many students who clearly are not poor.

If equity is the concern, an alternative to low reliance on tuition, and indeed an alternative to low reliance on user charges generally, is targeted assistance to lower-income consumers. Of course, this is already done in the world of higher education. The state or university can set tuition at a level that seems efficient given the perceived social benefits and costs, and lower-income students can then be assisted with some type of income-based financial aid. This method has the potential to be a more efficient way of improving equity because aid is given only to those consumers who society decides require and deserve assistance.[12]

/ *Financing water and sewer services*[13]

Water use fees are very common, whether the water service is provided by a local government or a privately operated water utility company. These fees actually comprise, either explicitly or implicitly, three separate charges—a water-supply charge, a capital and distribution charge, and a connection charge. The water-supply charge is intended to cover the marginal cost of additional gallons of water and therefore ideally should be based on amount of water used. Use is sometimes approximated by the number of water outlets per structure or by the number of persons per structure, but it is far more common for the actual number of gallons of water consumed to be measured by a water meter. Assuming that marginal cost per gallon of water is constant, which appears reasonable for all but some special industrial users, a use fee can be computed from the measured usage and the appropriate constant per gallon charge.

The capital and distribution charge is usually a fixed charge, which may depend on the location or size (front footage) of the structure served. A charge based on front footage is intended to represent the extra cost of the water-supply pipe, as distribution costs depend on user density. It is sometimes argued that these distribution charges should also depend on distance from the supply source, although application of that concept is problematical. The location of the supply source, the water-treatment plant, is not fixed but is selected by the government. Indeed, that

---

[12]It is also sometimes argued that lower-income students face a problem in financing higher education because the capital markets do not work properly; if these students will indeed earn higher incomes due to education, then financial institutions should be willing to make loans against those future earnings. If financial institutions will not, then an appropriate solution is government-sponsored education loans.

[13]For a more comprehensive discussion of these issues, see Paul Downing and Thomas DiLorenzo (1981).

location may be changed after many consumers have selected their locations. In addition, although a new and isolated development far from the supply source would entail large extra costs of service for running new supply lines, a new development next to an existing one would only require extension of the water line (unless an entirely new and larger supply line was required). In practice, this charge is most often a fixed, front-footage charge.

Water users are also often charged for the direct costs of hookup to the water system. This one-time connection charge may depend on the number of feet of pipe required or it may be a flat charge reflecting the large fixed costs to the utility.

Analysis of potential user charges for sewer services is essentially similar to that for water (indeed, sewer disposal is a result of indoor water consumption); costs depend on the amount and type of sewage disposed and on the size and location of the structure. However, actual metering of sewer discharge is not common, except for certain industrial users. Apparently, sewage flow meters are relatively expensive compared to water meters. The usual approach, particularly for residential users, is to assume that sewage flow is some percentage of water consumption and to compute a sewer-use fee from that number of gallons and a per-gallon charge. Of course, there is no reason for the sewer per-gallon charge to be the same as the water per-gallon charge. This method does not allow for variation among users in the purpose for which water is consumed, but it may still be the best option given the measuring costs.

These charges are usually collected from consumers through monthly or quarterly billings, much the same as electricity, natural gas, or telephone bills. The water and sewer charges are usually on one bill, and the capital/distribution charges may be combined into a single amount per front foot, paid through a monthly service charge, or included in the gallonage charge.

/ Financing refuse-collection services

The costs of refuse collection arise from both collection and disposal. Disposal costs depend on the amount and type of refuse and should include the cost of any environmental damage resulting from the disposal. A user charge to cover these disposal costs should therefore be a unit charge that varies by type of unit (the disposal cost of a pound of household garbage is different from that of a pound of used nuclear fuel). One difficulty in applying such a use fee is in measuring the amount of refuse. Possible measures include the number of specific-size cans collected or the weight of refuse collected. The first suffers because different amounts of garbage may be packed into a fixed-size container, and both entail substantial administrative costs in making and recording the measurement. Even if those problems could be overcome, individuals would have an incentive to deposit their refuse at a neighbor's location, which gives rise to all sorts of silly notions about enforcement and neighborhood wars.

One innovative solution to this measurement problem, used in Grand Rapids and Lansing, Michigan, among other localities, is to require that all refuse be deposited in plastic bags sold only by the local government. In the Michigan cases, the bags are delineated by unusual colors and insignia. The fee per bag charged by the government includes not only the cost of producing the bag (what would be charged in a store) but also the disposal cost per bag. This method avoids both the administrative costs of use measurement and the incentive for individuals to attempt to shift their costs to neighbors. There is a compliance cost to users, however, because they must arrange to purchase the special bags. To facilitate this and reduce those compliance costs, the local government may arrange to have the bags sold by private retailers rather than just at the government offices, although counterfeiting is a potential problem. This method could also be extended to provide different charges for different types of refuse (bottles and cans versus paper, for example) by having different color bags sold for different fees.

One should understand that *any* use fee based on actual amount of refuse generates an incentive for consumers to avoid the charge by littering and a corresponding cost to the government of enforcement. For instance, illegal dumping might occur on vacant land, in business dumpsters, or into surface-water sewer systems. It is possible for the costs from those externalities to outweigh any gains from the use of a refuse-collection fee. On the other hand, a use fee based on quantity also generates an incentive for consumers to avoid refuse through recycling, use of returnable containers, and substitution of reusable for disposable materials (such as cloth rather than disposable diapers). One alternative is to impose a fee on manufacturers or sellers to induce them to change the packaging or nature of products, such as a disposable-diaper tax recently proposed in Arizona. Another option is a recycling fee that is returned to the consumer if the product is recycled, such as bottle and can deposits.

Refuse-collection costs depend on the type of refuse and the density and location of the users. Obviously, collections requiring a special vehicle or extra trip (such as collection of household durables, for example, refrigerators) should ideally entail a specific charge. In practice, however, it is not clear that the absence of such a charge generates much inefficiency—replacement of those durables is probably insensitive to disposal costs. The argument for these special collection charges, then, must be fairness. Routine collection costs, on the other hand, depend mostly on time and the density of consumers. It takes longer to collect from widely spaced single-family residences, for example, than from multifamily residences with all refuse in one location, perhaps deposited in specially designed large containers. It may be appropriate therefore, as some localities evidently do, to charge a lower fee per unit of refuse for apartments and commercial establishments than for residences.

In practice refuse-collection services are provided both by local governments and private firms. In the first case, the service is usually financed out of general taxes, although fixed charges per structure per month are sometimes used. Among private firms, fixed monthly charges are most common, although the charge often applies to a fixed, maximum amount of service; extra service brings extra charges. In many rural areas, refuse disposal is still the responsibility of individual consumers who make the weekly trip to the dump, which may be operated by the government or a private firm and which is financed either from taxes or dumping charges.

/ Summary

User-charge refers to prices charged by state–local governments for specific services or privileges. They are to be distinguished from financing services through general taxes, with no direct relationship between tax payment and service received. User charges create an incentive for efficient choice because consumers face the true costs of their consumption decisions.

Financing methods that can be considered user charges include direct charges for use of a public facility or consumption of a service, license taxes or fees paid for the privilege of undertaking some activity (such as fishing license and driver license fees), and special property tax assessments levied for a specific service.

Charges and fees represented about 15.3 percent of the general revenue of state–local governments in 1986, with traditional user charges alone representing almost 13 percent of revenue. Education and hospitals are the two budget categories from which most state–local user charges arise. Total user charges of state–local governments, whether broadly or narrowly defined, have increased faster than other revenues since the later 1970s.

User-charge financing is more attractive, the greater is the share of marginal benefits that accrues to direct users, the greater the percentage of benefits of a service or facility that go to direct users, the more easily users can be identified and excluded (at reasonable cost) from consuming the service unless the charge is paid, and the more price elastic is demand.

Objection is raised to user fees on the grounds that they are a disadvantage for consumers with lower incomes and that the administration costs (to the government) and compliance costs (to the consumers) of collecting the charge may offset any expected efficiency gains.

Even if there is no additional cost to the government of providing a service to an additional consumer, an additional consumer may impose congestion costs on other users. The purpose of use fees in those situations is to allocate a scarce resource among competing demands and provide a measure of the demand for new capital investment.

Discussion Questions

1. In many large cities, the government operates a museum, library, and zoo that are visited by substantial numbers of people who are not residents of the city. They may come from the metropolitan area or from around the state. What economic reasons would justify the city financing these services through user charges? What problems would user-charge finance present in these cases? Consider how the charges might be structured for each service.

2. Suppose that your state provides a number of parks with majestic mountains, beautiful beaches, and unspoiled wilderness areas. These parks were acquired and operated in the past using the state's general tax revenue. Now the state

proposes to charge a daily entrance fee of $3 per vehicle, with the revenue earmarked for the ''state park fund''(to be used for operating expenses, capital improvements, and acquisition of new parks). At a public hearing on the proposal, one citizen complained ''It is unfair to require taxpayers who have paid for these parks with their tax dollars to now also pay a fee to use them.'' As director of the state parks department, how would you respond to this citizen?

3. Suppose that partly as a result of this type of complaint, the state park user-fee proposal is revised so that no fee will be charged for park use Monday through Friday, a $3 fee will be charged on weekends, and a $10 fee will be charged on holidays and holiday weekends (Memorial Day, Fourth of July, Labor Day, and so on). Is there any economic rationale for such a structure? Do you think it is fairer than charging the same fee at all times? More efficient?

4. Suppose that the apartment building you live in at college has only one water meter for the entire building. The landlord receives a water bill from the city each quarter based on the gallons of water used, but each apartment or tenant is not charged separately—the cost of water is effectively included in the rent. Now the water department decides to install separate meters for each apartment and to bill each separately rather than the landlord (so the rent is reduced by X per person for all tenants). The city justifies the cost of the extra meters and billings on the grounds that the city's scarce water resources will be used more efficiently. What is the price to a tenant or apartment per gallon of water before and after the new meters are installed? Do you think the new procedure will reduce water use? If so, how might the student tenants of these apartments act to conserve water? Will there be a gain in economic efficiency?

Selected Readings

''Costing and Pricing Local Government Services.'' *Governmental Finance,* 11 (March 1982): 3–27

Muskin, Selma, ed. *Public Prices for Public Products.* Washington, D.C.: The Urban Institute, 1972.

17 / Intergovernmental Grants

The basic economic justification for federal functional grants-in-aid is provided by the widespread, and ever-increasing, spillover of benefits from some of the most important state and local expenditure programs.[1]

George F. Break

Intergovernmental grants, sometimes called **grants-in-aid,** are transfers of funds from one government to another, most often from a higher-level government in the federal system to a set of lower-level governments. These grants are of many different types and are intended to improve the operation of a federal system of government finance. In this chapter, the purposes for grants, the economic effects of the different types of grants, and then an appropriate policy of grant use are considered.

/ Grants in the U.S. Fiscal System

In 1986 the federal government transferred more than $113 billion of aid to state–local governments, which represented about $.21 for every $1 raised by state–local governments from their own sources. Similarly, state governments transferred nearly $127 billion to local governments, or more than $.54 for every $1 collected by local governments from their own sources. As reflected by the data in Table 17.1, intergovernmental grants, both from the federal government to states and localities and from the states to localities, have been a dominant feature of the federal fiscal system in the United States for more than twenty years.

Although the absolute magnitude of these grants has generally increased annually over these years (1982 being an exception for federal aid), the relative importance of intergovernmental grants increased in the 1960s and early 1970s and peaked in the late 1970s. Intergovernmental grants, and particularly federal grants, have declined in relative importance since. For instance, federal aid increased from about 17 percent of state–local own-source revenue in 1964 to nearly 26 percent in 1974 and 34 percent by 1976. Over that same period, federal aid increased from

---

[1] *Intergovernmental Fiscal Relations in the United States.* Washington, D.C.: The Brookings Institution, 1967, 105.

TABLE 17.1

Federal and State Aid, Various Years, 1964–84

	Federal Aid			State Aid	
Year	Amount[a] (Billions of Dollars)	Percentage of Federal Outlay[b]	Percentage of State–Local General Revenue from Own Sources	Amount[a] (Billions of Dollars)	Percentage of Local General Revenue from Own Sources
1964	10.1	8.6	17.3	13.0	42.9
1969	19.4	11.0	20.4	24.8	54.0
1974	42.9	16.1	25.8	45.6	59.4
1976	69.1	15.9	34.4	56.7	60.8
1978	79.2	17.0	32.1	65.8	59.4
1980	90.8	15.5	30.4	82.8	63.6
1981	94.6	14.0	28.4	91.3	62.7
1982	86.0	11.8	23.3	97.0	59.4
1983	88.5	11.4	22.3	99.5	55.6
1984	99.0	11.5	22.2	106.7	54.3
1985	106.2	11.2	21.6	116.4	53.9
1986	113.1	10.7	21.4	126.8	54.3

Source: ACIR. Tables 8, 44, and 45. 1986.

[a]Census definition of aid amounts and general revenue.

[b]National income and product accounts definition of federal aid and outlay.

less than 9 percent of total federal government outlays to 17 percent by 1978. Since then, federal aid's share of the federal government budget has decreased to less than it was in 1969, and federal aid correspondingly provides a smaller fraction of state–local government revenue. Although state and local governments, on average, received $.34 of federal aid for every local dollar collected in 1976, they received $.21 in 1986. Similar decreases in the relative importance of state aid for local governments have also occurred in the 1980s, at least partly because states are receiving less federal aid to pass along to localities.

Still, intergovernmental grants are an important source of revenue for nearly all state–local governments, as suggested by the data in Table 17.2. In 1986 state governments received a quarter of their revenue through intergovernmental grants and local governments nearly 39 percent, with counties and school districts being the type of local governments most reliant on grants, at least on average. Although state aid is substantially more important than direct federal aid for all types of local governments except special districts, some of that state aid arises from federal grants to the states, which are effectively "passed on" to localities. The particularly high reliance on state aid by school districts reflects a growing role for state governments in financing local education, a topic discussed more comprehensively in Chapter 18.

More than 65 percent of federal aid to states and localities is nominally directed toward the three budget categories of education, highways, and public welfare, the last alone representing more than 37 percent, as shown in Table 17.3. In contrast, education is the dominant category of state aid to localities, accounting for about

TABLE 17.2

Intergovernmental Grants as a Percentage of General Revenue, by Type of Government, Various Years, 1962–84

Year	States	Local Governments					
		Total	Counties	Municipalities	Townships	School Districts	Special Districts
1962							
Federal	22.8	2.0	0.7	2.5	0.8	1.4	8.9
State	—	28.4	36.3	16.3	20.6	37.3	3.2
Total[a]	24.0	30.4	38.6	20.4	22.5	40.8	21.1
1967							
Federal	26.1	3.0	1.3	4.2	1.2	2.3	8.9
State	—	31.7	37.6	20.7	22.0	40.1	5.6
Total[a]	27.4	34.7	40.3	26.3	24.5	44.3	23.2
1972							
Federal	27.2	4.3	1.7	7.3	1.3	1.9	15.5
State	—	33.4	39.1	24.1	19.6	42.0	3.9
Total[a]	28.4	37.7	42.1	32.9	22.0	45.0	29.6
1977							
Federal	27.1	9.2	9.0	14.7	7.5	1.5	21.7
State	—	33.7	34.5	23.2	20.4	47.3	7.4
Total[a]	28.8	42.9	45.3	39.7	29.7	50.2	38.2
1982							
Federal	24.0	7.6	6.5	12.0	5.8	1.0	18.5
State	—	33.9	34.1	20.8	22.6	51.7	7.6
Total[a]	25.1	41.5	42.0	34.6	30.1	54.3	34.7
1986							
Federal	23.6	5.4	4.3	8.0	4.9	0.9	15.0
State	—	33.3	31.8	20.2	22.4	52.7	5.0
Total[a]	25.1	38.7	37.0	30.4	29.1	55.1	28.9

Sources: For 1962–82, U.S. Department of Commerce, Bureau of the Census. *Governmental Finances.* Table entitled "General Revenue by Source, by Level of Government" (1962, 1967, 1972, 1977, 1982). For 1986, U.S. Department of Commerce. *Governmental Finances, 1986* (1987).

[a]Includes grants from local governments.

64 percent of state aid. As a result of this aid along with direct expenditures by the federal and state governments, the federal government finances a little more than half of public-welfare expenditures, while state governments finance slightly less than half of expenditures on primary and secondary education.

/ *Purposes of Grants*

Traditionally, three potential roles for intergovernmental grants in a federal fiscal system are identified. Grants may be used to correct for externalities that arise from the structure of subnational governments and thus can improve the efficiency of

TABLE 17.3

Federal and State Aid, by Budget Category, 1986

	Federal		State	
Category	Category Aid as Percentage of Total Aid	Percentage of State–Local Expenditure in Category Financed by Federal Government[a]	Category Aid as Percentage of Total Aid	Percentage of State–Local Expenditure in Category Financed by State Government[a]
Education	16.0	9[b]	64.0	49[b]
Highways	12.5	28.6	4.9	45
Public welfare	37.3	56.5	11.7	39
Other	34.2	na	19.3	—
Total	100.0	19	100.0	54

Sources: U.S. Department of Commerce. *Governmental Finances in 1985–86* and *State Government Finances in 1986,* following procedure of ACIR, 1986, Table 18, p. 29.

[a]Expenditure measured as state–local direct general expenditure in category. Government share includes aid and direct expenditures, unless otherwise noted.
[b]Expenditures for elementary and secondary education only.
[c]Does not include welfare expenditure directly financed by the federal government, amounting to about $24 million in 1984.

fiscal decisions. Grants can be used for explicit redistribution of resources among regions or localities. And grants have been considered as a macroeconomic stabilizing mechanism for the subnational government sector.

Recall from Chapter 2 that the existence of interjurisdictional externalities, or spillovers, can cause service decisions by individual subnational governments to be inefficient from society's viewpoint. If nonresidents benefit from a state or local service, but those nonresident benefits are not considered in the decision about the amount of the service to provide, social marginal benefits will be underestimated and too little of the service provided. In such a case, an intergovernmental grant can be used to induce the subnational government to provide more of that specific service, as efficiency requires. Moreover, because the grant funds are generated from taxes collected by the granting government, those nonresidents who benefit from the service end up paying for part of the service through their state or federal taxes.

Recall from Chapter 4 that individual migration among local communities also may involve a type of externality, if that migration imposes costs on the other residents. Individuals may move to avoid subnational taxes or gain services. But if the new residents pay less than the average cost of services they consume, existing residents face either service reductions with constant taxes or higher taxes to maintain services. The potential migrants have no incentive to include those costs imposed on other residents in their decision about whether to relocate, so the distribution of population among localities may become inefficient. Again, intergovernmental grants may be used to resolve this difficulty. Grants to high-tax or low-service localities may forestall some of the migration in search of lower taxes or more services and contribute to a more efficient structure of local government.

Intergovernmental grants effectively substitute the granting government's tax revenue for that of the recipient government. If the taxes used by the granting government are more efficient than the ones they replace, this tax substitution is another way that grants may improve the efficiency of the federal system. Because mobility is so much greater among subnational jurisdictions than among nations, a nationally levied tax may generate fewer inefficiencies than a set of similar subnational taxes. The revenue can be generated nationally but spent locally, with a system of intergovernmental grants. This is at least part of the rationale for revenue-sharing programs.

Intergovernmental grants are also sometimes suggested as a method of explicit income redistribution for equity reasons. Taxes collected by the federal government or a state may be allocated to lower-level governments inversely proportional to income or property value, resulting in an implicit transfer from governments in higher-income jurisdictions to governments in lower-income jurisdictions. The effects of this type of income redistribution are not always clear, however, because jurisdictions are seldom completely homogeneous in income and because the local government determines how the grant funds are to be spent. Even jurisdictions that are low-income on average may have high-income residents, in some cases a substantial number. If the objective is to assist low-income individuals and families, it seems preferable in most cases to give grants directly to those individuals, rather than the state or local government where they reside.

/ Types of Grants

As depicted in Figure 17.1, intergovernmental grants are usually characterized by four factors: whether use of the grant is intended for a specific service or may be used generally, whether grants are automatically allocated by a formula or require an application associated with a specific project, whether the grant funds must be matched by recipient government funds, and whether the potential size of grant is limited.

Specific, or **categorical, grants** are the dominant type, both by number and amount of funds, offered by the federal and state governments. From the data in Table 17.4, the federal government had 392 different categorical grant programs in 1984, representing nearly 97 percent of the number of federal grant programs and nearly 82 percent of federal aid dollars. The dominant state program provides specific grants for local education.

If the amount of these specific grants does not change as a recipient government changes its taxes or expenditures, then they are said to be **lump-sum,** or **nonmatching grants.** The amount of grant cannot be altered by fiscal decisions of the recipient government. In 1984, 175, or about 45 percent, of federal categorical grants were nonmatching. **Matching grants,** on the other hand, do require recipient government taxes or spending, with the size of the grant depending on the amount

FIGURE 17.1 *Types of Intergovernmental Grants*

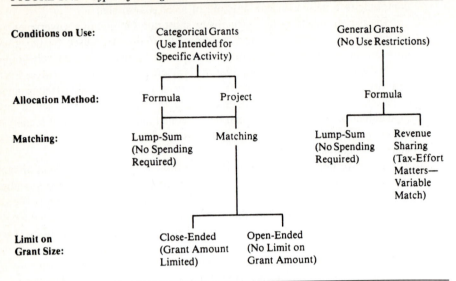

TABLE 17.4

Federal Grants, By Type, 1984 (Billions of Dollars)

Type	Amount	Percentage of Amount	Number	Percentage of Number
General assistance (revenue sharing)	$4.57	4.7	1	0.2
Block grants (for community development (two), health (four), social services (two), and one each for education, employment and training, low-income energy assistance, transportation	12.96	13.3	12	3.0
Categorical grants	80.05	82.0	392	96.8
Matching			217	55.4[a]
Formula			77	
Open-ended			11	
Project			140	
Nonmatching			175	44.6[a]
Formula			49	
Open-ended			7	
Project			126	
Total	97.58	100.0	405	

Sources: ACIR. (1984); U.S. Executive Office of the President (1985).

[a]Percentage of categorical only.

of those taxes or spending. Typically, a specific matching aid program offers to match each dollar of recipient tax or expenditure on that specific service with R grant dollars, intended to be spent on that service. R is called the matching rate. If $R = 1$, then each local dollar generates one grant dollar, so that the grant finances half of the expenditure. If $R = .5$, then each local dollar generates $.50 in grant funds, and the grant finances one-third of the expenditure ($.50/$1.50). Generally, then, the share financed by the grant (denoted by M), is

$$M = R/(1 + R)$$

For predicting the effects of matching grants, one needs to understand that through this matching rate, the grant reduces the price of additional amounts of the aided service to the recipient government. If $R = 1$, the grant finances one-half of expenditures, so the cost in local taxes of increasing spending by $1 is only $.50. In general, the local tax price (denoted by P) of an additional dollar of service (the local marginal cost) is

$$
\begin{aligned}
P &= 1 - M \\
&= 1 - [R/(1 + R)] \\
&= 1/(1 + R)
\end{aligned}
$$

If $R = 1$, each additional dollar of service costs local residents $.50 in local taxes. If $R = .5$, the local tax price of $1's worth of additional service is $.67. If $R = .25$, the local tax price is $.80; local residents pay $.80 for each additional dollar of expenditure on the specific aided service.

Both matching and nonmatching categorical grants may be allocated either by formula or a project-by-project basis and may be either open-ended (no limit on the grant amount) or close-ended (there is some limit on grant amount because the funds appropriated for the grant program are fixed). As shown in Table 17.4, however, project categorical grants outnumber formula grants by more than two to one, while less than 5 percent of categorical grants are open-ended. The class of open-ended, formula, nonmatching categorical grants (of which there were seven) should be clarified. In these cases, the formula allocating subnational government grants implies a fixed payment for factors outside of the recipient government's control, such as population or population characteristics, but there is no limit on the amount of aid. Programs in this class include unemployment compensation and some child nutrition grants.

General grants, those without use restrictions (or with only very loose restrictions), are rare among federal government grants, as shown in Table 17.4, although somewhat more common among state grants. These grants, which are sometimes said to provide general fiscal assistance, are almost always allocated by formula. If the formula includes factors outside of the direct control of the government, such as population or per-capita income, the grant is a pure lump-sum to the government. On the other hand, if the formula includes factors controlled by the recipient government, such as tax collections or tax effort, then the amount of the grant can be altered by recipient government decisions. This method, used for the federal and some state revenue-sharing grants, creates a type of matching grant, although the total amount of grant dollars are fixed and the matching rate varies, as discussed later in this chapter. Note that matching, open-ended, general-purpose grants are not a good idea because by redefining all consumption as part of government, all of consumption could be matched. It is obviously impossible for this to happen generally.

The best-known general-purpose grant was the U.S. General Revenue Sharing Program, begun in 1972, which initially provided grants totaling about $6 billion annually to state–local governments. The funds were first divided among the states by a formula that included population, per-capita income, and tax effort, with one-third of a state's funds allocated to the state government and the remaining two-thirds distributed to local governments in that state, again by formula. The size of the grant fund was increased slightly in 1976, while states were removed from receiving revenue-sharing grants and the fund decreased proportionately in 1984. The federal revenue sharing program for local governments expired in 1987.

A class identified as **block grants** is also listed in Table 17.4. This term is used to describe specific grants in categories that are very broadly or loosely defined. For instance, there are two separate block grants for community development. There is, correspondingly, a long list of approved activities that can be financed with these funds in that general category. The number and size of block grants has been growing in recent years as individual categorical grants have been combined into new block grants. The idea is that these fall in some intermediate area between narrowly defined categorical grants and ones with no use restrictions at all. As we will come to understand later in this chapter, in most cases these block grants are effectively general grants because the categories are broad enough to allow most recipient governments leeway for reallocating other funds.

/ Economic Effects: Theory

Intergovernmental grants may affect recipient government fiscal decisions either by increasing the resources available to provide government services, called an **income effect,** or by increasing resources and reducing the marginal costs of additional services, called a **price effect.** Either effect may influence the amount of government service demanded, although in different ways. In taking this approach to analyzing intergovernmental grants, economists retain the notion of individual demands for government services, as discussed in Chapter 14, which must be coordinated by a political choice system. If political decisions are made by voting, then the effect of the grant on a government's decisions is determined by the effect of the grant on the decisive voter.

Accordingly, most economic analyses of the expected effects of intergovernmental grants start with the effects of the grants on individual demands, as shown in Figure 17.2. An increase in available resources, which arises from a lump-sum grant, will cause the demand curve for government services to shift out (assuming that government services are normal goods, as supported by empirical evidence).

FIGURE 17.2   *The Income and Price Effects of a Grant*

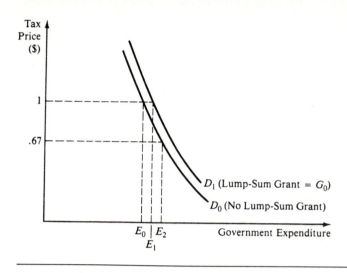

With the marginal cost of an additional dollar of expenditure remaining at \$1, desired expenditure increases from E_0 to E_1. On the other hand, a matching grant reduces the marginal cost (or price) of additional expenditure, which causes an increase in the amount of government service demanded, for instance, from E_0 to E_2. In economic parlance, lump-sum (nonmatching) grants increase demand via an income effect, whereas matching grants increase the desired amount of service due to a price effect. Given the characteristics of the grant program and the local political choice system, the economic effects of the grant can be predicted. Several general results follow.

/ Matching grants are more stimulative than lump-sum grants

Perhaps the most fundamental result of microeconomics is that a decrease in price will have a greater effect on consumption than an increase in income, if that increase is large enough to give a consumer the same choices as the price decrease. When the price of a product decreases, whether for hamburgers or education, consumers are influenced by two separate factors. The product whose price has fallen is now relatively less expensive compared to other goods than before the price change *and* the consumer's purchasing power has increased—even with constant income, more of all goods can be afforded. The first is called the substitution, or price, effect because it is an incentive for consumers to substitute more of the now relatively less expensive commodity. The second is the income effect. For normal goods, both of these influences are an incentive for consumers to consume more of the product whose price has decreased.

When consumers receive an increase in income, purchasing power rises, but there is no change in the relative price or cost of different products. Therefore, if the income effect that arises from a price decrease is of the same magnitude as the income effect from an increase in income, the price decrease should affect consumption to a greater degree. The income effects are the same, but the price decrease has an additional substitution effect. In essence, price changes are expected to stimulate greater changes in consumption than equivalent changes in income because price changes alter purchasing power *and* relative costs, whereas income changes alter only purchasing power (and the two changes in purchasing power are the same size).

The implication of this microeconomic principle is that *an open-ended matching grant is expected to increase government expenditure on the aided service by a greater amount than an "equal-size" lump-sum grant*, where "equal-size" is defined to mean a lump-sum grant large enough to allow the government the same expenditure as selected with the matching grant. Although the government could select the same expenditure in both cases, it does not because of the price incentive. The change depicted in Figure 17.2 represents this principle. A matching grant that provides $.50 for each $1 of locally financed expenditure reduces the local tax price per dollar of expenditure to $.67, thus inducing an increase in government expenditure on the specific service from E_0 to E_2. If a lump-sum grant equal to G_0 were offered instead, which would be large enough to allow the recipient government to select expenditure E_2, the theory argues that the actual expenditure selected would be smaller, for instance, equal to E_1.

This analysis applies directly to open-ended matching grants but must be modified for close-ended matching grants. Suppose, for example, that a matching grant is offered of $.50 for each $1 of locally financed expenditure up to a maximum local expenditure of $100 per capita. The maximum grant is $50 per capita. The local tax price is $.67 as long as local per-capita expenditure is less than $100; above $100, the local tax price is $1. In other words, this is initially a matching grant for recipient governments that spend less than $100 per capita before the grant program begins, but it is a lump-sum grant for governments that spend $100 per capita or more. Equivalently, this is a matching grant for governments that spend less than $150 per capita, *including the grant*. For instance, a government spending $135 per capita on the specific aided function (composed of $90 in local money and $45 of grant) can increase per-capita expenditure by $1 with an extra $.67 of local money. Once total per-capita expenditure reaches $150, the grant is at its maximum and is thus a lump-sum grant.

The close-ended nature of the grant complicates the analysis because (a) it is not possible to determine whether the grant is effectively matching or lump-sum without knowing the recipient government's position and (b) a recipient government's reaction to the grant can move its per-capita expenditure across the boundary, transforming an apparent matching grant into a lump-sum one, or *vice versa*. For governments "near" the expenditure cap on the grant, the full price effect of the grant may never apply. One expects, therefore, that *close-ended matching grants will be more stimulative, in aggregate, than pure lump-sum grants* (because some governments feel some price effect), *but less stimulative than open-ended matching grants* (because some governments reach the maximum).

/ Matching grants provide tax relief

The analysis above argues that matching grants will induce an increase in spending on the aided category, but will the increase be as large as the grant? If not, then the matching grant can also increase government spending in other budget categories or allow for local tax relief. As long as the demand for government service is price inelastic, a matching grant will increase expenditure by less than the amount of the grant, thus freeing local funds to be spent in other ways. Because the evidence, reported in Chapter 14, shows that demand for most state–local services is indeed price inelastic, matching grants are expected to be partially used for tax relief. The expenditure and tax effects of matching grants are demonstrated numerically in Table 17.5.

If an open-ended matching grant equal to $.50 for each $1 of local funds is offered, the local tax price falls from $1 to $.67, a decrease of 33 percent. If the price elasticity of demand for the aided service is less than one (inelastic), then expenditures will increase by less than 33 percent. Suppose that initial per-capita expenditures are $100 and the price elasticity is −.5. Then the 33-percent reduction in price would induce approximately a 16.5-percent increase in expenditure to $116.50. This would be financed by $77.67 of local money and $38.83 of grant money. The matching grant increases total expenditure but decreases the amount of local funds spent on the category by $22.33. This $22.33 can be spent by the government on other services or on local tax relief.

If demand is price inelastic, matching grants do stimulate increases in total expenditure but do not stimulate increases in locally raised money spent on the service. This has lead to some confusion as to whether matching grants are "stimulative," the confusion resulting from just what "stimulative" means.

TABLE 17.5

Matching Grants: Expenditure Effects, Tax Effects

Initial per-capita expenditure	$100
Initial local per-capita tax	$100
Price elasticity for per-capita expenditure	−0.5
Grant matching rate	0.50 ($.50 for each $1 of local tax)
Tax price with grant	$0.67 [$1/($1 + $.50)]
Percentage decrease in price	33%
Percentage increase in expenditure	16.5%
Per-capita expenditure with grant	$116.50
Per-capita grant	$ 38.83
Per-capita local tax	$ 77.67
Increase in expenditure	$ 16.50
Decrease in local tax	$ 22.33
Sum = grant	$ 38.83

/ Specific lump-sum grants may be no different than general grants

A lump-sum grant of $G that is restricted for use in a specific category may be no different, from the viewpoint of the recipient government, than a grant of $G with no use restrictions. That is, the two grants may have the same effect on a recipient government's fiscal behavior. This issue depends on whether the government can and does reallocate locally raised funds from the specific budget category to others as a result of the grant.

The possibilities are depicted in Figure 17.3, which shows the budget options for a community (or individual) between government expenditures on the aided category and expenditures on all other (government and private) goods. With no grant, this community can spend a maximum of $Z on other goods *or* a maximum of $V on the specific service *or* any combination on the budget line between those two points. A lump-sum grant expands the set of affordable options, that is, shifts the budget line out. A general lump-sum grant equal to ZY shifts the budget line to YW; the government receives ZY dollars that can be spent on anything, including entirely on "Other Goods." A lump-sum grant of the same size that must be spent on the aided category shifts the budget line to ZXW; the recipient government *must* buy ZX units of the aided service, the amount that can be purchased using all the grant funds. Thus, all the grant funds are spent on the intended service.

Two implications follow. First, *the restriction on use of the grant will "matter" to the recipient only if intended expenditures on the aided category are* less than E_G, that is *less than what the grant will buy.* If the recipient government would have spent more than E_G anyway, local funds equal to the amount of the grant can be shifted to other uses. Local funds are said to be *fungible* within the entire budget.

FIGURE 17.3 **Comparison of Alternative Lump-Sum Grants**

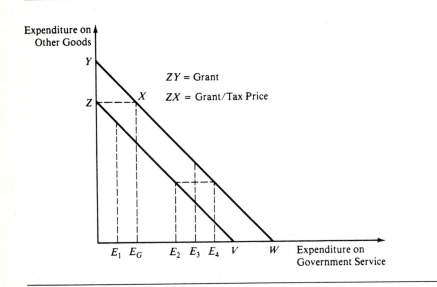

TABLE 17.6

Lump-Sum Grants: Expenditure Effects, Tax Effects

Initial per-capita expenditure	$100
Initial per-capita local tax	$100
Expenditure increase per grant dollar	$ 0.10
Per-capita grant	$ 38.83
Increase in per-capita expenditure	$ 3.88
Percentage increase in per-capita expenditure	3.88%
Per-capita expenditure with grant	$103.88
Per-capita grant	$ 38.83
Per-capita local tax with grant	$ 65.05
Increase in expenditure	$ 3.88
Decrease in local tax	$ 34.95
Sum = grant	$ 38.83

Put another way, beyond E_G, the budget choices from the two grant programs are identical. Second, a *lump-sum categorical grant does not guarantee that expenditures on the aided category will increase by the full amount of the grant.* A government initially spending E_2 on the specific service already spends an amount equal to the grant. Rather than increasing to E_4, the change from increasing expenditures by the full amount of the grant, the government more likely would increase expenditures to some intermediate level like E_3, freeing funds for increased spending in other areas as well.

Students are often experts on fungibility. Suppose your parents visit you at school and as they are leaving give you a gift of $5, which they insist *must* be spent on pizza. Even if you always obey your parents, does this mean you will spend $5 *more* on pizza this week than you usually do? Not necessarily. If you normally spend $10 per week on pizza, you might increase your pizza consumption to $11, including the $5 gift, and shift your own $5 you would have spent on pizza to some other necessity, perhaps books. You satisfied the restriction without having to increase consumption by the amount of the gift. In effect, you behaved in the same way as you would have if the gift came with no use limitation.

The expenditure and tax effects of lump-sum grants are shown in Table 17.6. Again assume that initial per-capita expenditures are $100, but that a lump-sum grant equal to $38.83 per capita is provided. Suppose further that the income elasticity is such that $.10 of each grant dollar is used to increase government expenditure on the aided category.[2] As a result of the grant, per-capita expenditure increases by $3.88 (.10 × $38.83) to 103.88, which is financed with $65.05 of locally raised money and the $38.83 grant. Accordingly, the amount of local funds spent on the category decreases by $34.95, which can be spent on other services or tax relief.

----

[2]Suppose that per-capita income is $500 and the income elasticity of demand is .5. The per-capita grant of $38.83 increases income by about 7.76 percent, causing an expenditure increase of 3.88 percent.

The potential for specific-purpose, lump-sum grant funds to be shifted to other uses in this manner has led to consideration of other types of use restrictions, particularly a requirement for maintenance of local effort. This restriction requires not only that the grant funds be spent on the aided category but also that local funds spent on the category not be reduced. But even this restriction may not be as severe as it seems because expenditure would normally increase annually without the grant. If a government spends $100 on a specific service in one year and plans to spend $110 in the following year, a $10 lump-sum grant with an effort maintenance restriction is the same as a $10 grant with no restriction. The grant can be spent on the specified service, and the additional $10 the government would have spent on that service can be reallocated to other uses. In general, the effort maintenance restriction is binding only if the grant is larger than the increase in expenditure that would be selected without the grant (which is not observed).

/ Tax effort grants are matching

One common factor in the allocation formula for revenue-sharing grants, used for the U.S. Federal Revenue Sharing Program and for about a one-quarter of state revenue-sharing funds in 1980, is tax effort, which is taxes as a fraction of some measure of ability to pay. Tax effort is usually measured either by tax revenue as a fraction of income or, for many local governments, property tax as a fraction of taxable value. In these revenue-sharing programs, a higher tax effort generates a larger grant, given no change in any other allocation factor. A high tax effort can reflect either a great demand for government service in a jurisdiction, a relatively low tax base, or a high production cost for government service. But because a subnational government chooses its tax effort, the size of the revenue-sharing grant can be affected by those recipient governments, similar to matching grants.

The operation of a representative state revenue-sharing program is demonstrated in Table 17.7, simplified with two equal-size recipient local governments. The state revenue-sharing program divides a fixed amount of state tax collections ($100) among the two localities based on population (POP_i) and tax effort, here defined as the effective property tax rate (T_i/V_i). Both jurisdictions initially collect equal property taxes, but because jurisdiction A's property value is lower, its tax effort is twice as great as jurisdiction B's. Because they have equal populations, A receives 66.7 percent ($66.70) of the revenue-sharing funds, and B receives the remaining 33.3 percent ($33.30).

What happens if one of these governments (B) increases property taxes by 20 percent to $600 while A holds taxes constant? Jurisdiction B's relative tax effort rises, and therefore its share of the revenue-sharing funds also rises. In this example, because B gains $4.20 in revenue-sharing funds from the $100 increase in taxes, the new local tax price is $.96. Jurisdiction A loses the $4.20 of revenue-sharing funds, a 6.3-percent decrease, even though it made no fiscal changes.

Several implications follow. A recipient jurisdiction can increase its revenue-sharing grant by increasing taxes at a greater rate than its competitor jurisdictions. Even if a jurisdiction does not seek a larger revenue-sharing grant, it will have to

TABLE 17.7

Sample Revenue-Sharing Program

Feature	Jurisdiction A	Jurisdiction B
Population	50	50
Property tax	$500	$500
Taxable value	$5,000	$10,000
Effective tax rate − tax effort	10%	5%
Relative tax effort (RTE)	1.50	0.75
$$\frac{T_i/V_i}{\sum_i T_i / \sum_i V_i}$$		
Grant share	66.7%	33.3%
$$\frac{RTE_i \times POP_i}{\sum_i (RTE_i \times POP_i)}$$		
Grant (fund = $100)	$66.70	$33.30
Effect of Property Tax Change		
New property tax	$500	$600
New relative tax effort	1.36	0.82
New grant share	62.5%	37.5%
New grant amount	$62.50	$37.50
Change in grant	− $4.20	+ $4.20
Percentage change in grant	− 6.3%	+ 12.6%
Price of tax increase	na	$0.96

increase taxes just to avoid losing grant funds if any other recipient jurisdiction raises its taxes. Each jurisdiction is in competition with all others for the limited revenue-sharing funds. Because all jurisdictions face these same opportunities and because each is uncertain about the behavior of its competitors, there is a general incentive for an increase in government expenditures. This program is different from a standard open-ended matching grant because the total amount of grant funds are fixed and because the rate at which local taxes are matched by increased grants changes as all the recipient jurisdictions react to the grant. As one special case, if all the recipient jurisdictions increase taxes at the same rate, no one's revenue-sharing grant changes, although all increase government spending.

/ Economic Effects: Evidence

It is difficult and somewhat dangerous to make generalizations about the estimated effects of intergovernmental grants because there seems to be substantial variation in how different governments respond to different grants and because the results of different economic studies often vary greatly even for the same grant program. Nevertheless, some conclusions about the general direction and relative magnitude of effects caused by different grants are broadly supported.

First, open-ended, categorical matching grants do seem to increase expenditures on the aided category and do so by a larger amount than equal-size specific lump-sum grants, as predicted by theory. Because the estimated price elasticities for most subnational government services are less than one (in absolute value), the expenditure increase from a matching grant is smaller than the grant, allowing funds to be diverted to other expenditure categories or to tax relief. The numerical examples of Tables 17.5 and 17.6 are generally representative, therefore, of the statistical evidence.

Although open-ended matching grants are not the most common type of federal grant, as previously noted, they are used for two well-known programs—Aid to Families with Dependent Children (AFDC) and Medicaid. Robert Moffitt's (1984) analysis of state government responses to federal AFDC grants supports the general conclusions noted above. Through grants to states, the federal government pays a percentage of state AFDC benefits, with that percentage differing in a complicated way both by state and the level of benefit chosen by the state. Using 1970 data, Moffitt estimated that the elasticity of a state's per-capita AFDC benefit with respect to the national subsidy rate is .15; a 10-percent increase in the subsidy rate increases per-capita benefits by 1.5 percent. In 1970 the average per-capita AFDC benefit was $45, with the federal government paying about 60 percent of the marginal cost (an additional $1 of benefit costs the state $.40). If the subsidy rate were increased to 70 percent, about a 16-percent increase, the per-capita benefit would increase by about 2.4 percent (16 × .15), or about $1. The average state would have received approximately $1.20 more in per-capita grant, with about $1 going for increased AFDC benefits.

Second, there is some evidence that closed-ended categorical matching grants sometimes have greater expenditure effects than open-ended matching grants, which seems contrary to theory. But closed- and open-ended grants are not used for the same services, so the different expenditure effects most likely result from differences in demand for the services. For instance, the closed-ended categoricals, which are the most common type of federal grant, may be used for services that state–local governments were not substantially providing or may include effort maintenance provisions. In either case, the opportunity to use grant funds to shift resources to other budget categories is limited, forcing a larger increase in spending on the aided category. Also, it may simply be that the demands for the services aided by closed-ended grants are more price elastic than those for which open-ended grants are used.[3]

Third, lump-sum grants also cause an increase in government expenditures, which seems in most cases to be smaller than the grant. There is a wide variance in the estimated expenditure effects of lump-sum grants, however, varying from an expenditure increase of $.20 up to $1 per dollar of grant received. Again, two reasons for this difference are differences in initial spending on the category by

---

[3]It does appear that demand for state–local welfare expenditures is less price elastic than the demand for state–local services generally.

subnational governments and different use restrictions among the grants. The majority of the estimates fall in the range of a $.25 to $.50 increase in expenditure per dollar of grant. If those results are representative, then $1 of lump-sum grant provides between $.50 and $.75 for expenditures in other budget areas or for local tax relief.

The evidence that a substantial portion of both matching and lump-sum grants are effectively diverted to uses other than those nominally intended raises the issue of which other budget categories benefit. This "leakage" of grant funds may occur both among different services and different local governments, which overlap in tax authority. As an example of the latter, aid to municipalities is expected to increase municipal expenditures and decrease local municipal taxes. The lower municipal taxes may, therefore, allow local school districts to also increase expenditures (by reducing opposition to increased local school taxes). In fact, there is evidence of just this sort of cross-government general-equilibrium effect; aid to either municipalities or independent school districts appears to cause increased spending by both.

The possibility of grant substitution among different budget categories for a single government has been examined in detail by Steven Craig and Robert Inman (1985), who studied state government expenditure responses to federal welfare and education grants. Craig and Inman concluded that although federal welfare and education grants to states do increase state expenditures in those categories, both influence expenditures in other areas by a larger amount. For instance, they estimate that an additional $1.21 from open-ended federal welfare grants to states would generate $.34 more in welfare spending, $.54 less in state education expenditures, $.63 less in state taxes, and thus $.78 more on other state services ($1.21 - .34 + .54 - .63 = .78$). Similarly, they find that $1 of additional lump-sum federal education aid to states increases state education expenditure by $.43, increases state welfare expenditures by $.23 (only $.09 of which is state money due to matching federal welfare aid), decreases state taxes by $.39, and thus allows $.09 to be spent on other state services. Although the specific magnitude of these estimates is surely not precise, it seems clear that intergovernmental grants do have some substantial unintended or unexpected effects on recipient government budgets.

Finally, there is evidence that suggests that an additional $1 of lump-sum grant money has a greater government expenditure effect than a $1 increase in residents' incomes. The results of a number of studies show that although $1 of increased income is expected to increase subnational government expenditure by about $.05 to $.10, $1 in lump-sum grant appears to increase expenditure by $.25 to $.50. This result has become known as the **flypaper effect,** reflecting the notion that money paid to a government tends to "stick" in the public sector. If true, this means that a $1 grant will have very different allocation effects than a $1 tax decrease by the granting government (which increases income by $1). These results have generated some controversy about whether they reflect important characteristics of political behavior or are illusory and caused by incorrect or imprecise economic analysis. That debate is presented next.

/ Is Grant Money Different Than Tax Money?

Do increases in lump-sum grants and increases in private personal incomes affect subnational government expenditures equally? If not, why not? These two issues have received increasing amounts of attention in recent years as a result of the empirical results mentioned above. The answers seem to fall into two categories. One position is that no flypaper effect really exists—that the empirical results result from incorrect statistical work or misinterpretation of those results. The other position, that the flypaper effect is real, is then divided on the cause—whether it reflects political power and control by government officials or behavior actually desired by voters, who may be misinformed.

First, why would economists think that grants and income *should* influence expenditures equally, anyway? That view arises from the belief that the public-choice process (voting) works to perfectly reflect the desires of various voters, or at least the decisive voter. The majority-voting/median-voter model so favored by economists is in this class; government selects the expenditures desired by the median voter, and if not, political competition will arise to move the government in that direction. For an individual voter, increases in income or grants to the voter's government are the same because both increase the resources available for consumption. An individual can convert grant funds into personal income through decreased local taxes.

The idea can be demonstrated through an individual's budget, which leads to that individual's demand for government services, as presented in Chapter 14. The budget is

$$Y_i = C_i + t_i(T)$$

Because local taxes must make up the difference between expenditures and grant funds,

$$Y_i = C_i + t_i(E - G)$$
$$Y_i = C_i + t_i E - t_i G$$
$$Y_i + t_i G = C_i + t_i E$$

where Y_i = income for person i
C_i = private consumption by person i
t_i = the local tax share for person i
T = total tax collected by person i's local government
E = expenditures by person i's government
G = the lump-sum grant to person i's local government

The left-hand side of the budget equation represents the resources available to be spent on either private consumption or government services. The individual's price for government services is the tax share, t_i. An individual voter's implicit share of lump-sum grants received by the government is the voter's tax share multiplied by the amount of the grant; this is the amount of local taxes the individual would have to pay to generate the same amount of revenue as the grant. Equivalently, if all the grant were used to lower local taxes, this represents the tax savings to that voter. With this view, it should not matter whether resources arise from an increase in Y_i or an increase in G; both expand the individual's budget and should increase demand for normal goods.[4] The same idea is illustrated by Figure 17.3. An increase of ZY in private income shifts the budget line in exactly the same way as a lump-sum grant equal to ZX.

The key to the argument, of course, is whether individuals do in fact have the option or desire to convert lump-sum grants received by the government into private income through tax reductions. If individuals suffer from some type of fiscal illusion or if budget-maximizing, monopoly government officials create such an illusion, then the grant funds may be treated differently than income. One possible type of illusion occurs because lump-sum grants reduce the *average cost* to residents of recipient government spending. A jurisdiction that spends $100 per capita and receives a $30 per-capita grant pays only 70 percent of the cost, on average. If individuals believe that this average cost is the price, then it appears that the lump-sum grant has reduced the price of government service similar to a matching grant. As a result, the expenditure effect would be greater than from the income effect alone. This is an illusion because the grant is lump-sum (constant). An increase in spending of $1 would cost the local jurisdiction $1; the marginal cost has not been reduced.

The flypaper effect could also result from the nature of the political process rather than incorrect perceptions by voters. By controlling the set of options from which voters choose, budget-maximizing officials may be able to have voters approve taxes to finance desired expenditures and then also spend the grant funds. The grant funds would therefore cause increased spending rather than tax relief. For this to work requires that voters not give grant funds the same careful consideration they do taxes and that political competitors not arise to give voters a different set of choices.

The competing position holds that the flypaper effect really does not occur, with the apparent evidence caused by statistical and analytical error. One possibility is that in studying grants, analysts may make mistakes in classifying grants as lump-sum or matching. Howard Chernick (1979) has argued, for example, that in choosing among competing projects applying for closed-ended lump-sum funds, officials of the granting government may favor those projects where the recipient government agrees to spend the largest amount of local funds. This converts a nominally lump-sum grant effectively into a matching one. If an analyst considers the grant lump-sum when it is in fact matching, it is not surprising to find an unexpectedly large expenditure effect. With some 400 different federal grant programs plus state grants to consider, many of these types of errors are possible.

Another possibility, suggested by Bruce Hamilton (1983), is that residents' income may affect the cost of providing government services as well as demand. For instance, it may require less government spending to bring students up to a

---

[4]From the budget equation, a $1 increase in Y_i should be precisely equivalent to an increase of $1/t_i$ in G.

given test-score level in a higher-income community than a lower-income one, due perhaps to nursery school or other educational services purchased privately by the families. If income does affect cost, then increases in income cannot be directly compared to increases in grants. Studies that ignore this possibility underestimate the expenditure effect of income increases, which can be part of the reason for the flypaper effect results. Similarly, other researchers have shown that analyses of the same grant to the same recipient governments in the same year will show a flypaper effect under some statistical procedures and not others.

Whether the flypaper effect is a political fact of life or a figment of imprecise analysis is, as yet, unresolved. In general, those who believe that substantial political competition between potential officials and economic competition among jurisdictions are prevalent, tend to believe that the flypaper effect must be small or weak. Those who believe government officials can maintain monopoly power and manipulate public opinion tend to believe that the flypaper effect is real and strong.

/ Intergovernmental Grant Policy

Economic theory and evidence about the effects of alternative types of intergovernmental grants lead to three major conclusions about grant policy. First, open-ended categorical matching grants are the best device if the objective is to increase recipient government expenditures on a specific function. A matching grant with a matching rate equal to the nonresident share of benefits will offset the effects of interjurisdictional externalities by reducing the local tax price. The lower price will induce the increase in expenditures necessary for efficiency. For instance, if the marginal social benefit of additional highway spending is half of the total, a matching grant to states that pays $1 for each $1 of state money reduces the state's cost by half and restores efficiency. Although other grants could also be used to increase expenditures, an open-ended matching grant will induce the desired expenditure response with the smallest possible grant; matching grants provide the largest expenditure effect per dollar of grant.

Second, general lump-sum grants are a better mechanism than matching grants to redistribute resources among subnational jurisdictions. There is no economic reason for such grants to go to all jurisdictions, of course; they should be targeted to low-income or high-cost jurisdictions. These grants should be lump-sum so as to not alter the relative price of government compared to private consumption. Although substantial tax relief is expected to result from such a program, these grants are not equivalent to federal tax reductions if the flypaper effect results are correct.

Third, categorical lump-sum and close-ended matching grants should generally be avoided. Close-ended matching grants become lump-sum once the maximum grant is reached, and categorical restrictions do not alter grant effects unless the grant is large compared to recipient government expenditures in the category. But if the objective is to increase expenditures or to induce recipient governments to begin spending on a specific function, open-ended matching grants are preferred.

As we have already seen, the actual intergovernmental grant system in the United States departs substantially from these rules. Categorical close-ended grants are the most common (both in number and dollars) form of federal grant. Revenue-sharing grants, the basic general-purpose grant, were given to all general-purpose local governments and included matching-grant effects due to tax effort allocation. And the specified categories for block grants are so broad that these are effectively general grants. Consequently, there is continual discussion about "reforming" the federal grant system. One such proposal is discussed in Application 17.1.

/ APPLICATION 17.1
Reagan's "New Federalism"

In his 1982 budget message, President Reagan proposed radically restructuring the federal intergovernmental grant system in the following ways:

1. The federal government would assume full financial responsibility for Medicaid (health insurance for the poor), a program which was, and still is, provided by states with federal assistance through open-ended matching grants. The matching rate for those grants is inversely proportional to state per-capita income.
2. State governments would assume full financial responsibility for AFDC and the food-stamp program. As noted previously, states also finance AFDC with federal assistance from open-ended matching grants. The food-stamp program is federally financed.
3. About sixty federal categorical programs would end with states having the option of continuing financing in those areas. Initially, states were to receive general lump-sum grants equal to the old categorical grants; after several years, those grants would end with states having the option of levying new excise taxes or other revenue sources to provide lost revenue.

After the merits of this proposal had been considered in detail, it was ultimately rejected by state and local governments. Although there are some quantitative differences among the analyses of the proposal, there is general agreement about the nature of its effects on states. First, by converting categorical matching grants initially into general lump-sum grants and then into new taxes, there would have been a decrease in state–local spending in the specific categories of those grants and ultimately a decrease in overall state–local spending. Second, the termination of matching grants for AFDC and full federal financing for food stamps would have led to a decrease in state expenditures on low-income assistance, despite the revenue gain to the states from federal takeover of Medicaid. With an average matching rate for AFDC grants of about 60 percent, the state tax price per dollar of benefit is only $.40. If the grants are eliminated, the price rises to $1. Even with inelastic demand, a price increase of this magnitude implies a substantial decrease in expenditures.

/ APPLICATION 17.1 Continued
Reagan's "New Federalism"

This would be offset by additional state income, but the income effect is much too small to offset the price effect.

Although this specific proposal was not adopted in its entirety, the Reagan administration did combine a number of small categorical grants into block grants. This was effectively a substitution of general lump-sum grants for categorical grants. Proposals for "turnbacks to the states," the term now used to characterize the ending of federal categorical programs in exchange for more state revenue authority, continue to be made.

/ Summary

Intergovernmental grants, sometimes called grants-in-aid, are transfers of funds from one government to another, most often from a higher-level government in the federal system to a set of lower-level governments.

In 1986 the federal government transferred $113 billion of aid to state–local governments, about $.21 for every $1 raised by state–local governments from their own sources. State governments transferred nearly $127 billion to local governments, or more than $.54 for every $1 collected by local governments from their own sources. Although the absolute magnitude of these grants has generally increased annually, the relative importance of intergovernmental grants increased in the 1960s and early 1970s and peaked in the late 1970s.

About 65 percent of federal aid to states and localities is nominally directed toward the budget categories of education, highways, and public welfare, the last representing more than 39 percent. In contrast, education is the dominant category of state aid to localities, accounting for more than 63 percent of state aid.

Grants may be used to correct for externalities that arise from the structure of subnational governments and thus can improve the efficiency of fiscal decisions. Grants can also be used for explicit redistribution of resources among regions or localities. And grants have also been considered as a macroeconomic stabilizing mechanism for the subnational government sector.

An open-ended matching grant is expected to increase government expenditure on the aided service by a greater amount than an equal-size lump-sum grant. If the demand for government service is price inelastic, a matching grant will increase expenditure by less than the amount of the grant, thus also freeing local funds to be spent in other ways.

A restriction on use of a lump-sum grant will "matter" to the recipient only if intended expenditures on the aided category are less than what the grant will buy. Effort maintenance restrictions are binding only if the grant is larger than the increase in expenditure that would be selected without the grant (which is not observed).

Lump-sum grants cause an increase in government expenditures, usually in the range of a $.25 to $.50 increase in expenditure per dollar of grant. One dollar of lump-sum grant thus provides between $.50 and $.75 for expenditures in other budget areas or for local tax relief.

Economic theory and evidence about the effects of alternative types of intergovernmental grants lead to three major conclusions about grant policy. A matching grant with a matching rate equal to the nonresident share of benefits is best if the objective is to offset the effects of interjurisdictional externalities. General lump-sum grants are a better mechanism than matching grants to redistribute resources among subnational jurisdictions. Categorical lump-sum and closed-ended matching grants should generally be avoided in favor of the other two.

Discussion Questions

1. Because nonresidents benefit from local government public-safety services, suppose that the federal government offers localities a public-safety grant equal to $1 for $1 of local tax money spent on that service.
   a. What is the effect of this grant on the price of public-safety spending to these localities? How might the grant correct for the spillover problem?
   b. Suppose that Central City currently levies a property tax for public safety at a rate of $10 per $1000 of taxable value on a base of $10 million of taxable property. If the price elasticity of demand for public safety in Central City is 0.2, calculate and explain the expected effect of the grant on public-safety spending, public-safety taxes, and tax rates in Central City.

2. Instead of the matching grant in the first problem, suppose Central City received a lump-sum grant of $55,000 that must be spent on public safety. If the total income of Central City residents is $2.2 million and the income elasticity of demand for public safety is 0.8, what is the expected effect of this grant on public-safety spending and taxes? Why does the matching grant increase spending more than the lump-sum grant?

3. Suppose that Central City received a lump-sum grant of $55,000 with no restrictions as to how that money must be spent. Do you think the effect on public-safety spending would be different than from the specific lump-sum grant in problem 2? Why or why not?

4. Periodically, it is proposed that the federal government reduce its role in intergovernmental fiscal relations by eliminating a number of smaller matching intergovernmental grants and simultaneously reducing federal taxes by an equal amount, particularly any that directly finance these grants. This concept was part of President Reagan's "New Federalism" and is sometimes referred to as "revenue turnbacks"—the idea being that individuals will retain the resources and states the option to tax those resources to continue the programs now financed by the grants. If such a change were made, how do you expect states would respond?

Selected Readings

Break, George. *Financing Government in a Federal System*. Washington, D.C.:
   The Brookings Institution, 1980. See Chapter 3, "The Economics of
   Intergovernmental Grants," and Chapter 4, "The U.S. Grant System."
Gramlich, Edward M. "Intergovernmental Grants: A Review of the Empirical
   Literature." In *The Political Economy of Fiscal Federalism,* edited by
   Wallace Oates, 219–39. Lexington, Mass.: Lexington Books, 1977.

Appendix   *Indifference-Curve Analysis of Grants*

One can also demonstrate the effects of different types of grants using the traditional
consumer-theory tools of indifference curves and budget lines, continuing the presentations in the appendices to Chapters 3 and 14. In Figure 17A.1, an individual
faces budget constraint *AF* in choosing between governmentally provided good G
and a composite good X, representing consumption on all other goods. The slope
of the budget line represents this individual's tax price. At the utility maximizing
bundle, this individual consumes G_0 units of good G and spends X_0 dollars on all
other goods.

   If this individual's jurisdiction receives an open-ended matching grant, the tax
price is reduced because of the match so that this individual's budget line shifts to
AD. Each unit of good G now costs less in local taxes because of the grant, so that
this individual can afford more G; as more G is consumed, the grant increases. At
allocation *D,* all of this individual's income is being spent on G, which is matched

FIGURE 17A.1   **A Comparison of Matching and Lump-Sum Grants**

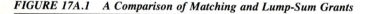

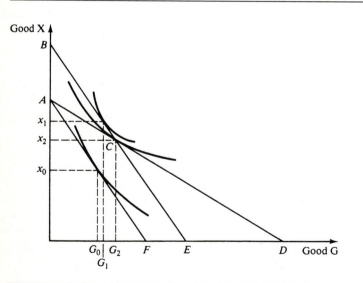

with grant funds at the matching rate. The individual's utility maximizing bundle with the matching grant is bundle C, involving G_2 units of G and X_2 dollars spent on X. In this case, the grant has induced an increase in consumption of the aided good G and an increase in spending on other goods as well.

Now suppose a lump-sum grant is offered instead of a matching grant, with the lump-sum grant just large enough to allow consumption of the same bundle as selected with the matching grant, that is, bundle C. A lump-sum grant equal to AB dollars shifts the budget constraint to BE, which goes through bundle C. A grant equal to AB is just large enough to allow this consumer to select bundle C. Because the lump-sum grant does not alter the prices of goods, this new budget line is parallel to the original. Faced with this lump-sum grant and budget line BE, this individual's utility maximizing bundle is G_1 and X_1.

The lump-sum grant increases consumption of the government good compared to that with no grant, but the increase in consumption of G is smaller with the lump-sum grant than under the matching grant. This is required, given the usual convex shape of indifference curves, because the bundles on budget line BE to the left of bundle C provide the consumer higher utility with lower consumption of G (but more spending on X). The absence of the price reduction on G means that fewer resources are allocated to consuming G. Therefore, the open-ended matching grant is more effective at increasing consumption of G than an equal-size lump-sum grant. The lump-sum grant, however, increases the recipient's utility more because the choice of consumption mix is not distorted by a price change.

Now consider a close-ended matching grant offered at the same matching rate as before but only applying to the first G_2 units of good G purchased with local funds. The budget line facing the consumer is now ACE. The matching grant lowers the price up to bundle C, which provides the maximum grant. Beyond consumption level G_2, the price of additional units of G returns to the original price with no grant. The budget line is thus parallel to the original but shifted out, due to receipt of the maximum grant. If the utility maximizing bundle is before G_2, the close-ended grant is matching; if it is after G_2, the grant is lump-sum. As Figure 17A.1 is drawn, the utility maximizing bundle is at C; the consumer takes advantage of the full matching potential of the close-ended grant.

Part 5

Applications and Policy Analysis

While the earlier parts of this book focus on detailed analysis and explanation of specific aspects of state–local government expenditure, revenue, and organization, Chapters 18–21 focus on specific policy issues that are of current interest. The four issues selected are provision of education and transportation services, the effect of constitutional and legislative budget restrictions on fiscal decisions, and the relationship between state–local fiscal policies and economic activity in the jurisdiction. Although this is clearly not an exhaustive list of current fiscal policy issues among subnational governments, all four have been very important over the past decade and continue to be so, and all involve substantial economic aspects that can be analyzed with the information and tools presented in the book. The discussion in these final four chapters draws on the theory and evidence discussed in previous chapters and tends to be less conclusive, reporting what is known about these complex policy questions as well as factual matters that are as yet unresolved.

Spending for education and transportation services together accounts for 45 to 50 percent of state–local general expenditure. Moreover, these are perhaps the most apparent state–local services, the ones that directly affect the greatest number of people on a day-to-day basis. For both, the discussion in these chapters is intended to report both how those services currently are financed and produced as well as what the expected effects of proposed changes in production and finance may be. Social services and income maintenance are other major categories of state–local spending that also might have been included in this section. It was not, partly because states serve mainly as agents of the federal government for many income-maintenance programs, partly because those programs affect fewer people on a daily basis, and partly because no book can cover every issue.

The last two chapters do not involve specific services or expenditures but rather focus on the overall fiscal decisions of individual state–local governments. Even before the tax-limit movement of the last decade, state–local governments had experimented with a variety of budget structures and restrictions. Understanding of those constraints and their effects on fiscal decisions helps to understand why some states respond to economic and fiscal changes differently than others and may suggest the advantages and disadvantages of similar fiscal constraints proposed for the federal government. Finally, although economic conditions in a jurisdiction are different and separate from fiscal conditions of the government for that jurisdiction, it is important to consider the relationship between economic and fiscal conditions. That states compete for economic activity is obvious, whether that competition is effective in increasing welfare is not.

18 / *Education*

. . . While we can take justifiable pride in what our schools and colleges have historically accomplished . . . , the educational foundations of our society are presently being eroded by a rising tide of mediocrity that threatens our very future as a Nation and a people.[1]

The National Commission on Excellence in Education

Education is, by almost any measure, the primary service provided by state–local governments in the United States. We have already learned that expenditures on elementary and secondary education represent the single largest category of state–local government spending, equal to nearly a quarter of aggregate subnational government general expenditure in 1985. Elementary and secondary education is an even larger fraction of local government spending, nearly 40 percent in 1985. This is five times as great as local spending for police and fire protection and nearly eight times as great as local spending on public welfare. Public elementary and secondary education teachers represent about 10 percent of full-time state–local employees and about 17 percent of local government employees.

In 1984–85 expenditures for public elementary and secondary schools were nearly $137 billion, equal to about 3.7 percent of GNP and $3449 per student in average daily attendance at those schools, as shown in Table 18.1. Public-school expenditures have increased substantially since 1970—by about 54 percent just between 1980 and 1985—but generally remained between 3.5 and 4.0 percent of GNP during that time. Expenditures per pupil have also increased substantially over the past twenty-five years, even in real terms (after adjustment for inflation). Indeed, real expenditures per pupil by public elementary and secondary schools were 2.5 times as great in 1985 than in 1960.

There were 39.5 million students enrolled in these public schools in the Fall of 1985. Public-school enrollment generally increased in the 1950s and 1960s—peaking in elementary schools in the late 1960s and in secondary schools in the mid-1970s, as noted by Eric Hanushek (1986). Since that time public- (and private-) school enrollment has decreased, largely because of demographic

---

[1]*A Nation at Risk: The Imperative for Educational Reform.* Washington, D.C.: The National Commission on Excellence in Education, 1983, 5.

TABLE 18.1

Overview of Public Elementary and Secondary Education, Various Years

Year	Spending (Billions of Dollars)	Pupils[a] (Thousands)	Spending as Percentage of GNP	Spending per Pupil[b] (Current Dollars)	Spending per Pupil (1985 Dollars)[b]	Teachers (Thousands)	Pupil–Teacher Ratio
1985	136.5	39,513	3.7	3449	3449	2210	18:1
1980	96.0	40,987	3.5	2272	3095	2162	19:1
1970	40.7	45,909	4.0	816	2285	2055	22:1
1960	15.6	36,281	3.0	375	1350	1408	26:1

Source: U.S. Department of Education (May 1987).

[a]Total enrollment in Fall of that school year.
[b]Current expenditures per pupil in average daily attendance.

factors, a trend that continued until the mid-1980s. Increases in total public-school enrollment in the 1980s are due to increases in elementary schools; increases in secondary public-school enrollments are not forecast until the early 1990s. It is important to note that total expenditures by these schools, per-pupil expenditures, and even real per-pupil expenditures continued to increase after 1970 when school enrollment was declining.

Salaries for teachers and other workers (administrators, librarians, counselors, maintenance persons, bus drivers) comprise the bulk of the expenditures by public schools. Recall from Chapter 15 that employee compensation represented about 66 percent of the noncapital direct expenditure of school districts in 1986. The number of public elementary and secondary school teachers has also increased over the past twenty-five years, again including the period since 1970 when the number of students was decreasing. As a consequence, the pupil–teacher ratio also decreased over the past twenty-five years, from nearly 26 students per teacher in 1960 to about 18 in 1985, a decrease of more than 30 percent.

Public-school services in the United States are provided both by independent school districts and by school systems, which are part of general-purpose local governments such as cities, townships, or counties. The number of school districts decreased substantially over the past twenty-five years, and particularly between 1960 and 1970, as shown in Table 18.2.[2] There were also substantial decreases in the number of public elementary schools before 1970 and to a lesser degree since. But the number of public secondary schools has remained relatively stable, though decreasing slightly. The picture that emerges from all of these data of the provision of public education over the past twenty-five years is one of increasing spending per pupil, in part because of decreases in class sizes and consolidation of both school districts and elementary schools within districts.

But budgetary data about education spending really do not capture the importance placed on public education and state–local government educational institu-

---

[2]The decreases in the 1960s were a continuation of the trend operating at least since 1930. See U.S. Department of Education (May 1987).

TABLE 18.2

Government Organization of Public Schools

Year	Number of School Districts	Percentage of Independent Districts	Number of Public Elementary Schools	Number of Public Secondary Schools
1984	15,747	90.6[a]	59,082	23,947
1980	15,912	91.7[b]	61,069	24,362
1970	17,995	91.5[c]	65,800	25,352
1960	40,520	93.7[d]	91,853	25,784

Sources: U.S. Department of Education (May 1987), U.S. Department of Commerce (1986).

[a]1982.
[b]1977.
[c]1972.
[d]1962.

tions. Education has been identified as an important means of altering the income distribution, generating social mobility, improving economic growth, increasing the "international competitiveness" of firms in the United States, and even improving the operation of the political public-choice system in a democratic society. A substantial amount of economic literature shows that the perception of local schools is an important factor influencing locational choices of both individuals and firms, and through that influencing property values in specific jurisdictions. And perhaps no local government fiscal or political issue generates as much or as intense public interest and comment as consideration of closing or consolidating local public schools.

/ Financing Education

/ Current practice

Nearly half of the revenue for financing public elementary and secondary schools in 1985 was provided by state governments, on average, with local governments—the school districts—generating a slightly smaller share from their own sources, about 44 percent of public-school spending. The federal government has a relatively minor role in financing elementary and secondary education, providing only 6.6 percent of public-school spending in 1985, and even private sources of spending (for private schools) represented less than 10 percent of total school spending in that year. As shown by the data in Table 18.3, the federal government's role has always been relatively small, increasing a bit from 1960 to 1980 but declining since. Similarly, the role of private schools has decreased in the past twenty-five years.

The relative roles of state and local governments in financing education changed dramatically in the 1970s, with the two levels of government effectively switching positions. Prior to the 1970s, state governments provided about 40 percent of school revenue, on average, and local governments more than half. Responding to a number of forces, state governments attempted to equalize educational opportunity across districts in the 1970s, which resulted in increased state financial commitments and

TABLE 18.3

Sources of Elementary and Secondary School Spending

	All Schools: Percentage Financed by				Public Schools: Percentage Financed by		
Year	Federal	State	Local	Private	Federal	State	Local
1985	6.3	44.1	41.0	8.6	6.6	49.6	43.7
1980	8.7	41.5	38.2	11.5	9.2	48.9	42.0
1970	7.4	34.6	47.5	10.5	7.2	40.9	51.8
1960	3.9	31.1	52.8	12.3	3.7	39.5	56.8

Sources: Hanushek (1986); ACIR (1987b); U.S. Department of Commerce (1987).

corresponding decreases in the financial responsibility of the localities. The increased state share was accomplished both by changing the magnitude and type of state grants to school districts, discussed in detail below. Because the primary local revenue source for schools (and the only source in many states) is the property tax, the increased state role in financing education reduced the demand for property tax increases in these years, and in some cases resulted in property tax reductions.

There is great diversity among state–local governments in the role of the state government in financing education. In fact, the variation in the roles state governments play in education is even greater than for most other services. At the opposite extremes, the public schools are almost entirely financed by local governments in New Hampshire where the state share is only 4.9 percent and the local share is 91.2 percent. In contrast, elementary and secondary education is a state government function in Hawaii where local school districts do not exist and the state generates 90.5 percent of revenue for school expenditures (the federal share is relatively large in Hawaii because of the substantial U.S. military presence in the state).

The distribution of states by the state government's share of public-school expenditures in 1985 is shown in Table 18.4. The median states in that distribution are Maine with 50.1 percent of school revenue provided by the state and Tennessee at 49.2 percent. But the state government provides more than 60 percent of revenue in thirteen states and less than 40 percent in another thirteen states. Considering these data, one might believe that Alaska, Hawaii, and even New Hampshire are special cases. Even if that is true, there is still the interesting comparison between New Mexico (77.4 percent state-financed), Washington (74.5 percent), and Alabama (70.7 percent) on the one hand and South Dakota (26.4 percent state-financed), Nebraska (28.1 percent), and Oregon (28.5 percent) on the other. There was also substantial variation among the states in the state government's share of education expenditures in 1970, although the entire distribution was shifted down reflecting the smaller role for states on average. The obvious conclusion is that there is no one or even typical way that states finance elementary and secondary education. As we will discover in this chapter, the economic, political, and social factors that underlie these financial differences extend as well to the states' role in regulating education.

TABLE 18.4

Distribution of States by State Share of Public Elementary and Secondary School Spending, 1985

State Share of Spending	Number of States	Examples	Number of States, 1970
> 90%	1	Hawaii, 90.5%	0
80–90%	0		1
70–80%	4	New Mexico (77.4%), Alaska (76.1%) Washington (74.5%), Alabama (70.7%)	1
60–70%	8		3
50–60%	12	Median: 50.1% in Maine and 49.2% in Tennessee	9
40–50%	12	U.S. average is 49.6%	10
30–40%	9		13
20–30%	3	S. Dakota (26.4%), Nebraska (28.1%) Oregon (28.5)	10
10–20%	0		2
< 10%	1	New Hampshire, 4.9%	1

Source: ACIR (1987b).

Just as there are differences among states in how elementary and secondary education is financed, there are also substantial differences among the states in the level of educational spending, as demonstrated in Table 18.5. As previously mentioned, per-pupil spending by all public schools in aggregate was $3449 in the 1984–85 school year, but per-pupil spending averaged less than $2500 in seven states and more than $4500 in five states. At the extremes, per-pupil spending was $2220 in Utah but $5492 in New York (the second highest) and $7843 in Alaska. The **coefficient of variation,** a comparative measure of variation in distributions equal to the standard deviation divided by the mean, was .28 for 1985, meaning that among the states there was an average of about 28-percent variation in per-pupil spending around the mean. There has perhaps been a small increase in the

TABLE 18.5

Distribution of States by Per-Pupil Spending, 1985

Per-Pupil Spending ($)	Number of States	Examples
2000–2500	7	Lowest is Utah at $2220
2500–3000	9	
3000–3500	14	Median states are Colorado at $3256 and Ohio at $3257; U.S. average is $3449
3500–4000	10	
4000–4500	5	
4500–5000	3	
> 5000	2	Alaska at $7843 and New York at $5492

Source: U.S. Department of Education (May 1987).

degree of difference among states in the level of education spending over the past twenty-five years, as the interstate coefficient of variation for per-pupil spending was .25 in 1980, .21 in 1970, and .22 in 1960.

The differences in per-pupil spending among different school districts within states appear to be about as large as the differences among states. William Neenan (1981, 186–89) reports, for example, that the ratio of per-pupil expenditures for districts at the 95th percentile to those at the 5th percentile had a median value of 1.69 in 1977 for those states with local school districts and varied from 2.2 to 1.2. Recall from Chapter 15 that differences in expenditures can result from differences in input prices and environmental conditions as well as from differences in demand, so that these differences in per-pupil spending may not correspond to equivalent differences in educational results.

/ Types of state aid

Unless state governments want to operate the public-school system directly (as in Hawaii), states have to rely on intergovernmental grants to assist local governments in financing public education, and those grants must be one of the two general forms—lump-sum or matching—described in Chapter 17. Prior to the 1970s, states generally used lump-sum per-pupil grants to support local education. Those grants were sometimes equal per-pupil amounts provided to all school districts, but more commonly the amount of the per-pupil grant for each district was directly related to educational costs in the district or inversely related to some measure of district wealth. Still, the grant is lump-sum because the size of the grant (per pupil) is independent of the district's choice about the level of spending (and thus taxes). These lump-sum school grants are usually referred to as **foundation aid** because the per-pupil grant represents a minimum expenditure level; the state aid is thought of as providing a basic foundation on top of which local revenue supplements may be added.

In general, then, a foundation aid program requires a basic grant per pupil and perhaps a way of reducing the grant for richer districts. A generic formula for a foundation aid grant is

$$G_i = B - R^* \cdot V_i$$

where G_i = per pupil grant to district i
   B = basic per-pupil grant or foundation level
   R^* = basic property tax rate set in the formula
   V_i = per-pupil property tax base in district i

Suppose, for instance, that a state establishes such a program with B = $1000 and R^* = $10 per $1000 of taxable property value. The largest (per-pupil) grant any district could receive is $1000, but that only if V_i is zero. Compare two school districts, one with per-pupil property value of $20,000 and the other $50,000. The first would receive a per-pupil grant of $800 [$1000 − ($10 × 20)] and the second $500 [$1000 − ($10 × 50)]. Because the only district-specific factor in the formula is the property tax base per pupil, which is outside of the direct control of the district, these are lump-sum grants. If both districts had identical property tax rates equal to the basic rate in the formula ($10), both would end up with $1000 per student to spend. The first would collect $200 in property taxes per pupil and receive $800 in grant funds; the second would generate $500 from property taxes and $500 from the grant program. Thus, all districts are guaranteed $1000 per pupil, the foundation amount. If districts wish to spend more than the guaranteed $1000 per pupil, they must collect local taxes to finance all of the additional spending.

Under what conditions would a district's grant be zero? A district would get no grant if its per-pupil property tax base is equal to or greater than B/R^*. If a district's per-pupil property value is $100,000 for the example, then the per-pupil grant is zero [$1000 − ($10 × 100)]. The reason is simple: With a per-pupil tax base of at least $100,000, the basic tax rate of $10 would generate the full foundation amount in taxes; no grant is required to bring such a district up to the foundation level.

Under foundation aid programs, however, districts may choose tax rates greater (but often not less) than the basic rate in the formula. Again compare two districts with $20,000 and $50,000 property tax bases per pupil. If they both select property tax rates of $30 per $1000 of taxable value, the first collects $600 of property taxes per pupil and receives a grant of $800, allowing spending equal to $1400 per pupil. The second collects $1500 per pupil in property taxes and receives a grant of $500, allowing spending of $2000 per pupil. The difference in grant amounts does not fully offset the difference in property taxes. Equal property tax rates do not generate equal amounts of per-pupil spending if those tax rates are greater than the basic rate in the aid formula. And there is no requirment or expectation that these two districts would select equal tax rates. In fact, it is possible that the wealthier district would select a higher tax rate.

Therefore, unless the basic tax rate in the foundation aid formula is set high relative to the actual rates employed by school districts, which requires that the foundation level of spending also be set high, foundation aid programs do not equalize resources across districts and thus are not expected to equalize spending. This general issue was the subject of a number of court cases in various states in the 1970s. In these cases it was argued that per-pupil spending on local education was dependent on and generally varied by the per-pupil taxable wealth of the school district and not exclusively on the wealth or income of the family. Because state aid programs did not offset this dependence, students were being denied equal protection under the law. These cases were successful in a number of states, the Serrano decision in California being the first and most often cited, with the state courts ordering the states to devise state aid programs that would eliminate (or at least reduce) the relationship between property wealth and per-pupil spending in school districts.

/ *Equalizing Aid.*   As a result of these decisions and other forces encouraging states to equalize educational opportunities, some states increased the basic grant amount in their foundation programs, while others adopted an entirely different type of state aid to education, called the **Guaranteed Tax Base (GTB)** or District Power Equalizing plan. As the name indicates, this aid program is intended to provide an equal, basic per-pupil property tax base to each district, rather than basic per-pupil minimum expenditure level of the foundation program. Per-pupil spending may still differ among school districts if they choose different property tax rates, but the aid program will effectively provide the same basic tax base to which their selected rate is applied. A GTB plan involves matching grants that reduce the price of education to the school districts, which is the important economic difference from foundation grants.

A GTB grant formula requires, at least, that the GTB and the allowed tax rate be specified. The general formula for grants of this type is

$$G_i = B + (V^* - V_i)R_i$$

where B = basic or foundation grant
  V^* = guaranteed per-pupil tax base
  V_i = per-pupil tax base in district i
  R_i = property tax rate in district i or maximum rate allowed for the guarantee

In a pure GTB program, $B = 0$, and R_i is the local tax rate without any maximum. In that case, districts receive positive grants if their per-pupil tax base (V_i) is less than the guaranteed tax base (V^*), with the grants being positively related to the tax rate selected by the district. Although there is no theoretical reason why these grants could not be negative, requiring that districts with $V_i > V^*$ transfer funds to the state for redistribution, in practice no state provides for such *recapture* of funds. In one variation on this program, some states mix the foundation and GTB styles by providing a basic per-pupil grant in addition to the guaranteed base, that is, they set $B > 0$. In that case, a district receives a per-pupil grant exactly equal to the foundation amount if $V_i = V^*$, with that grant being reduced if $V_i > V^*$ until G is zero (negative grants again are not used). In one other variation, the guaranteed base V^* applies only to some maximum, state-specified tax rate; districts may set a higher rate, but it will only generate more local tax revenue and not additional grant funds.

To illustrate the operation of the basic GTB formula, suppose that a state program guarantees a tax base of $50,000 per pupil ($V^* = $50,000$) and sets no maximum on the tax rate that is eligible for that guarantee. Districts with a per-pupil property tax base of $50,000 or more would receive no education grants from the state government. For districts with $V_i < $50,000$, the grant is inversely related to per-pupil wealth. For instance, a district with a per-pupil property tax base of $20,000 and a tax rate of $30 per $1000 of taxable value would collect $600 per pupil [$20,000 × ($30/$1000)] from property taxes and receive $900 per pupil [$30,000 × ($30/$1000)] from the state grant program. A district with a per-pupil tax base of $40,000 and the same tax rate would collect $1200 per pupil [$40,000 × ($30/$1000)] from property taxes and $300 per pupil [$10,000 × ($30/$1000)] in state aid. Both receive $1500 per pupil in total, which is the revenue generated from a base of $50,000 and a tax rate of $30. In essence, all districts are guaranteed $50 per pupil for each $1 of property tax rate selected. Any portion of that amount that is not provided by the local property tax base is made up by a state grant.

It follows from this discussion that an increase in a district's tax rate will also lead to a larger grant per pupil for districts with $V_i < V^*$. Continuing the numerical illustration, suppose that the district with a per-pupil tax base of \$20,000 increases its property tax rate to \$31 per \$1000 of taxable value. That additional \$1 in the tax rate generates an additional \$20 per pupil from local property taxes and \$30 per pupil from state aid; again, the net effect is an increase of \$50 per pupil for each \$1 of tax rate, the guarantee amount. The local district's share of the additional per-pupil revenue is V_i/V^*, generally, and 0.4 in this specific example. The district with a per-pupil value of \$20,000 pays only 40 percent of the cost of increased school expenditures per pupil, the remainder financed by the aid program. In contrast, the district with per-pupil value of \$40,000 would pay 80 percent of the cost of increasing per-pupil spending (\$40,000/\$50,000). As previously mentioned, one effect of a GTB aid program is to reduce the local price of providing education. *The marginal cost or price to the local district of increasing per-pupil spending by \$1 is* V_i/V^* *if* $V_i < V^*$, *and \$1 otherwise.*

It is difficult to summarize the actual types of aid programs used by the states because each typically has a number of different components and because the structure of the aid programs often includes fiscal features specific to each state. The Education Commission of the States (1986) does provide a description of the school aid program in each state, and based on their report for the 1985–86 school year, some approximate characterizations can be made. Foundation aid programs remain most common, being used by about twenty-eight states in 1985–86, with most of those (about nineteen) determining the per-pupil grant based on the tax wealth of the districts. Power-equalizing grants of either the guaranteed-yield or tax-base type were used by about thirteen states, while another eight states had aid programs that substantially included both foundation and equalizing components.

/ Economic effects of equalizing state aid

Although the focus of the discussion about different state aid programs so far has concentrated on their distributional properties, another important economic and policy issue is their expected effects in influencing recipient school districts to alter educational expenditures. In short, do state education grants induce school districts to spend more on education, and if so, by how much? Perhaps the best way to understand the potential economic effects of different grant types is to actually work through the responses of specific districts given some assumptions about economic and fiscal conditions. The following educational grant simulation does just that. Information about the demand for educational service and the initial expenditure choices of several representative schools is first presented, and then a new proposed state education grant program is described. The effect of that grant program on each school district's behavior is then analyzed, given the demand restrictions. The simulation will be most useful if you attempt to analyze the expected outcomes before reading the analysis in the text. Some suggestions about how you might proceed to do that are offered after the simulation is set up.

Education Grant Simulation.   Suppose that a state consists of four school

districts, denoted A through D, each financing education solely with local property taxes. The initial fiscal situation in each of those districts is shown below, with V equaling the per-pupil taxable property value in each district, R equaling the property tax rate in each district specified in dollars of tax per $1000 of taxable value, and E equaling the per-pupil school expenditure in each district:

A	B	C	D
$V = \$36,360$	$V = \$50,000$	$V = \$51,000$	$V = \$60,000$
$R = \$55$	$R = \$50$	$R = \$50$	$R = \$60$
$E = \$2000$	$E = \$2500$	$E = \$2550$	$E = \$3600$

Thus, district A is the low-wealth, low-spending district while D is the opposite—high-wealth, high-spending. The variation in per-pupil spending magnitudes represented here is consistent with evidence about the actual variation among districts within states as reported by Neenan (1981). Note also that the product of the per-pupil value and tax rate equals the per-pupil expenditure in each district, which is required if local property taxes fully finance the schools.

Suppose it is known that the (absolute value of the) price elasticity of demand for educational spending is the same in each district and equal to .5, so that demand for education is price inelastic. This value is consistent with the evidence reported in Chapter 14; if anything, it may be relatively high. Similarly, suppose that the income elasticity of demand for education in each district is 1.0 and that the average family income in each district is half as large as the per-pupil property value (such would be the case if all the property is residential and consumers buy houses valued at twice their income, so a consumer with a $25,000 income has a $50,000 house).

The state government is considering introducing a program of state education grants to these school districts, to be determined by the following formula:

$$\text{Grant per Pupil} = \$100 + (\$50,000 - V)R$$

where V and R correspond to the per-pupil value and tax rate in each district and the per-pupil grant may not be smaller than zero (no recapture). The policy question is to analyze what the expected effect of such a grant program would be on educational spending and property taxes in each district, and given that, what the potential advantages might be from the state's point of view.

At this point you should stop reading and think about how you would do such an analysis if you were assigned this task as an economic or policy analyst for the state. The following suggestions may be helpful:

1. Determine whether the grant for each separate district is matching or lump-sum. Lump-sum grants are a fixed amount that do not change in response to a recipient government's fiscal reactions, whereas matching grants explicitly depend on the fiscal decisions of those governments.

2. If the grant is lump-sum, use the income elasticity to determine the effect on per-pupil spending and the required local property tax rate.

3. If the grant is matching, determine the marginal cost or "price" to the locality of increasing education spending and note how the grant has changed that "price." Use the price elasticity to compute the expected effect on per-pupil spending and the tax rate in the district.

4. If you follow steps 1–3, you will estimate new levels of spending and taxes in each district. Now evaluate those changes. Has education spending increased on average? Has spending become more equal? To what degree? Have local taxes decreased on average? What's happened to the distribution of tax rates? Has the state received a good return on the use of its funds? Would you recommend the adoption of this grant program?

Now let's see how you did. Consider the districts in order of ease of the analysis. **District D** receives no grant because its per-pupil value is greater than the $50,000 base guaranteed in the grant formula (D's grant from the formula is negative, but the smallest a grant can be is zero). Therefore, it is expected that the grant program will have no effect on education spending or property taxes in district D.[3]

District B receives a lump-sum grant of $100 per pupil because its per-pupil value exactly equals the guarantee amount $[G = \$100 + (O)R]$. Thus, district B receives the foundation amount but no matching aid from the GTB component of the formula. The lump-sum aid means that this district now has $100 more per pupil in income, which can be spent to buy more education service or other things. The per-pupil income in district B is $25,000, so the $100 grant represents an income increase of 0.4 percent $[(\$100/\$25,000) \times 100\%]$. With an income elasticity of demand for education equal to 1, an increase in income of .4 percent will cause an increase in educational spending of .4 percent. Thus, per-pupil spending is expected to increase by $10, from $2500 to $2510. Although the district receives a grant of $100 per pupil, only $10 of that amount gets spent on more educational spending. What happens to the rest of the grant? It goes for lower local property taxes and thus more private spending by taxpayers. The new level of spending will be financed both by property taxes and the grant, so that

$$E' = \$100 + (V)R'$$
$$\$2510 = \$100 + \$50,000 \times R'$$
$$R' = \$48.20 \text{ per } \$1000 \text{ of taxable property value}$$

---

[3] D would get a positive grant if it lowered its tax rate to less than $10 per $1000 of value, but education spending per pupil would fall drastically.

The grant allows district B to lower its property tax rate to $48.20 from $50.00. The district collects $2410 per pupil in property taxes and receives $100 per pupil in state aid for per-pupil education expenditures of $2510. Spending rises slightly, but local property taxes decline by a greater amount.

District A receives both the full foundation amount of $100 per pupil and matching aid from the GTB part of the formula because its per-pupil value is less than the guarantee amount. The grant to A given the initial conditions is $750 [$100 + ($13,640)($55/$1000)], but that grant amount will change as district A changes its property tax rate in response to the grant itself. The matching grant from the GTB formula reduces the "price" of educational spending to the residents of district A. Following the discussion of the previous section, the new price is $V_A/\$50,000$, or 0.727. To increase per-pupil spending by $1, district A must collect an additional $.727 in local property taxes per pupil and would receive an additional $.273 per pupil in state aid. Without the grant program, the local price was $1, so that the effect of the grant is to lower the education price in A by 27.3 percent. If the price elasticity of demand for education spending is .5, then per-pupil spending is expected to increase by 13.65 percent as a result of the matching grant. If that was the only effect, per-pupil spending in A would increase by $273 to $2273.

But district A also receives the $100 of foundation aid, which they would continue to receive even if their property tax rate was zero. That $100 grant represents a .5-percent increase in per-pupil income [($100/$20,000) × 100%], which is expected to further increase per-pupil spending by .5 percent because the income elasticity of demand for education spending is assumed to be 1. Thus, the new level of per-pupil education spending in district A is expected to be about $2284, an increase of about $284 due to the grant. Again, district A will finance that expenditure with property taxes and the grant, so that

$$\$2284 = (\$36,360)R' + \$100 + (\$13,640)R'$$
$$R' = \$43.68 \text{ per } \$1000 \text{ of taxable value}$$

District A lowers its property tax rate to $43.68 from $50 as a result of the grant. The district collects $1588.20 per pupil in property taxes and receives $695.80 per pupil in state aid, allowing spending of $2284 per pupil. Of the total education grant of about $696, only about $284 goes for higher education spending and the rest into lower taxes. The grant causes a larger expenditure increase in district A than B because A receives a matching grant in addition to the foundation amount.

District C also receives a type of matching grant, although in this case an increase in the district's tax rate causes a decrease in the district's grant. This occurs because C has a per-pupil property value greater than the guarantee amount but not so much larger than its grant is zero. The grant to C given its initial tax rate is $50, as shown below:

$$G = \$100 + (-\$1000) \times (\$50/\$1000)$$
$$G = \$100 - \$50$$
$$G = \$50$$

As district C raises its tax rate above $50, the grant decreases by $1 for each $1 increase in the rate, and thus equals zero at a tax rate of $100. On the other hand, if district C lowers its tax rate, the per-pupil grant increases. District C's grant is therefore matching, but the matching rate is negative. The new "price" of educational spending for the residents of district C is $V_C/\$50,000$, or 1.02. To spend an additional $1 per pupil on education, district C must increase local property taxes by $1.02 per pupil; the extra $.02 cents in tax offsets the lower grant that results. In other words, the effect of this grant program on district C is to increase the price of educational spending and thus create an incentive for C to lower educational spending. If the price elasticity of demand is .5, the 2-percent increase in price will cause a 1-percent decrease in education spending. Per-pupil spending in C is expected to fall by $25.50 to $2524.50. Per-pupil taxes in C are also expected to fall; a tax rate of $48.49 per $1000 of value will generate about $2473 in property taxes per pupil and about $51.50 per pupil in state aid, allowing per-pupil expenditure of $2524.50.

The expected effects of the grant program on these school districts are summarized below:

	A	B	C	D	Average
Initial spending	$2000	$2500	$2550	$3600	$2663
New spending	$2284	$2510	$2525	$3600	$2730
Per-pupil grant	$695.8	$100.0	$51.5	$0.0	$211.8
Initial tax	$2000	$2500	$2550	$3600	$2663
New tax	$1588	$2410	$2473	$3600	$2518
Initial tax rate	$55.00	$50.00	$50.00	$60.00	$54.00
New tax rate	$43.68	$48.20	$48.49	$60.00	$50.09

On the basis of this analysis, the proposed education grant program is expected to have the following effects in the state:

1. Per-pupil education spending increases slightly by about 2.5 percent, on average, although spending rises in only half the districts and falls in one. A little more than 30 percent of the state grant funds go for higher spending on education.
2. The variance in per-pupil spending among the districts in the state is reduced only slightly. The ratio of the highest to lowest spending level is reduced to 1.58 from 1.8, about a 12-percent change. But the dollar difference between those districts is still more than $1300.
3. Property taxes are reduced in all districts that receive state grants resulting in about a 7-percent decrease in property tax rates, on average. A little less than 70 percent of the state education grant funds go to reduce local property taxes.
4. Property tax rates are reduced more in districts with lower per-pupil property values, so that effective tax rates now increase with property

value. The ratio of tax rate to per-pupil expenditure—which represents the tax rate required to provide per-pupil spending of $1—is made much more equal across the districts. Without the grants, those ratios were .025 for A, .020 for B, .0196 for C, and .0167 for D. Thus a tax rate of $.025 per $1000 of taxable value was required in order to spend $1 per pupil in A, but a rate of only about $.02 was required in B and C. With the grants, the required rates are $.0191 in A and $.0192 in B and C.

It is also interesting to note what the effect would have been on district D if recapture—that is, negative grants—were allowed. In that case, the price to local residents per dollar of per-pupil spending would have been $1.20 ($60,000/$50,000). Residents of district D would have had to increase local property taxes by $1.20 per pupil in order to increase spending by $1 per pupil because the district would also have to pay additional funds to the state. Thus, the price of education to residents of D rises by 20 percent, which is expected to cause a 10-percent decrease in per-pupil spending if the price elasticity is .5. Thus, per-pupil spending in D would have fallen to $3240. While that would have generated more spending equality than without recapture, the interdistrict differences would still be large and the increased equality would be achieved by worsening educational opportunity in one district.

/ Policy implications

The results of this simulation represent quite accurately the actual results obtained in states that have adopted grant programs of this type. There simply has not been a substantial equalization of per-pupil spending among school districts in states since reform of state aid programs began in the early 1970s. The economic reasons for this are clear. Because the demand for education spending is price inelastic, the price reductions that are caused by the matching grants do not influence consumption very much. Similarly, given the magnitude of income effects, lump-sum grants also do not influence education-spending levels substantially. As a result, most of the state education grant funds go to reduce local property taxes rather than to increase education spending. As Richard Murnane (1985, 133) has noted,

> . . . It seems clear that the main lesson from the first ten years of school finance [reform] is that GTB finance plans which lower the price of education to property-poor communities, but leave the communities free to choose between more spending on education or lower tax rates, will not produce an equalization of per-pupil spending levels across school districts and will not result in districts spending enough to provide their students with a strong basic academic program.

It is important to understand that this difficulty cannot be changed by increasing the size of state aid programs if the structure of those programs remains the same. If demand is price inelastic, a substantial portion of the grants will go to reduce taxes regardless of how much the price of education spending is reduced. The simulation understates the magnitude of the problem in at least one way, as well, because it is static. If incomes are increasing over time, then the demand for education spending will also be rising in many and perhaps all districts. Those economic forces may serve to widen the spending disparities, so that the modest equalizing force from state aid may serve only to preserve the existing distribution and prevent the increased variance that would otherwise occur.

What are the options for state policymakers who wish to equalize education opportunities or spending among school systems in their state or who wish to increase the level of spending throughout the state? In general, there are three approaches. First, a state government can assume the responsibility for directly providing elementary and secondary education, effectively having a single state school district as in Hawaii. This would certainly involve the most dramatic and traumatic change to the fiscal system among the alternatives. There are at least two economic reasons why this alternative may not be desirable. If there are cost differences among different school districts, then equal per-pupil expenditures may not generate equal educational service. And politically, it would likely be very difficult not to have equal per-pupil spending in all areas with a state system. The advantage of local districts is that such cost differences and differences in individual desires about emphasis in education can be recognized and acted on.

The second option is for states to mandate a minimum amount of per-pupil spending through their aid programs and to set that minimum relatively high compared to actual spending levels in that state. The second prescription is crucial because unless the minimum applies to a number of school districts, there will be little equalization. States can do this using either a foundation or GTB program. With foundation aid, the state can require that districts at least levy the specified tax rate in the formula, with both that rate and the foundation amount set relatively high. For instance, if the foundation amount is set at $2500 per pupil and the required tax rate is $40 per $1000 of taxable value, districts with per-pupil values less than $62,500 per pupil ($2500/$40) would receive foundation grants. But the minimum any district could spend is $2500 per pupil. With GTB aid, this result can similarly be accomplished by setting a relatively high minimum required tax rate. Returning to the simulation, if the minimum were set equal to the average rate of about $50 that prevailed after the grants were received, districts A, B, and C would have had to increase their tax rate and per-pupil spending. By requiring a number of local districts to increase spending up to the minimum amount, the state government is restricting local choice but to a lesser extent than results from direct state provision of education.

The third alternative is for states to mandate minimum educational conditions but not minimum spending levels in local school systems. For instance, a state might set minimum standards all teachers must satisfy, or a state might establish minimum course requirements that students must satisfy in order to graduate. If those minimum standards are set relatively high compared to the actual performance of many districts in the state, then those local districts will be required to adjust the educational service provided, which might require increased per-pupil expenditures in some districts. The difficulty with this alternative, as we will examine next, is discovering just what conditions matter for educational results and thus how to set the minimum standards.

/ Producing Education

/ The paradox of declining performance

We have learned that per-pupil spending in real terms by public schools continually increased over the past twenty-five years, in part because average class sizes declined. The paradox, however, is that student performance, measured by a variety of average test scores, generally declined during the last half of the 1960s and the decade of the 1970s. Changes in the scores on the Scholastic Aptitude Test (SAT)—a test purporting to measure preparation for college given to high school seniors and with which many of the readers of this book are intimately familiar—were given prominent attention. The now well-known story is that those average scores, for both verbal and mathematics skills, declined from 1963–80. Over that period, the average SAT verbal score declined by more than 11 percent from 478 to 424 and the average math score by more than 7 percent from 502 to 466 (possible SAT scores range from 200–800 on each component of the test). Similarly, American College Testing Program (ACT) average scores also declined from 1966–76.

It is now generally understood, although not as widely reported, that the SAT score changes were also being reflected by changes in scores of other standardized tests given to students at various grade levels over this period. For instance, Hanushek (1986) notes that scores on the Iowa Tests (standardized tests used in many states and given to students in grades 5, 8, and 12) also declined beginning in the mid-1960s through the 1970s. Interestingly, Hanushek also notes that the timing of improvements in those test scores and others he discusses are consistent: Fifth-grade scores started to rise in 1975, eighth-grade scores in 1977, and twelfth-grade scores in 1980. These average scores do mask some differences by subject matter. Murnane (1985) discusses a set of tests sponsored by the national government called the National Assessment of Educational Progress (NAEP) given to students aged nine, thirteen, and seventeen in 1971, 1975, and 1980. Those results showed that reading skills improved over the decade for the nine and thirteen year olds and declined for seventeen year olds, while students' mathematics skills remained stable or declined over the period and science skills generally declined.

What are the possible explanations for these widespread decreases in student-achievement test scores over the same period when public-school spending was rising relative to both enrollment and inflation? Part of the explanation for the change in college-entrance test scores lies in changes in the number and mix of students who were taking the test and going on to college, which was important in the 1960s but not the 1970s. Some of the explanations offered for the broader trend include shortages of qualified teachers, especially in mathematics and science, the nature of teacher-training programs emphasizing education over academic classes, social factors that altered interest or participation in education, and changes in the characteristics of schools and public-school programs themselves, such as introduction of broader, less academic curricula or new teaching methods. But the evidence is inconclusive or even negative on some of these factors. The real task in resolving the paradox is discovering in a general sense just what inputs into the education process affect educational outcomes and by what magnitude. With that information, it may be possible both to understand what happened in the 1960s and early 1970s and to improve the provision of education in all types of schools in the future.

/ A production function approach to education

Recall from Chapter 15 that a production function characterizes the relationship between inputs and the range of possible outputs that can be produced with each input combination. If that technology of producing "education" can be identified and quantified—that is, if the effect of different educational inputs on educational results can be determined—then one would have a mechanism to evaluate how different schools go about educating and why educational results differ for different students or at different times. The concept of education production analysis by economists, then, is to statistically relate education outputs to education inputs. Mathematically,

$$Q = q(I_1, I_2, I_3, \ldots)$$

where Q = the educational outcome
  I = educational inputs

Although it seems natural to economists to examine the "production of education" in the same way that one might study production of automobiles, computers, or agricultural products, this approach when applied to education remains controversial, and it and its results are therefore not accepted by some.

/ Measuring Outcomes.
The necessary first step in analyzing and evaluating production decisions is identifying both the *objective* of the organization and some way of *measuring output*. As discussed in Chapter 15, neither of these decisions is straightforward in the case of many services provided by governments, including, and perhaps especially for, education. Moreover, the appropriate way to measure output depends on what the objective of the government is in providing the service. For instance, a discovery that schools do not do a good job of improving students' scores on standardized tests may not be surprising or very useful if, in fact, schools do not care about test scores and thus do not try to improve them.

In doing production analysis for private firms, particularly those in manufacturing, these decisions seem clearer. Economists typically assume that the objective of the firms is to produce that amount of product that generates the highest possible profit. Output can either be measured by the number of physical units produced or by the dollar volume of sales. If profit rises, then the firm is moving in the direction of achieving its goal. Production changes that increase profits are deemed desirable. Economists also sometimes consider objectives other than maximizing profit, such as increasing market share or maximizing sales subject to a minimum-profit restriction, but even in those cases the objective is clear and easily quantifiable.

With respect to government services and education particularly, the objective of the government is not so easily defined. And even if an objective can be agreed on, the measures of output and thus success in meeting the objective are imprecise. The output or result of education is usually measured in one of four ways: by scores on standardized tests, by numbers of students achieving a particular level of education (number graduating from high school and number entering college, for example), by economic achievements such as rate of employment or level of income, or by subjective measures (often through surveys) of individual satisfaction. Among the numerous studies attempting to relate education inputs and methods to educational results, test scores are easily the most commonly used measure of performance or output, partly because they are readily available for many students and because they make comparisons over time relatively easy.

Analyses relating economic achievements to education level certainly suggest, at least on the surface, that more education leads to economic gains. For instance, the basic data shown in Table 18.6 indicate that unemployment rates are lower and incomes higher among those who have completed more years of school. There are two qualifications to these correlations, however. First, some have argued that rather than producing education, the primary effect of the school system is to serve as a *screening device,* identifying more able individuals by the fact that they are allowed to pursue more education. By this viewpoint, the role of schools is to select the more able and provide that information to the market. If that is the case, those with more education do better economically because they are more able, not because additional years of school made them more skilled.

Second, these correlations do not distinguish the *quantity* of education from the *quality* of result. Measures of numbers of students graduating on time, the percentage entering college, the number of school years completed, or the number who are employed x years after graduating are predominately quantity measures, which do not distinguish very well the quality of education. After all, there are a wide variety of colleges and the fact that someone is employed does not indicate the type of job or level of satisfaction. This is, of course, another reason for the attractiveness of test scores that can be interpreted as reflecting an entire range of outcomes. Whether test scores do, in fact, reflect educational "quality" is contro-

TABLE 18.6

Education and Economic Achievement

Years of School Completed	Unemployment Rate March, 1986 (%)	Median Family Income, 1985[a] ($)
Elementary school	12.4	15,370
4 years high school	8.1	27,472
1–3 years college	5.3	32,177
4 years college	2.5	43,187
5 years college or more	2.5	50,525

Sources: U.S. Department of Education (May 1987); U.S. Department of Commerce (Aug. 1986).

[a]For households headed by someone with this educational level.

versial and problematic. The evidence shows, for instance, that test scores are not necessarily correlated with later economic success by students.

But even if a measure (or several measures) of educational output from this list can be agreed on, it is not clear what the objective of the school system is or should be. This difficulty arises because there is typically a wide range of students in any school system, so that one might be interested in the distribution of results among those students as well as the average result. This point has been emphasized by Byron Brown and Daniel Saks (1975) who suggest that schools might be interested in both the mean and variance of test scores, for instance. Suppose that the two alternative sets of test scores shown in Table 18.7 are both possible outcomes, which arise from different allocations of the teacher's time and other resources, for a school or class. The average test score (or equivalently, the sum of scores) is maximized in case A by applying more of the educational resources to the better students. Although the resulting average score is high, the variation among the students is also very large; the coefficient of variation is 30.2, meaning an average of 30.2-percent variation in scores around the mean score. Case B represents the results of an alternative application of the same educational resources, perhaps applying those resources more evenly among the students. The result is a 2-percent lower average score but much less variation among the students (about 20 percent around the mean). In essence, what has happened is that the top scores have fallen by more than the bottom scores have risen, but the percentage gains by the students at the bottom of the distribution outweigh the percentage decreases by those at the top.

Which distribution is better? Which do *you* prefer? There may be no clear answer. One often hears about equal opportunity in education or society, and an explicit economic objective of government is to alter the distribution of income or resources in society. If that is the case, then individuals and government may be willing to accept lower average test scores or educational outcomes in exchange for a more even distribution of those outcomes. This issue implies one of the

TABLE 18.7

Sample Alternative Test-Score Distributions

Student	Case A	Case B	A − B		Percentage Change
1	700	600	− 100		− 14.3
2	650	570	− 80		− 12.3
3	600	550	− 50		− 8.3
4	550	520	− 30		− 5.5
5	500	490	− 10		− 2.0
6	450	450	0		0.0
7	400	410	+ 10		+ 2.5
8	350	380	+ 30		+ 8.6
9	300	350	+ 50		+ 16.7
10	250	320	+ 70		+ 28.0
Average	475	464.	− 11	(Loss)	− 2.3
Standard deviation	143.6	92.1	− 51.5	(Gain)	− 35.9
Std. Dev./Ave.	30.2%	19.8%	− 10.4		− 34.4

difficulties in evaluating teachers or schools. If teachers are evaluated or paid or districts rewarded with state aid based on the average score of their students on some standardized test, then there is an incentive to maximize those average scores by allocating teaching time or resources to those students whose test scores improve the most. But the resulting distribution of student performance may not be that which is most desired.

Another important issue in measuring and evaluating educational outcomes is whether to focus on the *level* of outcome or result by a student or school or on the *change in that level* by a student or school over some time. The distinction is important because factors specific to a student (innate ability, effort) are expected to influence the level of achievement by that student and those factors may be difficult to measure and thus control for in studies of educational outcomes. By focusing on the change in achievement for a given student or set of students over time, those other student specific factors are held constant, so that the change in achievement may reflect the value added by the educational system.

Often the same standardized test is given to students at different times—for instance, in grades 5, 8, and 12—and the scores at each grade level compared to some average or norm for that level. The student's score relative to the norm at one grade level (90 percent of the norm in grade 5) compared to the same student's score in a later grade (110 percent of the norm in grade 12) may reflect the improvement caused by the school system. The fact that the average twelfth-grade score for two schools is both 110 percent of the norm may not mean that both schools are doing an equally good educational job if the students in one school started at a lower level. The change in scores for the same students may be the preferable measure. In fact, it may be that a school with a lower average twelfth-grade score has a greater value added than some other school with a higher average score, but one whose students started at a higher level.

/ Measuring Inputs. The second requirement for analyzing educational production is to identify and measure the inputs into the production process, those factors that are expected to influence educational results. In general, one can identify three types of inputs: those provided by the schools, those provided by society (broadly defined), and those provided by the student. Thus,

$$Q = q(\textit{School Inputs, Social Inputs, Student Inputs})$$

with examples of each type of input shown below:

School Inputs	Social Inputs	Student Inputs
Teachers	Family experiences	Innate ability
Books	Cultural factors	Effort
Classroom hours	Nonschool learning	
Curricula		
Other students		

At least three important issues must be resolved before this general model can be applied. First, one factor that differentiates the production of education from production of many other commodities is that the inputs are expected to have a cumulative effect. The educational achievement of a student at a particular grade or age is expected to depend on all the previous education inputs applied to that person, not just on the most recent or those from a particular grade. In other words, for a statistical analysis based on test scores, one should not relate the score at a particular grade to the inputs provided by that year's class, but rather to all past education received by that student. This is another difficulty in using test scores or achievement results to evaluate teachers or school systems because a student's achievement at one time may depend on the work of past teachers or other schools. This is another reason why focusing on the change in achievement in a particular period may be more useful.

Second, the school inputs can either be measured by the actual numbers of inputs used (number of teachers per student, number or percentage of teachers with a Master's degree, number or percentage of teachers with more than five year's experience, number of school days per year, types of subjects taught) or by the amount of money spent by the school on those inputs (instructional expenditures per student). However, it may be that additional spending will improve educational outcomes only if those resources are applied in particular ways. Finally, it must be decided whether the unit of analysis is to be the classroom, thus focusing on specific teachers, or on the school or school system.

/ Evidence on educational production: What matters?

Hanushek (1986) has identified about 150 different studies prepared over the past twenty years using the basic approach outlined above, of the factors influencing educational production. Although these studies use different data sources and different theoretical and statistical models, some relationships among inputs and results have been noted consistently while other hypotheses about relationships have consistently not been supported by the research. Accordingly, a consensus has developed about what factors appear to be important in improving educational results.

First is a surprising result about some factors that apparently have not been associated with improved educational outcomes. As stated by Hanushek (1986, 1162), "There appears to be no strong or systematic relationship between school expenditures and student performance." As we have previously learned, the instructional expenditures of schools are largely composed of the costs of teachers. So higher per-pupil expenditures would most likely be expected to arise from smaller class sizes, paying all teachers higher salaries, or hiring teachers with more education (which would require higher salaries). The absence of a relationship between per-pupil expenditures and student performance is also found when expenditures are decomposed into these characteristics. So there also appears to be no strong or systematic relationship between smaller class sizes, teachers with more graduate education, or higher teacher salaries generally and student performance.

That per-pupil expenditures *per se* do not appear to matter for student performance is certainly surprising, at least to economists, because it implies that additional inputs do not lead to additional output. It is important to note, however, that
although the result suggests that increased per-pupil expenditures *have not* led to
improved performance, increased spending still *might* lead to improved performance
if those additional resources were spent differently, that is, on different inputs that
do affect performance. For instance, smaller classes might improve performance if
the time in those classes was used differently than it is in larger ones, whereas the
finding that graduate education of teachers does not improve performance may say
more about the current nature of graduate education than it does about the value
of more training generally. Therefore, what these studies suggest about how to
improve educational performance is particularly important.

Second, the "skill" of the teacher is one factor that apparently is related to
student performance. As Murnane has noted (quoted in Brown and Saks 1981,
222), "Virtually every study of school effectiveness finds that some attributes of
teachers are significantly related to student achievement. . . . In particular, the
intellectual skills of a teacher as measured by a verbal ability test or the quality of
college the teacher attended tend to be significant." A similar theme is cited by
Hanushek (1986, 1164) who writes that "The closest thing to a consistent finding
among the studies is that 'smarter' teachers, ones who perform well on verbal ability
tests, do better in the classroom . . . ." The practical difficulty with this finding is
that it may not always be easy to identify ahead of time "more skilled" or "smarter"
people and then to induce more of those people into teaching. In fact, it may be
that there are several ways for individuals to be successful teachers, so that identifying a single characteristic to indicate that someone will be a "good" teacher is
not feasible.

The third general conclusion of these studies is that the school curriculum can
be related to student performance, at least on standardized tests. As noted by
Murnane (1985, 120), "The best documented schooling change contributing to the
[SAT] score decline is a reduction in the number of academic courses students take.
. . . Subsequent research supports the link between the number of academic courses
students take and their scores on standardized tests." By "academic courses," this
finding refers to the so-called basics—reading and writing, mathematics, science,
social studies—as opposed to vocational and other courses students can select (the
arts, sports, and so on). This finding should not be surprising because it is these
academic skills that are primarily tested by standardized tests. Nonetheless, it is
comforting that the statistical studies come to such a commonsense conclusion: If
one wants students to read and write well and do mathematics, then those are the
courses students must take and the skills they must practice in school.

/ Policy implications

In large measure, these results have spurred many of the actual and proposed changes
in state education policies in recent years. Most of these changes and proposals

focus on teachers and courses. Regarding teachers, the policy issues concern how teachers are trained, certified and evaluated, and paid. A number of colleges and universities have now agreed that students working to become teachers will take fewer education classes and more classes in the specific disciplines they plan to teach. Thus, for example, someone who plans to be a high school math teacher will major in mathematics in college and take some specialized education classes in addition (rather than majoring in education and taking a few math classes). All states have some procedure to certify teachers as eligible to teach in that state. A number of states have acted to toughen certification requirements by raising the basic education requirement, creating certification exams, and/or using a probation period coupled with on-the-job evaluation.

Regarding teacher pay, the two common proposals are for higher teacher salaries generally and for adoption of a merit-pay system for salary increases, with those increases depending on some measure of a teacher's "success." The first is intended to attract more skilled people into teaching, whereas the second is intended both as an incentive for teachers to be more successful and as a reward for teachers who are. The average annual salary of public elementary and secondary school teachers was $23,595 in 1984–85 and $25,313 in 1985–86 (U.S. Department of Education, May 1987).[4] Although the average salary of teachers increased throughout the 1970s and 1980s, it did not increase as fast as the general level of prices in the 1970s. Consequently, in real terms the average salary decreased in the 1970s: Indeed, it was not until 1985–86 that the average real salary exceeded that in 1970 ($24,878 in 1985–86 dollars). Of course, the average real salary of all workers declined some in the 1970s, although Hanushek (1986) presents evidence that suggests that the real salaries of teachers declined slightly more than those of all workers in those years.

There seem to be at least three important economic issues about these proposals to alter teacher pay. First, increased salaries may not be successful in attracting more skilled people into teaching soon if there is no mechanism to create job vacancies for these individuals and if teacher certification requirements prevent some people from moving into teaching without additional specialized training. Second, increases in teacher pay generally may not succeed in attracting more of the most scarce teachers, those in mathematics and science. The opportunity costs for people trained in those disciplines may require paying different salaries to teachers of different subjects, even if they have the same education and experience. Third, although merit pay is likely to induce teachers to spend more time generating the results on which the merit evaluation is based, that will improve education only to the extent that the performance test is valuable or appropriate. If the merit pay is based on the average performance of students, then teachers have an incentive to maximize test scores and may be less concerned with the distribution of those scores, as previously discussed.

---

[4]In contrast, the median annual income (not just salary) in 1985 of full-time workers with four years of college was about $33,000 for men and $22,000 for women.

/ APPLICATION 18.1
Private Versus Public Schools

What is and what should be the relative role of private schools in the primary and secondary education system? This question is the source of controversy concerning several issues. For instance, are private schools more successful at "educating" students than public schools? Would the educational system operate better or at lower cost if there was more direct competition not only between private and public schools but also among the public schools? Should a system of educational vouchers or tuition tax credits be adopted, allowing all students to freely choose the school to attend? Should private schools be used to supplement public education?

Under an educational voucher system, proposed by Milton Friedman in 1962, all students would receive a voucher worth $X per year from the government, which could only be spent on education at any school of the student's choice. For instance, a voucher worth $3000 might fully cover the cost of attending the local public school or could be supplemented with private funds to cover tuition at a competing private school. In fact, it would be possible that there be only private schools. A tuition tax credit plan would have a similar effect. Families would receive a tax credit for all or part of private-school tuition, so that the government would provide for a minimum amount of education for all students regardless of the school selected. The concept behind these plans is that the combination of individual choice of schools coupled with direct competition among them would serve to improve the overall educational system. There are at least two concerns about these plans. One is that a greater division of schools based on class or student ability would arise than exists now. Secondly, some argue that one important function of public schools is to educate students about differences among people partly by bringing together students from very different backgrounds. Less of that might occur if individuals choose schools directly rather than indirectly through the choice of residential community.

Do private schools, in fact, do a better job of educating students than the public schools? The evidence from research on this issue is inconclusive. This is an inherently difficult question to examine because under the current system the students who choose private schools are typically from very different backgrounds than many students who have no choice but to attend public

States have also acted to change the types of courses students take, both by altering graduation requirements imposed by state governments and by introducing competency examinations for students (used by seventeen states). According to the U.S. Department of Education, since 1980 thirty-eight states have acted to raise or impose state government minimum course requirements for high school graduation. Only three states (Massachusetts, Michigan, and Nebraska) do not have substantial state standards, leaving those as an option for local districts. Among those states with course requirements imposed by the state government, common

---

/ APPLICATION 18.1 Continued
Private Versus Public Schools

schools. Even if one discovers that private-school students do better, on average, than public-school students, it is difficult to discover whether that difference arose from something the schools did or because of differences in the students' background. And as previously discussed, it may be difficult to even identify and measure those background factors that might differentiate the students. How does one quantify the "importance placed on education" by a family and thus the attitudes imparted to the students by families? The relevant question is whether private schools would do a better job than public schools *if the private schools had the whole mix of public-school students.* And that question remains unresolved.

Rather than thinking about private and public schools as potential substitutes in providing education, in many ways it is more accurate to think of them as complementary. Education provided by or through government is really a minimum or floor amount because individuals can and do supplement their public education with private preschools or nursery schools, after-school tutoring, private extracurricular activities, and special summer education programs. From an economic perspective, if individuals demand a given amount of education and if that amount is not being provided through the government, then individuals are free to buy more.

In fact, there is evidence that these kinds of activities have been increasing in recent years. The Census Bureau reports that 39 percent of all three- and four-year-old children attended nursery school in 1986, compared to 31 percent in 1975 and 11 percent in 1965. No doubt this is partly due to and financed by the tremendous growth in the labor force participation of women. In 1985 the *Wall Street Journal* (1985a) reported on the development of three private firms offering after-school instruction in basic reading and math skills. These firms, through company-owned or franchised outlets in many communities, sell private instruction in very small groups for either remedial or enrichment purposes. In 1985 prices averaged about $20 to $25 per hour. Many colleges and universities, and even public elementary and secondary schools in some communities, have developed summer programs not just in sports and music but also in science, computers, mathematics, and language, which are attracting increasing numbers of students.

---

requirements are three to four units (years) of English and two to three units of mathematics, science, and social studies each. One of the most dramatic changes occurred in Florida, which now has among the most stringent requirements. Local school districts previously determined requirements, but now all high school graduates are required to have four units of English and three each of social studies, mathematics, and science. Whether these changes will help in improving student performance depends partly on the simultaneous changes regarding teachers. Requiring students to take more classes in reading, writing, mathematics, and science is likely to improve educational results only if there are well-trained and skilled teachers willing to teach those specific subjects.

/ Summary

In 1985 public elementary and secondary schools served about 40 million students. Public school spending amounted to about $3449 per student, 3.7 percent of GNP and 40 percent of local government spending. Expenditures per pupil, even after adjustment for inflation, increased substantially in the past twenty-five years.

Nearly half of the revenue for financing public elementary and secondary schools in 1985 was provided by state governments with local governments generating about 44 percent of public-school revenue. The federal government provided the remaining 6 percent. The relative role of state–local governments was approximately reversed in the 1970s.

The variation in the roles state governments play in financing education is even greater than for most other services. The median state provided about 50 percent of school revenue in 1985, but the state government provided more than 60 percent of revenue in thirteen states and less than 40 percent in another thirteen states.

Prior to the 1970s, states generally used lump-sum per-pupil grants to support local education. Such grants are usually referred to as foundation aid because the per-pupil grant represents a minimum expenditure level and the state aid is intended to provide a basic foundation on top of which local revenue supplements may be added.

Guaranteed Tax Base or District Power Equalizing aid plans are intended to provide an equal, basic per-pupil property tax base to each district, rather than basic per-pupil minimum expenditure level. A GTB plan involves matching grants that reduce the price of education to the school districts. Because the demand for education spending is price inelastic, the price reductions that are caused by the matching grants do not influence education spending very much.

There appears to be no relationship between rising school expenditures and improved student performance, given how those funds have been used, including spending for smaller classes or higher teacher salaries. But the intellectual skills of a teacher as measured by a verbal ability test or the quality of college the teacher attended tend to have a significant effect on student performance. And school curriculum can matter because of the link between the number of academic courses students take and their scores on standardized tests.

In the 1970s, the primary educational policy issue concerned the differences in per-pupil spending among districts. States altered their educational grant programs and spent more money on education, but spending differences among districts were not reduced and educational performance generally did not improve. In the 1980s, the primary issues moved from focusing on educational spending to educational results. Expenditures are a very imperfect measure of the output of government in providing services, and consistent with that observation, increasing expenditures may be necessary, but certainly are not sufficient, for improving service results.

Discussion Questions

1. Per-pupil spending often varies among school districts in a given state. Suppose that one district spends $2500 per pupil for instruction (excluding transportation, lunches, administration, and so on) while another district of about the same size spends $4000 per pupil. What could account for this difference? Consider factors in the categories of the quantity of inputs, the type of inputs, the prices of inputs, and the type of output.

2. The role of state governments in providing public primary and secondary education varies greatly. In one case, the state government operates the school system; in a number of others, the state government provides a substantial amount of the revenue for local schools (half or more) and sets minimum graduation or teacher requirements; and in other cases, the state provides either a relatively small amount of revenue or sets few standards or both. What are the economic arguments for and against state involvement in financing and producing education? What social and economic characteristics of a state might influence the choice of how to produce education? Do these help explain the cases of Hawaii and New Hampshire or Washington compared to Oregon?

3. Refer back to the Education Grant Simulation case beginning on page 380. In that illustration, a program of matching grants was not effective in equalizing per-pupil spending because demand was relatively inelastic. What other means might be used to narrow these spending differences? Outline the specifics of a state program that you believe would be successful in setting a minimum per-pupil spending level of $2662.50, the average level in the illustration. Explain the effect of that program on each district and discuss whether you would support such a change in your state.

4. Suppose that your college or university decides to evaluate its undergraduate program to determine how successful it is at educating students. How should the output of a university be measured? In terms of education only, what characteristics do you think show how good of a job a college does? How should the teaching output or quality of individual professors be measured? Does your university attempt to measure education output or teaching success? Does your university have a merit-pay system for faculty, and if so, what role does education output or teaching quality play?

Selected Readings

Hanushek, Eric A. "The Economics of Schooling." *Journal of Economic Literature* 24 (Sept. 1986): 1141–77.

Murnane, Richard J. "An Economist's Look at Federal and State Education Policies." In *American Domestic Priorities: An Economic Appraisal,* edited by J. Quigley and D. Rubinfeld, 118–47. Berkeley: University of California Press, 1985.

19 / *Transportation*

> . . . In no other major area are pricing practices so irrational, so
> out of date, and so conducive to waste as in urban transportation.[1]
>
> *William S. Vickrey*

Although education may be the dominant single service provided by subnational
governments, transportation is surely the most apparent service, the one more
individuals directly interact with on a day-to-day basis. In fact, transportation
facilities provided by state and local governments may be so apparent that they are
sometimes taken for granted, without an understanding of what they cost or how
they are financed. Once while making a presentation about state government spending to a local citizens group, I was confronted by an individual who asserted that
he did not get any benefits from state taxes. I asked the fellow how he had gotten
to the meeting that day. He responded that he had driven and then said "Well,
obviously I use the roads, but except for that . . . ." Except for the roads? It is
estimated that in 1984 one mile of interstate highway cost between $2 and $3.5
million for construction alone, plus the cost of engineering and acquisition of land.
And even though primary, secondary, and most urban roads cost less, it is clear
that even a short automobile trip requires the use of many millions of dollars worth
of capital infrastructure provided through governments.

It has also been noted that transportation is somewhat of a unique service
because inputs provided both publicly and privately are often combined to produce
transportation service. Individuals own private automobiles, which they drive on
public roads and bridges. Private airline firms fly privately owned airplanes among
publicly provided airports using a publicly provided air traffic control system.
Privately owned and operated boats travel on publicly owned and maintained water-
ways and harbors. In essence, the supply of transportation service is provided jointly
by the private and public sectors, with the public sector primarily responsible for
providing and maintaining transportation routes. The demand for transportation
service—both for routes and vehicles—arises almost entirely from private choice,
however. As a result of the complementary nature of the public- and private-
transportation inputs, government must consider private demand for transportation
in providing facilities. But it is also true that those publicly provided facilities—

---

[1]"Pricing in Urban and Suburban Transport." *American Economic Review* (May 1963): 452.

and their prices—can influence private decisions about the amount and type of transportation individuals demand.

The emphasis in this chapter is on the role of government in providing and financing those public facilities. Roads and highways are the largest category, measured both by dollars and use, of transportation facilities provided by government. And in the provision of highways, state governments play the dominant role by receiving aid funds from the federal government, collecting substantial own-source revenues, spending directly on the construction and maintenance of roads, and transferring aid funds to local governments for their direct spending.

/ Financing Transportation: Current Practice

/ Types of transportation service

Governments provide transportation facilities or service for air, rail, road, and water transit. Of the total expenditures by all levels of government on these transportation services in 1986, about 80 percent (nearly $50 billion) went for highways, as shown in Table 19.1. In contrast, about 12.6 percent of government transportation spending went for air transit and about 5.5 percent for water transportation. Of the $50 billion spent on highways, more than half—$27 billion, or 55 percent—represented new capital expenditure, that is, construction of new roads and highways. On the other hand, capital expenditures accounted for only a bit more than a third of spending on air and water transit and parking facilities in 1986.

The dominance of spending on highways among all government transportation spending is certainly not surprising because it reflects the dominance of the automobile and the scope of highway transportation in general. In 1985 there were nearly 4 million miles of roads in the United States on which the nearly 170 million registered motor vehicles were driven about 1.8 trillion vehicle-miles by the 155 million licensed drivers. The Nationwide Personal Transportation Study for 1983 showed that about one-third of households in the United States have one motor

TABLE 19.1

Transportation Expenditure by All Levels of Government, 1986[a]

	Total Expenditures		Capital Expenditure Only	
Function	Amount (Millions of Dollars)	Percentage of Total	Amount (Millions of Dollars)	Percentage of Function Total
Highways	49,936	80.3	27,011	55.1
Air transportation	7,856	12.6	2,574	32.8
Water transportation	3,415	5.5	1,156	33.9
Parking facilities	682	1.1	268	39.2
Transit subsidies[b]	276	0.4	na	na

Source: U.S. Department of Commerce. *Governmental Finances in 1986.* Table 8.

[a]Does not include expenditures on police protection, debt service, and general government regulation.
[b]Operating subsidies only; capital expenditure excluded.

vehicle, another third own two vehicles, while only about 13 percent have none. The purposes for automobile travel by individuals are almost equally divided among work (34 percent of vehicle-miles), family and personal business (30 percent), and social and recreational trips (30 percent).

/ The role of the federal and subnational governments

The general pattern for financing transportation services involves both direct spending on purchases and payment of intergovernmental aid by each of the three primary levels of government. Total spending and intergovernmental aid payments by each level of government for each major category of transportation service are shown in Table 19.2. The federal government's role concerning highways is primarily in providing grants to subnational governments, whereas for air and water transit the federal government has a substantial role in directly purchasing and providing services and facilities. In all cases except transit subsidies, state governments are both substantial direct purchasers of services and facilities and transmitters of aid to local governments. Local governments mostly serve as direct purchasers and providers of facilities and services, using both their own revenues and the intergovernmental aid.

For instance, of the approximately $15 billion spent by the federal government for highways in 1986, about $14.4 billion, or 96 percent, was composed of highway grants paid to state–local governments. Thus, although the federal government has a substantial role in financing highways, the federal government spends very little directly purchasing highway facilities. In contrast, state governments spent about $37 billion on highways in 1985 with about 18 percent ($6.5 billion) representing grants paid to local governments, while nearly all of the approximately $19 billion spent by local governments went for direct purchases of facilities and services. For air and water transportation, however, both the level of federal government spending and the share going for direct purchases is greater than that by state governments.

A truly accurate picture of the roles of the different levels of government in financing transportation requires both the distribution of final spending and the

TABLE 19.2

Transportation Expenditure by Level of Government, 1985 (Amounts in Millions of Dollars)

	Federal		States		Local	
Function	Total Spending	Intergovernmental Aid Paid	Total Spending	Intergovernmental Aid Paid	Total Spending	Intergovernmental Aid Paid
Highways	14,938	14,370	36,661	6,470	19,220	63
Air transportation	4,452	853	599	145	3,805	2
Water transportation	1,712	22	572	24	177	—
Parking facilities	—	—	—	—	682	0
Transit subsidies[a]	—	—	1,880	1,739	844	709

Source: U.S. Department of Commerce. *Governmental Finances in 1986.* Table 8.

[a]Operating expenses only. Duplicative intergovernmental transactions are excluded.

distribution of own-source revenue used for purchases and intergovernmental grants in each transportation category. About 98 percent of the actual spending on highway facilities and services is done by state–local governments, states alone accounting for more than 60 percent. But states generated only slightly more than half of the revenue spent on highways. The federal government provided about 25 percent of the funds spent on highways in 1985 but spent less than 2 percent directly itself. Local governments generated slightly less than 25 percent of revenues spent on highways but accounted for nearly 37 percent of direct spending. The conclusion from these analyses is that state governments are dominant in both generating and spending funds for highways. For air and water transportation, in contrast, about half of the spending is done directly by the federal government and the other half by subnational governments.

/ Transportation revenues

Although governments generate revenues for transportation spending from a variety of sources, taxes and tolls collected from users are the major component. For instance, Department of Transportation (DOT) data show that about 60 percent of all government revenues spent on highways in 1986 arose from taxes and tolls collected directly from highway users. The revenue amounts and tax rates for the larger transportation taxes and charges are shown in Table 19.3. The federal government levies excise taxes on the sale of motor fuels ($.09 per gallon of gasoline

TABLE 19.3

Transportation Revenues, 1985–86

Source	Tax Rate	Amount (Millions of Dollars)
Federal Government		
Motor fuel tax	$.09/gal. (gasoline)	11,641
	$.15/gal. (diesel fuel)	
Truck and trailer tax	12% retail price	1,290
Tire tax	$.15–$.50/pound	243
Road use charges for trucks	$100–$550/truck	
Air transportation tax	8% of ticket price	2,308
Airport charges		68
Water transport use charges		527
State–Local Governments		
Motor Fuel Tax[a]	$.04–$.20/gal.	14,400
Motor vehicle license fees		8,247
Motor vehicle operator license fees		695
Highway use and toll charges		2,918
Parking charges		632
Airport use charges		3,454
Water transport use charges		1,230

Sources: U.S. Department of Commerce. *Governmental Finances in 1986;* U.S. Department of Transportation (1986a).

[a]Does not include state and local general sales taxes on gasoline and motor vehicles.

and $.15 per gallon for diesel fuel), tires, trucks and trailers, and airline tickets and also collects user charges for road use (from trucks weighing more than 55,000 pounds) as well as for airport and waterway use. State and some local governments also levy excise taxes on the sale of motor fuels (varying from $.04 to $.20 per gallon of gasoline for the states only, as shown in Table 9.3), and some states apply their general sales tax to the sale of gasoline as well, often with that revenue earmarked for transportation. State–local governments collect fees, which serve both a regulation function and a transportation revenue source, for licensing both vehicles and drivers. State–local government also collect tolls and charges for highway, airport, and waterway use and for parking. Even if the notion of transportation-user taxes and charges is broadly defined to include all of these, motor fuel taxes comprise roughly two-thirds of the revenue collected from users.

/ Financing Transportation: Theoretical Issues and Alternative Practices

/ Role for user charges

Recall from Chapter 16 that user-charge financing is attractive if the share of marginal benefits accruing to direct users is relatively large, the users can be identified easily, and the direct users can be excluded (at reasonable cost) from consuming the service unless the charge is paid. Does it seem that these conditions

FIGURE 19.1   Allocation of Transportation Costs to Users and Nonusers

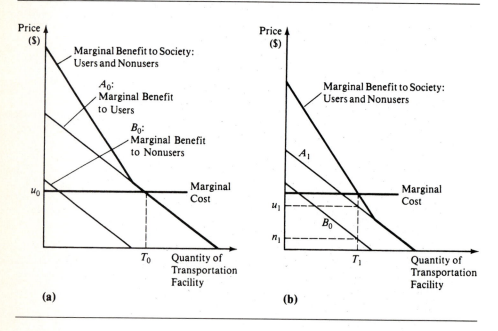

(a)   (b)

are satisfied by transportation facilities and services provided by state–local governments? Typically the answer is yes, with one qualification. Although external benefits from transportation systems undoubtedly exist, they may be swamped by the substantial demand by and benefits to direct users. Direct users identify themselves by purchasing and registering vehicles, by purchasing fuel and other supplies, and by taking trips. The potential qualification is that while exclusion of users who do not pay is possible, it may be costly, particularly for some forms of transportation-user charges. This suggests that transportation-user charges will be attractive only when they can be collected and enforced in a relatively low-cost manner.

One issue in applying user charges to transportation is whether users—through direct charges—should pay part or all of the capital cost of facilities. The answer depends on the distribution of *marginal benefits* between those who are direct users and those who are not, not simply on the existence of benefits to nonusers. Surely benefits from the transportation network provided by state–local governments do flow to individuals for reasons other than their direct use of those networks; there are general social benefits from a transportation system. The transportation networks are used to bring individuals and goods to those who are not direct users (in those instances). In general, a basic transportation network enables the economy to function smoothly and assists government in carrying out its defense and public-safety responsibilities. But the relevant question is whether those social purposes are enhanced by expanding the transportation network. Are there social or external benefits at the margin?

The possibilities are illustrated in Figure 19.1a. Demand curve A_0 represents the private marginal benefits that go to individuals as a result of their direct use of the transportation network, and B_0 represents the general social marginal benefits that go to all of society. Remember that marginal benefit means the additional gain from an additional unit of transportation facility, perhaps another mile of highway. The efficient amount of this transportation facility is T_0, where the marginal cost of another unit of the facility equals the sum of the marginal benefits that go to direct users and generally to society. But at that size transportation system, there are no additional benefits to society generally, only additional benefits for direct users. Apparently, a smaller transportation network would be sufficient to allow the economy and government to function as well, at least in providing general benefits to all of society. Expansion of the transportation network beyond that size benefits specific individuals due to their use of that facility but does not provide any additional general benefits to all. In that case, those direct users who benefit from the expansion of the transportation facility should pay all of the capital cost.

A second possibility, perhaps representing an earlier time, is shown in Figure 19.1b. Although the general social marginal benefits from this transportation facility are the same as in Figure 19.1a, the private, direct benefits to users are lower; that is, the private demand for this transportation facility is less than in Figure 19.1a. In this case, there are marginal gains both to direct users and generally to the society at the efficient amount of the facility, T_1. Appropriate financing in this case requires that direct user charges be u_1 per unit of the facility, with the remainder of the cost, $MC - u_1$, coming from general taxes paid by all of society. User charges are still appropriate but only to cover a portion rather than all of the capital costs.

In other words, if the transportation system is already large enough to provide all the general benefits that arise from having a transportation network, then any further expansion of that system will only generate private benefits and should be entirely financed by users of that expansion. It is often suggested that this is the current situation regarding highways, so that it is appropriate to finance more road building entirely from user charges. But if full user-charge financing is used when there are still additional social benefits to be had, society will end up underinvesting in transportation facilities. If users were charged the full marginal costs in Figure 19.1b, they would demand less than the efficient amount of facility. In short, user charges should cover the same portion of costs as direct-user benefits represent of the aggregate marginal benefits.

/ User Charge Practice. How well does the actual transportation financing system correspond to this theory? For highways, at least, it seems fairly well. According to DOT, about 75 percent of the revenue for highway expenditures for all purposes in 1985 came from highway user taxes and tolls (59 percent), income from invested funds (7 percent), and proceeds of transportation bond sales (9 percent). The latter two primarily represent past and future highway-user taxes and tolls, respectively. The other 25 percent of highway revenues came from other taxes, fees, and assessments, especially property taxes. In fact, two-thirds of the highway revenue not collected directly from users arose at the local government level. And some local government property taxes were special assessments for streets and roads. When coupled with the fact that not all total highway expenditures actually go for the facilities (some of the money goes for law enforcement and safety programs, for instance), it seems clear that funds collected directly from highway users account for almost all expenditures on road and highway facilities.

Motor fuel taxes on gasoline and diesel fuel account for the great bulk, about 70 percent, of highway-user taxes and tolls. And because highway-user taxes and tolls cover about 75 percent of total highway expenditures, it follows that motor fuel taxes represent a bit more than half of total highway spending for all purposes. It is important to ask therefore how well motor fuel taxes work as user charges. Most importantly, motor fuel taxes do vary by the amount and type of road use. The more miles an individual goes, the more gasoline required and thus the more gasoline excise tax implicitly paid. Similarly, larger or heavier vehicles generally require more gasoline than smaller or lighter ones to travel a given distance, which corresponds to road "use" if larger and heavier vehicles impose greater maintenance or safety costs on the highway system. Collection of motor fuel taxes also entails relatively low administrative costs, partly because they are usually collected at the wholesale or distributor level where there are fewer firms than at retail.

But motor fuel taxes are imperfect user charges for at least three reasons. First, all gasoline and diesel fuel is not used on highways; some is used for boats, airplanes, agricultural machinery, off-road vehicles, and lawnmowers, for example. Because of this, some motor fuel taxes are often earmarked for waterway or natural-resources uses, and some states exempt fuel for agricultural purposes from the tax. Second, fuel usage is not expected to correspond perfectly to road and highway "use" because vehicles (and drivers) differ in their fuel economy. Third, fuel taxes do not do a good job of differentiating highway use by location and time, so they do not adequately represent congestion costs created by highway users. Fuel taxes may have to be supplemented with some form of congestion charge therefore, as discussed later in this chapter. Despite these difficulties, motor fuel taxes have come to be accepted and used as the primary highway-user charge.

It may be worth noting that many of the other fees and taxes collected from highway users do not correspond to use nearly as well as fuel taxes. Driver's license and vehicle registration fees, for instance, are usually not based on an accurate measure of road "use." Driver's license fees are usually lump-sum charges and vehicle registration fees are usually based either on vehicle value or weight, neither of which correspond to actual road use. These fees are intended more as a regulatory device than as a source of revenue for highway facilities. A similar argument also applies to road-use fees for trucks and excise taxes on tires, which are also based on weight. On the other hand, road tolls can be tailored to road use, differentiating by distance traveled, vehicle type, and time and place of trips, although tolls can entail high administrative and compliance costs as discussed later.

Spending on transportation facilities for air and water travel is also heavily financed through taxes and charges collected from direct users. On the other hand, spending on mass-transit services—urban bus, rail, and subway systems—is not as heavily reliant on user taxes and charges. According to Jose Gomez-Ibanez (1985, 191),

> Passenger fares had been enough to cover operating costs and make a small contribution to capital expenses through the 1950s, despite the fact that the [mass-transit] industry was contracting. In 1964 passenger receipts fell below operating expenses for the industry as a whole and by the 1980s covered only about 40 percent of operating costs and made no contribution to capital expenses.

The share of operating costs covered by passenger fares is surely even less than 40 percent today. Mass-transit expenditures, which are almost all made by local governments, are financed by substantial amounts of federal and state aid. For the federal government and many states, gasoline taxes are a major source for at least part of the mass-transit grant funds. This may serve as an indirect form of benefit charge if highway users do in fact benefit from the existence of mass-transit systems, an issue considered in the later section on transportation pricing.

/ Role for federal aid

Even if it is agreed what share of transportation costs should be born directly by users, the appropriate level of government to collect those user taxes and charges and the appropriate level to provide any general funds also must be resolved. Recall that federal aid plays an important role in financing transportation, particularly for highways and investment in mass-transit facilities. The federal government finances about a quarter of all expenditures on highways, almost all through grants to the states, and 80 percent of new capital expenditures on mass-transit facilities. What economic rationale is there for the federal government's role in financing transportation facilities and services, and does the federal aid system as structured correspond to that theory?

Recall from Chapter 17 that the chief economic rationale for intergovernmental grants is to correct for inefficient service choices by subnational governments, which arise because consideration is given only to local or state benefits. If there are benefits external to the government providing a service and those benefits are not considered, then too little of the service is provided from the broader viewpoint of the entire society. One way to correct that problem is to provide a matching grant for the service, which reduces the cost of the service to the providing government and thus induces an increase in the amount provided. The matching rate should correspond to the ratio of nonresident to resident benefits at the margin. A matching grant also achieves a degree of fairness by effectively requiring nonresidents of a jurisdiction to help finance services provided by that jurisdiction from which they benefit.

In theory this notion also provides a reason for federal government involvement in transportation finance. There are presumably national reasons for wanting to have a relatively uniform transportation network covering the breadth of the nation and connecting various metropolitan areas and states. At the very least, it has been argued that such a transportation network is necessary for the federal government to carry out its national defense responsibilities. To the extent that the benefits of interstate transport are underestimated or neglected by the states or to the extent that intrastate transport is underappreciated by local governments, the federal government has the responsibility of resolving those externality problems. Because nonresidents substantially use transportation facilities directly provided by states and localities, some nonresident contributions—through federal aid—are called for.

/ Aid Structure.   Initially at least, these reasons did seem to correspond closely to the structure of federal aid for transportation, and especially for highways, as suggested by the abbreviated history of federal transportation aid in Table 19.4. Federal aid was initially limited to principal roads connecting states or counties within states, and even until 1954, the roads eligible for federal highway grants were limited to rural primary and rural secondary roads and urban extensions of rural primary roads. For those types of roads, federal matching grants resulting in a 75-percent federal cost share and 25-percent state share were available. Urban extensions of rural secondary roads were added to the federal aid highway system in 1954, and financing of the Interstate and Defense Highway System began in 1956, with federal grants covering 90 percent of capital costs. Even then, the focus of federal transportation grants remained on transport among states or regions within states.

The role of federal aid was expanded somewhat in the 1960s and 1970s, however, by the creation or expansion of grant programs for road maintenance and mass-transit services. A separate grant program for bridge repair and replacement was instituted in 1970, and specific grants for resurfacing, restoration, and rehabilitation of interstate highways were first offered in 1976. As more and more of the primary and interstate highway system was in place, a change in spending away from additional construction and toward maintaining the existing structure is certainly expected. The issue, however, is whether the federal government should play a similar role for maintenance as it did for construction. The federal government

TABLE 19.4

History of Federal Transportation Aid to States and Localities

Year	Federal Aid Structure and Uses
Early 1900s	Federal highway aid begins.
1921	Federal aid restricted to principal roads connecting states or counties within states.
1944	Rural secondary roads and principal urban highways added to federal aid system by Federal Highway Aid Act. Matching grants used with 75% federal and 25% state–local shares. Federal aid road system includes rural primary roads, rural secondary roads, and urban extensions of rural primary roads.
1954	Urban extensions of rural secondary roads added to federal aid system.
1956	Substantial grants for Interstate and Defense Highway System begun with 90% federal and 10% state shares. Highway Trust Fund created by the Highway Revenue Act to receive transportation-related taxes and charges.
1964	Grants for mass-transit capital costs instituted, to cover up to two-thirds of the cost.
1970	Separate grants for bridge rehabilitation and replacement instituted.
1973	Maximum federal grant share for mass-transit capital costs increased to 80%, still the current rate.
1974	Grants for mass-transit operating costs at a 50/50 share instituted.
1976	Specific grants for resurfacing, restoration, and rehabilitation of interstate highways provided.
1983	Surface Transportation Assistance Act increased federal gasoline tax from $.04 to $.09 per gallon with $.04 of the increase restricted to aid for interstate and rural primary roads only and $.01 earmarked for mass-transit capital grants.

Sources: U.S. Department of Transportation (1986a); Gomez-Ibanez (1985).

also began to support mass-transit services in this period. Grants for up to two-thirds of capital expenses were started in 1964, with the federal share increased to 80 percent in 1973. And matching grants for mass-transit operating costs at a 50-percent federal share were started in 1974. Thus, a federal aid system that had started out to assist states in financing construction of major roads connecting states and population centers was, by the late 1970s, also substantially assisting in the construction and operation of roads and transit systems mostly used for transport within metropolitan areas.

Although the Reagan administration proposed a major restructuring of federal transportation aid in 1981 in the direction of the original notion of financing transport only among states and regions, a less radical alteration was adopted. With the Surface Transportation Assistance Act of 1982, the federal gasoline tax was increased from $.04 to $.09 per gallon with all of the $.05 per-gallon increase in the tax earmarked for limited purposes. The additional revenue from $.04 of the increase was restricted for aid for interstate and rural primary roads only, while the revenue from the additional $.01 increase was earmarked for the Federal Mass Transportation Trust Fund to be used for mass-transit capital expenses only. As a result, the portion of federal aid going for highways used for transport among states and areas was substantially increased, consistent with the original intent of federal transportation aid.

The current structure of federal highway aid can be seen by examining both the roads eligible for aid and the distribution of aid dollars among various purposes. In 1985 roads that were part of the federal aid system represented only about 22 percent of the total mileage of roads in the United States but accommodated more than 80 percent of the number of vehicle-miles traveled, as shown in Table 19.5. In contrast, rural roads not eligible for federal aid represented about 65 percent of road mileage but only 8 percent of motor vehicle travel. Among the various categories of roads within the federal aid system, rural primary roads accounted for about 29 percent of vehicle-miles, urban roads about 22 percent, interstate highways about 21 percent of vehicle travel, and rural secondary roads only about 9 percent.

Of the more than $13 billion of federal highway aid administered by the Federal Highway Administration (FHA) in 1985, about 75 percent went directly for construction and maintenance of federal aid system roads, about 11 percent of the FHA aid went for repair and replacement of bridges, and about 3 percent for highway safety programs. Despite the expansion in scope of federal highway aid over the years, federal highway aid is still heavily skewed toward roads used for interstate and interregional travel, as shown by the comparison of the distribution of federal aid funds used directly for road construction and maintenance with the distribution of vehicle-miles traveled by type of road in Table 19.6. In 1985, 63 percent of FHA grant funds for road construction and maintenance were used for interstate highways although they accounted for only about a quarter of the total vehicle-miles traveled on all the federal aid system roads. For all other categories of federal aid roads, the share of construction and maintenance aid is less than the share of motor travel. More than 85 percent of federal highway grants administered by the FHA are intended for the interstates and other primary roads together. Moreover, the share of aid relative to travel declines as one goes from interstate highways to primary roads to secondary roads and is lowest for urban roads, which account for

TABLE 19.5

Public Road System in the United States, 1985

Type of Road	Miles (Millions)	Percentage of Total Miles	Vehicle-Miles (Millions)	Percentage of Vehicle-Miles
Federal aid system	843,309	21.8	1,427,915	80.5
Interstates	43,593	1.1	370,589	20.9
Rural Primary roads	257,413	6.7	518,632	29.2
Rural Secondary roads	398,248	10.3	155,959	8.8
Urban roads	144,055	3.7	382,735	21.6
Outside of the federal aid system	3,018,625	78.2	346,847	19.5
Rural roads	2,515,304	65.1	141,870	8.0
Urban roads	503,321	13.1	204,977	11.5

Source: U.S. Department of Transportation (1986a).

TABLE 19.6

Comparison of Federal Aid and Vehicle Travel by Type of Road, 1985

Road Type	Distribution of FHA Construction and Maintenance Aid	Distribution of Vehicle-Miles Among Federal Aid Roads[a]	Ratio of Aid Share to Travel Share
Interstate	63.0	26.0	2.42
Rural primary	22.6	36.3	.62
Rural secondary	6.0	10.9	.55
Urban	8.4	26.8	.31

[a]Vehicle-miles of travel from Table 19.5 for each category as a percentage of the sum of vehicle-miles for all four categories.

nearly 27 percent of vehicle travel on federal aid system roads but receive only about 8 percent of grant funds.

It is important to remember, of course, that this is only the distribution of the nominal or intended categories of grant funds. Recall from Chapter 17 that the actual effect of categorical grants on spending may differ from the specified categories. For instance, even though 63 percent of FHA aid goes for interstate highways, that does not mean all of those funds represent spending that states would not otherwise undertake. If a state spends $50 million on resurfacing of interstate highways involving $45 million of federal funds and $5 million of state money but would have spent, say, $30 million without the federal aid, then the $45 million federal grant increased spending on interstate resurfacing by only $20 million ($50 − $30). Still, because the matching grant involves a 90-percent federal government share and thus a 90-percent decrease in the price of interstate construction and maintenance to states, a substantial increase in spending is possible even if demand is relatively price inelastic. (If the elasticity is − .5, a 45-percent increase in spending results.) In fact, the evidence from demand studies shows price elasticities between − .5 and − 1.00.

The notion that federal transportation aid is intended to offset interstate or interregional benefit externalities is still the reason usually cited by economists opposed to federal aid for urban mass transit at current levels. As noted, the federal government pays 80 percent of the capital costs of local mass-transit systems and for a time paid up to 50 percent of operating costs. Because these urban (rail and subway) mass-transit systems largely transport individuals only within metropolitan areas, the nature of the national interest in these systems is problematic, at best. There may well be interjurisdictional spillovers from mass-transit systems, but because they are nearly all contained within specific metropolitan areas, perhaps they could be better addressed by state governments. Yet attempts to reduce or eliminate this type of federal transportation assistance are met with great opposition. The explanation may be that while economists cite externalities as a theoretical reason for federal grants, more often the actual political reason for grants is distributional. Federal mass-transit aid is justified because aid is implicitly given to individuals who use other transport modes (cars), because the central cities where most mass-transit systems are located may have fiscal or economic difficulties, and because certain states or localities are perceived as being "shortchanged" in receipt of federal government spending. Certainly, the federal government has distributional responsibilities, and those are legitimate concerns. But it is also important to explicitly recognize that those are the reasons for federal mass-transit aid rather than the national interest arguments more appropriate for highways.

/ *Matching Rates.*   When interstate or regional transportation externalities justify federal grants for efficiency reasons, the second economic issue concerns the appropriate matching rate for those grants. Recall from Chapter 17 that the theoretical answer is that the grant should cover that fraction of marginal benefits that spill over to nonresidents. If, for instance, 30 percent of the benefits from a new highway project in one state will directly go to nonresidents of that state or to society generally, then a federal matching grant with a 30-percent federal share and 70-percent state share is appropriate. By focusing only on direct benefits to residents, the state underestimates aggregate benefits by 30 percent, which then can be offset by a grant that reduces the price to the state also by 30 percent. If the grant-matching rate is set above the share of marginal external benefits, then the price reduction to the state or local government causes overinvestment in that transportation facility.

The current federal government share for the major transportation grants is 90 percent for both construction and maintenance of interstate highways; 75 percent for other primary, secondary, and urban roads in the federal aid system; 0 percent for roads not in the federal aid system; and 80 percent for the capital costs of new or expanded urban mass-transit systems. It seems unlikely, however, that the share of general social and nonresident benefits are anywhere near that high. In fact, if the federal government will pay 90 percent of the cost of interstate highways and 80 percent of the cost of subways, you might wonder why states and cities are not building new highways and transit systems all over the place.

The answer, of course, is that these are not open-ended grants; the matching rates do not apply to any-and-all expenditures on these services by states and localities, only those approved by the granting federal agencies. You have already seen that the roads eligible for federal aid in each state—the federal aid highway system—are specifically defined and represent a small fraction of the total road system. Similarly, the Interstate and Defense Highway System begun in 1956 includes only a planned set of interconnected highways. There are divided, four-lane or larger highways, some of which predate the interstate system and some of which are toll roads, which are not part of the interstate system and not eligible for the matching grants at the 90-percent rate.[2] For mass-transit systems, cities must apply to the Urban Mass Transit Administration and satisfy a number of federal regulations concerning the cost of potential alternatives to the proposed transit system, treatment of potential cost overruns, and timing of the development.

Because of the limitations on the magnitude of these transportation grants, the full effect of the large price reductions is not expected to be realized. If the grant

---

[2]These are likely to be primary roads, however, eligible for matching grants at the 75-percent rate.

to a state is capped at an expenditure level below that which the state actually selects, then the last dollar spent by the state is not matched and the price of the marginal expenditure not reduced. For those states, these are effectively lump-sum rather than matching grants. The irony is that the caps are required because of the very high matching rates, rates well beyond the expected magnitude of external benefits. But the caps also negate the spending effect that the high matching rates are intended to bring about.

The common prescription of economists for this problem is to return to the original notion of matching grants to offset only benefit spillovers. As proposed by Edward Gramlich (1985b, 57),

> . . . If there is a valid spillover rationale for categorical grants, a better way to improve the grant than by simply converting it to block form . . . is simply to lower federal matching shares until the ratio of internal to total program costs at the margin equals the ratio of internal to total program benefits at the margin. . . . My own preference would be to assume an internal share of 80 percent unless it could be shown to be significantly lower.

If Gramlich's prescription were applied to transportation grants, the relative cost shares of the federal and state governments effectively would be reversed from the current status. Paradoxically, such a change could actually increase spending on these transportation services, however. In at least some cases, the caps on the current transportation grants mean that they have no effect on the marginal cost of transportation facilities in some states; the price of the marginal dollar spent is $1. If a 20-percent federal grant without any spending limits were substituted, the marginal cost or price to states of these transportation facilities would be reduced by 20 percent. Because a small price reduction is expected to have more effect than no price reduction, state–local spending on these transportation facilities could be expected to rise in those cases. On the other hand, the amount of federal aid would fall, and states would pay a larger share of the average cost of these facilities than now. In other words, the appropriate role for the federal government in financing transportation is reflected not just by the amount of federal aid but also by the structure of those grant programs.

/ Optimal transportation pricing

Although the use of charges and taxes to finance construction and maintenance of transportation facilities has been considered, user charges also may be appropriate to bring about *efficient use* of public facilities after they have been constructed, if those facilities experience congestion. If a facility is congested, an additional consumer imposes extra costs on all other users. The purpose of use fees or prices for those facilities is to make those costs apparent to potential users, that is, to allocate the scarce facility among competing demands. In fact, because congestion on roads and in mass-transit systems and airports is common, economists have long suggested that a more efficient transportation system would result if users were charged prices for transportation services that reflected congestion costs.

/ APPLICATION 19.1
Gasoline Prices, Consumption, and Taxes

The bulk of state–local own-source revenues spent on transportation comes from state excise taxes on the sale of motor fuels, especially gasoline. Because each of those states' taxes is a specific tax at a rate of so many cents per gallon, the revenue generated by those taxes for any set of rates depends on the number of gallons consumed. As gasoline prices increased in the 1970s after OPEC–led moves to hold down world oil output, consumers eventually responded by altering behavior in a number of ways to hold down consumption of gasoline. Those changes put a squeeze on highway and other transportation funds in a number of states because reductions or slow growth in the gallons of fuel consumed directly affected excise tax revenues.

The average price of gasoline in the United States more than tripled between 1970–80, with the largest increases coming in 1973 and 1979. As a result, the price of gasoline was increasing much faster than the average level of prices; the price of gasoline in "real terms'" (after adjustment for inflation) rose nearly 65 percent in that decade. Consumer use of gasoline proved to be more sensitive to the price than was often believed. After the large price increases in 1973 and 1979, both highway use of gasoline and consumption of all motor fuels (diesel fuel, gasohol, as well as gasoline) actually declined in the next several years. Indeed gasoline consumption for highway use in 1980, about 101 billion gallons, was not substantially different from the 100.6 billion gallons consumed in 1973 despite increases in population, income, and highway travel over those years. Part of the explanation lies in a switch to more fuel-efficient vehicles and part in a switch to other fuels. The first effect dominated though, as shown by the information about highway use and fuel consumption since 1973 in Table 19.7. A 35-percent increase in the number of vehicle-miles traveled on highways was accomplished with only an 11-percent increase in fuel consumption due to a substantial increase in fuel efficiency.

TABLE 19.7

Highway Travel and Fuel Consumption, 1973–85[a]

Year	Vehicle-Miles of Travel (Billions)	Fuel Consumption (Millions of Gallons)	Average Miles per Gallon
1973	1313	110.5	11.89
1975	1328	109.0	12.18
1979	1529	122.1	12.52
1981	1553	116.1	13.57
1985	1774	121.3	14.62
Percentage change, 1973–85	35	11	23

Source: U.S. Department of Transportation (1986b).

[a]Travel and consumption for all vehicles, including passenger cars, motorcycles, buses, and trucks.

/ APPLICATION 19.1 Continued
Gasoline Prices, Consumption, and Taxes

State highway funds felt the effect of these changes. The number of gallons of motor fuel taxed by states was lower in 1974 and 1975 than in 1973, and was lower in all of the years 1980–84 than in 1979. By 1985 slightly more than 123 billion gallons of motor fuel were taxed by the states, about the same as the 122.7 billion in 1979. It is clear that unless motor fuel tax *rates* were increased, reductions in motor fuel consumption would lead to reductions in state transportation revenue. In fact, state motor fuel tax collections remained about constant in 1973–75 and went down in the 1980–81 period. Yet over these years, the amount of highway use and the cost of highway construction and maintenance continued to increase, creating something of a crisis in some states. State governments reacted to this financial problem in several ways. Many states simply increased, some more than once, the magnitude of their motor fuel tax rate. A few states adopted a variable motor fuel tax rate that would automatically increase if consumption of fuels in gallons went down. Some states considered switching from a specific per-gallon tax structure to an *ad valorem,* or percentage tax, system; because the prices were rising faster than consumption was falling, total expenditure on fuels was rising.

The overall effects of changes in fuel consumption and state tax rates for state highway finance since 1973 are shown in Table 19.8. The average state tax rate on all motor fuels increased continually over these years and ended up about 48 percent higher in 1985 than in 1973. That increase in rates, coupled with the very small growth in fuel consumption, led to a 65-percent increase in state revenue from motor fuel taxes. But that increase in revenue was dwarfed by the increases in the cost of road maintenance and construction, about 164 percent and 143 percent, respectively, over these years. This situation illustrates two important features about government finance. Earmarking of

TABLE 19.8

State Motor Fuel Taxes and Highway Costs, 1973–85

Year	Average State Motor Fuel Tax (Cents per Gallon)	State Motor Fuel Tax Revenue (Billions of Dollars)	Cost Index for Highway Maintenance and Operation	Cost Index for Highway Construction[a]
1973	7.53	8.1	69.86	70.8
1975	7.65	8.3	85.24	96.7
1979	8.01	10.0	118.17	142.6
1981	9.11	9.7	146.29	156.7
1985	11.11	13.4	184.37	172.1
Percentage Change, 1973–85	48	65	163.9	143.1

Sources: U.S. Department of Transportation (1986b). U.S. Department of Commerce. *State Governmental Finances,* various years.

[a]1977 base year = 100.

**/ APPLICATION 19.1 Continued
Gasoline Prices, Consumption, and Taxes**

revenues reduces budget flexibility for government and can create short-run disruptions. Because highway finance is tied to motor fuel taxes, other revenues were not available. Fuel tax rates had to be increased, but in some cases not before a highway finance crisis resulted. Second, focusing on tax rates alone can be misleading because it is the change in the rates and base that determines what happens to the amount of tax revenue. In this case, holding tax rates constant would have meant decreases in revenue and an even wider gap between the growth of revenue and costs.

/ Congestion Prices. A facility is said to be congested when an additional user reduces the benefits for all other users. In the case of transportation, this usually means that it takes more time to travel between two given points. As a road or highway becomes congested, for instance, the traffic speed is reduced, increasing the travel time required for a given trip. It is that increase in travel time, rather than an increase in vehicle-operating costs, that accounts for most of the increase in travel costs to users due to congestion.

This notion of highway congestion is represented in Figure 19.2. Up to traffic quantity T_c, sometimes called the travel "capacity" of the road, there is no congestion. The operating and time costs for one vehicle to travel one mile are constant at c_0, assuming some value of time. If traffic exceeds T_c, congestion begins. The operating and time costs for one vehicle to travel one mile, the average cost, which each individual driver faces, increases as the amount of traffic increases—travel speed goes down and travel time increases the more traffic there is. The marginal social cost, on the other hand, represents the extra cost to all travelers from one more vehicle using the road: It is the extra time cost imposed on all travelers because

FIGURE 19.2   Pricing Traffic Congestion

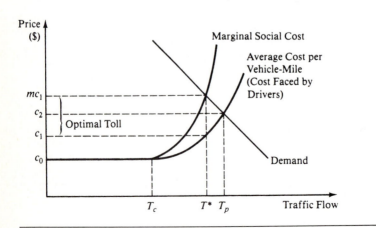

the additional vehicle slows traffic. As with all marginal and average cost curves, for average cost per vehicle to increase requires that the extra cost created by each additional vehicle be greater than the old average (the marginal cost is above the average cost in Figure 19.2).

The existence of congestion creates inefficiency because each user is concerned only with the travel costs to him or her and does not consider the costs imposed on other travelers by the additional congestion. Because users perceive the costs to be lower than they truly are, the road is overused or too crowded. If the demand for this road is as shown, then T_p vehicles would use this road at an average cost of c_2, although the cost imposed on all users by the last vehicle to enter this road, the marginal cost, is much greater. Thus, use of this road at peak demand is inefficiently too high—the marginal cost imposed by the last vehicle is greater than the marginal benefit to that user, as shown by the demand curve. The efficient amount of use of this road is T^*, where marginal cost equals marginal benefit or demand. Reducing the number of vehicles on this road from T_p to T^* reduces travel time, and the gains to the remaining users are greater than loss to those who no longer use the road at this time.

Efficient use of this road requires that all potential users fully perceive all the costs of their road use, including the congestion costs imposed on others. In short, users must face a "price" that reflects all costs. The economic solution to this congestion problem therefore is to levy a congestion fee or toll equal to the difference between average and marginal cost at the efficient quantity. For the case in Figure 19.2, a congestion fee equal to $mc_1 - c_1$ would mean that users would face a price per vehicle-mile of mc_1 at quantity T^*. A price equal to true marginal cost would result in T^* vehicles using the road at this demand time. Note first that with the efficient price, congestion is not necessarily eliminated, but it is reduced until the benefits from use of this road are in line with the true costs. Second, because the optimal congestion fee equals the difference between average and marginal costs, the fee should be greater for facilities or times when the congestion is worse. Indeed, if demand is such that road use is below T_c, no congestion toll is required because there is no congestion.

Application of this transit-pricing theory to real situations is obvious. Many roads, highways, and bridges are very congested during the work commuting periods in the morning and early evening but not crowded during other parts of the day. Roads in some parts of urban areas seem congested all day—midtown Manhattan or the Loop in Chicago come to mind—while roads in other parts of those metropolitan areas are congested only at some times or perhaps not at all. Mass-transit systems may be congested during commuting periods and airports congested during certain times of day and during holiday periods. All these situations might be resolved through the use of congestion pricing, but actual use of that tool so beloved by economists is rare. Two reasons seem to account for the general absence of congestion pricing. The first is public opposition to "paying twice" for facilities, a misperception because the costs of construction and the costs from congestion are separate and different. As noted by William Vickrey (1963, 455) over twenty-five years ago, "The delusion still persists that the primary role of pricing should always be that of financing the service rather than that of promoting economy in its use.'' The second reason arises from difficulties in administering and enforcing congestion charges, the issue to which we now turn.

/ *Methods Of Levying Congestion Charges.*

The most obvious way to levy a congestion charge is by a road or bridge toll paid at a booth either just before or just after traveling on the facility. Such use tolls can reflect both the costs of construction and maintenance as well as congestion and can vary by vehicle type, place, time of day, and time of year. The disadvantage of toll booths is that they can entail both high administration costs (wages of collectors) and high compliance costs (delay). Indeed, use of toll booths to relieve congestion can be counterproductive because stopping to pay the toll may only create more congestion. On the other hand, where tolls are already being collected, such as for buses, subways, and airports, changing the structure of those tolls to levy congestion charges may not increase collection costs much. If the current subway price is $.50 per trip, it would not cost more to charge $1.00 per trip during congested periods.

Motor fuel taxes, while a relatively good way of collecting charges for construction and maintenance of roads, do not make very good congestion charges. If gasoline taxes were increased so that drivers faced the full costs of travel, including congestion costs at the most congested time of day, then the cost of travel would be inefficiently too high for uncongested times. This simply substitutes a new efficiency problem for the other. And it would be nearly impossible to enforce higher gasoline prices in congested areas than in uncongested ones, because individuals may simply adjust where they buy the gasoline.

A third alternative, one often favored by economists, is metered usage, which entails some method of measuring and recording use of transit facilities coupled with a billing procedure. A number of variations of this alternative have been suggested, but one of the first and still among the most interesting is that proposed by Vickrey in 1963:

> My own fairly elaborate scheme involves equipping all cars with an electronic identifier . . . [which] would be scanned by roadside equipment at a fairly dense network of cordon points, making a record of the identity of the car; these records would then be taken to a central processing plant once a month and the records assembled on electronic digital computers and bills sent out. Preliminary estimates indicate . . . the operating cost would be approximately that involved in sending out telephone bills. Bills could be itemized to whatever extent is desired to furnish the owner with a record that would guide him in the further use of his car. In addition, roadside signals could be installed to indicate the current level of charge. . . .

In other words, just as we are billed for our metered use of electricity, natural gas, water, and telephone, so too would we receive a monthly bill for road or transit use. The comparison to telephone bills is apt. The charge for traveling on a particular segment of a particular road could vary by vehicle type and time of day or year, although any differences in prices for different times would have to be known by the users so that travel decisions can be altered. Individual drivers could use congested roads at congested times if they were willing to pay the full price, or they would have the option of using a less congested (and thus lower-priced) alternative road, changing to a mass-transit system, changing the time of their trip, or foregoing the trip altogether.

When Vickrey advanced this idea more than twenty-five years ago, questions about technological feasibility and cost were a legitimate concern, but no longer. Jonathan Marshall (1986) reports that since 1984 Oregon has used an electronic identification system at some truck-weigh stations and that the New York–New Jersey Port Authority intends to use electronic license plates to bill buses for use of the Lincoln Tunnel between New York and New Jersey. Indeed, an electronic road-pricing system similar to Vickrey's was apparently tried out in Hong Kong from 1983–85. Although economically successful, the experiment was not permanently adopted both because consumers objected to "paying twice" through taxes and the charges and because of concerns about privacy. Concern about government acquiring and using travel records of individuals is the other potential difficulty with this version of metered usage, although it is not clear that those records would be any more sensitive than the telephone and tax records maintained now and available to the government.

A simplified version of metered usage is the sale of travel permits for driving in a specific area during congested hours. Under such a system, any vehicle entering the restricted zone during established hours would have to display a nonremovable sticker purchased by the operator. In effect, anyone wishing to drive anywhere in the zone for any period would have to pay the single extra charge for the permit. Such a system was adopted in 1975 in Singapore. Windshield stickers were required to enter a restricted zone between 7:30 A.M. and 9:30 A.M. from any of twenty-two entry points. The price of the dated stickers was about $1.30 (U.S.) per day or $26 per month. Cars with at least four occupants and public-transit vehicles were exempt, and fourteen park-and-ride lots were established just outside the zone for transfer to relatively inexpensive minibuses. Enforcement was encouraged by guards located at the twenty-two entry points to the zone who recorded the license numbers of vehicles violating the rules for subsequent arrest.

According to a World Bank Study reported by K. J. Button and A. D. Pearman (1986), the Singapore congestion pricing scheme had dramatic immediate effects. After about one month, the number of vehicles entering the zone during the two-hour period decreased by about 45 percent and average speeds increased by about 22 percent. The reduction in vehicles resulted from a large increase in the use of car pools, a shift to travel routes just outside the zone (which increased traffic congestion in those areas), and from expansion of commuting into the 7:00 A.M. to 7:30 A.M. period (eventually the time a permit was required was expanded to include this half-hour as well). In contrast, very few individuals switched from cars to the buses, so the park-and-ride lots were eventually largely abandoned. The travel-permit system generated substantial revenue for the government, so much so that fees were substantially increased in early 1976 to levels that may not have been justified purely on congestion grounds. While it is not clear that this particular method could be applied equally effectively in larger or more diverse urban areas, the responses to congestion prices in Singapore suggest that there is substantial elasticity to commuting travel demand. Consumers *do* respond to prices by altering their travel behavior.

/ *Pricing Of Competing Transportation Facilities.* An alternative to direct congestion pricing is available if consumers have the choice of a competing mass-transit system or uncongested road as an alternative to a congested road. If it is technologically or politically infeasible to levy a congestion charge on the congested road, a reduction in the cost of the competing transit mode may have an equivalent effect. In both cases, the relative cost of the congested road rises. This possibility is illustrated in Figure 19.3, which shows T_0 use of the uncongested transit mode at an average cost of c_0 and T_p use of the congested road at the peak travel time. The efficient use of the congested road is T^*, which could be accomplished by an efficient congestion charge, as previously argued. But if the congestion charge is not feasible, a similar effect can be accomplished if the modes are substitutes by lowering the cost of the uncongested travel mode. If travel on mode I is subsidized so that the cost falls to c_1, the demand for the now relatively more expensive mode II is reduced. Theoretically, there is some subsidy that would reduce demand for mode II just enough so that use falls to T^*.

This argument has been applied to justify the use of gasoline excise tax revenue to subsidize mass-transit costs. If lower transit fares induce travelers to switch from cars to transit, then the remaining drivers who pay the gasoline tax benefit from the reduced highway congestion. In essence, the share of the gasoline tax that goes for mass transit is a type of congestion charge. Of course, the validity of this

FIGURE 19.3 *Pricing of Substitute Transit Modes*

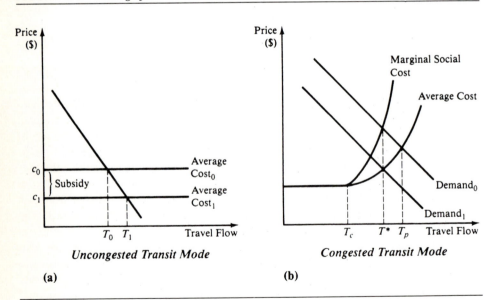

argument depends on the willingness of some travelers to switch from cars to mass transit. The evidence is not encouraging, as it suggests that very large subsidies— sometimes even larger than the transit fares—are often required to induce a substantial switch to transit. This is consistent with the experience in Singapore as well. If the competing mode I is an uncongested road, the switch may be easier. To induce travelers to switch to the uncongested road (even though it may require a longer distance trip), the cost might be reduced by raising the speed limit, removing some traffic lights, and resurfacing, for example. It is important to understand why transferring travelers from an existing congested to uncongested transportation facility increases economic efficiency. Because the uncongested road already exists, more vehicles can be accommodated there at no additional cost, whereas less use of the congested road reduces social costs. Not using the uncongested road up to capacity means that society is effectively wasting resources invested in that facility.

/ Optimal transportation investment

One alternative for dealing with a congested transportation facility, which was not discussed above, is simply expanding that facility. If a two-lane road is crowded, build a four-lane road; if that becomes crowded, expand it to six lanes; if that becomes congested, build a new road parallel. Indeed, more often than not that has been the approach to transportation investment in the United States. But this concept raises the issues of just what determines the optimal amount of investment in transportation facilities by the society and how that determination is related to the use (or absence) of efficient transportation prices.

The simplistic and standard economic answer to the question about the optimal amount of investment in transportation facilities is that more facilities should be built if the marginal benefit to society exceeds the marginal cost. The marginal cost includes the cost of the land for the facility and the actual cost of construction. The marginal benefit includes both the amount of time that would be saved in making current trips and the value of any new trips that would be made on the expanded facility. The difficulty in applying this rule is knowing what the marginal benefit of road or transit expansion is if individuals are not charged the true cost of using those facilities now. Thus, the first step in determining the optimal investment in transportation facilities is setting an efficient price for the current capacity.

The cost curves in Figure 19.4 represent a transportation facility, say a road, with a "capacity" of T_0^c; that is, there is no congestion until use rises above that quantity. If demand is D_1 and there is no congestion pricing, the amount of traffic using the road is T_1, so the road is congested. How much would the road have to be expanded to eliminate congestion given Demand$_1$? The road would have to be expanded so that it has capacity T_1^c; that amount of traffic could use the road at the constant average cost of c_0. Note that the amount of traffic using the road after expansion, T_1^c, is greater than the amount using the road before expansion, T_1. The expansion of the road itself lowers travel costs and attracts more traffic.

A similar argument applies if an expansion is justified by a forecast increase in demand to Demand$_2$. To maintain the target average travel cost of c_0 with the

FIGURE 19.4 The Relation Between Highway Capacity and Use

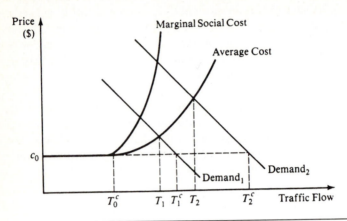

higher demand, the road capacity would have to be increased to T_2^c. But if demand increased and the road was not expanded, average travel cost would rise due to the congestion, and use of the road would stop at T_2. The congestion serves to hold down use of the road, while expansion of the road attracts more traffic by reducing congestion and thus lowering travel costs. Note that if an efficient congestion charge were levied (price equals marginal social cost), use of this road would stop at T_1 even if demand rises to the higher level Demand$_2$. The basic point is that *use of a road or other facility is not an appropriate measure of the "need" for or benefits from expansion of that facility if users do not pay the full costs.*

This point emphasizes again why efficient use charges are important. If use and congestion of a transportation facility continue to increase even when the consumers are paying charges reflecting all the costs, then there is evidence of substantial benefits from additional investment in those facilities. Indeed, Herbert Mohring and Mitchell Harwitz (1962) have shown that if the production of the transportation facility exhibits constant returns to scale (the cost of producing another unit of the facility is constant) and if users are charged the full costs including congestion costs, then the revenue generated by the congestion tolls will be exactly sufficient to pay the cost of an efficient-size facility. Under those conditions, if revenues greater than costs are being generated, then the facility should be expanded using those surplus funds. When the facility is at the efficient size, toll revenues will just cover costs. If production of the facility exhibits increasing or decreasing returns, the results of this type analysis are different although the concept is the same. If consumers are charged appropriate congestion fees and if the cost conditions for expansion of the facility are known, then the revenue from the congestion charge can be a guide to the efficient amount of investment. Without efficient congestion fees, government officials are effectively flying blind in trying to evaluate the demand for expansion of transportation facilities.

/ APPLICATION 19.2
Airport Congestion and Airline Delays

The analysis of highway congestion applies equally well to congestion at airports, an issue causing increasing concern and consternation in the 1980s. Since federal government deregulation of airline routes and fares in 1978, there has been an increase in the number of airline firms, general decreases in air travel prices, and a resulting substantial increase in the amount of airline travel, with more passengers traveling more miles. Airlines are expected to carry about 450 million passengers in the United States in 1987 compared to only 275 million in 1978, and the number of passenger-miles in 1987 is expected to be more than double that in 1978. In contrast to the increase in air travel, the number and size of airports has not increased substantially at all since deregulation. The last major new airport built in the United States—at Dallas–Fort Worth—was in 1974. The result is apparent to anyone who has flown at a major U.S. airport recently—crowded or even full parking lots, congested waiting and baggage-handling areas, a shortage of departure gates, and flight delays.

Airports serving commercial airline flights are owned and operated by local governments and financed by a combination of federal government grants and locally generated revenues. The federal government levies an 8-percent tax on the price of domestic airline tickets with the revenue earmarked for the aviation trust fund and used for airport construction grants as well as other air services. In 1987 the fund had an unallocated balance of about $5.6 billion. The local airports generate revenue from parking and concession charges, aircraft-landing (or takeoff) fees, and sometimes property taxes. Aircraft-landing fees are charged per 1000 pounds of maximum gross weight, which averaged about $.40 per 1000 pounds in 1978 according to Steven Morrison (1983). At that rate, the fee is about $62 for a Boeing 727 and $226 for a Boeing 747, in both cases less than $1 per passenger.

The nature of airport congestion is remarkably similar to that for highways. The large airports in major metropolitan areas and a few others that the airlines use as hubs are very congested, especially at certain hours of the day, while most other airports in smaller cities are never congested. Thus, crowded facilities in some places are balanced by an excess capacity at others. And where congestion does exist, typically there are peak and offpeak periods. Just as with highways, there are two major economic issues. The short-run issue concerns the efficient use of all existing facilities. All airlines tend to want to offer flights to the major metropolitan areas at the same times because those are the areas and times of greatest demand. But the peak-time and -place users are not charged fees for the congestion they create because landing fees are not higher at those congested times or even at the more congested airports.

The solution proposed by economists should not be surprising: Congestion tolls should be charged. Specifically, it is argued tthat landing fees should be higher at congested than uncongested airports and at those crowded airports, higher at the more congested times. Such a pricing strategy would create an incentive for the airlines to schedule and consumers to prefer more flights at the

/ **APPLICATION 19.2 Continued**
Airport Congestion and Airline Delays

less congested times and airports, making better use of the existing airport capacity. For instance, Morrison (1983) estimated that the efficient landing fee at peak times in 1978, given existing capacity, should have been $654 at LaGuardia compared to the actual $286 for a 727 and $283 at Washington National rather than the actual $49. Both were and still are among the more congested of U.S. airports.

The long-run issue concerns the appropriate amount and location of new investment in airport facilities. The optimal amount of airport investment in an area depends on the cost of construction compared to the benefits from reduced delays. Because both the cost of airport construction (largely due to land price differences) and the benefits from reduced congestion will vary for different areas, some of the congested airports should be expanded more than others, while some of the uncongested airports should be closed or allowed to depreciate. On this issue Morrison estimates, for instance, that LaGuardia's size should be tripled or quadrupled and that Washington National's should be roughly doubled. On the other hand, the airports at Albuquerque, Mobile, and Oklahoma City seem to be much larger than is necessary or efficient.

Part of the reluctance to use efficient airport pricing and the difficulty in achieving efficient airport investment may be partly due to the fact that this service is provided by local governments. If a congested airport charged landing fees that reflected true costs, some flights and passengers might be switched to other less congested airports in nearby cities. The locality operating the congested airport would then fear the loss of jobs, income, and tax revenue. The local government may prefer to impose the congestion costs on travelers in the short run and expand the airport in the long run. But if many localities follow this strategy, excess airport capacity in some areas seems a likely result. Thus, a fundamental issue of federalism is raised. To achieve a more efficient air travel system, it may be necessary to reexamine whether local government is the appropriate level in the federal system to have the primary responsibility for providing airport services.

/ Summary

Of the total expenditures by all levels of government on transportation facilities or services for air, rail, road, and water transit in 1985, about 80 percent (nearly $46 billion) went for highways.

Taxes and tolls collected from users, including motor fuel taxes, vehicle and driver license fees, taxes on airline ticket prices, aircraft-landing fees, and a variety of user tolls, are the major component of revenues for transportation spending.

The federal government provided about 25 percent of the funds spent on highways in 1985 but spent less than 2 percent directly itself. States generated slightly more than half of the revenue spent on highways, but with the addition of federal aid accounted for about 60 percent of direct spending on highways. Local governments generated slightly less than 25 percent of revenues spent on highways but accounted for nearly 37 percent of direct spending.

If the transportation system is already large enough to provide all the general benefits that arise from having a transportation network, then any further expansion of that system will only generate private benefits and should be entirely financed by users of that expansion. About 75 percent of the revenue for highway expenditures for all purposes in 1985 came from highway users, with motor fuel taxes representing a bit more than half of total highway spending.

Motor fuel taxes are good proxies for highway-user charges because motor fuel taxes vary by the amount and type of road use and because they can be collected at relatively low administration costs. But motor fuel taxes are imperfect user charges because all gasoline and diesel fuel is not used on highways, vehicles (and drivers) differ in their fuel economy, and fuel taxes do not differentiate highway use by location and time.

The argument for federal highway aid is that nonresidents substantially utilize transportation facilities directly provided by states and localities. Despite the expansion in scope of federal highway aid over the years, federal highway aid is still heavily skewed toward roads used for interstate and interregional travel.

The appropriate matching rate for federal grants should cover that fraction of marginal benefits that spill over to nonresidents. The current federal government share for the major transportation grants is 90 percent for both construction and maintenance of interstate highways; 75 percent for other primary, secondary, and urban roads in the federal aid system; 0 percent for roads not in the federal aid system; and 80 percent for the capital costs of new or expanded urban mass transit systems.

The existence of congestion creates inefficiency because each user is concerned only with the travel costs to him or her (the average cost) and does not consider the costs imposed on other travelers by the additional congestion (the marginal cost). The economic solution to any traffic-congestion problem is to levy a congestion fee or toll equal to the difference between average and marginal cost at the efficient quantity. The congestion fee can be levied through tolls, fuel taxes, or metered usage.

The degree of congestion of a road or other facility is not an appropriate measure of the "need" for or benefits from expansion of that facility if users do not pay the full costs. Thus, the first step in determining the optimal investment in transportation facilities is setting an efficient price for the current capacity. The facility should then be expanded if that price generates sufficient revenue.

Discussion Questions

1. Congestion is a common problem on roads and other transportation systems. Carefully explain what an economist means by "congestion" and why it is an economic problem. What type of user charge can "solve" a congestion problem?

2. "If a road is congested, then it is too small for the demand. The road should be expanded or replaced." True, false, or uncertain? Explain.

3. Suppose that Your College Town has two parallel four-lane roads connecting the college to the rest of the city. One goes from the college directly into the heart of town and is usually congested, particularly so at rush hours and other times when there are special activities on campus (such as a concert or athletic event). There are no special tolls or charges for this road. The other runs two miles south of the first with a number of connecting streets and is seldom crowded. The state highway department would like to use the revenue from a gasoline tax increase to expand the first road to six lanes. Would such an expansion be called for on economic efficiency grounds? Does society lose anything if the second road is not used to capacity? How else might the congestion on the first road be alleviated? What if congestion tolls were not feasible?

4. Besides gasoline taxes, most states also generate revenue from vehicle registration fees and drivers' license charges. If these are to serve as user charges, what types of transportation service should be financed by the gas tax and what types by these fees? Recently, some states have considered levying special-use fees on each driving infraction conviction. For instance, in addition to the existing fines, there could be an additional $5 charge for each case of speeding. If this was to be a user charge, what type of service might it finance?

Selected Readings

Gomez-Ibanez, Jose A. "The Federal Role in Urban Transportation." In *American Domestic Priorities: An Economic Appraisal,* edited by J. Quigley and D. Rubinfeld, 183–223. Berkeley: University of California Press, 1985.
Vickrey, William S. "Pricing in Urban and Suburban Transport." *American Economic Review* (May 1963): 452–65.

20 / The Budget Process

> Unbalanced budgets are almost always possible in real-world fiscal
> systems.[1]
>
> *James M. Buchanan*

A budget is the blueprint for how government intends to achieve its objectives in influencing and altering the society. The process by which that budget is formulated is important because the process may impose restrictions on the outcome and because the process reflects the inherent economic difficulties of government budgeting. In this chapter therefore, we consider the budget process of state–local governments, including typical budget timetables, problems of revenue and expenditure forecasting, types and effects of budgeting rules including balanced budget requirements and tax or expenditure limits, budget treatment of different types of expenditures, and the degree of and reasons for earmarking of revenues for specific expenditure categories. As we will see, the diversity that is so characteristic of state–local government finance extends as well to budget practices.

/ The State Budget Schedule

State governments budget on either a one- or two-year cycle, with twenty-nine states adopting annual budgets and the other twenty-one adopting biennial (that is, two-year) budgets. Of the twenty-one states with a biennial budget cycle, eight also have biennial legislative sessions, so that the legislature theoretically meets once in two years and adopts a budget for the following two years. In some of these biennial budget–cycle states, the budget may be reviewed and revised annually, whereas in others there is effectively no opportunity for revision during the period. Finally, thirteen states budget over a biennial cycle but have annual legislative sessions so that annual review and revision of the budget is possible and in some cases expected. The grouping of states according to budget cycle is shown in Table 20.1.

All states but four begin their fiscal years on July 1, with Alabama and Michigan following the practice of the federal government in beginning the fiscal year on

---

[1]*Public Finance in Democratic Process: Fiscal Institutions and Individual Choice*. Chapel Hill: University of North Carolina Press, 1967, 98.

TABLE 20.1

State Budget Cycle and Fiscal Year Schedule[g]

Annual Legislative Sessions and Annual Budget Cycles	Biennial Legislative Sessions and Biennial Budget Cycles[a]	Annual Legislative Sessions and Biennial Budget Cycle
Alabama	Arkansas	Florida
Alaska	Texas[d]	Hawaii
Arizona	Montana	Indiana
California	Kentucky[e]	Iowa
Colorado	N. Carolina[b,c]	Maine
Connecticut	Nevada	Minnesota[b]
Delaware	N. Dakota[d]	New Hampshire
Georgia	Oregon[d]	Ohio
Idaho		Vermont[f]
Illinois		Virginia[e]
Kansas		Washington[c]
Louisiana		Wisconsin
Maryland		Wyoming[e]
Massachusetts		
Michigan		
Mississippi		
Missouri		
Nebraska		
New Jersey		
New Mexico		
New York		
Oklahoma		
Pennsylvania		
Rhode Island		
S. Carolina		
S. Dakota		
Tennessee[b]		
Utah		
W. Virginia		

continued

October 1 and New York (April 1) and Texas (September 1) being still different. In most cases, local government fiscal years follow the schedule of the state in which they are located.[2] With the exception of Kentucky, Virginia, and Wyoming, biennial budget states begin the budget cycle in odd-numbered years. Thus, for instance, a budget would be adopted for the July 1987 through June 1989 biennium.

A representative budget cycle and process for a state government on an annual budget cycle is shown by Table 20.2, which centers on a budget for fiscal year (FY) 1987–88. The governor's formal budget proposal for that year would be formulated by the executive departments in the Fall of 1986, although individual departments of state government would have begun the process of developing and

---

[2]There are exceptions. For instance, local governments in Michigan and New York begin the fiscal year on July 1, rather than with the state government; New Jersey municipalities operate in calendar years.

TABLE 20.1

Continued

Since 1969 ten states have changed their budgeting cycle. Hawaii, Vermont, and Florida have all changed from annual to biennial budgets. In that same time, Connecticut, Idaho, Illinois, Missouri, and Nebraska have all gone from biennial to annual budgets. Indiana experimented with annual operating budgets in fiscal years 1975–76 and 1976–77, but operated with a biennial capital and highway budget. It returned to full biennial budgeting in 1977.

Currently, twenty-nine states have annual budgets and, of course, annual legislative sessions. Another eight states have biennial budgets with biennial sessions, and thus lack any opportunity for annual changes or revisions. (The exception is Oregon, whose joint Ways and Means committees meet during the interim as the Emergency Board, a constitutional board with authority over supplemental appropriations, federal funds, and transfers.) The remaining thirteen states have biennial budgets, but meet annually. This last group has some review of the budget annually, but it varies from full reviews to occasional amendments.

Of those states with biennial budgets, only North Carolina, North Dakota, Oregon, Texas, Washington, and Wyoming actually make appropriations for the full biennium rather than by fiscal year, and North Carolina, Washington, and Wyoming review the budget for possible changes annually.

Source: National Conference of State Legislatures, Denver. Adapted from ACIR (1986b, Table 86, 140).

[a]Unless otherwise noted, biennial budget states make appropriations for each fiscal year separately and begin their two-year budget cycles in odd-numbered years.

[b]Technically a biennial session, but in practice meets annually.

[c]Appropriations are made for the biennium, but reviewed annually.

[d]Appropriations are made for the biennium.

[e]Biennial budget cycle begins in even-numbered years.

[f]In 1979 language was included in the appropriations bill allowing the governor to submit an annual or biennial budget depending on the discretion of the governor.

[g]All state fiscal years begin on July 1 except for Alabama (October 1), Michigan (October 1), New York (April 1), and Texas (September 1).

TABLE 20.2

Representative State Budget Cycle, Fiscal Year 1987–88

October–December 1986	Formulate budget for fiscal year 1987–88; prepare economic and budget forecasts through June 1988.
January 1987	Governor presents FY 1987–88 budget proposal.
January–June 1987	Legislature reviews and reworks budget proposal; forecasts redone, as new information becomes available; legislature adopts FY 1987–88 budget; governor signs FY 1987–88 budget.
July 1 1987	Fiscal year 1987–88 begins.
July 1987–June 1988	Expenditures and revenues monitored, with differences from budget estimates noted, corrective action taken if deficits appear.
October–December 1987	Formulate fiscal year 1988–89 budget; prepare forecasts through June 1989.
January 1988	Governor presents FY 1988–89 budget proposal.
June 30 1988	Fiscal year 1987–88 ends.
July 1 1988	Fiscal year 1988–89 begins.
July–September 1988 or later	Expenditures and revenues for FY 1987–88 audited; final FY 1987–88 accounting prepared and presented.

honing their budget requests well before that. Once the governor's priorities for the following fiscal period are decided, the budget will be developed based on revenue and expenditure forecasts for that coming fiscal period, which in turn depend on an economic forecast for that period. An economic and budget forecast must be made in the Fall of 1986 therefore, for a period eighteen to twenty-one months in the future (through June 1988). It is not surprising therefore that those forecasts are often not very accurate. The magnitude of this difficulty is substantially greater if the state adopts a biennial budget.

After the governor presents the budget proposal for FY 1987–88, usually in the form of a budget or state-of-the-state message to the state legislature in January 1987, the relevant legislative committees review that proposal and almost always revise it. The revision may reflect differences between the executive and legislative branches in priorities for state action and/or differences in economic and budget forecasts. If, for instance, the legislators believe there will be greater economic growth and thus more revenue than does the governor, the legislature may propose different amounts or types of expenditures or perhaps a tax cut. Eventually a budget is adopted by the legislature and sent to the governor.

The governor may sign that budget (signifying approval), veto the budget (requiring the legislature to try again), or, in forty-three states, veto part of the budget. In the last instance, the governor has "*line-item veto authority,*" the option of vetoing individual "lines" or specific expenditures in the budget. When the governor has authority to veto the entire budget or individual lines, the legislature may override that veto, usually by vote of more than a majority of the legislators.[3] As a result of this process, a final budget is finally agreed on, and the fiscal year begins on July 1, 1987.

It is worth noting here that a line-item veto may give the executive substantially different influence over the final budget than an overall veto does. At the federal level, the president may veto any individual appropriations bill, although each bill may contain the budget for an entire department or several department's activities in a specific program area. Thus, the executive must choose or reject the appropriation as a package. If legislators are willing to trade votes because the bill includes something that each want (even though it may also contain some things each do not want), then the legislature may be able to override an executive veto. If the executive has a line-item veto, individual parts of the appropriation or budget may be rejected—say a new dam for one state or a new building at one particular state college campus. In that case, it may be harder for legislators to build coalitions to override the veto because those legislators whose favorite projects are not vetoed are unlikely to support the override.

As the fiscal year unfolds, both expenditures and revenues are monitored, the budget forecast is reestimated as actual data become available, and adjustments to the budget may, and often are, made. One common type of adjustment is a "supplemental appropriation," which is to say that the governor and legislature agree to add expenditures in some area to the initially approved budget. On the other

---

[3]The governor has no veto authority in North Carolina.

hand, if the revised forecast suggests that the fiscal year is likely to end with a budget deficit, the governor and/or legislature may act to increase revenue or decrease expenditures or both in an attempt to avoid the deficit. In fact, in many states this type of action is required, as discussed later in this chapter. Before the fiscal year ends, the process starts again with planning for the next year's budget. Finally, the ultimate revenue and expenditure statement for FY 1987–88 will not be completed until well after the start of FY 1988–89. This final accounting is delayed partly because some taxpayers have not settled accounts due to filing extensions or compliance reviews, partly because some bills that are incurred during the year may not be settled until after, and partly simply because of the time required to collect, review, and tabulate all the material.

The length and inherent overlap of the budget process—the time from the start of budget formulation to the final accounting for a single fiscal year is usually at least two years—creates several economic problems. First are forecasting problems. A budget forecast requires both a tax and expenditure forecast, which in turn depend on expected economic conditions—that is, an economic forecast. State (and local) taxes (on income, sales, profits) are obviously sensitive to changes in economic conditions, although to different degrees. Because states generally rely on a much broader mix of taxes than does the federal government, the revenue forecasting problem for states may be greater than at the federal level. But state expenditures— for instance, for Medicaid, public assistance, or even public safety—may also change with economic conditions. Accordingly, it is often suggested that a forecasting error of 1 to 2 percent is excellent for states; but a 2-percent overestimate of revenues combined with a 2-percent underestimate of expenditures generates a 4-percent budget deficit.

Intergovernmental aid also creates difficulties in forecasting because a state may not be certain about the amount or type of federal aid it will receive during a fiscal year. This difficulty is often even worse for local governments who may be uncertain about both federal and state aid, which together often account for more than a third of a local government's general revenue. A school district or a city may be planning a budget for the fiscal year beginning July 1 at the same time that the state is planning and debating its own budget for the same time period. The final state budget may not be approved until just before the fiscal year starts (or in some cases even after). Adoption of the locality's final budget may also have to be delayed or a budget will have to be adopted based on an expected amount of state aid. If the expectation turns out to be wrong, a midyear budget correction may be required. This difficulty can be exacerbated by differences in fiscal years, for instance, if the local government fiscal year starts before the state's fiscal year.

Another problem is that the deficit or surplus from one fiscal year is not known exactly before the next fiscal year begins. In most cases, states are prevented from ending a year with an operating deficit or must eliminate the deficit in the next year. A budget surplus from one year in most cases becomes a starting balance, which can be applied to the next year. A budget surplus from one year, then, provides a cushion against forecasting error for the subsequent year.

/ State Budgeting Rules

As mentioned, most state governments face some type of legal (as opposed to economic) restrictions regarding budget deficits, as shown in Table 20.3. In thirteen states, the requirement is that the governor must *submit* or the legislature must *pass* a balanced budget. While this may require the parties to think in balanced budget terms, this alone imposes little restraint because a budget balanced when adopted can quickly become a budget in deficit in practice. Therefore, in some cases, the requirement for an initially balanced budget is combined with a requirement that expenditures be reduced if a deficit arises.

Another thirty-six states (only Oregon and Hawaii are in both this and the above category) are prohibited, either constitutionally or statutorily, from carrying over a budget deficit into the next fiscal year or budget biennium. This is somewhat more restrictive than merely requiring an initially balanced budget because it requires that states do something to offset an actual budget deficit before the next fiscal period. Theoretically, however, that something could be borrowing, that is, selling bonds to raise funds to cover the operating deficit. In that case, the debt service and repayment schedule on those bonds would appear in subsequent budgets, but there would be no deficit to carry over. Consequently, tight constitutional debt limitations are imposed in sixteen of these thirty-six states. Because these limitations are very small (for instance, $150,000 in Ohio), the option of converting operating deficits into bonded debt is effectively legally blocked. Of course, such action may also be economically blocked if the credit markets are unwilling to accept such bonds.

Only one state, Vermont, has no type of balanced budget restriction. The governor is required to recommend in the proposed budget methods to correct deficits that occurred in past years, but the proposed budget need not be balanced.

/ Procedures when a deficit arises

According to research by the Council of State Governments (1976), fifteen states (three constitutionally) *require* action to reduce expenditures if budget deficits appear to be developing during a fiscal period.[4] For example, the operative sections of the current Michigan Constitution, adopted in 1963, read, in part:

> **Art. 5, Sec 18.** The governor shall submit to the legislature . . . a budget for the ensuing fiscal period setting forth in detail, for all operating funds, the proposed expenditures and estimated revenues of the state. Proposed expenditures from any fund shall not exceed the estimated revenue thereof.

> **Art. 5, Sec. 20** . . . The governor, with the approval of the appropriating committees of the house and senate, shall reduce expenditures authorized by appropriations whenever it appears that actual revenues for a fiscal period will fall below the revenue estimates on which appropriations for that period were based.

---

[4]According to The Council of State Governments (1976), of these fifteen only the provisions in Michigan and Oklahoma are both constitutional and mandatory, the others being either statutory or permissive or both.

TABLE 20.3

State Balanced Budget Restrictions

Areas and Region	Category I Statutory(S) or Constitutional(C)? (1) Statutory	(2) Constitutional	Governor Only Has to Submit a Balanced Budget	Legislature Only Has to Pass a Balanced Budget	May Carry Over a Deficit but Must Be Corrected in Next Fiscal Year	State Cannot Carry Over a Deficit into Next Biennium	State Cannot Carry Over a Deficit into Next Fiscal Year
New England							
Connecticut	X		S	S	S		
Maine	X						S
Massachusetts		X	C				
New Hampshire	X		S				
Rhode Island		X					C
Vermont				No Requirement			
Mideast							
Delaware		X					C
Maryland		X	C	C	C		
New Jersey		X					C
New York		X	C				
Pennsylvania	X	X	S,C	S	S,C		
Great Lakes							
Illinois		X	C	C			
Indiana		X					C
Michigan		X			C		
Ohio	X	X					S,C
Wisconsin		X			C		
Plains							
Iowa		X					C
Kansas		X					C
Minnesota	X	X				S,C	
Missouri		X					C
Nebraska		X					C
S. Dakota		X				C	
N. Dakota	X	X					S,C
Southeast							
Alabama		X					C
Arkansas	X						S
Florida	X	X					S,C
Georgia		X					C
Kentucky	X	X				C	S
Louisiana		X		C			
Mississippi	X						S
N. Carolina	X	X					S,C
S. Carolina	X	X			S,C		C

continued

TABLE 20.3

Continued

	Category I Statutory(S) or Constitutional(C)?		Category II Nature of Requirement ( ) = Number of Points				
Areas and Region	(1) Statutory	(2) Constitutional	Governor Only Has to Submit a Balanced Budget	Legislature Only Has to Pass a Balanced Budget	May Carry Over a Deficit but Must Be Corrected in Next Fiscal Year	State Cannot Carry Over a Deficit into Next Biennium	State Cannot Carry Over a Deficit into Next Fiscal Year
Tennessee		X			C		C
Virginia	X	X				S,C	
W. Virginia		X					C
Southwest							
Arizona		X					C
New Mexico		X					C
Oklahoma		X					C
Texas		X		C		C	
Rocky Mountain							
Colorado		X					C
Idaho		X					C
Montana		X		C		C	C
Utah	X	X					S,C
Wyoming		X				C	
Far West							
California		X	C		C		
Nevada	X	X	S	C			
Oregon	X	X	S			C	
Washington	X	X				S,C	
Alaska	X	X	S		C		
Hawaii	X	X	S,C			C	C

Source: ACIR staff compilation based on 1984 surveys of executive and legislative fiscal directors, and *Limitations on State Deficits,* Council of State Governments, Lexington, Kentucky, May 1976. Reprinted from ACIR, 1986b, Table 87, 141-42.

Note that Section 20 states that "the governor . . . *shall* reduce expenditures . . . ." In Michigan, therefore, the governor is required to submit a balanced budget *and* to reduce expenditures if an actual deficit arises. Procedures for dealing with impending deficits vary widely among the other states.

According to ACIR (1986b), in twenty states the authority to adjust expenditures when deficits appear likely rests entirely with the executive branch, in most cases the governor. In those states, the executive may reduce expenditures selectively or across the board without consulting the legislature, usually with some relatively small exceptions. In eleven states, the executive can unilaterally reduce the budget across the board only. Another eight states give the governor authority to reduce the budget, but only up to some maximum amount, specified either as a percentage of the total budget or as a maximum percentage for each category of the budget. In Virginia, for instance, the governor's reductions are limited to no more than 25 percent of an agency's appropriation and 15 percent of employee salaries with appropriations for interest payments, certain pensioners, some employee benefits, and some capital construction projects protected. Another eight states require that the governor consult with or obtain the approval of the legislature before budget reductions can be made. In those cases, the governor usually proposes changes to the legislature. Michigan's procedure, noted above, is representative of this group, although some states require approval of the full legislature rather than just the budget committees.

/ Planning for deficits: State contingency funds

One possible way for state governments to deal with unanticipated deficits is for the state to maintain a contingency fund, which can be used to augment revenue as needed. Following the old adage that "the time to fix your roof is when the sun is shining," such a fund can be added to in good economic years for use in years with slow or nonexistent economic growth, thus serving as a type of "state savings account." In fact, these contingency funds are sometimes referred to as "Rainy Day Funds." Historically, it has been considered good budgeting practice to maintain a reserve balance equal to 5 percent of a state's general spending, and some states have used this as an objective. Although these contingency funds may be good budgeting practice, they often create political difficulties. Some groups will always want to spend all the government's available funds on favorite programs now, while others will object to the government holding surplus funds rather than returning them to taxpayers through a tax cut.

In recent years, many states have formalized these contingency funds by creating separate accounts in the state budget by statute. The statute typically specifies when and from what source money is to be added to the account, the maximum size of the account, and when and for what purposes account funds may be withdrawn and spent. According to ACIR (1986b), twenty-nine states have now authorized such formal rainy day funds, although not all of them may have actually established a balance. The expectation is that by formalizing the contingency fund procedures and placing the money in a special account, there will be less of an incentive to raid the funds for additional spending or tax cuts in good times.

Money is added to these rainy day funds either by specific appropriation of the legislature or according to a specified formula; twelve states generally fall into the first category and seventeen into the second. For example, in Florida all surplus money in the state general fund is transferred to the working capital fund, up to a maximum of 10 percent of the general fund revenue, while in Michigan, a transfer is made to the countercyclical budget and economic stabilization fund if the growth of inflation-adjusted personal income is greater than 2 percent. The amount transferred is the growth rate minus 2 percent times total general fund revenue. The maximum size of the rainy day funds is sometimes specified, with 2 to 5 percent of the state government general fund being the most common limits.

Similarly, rainy day funds may be spent either by appropriation of the legislature or automatically when certain conditions are met: fifteen states use the appropriation method for spending, and the other fourteen have some spending formula. For example, in Connecticut the budget reserve fund may be automatically spent to cover a state operating deficit, and in Ohio the budget stabilization fund is automatically used if state inflation-adjusted personal income falls in any year.

Whether rainy day funds are successful at protecting state governments from unanticipated economic difficulties and thus smoothing the pattern of state expenditures across economic expansions and recessions depends on the magnitude of the fund compared to the magnitude of the economic difficulty. If states are unwilling to maintain balances, either because of the absence of appropriations or raids on funds that are automatically built up, then obviously the funds will have not avoided the political pressures and cannot solve the budget uncertainty problems.

/ State Budget Flexibility

In most states and localities, the budget is separated into different funds representing expenditures for various purposes, in many cases with specific revenue sources earmarked for specific expenditures or funds. The general fund receives state revenues not earmarked for specific purposes and is the fund from which expenditures can be made on any service. Earmarking serves as a way of codifying, either constitutionally or by statute, how state revenues are to be spent, and thus generally reduces the flexibility of state officials in changing the nature of the budget. As always in state–local finance, there is substantial variation among the states, this time in the degree of earmarking, as reflected by the relative size of the general fund shown for selected states in Table 20.4.

When all the states are combined, state general funds represent only slightly more than half of total state government expenditures and about 80 percent of state expenditures excluding state government intergovernmental aid payments. Connecticut and Wyoming represent the opposite budget approaches. Nearly 80 percent of Connecticut's budget and all of its budget excluding state aid are part of the general fund and thus not earmarked to specific uses. In contrast, the general fund represents only 28 percent of Wyoming's total budget and 48 percent of the total expenditures excluding state aid payments. Most state revenues in Wyoming are therefore earmarked to specific purposes. Among the states shown in Table 20.4, California, Florida, Illinois, New York, and Minnesota are similar to Connecticut in having largely general budgets; Michigan, South Dakota, Texas, and Virginia have very restricted budgets, with Massachusetts falling between those two groups. There tends to be a greater degree of earmarking in states with biennial budgets than in those with annual budget review, perhaps because the earmarking limits

TABLE 20.4

State General Fund Budgets Compared to Total Budgets, Selected States, Fiscal Year 1984

State	State General Fund Ependiture as Percentage of Total Expenditure	State General Fund Expenditure as Percentage of Total Expenditure Less Intergovernmental Expenditure
All states	54	83
California	58	100
Connecticut	79	100
Florida	59	94
Illinois	66	93
Massachusetts	55	78
Michigan	41	57
Minnesota	65	100
New York	59	100
S. Dakota	32	39
Texas	32	48
Virginia	44	62
Wyoming	28	48

Source: ACIR, 1986b, Table 88, 143.

administrative discretion in spending in the relatively long time between legislative or budget sessions.[5]

Some types of revenue earmarking are common. In most states, gasoline tax revenue is earmarked for roads and highways and allocated to a separate transportation fund. Hunting and fishing license revenue is often earmarked for wildlife management or recreation. State aid payments to local governments are usually specified in statute and connected to specific revenue sources. As we have seen, federal grants to states often carry categorical use restrictions. In recent years, state governments that have adopted lotteries have tended to earmark lottery revenue for a specific purpose such as education. Among local governments, all the revenue to independent school districts is explicitly earmarked to primary and secondary education.

The practice of a specific state with a very restricted budget, Michigan, is illustrative. Table 20.5 shows the governor's proposed Michigan state government budget for FY 1985–86, as sent to the legislature in the January 1985 budget message. Total estimated general fund–general purpose revenue—the only completely unrestricted part of the budget—is $5895.5 million, or about 43 percent of the net total revenue of $13,777.5 million. General fund–special purpose (GF–SP) revenues represent restricted revenue for which there is no separate state budget

---

[5]The general fund is a smaller fraction of state expenditures than the national average in fourteen of the twenty-one biennial budget states, and in six of the eight states that also have a biennial legislative session.

TABLE 20.5

General and Special Revenue Funds Estimates, Fiscal Year 1986 (Classified by Fund)

	General Fund		Special Revenue Funds	
Revenue Source	General Purpose	Special Purpose	Employment Security Administration	Game and Fish Protection
Taxes				
Individual income	$3,919,600,000	$ 284,500,000	$	$
Less: Refunds	970,300,000			
Net individual income	2,949,300,000	284,500,000		
Sales	514,800,000	335,000,000		
Single business tax	1,231,000,000	216,300,000		
Gasoline				
Use	365,400,000			
Motor vehicle registration				
Cigarette excise	105,400,000	19,400,000		
Telephone and telegraph company	114,100,000			
Insurance company premium	109,100,000			
Oil and gas severance	82,000,000			
Inheritance	64,500,000			
Beer and wine excise	53,000,000			
Liquor excise and specific	20,900,000			
Diesel fuel				
Intangibles	52,000,000	9,500,000		
Commercial and industrial facilities				
Horse-race wagering	9,890,000	13,010,000		
Watercraft registration				
Aviation fuel				
Car loaning	1,550,000			
Liquefied petroleum				
Railroad company	250,000			
Penalties and interest	35,000,000			
Other	1,000,000			
Total Taxes	$5,709,190,000	$ 877,710,000	$	$
Nontax Revenue				
Federal aid	$ 10,000,000	$3,159,028,800		$ 700,000
Local agencies	3,562,000	105,588,300		
Services	3,488,000	64,014,000		
Licenses and permits	21,156,600	61,124,200		21,501,900
Miscellaneous	81,500,000	39,638,200	37,100	9,765,500
Lottery				
Other	66,613,000	151,607,900	393,500	
Total Nontax Revenue	$ 186,319,600	$3,581,001,400	$ 430,600	$ 31,967,400
Grand Total	$5,895,509,600	$4,458,711,400	$ 430,600	$ 31,967,400
Interfund transfers	1,315,000	117,159,800	393,500	
Net Total				

continued

TABLE 20.5

Continued

	Special Revenue Funds			
School Aid	Transportation	Waterways	Other[a]	Total
$	$	$	$	$4,204,100,000
				970,300,000
				3,233,800,000
1,340,100,000	43,600,000			2,233,500,000
				1,447,300,000
	582,900,000			
				365,400,000
	283,500,000			283,500,000
121,200,000				246,000,000
				114,100,000
				109,100,000
				82,000,000
				64,500,000
				53,000,000
20,900,000				41,800,000
	54,700,000			54,700,000
				61,500,000
56,596,000				56,596,000
				22,900,000
		550,100	1,650,400	2,200,500
	3,700,000			3,700,000
				1,550,000
	1,400,000			1,400,000
				250,000
				35,000,000
1,100,000		43,000		2,143,000
$1,539,896,000	$ 969,800,000	$ 593,100	$ 1,650,400	$ 9,098,839,500
$ 34,989,000	$ 319,192,100	$400,000	$ 700,000	$ 3,525,009,900
	12,873,000			122,023,300
	728,100			68,230,100
	12,564,500	29,000	4,225,000	120,601,200
	37,143,100	875,000	570,567,600	739,526,500
372,000,000				372,000,000
440,123,200	403,289,300	5,963,000	187,200,000	1,255,189,900
$ 847,112,200	$ 785,790,100	$ 7,267,000	$ 726,692,600	$6,202,580,900
$2,387,008,200	$1,755,590,100	$ 7,860,100	$ 764,343,000	$15,301,420,400
812,123,200	403,278,000	5,963,000	183,700,000	1,523,932,500
				$13,777,487,900

Source: Budget Message of the Governor (1985).

[a]Includes grand totals for Budget Stabilization, $230,200,000; Children's Trust, $890,000; Construction Code, $2,939,000; Construction Lien Recovery, $312,300; Justice Training, $4,900,000; Lottery, $476,700,000; Marine Safety, $1,855,400; Motor Vehicle Accident Claims, $565,000; Nongame Fish and Wildlife, $325,000; Park Improvement, $3,880,000; Recreational Land Acquisition, $29,802,100; Safety, Education and Training, $2,946,000; and Veterans' Trust, $8,928,200.

fund; $3159.0 million, or 71 percent of the total $4458.7 million GF–SP revenue, is federal aid to the state government. In Michigan's case, $1539.9 million of state taxes and $847.1 million of nontax revenue, including lottery revenues, are earmarked for state aid to local schools, and an additional $1755.6 million of revenue, most of it from gasoline taxes, vehicle registration fees, and federal aid, is earmarked for transportation. The "other" category of special funds includes thirteen different revenue funds, including the state's budget stabilization fund noted previously in this chapter.

This look at a specific state budget also points out some other aspects of state budgeting. Note the great number of different taxes, although three—income, sales, and business—provide most of the revenue. As noted previously, the great variety of taxes complicates state revenue forecasting. And any individual tax may be allocated to several different spending categories. In Michigan the state's sales tax provides the second largest amount of tax revenue to the state government, but only 23 percent of that amount is general revenue; 60 percent of the state's sales tax revenue is earmarked for local school aid, 15 percent is earmarked for general aid to other local governments and listed as GF–SP revenue, and 2 percent (from the sale of gasoline) goes for transportation.

/ What are the advantages and disadvantages of earmarking?

Earmarking revenues for a specific purpose can have economic advantages by establishing a benefit tax system and providing some revenue certainty to assist in long-run planning. If the revenue is generated in relation to the benefits of the service provided, then the revenue source is serving as a benefit tax and tying revenues and expenditures together may be reasonable. This is usually the argument regarding gasoline taxes and transportation expenditures, as described in Chapter 19. If earmarking makes it more difficult, either procedurally or politically, to reduce expenditures in an area, then there is more certainty for providers and recipients of services in that area. When gasoline taxes are earmarked to transportation, expenditures are affected during an economic downturn proportional to the decrease in gasoline consumption, but it is difficult to reduce transportation expenditures more and transfer those taxes to other purposes.

Earmarking is often also said to provide political benefits. There is ample evidence that taxpayers often do not have a good understanding of government budgets, both the magnitude of different revenue sources and the types of services provided by expenditures. When a particular revenue source is tied to specific expenditures, understanding of that aspect of the budget is often improved. Government officials sometimes use this procedure in an attempt to increase the attractiveness of some revenue sources by earmarking that revenue source to a service with easily identified and highly valued benefits. As noted in Chapter 13, that method has been used with many state lotteries.

The main problem caused by earmarking is a reduction in budget flexibility for the government, which, of course, is the other side of the revenue certainty point noted as an advantage. Earmarking may make it more difficult to change the priorities in the state budget over time and to respond, in the short run, to economic fluctuations. This may be particularly true if the earmarking is constitutionally specified because amending the state constitution usually requires either a supra-majority vote of the legislature or a vote of the electorate or both. Earmarking may also make it politically difficult to alter the budget simply because the revenue–expenditure tie becomes well known and accepted. It is not uncommon for a state government to have surpluses in one or more earmarked funds while it faces an operating deficit in the general fund.

It is also important to note, however, that earmarking does not necessarily guarantee that a state will spend more on the earmarked service than if it was financed with general revenues. In some cases, states augment the earmarked revenues for a service with general fund revenue as well, thus choosing to spend more than the earmarked source provides. The state government is responding to the demand for that particular service, so the earmarking is effectively not a constraint. The state would, in all likelihood, continue the spending in that area even without an earmarked revenue source. In the Michigan budget shown in Table 20.5, the state transfers $812 million of general revenues to the school aid fund to supplement the revenues earmarked to that fund.

/ Tax and Expenditure Limits

Although most of the discussion in this chapter so far has concentrated on state government budgeting rules and procedures, most of that material is directly applicable to local governments as well. But there are also some important differences in state and local budgeting. One important difference between states and localities has already been noted—local governments are typically more reliant on intergovernmental aid than are states. The other important factor is that local governments are, in most cases, created and regulated by states as a legal matter. Therefore, the budget options that localities have—types of revenue sources, some required or mandated expenditures, restrictions on tax rates, tax levels, or tax and expenditure growth—all are specified by the state government.

Nearly all local governments and about a third of state governments are constrained in their budgeting by statutory or constitutional limits on taxes or spending or both. Local government tax limits (imposed by state governments) date at least since the late 1800s. Prior to 1970, the most common form of state-imposed local tax limit was a maximum property tax rate either for specific services, for specific types of local governments, or for overall local government taxes. Beginning around 1970, a number of state governments acted to add new or different tax and expenditure limits on local governments under their authority. And in the later 1970s and early 1980s, taxpayer-initiated tax and expenditure limits affecting both local and state governments were adopted in a number of states, with California's Proposition 13 in 1978 often identified as the start. These limits—and the tax revolt they were said to represent—have altered the way in which state and local tax and expenditure decisions are made in many cases. Still, the effectiveness of these limits in reducing the level or growth of spending is unsettled and their desirability still questioned.

/ Types and use of limits

/ *Local Tax Rate Limits.* In general, limits may be directed at tax rates, tax revenue, amount of expenditure, or the rate of growth of revenue or expenditure. Indeed, all these types are applied to local governments by states. The oldest and most common form of local limit is a **maximum property tax rate,** either for overall property taxes or only those for specific purposes. According to the tabulation of the ACIR (1987a), thirty-three states imposed either an overall or specific property tax rate limit or both on local governments in 1985. Such a maximum rate obviously has no restricting effect when tax rates are well below the maximum. And if tax rates are at the maximum, property tax revenue can increase only to the extent that the property tax base increases (because revenue equals the rate multiplied times the base). Thus, rate limits do not prevent increases in revenue but may restrict increases in revenue to the rate of growth of the tax base. This is the type of limit adopted when California voters approved Proposition 13—the local property tax rate is limited to no more than 1 percent of assessed value, and assessed value is defined to be the market value in 1975–76 plus a maximum annual 2-percent increase for inflation.[6] Similarly, the limit adopted in Massachusetts was called Proposition 2½ and limited the property tax rate to no more than 2.5 percent of value. In addition to limits on property tax rates, local governments with the authority to levy local income or sales taxes also are restricted by state-imposed maximum rates.

/ *Local Revenue Limits.* A second relatively common form of local tax limit is a **limit on tax revenue,** either for a specific tax or overall—what is often called a **levy limit** in the case of local property taxes. Revenue, or levy, limits are usually specified as a maximum allowed percentage increase from the prior year or by a maximum percentage of income that tax revenue can take. For instance, some local governments are restricted to property tax increases of no more than 5 percent (for instance) per year or to percentage increases no greater than the percentage growth in the Consumer Price Index (the inflation rate) and the percentage growth in population. Property tax levy limits were used in twenty-two states in 1985 (ACIR 1987a). In five states, local governments face overall limits on own-source revenue, specified either as an allowed percentage increase or a maximum share of income. In the case of overall revenue limits, individual revenue sources may increase more than the limit allows if that increase is balanced by some other revenue source increasing less than is allowed.

/ *Local Expenditure Limits.* The third type of state-imposed local limit is a restriction on the **maximum allowed level of expenditure,** usually set as a maximum allowed annual percentage increase. General local expenditure limits were

---

[6]However, properties can be reassessed at their full market value when sold. See Chapter 7.

used in six states in 1985 (ACIR 1987a), although the limit applied only to school districts in three of those states. School expenditure limits were sometimes used in conjunction with state education aid programs in an attempt to equalize per-pupil school spending among different districts in a state. General local expenditure limits applying broadly to general-purpose local governments persist today in only two states, Arizona and California.

/ State Revenue and Expenditure Limits. In contrast to many local government tax and expenditure limits, all of the eighteen current state government tax or expenditure limits were adopted since 1976, when New Jersey adopted a general limit on the growth of state government expenditures (New Jersey's limit expired in 1983). The eighteen state governments currently with general tax or expenditure limits are Alaska, Arizona, California, Colorado, Hawaii, Idaho, Louisiana, Michigan, Missouri, Montana, Nevada, Oregon, Rhode Island, South Carolina, Tennessee, Texas, Utah, and Washington (ACIR 1987a). These limits generally restrict the annual growth in own-source revenue or expenditures to the percentage growth rate of state personal income (which is most common) or to the percentage growth in population and the general price level (inflation) or to fixed percentage limit (7 percent in Colorado, for instance).

Most of these state government limits were adopted between 1978–82. In several cases, the limits were initially proposed by taxpayers using the initiative and referendum process, although in most cases the limit was proposed by the state legislature perhaps prodded by an actual or threatened citizen-inititive proposal. Regardless of how proposed, about half of these state limits were eventually directly approved by the voters with the others adopted by vote of the state legislature. In describing these state government limits, Daphne Kenyon and Karen Benker (1984) note that none of these limits apply to all state expenditures or revenues, that several of the limits are not very restrictive in that they apply only to *proposed* expenditures, and that some provision for exceeding the limit exists in each case. As with local government limits, some of these limits require supramajority votes to exceed the limit.

/ Objectives of tax and expenditure limits

In general, fiscal limits can be designed to set a maximum level for taxes or expenditures, to reduce the level or alter the growth of taxes or expenditures, or to require some specific action to alter taxes or expenditures. The ultimate intent of these types of limits can be to reduce the level of government taxes and spending, to impose more political control over changes in taxes and spending, to alter the mix of government revenue sources, or to alter the relative fiscal roles of state compared to local governments. These ultimate objectives are not mutually exclusive—some limit proposals are intended to accomplish more than one objective, while others are perceived that way by voters. In one analysis of state limits on local governments adopted in the 1970s, Helen Ladd (1978) reported that states with higher per-capita property taxes and those with higher rates of growth of per-capita expenditures were more likely to have adopted limits, suggesting that lower expenditures and property taxes were likely objectives.

Consistent with Ladd's results, of all the potential objectives of tax limits, the one receiving the most attention has been the attempt to reduce the level of taxes and spending. But why would individual voters attempt to use the political process to reduce government taxes and spending when the level of taxes and spending was originally chosen through that same political process? The answer must be that there is a perception that the political system is imperfect so that government is not providing the magnitude of taxes and spending that the public desires. Of course, as you learned in Chapter 3, this conclusion can be consistent with several different economic models of voting on government fiscal issues. In one of those cases, the monopoly bureaucrat model, the government acts as a monopolist in offering voters the choice between two alternative expenditure levels—one at a level higher than that most desired by the median voters and the other at a very low level. Given that and only that choice (because political competition has been eliminated by the government officials), voters select the higher expenditure level. From this viewpoint, tax and expenditure limits can be seen as an attempt to create political competition—to lower spending levels by reducing the monopoly government's ability to control the choices proposed to voters.

But suppose that political competition does exist (either from viable alternative political candidates or from interjurisdictional competition for residents and businesses) and that fiscal choices are made by majority voting. Recall that in this case voters will select the median-desired level of taxes and spending—indeed, this is called the median-voter model. Might fiscal limits make sense even when fiscal decisions are made by majority voting with political competition? The answer is yes because there is no guarantee that majority voting will result in the economically efficient level of expenditure being selected. This possibility is illustrated in Figure 20.1. If the voting groups with the three different demands shown all face the same tax price, then their desired levels of spending are A^*, B^*, and C^*. With majority-voting expenditure, level B^*,—the median level—is selected.

Now suppose that a fiscal limit is imposed that has the effect of reducing expenditures to E_C. Groups B and C are made worse off because the new spending level is farther from their desired levels than B^* is, but group A is made better off because E_C is closer to A's desired spending level than B^* is. The welfare gain by group A would be greater than the sum of losses by B and C if the original spending level B^* was inefficiently too high. In Figure 20.1, the loss of consumer surplus by B is represented by triangle yxu, which is the difference between the value of government service to B and the cost to B for the quantity eliminated by the limit. For each \$1 of spending between E_C and B^*, the value to B is greater than B's tax cost. Similarly, the welfare loss to group C is represented by area ywv. On the other hand, group A gains because each \$1 spent beyond A^* is worth less to A than the tax cost. The gain to A is represented by area $zyut$. Depending on the nature of demand, the tax price, and the level of the limit, the gain to A may be greater than, equal to, or less than the sum of welfare losses by B and C.

This also can be seen by comparing the value of the marginal unit of public expenditure at the controlled level, E_C, for each group to the tax cost of each group. The marginal value of additional public expenditure is c', b', and a', respectively,

FIGURE 20.1   A Spending Limit May Increase Economic Efficiency

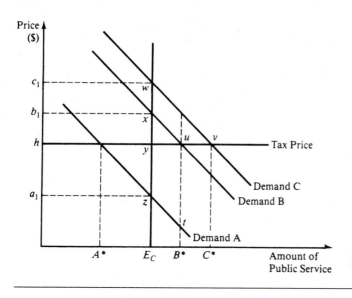

with $(c' - h) + (b' - h) \gtreqless (a' - h)$ depending on the nature of the demands at E_C. As explained by Michael Bell and Ronald Fisher (1978, 391–92), the possibility that a fiscal limit can improve economic efficiency and increase welfare "occurs because majority voting takes account only of each group's rank-order of expenditures and does not compensate for different magnitudes of preference. Thus a net welfare gain would be possible if the difference in provided and desired service levels was much greater for the group desiring less than the median amount than the group desiring more. . . ." In any case, tax and expenditure limits may be intended to correct for inefficiencies that result from the political choice process.

A similar argument can be made concerning limits intended to alter the relative use of different revenue sources or the roles of the state government compared to local governments. Voters who desire a very different fiscal environment than the one in place may seek such limits, and those voters would be made better off if the limit is adopted and is effective. Other voters would be made worse off. For instance, homeowners and other capital owners might seek a limit on local property tax revenues with the expectation that the state government would substitute state aid collected through the state sales tax. Such a change might reduce the relative tax share of substantial capital owners. Whether there is an overall gain in economic efficiency depends on the choice selected by voting or some other political system and on the differences in the desired nature of fiscal policy among the different voting groups.

In some cases, fiscal limits are supported because of voter's perceptions about the expected effects, even if some of those perceptions are contradictory. Suppose, for instance, that a limit to reduce local property taxes is proposed with no provision for substituting a different source of revenue. A logically correct and economically defensible position (for some voters, at least) is that a reduction in local government or state government services would result, which would be desirable if the voter preferred private choice and provision of those services. But research about voters' perception of tax limits shows that three other often faulty perceptions are common:

1. **Free Lunch Perception:** Voters believe that the effect of the limit will be to reduce taxes but have no effect on government-provided services. The notion is that the limit will induce government officials to "reduce waste." This perception is usually faulty either because "waste" in the sense of unnecessary expenditures may not exist or because if it does, there is no reason for government officials to reduce it. If government officials are budget-maximizers, as is often claimed by proponents of limits, then reducing services in response to the limit may be the most effective way to eliminate the limit.

2. **Head-in-the-Sand Perception:** Voters believe that the effect of the limit will be to reduce taxes and government services, which is fine, because those voters do not believe they get any benefits from government services. These voters have their heads in the sand because such a perception is nonsense—everyone benefits from some services provided by state–local governments.

3. **Optimist Perception:** Voters believe that the effect of the limit will be to reduce taxes and government services, but these voters are confident that the services to be cut will not be those that give them benefits—only other voters' favorite services will be cut. Again, this perception seems contrary to the political notion that makes limits attractive in the first place. If government officials are trying to maintain expenditures higher than the voters desire, then the politically strategic response of such officials to the limit is to reduce services enjoyed by most voters—so that the limit might be rejected or overturned.

Several surveys of voter attitudes about government taxes and spending and about proposed fiscal limits support the existence of these faulty perceptions. Jack Citrin (1979) analyzed survey data that included California voters' positions on Proposition 13, their socioeconomic characteristics, and their preferred change in taxes and spending on a variety of different services. Citrin reported that in most cases a majority preferred the status quo level of taxes and spending despite the approval of the proposition. He argued (p. 127) that his findings "confirm that the main intention of California voters in passing Proposition 13 was to cut taxes rather than eliminate a wide range of government services." Paul Courant, Edward Gramlich, and Daniel Rubinfeld (1980) analyzed a survey of Michigan voters from 1978 taken at a time three different constitutional tax limitation proposals were on the ballot. In the survey, voters were asked about how they voted on each proposal, about their desired changes in state–local taxes and services, and about their perceptions of the likely effects of each proposal. Voters who perceived that the limit would reduce taxes were more likely to vote for the amendments, *even if they did not desire a reduction in spending.* Courant and his colleagues concluded (p. 19) that "it appears that voters are perceiving that their own taxes will be cut without expenditures being cut, either because of supposed efficiency gains, greater uncertainty about the spending side of the budget, or the unending search for a free lunch."

/ Effectiveness of tax and expenditure limits

Although it is difficult to evaluate the effectiveness of tax and expenditure limits because the objective is not always clear, several studies have examined the changes in taxes and spending that occur after limits are imposed and compared those changes to states without limits. The results are somewhat ambiguous. Regarding local government limits, the ACIR (1977) analyzed local government expenditures and local property tax reliance for all states in 1974, with the states divided into those with rate limits, those with levy limits, and those with no limits. Those results showed that local per-capita own-source expenditures tended to be lower in states with limits than those without, but that there was no general difference in property tax reliance. These results are consistent with two possible hypotheses—either the existence of limits held down spending but did not induce a shift away from property taxes or those states whose citizens preferred a lower level of spending adopted fiscal limits to reflect their viewpoint.

Kenyon and Benker (1984) examined the change in state spending relative to state personal income for the states between 1978–83 to see whether there was a difference in those states with state government tax or expenditure limits compared to those with no state limits. They concluded that tax or expenditure limits have not restricted growth in taxes and spending in most cases, a conclusion borne out both by the opinions of state budget officers and actual expenditure data. As previously noted, most state limits restrict some components of state taxes or spending to a fixed maximum percentage of state personal income. Kenyon and Benker report that expenditures increase faster than income in some years and slower than income in others for states with and without limits. Over the entire period, state expenditures in aggregate remained at a nearly constant share of personal income.

The fact that limits that restrict the growth of own-source expenditures or revenue to the growth rate of personal income would not be effective is consistent with the common finding of an income inelastic demand for state–local government services. In that case, expenditures would not increase faster than income if that was the only factor changing. A growing economy, then, would be consistent with a constant or declining share of income going to own-source state–local spending if the relative costs of providing government services were not also rising.

The Kenyon–Benker results about the general ineffectiveness of state government tax and expenditure limits are confirmed by a recent ACIR study (1987a) focusing on state spending, taxes, deficits, and overall debt for 1984. Those statistical results show that the existence of state tax or expenditure limits does *not* result in lower per-capita own-source expenditures, lower per-capita state taxes, a lower level of per-capita state debt, or fewer state deficits.

/ State Budget Results

Surprisingly, there has been little research concerning the effects of the various budget rules (other than fiscal limits) on state government budgets. This is partly because of difficulties with interstate comparisons due to wide differences among states in accounting practices and definitions of "the general fund." Still, some generalizations are possible.

State–local governments generally do not have operating budget deficits, at least by the definitions states use. Most states do not count in these deficits so-called bonded indebtedness, borrowed funds for capital expenditures, because those debts are balanced by the capital asset purchased with the funds. The aggregate budget surplus or deficit for state–local governments for various years, as defined in the National Income and Product Accounts (the GNP statistics), is shown in Table 20.6. There is an aggregate budget surplus in most years, although the magnitude varies some according to national economic conditions. Even when states' balances in social insurance funds (mostly pension funds) are excluded (which may make sense because the current balances in those funds are for future liabilities), the pattern shows surpluses in some years offset by deficits in others. Whether the general absence of deficit financing of current expenditures among state–local governments results from the budget restrictions or from capital market constraints is problematical. The recent ACIR study (1987a) previously mentioned does find evidence that state expenditures, taxes, deficits, and debt are lower in states with stringent balanced budget requirements than those without, at least for the one year

TABLE 20.6

State–Local Government Budget Balance, Selected Years

Year	Expenditures[a]	Receipts[a]	Surplus or Deficit[a]	Surplus or Deficit Excluding Social Insurance[b]
1960	$ 49.9	$ 50.0	$ 0.1	$ −2.2
1962	58.2	58.6	0.4	−2.1
1965	75.5	75.5	0	−3.4
1967	95.2	94.1	−1.1	−5.8
1970	134.0	135.8	1.8	−5.1
1972	165.8	179.3	13.5	4.8
1975	235.2	239.6	4.5	−8.9
1977	273.2	300.1	26.9	9.0
1980	363.2	390.0	26.8	−0.2
1982	414.3	449.4	35.1	−1.8
1984	475.9	540.5	64.6	15.8
1986	561.9	618.8	56.8	7.4

Sources: Economic Report of the President (Jan. 1987); U.S. Department of Commerce. *Survey of Current Business* (May 1986 and July 1987).

[a]As defined in the National Income and Product Accounts.

[b]Surplus or deficit excluding employee pension funds and funds for workers' compensation or unemployment, and so on.

examined. But these results are weakened by the fact that states have a number of ways to "hide" deficits, as described next. Also as before, correlation does not imply causation—those states that adopt balanced budget restrictions may simply be those where voters prefer lower spending and conservative budgeting.[7]

It is clear that despite the restrictions, state and local governments are *sometimes* able to build up substantial operating deficits in practice while meeting the letter of the restrictions. Steven Gold (1983, 6) has noted one way this is accomplished:

> If a state is close to a deficit, it usually has considerable latitude to accelerate tax collections, defer outlays, and adopt accounting practices which avert a deficit. The number of states with deficits in fiscal year 1982 would have been considerably greater if it were not for accounting devices employed to "paper over" potential deficits.

For instance, a switch from cash to accrual accounting for taxes (counting the taxes in the year in which they become due rather than when actually paid) and deferring a state aid payment for local governments into the next fiscal year (perhaps a payment scheduled for April 1 is not made until July 1) could serve to "balance" the first fiscal year's budget, of course, at the cost of moving the problem into the next fiscal year.

States can also sometimes avoid general fund deficits by borrowing money from another state government fund that has a surplus or carryover balance. In this way, a state effectively avoids the earmarking of revenue to the fund with a surplus, at least in the short run. But if the earmarking law is to be ultimately followed, that money must be eventually repaid to the earmarked fund from general revenues. Besides avoiding the earmarking law, interfund transfers of this type can be an expensive way for state governments to borrow money. The surplus funds in an earmarked account can be invested to earn the highest possible interest rate (subject to state laws on allowed risk), usually the rate of return available on fully taxable investments. The opportunity cost of using those surplus funds to finance general expenditures is the lost investment income. But because the interest rate on non-taxable state–local government bonds is usually less than the rate available on taxable securities (and because states are not subject to federal or state taxes), it would be cheaper for the state to sell short-term notes rather than to borrow its own funds. But, as previously noted, many state governments are prohibited from this option.

If accounting gimmicks are used at the end of successive fiscal years to generate "balanced budgets," the implicit deficit can quickly pyramid. The state government in Michigan, over the period 1975–82, accumulated general fund budget deficits of about $850 million, an amount equal to about 15 percent of the state's 1982 general fund–general purpose budget. This deficit arose despite the apparently strict constitutional balanced budget requirement noted previously. In early 1983, this accumulated deficit precipitated a fiscal crisis, as the state was effectively excluded from the credit markets.[8] Similarly, a long period of improper accounting allowed

---

[7]As another example of the difficulty of determining causation, does the adoption of a state lottery "cause" a state's voters to want to gamble, or do those states whose voters are interested in gambling adopt lotteries?

[8]See *Budget Message of the Governor* (Jan. 1985).

New York City to maintain balanced budgets on paper while accumulating large budget deficits, which resulted in a city fiscal crisis in 1975. In both of these cases, the ultimate economic and financial restrictions (the unwillingness of investors to lend these governments additional amounts) did more to force balanced budgets than did the legal restrictions.

One reason these types of problems have been able to develop is that states (and sometimes even local governments in a single state) have not abided by any uniform accounting rules. In recent years, there has been a movement to develop and have states apply "generally accepted accounting principles" (GAAP) in their budgeting. If states do so, it may be easier to recognize changes in the true fiscal condition of state–local government budgets.

/ Summary

State governments budget on either a one- or two-year cycle, with twenty-nine states adopting annual budgets and the other twenty-one adopting biennial (that is, two-year) budgets.

The length and inherent overlap of the budget process creates difficult forecasting problems. And the deficit or surplus from one fiscal year is often not known exactly before the next fiscal year begins.

State budgets are usually separated into different funds representing expenditures for various purposes, in many cases with specific revenue sources earmarked for specific expenditures or funds. The general fund receives state revenues not earmarked for specific purposes and is the fund from which expenditures can be made on any service. State general funds represent only slightly more than half of total state government expenditures and about 80 percent of state expenditures excluding state government intergovernmental aid payments.

Earmarking revenues for a specific purpose can be used to establish a benefit tax system and provide some revenue certainty to assist in long-run planning. The main problem caused by earmarking is a reduction in budget flexibility for the government, making it more difficult to change the priorities in the state budget over time and to respond, in the short run, to economic fluctuations.

Most state governments face some type of legal (as opposed to economic) restrictions regarding budget deficits. In thirteen states, the requirement is that the governor must submit or the legislature must pass a balanced budget. Another thirty-six states prohibit, either constitutionally or statutorily, carrying a budget deficit over into the next fiscal year or budget biennium, with tight constitutional debt limitations imposed in sixteen of these thirty-six states.

Fifteen states (three constitutionally) require action to reduce expenditures if budget deficits appear to be developing during a fiscal period. The authority to adjust expenditures when deficits appear likely usually rests with the executive branch, sometimes only up to some maximum amount. State governments may also prepare for unanticipated deficits by maintaining a contingency fund to augment revenue as needed.

Nearly all local governments and about a third of state governments are constrained by statutory or constitutional limits on taxes or spending or both. Property tax rates are limited in thirty-three states, property tax amounts in twenty-two, local general revenues or expenditures in eleven, and state own-source revenue or expenditures in eighteen.

States can sometimes avoid general fund deficits or get around budget restrictions by borrowing money from another state government fund that has a surplus or balance or by altering accounting practices. As a result of some difficulties from these practices, there has been a movement to develop and have states apply generally accepted accounting principles in their budgeting.

Discussion Questions

1. From your library or state budget office get a summary of a recent state government budget and examine the degree to which state revenues are earmarked to specific budget categories or funds. How restricted is your state's budget as to how revenues must be spent? If all earmarking of revenues were ended today, how do you think your state's spending mix would change, if at all?

2. Unlike the federal government, most state governments are limited in their ability to engage in deficit finance either by an explicit requirement that the state budget be balanced each fiscal period or by a tight limit on the issuance of state debt. How might a budget be balanced at the start of a fiscal year and not at the end? What options does a state have to balance a budget during a fiscal period without reducing spending? How might a state ''borrow'' to finance a deficit without actually issuing bonds or other financial instruments—that is, how can a state borrow internally?

3. A number of states have now established contingency funds that are paid into in years when the state's economy is strong and drawn from when the state's economy is in recession. This means that state taxes are greater than spending in good economic years and less than spending in bad years. How can these contingency funds actually stabilize a state's economy? An alternative would be for states to have lower tax rates in good economic years and to increase rates to maintain spending during recessions. What are the economic and political advantages and disadvantages to saving as opposed to periodic adjustment of tax rates?

4. Suppose a state is considering three different types of fiscal limits for local governments in the state—a maximum property tax rate, a limit that property tax revenue may not increase more than population and inflation together, or a limit that spending may not increase more than 5 percent. In each case, the limit may be exceeded by majority vote. Which limit is most restrictive and why?

Contrast the three in terms of the sources of allowed increases in taxes or spending and the potential effect on local services.

Selected Readings

Brennan, Geoffrey and James Buchanan. "The Logic of Tax Limits: Alternative Constitutional Constraints on the Power to Tax." *National Tax Journal Supplement* 32 (June 1979): 11–22.

Friedman, Lewis, "Budgeting." In *Management Policies in Local Government Finance,* edited by J. Aronson and E. Schwartz, 91–119. Washington, D.C.: International City Management Association, 1981.

Gold, Steven D. "Contingency Measures and Fiscal Limitations: The Real World Significance of Some Recent State Budget Innovations." *National Tax Journal* 37 (Sept. 1984): 421–32.

Suits, Daniel B. and Ronald C. Fisher. "A Balanced Budget Constitutional Amendment: Economic Complexities and Uncertainties." *National Tax Journal* 38 (Dec. 1985): 467–77.

21 / Economic Development

... State and local governments have been engaged for some time in an increasingly active competition among themselves for new business.[1]

George F. Break

Competition among states and localities for new investment or business expansion has received much public attention in recent years—even the ''Phil Donohue Show'' featured a number of governors ''competing'' for the proposed new manufacturing plant of the Saturn Corporation, a General Motors subsidiary. Although there has always been interstate competition for businesses, there seems to be more competition, or at least greater attention to that issue by state–local government officials recently. Perhaps this is because the range of incentives offered to potential investors has grown to include tax-exempt financing and government provision of special services to businesses besides the more traditional business tax incentives. The increased use of investment incentives and heightened competition among subnational governments has also generated some controversy about the equity and efficiency of these policies for influencing business investment decisions.

There are also, and always have been, substantial differences among states and different localities in economic conditions. Part of the reason for these differences in employment and income among areas may be the fiscal policies—taxes and spending—carried out by the governments in those places, although you have learned in this book that the opposite is also true: Economic conditions influence the demand for state–local government services. Moreover, differences in economic conditions among states or regions may themselves influence business investment and location decisions and thus a change in future economic conditions. For instance, a firm might be attracted to an area with relatively high unemployment because of the availability of workers at lower wages than in other places.

The fundamental question, then, is what accounts for differences in economic conditions such as employment and income among different states and regions? With some understanding of that issue, it is possible to examine why and how economic conditions in various places change over time. And that understanding directly leads to a series of questions concerning the appropriate policy of state–

---

[1]*Intergovernmental Fiscal Relations in the United States.* Washington, D.C.: The Brookings Institution, 1967, 23.

local governments toward economic development. Do firms and consumers change the location of their economic activity because of general state–local government fiscal policies? Do specific state–local business investment incentives "succeed" in attracting new businesses or investment? If so, who receives the bulk of the final economic benefit of that new investment? And if tax and financial incentives do "succeed" in attracting new investment, are they cost-effective and fair? These are the public policy issues being debated by the business community and government officials and the issues considered in this chapter.

/ Interstate Differences in Economic Conditions

In any given year, there are substantial differences in per-capita incomes and un-employment rates among the states, as shown in Table 21.1. In 1986 state per-capita incomes varied from $19,208 in Connecticut to $9552 in Mississippi, with the average for the nation at $14,461. The coefficient of variation (standard devia-tion/mean) for state per-capita income is .165, meaning that state per-capita income varies 16.5 percent on average around the mean. Relatively big income differences remain even if states are grouped together in regions, with regional per-capita income varying from $16,952 in New England to $12,504 in the Southeast states, although in some cases there is as much variation within those regions as among them. It is useful to remember that personal income includes all income regularly received by persons, including wages and salaries and other labor income, rent, interest, div-idends, and transfer payments. The last means that personal income may be main-tained or even increase in periods when economic activity declines because of transfer payments such as Social Security, unemployment compensation, welfare programs, and government subsidy payments. In essence, those transfer payments reduce income differences that would otherwise occur.

Of course, the differences in nominal incomes reported in Table 21.1 may actually overstate the real differences in purchasing power if the prices of consumer goods (the "cost of living") are generally higher in the higher-income states and regions. Not surprisingly, that seems to be the case. An analysis of that issue by Peter Mieszkowski (1979) suggests that regional per-capita income differences are reduced by about one-third because of cost-of-living differences. But regional in-come differences, even in real terms, still do exist, and the state-by-state differences are not reduced nearly as much by consideration of price differences for consumer goods.

The variation in state and regional unemployment rates is similar to that for income. In 1986 state unemployment rates varied from 2.8 percent in New Hamp-shire to 13.1 percent in Louisiana, with the national average at 7.0 percent. Among the Census regions, unemployment was lowest in New England and highest among the Southeast and Southwest states. You should recall that the unemployment rate is the ratio of the number of unemployed persons (those not working but looking for work) to the number of unemployed plus employed persons (what is called the labor force). The unemployment rate therefore reflects both the supply of labor in

TABLE 21.1

State and Regional Variation in Per-Capita Income and Unemployment Rates, 1986

State and Region	Per-Capita Income ($)	Rank	Unemployment Rate (%)	Rank
United States	14,461	—	7.0	—
New England	16,952			
Connecticut	19,208	1	3.8	49
Maine	12,709	34	5.3	38
Massachusetts	17,516	4	3.8	48
New Hampshire	15,922	8	2.8	50
Rhode Island	14,670	16	4.0	47
Vermont	12,845	33	4.7	43
Mideast	16,388			
Delaware	15,010	13	4.3	46
Maryland	16,588	7	4.5	45
New Jersey	18,284	2	5.0	40
New York	17,118	5	6.3	38
Pennsylvania	13,944	21	6.8	23
Great Lakes	14,178			
Illinois	15,420	9	8.1	18
Indiana	12,944	32	6.7	25
Michigan	14,064	20	8.8	10
Ohio	13,743	24	8.1	16
Wisconsin	13,796	22	7.0	21
Plains	13,832			
Iowa	13,222	29	7.0	22
Kansas	14,379	18	5.4	35
Minnesota	14,737	14	5.3	37
Missouri	13,657	25	6.1	30
Nebraska	13,777	23	5.0	41
N. Dakota	12,284	36	6.3	27
S. Dakota	11,850	39	4.7	44
Southeast	12,504			
Alabama	11,115	44	9.8	5
Arkansas	10,773	47	8.7	12
Florida	14,281	19	5.7	34
Georgia	13,224	28	5.9	33
Kentucky	11,129	43	9.3	6
Louisiana	11,227	42	13.1	1
Mississippi	9,552	50	11.7	3
N. Carolina	12,245	37	5.3	36
S. Carolina	11,096	45	6.2	29
Tennessee	11,831	40	8.0	19
Virginia	15,374	10	5.0	39
W. Virginia	10,530	49	11.8	2
Southwest	13,180			
Arizona	13,220	30	6.9	23
New Mexico	11,037	46	9.2	7
Oklahoma	12,368	35	8.2	15
Texas	13,523	26	8.9	9

continued

TABLE 21.1

Continued

State and Region	Per-Capita Income ($)	Rank	Unemployment Rate (%)	Rank
Rocky Mountain	13,109			
Colorado	15,113	11	7.4	20
Idaho	11,432	41	8.7	11
Montana	11,904	38	8.1	17
Utah	10,743	48	6.0	31
Wyoming	13,230	27	9.0	8
Far West				
Alaska	17,744	3	10.8	4
California	16,778	6	6.7	26
Hawaii	14,691	15	4.8	42
Nevada	15,074	12	6.0	19
Oregon	13,217	31	8.5	13
Washington	14,498	17	8.2	14

Source: U.S. Department of Commerce. *Survey of Current Business,* April 1987; U.S. Department of Labor (May 1987).

each market as well as the demand for workers in those markets. And while demand for workers depends on the economic conditions of the industries and the wages in each region, the supply of workers reflects demographic characteristics of the population as well as economic opportunities. Thus, economic growth and higher incomes in a region might not lead to substantial decreases in the unemployment rate if more people begin looking for work or migrate to the region, thus increasing the size of the labor force.

Throughout this century, the differences in per-capita income among the states and regions have been continually reduced, dramatically since 1930, as depicted in Figure 21.1. This narrowing of income differences has been accompanied by a general realignment of population and economic activity. While per-capita income in the Southeast was less than half of the national average in 1930, it is about 86 percent of the national average today. At the other end of the distribution, per-capita income in the Mideast states was about 40 percent greater than the national average in 1930 but only about 13 percent higher today. Although the income differences have narrowed substantially, the relative position of the various regions has remained pretty stable. For instance, the New England, Mideast, and Far West regions have generally had above-average income while the Southeast, Southwest, and Plains regions have had below-average incomes.

This narrowing of income differences is undoubtedly due to a number of factors. Because wages and salaries account for about 60 percent of personal income, one attractive economic explanation might be a flow of new investment to regions with relatively low wages, resulting in an increase in economic activity, population, and

FIGURE 21.1 *Regional per-Capita Income as a Percentage of U.S. Average, Selected Years, 1900–84*

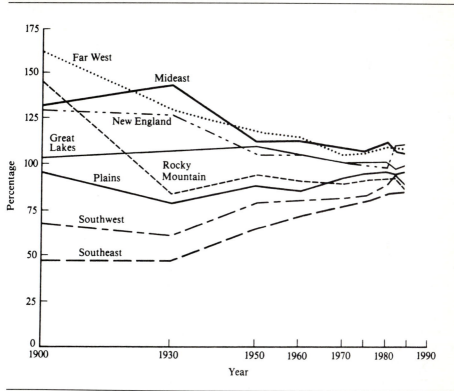

Source: ACIR (1981b) updated by author.

ultimately wages and incomes. At the same time, workers may migrate from low-wage to high-wage regions, reducing the supply of labor in the lower-wage areas. This is certainly what would be expected in the standard competitive economic model, with investors allocating mobile capital to those regions where the highest returns are possible and workers moving, perhaps to a lesser degree, to take advantage of job opportunities. If low wages in a region truly mean low costs (that is, the workers are equally productive as in higher-wage areas), then higher profits might be earned by capitalists who invest in those low-wage areas.

The evidence on this theory is somewhat inconclusive, however. George Borts and Jerome Stein (1964) examined the growth of employment and capital investment among states for the periods 1918–29, 1929–48, and 1948–53 and found that wage differences were only weakly related to changes in investment and not at all related to employment growth. The first issue is more important because a constant level of employment is still consistent with rising wages (and incomes) if the demand for labor is increasing due to new investment. More recently, Michael Wasylenko and Therese McGuire (1985) studied the change in employment among states between 1973–80 for various industries and reported that lower wages contributed to greater employment growth over the period for all industries studied. Again, the combined effect of an out migration of workers from low-wage areas (a decrease in labor supply) coupled with new investment in the region (an increase in the demand for labor) is expected to be an increase in wages, although employment (the quantity of labor) may rise or fall. From this viewpoint, a narrowing of income differences is the natural result of economic forces.

Among the other factors that have likely contributed to this narrowing of income differences are differences in the prices of other important inputs into production, especially land, energy, and transportation services. As with labor, areas with little development and thus relatively low prices for these goods may be attractive to some investors. Capital movements in response to those price differences would again naturally serve to equalize those price differences and thus income differences. Some fiscal policies of the federal government are also thought to have played a role in promoting economic growth in various regions of the country. On one hand, the growth of transfer programs such as Social Security, health insurance, and welfare payments, which stimulate economic growth through demand, have added income in some areas. On the other hand, attention has also been directed at federal decisions about the location of federal (especially military) installations as well as federal government purchases of goods and materials. The regional pattern of federal government expenditures is believed to have particularly stimulated growth in the Southeast and Southwest states. Finally, some analysts have suggested that various social and historical changes such as changes in the pattern of immigration to the United States, the introduction of air conditioning, and improvement in racial relations have also contributed to the dispersion in economic activity.

It is worth noting that there are also substantial differences in economic conditions among various regions or areas within states. This is demonstrated by the 1986 unemployment rates for the metropolitan areas in California, Michigan, and New York, shown in Table 21.2. In such a large and diverse state as California, unemployment rates varied from 4.5 percent in the San Francisco area to more than 14 percent in the Modesto area. Although the variation was smaller in Michigan and New York, it was still substantial. Similar differences exist for other measures such as per-capita incomes and in other states. As with differences among states, the mobility of capital and labor is apparently not sufficient to fully eliminate economic differences among regions within states.

The long-term dispersion of population and economic activity in the United States from the older industrialized areas to regions that were primarily rural and the resulting narrowing of income differences serves as a background against which the role of state fiscal policies can be examined. The issue in the remainder of this chapter is whether state–local taxes and services contribute to interstate reallocations of economic activity, and if so, how states might alter their fiscal decisions to induce more investment.

TABLE 21.2

Variation of Unemployment Rates Within Selected States, 1986

Unemployment Rate for Each Metropolitan Area					
California (%)		Michigan (%)		New York (%)	
Anaheim	4.0	Ann Arbor	4.7	Albany	5.2
Bakersfield	12.0	Battle Creek	9.1	Binghampton	6.1
Fresno	12.3	Benton Harbor	9.0	Buffalo	7.2
Los Angeles	6.7	Detroit	8.2	Elmira	6.8
Modesto	14.1	Flint	10.6	Glens Falls	6.9
Oakland	5.8	Grand Rapids	7.4	Nassau	4.3
Oxnard	6.9	Jackson	9.1	New York	6.7
Riverside	6.4	Kalamazoo	6.0	Poughkeepsie	3.8
Sacramento	6.2	Lansing	7.0	Rochester	5.7
Salinas–Monterey	10.3	Muskegon	11.0	Syracuse	7.4
San Diego	5.0	Saginaw	10.0	Utica	7.1
San Francisco	4.5				
San Jose	5.8				
Santa Barbara	5.1				
Santa Rosa	5.7				
Stockton	11.6				
Visalia	6.5				
State	5.4	State	8.8	State	6.3
United States 7.0%					

Source: U.S. Department of Labor (1987).

/ Interstate Differences in Fiscal Policy

/ Magnitude of tax costs

To evaluate whether tax differences among the states influence investment decisions, it is first necessary to determine the magnitude of those tax differences. The degree of business taxation in different states has been measured in three primary ways: by the share of total taxes collected from businesses, by the ratio of total business taxes in a state to some measure of total business size or income for a particular year, and by the comparative profitability of "identical" firms located in different states and thus paying different taxes. Each method has advantages and disadvantages, so that the information conveyed by each measurement is different and often not consistent with the results of the other methods.

/ Business Tax Share.
ACIR (1981a) estimated the state–local government taxes with "an initial impact on business" for each state for 1977 and then calculated the share of state–local taxes initially collected from business. The list of taxes with "an initial impact on business" included property taxes on business property, sales taxes collected on business purchases of goods and services, gross receipts taxes, business income and value-added taxes, license fees, and taxes on specific business

activities, such as severance taxes. ACIR reported that these ''business'' taxes represented about 31 percent of total state–local taxes (34 percent if unemployment insurance taxes were included) and that the business tax share of total taxes had declined steadily from 1957, when taxes with an initial impact on business represented about 37 percent of total state–local taxes. Among the various regions, business taxes were relied on relatively most heavily in the Southwest (41 percent) and least heavily in the Plains states and New England (27 percent). Taxes with an initial impact on business (many of which are severance taxes) accounted for half or nearly half of total state–local taxes in Wyoming (50.9 percent), Louisiana (49.6 percent), West Virginia (45.4 percent), Alaska (45.1 percent), and Texas (44.1 percent), but less than a quarter of total taxes in Massachusetts and Michigan (23.6 percent), South Dakota (22.4 percent), Wisconsin (22.3 percent), Iowa (21.5 percent), and Nebraska (19.1 percent).

The ACIR approach shares one problem common to many business tax studies, the inability to distinguish between the initial and final burden of a tax. If the ability of businesses to alter behavior and thus shift taxes to consumers or factor suppliers differs among states, then the share of taxes with an initial impact on business will be misleading as to the final tax burdens on business from a state's taxes. In addition, the *share* of taxes with an impact on business does not necessarily correspond to the *level* of taxes on business. Obviously, even if a state collects a large share of its taxes from businesses, the tax burden on businesses in such a state with a low level of total taxes may be smaller than that in some other state with higher taxes generally, but with a smaller business share. But if the share of state service benefits enjoyed by businesses is known or at least similar in different states, then the share of taxes does convey information about the potential fiscal advantage of businesses in some states. If businesses ''pay'' 40 percent of taxes in a state and receive benefits from only 30 percent of state–local expenditures, they may not care that the level of business taxes in that state is low.

/ *Business Taxes Compared to Business Income.*   An alternative approach is taken by William Wheaton (1983) who estimates the level of business tax collections from a set of specific taxes compared to the level of net business income in the state. Net business income is sales less expenses but before federal taxes. Wheaton includes all tax payments for which a business is legally liable—including property, corporate income, unemployment insurance, and specific output taxes—except for sales taxes on business purchases because he believes that there is no reliable estimate of the fraction of state sales taxes that arise from intermediate-goods transactions. The estimates are made for both all business taxes and all business income in each state (which requires an estimate of total net business income) and for taxes and income of manufacturing firms only (which requires an estimate of manufacturing taxes only but not manufacturing net business income, which is available from the Census of Manufacturing). The estimates are based on 1977 data.

Wheaton reports that state–local taxes collected from business represented 7.7 percent of net income for all firms in 1977, on average, and 7.9 percent for manufacturing firms alone. Wheaton also found substantial interstate variation in business tax levels. For all businesses, the level of taxation varied from 20.2 percent of net income (in Delaware) to 4.8 percent (in Utah), with an average of about 36-percent variation in state business tax levels around the median level. On a regional basis, the highest level of business taxation occurred in New England (10.2 percent), the Mid-Atlantic states (9.5) and the Pacific Coast (8.7), while the lowest levels were in the East South Central (5.6 percent) and South Atlantic (5.7) states. The pattern for manufacturing firms alone was similar, although the degree of interstate and regional variation in effective business tax rates was greater for manufacturing firms than for all businesses. For instance, manufacturing taxes varied from 14.8 percent of net income in New England to 3.8 percent in the East South Central states.

Wheaton's estimates also are based on the initial magnitude of taxes collected from business rather than the final burden of those taxes. In addition, one might compare the taxes to some other measure of business activity rather than net income, such as sales or value added. Because sales equals the total costs of a firm plus profits, sales might be the most appropriate base against which to compare taxes, particularly if firms can shift business taxes to suppliers, by paying lower wages for instance. In fact, Wheaton does include business taxes such as those for unemployment compensation, which might be considered an implicit factor payment. Because net income is usually between 5 and 10 percent of sales, and given Wheaton's estimate that business taxes are about 8 percent of net income, state–local business taxes would amount to less than 1 percent of total sales, on average.

It is worth noting that Wheaton's results support the notion that business tax rates tend to be higher in those states and regions where there is substantial business activity and where income is relatively high. This again raises the issue of the direction of causation for tax rates; do low tax rates contribute to business growth or does business growth contribute to an increased demand for government services? For instance, the ACIR computations show that the New England states collect the smallest *share* of their taxes from business of all the regions, while Wheaton's results show that the New England states have the highest *level* of business taxes. The high level of business taxes in New England resulted from the high level of taxes and expenditures generally in those states, rather than any decision to adopt a tax structure designed to impose a relatively heavy tax burden on business. Similar uncertainties arise in specific states such as Michigan, perhaps the most classic "manufacturing" state. Michigan has the fifth lowest share of taxes collected from business of all states according to ACIR, but the second highest level of business taxes according to Wheaton's measure. Businesses in Michigan enjoy a relatively favorable tax position compared to other taxpayers *within the state,* but apparently relatively high taxes compared to businesses in other states.

/ Business Taxes and Profitability. A third approach to measuring interstate tax differentials does not focus on the tax differences *per se* but rather on the profit differences that result from operating in different places with different taxes. One common method of doing this is to create some hypothetical firms and then calculate their profitability under some assumptions about operating procedures for sets of different states' taxes. Most often these calculations are made for a single year. The single-year tax differences for these representative firms may not be very accurate measures of profit differences over the life of a capital investment, however, because many state and local taxes have time-dependent features which vary from place to place.

A more sophisticated approach to measuring business profitability at various locations has been developed by James Papke and Leslie Papke (1984). The Papkes (who, by the way, are father and daughter) focus on the profitability of a new investment at various locations over the entire productive lifetime of that investment. For an assumed set of characteristics of a representative firm, Papke and Papke compute the change in profitability that results from a new investment at one location, which allows calculation of the rate of return on that new investment. Because the taxes at that location are carefully modeled, the rate of return from investment at one location can be compared to the return from investment at another, with any difference arising from the tax differences.

Because the Papke measure of the rate of return depends on the assumed characteristics of the sample firm, it is not possible to get one single estimate for each state but rather a different estimate for a given type of firm in different states. For illustration, Leslie Papke (1987) reported the after-tax rates of return on new investment for both the furniture and electric components industries in twenty different states. For furniture, the rates of return varied from 11.9 percent (in New Jersey) to 13.7 percent (in Texas), an average difference of about 14 percent from the highest to lowest. Thus, it does seem that interstate tax differences can result in different profits on new investments in different states, even for similar firms, although those differences are not huge and could easily be offset by differences in other costs or government services. Also, it is worth noting that because state–local taxes are a relatively small fraction of a firm's total costs, relatively large differences or changes in state–local taxes are required to bring about even small differences or changes in after-tax rates of return.

In terms of reflecting the relative degree of business taxation in different states, the Papke measures of profitability tell a somewhat different story than either the ACIR or Wheaton measures. For instance, among the twenty states examined by Papke, Michigan had the highest level of business taxes according to the Wheaton measure but the fifth highest (out of twenty) return on new investment. On the other side, Tennessee had the fourth lowest level of business taxes by the Wheaton measure but the seventh highest by the Papke measure. A large part of the difference in these two measures of comparative business taxes arises from a fundamental difference in concept, which is emphasized in every introductory economics class and should be familiar to you. Wheaton's method measures the *average cost* imposed by state–local taxes because it compares all business taxes to net income. In contrast, Papke's method is intended to reflect the influence of taxes on the *marginal cost* of investment, that is, how much would taxes increase as a result of new investment.

/ *Effect of federal taxes on interstate tax differences*

The magnitude of nominal interstate tax differences shown by some measures greatly overstates the effective differences because state–local business taxes are a deductible expense for firms in computing their federal income tax liability. As a result of the deductibility of state–local taxes, part of any difference in state–local taxes in different locations is offset by higher federal taxes for firms in the lower state–local tax areas. This point is demonstrated in Table 21.3, which shows a comparison of the net income after local property taxes and federal income taxes for two identical firms located in different states. The firm in state A pays $50,000 in property taxes, which is then deducted from the $200,000 of operating profits to compute federal taxable income, resulting in a federal income tax liability of $51,000 (at a rate of 34 percent and ignoring exemptions and credits). The same firm in state B pays only $30,000 in property taxes but then has a federal tax liability of $57,800. The net effect is that although there is a $20,000 difference in property taxes, there is only a $13,200 difference in net after-tax income. Fully 34 percent of the property tax difference has been offset by the additional federal income tax deduction.

As part of the Tax Reform Act of 1986, the maximum federal corporate income tax rate was reduced from 46 percent to the current 34 percent, which had the effect of reducing the value of the federal deduction for state–local taxes and increasing the effective difference in state taxes. Steven Galante reported in *The Wall Street Journal* (1987) that as a result, more and more firms are focusing on their state income tax liability. Galante quoted Joseph J. Nugent, the regional director for state and local taxes in Coopers and Lybrand's Philadelphia office as stating that "A dollar in state taxes used to cost you 54 cents out of pocket. Now its going to cost 66 cents."

TABLE 21.3

Effect of the Federal Tax Deduction for State–Local Taxes on Interstate Tax Differences: Property Value, Taxes, and Profits for an Identical Firm in Two States

Fiscal Characteristic	State A ($)	State B ($)
Property value	1,000,000	1,000,000
Property tax rate	50 per 1000	30 per 1000
Property tax	50,000	30,000
Profit before property tax	200,000	200,000
Federal taxable income	150,000	170,000
Federal income tax (34% rate)	51,000	57,800
Net after-tax income	99,000	112,200
Difference in property tax	+ 20,000	
Difference in federal tax		+ 6,800
Difference in after-tax income		+ 13,200

Not only does federal tax deductibility of state–local business taxes serve to reduce effective interstate tax differences, but it also works to negate some of the benefits of state or local tax incentives. In Table 21.3, if state A gave this firm a property tax abatement reducing taxes from $50,000 to $30,000, the firm's federal income tax would increase from $51,000 to $57,800. Thus, the state or local government would have given up $20,000 of property tax revenue, but the firm would only have gained $13,200 in net income; the remaining $6800 goes to the federal government in the form of a larger federal tax payment. The magnitude of the effect of federal income tax deductibility of state–local business taxes depends directly on the federal marginal tax rate; the higher the rate, the more federal deductibility offsets interstate tax differences and reduces the value of state and local tax incentives.

/ Types of fiscal incentives

The fiscal incentives offered by state–local governments to offset real or perceived business cost differences, whether they arise from tax differences or other factors such as energy or transportation cost differences, are of three basic types: capital financing, usually at below market interest rates; tax reductions through the use of credits, deductions, abatements, or specialized rates; and direct grants of goods or services such as land, labor training, or management advice. Most states offer these incentives in one way or another, developing a package of specific incentives from the general list for each potential investment project. Each of these general types of incentives is briefly described next, whereas a selected list of specific types of incentives and the number of states using each is shown in Table 21.4.[2]

/ Financing.

Recall from Chapter 12 that nearly all state–local governments use their ability to sell tax-exempt revenue bonds to provide low-interest loans to private investors. State or local governments or their development agencies sell bonds at relatively low tax-exempt rates and provide those funds to private firms at either a slightly higher rate (although still less than the firm would pay if it borrowed in the private market on its own) or in exchange for some service fee. Although the ability of state–local governments to issue these ''private-purpose revenue bonds'' was reduced by the Tax Reform Act of 1986, it was not eliminated, at least for many purposes.

Another form of subnational government financial assistance to investors takes advantage of the fact that most states and localities have major pension funds to finance retirement benefits for government employees. In some cases, both employees and the employer governments contribute toward future retirement benefits; in others, the funds are established entirely by employer contributions. Some state retirement funds are managed by the states themselves, others are managed by private financial investment firms hired by the states. In either case, the pension

---

[2]For more detail on the specific incentives available in each state, see the *Directory of Incentives for Business Investment and Development in the United States: A State-by-State Guide* (1986).

TABLE 21.4

Major State Economic Development Incentives, 1986

Type of Incentive	No. of States Offering[a]
Capital Financing Incentives	
Direct state loans	27
Loan guarantees	16
Local industrial development bonds	45
State industrial development bonds	26
Industrial development bond guarantees	9
Privately sponsored credit corporations	11
State equity/venture capital corporations	8
State fund grants	14
Tax Incentives	
Property tax abatement	31
Business inventory exemption	35
Investment income tax credit	20
Job creation income tax credit	17
Research and development income tax credit	14
Sales tax exemption for industrial fuels and materials	43
Sales tax exemption for industrial machinery and equipment	42
Direct Goods and Services	
Customized industrial worker training	42
Management and technical assistance	na
Combination of Incentives	
Enterprise zones	22

Source: National Association of State Development Agencies. *Directory of Incentives for Business Investment and Development in the United States: A State-By-State Guide. Washington, D.C.:* The Urban Institute Press, *1986.*

[a]List includes the fifty states and Puerto Rico. The number may be somewhat deceiving because no account is taken for the degree of use of each incentive. The jurisdiction is counted if the incentive is available at all.

fund monies are invested in bonds (both government and corporate), stocks, bank certificates of deposit, money market funds, and other investments; the idea being to earn a reasonable return on the funds without incurring inordinate risk of loss of the funds so that the planned retirement benefits can be paid. A number of states have now specified that a certain percentage of the pension fund money may be used to finance new businesses in that state or locality. The pension fund either loans the money to the potential investor in the state or exchanges it for an equity position in the firm. At least in those states with relatively large pension funds, the idea is to increase the available money for new investment in that state.

Government loans to or investment in a new business venture is attractive to the firm if the loan is at a low-interest rate or if the government will accept a lower return on investment than in the private market or if private loans or investment are simply not available to this firm. In the last instance, a firm may have difficulty getting private financing because the management has little experience or insufficient collateral or because the product is so new that that is no track record. In essence, the venture is judged "too risky" by private investors. For all of these types of financing assistance, then, there is a real cost to the government, either in the form of foregone income (a lower return than available elsewhere) or additional risk.

/ *Tax Incentives.* Nearly every state offers some type of specific tax reduction to at least certain types of businesses. The most common form of tax incentive is probably property tax abatement, offered now in thirty-one states for firms building new facilities or rehabilitating existing ones. Although the structure of the various plans differs, the common approach is a reduction in property taxes of some specified percentage for a certain number of years. The decision about granting property tax abatements and the ultimate financing of their cost may be the responsibility of state government or local governments or both. Other typical types of tax incentives include income tax credits for investment or research and development expenses and sales tax exemptions either for a business's purchases or its sales.

One criticism of tax incentives is that most, such as property tax abatements and corporate income tax credits, serve to reduce capital costs (or equivalently, increase the return to capital owners). Consequently, the tax reductions will be relatively more valuable for capital intensive firms and will provide an incentive for all firms to increase the amount of capital used in production compared to other inputs, particularly labor. This potential problem is a particular concern if one of the main objectives of the incentives is to increase employment in the state or locality. If the incentives only attract capital intensive firms or if the incentives induce firms to use relatively less labor and more capital in production, then the employment gains from the fiscal incentives may be much less than anticipated.

One possible fiscal incentive, of course, is a reduction in the overall level of business taxes in a state for all businesses, for instance, by the substitution of a personal tax (on consumption or income) for those collected from businesses. But it is more common for states to offer "targeted tax incentives," which are available only for specific types of firms or firms in specific circumstances. The idea is that general business tax reductions would provide benefits to some firms who have no intention of either expanding or relocating their business; thus, some of the tax reduction is thought to be "wasted" as an economic development device. But it is important to understand that targeting tax incentives requires government and the political process to make decisions about what firms are to receive the incentives. And because officials never have complete information about investment options, those governmental decisions may also entail "waste" or error of two types. Government officials may decide to grant tax reductions to firms who would invest in the state or locality anyway and tax reductions may be denied to firms when the incentive would have influenced the investment location decision. It is not clear, therefore, that targeted tax incentives are any different or any more efficient than general business tax reductions.

/ *Direct Grants.* States and localities also may provide direct grants of goods or services to firms specific to a firm's production requirements. Governments have long used their eminent-domain power to assemble tracts of land for public projects such as roads but in recent years have also done so to provide large blocks of land for commercial or industrial development. In some of these so-called urban renewal projects, the government acquires the land and then gives it or sells it to the private investor at a below-market price. State or local governments may also provide or finance specific training for the new employees of a business willing to invest, expand, or remain in the state or area. Because of a number of studies suggesting that many new small businesses lack managerial or financial experience, some states and localities have begun "incubators," a term for a facility that houses new businesses and provides technical or management assistance for all the firms. The idea is that after the firms are established and the operators gain experience, they have greater likelihood of success on their own.

As part of the targeting of fiscal incentives, many states have also acted to identify specific areas within states where the incentives are to be used particularly intensively. About twenty-two states have now created **enterprise zones,** which may be either the only areas where some incentives are available or areas where greater incentives are available than elsewhere in the state. In that way, a state may not only attempt to increase investment in the state but also attempt to influence the location of that investment toward areas with lower incomes or less economic growth.

/ Effects of Fiscal Factors: Theory

/ Intergovernmental interaction

One fundamental fact about fiscal incentives is that they are offered by most states and at least most of the larger counties and municipalities. But if fiscal incentives are available in most locations, then they do not affect the *relative cost* for businesses in those different locations. Rather, the cost *differences* among locations that existed without incentives are preserved, although the level of business tax and financing costs is decreased at all locations. The fact that similar fiscal incentives for business come to be offered by nearly all states seems a natural result of interstate competition. The number of states is large enough that collusion among states not to offer fiscal incentives is difficult, but not so large that states are unaware of the nature and magnitude of incentives offered by competitors. The result seems to be equivalent to an oligopolistic market in which competitor's offers of lower prices (fiscal incentives) are always matched.

A simplified version of the process as it seems to have worked is shown in Figure 21.2. Beginning in Figure 21.2a, state A offers some set of business incentives that lowers business costs in the state, shown by a downward shift in the supply curve (recall that supply represents marginal costs). If the incentives are successful and capital is mobile, production costs in A decrease, and output in the state increases. The effect of the lower costs and prices of production in state A is to lessen the demand for production in state B, causing a corresponding decrease in output there. In essence, if state A's incentives are successful, they move economic activity from the competitor state B to state A.

But state B is expected to either respond to the effect of the incentives offered by state A or to see the same opportunity in incentives as state A did. The result, shown in Figure 21.2d, is that state B also offers fiscal incentives that reduce

FIGURE 21.2   *State Interaction in Offering Investment Incentives*

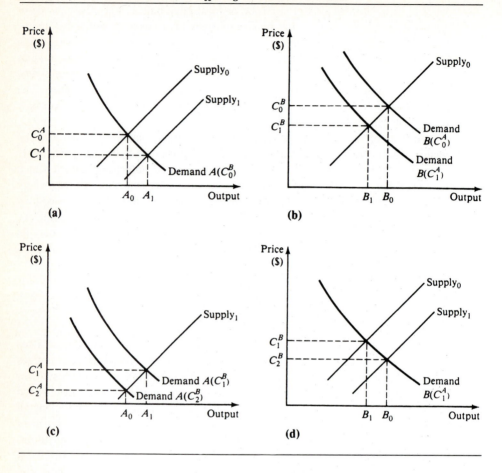

(a)

(b)

(c)

(d)

business costs in that state. Thus, the supply curve in B is shifted downward, and production rises. In Figure 21.2c, the incentives offered by B exactly offset those offered by A, so that output in B returns to the level that existed before the incentives were offered. In addition, the cost reduction caused by B's fiscal incentives reduces the relative attractiveness of production in state A, causing output in A to also return to its original level. Before the process began, costs in B were higher than in A (C_0^B is greater than C_0^A), and after the incentives are offered costs in B are still higher than in A (C_2^B is greater than C_2^A). Neither state has gained a *relative advantage,* although business costs have been lowered in both states. Both states were forced to adopt incentives to avoid losing economic activity to the other, however.

It might be incorrect to conclude, however, that nothing has changed in the world depicted by Figure 21.2. If these governments are providing the same amount of government services after the incentives as before, there has been a redistribution of tax burden; direct business taxes account for a smaller share of total taxes than previously. That redistribution of tax burden could alter economic decisions in the overall society. Suppose, for instance, that the tax burden on capital ownership has been reduced and that the tax burden on consumption increased. The expected result is a modest increase in saving and thus a larger capital stock in the future than would have been the case without the tax redistribution. In that case, the subnational government fiscal incentives, which resulted from interstate tax competition, would have been equivalent to a federal reduction in capital taxes, such as a reduction in the federal corporate income tax. Although each state acted to improve its competitive position compared to the other states, the result is maintenance of relative costs but a reduction in national business costs. The combined reactions of all states and localities effectively comprises a national policy of providing business incentives.

/ Role of consumer and factor mobility

If individual states or localities are successful in using fiscal incentives to reduce the relative cost of investment or business in those locations, the ultimate economic effects and beneficiaries of the incentives depend mostly on the mobility of consumers and factor suppliers.

The mobility case most often considered by economists, at least theoretically, is that in which suppliers of capital (investors) are fully mobile among different locations, whereas suppliers of other factors, especially labor, and consumers do not move among locations in response to economic differences. In this special case, the expected effects of fiscal incentives that lower investment or capital costs in one location compared to others are straightforward. The incentive increases the rate of return to investment in that location and thus attracts more capital. Because the increased supply of capital investment at that location reduces the rate of return, the capital inflow will continue until the rate of return is reduced to that available at those other locations without any incentives. The obvious result of the incentive is an increased amount of investment in the jurisdiction offering the incentive and a decrease in the quantity of investment at the other locations. The increased amount of investment in the jurisdiction is expected to increase the demand for other factors of production such as labor, which increases the wage in that jurisdiction. If workers are not mobile, then those wage differences persist. If workers are mobile, then the higher wages in the jurisdiction attract new workers from other locations until wages are equalized. Because of the increased investment and production in the jurisdiction with the incentive, the prices of local consumer goods are expected to decrease. If consumers are not mobile, then local consumers benefit from these lower prices.

Suppose, for instance, that one locality provides a property tax reduction that is not matched by surrounding communities for new commercial investment. The new lower taxes on new commercial buildings make it more attractive than previously to build in that locality, so an increase in the supply of apartment buildings, retail store space, and office buildings is expected. The increase in commercial building has two subsequent effects. First, there is more demand for workers, which results in an increase in wages if more workers do not appear (labor is immobile).

Second, the increase in commercial building is expected to reduce commercial rents if more consumers of commercial space do not appear (consumers are immobile). So if apartments and office buildings rented for equal amounts in all the communities before the tax abatement, rents are now lower in the community with the abatement.

This story shows why the assumption of immobile workers and consumers is implausible, at least for regions within states or for metropolitan areas. If apartment and office building rents are reduced in one location because of new construction or conversion from other uses, one certainly expects that some individual renters of housing or businesses that lease office space will move to the locality offering lower rents; that is, consumers are mobile. But as consumers move to take advantage of the lower rents, the demand for the apartments and office space increases, driving rents up. The movement of consumers is expected to continue until rents are again equal in all locations.

If consumers move to take advantage of the lower rents, what does that do to the profit position of the investors? If investors or owners of the buildings charge the same rent at all locations, then those in the higher-tax areas (those without abatements) must be earning lower rates of return than those in the lower-tax areas (those with the abatement). That difference in profitability should start another round of capital movement, again toward the jurisdiction with the tax incentive. That increases the supply of capital and reduces rents, which should then start another round of consumer moves.

What force exists that might stop this process before all the investment and economic activity is in one locality? There is one factor of production that is generally very immobile, namely land. The increase in the amount of investment in the jurisdiction with the tax incentive and any subsequent increase in demand for space by mobile consumers both serve to increase the demand for the available land in the jurisdiction, thus increasing the price of that land. Eventually, land becomes so expensive that additional investment and location in the locality is unattractive, even with the tax abatement.

/ *Incidence of Benefits.*   Who benefits, then, from this process that was instituted by the granting of tax abatements in one locality? Clearly, those who own land in the jurisdiction at the time when the tax abatement is granted (regardless of where they live) benefit from the increase in the value of their land. Whether consumers of local goods in that jurisdiction, such as individual tenants in rental housing and commercial tenants in office buildings, benefit depends on the mobility of those consumers. If new tenants move into the jurisdiction, then rents are not lowered by the abatement. (Similarly, if tenants move out of the jurisdictions without the abatement, then those that remain are not hurt by the relatively higher taxes that exist in those locations.) Aside from the benefits to landowners, whether benefits go to property owners or property consumers depends on which group is relatively more mobile.

This story of the **capitalization of the fiscal incentive** should be familiar to you because it is the same one discussed in Chapter 8 concerning property tax incidence. It doesn't matter what the source of the higher cost is in some localities—

higher property tax rates, lack of a tax abatement program, an absence of subsidized interest rate for borrowing, or higher costs for worker training—the process of reaction and adjustment to those cost differences is the same. But remember two warnings about this analysis. First, the process starts only if some jurisdictions obtain a cost advantage over others and if investors respond to that advantage, which might not happen if all communities offer equivalent incentives or if the incentives generate only relatively small cost differences. Second, how smoothly the process actually proceeds compared to the theory depends on many other factors including moving costs, perceptions of market conditions for buyers of a firm's product, the public services available at different locations, the accuracy and cost of information about cost and market differences at various locations, the personal preferences of business owners and managers, and perhaps even inertia. The degree to which investors, workers, and consumers will actually respond to regional or interstate fiscal differences is uncertain and can only be resolved by looking at some evidence.

Before we turn to that review of the evidence about fiscal differences and incentives, it may be helpful to review the theoretical possibilities again by referring to Figures 21.3–21.5. The effect of a capital subsidy, either from a tax abatement or a tax-exempt revenue bond, is shown in Figure 21.3. If the rate of return available in the economy is r_0, the subsidy increases the return available in this jurisdiction to r_1. The higher rate of return available in this jurisdiction attracts more investment, so the amount of capital increases from K_0 to K_1 until the rate of return in the jurisdiction returns to the average level of r_0. (This is equivalent to the analysis of a property tax decrease by one locality discussed in Chapter 8.)

The expected effect of the capital subsidy on the markets for other inputs is shown in Figure 21.4. The increased investment is expected to increase the demand

FIGURE 21.3   *Effect of a Capital Investment Subsidy*

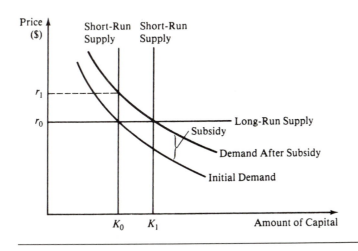

FIGURE 21.4   *Effect of an Increase in Investment in the Markets for Other Inputs*

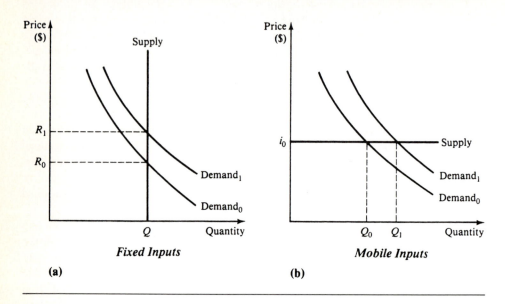

Fixed Inputs

(a)

Mobile Inputs

(b)

for other inputs, which will increase the price of other inputs that are not mobile—that is, those with a fixed quantity in the jurisdiction—and will increase the quantity of those other inputs that are mobile. For instance, if labor is mobile, then an increase in employment is expected to accompany the increase in investment, whereas because land is not mobile, the rents on land are expected to increase because of the new investment.

If the net effect of the capital subsidy and related input market changes is a reduction in production costs, as intended, then the effects on the prices and quantities of outputs are shown in Figure 21.5. For nationally traded goods, those sold outside the local jurisdiction with a price determined in a broader market, the cost decrease causes an increase in production in the jurisdiction but no decrease in price. For local goods, those whose price is determined entirely in the jurisdiction, the cost decrease is expected to induce both an increase in production and a decrease in the price of these local goods.

/ Effects of Fiscal Factors: Evidence

/ Investment among regions

The evidence concerning the effect of state–local government fiscal policies on investment among states or regions is mixed, with the one consistent conclusion perhaps being that there is no general result—fiscal policies have very different effects for industries with different characteristics. Most of the research on this

FIGURE 21.5 *Effect of an Investment Subsidy on Prices of Consumer Goods*

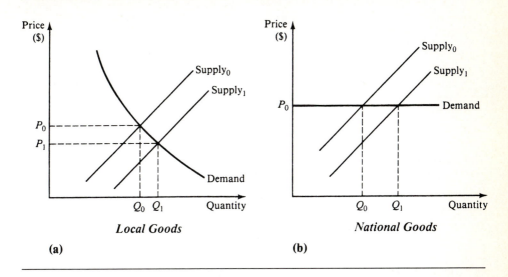

Local Goods

(a)

National Goods

(b)

issue has been focused on manufacturing industries and carried out by relating variation in the number of firms or amount of employment or changes in those measures across states to variations in market, cost, and fiscal factors among the states. Most of the earlier studies of these issues, such as those by Dennis Carlton (1979) and Roger Schmenner (1982), found that differences in wages, energy costs, labor skills, and the amount of manufacturing already carried out in a state influenced firms' decisions to locate or expand in a state but that the level of state and local taxes did not have much influence. The amount of a specific economic activity already being carried out represents what are called **agglomeration economies**, cost advantages that arise when firms producing the same thing are located near each other. For instance, it may be possible to have inputs delivered at lower cost if the supplier can deliver to several firms in one trip.

Other more recent studies have found that subnational government taxes do influence business decisions. Timothy Bartik (1985) examined investment in branch plants in the forty-eight continental states by the 500 largest companies (according to *Fortune* magazine) from 1972–78. He reported that besides transportation and agglomeration factors, investment decisions were affected negatively by the state effective corporate income tax rate and the degree of unionization in a state. It is not clear whether the concern with unionization was about the level of wages, the possibility of strikes, or something else, but Bartik also reported that differences in wages and energy prices apparently did not affect these branch plant investment decisions.

Michael Wasylenko and Therese McGuire (1985) examined the percentage change in employment in states from 1973–80 for six industries—manufacturing, wholesale trade, retail trade, utilities, finance, and services. They report that the wage level, electricity prices, and the educational attainment of workers generally affected investment in these industries. Among fiscal factors, the overall level of state–local taxes seemed to influence employment growth negatively for manufacturing, retail trade, and services (although the level of any particular tax had no effect), whereas the level of state–local spending on education seemed to affect employment growth positively for the retail trade and financial industries. These results certainly suggest that the magnitude of the effect of fiscal policies on investment will vary by industry, although it is not clear how to explain the specific pattern of effects found by Wasylenko and McGuire. Why the level of state–local taxes would influence retail and service investment, industries that are generally dependent on local markets, but not investment in wholesale trade and finance, where more flexibility in locations are expected, is unclear.

Leslie Papke (1987) examined the relationship between the after tax rate-of-return on new investment in a state and the amount of new capital expenditure per worker in the state for a number of different industries in 1978. The effect of state–local taxes is to reduce the rate of return available in a state. She reported that a ''significant part of the geographic pattern in investment across industries and states can be accounted for by differences in net profit rates,'' that is, returns net of state–local and federal taxes. On average, a 1-percent variation in after-tax rate of return is expected to cause about a 2-percent difference in new investment per worker. The sensitivity of new investment to the net return varies greatly by industry, with manufacturing of drugs (elasticity of .75) and blast furnaces being relatively insensitive (elasticity of 1.08) and manufacturing of furniture (elasticity of 3.91) and apparel (elasticity of 4.1) being very sensitive.

Because higher state–local taxes are expected to reduce net profits, the Papke results suggest that higher state–local taxes are expected to also reduce new investment. But Papke cautions that large changes in state–local tax rates are required to bring about even modest changes in rates of return. For instance, her computations suggest that a 1-percent reduction in the rate of return would require an increase in a state corporate income tax rate from 7 to 15 percent or an increase in effective property tax rates from .7 percent to 5.0 percent (assuming a 7-percent corporate income tax rate). And even those large state tax–rate differences would reduce new investment per worker by only about 2 percent in the higher-tax state, on average.

It appears therefore that interstate tax differences may influence new investment decisions for branch plants or expansions in some industries. For other industries, interstate tax differences are just too small to have any substantial effect on net profitability in different states or tax differences are simply not as important as differences in other cost or market factors. There is also at least some evidence that state–local government spending, particularly on education or worker training, may serve to attract new investment to a state. Other than the direct fiscal policies of state–local governments, there is relatively consistent evidence that labor costs and skills, energy costs, and advantages brought about by a concentration of manufacturing in a location all are important factors in influencing interstate manufacturing investment decisions.

/ Investment within regions

Studies of business investment decisions within states or metropolitan areas are more consistent in finding that local fiscal policies, and especially property taxes, influence the location of new investment. As stated by Michael Wasylenko (1986) in a review of the evidence concerning intraurban location of business, "Tax differentials probably have significant effects on the location of firms and differences in intraregional employment growth" (p. 227). The other factors that are consistently found to affect business location decisions within metropolitan areas, at least for manufacturing firms, are the availability of labor with suitable skills, the availability of sufficient quantities of (usually vacant) land, the quality of the transportation network for transporting both goods and workers, and agglomeration economies.

Analyzing the effect of local tax differentials on business investment decisions is complicated by the fact that some communities in almost every metropolitan area choose to effectively zone out some types of industry. Those communities may find any noise, congestion, or environmental pollution, which accompanies industrial development, to be particularly undesirable and thus respond by not supplying many or any industrial development sites. Other communities may allow industrial development but not encourage it by offering tax or other incentives. If communities that effectively preclude development are included with those seeking development in studies of the effect of tax differentials, biased results are expected. If the communities that exclude industrial development by zoning have high-tax rates, for instance, statistical studies might attribute the lack of investment to the tax rates when the actual cause is the community's unwillingness to allow development.

To correct for this problem, studies of business investment within an area must consider the supply of land by a community for industrial development in addition to the demand for locations or land for development by business firms. This adjustment may be accomplished either by excluding those communities that do not allow development from the studies or by explicitly modeling a community's decision about the amount of development to allow. When either of these adjustments are made in studies of intraurban location decisions, local tax differences are consistently found to be even more important factors in influencing business investment decisions within areas.

Besides any direct effects of local business taxes on business location, local taxes may have indirect effects by affecting population and local labor markets. A number of studies, starting with that by Wallace Oates (1969) and followed by many others, have found a negative relationship between local property tax rates and residential housing values and a positive relationship between local government services (especially education) and housing values. These studies have been interpreted as confirming at least the process envisioned by Tiebout where individuals move among communities based on fiscal packages. Put another way, the results of these studies are consistent with an outflow of population and thus a decrease in demand for housing in relatively high-tax communities. The results of local

/ APPLICATION 21.1
A Tale of Two Regions: New England and the Southwest

In 1975 the unemployment rate in the six New England states was 10.4 percent, much above the national average of 8.5 percent and the highest of any region in the country. Massachusetts and Rhode Island tied for the third highest unemployment rate of all states in the country at 11.1 percent. Regional per-capita income was about equal to the national average, a reversal of New England's traditional relatively high-income position. The economy of the New England states had deteriorated from high manufacturing costs, particularly in such traditional industries as textiles, and was particularly hard hit by the 1972–75 national recession. But by June 1987, just twelve years later, the New England economy was humming. Regional unemployment was 3.2 percent, less than half the national average and the lowest of all regions, and the New England state with the highest unemployment rate, Maine at 4 percent, was still the eighth lowest of all states. Per-capita income in New England in 1986 was 17 percent greater than the national average.

The economic turn-around in the New England states illustrates many of the theories about the process of economic reallocation among regions discussed above, the potential effects of forces that arise outside the region, and just how quickly economic changes can occur. The relatively high unemployment and slow growth of incomes in those states in the 1970s caused by the decline or departure of past dominant industries was the incentive to reduce relative wages, and thus labor costs, in those states. That, in turn, made the region more attractive to other industries, including computers and other electronics, financial services, and education, which expanded to replace those lost. Among outside forces, a decline in worldwide energy costs helped the region relatively, and some have noted that the expansion in defense spending by the federal government in the 1980s contributed to the growth of many electronics firms.

An increase in the demand for labor has accompanied the economic expansion in New England, but there has not been a substantial population migration to the region. The predictable result has been an increase in wages, reflected by the very high per-capita income in the region currently and popular comments about a "later shortage." The real complaint, of course, is that labor costs would be lower if there were more workers. Between 1981–85 wages in the Northeast increased by nearly 27 percent. Why hasn't the increase in incomes attracted many more workers? Apparently one reason is another result of the expansion—a substantial increase in housing prices—partly from the increase in individual incomes and partly from the increase in land values caused by the demand for land for commercial and industrial as well as residential uses. As Eugene Carlson (1986c) noted in *The Wall Street Journal,* "This modest supply of new homes is bumping up against unprecedented demand caused by the region's prosperity. . . . The average home price in Boston has soared to $156,000 from $96,500 in two years."

How have firms reacted to the "labor shortage," or more correctly the rise in wages? One interesting effect has been the movement of some economic

/ APPLICATION 21.1 Continued
A Tale of Two Regions: New England and the Southwest

activity from the metropolitan areas, where the economic expansion began, to the rural areas of these states. *The Wall Street Journal* (Carlson 1987b) reported that a number of firms have expanded to northern New England to take advantage of the available labor and relatively lower wages in the rural areas. For instance, Bose Corporation, a loudspeaker manufacturer, opened a plant in northern New Hampshire just south of the Canadian border in 1985 to supplement its headquarters just outside of Boston. As a result of this trend, the unemployment rate in rural New England has also declined and incomes risen. Economic activity has been dispersed within these states by the same forces seen to move activity among states. And so New England has come full circle in the process. High unemployment and falling wages coupled with other factors made it an attractive place for investment. The resulting growth reduced unemployment and increased wages and housing costs, which will impose a natural constraint on additional economic growth in the region.

Although some have suggested that changes in state fiscal policies contributed to the increased economic activity in the New England states, the average fiscal characteristics of the region really have changed little since the mid-1970s. For instance, in 1975 per-capita state and local expenditure by all the New England states together was just slightly above the national average ($1101 versus $1077), and per-capita taxes were about 10 percent above the national average ($727 versus $664). In 1985 per-capita expenditure was still about equal to the national average ($2743 versus $2757), and per-capita taxes were about 11 percent above the national average ($1627 versus $1465). Although some individual states in New England have changed their relative level of taxes and spending (Massachusetts being the best known), the relative average fiscal picture in the region has not changed, and the increase in economic activity has occurred throughout the region.

The continual dynamic nature of regional economic growth and decline is also illustrated by the current problems in some Southern and Southwestern states, particularly those dependent on the production of oil and natural gas. Just opposite from the New England states, unemployment in such states as Louisiana, Oklahoma, and Texas was below the national average in the 1970s and early 1980s, and incomes were rising relatively quickly, fueled by the increase in energy prices. But by June 1987, all three states' unemployment rates were above the national average, with Louisiana's the highest of any state at 11.2 percent. Changes in energy usage as a result of the price increases in the 1970s coupled with increased oil production by OPEC and other producers led to large decreases in energy prices in the mid-1980s. As energy-related industries stopped growing and even shrunk, these states suffered a decline in wealth and economic activity. As a result, demand for labor and land fell, unemployment and vacancies increased, and income and land values declined. But as with the experience of the New England states, these price decreases are expected to provide the incentive for new investment in those states and subsequent economic growth in the future.

business location studies show that firms are attracted to communities where labor is readily available. Relatively high property or personal income taxes may therefore reduce the available supply of labor in a region or raise the wage that employers must pay for a given quantity or quality of workers. In either case, the local personal taxes may indirectly influence business location decisions in that manner.

The results of the studies about housing values suggest that consumers move among communities within a region in response to price differences caused by tax differences. Mobility of consumers of capital was also found in research by William Wheaton (1984) examining the relationship between rental rates for space in commercial buildings in the Boston metropolitan area in 1980 and community effective property tax rates. Wheaton reported that differences in tax rates had no effect on the relative level of commercial rents in the communities. In other words, it appears that if landlords attempted to charge higher rents for commercial space in communities with higher taxes, tenants were willing to move to lower-tax, and thus lower-rent, communities. If rents are the same for similar buildings in high and low property tax communities, then the tax difference is being born by owners— landlords earn lower rates of return in higher-tax communities. For that to occur requires that consumers of commercial office space be more willing to move within the region than owners of capital are willing to relocate their investments. Although Wheaton's research showed that tax-rate differences did not affect rents, differences in building characteristics (age, size, whether located in a complex) and community characteristics (public transit, highways, labor skills) did affect commercial rents in the ways expected.

/ Policy Issues

Even if fiscal incentives are effective in attracting new investment to a state or locality, there are several other issues that should be considered in order to fully evaluate incentives. First, the use of targeted fiscal incentives rather than general business–tax decreases means that some businesses in a jurisdiction will be taxed at lower effective rates than others. If the incentives are applied on a case-by-case basis, it is even likely that otherwise similar businesses—for instance, similar size firms in the same business—will pay different taxes if one is granted an incentive to avoid a threatened move or to retain an expansion. Although it is a fundamental principle of optimal tax theory that taxpayers who respond to taxes differently should be taxed at different rates, differential taxation of similar businesses creates difficult equity and political concerns.

Second, granting tax reductions to some or even all businesses may create an external cost on other taxpayers. If those businesses consume government-provided goods or services that are not pure public goods—that is, that require additional cost to provide—then the tax structure is moved further away from a benefit tax. Essentially, other taxpayers must bear the marginal costs of services that exclusively benefit the firm's owners. This means that the tax costs imposed on the other taxpayers—individuals only or individuals and some businesses—must be greater

/ APPLICATION 21.2
Business Climate Studies and Rankings

As a result of the increased attention to state–local taxes and their effect on economic development by both business and government, a number of attempts have been made to evaluate and compare business costs—or what is often called the "business environment"—in the various states. Among the best-known and thus perhaps most controversial of these comparisons is the annual study of general manufacturing climates among the states done since 1979 by Grant Thornton, an accounting and management consulting firm. Grant Thornton surveys state manufacturer associations, chamber of commerce representatives, and government officials to determine the factors that are thought to be important for manufacturing investment decisions, attaches weights to each of the factors selected based on the survey, collects data for each factor for each state, and computes an overall index of manufacturing business climate for each state.

For the 1986 study[3], twenty-one different factors were measured representing the five major categories of state–local government fiscal policies, state-regulated employment costs (unemployment and workers' compensation), labor costs, availability and productivity of resources, and quality of life (education, health care, cost of living, transportation). The five factors with the heaviest weight of the twenty-one, all reflecting the labor market in the state, were the average annual hourly manufacturing wage (7.14 percent of the total index), the percentage of manufacturing workers who were unionized (6.81 percent), an index representing the size and education level of the labor force (5.78 percent), the average workers' compensation insurance rate per $100 of payroll (5.38 percent), and the percentage change in the average hourly manufacturing wage over the previous five years (5.36 percent). These five factors accounted for more than 30 percent of the overall manufacturing climate index of a state, therefore. The five state fiscal policy factors—the level of taxes; the change in taxes, expenditures, and debt over the previous five years; and the level of state business incentives—represented about 20 percent of the overall index. Other major factors included the educational attainment of the population, energy costs, and the productivity of manufacturing workers.

The states ranked as having the highest and lowest manufacturing climate scores by this process for 1986 were as follows:

Best Climate		Worst Climate	
1	North Dakota	48	Michigan
2	Nebraska	47	Ohio
3	South Dakota	46	Montana
4	Virginia	45	Louisiana
5	Colorado	44	Wyoming
6	Missouri	43	West Virginia
7	Arizona	42	Illinois
8	Kansas	41	Maine
9	North Carolina	40	Washington
10	Nevada	39	Oregon

It has not gone unnoted that many of the states with supposedly the best manufacturing climates actually have little manufacturing activity and weak state economies (such as the Dakotas and Nebraska), while some of the states with the supposedly worst climates are the manufacturing centers in the United States and had relatively strong economies at the time of the study (such as Michigan, Ohio, Illinois, and Washington). This is not surprising because it reflects both the factors included in the index and the process of movement of economic activity discussed in this chapter. In a state with little economic activity and substantial unemployment, the demand for labor is relatively low and thus one expects wages and other labor costs to be relatively low and perhaps even falling. For instance, Eugene Carlson reported in *The Wall Street Journal* (1987a) that both North Dakota and Nebraska have lost manufacturing jobs since 1980. In fact, Nebraska's lack of success in attracting new business induced the state to adopt a new set of business tax incentives in 1987 (Farney 1987).

The same economic argument helps to explain why states with a large amount of manufacturing activity and relatively high incomes show up with an unfavorable manufacturing business climate. Where there is substantial manufacturing activity, demand for labor is high and thus wages and other labor costs are expected to be relatively high and perhaps even rising. In addition, workers in the larger manufacturing firms are more likely to be unionized than in smaller firms, and manufacturing workers in many cases tend to have a lower overall level of educational attainment than in other commercial activities. Not surprisingly, with high wages and incomes these states appear as high-cost states. Given the importance of labor market factors in the business climate index, these labor market conditions translate into a corresponding manufacturing business climate. The logic of the analysis is consistent with the observed long-term trend of equalization of regional incomes in the United States—economic activity moves to the low-wage/low-income areas from the high-wage/high-income areas.

But the fact that manufacturing activity continues to decline in states with a high manufacturing climate rating and increase in some with a low rating raises an important issue of causation. Do low labor costs attract more investment, or does new investment (because of some other factor) cause an increase in demand for labor and wages? There must be some reason why manufacturing employment continues to decline in North Dakota and Nebraska and increase in Michigan and Ohio. The answer, it seems likely, is that some other factors not captured as well by the index are more important for some types of manufacturing. Among these might be the location of production compared to the location of markets (transportation costs) and to the location of financial market centers. Thus, the manufacturing business climate index shows that a state with North Dakota or Nebraska's labor market conditions and New York or Michigan's location would be great for manufacturing. But even the labor market advantages in such states as North Dakota and Nebraska apparently are not sufficient to offset other disadvantages, perhaps due to those market and transportation factors.

---

[3]*The Eighth Annual Study of General Manufacturing Climates of the Forty-Eight Contiguous States of America* (1987).

than the marginal benefits received by those taxpayers. The external cost therefore leads to inefficient decisions about the amount and mix of government services to provide.

Third, some states and localities elect to offer fiscal incentives because other competing jurisdictions are doing so. By acting to counteract others' fiscal incentives, a state or locality intends to maintain relative business costs at the level before any incentives were granted. As previously discussed, this intergovernmental competition leads to a lowering of overall business costs but does not create any incentive for the pattern of investment among the jurisdictions to change. One option for states and localities to consider in this case is collusion—mutual agreements not to offer certain types of incentives to certain types of businesses. Such collusion could improve economic efficiency if it prevents the kind of external cost effects noted above without altering the relative costs of business in different jurisdictions. Of course, as with all attempts at collusion when there are more than just a few players, enforcement of the agreements would be nearly impossible. And given some recent antitrust decisions concerning the market power and actions of subnational governments, such agreements might be found to be illegal.

/ Summary

Differences in per-capita income among the states and regions have been continually reduced this century, a change that has been accompanied by a general realignment of population and economic activity from the urban industrialized areas to the more rural regions. One possible economic explanation is a flow of new investment to regions with relatively low wages, resulting in an increase in economic activity, population, and ultimately wages and incomes.

State–local taxes with an initial impact on business represented about 31 percent of total state–local taxes in 1977, a share that has declined steadily from 1957. State–local taxes collected from business also represented about 8 percent of net income for all firms in 1977. Interstate differences in state–local business taxes are reduced because those taxes are a deductible expense for firms in computing their federal income tax liability.

Fiscal incentives for investment are offered by most states and at least most of the larger counties and municipalities, so that they do not affect the relative cost for businesses in those different locations.

The evidence concerning the effect of state–local government fiscal policies on investment among states or regions is mixed, with the one consistent conclusion perhaps being that there is no general result—fiscal policies have very different effects for industries with different characteristics. There is relatively consistent evidence that labor costs and skills, energy costs, and advantages brought about by a concentration of manufacturing in a location are generally important factors in influencing interstate manufacturing investment decisions.

Studies of business investment decisions within states or metropolitan areas are more consistent in finding that local fiscal policies, and especially property taxes, influence the location of new investment. Relatively high property or personal income taxes may also reduce the available supply of labor in a region or raise the wage that employers must pay for a given quantity of workers, thereby indirectly influencing business location decisions.

Discussion Questions

1. In thinking about the effects of state–local government fiscal policy on economic development, attention is usually focused on what government can do to attract economic activity. But some communities actually discourage or prohibit new industrial or commercial investment. What are the gains to the community from new business investment? What are the costs or problems to a community from a new shopping center, for instance? What about a new manufacturing plant? When would a community discourage these types of activities?

2. If localities offer incentives such as tax breaks or tax-exempt financing to firms that provide new investment in the community, a common complaint is that this disadvantages existing firms that receive no similar incentives and yet may be in the same business. Is this correct? Suppose that one community offers an incentive for new investment that is successful in actually attracting new investment. Work through the effects on the return to capital in the community, on the local labor market, and on the land market in the community.

3. If all states offer essentially the same economic development incentives, then no state gains an advantage. Yet this is exactly what seems to happen. Why do states continue to offer these incentives when it is not to their collective advantage?

4. The evidence about interstate investment decisions seems to show that state incentives have very different effects for different industries. In some industries, investment is greatly influenced by state incentives; in others, state incentives seem to have little effect. What types of industry would seem to be most likely to have investment decisions easily influenced by tax or financing incentives?

Selected Readings

Advisory Commission on Intergovernmental Relations. *Regional Growth: Interstate Tax Competition.* Washington, D.C.: Author, March 1981.

Mieszkowski, Peter. "Recent Trends in Urban and Regional Development." In *Current Issues in Urban Economics,* edited by P. Mieszkowski and M. Straszheim, 3–39. Baltimore: Johns Hopkins University Press, 1979.

Wolkoff, Michael J. "Chasing a Dream: The Use of Property Tax Abatements to Spur Economic Development." *Urban Studies* 22 (Aug. 1985): 305–15.

References

Aaron, Henry J. "What Do Circuit-Breaker Laws Accomplish?" In *Property Tax Reform*, edited by G. Peterson, 53–65. Washington, D.C.: The Urban Institute, 1973.

Aaron, Henry J. *Who Pays the Property Tax?* Washington, D.C.: The Brookings Institution, 1975.

Advisory Commission on Intergovernmental Relations. *State Limitations on Local Taxes and Expenditures*. Washington, D.C.: Author, February 1977.

Advisory Commission on Intergovernmental Relations. *Regional Growth: Historic Perspective*. Washington, D.C.: Author, 1980.

Advisory Commission on Intergovernmental Relations. *Regional Growth: Interstate Tax Competition*. Washington, D.C.: Author, 1981a.

Advisory Commission on Intergovernmental Relations. *Significant Features of Fiscal Federalism, 1980–81*. Washington, D.C.: Author, December 1981b.

Advisory Committee on Intergovernmental Relations. *A Catalog of Federal Grant-in-Aid Programs to State and Local Governments*. Washington, D.C.: Author, 1984a.

Advisory Commission on Intergovernmental Relations. *Changing Attitudes on Governments and Taxes*. Washington, D.C.: Author, 1984b.

Advisory Commission on Intergovernmental Relations. *Strengthening the Federal Revenue System: Implications for State and Local Taxing and Borrowing*, Report A–97. Washington, D.C.: Author, 1984c.

Advisory Commission on Intergovernmental Relations. *Cigarette Tax Evasion: A Second Look*, Report A–100. Washington, D.C.: Author, March 1985a.

Advisory Commission on Intergovernmental Relations. *Intergovernmental Service Arrangements for Delivering Local Public Services: Update 1983*. Washington, D.C.: Author, October 1985b.

Advisory Commission on Intergovernmental Relations. *Preliminary Estimates of the Effect of the 1986 Federal Tax Reform Act on State Personal Income Tax Liabilities*. Washington, D.C.: Author, December 8, 1986a.

Advisory Commission on Intergovernmental Relations. *State and Local Taxation of Out-of-State Mail Order Sales*, Report A–105. Washington, D.C.: Author, April 1986b.

Advisory Commission on Intergovernmental Relations. *Significant Features of Fiscal Federalism, 1985–86 Edition*. Washington, D.C.: Author, 1986c.

Advisory Commission on Intergovernmental Relations. *Fiscal Discipline in the Federal System: National Reform and the Experience of the States*. Washington, D.C.: Author, July 1987a.

Advisory Commission on Intergovernmental Relations. *Significant Features of Fiscal Federalism, 1987 Edition*. Washington, D.C.: Author, 1987b.

Advisory Commission on Intergovernmental Relations. *Significant Features of Fiscal Federalism, 1988 Edition, Volume 1*. Washington, D.C.: Author, 1988.

Alper, Neil O., Robert B. Archibald, and Eric Jensen. "At What Price Vanity?: An Econometric Model of the Demand for Personalized License Plates." *National Tax Journal* 40 (March 1987): 103–109.

Anderson, John E. "Property Taxes and the Timing of Urban Land Development." Ypsilanti: Eastern Michigan University, 1986.

Aronson, J. Richard and John L. Hilley. *Financing State and Local Governments*. Washington, D.C.: The Brookings Institution, 1986.

Bahl, Roy. *Financing State and Local Government in the 1980s*. New York: Oxford University Press, 1984.

Bahl, Roy W. and Walter Vogt. *Fiscal Centralization and Tax Burdens: State and Regional Financing of City Services*. Cambridge, Mass.: Ballinger, 1975.

Baldwin, Robert R. "Domestic Preference Litigation: A Review of Developments Since the Decision in *Metropolitan Life Insurance Company v. Ward*." Paper presented at the National Tax Association–Tax Institute of America Conference in Hartford, Conn., November 1986.

Ballard, Charles L. and John B. Shoven. "The V.A.T.: The Efficiency Cost of Achieving Progressivity by Using Exemptions." In *Modern Developments in Public Finance: Essays in Honor of Arnold Harberger*, edited by M. Boskin, 109–29. Oxford, England: Basil Blackwell, 1985.

Barr, James L. and Otto A. Davis. "An Elementary Political and Economic Theory of Local Governments." *Southern Economic Journal* 33 (Oct. 1966): 149–65.

Bartik, Timothy J. "Business Location Decisions in the U.S.: Estimates of the Effects of Unionization, Taxes, and Other Characteristics of States." *Journal of Business and Economic Statistics* 3 (1985): 14–22.

Bator, Francis M. "A Detailed Analysis of Tax Pyramiding." *Quarterly Journal of Economics* 72 (Aug. 1958): 351–79.

Baumol, William J. "Macroeconomics of Unbalanced Growth: The Anatomy of the Urban Crisis." *American Economic Review* 62 (June 1967): 415–26.

Beaton, W. Patrick, ed. *Municipal Expenditures, Revenues, and Services*. New Brunswick, N.J.: Rutgers University, Center for Urban Policy Research, 1983.

Beck, John H. "Nonmonotonic Demand for Municipal Services." *National Tax Journal* 37 (March 1984): 55–68.

Beckmann, Martin. *Location Theory*. New York: Random House, 1968.

Bell, Michael E. and John H. Bowman. "The Effect of Various Intergovernmental Aid Types on Local Own-Source Revenues: The Case of Property Taxes in Minnesota Cities." *Public Finance Quarterly* 15 (July 1987): 282–97.

Bell, Michael E. and Ronald C. Fisher. "State Limitations on Local Taxing and Spending Powers: Comment and Re-evaluation." *National Tax Journal* 31 (Dec. 1978): 391–95.

Bergstrom, Theodore C. and Goodman, Robert P. "Private Demand for Public Goods." *American Economic Review* 63 (June 1973): 280–96.

Biddle, Jeffrey. "Searching for a Bandwagon Effect in the Market for Personalized License Plates." Working paper, Michigan State University, Sept. 1987.

Billings, R. Bruce. *Report of the First Review Commission.* Hawaii Tax Review Commission, 1984.

Board of Governors of the Federal Reserve System. *Federal Reserve Bulletin,* various years.

Board of Governors of the Federal Reserve System. *Flow of Funds Accounts,* various years.

Borcherding, Thomas E. and Deacon, Robert T. "The Demand for the Services of Non-Federal Governments." *American Economic Review* 62 (Dec. 1972): 891–906.

Borts, George H. and Jerome Stein. *Economic Growth in a Free Market.* New York: Columbia University Press, 1964.

Bowen, Howard R. "The Interpretation of Voting in the Allocation of Economic Resources." *The Quarterly Journal of Economics* 58 (Nov. 1943): 27–64.

Bradbury, Katherine L. et. al. "State Aid to Offset Fiscal Disparities Across Communities." *National Tax Journal* 37 (June 1984): 151–170.

Bradford, David F., R. A. Malt, and Wallace E. Oates. "The Rising Cost of Local Public Services: Some Evidence and Reflections." *National Tax Journal* 22 (June 1969): 185–202.

Bradford, David F. and Harvey S. Rosen. "The Optimal Taxation of Commodities and Income." *American Economic Review* 66 (May 1976): 94–101.

Brazer, Harvey E., ed. *Michigan's Fiscal and Economic Structure.* Ann Arbor: University of Michigan Press, 1982.

Brazer, Harvey E., Deborah S. Laren, and Frank Yu-Hsieh Sung. "Elementary and Secondary School Financing." In *Michigan's Fiscal and Economic Structure,* edited by H. Brazer, 411–46. Ann Arbor: University of Michigan Press, 1982.

Break, George F. *Intergovernmental Fiscal Relations in the United States.* Washington D.C.: The Brookings Institution, 1967.

Break, George F., ed. *Metropolitan Financing and Growth Management Policies.* Madison: University of Wisconsin Press, 1978.

Break, George F. *Financing Government Expenditure in a Federal System.* Washington D.C.: The Brookings Institution, 1980.

Brennan, Geoffrey and James Buchanan. "The Logic of Tax Limits: Alternative Constitutional Constraints of the Power to Tax." *National Tax Journal Supplement* 32 (June 1979): 11–22.

Brown, Bryon W. and Daniel H. Saks. "The Production and Distribution of Cognitive Skills." *Journal of Political Economy* 83 (June 1975): 571–93.

Brown, Byron W. and Daniel H. Saks. "The Microeconomics of Schooling." In *Review of Research in Education* 9, edited by D. Berliner. American Educational Research Association, 1981.

Brown, Byron W. and Daniel H. Saks. "Spending for Local Public Education: Income Distribution and the Aggregation of Private Demands." *Public Finance Quarterly* 11 (Jan. 1983): 21–45.

Buchanan, James M. "The Economics of Earmarked Taxes." *Journal of Political Economy* 71 (Oct. 1963): 457–69.

Buchanan, James M. "An Economic Theory of Clubs." *Economica* 32 (Feb. 1965): 1–14.

Buchanan, James M. *Public Finance in Democratic Process: Fiscal Institutions and Individual Choice*. Chapel Hill: University of North Carolina Press, 1967.

Buchanan, James M. and Charles J. Goetz. "Efficiency Limits of Fiscal Mobility: An Assessment of the Tiebout Model." *Journal of Public Economics* 1 (1972): 25–45.

Budget Message of the Governor, 1985–86 Fiscal Year, State of Michigan, Lansing, January 1985.

Button, K. J. and A. D. Pearman. *Applied Transport Economics*. Great Britain: Gordon and Breach Science Publishers, 1986.

Carlson, Eugene. "Los Angeles County Discovers Benefits in Taxable Securities." *The Wall Street Journal,* 10 December 1986a, 33.

Carlson, Eugene. "Good Times in New England: How Long Can They Go On?" *The Wall Street Journal,* 19 August 1986b, 27.

Carlson, Eugene. "Manufacturing-Climate Rating Sparks Usual Storm in States." *The Wall Street Journal,* 23 June 1987a, 33.

Carlson, Eugene. "Outlying New England Areas Now Feeling the Labor Pinch." *The Wall Street Journal,* 29 September 1987b, 33.

Carlton, Dennis. "The Location and Employment Choices of New Firms: An Econometric Model with Discrete and Continuous Endogenous Variables." *The Review of Economics and Statistics* 65 (1983): 440–49.

Chernick, Howard A. "An Econometric Model of the Distribution of Project Grants." In *Fiscal Federalism and Grants-in-Aid,* edited by P. Mieszkowski and W. H. Oakland. Washington, D.C.: The Urban Institute, 1979.

Citrin, Jack. "Do People Want Something for Nothing: Public Opinion on Taxes and Government Spending." *National Tax Journal Supplement* 32 (June 1979): 113–29.

Clark, Phil. "Private Activity Tax-Exempt Bonds, 1984." U.S. Department of Treasury, *Statistics of Income Bulletin* 5 (Winter 1986): 55–63.

Clotfelter, Charles T. and Phillip J. Cook. "Implicit Taxation in Lottery Finance." *National Tax Journal* 40 (Dec. 1987): 533–46.

Cohn, Gary. "As Jackpots Grow at Tracks and Frontons, Bettors Form Syndicates to Even the Odds." *The Wall Street Journal,* 23 September 1986, 33.

Container Corporation of America v. Francise Tax Board (463 U.S. 159 1983).

"Costing and Pricing for Local Governmental Services." *Governmental Finance* 11 (March 1982): 3–27.

Courant, Paul N., Edward M. Gramlich, and Daniel L. Rubinfeld. "Why Voters Support Tax Limitation Amendments: The Michigan Case." *National Tax Journal* 33 (March 1980): 1–20.

Craig, Steven and Robert P. Inman. "Federal Aid and Public Education: An Empirical Look at the New Fiscal Federalism." *Review of Economics and Statistics* (Nov. 1982): 541–52.

Craig, Steven and Robert P. Inman. "Education, Welfare and the 'New' Federalism." In *Studies in State and Local Public Finances,* edited by H. Rosen. Chicago: University of Chicago Press, 1985.

Davies, Daniel G. "The Significance of Taxation of Services for the Pattern of Distribution of Tax Burden by Income Class." *Proceedings of the Fifty-Second Annual Conference,* National Tax Association, Columbus, Ohio, 1969, 138–46.

Deasey, John A., Jr. "An Update on National Survey of Production Exemptions Under Sales and Use Tax Laws." *Proceedings of the Seventy-Ninth Annual Conference,* National Tax Association, Columbus, Ohio, 1987, 296–310.

DeBoer, Larry. "Administrative Costs of State Lotteries." *National Tax Journal* 38 ((Dec. 1985): 479–87.

Distilled Spirits Council of the United States, Inc. *Annual Statistical Review,* 1984–85. Washington, D.C., 1985.

Downing, Paul B. and Thomas J. DiLorenzo. "User Charges and Special Districts." In *Management Policies in Local Government Finance,* edited by J. R. Aronson and E. Schwartz, 184–210 Washington, D.C.: International City Management Association, 1981.

Due, John F. *State and Local Sales Taxation.* Chicago: Public Administration Service, 1971.

Due, John F. and John L. Mikesell. *Sales Taxation, State and Local Structure and Administration.* Baltimore: Johns Hopkins University Press, 1983.

"The Economic Case Against State-Run Gambling." *Business Week,* 4 August, 1975, 67–68.

Economic Report of the President. Washington, D.C.: Council of Economic Advisors, Feb. 1986, 1988.

The Eighth Annual Study of General Manufacturing Climates of the Forty-Eight Contiguous States of America. Chicago: Grant Thornton, June 1987.

Farney, Dennis. "Nebraska, Hungry for Jobs, Grants Big Business Big Tax Breaks Despite Charges of 'Blackmail,' " *The Wall Street Journal,* 23 June 1987, 66.

Feldstein, Martin. "Wealth Neutrality and Local Choice in Public Education." *American Economic Review* 65 (1975): 75–89.

Fischel, William A. "A Property Rights Approach to Municipal Zoning." *Land Economics* 54 (1978): 64–81.

Fisher, Ronald C. "The Combined State and Federal Income Tax Treatment of Charitable Contributions." *Proceedings of the Seventieth Annual Conference,* National Tax Association–Tax Institute of America, Columbus, Ohio, 1978.

Fisher, Ronald C. "A Theoretical View of Revenue-Sharing Grants." *National Tax Journal* 32 (June 1979): 173–84.

Fisher, Ronald C. "Expenditure Incentives of Intergovernmental Grants: Revenue Sharing and Matching Grants." In J. V. Henderson, ed., *Research in Urban Economics* 1 (1980a): 201–18.

Fisher, Ronald C. "Local Sales Taxes: Tax Rate Differentials, Sales Loss, and Revenue Estimation." *Public Finance Quarterly* 8 (April 1980b): 171–88.

Fisher, Ronald C. "Income and Grant Effects on Local Expenditure: The Flypaper Effect and Other Difficulties." *Journal of Urban Economics* 12 (1982): 324–45.

Fisher, Ronald C. and Robert H. Rasche. "The Incidence and Incentive Effects of Property Tax Credits: Evidence from Michigan." *Public Finance Quarterly* 12 (July 1984): 291–319.

Fisher, Ronald C. "Taxes and Expenditures in the U.S.: Public Opinion Surveys and Incidence Analysis Compared." *Economic Inquiry* 23 (July 1985): 525–50.

Fisher, Ronald C. "Intergovernmental Tax Incentives and Local Fiscal Behavior." Working paper, Michigan State University, 1986.

Flatters, Frank J., Vernon Henderson, and Peter Mieskowski. "Public Goods, Efficiency, and Regional Fiscal Equalization." *Journal of Public Economics* 3 (1974): 99–112.

Fox, William F. "Tax Structure and the Location of Economic Activity Along State Borders." *National Tax Journal* 39, (Dec. 1986): 387–401.

Friedman, Lewis. "Budgeting." In *Management Policies in Local Government Finance,* edited by J. R. Aronson and E. Schwartz, 91–119. Washington, D.C.: International City Management Association, 1981.

Gade, Mary N. *Optimal State Tax Design.* Unpublished Ph.D. dissertation, Michigan State University, 1986.

Gade, Mary N. "Tax Exporting and State Revenue Structures." Oklahoma State University, December 1987.

Galante, Steven P. "Companies Shifting Tax Focus as State Levies Loom Larger." *The Wall Street Journal,* 20 April 1987.

Getz, Malcolm. *The Economics of the Urban Fire Department.* Baltimore: Johns Hopkins University Press, 1979.

Goddeeris, John. "User Charges as Revenue Sources." In *Michigan's Fiscal and Economic Structure,* edited by Harvey E. Brazer, 765–87. Ann Arbor: University of Michigan Press, 1982.

Gold, Steven D. *Property Tax Relief.* Lexington, Mass.: Lexington Books, 1979.

Gold, Steven D. "Contingency Measures and Fiscal Limitations: The Real World Significance of Some Recent State Budget Innovations." *National Tax Journal* 37 (Sept. 1984): 421–32.

Gold, Steven D., ed. *Reforming State Tax Systems.* National Conference of State Legislatures, Denver, 1986.

Gold, Steven D. "The State Government Response to Federal Income Tax Reform: Indications from the States That Completed Their Work Early." *National Tax Journal* 40 (Sept. 1987): 431–44.

Gomez-Ibanez, Jose A. "The Federal Role in Urban Transportation." In *American Domestic Priorities: An Economic Appraisal,* edited by J. Quigley and D. Rubinfeld, 183–223. Berkeley: University of California Press, 1985.

Gordon, Roger H. and Joel Slemrod. "An Empirical Examination of Municipal Financial Policy." In *Studies in State and Local Finance,* edited by H. Rosen. Chicago: University of Chicago Press, 1986.

Gordon, Roger H. and John D. Wilson. "An Examination of Multijurisdictional Corporate Income Taxation Under Formula Apportionment." *Econometrica* 54 (1986): 1357–73.

Gramlich, Edward M. "Alternative Federal Policies for Stimulating State and Local Expenditures: A Comparison of Their Effects." *National Tax Journal* 21 (June 1968): 119–29.

Gramlich, Edward M. "Intergovernmental Grants: A Review of the Empirical Literature." In *The Political Economy of Fiscal Federalism*, edited by Wallace Oates. Lexington, Mass.: Lexington Books, 1976.

Gramlich, Edward M. "Deductibility of State and Local Taxes." *National Tax Journal* 38 (Dec. 1985a): 447–66.

Gramlich, Edward M. "Reforming U.S. Federal Fiscal Arrangements." In *American Domestic Priorities: An Economic Appraisal,* edited by J. Quigley and D. Rubinfeld, 34–69. Berkeley: University of California Press, 1985b.

Gramlich, Edward M. and Harvey Galper. "State and Local Fiscal Behavior and Federal Grant Policy." In *Brookings Papers on Economic Activity.* Washington, D.C.: The Brookings Institution, 1973, 15–58.

Gramlich, Edward M. and Deborah S. Laren. "Migration and Income Redistribution Responsibilities." *Journal of Human Resources* 19 (1984): 489–511.

Greene, Kenneth V. and Thomas J. Parliament. "Political Externalities, Efficiency, and the Welfare Losses from Consolidation." *National Tax Journal* 33 (June 1980): 209–17.

Guttman, George. "The Taxmen Could Have Made It Easier." *The Wall Street Journal,* 15 April 1986.

Hamilton, Bruce W. "Zoning and Property Taxation in a System of Local Governments." *Urban Studies* 12 (June 1975): 205–11.

Hamilton, Bruce W. "The Effects of Property Taxes and Local Public Spending on Property Values: A Theoretical Comment." *Journal of Political Economy* 84 (June 1976a): 647–50.

Hamilton, Bruce W. "Capitalization of Interjurisdictional Differences in Local Tax Prices." *American Economic Review* 66 (Dec. 1976b): 743–53.

Hamilton, Bruce W. "The Flypaper Effect and Other Anomalies." *Journal of Public Economics* 22 (Dec. 1983): 347–61.

Hansen, W. Lee and Burton A. Weisbrod. "The Distribution of Costs and Direct Benefits of Public Higher Education: The Case of California." *Journal of Human Resources* 4 (Spring 1969): 176–91.

Hanushek, Eric A. "The Economics of Schooling." *Journal of Economic Literature* 24 (Sept. 1986): 1141–77.

Hellerstein, Walter. "Florida's Sales Tax on Services." *National Tax Journal* 61 (March 1988): 1–18.

Henderson, J. Vernon. "The Tiebout Model: Bring Back the Entrepreneurs." *Journal of Political Economy* 93 (April 1985a): 248–64.

Henderson, J. Vernon. "Property Tax Incidence with a Public Sector." *Journal of Political Economy* 93 (Aug. 1985b): 648–65.

Herbers, John. "States Consider Adjusting Taxes To Federal Code." *The New York Times,* 1 February 1987, 1, 18.

Hettich, Walter and Stanley Winer. "A Positive Model of Fiscal Structure." *Journal of Public Economics* 24 (1984): 67–87.

Hirsch, Werner Z. *The Economics of State and Local Government.* New York: McGraw-Hill, 1970.

Holcombe, Randall G. "Concepts of Public Sector Equilibrium." *National Tax Journal* 34, no. 1 (March 1980): 77–80.

Holtz-Eakin, Douglas and Harvey S. Rosen. "Tax Deductibility and Municipal Budget Structure." In *Fiscal Federalism: Quantitative Studies,* edited by H. Rosen. Chicago: University of Chicago Press, 1988.

Hulten, Charles R. "Productivity Change in State and Local Governments." *Review of Economics and Statistics* 66 (1984): 256–266.

Inman, Robert P. "Testing Political Economy's 'As If' Proposition: Is the Median Voter Really Decisive?" *Public Choice* 33 (Winter 1978): 45–65.

Inman, Robert P. "The Fiscal Performance of Local Governments: An Interpretive Review." In *Current Issues in Urban Economics,* edited by P. Mieskowski and M. Strasheim. Baltimore: Johns Hopkins University Press, 1979a.

Inman, Robert P. "Subsidies, Regulations, and the Taxation of Property in Large U.S. Cities." *National Tax Journal* 32 (June 1979b): 159–168.

Inman, Robert P. "Does Deductibility Influence Local Taxation?" Working paper No. 85–86, Federal Reserve Bank of Philadelphia, May 1985.

Jay, Christopher. "NSW Crackdown on Bootleg Cigarettes." *Financial Review,* 6 August, 1987, 6.

Kaufman, George C. and Philip Fischer. "Debt Management." In *Management Policies in Local Government Finance,* edited by J. R. Aronson and E. Schwartz, 287–317. Washington, D.C.: International City Management Association, 1987.

Kelejian, Harry H. and Wallace E. Oates. *Introduction to Econometrics.* New York: Harper & Row, 1981.

Kenyon, Daphne. "Implicit Aid to State and Local Governments Through Federal Deductibility." In *Intergovernmental Fiscal Relations in an Era of New Federalism,* edited by M. Bell. Greenwich, Conn.: JAI Press, 1986.

Kenyon, Daphne A. and Karen M. Benker. "Fiscal Discipline: Lessons From the State Experience." *National Tax Journal* 37 (Sept. 1984): 433–46.

King, A. Thomas. "Estimating Property Tax Capitalization: A Critical Comment." *Journal of Political Economy* 85 (April 1977): 425–32.

Kohler, Heinz. *Intermediate Microeconomics.* Glenview, Il.: Scott, Foresman, 1982.

Ladd, Helen F. "Local Education Expenditures, Fiscal Capacity and the Composition of the Property Tax Base." *National Tax Journal* 28 (June 1975): 145–58.

Ladd, Helen F. "An Economic Evaluation of State Limitations on Local Taxing and Spending Powers." *National Tax Journal* 31 (March 1978): 1–18.

Lankford, R. Hamilton. "Efficiency and Equity in the Provision of Public Education." *The Review of Economics and Statistics* 67 (Feb. 1985): 70–80.

Limitations on State Deficits. The Council of State Governments, Lexington, Ky., 1976.

Lynch, Carolyn D. "The Treasury II Tax Reform Proposal: Its Impact On State Personal Income Tax Liabilities." *Proceedings of the Seventy-Ninth Annual Conference,* National Tax Association, Columbus, Ohio, 1987, 310–16.

Marshall, Jonathan. "How to Break Up Traffic Jams." *The Wall Street Journal,* 15 September, 1986.

Martinez-Vasquez, Jorge. "Selfishness Versus Public 'Regardingness' in Voting Behavior." *Journal of Public Economics* 15 (June 1981): 349–61.

Maxwell, James A. *Financing State and Local Governments.* Washington, D.C.: The Brookings Institution, 1965.

McDavid, James C. "The Canadian Experience with Privatizing Residential Solid Waste Collection Services." *Public Administration Review* (Sept. 1985): 603–04.

McEachern, William A. "Collective Decision Rules and Local Debt Choice: A Test of the Median-Voter Hypothesis." *National Tax Journal* 31 (June 1978): 129–36.

McGinley, Laurie. "How Some U.S. Areas Cope with Anomaly: Surging Economies." *The Wall Street Journal,* 12 December 1985, 1.

McLure, Charles E. "Commodity Tax Incidence in Open Economics." *National Tax Journal* 17 (June 1964): 187–204.

McLure, Charles E. "Tax Exporting in the U.S.: Estimates for 1962." *National Tax Journal* 20 (March 1967): 49–77.

McLure, Charles E. "The 'New View' of the Property Tax: A Caveat." *National Tax Journal* 30 (March 1977a): 69–75.

McLure, Charles E. "Taxation of Multijurisdictional Corporate Income: Lessons of the U.S. Experience." In *The Political Economy of Fiscal Federalism,* edited by W. Oates, 241–59. Lexington, Mass.: Lexington Books, 1977b.

McLure, Charles E. "The State Corporate Income Tax: Lambs in Wolve's Clothing." In *The Economics of Taxation,* edited by H. J. Aaron and M. J. Boskin. Washington, D.C.: The Brookings Institution, 1980.

McLure, Charles E. "The Elusive Incidence of Corporate Income Tax: The State Case." *Public Finance Quarterly* (Oct. 1981): 395–413.

Megdal, Sharon B. "A Model of Local Demand for Education." *Journal of Urban Economics* 16 (1984): 13–30.

Megdal, Sharon B. "The Flypaper Effect Revisited: An Econometric Explanation." *The Review of Economics and Statistics* 69 (May 1987): 347–51.

Michigan Department of the Treasury. *Analysis of the Michigan Single Business Tax,* January 1985.

Mieszkowski, Peter M. "The Property Tax: An Excise Tax or a Profits Tax?" *Journal of Public Economics* 1 (1972): 73–96.

Mieszkowski, Peter. "Recent Trends in Urban and Regional Development." In *Current Issues in Urban Economics,* edited by P. Mieszkowski and M. Straszheim, 3–39. Baltimore: Johns Hopkins University Press, 1979.

Mieszkowski, Peter M. and Zodrow, George R. "The Incidence of a Partial State Corporate Income Tax." *National Tax Journal* 38 (Dec. 1985): 489–96.

Mikesell, John L. and C. Kurt Zorn. "Impact of the Sales Tax Rate on its Base: Evidence from a Small Town." Mimeograph, Indiana University, 1985.

Mikesell, John L. and C. Kurt Zorn. "Revenue Performance of State Lotteries." *Proceedings of the Seventy-Eighth Annual Conference,* National Tax Association–Tax Institute of America, Columbus, Ohio, 1986, 159–69.

Miller, Merton H. "Debt and Taxes." *Journal of Finance* 32 (1977): 261–75.

Moffitt, Robert A. "The Effects of Grants-in-Aid on State and Local Expenditures: The Case of AFDC." *Journal of Public Economics* 23 (April 1984): 279–305.

Mohring, Herbert and Mitchell Hartwitz. *Highway Benefits: An Analytical Framework.* Evanston, Ill.: Northwestern University Press, 1962.

Morgan, William E. and John H. Mutti. "The Exportation of State and Local Taxes in a Multilateral Framework: The Case of Business Taxes." *National Tax Journal* 38 (June 1985): 191–208.

Morrison, Steven A. "Estimation of Long-run Prices and Investment Levels for Airport Runways." In *Research in Transportation Economics,* edited by Theodore E. Keeler, 103–130. Greenwich, Conn.: JAI Press, 1983.

Murnane, Richard J. "An Economist's Look at Federal and State Education Policies." In *American Domestic Priorities: An Economic Appraisal,* edited by J. Quigley and D. Rubinfeld, 118–47. Berkeley: University of California Press, 1985.

Musgrave, Richard A. and Peggy B. Musgrave. *Public Finance in Theory and Practice.* New York: McGraw-Hill, 1984.

Mushkin, Selma, ed. *Public Prices for Public Products,* Washington, D.C.: The Urban Institute, 1972.

Mutti, John H. and William E. Morgan. "The Exportation of State and Local Taxes in a Multilateral Framework: The Case of Household Type Taxes." *National Tax Journal* 36 (Dec. 1983): 459–76.

Nafziger, Richard. "Taxation of Business in Washington: An Examination of the B & O, Corporate Profits, and Value-Added Taxes and their Potential Impact on Washington Business." Ways and Means Committee, Washington State House of Representatives, Olympia, Wash., 1985.

National Association of State Development Agencies. *Directory of Incentives for Business Investment and Development in the United States: A State-by-State Guide.* Washington, D.C.: The Urban Institute Press, 1986.

National Bellas Hess v. Illinois Department of Revenue (386 U.S. 753 1967).

Neenan, William B. *Urban Public Economics.* Belmont, Calif.: Wadsworth, 1981.

Nelson, Richard R. "Roles of Government in a Mixed Economy." *Journal of Policy Analysis and Management* 6 (Summer 1987): 541–57.

Netzer, Dick. *Economics of the Property Tax.* Washington, D.C.: The Brookings Institution, 1966.

Niskanen, William A. "The Peculiar Economics of Bureaucracy." *American Economic Review* 58 (May 1968): 293–305.

Oates, Wallace. "The Effects of Property Taxes and Local Public Spending on Property Values: An Empirical Study of Tax Capitalization and the Tiebout Hypothesis." *Journal of Political Economy* (Nov. 1969): 957–71.

Oates, Wallace E. *Fiscal Federalism.* New York: Harcourt Brace Jovanovich, 1972.

Oates, Wallace E. "The Effects of Property Taxes and Local Public Spending on Property Values: A Reply and Yet Further Results." *Journal of Political Economy* 81 (July 1973): 1004–1008.

Oates, Wallace E., ed. *The Political Economy of Fiscal Federalism.* Lexington, Mass.: Lexington Books, 1977.

Pack, Janet Rothenberg. "Privatization of Public-Sector Services in Theory and Practice." *Journal of Policy Analysis and Management* 6 (Summer 1987): 523–40.

Papke, Leslie. "Subnational Taxation and Capital Mobility: Estimates of Tax-Price Elasticities." *National Tax Journal* 40 (June 1987): 191–203.

Papke, James A. and Leslie A. Papke. "State Tax Incentives and Investment Location Decisions." In *Indiana's Revenue Structure: Major Components and Issues, Part II,* edited by J. Papke. West Lafayette, Ind.: Purdue University Press, 1984.

Pechman, Joseph A. *Who Paid the Taxes, 1966–85.* Washington, D.C.: The Brookings Institution, 1985.

Peers, Alexandra. "Tax Bill's Crackdown on Municipal Bonds Angers Local Officials." *The Wall Street Journal,* 22 October 1986.

Phares, Donald. *Who Pays State and Local Taxes*. Cambridge, Mass.: Oelgeschlager, Gunn, and Hain, 1980.

Poole, Robert W., Jr. and Philip E. Fixler, Jr. "Privatization of Public-Sector Services in Practice: Experience and Potential." *Journal of Policy Analysis and Management* 6 (Summer 1987): 612–25.

Poterba, James M. "Explaining the Yield Spread Between Taxable and Tax-Exempt Bonds: The Role of Expected Tax Policy." In *Studies in State and Local Public Finance*, edited by H. Rosen. Chicago: University of Chicago Press, 1986.

Ramsey, Frank P. "A Contribution to the Theory of Taxation." *Economic Journal* 37 (1927): 47–61.

Raphaelson, Arnold H. "The Property Tax." In *Management Policies in Local Government Finance*, edited by J. R. Aronson and E. Schwartz, 123–51. Washington, D.C.: International City Management Association, 1987.

Reischauer, Robert P. "General Revenue Sharing—The Program's Incentives." In *Financing the New Federalism*. Baltimore: Johns Hopkins University Press, 1975.

Rodgers, James D. "Sales Taxes, Income Taxes, and Other Revenues." In *Management Policies in Local Government Finance*, edited by J. R. Aronson and E. Schwartz, 152–83. Washington, D.C.: International City Management Association, 1981.

Romer, Thomas and Howard Rosenthal. "Bureaucrats Versus Voters: On the Political Economy of Resource Allocation by Direct Democracy." *Quarterly Journal of Economics* 93 (1979a): 563–87.

Romer, Thomas and Howard Rosenthal. "The Elusive Median Voter." *Journal of Public Economics* 12 (1979b): 143–70.

Rosen, Harvey S. *Public Finance*. Homewood, Ill.: Richard D. Irwin, 1988.

Rosen, Harvey S. and David J. Fullerton. "A Note on Local Tax Rates, Public Benefit Levels, and Property Values." *Journal of Political Economy* 85 (April 1977): 433–40.

Samuelson, Paul A. "The Pure Theory of Public Expenditure," *Review of Economics and Statistics* 36 (Nov. 1954): 387–89.

Sappington, David E. M. and Joseph E. Stiglitz. "Privatization, Information, and Incentives." *Journal of Policy Analysis and Management* 6 (Summer 1987): 567–82.

Savas, E. S. *Privatization: The Key to Better Government*. Chatham, N.J.: Chatham House Publishers, 1987.

Savas, E. S. and Barbara Stevens. *The Organization and Efficiency of Solid Waste Collection*. Lexington, Mass.: Lexington Books, 1977.

Schmenner, Roger W. *Making Business Location Decisions*. Englewood Cliffs, N.J.: Prentice-Hall, 1982.

School Finance at a Glance, 1985–86. Education Commission of the States, Denver, Colo., 1986.

Shribman, David. "Colorado Business Groups Leave Ranks Of Anti-Tax Forces, Urge Higher Taxes." *The Wall Street Journal*, 14 April 1986.

Slemrod, Joel. "The Optimal Progressivity of the Minnesota Tax System." In *Final Report of the Minnesota Tax Study Commission, Vol. 2*. Minneapolis: Butterworth Legal Publishers, 1986, 127–37.

Steiner, Peter O. "The Public Sector and the Public Interest." In *Public Expenditure and Policy Analysis*, edited by R. Haveman and J. Margolis, 3–41. Boston: Houghton Mifflin, 1983.

Strauss, Robert P. "Business Taxes in West Virginia: A Research Report to the West Virginia Tax Study Commission." West Virginia Tax Study Commission, Charleston, 1983.

Suits, Daniel B. "Gambling Taxes: Regressivity and Revenue Potential." *National Tax Journal* 30 (March 1977): 19–35.

Suits, Daniel B. "The Elasticity of Demand for Gambling." *Quarterly Journal of Economics* 93 (Feb. 1979): 155–62.

Suits, Daniel B. and Ronald C. Fisher. "A Balanced Budget Constitutional Amendment: Economic Complexities and Uncertainties." *National Tax Journal* 38 (Dec. 1985): 467–77.

Sunley, Emil. "State and Local Governments." In *Setting National Priorities, The Next Ten Years,* edited by H. Owen and C. Schultze, 371–409. Washington, D.C.: The Brookings Institution, 1976.

Tannenwald, Robert. "The Aftermath of Federal Tax Reform: The Effects of Federal Tax Reform on Interstate Tax Competition." Paper presented at the Conference on Interjurisdiction Tax and Policy Competition, The Urban Institute, Washington, D.C., 1988.

Tiebout, Charles M. "The Pure Theory of Local Expenditures." *Journal of Political Economy* 64 (Oct. 1956): 416–24.

Toder, Eric and Thomas S. Neubig. "Revenue Cost Estimates of Tax Expenditures: The Case of Tax-exempt Bonds." *National Tax Journal* 38 (Sept. 1985): 395–414.

U.S. Department of Commerce, Bureau of the Census, Census of Governments. *Compendium of Government Finances.* Washington, D.C., 1962, 1967, 1972, 1977, 1982.

U.S. Department of Commerce, Bureau of the Census, 1982 Census of Governments. *Taxable Property Values and Assessment-Sales Price Ratios.* Washington, D.C., 1984.

U.S. Department of Commerce, Bureau of the Census. *Current Population Reports,* P–60 series. Washington, D.C., Aug. 1986a.

U.S. Department of Commerce, Bureau of the Census. *Finances of School Districts, 1984–85.* Washington, D.C., 1986b.

U.S. Department of Commerce, Bureau of the Census. *State Government Tax Collections in 1985,* Series GF85, no. 1. Washington, D.C., 1986c.

U.S. Department of Commerce, Bureau of the Census. *City Government Finances.* Washington, D.C., various years.

U.S. Department of Commerce, Bureau of the Census. *County Government Finances.* Washington, D.C., various years.

U.S. Department of Commerce, Bureau of the Census. *Survey of Current Business.* Washington, D.C., various issues.

U.S. Department of Commerce, Bureau of the Census. *Governmental Finances,* Washington, D.C., various years.

U.S. Department of Commerce, Bureau of the Census. *State Government Finances.* Washington, D.C., various years.

U.S. Department of Commerce, Bureau of the Census. *U.S. Statistical Abstract,* Washington, D.C., 1987.

U.S. Department of Education. *Digest of Education Statistics, 1987.* Washington, D.C., May 1987.

U.S. Department of Labor. *Consumer Expenditure Survey, Interview Survey.* Washington, D.C., 1984.

U.S. Department of Labor. *Employment and Earnings*. Washington, D.C., various issues.

U.S. Department of Transportation, Federal Highway Administration. *Highway Statistics, 1985*. Washington, D.C., 1986a.

U.S. Department of Transportation, Federal Highway Administration. *Highway Statistics Summary to 1985*. Washington, D.C., 1986b.

U.S. Department of the Treasury. *Economic Analysis of Gross Income Taxes*. Washington, D.C., 1986.

U.S. Executive Office of the President, Office of Management and Budget. *Special Analyses, Budget of the U.S. Government, Fiscal Year 1986*. Washington, D.C., 1985.

Vickrey, William S. "Pricing in Urban and Suburban Transport." *American Economic Review* (May 1963): 452–65.

The Wall Street Journal. "Growth of Franchised Education Outlets Reflects Concerns About Public Schools," 15 October 1985a.

The Wall Street Journal. "New Hampshire Tries Harder Marketing Liquor With Spirit," 8 October 1985b.

The Wall Street Journal. "State and Local Governments See Pluses in Borrowing Overseas," 28 October 1986.

The Wall Street Journal. "Quality of Life," 19 June, 1987a, 19.

The Wall Street Journal. "Traverse City Whacks Washington," Editorial, 28 July 1987b, 28.

Walsh, Michael J. "A Note on Border Tax Effects: Additional Evidence." Working paper, Michigan State University, 1986.

Wasylenko, Michael. "Local Tax Policy and Industry Location: A Review of the Evidence." *Proceedings of the Seventy-Eighth Annual Conference*, National Tax Association, Columbus, Ohio, 1986, 222–28.

Wasylenko, Michael and Therese McGuire. "Jobs and Taxes: The Effect of Business Climate on States' Employment Growth Rates." *National Tax Journal* 38 (Dec. 1985): 497–512.

Weinstein, Barbara. "The Michigan Liquor Control Commission and the Taxation of Alcoholic Beverages." In *Michigan's Fiscal and Economic Structure*, edited by H. Brazer, Ann Arbor: University of Michigan Press, 720–54.

West Virginia Tax Study Commission. *A Tax Study for West Virginia in the 1980's* (March 1984).

Wheaton, William C. "Interstate Differences in the Level of Business Taxation." *National Tax Journal* 36 (March 1983): 83–94.

Wheaton, William C. "The Incidence of Interjurisdictional Differences in Commercial Property Taxes." *National Tax Journal* 37 (Dec. 1984): 515–28.

Wilde, James A. "The Expenditure Effects of Grants-in-Aid Programs." *National Tax Journal* 21 (Sept. 1968): 340–48.

Wiseman, Michael. "Proposition 13 and Effective Property Tax Rates in San Francisco." *Research Papers in Economics*, no. 86–88, University of California at Berkeley, Feb. 1986.

Zimmerman, Dennis. "Resource Misallocation from Interstate Tax Exportation: Estimates of Excess Spending and Welfare Loss in a Median Voter Framework." *National Tax Journal* 36 (June 1983): 183–202.

Selected
End-of-Chapter
Questions

/ Chapter 1

1. The change in federal aid was one of several factors that may have contributed to the slowdown in the growth of the state–local sector, although state–local spending from own sources also stopped growing. Other factors include the decline in national income, the decreased demand for state–local services, and the slowdown in the growth of state–local labor costs.

3. Local services might include police protection, fire prevention and protection, streets, parks, garbage collection, education, library, public transit. State services could include higher education, highways, state courts, prisons, parks, environmental protection, income-support programs.

/ Chapter 2

1. Because the two services appear to have the same public good characteristics, the decision concerning public versus private provision may hinge on other factors such as the range of benefit spillover. Property owners likely provide a benefit to a larger number of people by clearing the streets along their property than by clearing their sidewalks. Sidewalk cleaning may give mostly neighborhood benefits. If the spillover involves a large number of people, cooperation is more difficult (and free-riding more likely). In addition, the relatively larger expense involved in operating a snowplow compared to individual snow shovels may make government provision of street-clearing services more likely.

2. Efficiency in the provision of public goods requires that the marginal cost of producing another unit equal the sum of all individual marginal benefits.

3. The provision of some public services generates positive externalities to residents outside of the jurisdiction who will not be charged for the benefits they receive. These services will be underprovided from society's viewpoint if jurisdictions base their decisions concerning how much of a service to provide solely on the basis of benefits and costs accruing to the residents of the jurisdiction. Spillovers in the case of public safety might take the

form of there being fewer criminals in the entire area, safety for visitors to a jurisdiction, or smoother traffic flow for commuters.

/ Chapter 3

1. Although the selected amount of spending received majority support, it most likely is not the most preferred level of spending for all of those in the majority. Only the median voter is perfectly happy with the outcome.

2. Majority voting does not ensure that the amount of spending chosen is efficient. The spending level chosen will be the level at which the median voter's marginal benefit equals marginal tax cost. It would only be by accident that the amount selected would be the efficient level.

3.   a. The preferences of group 1 and group 2 are single-peaked, but the preferences of group 3 are not.
   b. The level of spending selected will depend on the order in which the votes are taken. No equilibrium exists because group 3's preferences are not single-peaked; cycling results.
   c. Taking into account the relative strengths of the voters' preferences in addition to their order might reduce the likelihood of an inconsistency occurring. Alternatively, a level could be selected, and voters could move if they preferred.

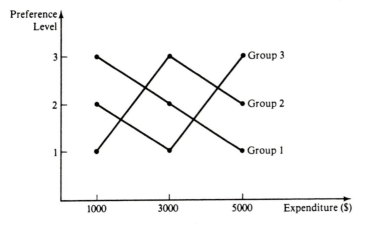

/ Chapter 4

1.   a. No. A voter in B would not prefer to live in a big house in A. The tax cost is the same in either district, and the voter has already indicated a preference for a small house in B.
   b. Yes. The move to a small house in A would allow (approximately) the same school benefits with a lower tax cost.
   c. The required tax rate is $32 per $1000 of value. Small-house consumers are better off in the mixed district, but big-house consumers are better off in A.

    d. Without complete capitalization, big-house consumers would not like to live in the mixed community. Demand for big houses and the price of big houses would fall, while demand for small houses and their price would rise.

    e. Big and small houses can exist in the same community if the tax advantage enjoyed by a small-house consumer in a big-house community is capitalized into the price of that small house. As a result, each household will pay the full cost of the services provided. In that instance, tax-rate differences are corrected for by housing price changes.

2. In a world without mobility, communities will be made up of residents with greatly varying demands for public services. The equilibrium level of spending determined by majority voting is inefficient and will not perfectly satisfy a majority of voters. In a world with mobility, communities will be made up of residents who have similar demands for public goods and services. All residents will be satisfied and the level of provision determined by majority voting will be efficient.

3. Consumers will vote with their feet and move to communities that best satisfy their preferences. But barriers to mobility, such as moving costs and information costs, often prevent the consumers in a community from having exactly similar preferences. If so, then political voting will play a role in determining the level of expenditure.

/ Chapter 5

1. A major advantage of local provision of government goods and services is that it may allow communities to exactly satisfy the demands of their residents. Economies of scale are not relevant if communities can purchase services from other governments or private firms.

2.   a. Economic reasons for consolidation might include: economies of scale in the production, financing, or administration of public goods and services; efficiency gains in reducing externalities that arise as benefits or costs from one community's provision of a public good spill over into another community; and the ability to reduce the inequality of provision across communities due to differences in per-capita income.

    b. Consolidation may be less desirable when demands for services vary greatly across municipalities. Large income differences suggest that there may be substantial demand differences, but also raise the equity issue. Consolidation may not be necessary if economies of scale are achieved by contracting.

/ Chapter 6

1.   a. The price of beer rises from P_0 to P_1 + tax in the short run but remains at P_0 in the long run. The quantity of beer sold falls from Q_0 to Q_1 in the short run and to Q_2 in the long run. In the long run, the number of beer stores and bars will fall.

    b. Beer demand in YCT may be elastic because of the proximity of lower-tax cities where beer can also be purchased. Beer sales in nearby cities will increase, as will the number of stores and bars.

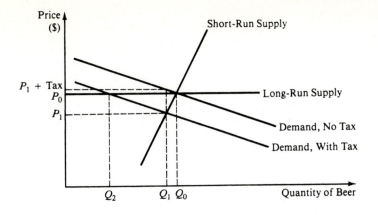

2. Sellers will bear the revenue burden of a tax when supply is perfectly inelastic. The sellers' burden will be distributed among the factors of production. Some examples of inelastically supplied goods include land and air (though not clean air).

3. Efficiency costs depend on the tax rate squared. As the tax rate increases, the efficiency cost rises at a faster rate.

4. An excise tax could have no efficiency cost and even could increase economic efficiency if marginal social costs exceed marginal private costs. An example is an excise tax on cigarettes. Smoking imposes costs on others that are not incorporated into the price of cigarettes. An excise tax would ensure that marginal private costs more closely approximate social costs.

/ Chapter 7

1. Property tax revenues will increase if market values and/or assessed values increase, even when property tax rates remain constant.

2.   a. $2000.
   b. A 10-percent increase in market value will lead to a 10-percent increase in the tax bill. The new tax bill will be $2200. If the tax rate also rises 10 percent, the new tax bill would be $2420.
   c. The new taxable value of $40,000 would lead to a reduction of the tax bill of $400 (from $2000 to $1600.) The tax savings from the exemption remain the same as value increases. The tax savings increase as the tax rate increases.
   d. The original property tax bill is $2000, and 5 percent of your income is equal to $1500. The tax credit is equal to one-half of the amount by which your tax bill exceeds $1500, or $250. The tax savings from the credit increase as value increases and as the tax rate increases.

4. The annual net income is $50,000 ($250,000 − 200,000). With a discount rate of 10 percent, the current market value of the building is (50,000/ .10 [1 − (1/1.10) exp (−20)], or $425,700. With a discount rate of 5 percent, the current market value is $623,110.

/ Chapter 8

1. True if capital and labor are mobile while land is not. The amount of capital investment will increase in the city, with the effect of increasing the demand for the complementary inputs land and labor. More labor will enter, holding wages down. The increase in the demand for land will increase the price of land. Landowners in the city benefit, but owners of capital in other cities also benefit from the reduced supply of capital (and the higher rate of return) in their communities.

2. Across-the-board reductions in property taxes will not cause any changes in the allocation of capital among communities. An increase in demand for property will increase the net-of-tax return on capital overall. Owners of property will benefit from the tax reduction, (and so may owners of factors of production that are complements with property in the long run). It is likely that the tax structure will become less progressive.

3.   a. The amount of industrial property will increase from Q_0 to Q_1 due to changes in how capital is used and an inflow from other jurisdictions. The amount of commercial and residential property will fall to Q_1. If capital is mobile in use, then all types of property will earn a net-of-tax return of R_2.

   b. Commercial and residential property would have to be taxed at a higher rate to keep revenue the same. The tax differential between industrial property on the one hand and commercial and residential property on the other would increase. One could use the graphs above, and assume that the demand for industrial property will increase by a larger amount. The quantity of industrial property will be greater than Q_1, and the amount of commercial and residential property will fall below Q_1. The net-of-tax returns in both markets would rise above R_2.

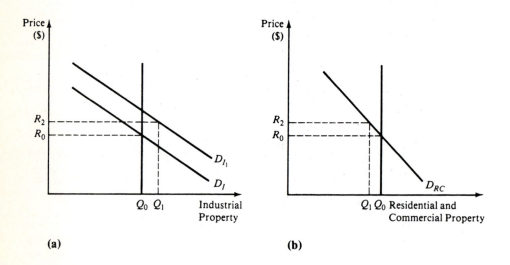

(a)   (b)

4.   a. The marginal property tax price falls by 20 percent for taxpayers with income less than $30,000. For taxpayers above this income level, the tax credit does not affect the marginal property tax price.

b. Yes. Taxpayers below the $30,000 income level have a net cost of $.80 for each $1 increase in their property tax. The increase in the property tax (and presumably services) of $400 actually costs them $320. With a price elasticity of 1.5, the 20-percent decrease in price would induce a 30-percent increase in desired spending, or $450.

/ Chapter 9

1. An individual could reduce liability by consuming relatively fewer goods and more services, by consuming less of all goods and services and increasing saving, by purchasing goods in or from states with lower sales taxes, or by purchasing intermediate goods with the intent of producing the final good by one's self. Economic costs include the efficiency losses that occur as the tax causes individuals to alter their consumption patterns, and the costs (time and out-of-pocket) spent attempting to avoid the tax.

2. Many legal and medical services are purchased by individuals to deal with problems that occur during a typical lifetime. Legal and medical expenditures can serve to prevent misfortune, and the same is true of spending on car repairs, fire extinguishers, and child car seats. If one were concerned about the fairness involved in taxing a person's misfortune, it might make more sense to provide a tax credit or exemption to help those with "excessive" medical or legal bills.

3. Sales taxes are generally viewed as regressive because consumption expenditures as a fraction of income are greater for lower-income taxpayers. A sales tax could be made more progressive by exempting certain "necessity" items from the tax base, by establishing a personal exemption for individual taxpayers, by applying higher rates to goods particularly consumed by higher-income persons, or by creating a progressive rate structure.

/ Chapter 10

1. a. With no deductibility, the combined marginal tax rate is 20 percent. If the state tax is deductible from the federal tax, the marginal rate is 19.25 percent. With reciprocal deductibility, the tax rate is 18.6 percent.
   b. 25 percent, 23.5 percent, and 22.3 percent.

2. a. The net, after-tax cost of property taxes is $(1 - .15)(2000)$, or $1700 (85 percent).

/ Chapter 11

1. The general perception is that a firm's benefits from government services are proportional to its amount of production, which is better measured by capital and employment than sales. Benefits may arise from transportation facilities, utilities, public-safety services, education, courts, and other state regulatory functions. Firms with only (or nearly only) sales in a state may benefit from transportation and regulatory services, but not from those services that apply physically to production.

2.

Tax Type		Tax Base
Gross receipts	=	Revenue
Value-added (consumption)	=	Revenue − material purchases − capital purchases
Net income	=	Revenue − material purchases − wages − interest − rent − depreciation

The base of the gross receipts tax is the largest followed by that for the value-added tax. The difference between the value-added and net-income tax bases depends largely on the relative importance of wages in a firm's costs.

3. Most state sales taxes are intended to be "destination based"—taxing sales where consumption occurs. A state's VAT base may be different if firms buy intermediate goods in other states where no VAT is collected and then deduct those costs. Also, most state VATs are "origin-based"—taxing sales where they are made.

   If every state adopted a consumption-type VAT, the cumulative base of this tax would be the same as a national sales tax if exemptions were the same, except perhaps for the treatment of international transactions. But because of the difference between taxing at origin and destination, the distribution of tax among states would not necessarily be the same.

4. A firm pays state income taxes based on the percentage of its total capital, employment, and sales it has in a state. Unless capital is immobile and the producer has monopoly power, the burden of an increase in state income taxes paid by firms would fall entirely on the state's immobile land, labor, and capital and not on consumers in another state. One state cannot shift the burden of an income tax increase to another state's consumers if there are competitive markets and capital is mobile.

/ Chapter 12

1. Economists typically prefer to time the payments for services to coincide with the benefits received. That is the major advantage of debt financing. Similarly, the big disadvantage with the temporary tax increase or the payment out of current revenues is that residents (either today's or next year's) pay the entire cost of the project. The choice is between a one-time 20-percent tax increase or a less than 1-percent increase over thirty years.

2. Exempting municipal interest from federal taxes is a fairly costly method of subsidizing state–local government borrowing costs. Recent evidence shows that the revenue loss exceeds the interest savings to borrowers. Direct loan subsidies might prove to be more efficient.

3.   a. A reduction in marginal tax rates will increase municipal bond interest rates. Investors have to be offered higher municipal yields to remain indifferent between tax-exempt and taxable securities.

    b. A reduction in the supply of municipal bonds will lead to lower interest rates. A leftward shift in the supply of bonds causes the price to increase and yields to fall.

    c. The elimination of alternative tax shelters will lead to an increase in municipal bond demand. Interest rates will tend to fall.

    d. An increase in the supply of municipal bonds will increase municipal yields. Investors have to be "bribed" into holding more bonds.

4. The increased supply of revenue bonds increases interest rates on municipal bonds that each state issues for traditional governmental purposes. The tax-exempt status of revenue bond interest results in fairly large revenue losses for the federal government. No individual state would willingly reduce its use of revenue bonds. Each state perceives its costs (the impact of that state's borrowing on the tax-exempt interest rate) to be small, while the benefits (in the form of increased private development) are perceived as large.

/ Chapter 13

1. Voters may not have realized that a state lottery is a regressive revenue source. Even if someone never intends to buy a lottery ticket, he or she might vote for the state lottery if it would reduce his or her state tax bill. The lottery vote is really a vote about the state's revenue structure.

2. All these tax bases arise from individual choice—the choice of whether and how much to smoke, work, or buy lottery tickets. Because the demand for cigarettes is quite inelastic and considering the external cost of smoking, cigarette excise taxes seem quite efficient. Even if gambling taxes are similarly efficient, the lottery involves both a tax and government production. The efficiency of income taxes depends on how much workers and investors respond. Both cigarette taxes and lotteries are regressive revenue sources, while income taxes are generally proportional or progressive. The administrative cost of collecting both cigarette and income taxes is lower relative to revenue than for lotteries.

3. Because both involve generating revenue from gambling, the difference in method might either reflect historical factors or economic differences in how the services are produced. For instance, concern about organized crime is often mentioned concerning lotteries and number games, but there also has been concern about fixing of horse races. There may be more economies of scale for lotteries than race tracks, but that only calls for monopoly in lottery producers, not necessarily government monopoly. The difference may also reflect public perception that one is "bad" and thus needs closer government supervision or regulation.

/ Chapter 14

1. E_D^Y = percentage change in quantity/percentage change in income; .80 = percentage change in quantity/.20; .16 = percentage change in quantity of state expenditures. Because state per-capita income increases by more than state expenditures, state spending as a percentage of income falls.

2. For desired local services to be the same for all voters, the voter's tax must increase with income in the same proportion as demand does. With tax prices, t_0^R, t_0^M, and t_0^R, all three have the same level of desired government expenditure (P_0, M_0, and R_0). Although tax prices will increase with income, it is not clear whether they will increase faster, proportional to, or less than income. The necessary tax structure depends on the income elasticity of demand.

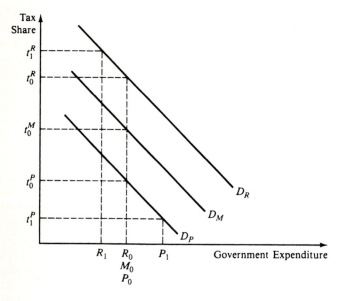

This requires a very low tax price for the poor and a very high tax price for the rich. With tax shares t_1^P, t_1^M, and t_1^R, the poor demand P_1, the medium-income group demands M_1, and the rich demand R_1.

3. Coalitions of rich and poor may result both from economic and taste factors. Economically, the rich demand substantial services because they have high income, while the poor may face very low (even zero) prices due to the structure of taxes and state and federal subsidies.

/ Chapter 15

1. The incidence of crime in a city is a consumer output that is a function not only of city expenditure on police services but also the size of the city's population and its environment. One city may spend more on police protection but have a larger population and/or environment that causes a greater incidence of crime.

2. Education expenditures could rise in the face of declining student enrollment because of increases in the price of inputs such as teachers, books, and utilities. The district also could have decided to attempt to improve the education given in the district by lowering class sizes. Or the quality of students entering school could be declining, requiring more inputs to provide the same level of educational output.

3. The Baumol story is that government wages increase to keep pace with private sector wages leading to cost increases in the public sector. If demand for government goods is price inelastic, larger and larger expenditures on government goods are required. As long as government expenditures rise no faster than national income, a rising government share may not result. The connection could be broken by productivity gains in producing government goods or by more consumer resistance.

4. Professors could be substituted for or perhaps made more productive by combining them with more capital, including such things as audiovisual technology enabling the broadcast of lectures to more students or self-teaching computer programs. Graduate students and part-time teachers from industry might also be used. This may lower the total cost but is unlikely to lower the rate of increase of professors' salaries. These changes may affect the nature of a university education by reducing its human element and the important interactions between student and professor. This problem applies equally to private and public universities.

/ Chapter 16

1. City services provided by a museum, library, or zoo are not pure public goods. For both residents and nonresidents, the city is justified in instituting user charges to finance them. The problems with user charges are that city services of cultural value are restricted to people who are willing to pay the user charge and the administrative and compliance costs of collecting the charges.

   These services exhibit high fixed costs and low marginal costs. If the city sets the user charge at average cost, it covers full cost but discourages many from using. If it prices at marginal cost, it creates deficits that must be covered by taxes. One possibility is a monthly or yearly pass to cover fixed costs and a small fee upon each visit to cover marginal cost. To make the user charge "fair," city residents who pay taxes that support the service or the poor could be waived of the fixed fee. The city might also consider price discrimination based on demand—higher prices at peak demand times.

2. Some operating costs depend on the number of visitors and that congestion reduces the enjoyment of all visitors. A charge can cover these variable costs and allocate this scarce resource to those who value it most. Also, the fees help to measure the demand for more parks and provide revenue to acquire new ones.

3. An efficient user fee equals the marginal benefit derived from use. Because demand is greatest on holidays, followed by weekends, and then weekdays, marginal benefit is also. A variable rate user fee seems efficient. The user fees effectively allocate the scarce park resource among competing demands, which are different at different times. This may be fairer in the sense that parks are "free" on weekdays when they are not crowded and crowding is controlled at peak demand times. An alternative is to set a limit on visitors and allocate on a first-come first-served basis.

4. With only one meter, each tenant pays the average cost of water use among all tenants. Thus, each tenant would correctly perceive that more water use would cost that individual little extra. After the installation of water meters for each apartment, each tenant pays the marginal cost of water use. Because of that, tenants will have an incentive to conserve on water usage. Tenants could conserve water by taking shorter and less frequent showers, substituting baths for showers, taking showers together, showering on campus, using

paper plates, and filling up dishwasher or sink before doing dishes. There may be a gain in economic efficiency, but one also has to consider the administrative cost (installing, monitoring, and sending bills to each tenant) of individual water metering.

/ Chapter 17

1. a. Price of public safety $= 1/(1 + R); R = 1$, so price $= 0.5$. The spillover caused the community to spend too little on public safety. By reducing the price for public safety, voters have an incentive to increase spending on public safety.
    Public-safety tax revenue $= \$10$ per $\$1000 \times \$10,000,000 = \$100,000$; *EDP* $=$ percentage change in quantity/percentage change in price, $0.2 =$ percentage change in quantity/0.5, and $0.1 =$ percentage change in quantity. Before the grant, public-safety spending is $\$100,000$. After the grant, public-safety spending increases 10 percent to $\$110,000$—$\$55,000$ from local taxpayers and $\$55,000$ from the grant. Now Central City has to raise only $\$55,000$ in property taxes and can lower their tax rate to $\$5.50$ per $\$1000$ of taxable value.

2. Percentage change in income $=$ income change/total income $= \$55,000/\$2,255,000 = 0.024$; *EDY* $=$ percentage change in quantity/percentage change in income, $0.8 =$ percentage change in quantity/0.024, and $0.0192 =$ percentage change in quantity. Before lump-sum grant Central City was spending $\$100,000$; now it spends 1.92 percent more, or $\$101,920$. Of that, $\$55,000$ comes from the grant and $\$46,920$ in taxes. The new required tax rate is $\$4.692$ per $\$1000$ of taxable value. The matching grant reduced the tax price of public safety and provided more revenue, while the lump-sum grant does nothing to reduce the price of public safety.

3. Because Central City spends more than $\$55,000$ on public safety, both a restricted and nonrestricted grant are ''fungible'' and can be spent on any service in Central City's entire budget or for tax relief.

4. States and localities would most likely respond by reducing expenditures on the specific categories previously supported by matching grants because the tax price per dollar of expenditure on these categories would rise drastically. The reduction in federal taxes effectively represents additional income that can be spent on all goods and services.

/ Chapter 18

1. One district could spend more because it uses more teachers (smaller classroom size), more books, more personal computers, and more audiovisual equipment. Or the district may use the same number of teachers, but require that they have additional degrees or more years of experience. Those differences in education method may be called for because of social, cultural, and environmental characteristics of the students. Teacher and administrator salaries may be higher in one district than another because of labor market differences. Finally, the districts may have different educational objectives (score on standardized tests, pass or graduation rate, and parental satisfaction) that require spending different amounts of money.

2. The arguments for state involvement in financing and producing education essentially boil down to problems due to externalities (general social benefits of education from basic

uniformity of knowledge and spillovers across jurisdiction boundaries from mobility) and attempts to equalize incomes. The arguments against state involvement include the loss of local control in choice of curriculum and level of spending and a potential reduction of competition that might induce schools to operate efficiently and at lower cost.

State governments would be more likely to take a larger role in public education, the more homogenous the state's population, the stronger the value residents place on equal education for all state residents, and the greater the mobility of residents within the state. It is not clear that such arguments explain the differences between Hawaii and New Hampshire or Oregon and Washington; historical and noneconomic factors may also be important.

3. One solution would be to institute a system of guaranteed tax base aid in which the key component would be that a locality's property tax rate could not fall below $50 per $1000 of taxable property. The foundation grant could be set at $162.50 and the guaranteed per-pupil tax base at $50,000.

The effects of this grant program are summarized below:

	A	B	C	D	Average
Initial spending	$2000.0	$2500.0	$2550.0	$3660.0	$2663.0
New spending	2662.5	2662.5	2662.5	3600.0	2898.9
Initial tax	2000.0	2500.0	2550.0	3600.0	2663.0
New tax	1818.0	2500.0	2550.0	3600.0	2617.0

This plan operates by requiring a high minimum tax rate. Although state government is restricting local choice, it is less restrictive than the other options of a statewide school district or minimum education standards for each local district.

4. University output includes undergraduate, graduate, and professional education, research, consulting, and other forms of public service. The educational output of a university can be measured by scores on standardized tests, the later economic achievements of students (job types, employment level, salaries, number continuing education, and advanced degrees) and subjective surveys of students' satisfaction with education. Measuring the teaching results of individual professors is more difficult because a student's achievements are the result of many professors. Many universities attempt to measure a professor's teaching quality through student evaluations and peer reviews conducted by other professors.

/ Chapter 19

1. Congestion occurs when the marginal cost of accommodating an additional consumer is greater than zero. An example is a busy road where one more driver decreases the benefits (slows down traffic and increases accident chances) other drivers receive from using the road. A user charge specific to the amount of congestion is necessary. A charge equal to the marginal cost of the additional user solves a congestion problem.

2. A congested road is too small because the demand for the road is too great at the existing price. An existing price of zero for road use does not include the social marginal cost an additional user places on existing users. Congestion suggests that capacity is too small only if all users are already paying all private and social costs.

3. Because there is no congestion charge, drivers choose to use the more direct road. It is not efficient to use gasoline tax revenue to expand the more direct road because drivers are overusing the direct road and underusing the indirect road. This is a waste of a resource. The solution to this problem is to provide incentives for drivers to use the indirect road and to not use the direct road. If congestion gets bad enough on the direct road, the opportunity cost of using that road will be high enough that drivers of their own choice will switch to the other road. To help this process along, a state or locality could use stop lights, speed limits, not fix potholes, or use an advertising campaign or road signs that make drivers more aware of the uncongested route. A second possibility is to charge a user fee to use the direct road. Expansion of the direct road would increase its use and lead to a greater waste of the indirect road.

4. Gasoline taxes go for road maintenance and construction, things that are proportional to type and amount of road use. Registration and license fees, on the other hand, are not proportional to road use and thus should go to cover some fixed costs of the highway system, such as courts, traffic safety and enforcement, or general administration. A similar argument applies to infraction fees, which might apply to the general public-safety structure.

/ Chapter 20

2. If revenue and expenditure forecasts turn out to be inaccurate for economic or political reasons, the state's budget could be balanced at the start of the fiscal year and fall into deficit during the year. States can avoid a deficit by increasing taxes and fees, by borrowing, or by altering accounting procedures. Internal borrowing means borrowing money from other state funds displaying a surplus.

3. Contingency funds allow states to maintain a relatively constant level of real services in both bad and good economic times. Without a fund, the increase in tax rates needed during recessions collects more revenue from individuals still working and businesses still producing, potentially further hurting the state's economy. The political advantage of a variable tax rate is that it would allow a state politician to gain favor in an economic upswing by reducing state taxes, whereas the disadvantage is that tax-rate increases would be necessary when recession strikes, the least likely time that voters would approve of them.

4. The most restrictive limit restricts expenditure increases to no more than 5 percent per year. This limit makes no allowance for inflation and/or the growth in the tax base and could cause real per-capita local expenditure to fall. The second most restrictive limit would be a maximum local property tax rate, which allows expenditure to increase only if the property tax base expands or voters approve. But an increase in tax base may mean more residents and firms to serve. If the assessed value of the locality's property tax base does not keep up with inflation, this restriction means a reduction in the locality's real per-capita expenditure. The least restrictive limit would be that property taxes cannot increase more than the combined rate of a locality's population growth (property tax base) and inflation.

/ Chapter 21

1. The gains to a community from new business investment are increased tax revenue that can be used to provide more services or reduce taxes, increased local employment and income, and shopping or service convenience (decreased price of local goods). The costs to a community from a new shopping center include the cost of locally provided goods and services to shopping center (roads, sidewalks, utility hookup, and sanitation) and noise, traffic congestion, and unsightliness. The costs of a manufacturing plant would include all of the above perhaps plus greater water and air pollution. A community would discourage new business investment when its perceived costs are greater than its perceived benefits.

2. The rate of return to capital initially increases, which attracts new capital until its rate of return is reduced to that available elsewhere. The additional investment causes an increase in the demand for labor, which raises local wages. If labor is mobile, those wages attract new workers until local wages are equal to wages available elsewhere. Because of new investment, the demand for local land also increases. If the supply of local land cannot increase, the local rate of return or price of land increases. Local businesses that do not receive the same incentives as new businesses may not be at a disadvantage therefore, because they receive a capital gain on the land they own and a lower local property tax rate or increased local services.

3. One possibility is that states continue to offer development incentives because they believe that other states will not match theirs. Even if this is not the case, there may be short-run advantages that the state gains until other states react. The ultimate objective of development incentives may be to enrich local landowners.

4. Industries that have national markets for their output are more likely to be influenced by state tax or financing incentives. Firms in national industries are not tied to a local market and are free to locate anywhere. A firm tied to a local market is less likely to locate away from that market. A similar argument applies to industries which have inputs tied to specific local markets (coal, iron ore, water).

Name Index

The letter *n* following a page number indicates that the name will be found in a footnote or a source line.

Subject Index